LITERACY
IN GRADES 4-8

BEST PRACTICES FOR A COMPREHENSIVE PROGRAM

Third Edition

Nancy Lee Cecil

CALIFORNIA STATE UNIVERSITY, SACRAMENTO

Joan P. Gipe

CALIFORNIA STATE UNIVERSITY, SACRAMENTO (PROFESSOR EMERITUS)
WALDEN UNIVERSITY, MINNEAPOLIS

Marcy Merrill

CALIFORNIA STATE UNIVERSITY, SACRAMENTO

Holcomb Hathaway, Publishers
Scottsdale, Arizona

Library of Congress Cataloging-in-Publication Data

Cecil, Nancy Lee.
  Literacy in grades 4-8 : best practices for a comprehensive program /
Nancy Lee Cecil, California State University, Sacramento; Joan P. Gipe,
California State University, Sacramento (Professor Emeritus); Walden
University, Minneapolis; Marcy Merrill, California State University,
Sacramento. — Third Edition.
      pages cm
  ISBN 978-1-934432-83-9 (print) — ISBN 978-1-62159-025-5 (ebook)   1.
Reading (Elementary) 2. Reading (Middle school) 3. Literacy programs. I.
Gipe, Joan P. II. Merrill, Marcy. III. Title. IV. Title: Literacy in grades
four through eight.
  LB1573.C4334 2014
  372.4—dc23
                                                              2014000379

To my daughter, Chrissy—
my most powerful literacy teacher

NC

To Mom, who instilled in me a love of books

JPG

I dedicate this to my daughters, Miriam and Natalie,
who teach me to read the world in a whole new way

MM

Holcomb Hathaway, Publishers, Inc.
8700 E. Via de Ventura Blvd., Suite 265
Scottsdale, Arizona 85258
480-991-7881
www.hh-pub.com

10 9 8 7 6 5 4 3 2 1

Print book ISBN: 978-1-934432-83-9
Ebook ISBN: 978-1-62159-025-5

CHAPTER Three

Fostering Oral Language   63

CHAPTER Four

Vocabulary Instruction   91

CHAPTER Five

Reading Comprehension   131

CHAPTER Six

Writing Instruction   179

CHAPTER

Seven

Literacy in the Content Areas
LEARNING FROM INFORMATIONAL TEXT   209

CHAPTER

Eight

Fluency   249

CHAPTER

Nine

Differentiating Instruction for Diverse Classrooms   263

CHAPTER
Ten

Fostering Literacy In and Beyond the Classroom 289

CHAPTER
Eleven

Connecting School and Home 313

CHAPTER
Twelve

Literacy in Grades 4–8
ORCHESTRATING A BALANCED AND COMPREHENSIVE PROGRAM 329

Appendices

Today's intermediate- and middle-grade teachers face many critical issues. Among the most pressing are the following: What strategies should teachers use to foster literacy in their diverse students, helping them to read and write, to comprehend (and create) text in its many formats? How do teachers help all students become capable, fluent readers and writers who choose to read and write beyond the classroom? What practices and instructional materials has research found to be the most effective? How can assessment inform instruction? In what ways do family and community influence literacy success? And how can standards be used as a road map to guide effective instruction?

The need for answers to such questions resulted in this book, *Literacy in Grades 4–8: Best Practices for a Comprehensive Program,* now in its third edition. Clearly, the answers to these and similar questions profoundly affect what teachers do in the classroom. For example, if research findings, coupled with objective observations, identify certain strategies or materials as significantly more effective than others, we as teachers can make more intelligent decisions about day-to-day classroom activities.

Our challenge in writing *Literacy in Grades 4–8* has been to show preservice and practicing teachers how to teach the language arts in a skillful yet motivational way; how to create a classroom climate where the joy of language, literacy, and learning thrives; and most important, how to inspire the heterogeneous garden of learners in today's classrooms to want to engage in literate behaviors, while believing they can.

A wealth of evidence from literacy and other educational researchers suggests that a comprehensive and balanced, language-based, interactive program of direct instruction in the skills of literacy combined with an abundant exposure to quality children's and young adult literature create a program that has an extraordinary chance of developing learners who can read and write, and choose to do so. Instead of emphasizing bits and pieces of fragmented reading and writing skills, a comprehensive, balanced program focuses more on reading, writing, listening, speaking, viewing, visually representing, and thinking as interrelated communication processes—processes that are pivotal to all learning.

Readers of this book will be given strategies and procedures that suggest how to implement a balanced, comprehensive literacy program by integrating direct and indirect instruction in word study, vocabulary, comprehension strategies, and speaking, listening, and writing skills within the context of rich and varied language arts experiences. *Literacy in Grades 4–8* addresses such issues as teaching to standards—including the Common Core State Standards—differentiating instruction for readers of all levels, motivating students to want to read, using assessment to inform instruction, integrating technology, working with English learners and struggling readers, and connecting with caregivers.

The book presents many topics of particular interest to teachers, including content area literacy; developing motivated, lifelong readers and writers; listening to learn; formal and informal speaking instruction; planning and implementing a differentiated lesson; and developing authentic learning experiences.

Countless programs, procedures, and strategies are available for literacy instruction in grades 4–8 today, and choosing among them can be challenging to the seasoned teacher and overwhelming to the beginning one. Therefore, we have selected prototypes that seem to represent the most effective practices according to current research and the reinforcing testimonies of a host of outstanding teachers who were observed and interviewed for the writing of this book.

The order of this text's chapters represents only one possible approach to teaching this material—the final order of presentation will be determined by you as you teach your course. For example, we feel the placement of the assessment chapter early in the text supports efforts to differentiate instruction, as assessment needs to occur prior to effective planning for differentiation. We recognize, however, that others might prefer to teach assessment later in the term. Therefore, with the possible exception of Chapter 1, the order in which the chapters are studied can be determined by the unique needs of your students.

New to This Edition

We have added and expanded coverage of many topics. You will find:

- Added material connecting the Common Core State Standards and the instruction and assessment of literacy skills.
- A combined word study and vocabulary chapter to help readers integrate these important topics in their teaching.
- More on technology, including comprehension of multimodal texts, enhancing writing instruction with technology tools, and teaching activities with an added technology component.
- Added discussion of teacher techniques during text discussions, strategic moves that help students become more strategic readers.

The Book's Special Features

Some of the special features of *Literacy in Grades 4–8* aid readers in understanding new concepts and vocabulary. Other features are designed to foster reflection and mastery of the material and to encourage readers to try out ideas in the classroom. The following features are particularly noteworthy:

In the Classroom. Each chapter begins with a vignette in which readers observe an authentic classroom setting and see how a practicing teacher deals with the subject addressed in the chapter. These small glimpses of literacy instruction build vicarious background and trigger readers' prior knowledge about the chapter's topic. We refer to the vignette throughout the chapter and in some of the activities, helping readers make the connection between new concepts and classroom instruction. (See page 64 for an example of this feature.)

Activities. More than 50 activities designed for use in classrooms are included in selected chapters. These specific, step-by-step procedures allow readers to put into practice—in their field placement, practicum, or school—the ideas and strategies they encounter in the chapter.

Concept Guides. To help readers follow extended discussions of a topic, we've used special numbered headings that correspond to an introductory list; thus, readers will know, for example, when they've reached item 2 of 4 total discussion points. See page 10 for an example of this feature.

Troubleshooting sections. Many chapters end with a brief section intended to help teachers consider alternative suggestions and activities appropriate for students for whom the literacy focus discussed in the chapter is a particular challenge. Ideas for corrective instruction are offered.

Questions for Journal Writing and Discussion. Questions at the end of each chapter help readers reflect on and internalize key ideas. These questions are suitable for response in journal form or for stimulating lively discussion.

Suggestions for Projects and Field Activities. This special section makes the connection from research and theory to real classroom practice. At the end of each chapter, readers find several suggestions for surveying, interviewing, or observing local teachers to compare strategies presented in the chapter with actual practice. Other activities ask readers to try out a strategy or activity in the chapter with a small group of learners.

Chapter on literacy and the family. Understanding the vast array of literacy practices in students' homes can lead to a partnership between home and school that will greatly enhance the literacy program at school. In exploring this connection, we look at the best ways to communicate with diverse families and foster their active involvement in helping their children become truly literate beings.

Chapter on "orchestration." In the final chapter of the book, we provide an intimate view of the urban classroom of an exemplary teacher who demonstrates many of the procedures, strategies, and ideals presented in the rest of the book. The reader receives a rare insider perspective on how a seasoned teacher makes decisions about classroom climate, materials, and room arrangements, and about how to maximize limited instructional time.

Glossary. An extensive book-end glossary is included, allowing readers to review critical terms and concepts highlighted throughout the text.

Appendices. Book appendices include references for children's and adolescent literature; literacy-related websites suitable for teachers, parents, or students; and a variety of literacy checklists and assessment tools for classroom use.

Student Website: www.hhpcommunities.com/literacyingrades4-8. This interactive, web-based student resource and study guide includes chapter objectives, key concepts, questions and projects, relevant websites, and teaching activities.

Ancillaries. A PowerPoint presentation and Instructor's Manual are available to adopters of this text. The Instructor's Manual provides several valuable tools for each chapter: a summary of key concepts, a list of key vocabulary, suggestions for in-class discussions and activities, and a range of assessment devices, including objective and subjective questions.

Our goal is to offer a text that facilitates the development of reflective teachers who are empowered to think critically about the complicated task of teaching students to become literate. We present evidenced-based perspectives in literacy education, describe a comprehensive range of instructional practices, and show preservice and practicing teachers how to select practices that conform to the individual needs of their students. A caring teacher, armed with the knowledge of how to carry out the most effective practices in literacy, is what is most needed to develop eager and proficient young readers and writers.

Acknowledgments

We wish to extend sincere thanks to the reviewers of this edition in its various stages. They include: Susan Bishcel, University of San Francisco; RoseAnn Donovan, Carroll University; Susan Gebhard, Salem College; Donna Harkins, University of West Georgia; Tamara Hillmer, University of Mississippi; Elizabeth Hommel, Western Illinois University; Helen Maniates, University of San Francisco; Laurie McAdams, Tarleton State University; Betty Murphy, Tarleton State University; Mary Paxton, Shippensburg University; Leslie Potter, Daytona State University; Kathy Rosebrock, University of San Francisco; and Zaline M. Roy-Campbell, Syracuse University. Their comments were insightful and helpful, and the book is better as a result of their efforts.

Special thanks to Colette Kelly and Gay Pauley of Holcomb Hathaway for their expertise, gentle pushing, and careful attention to detail. Thanks, too, to Sally Scott of Holcomb Hathaway for her work in constructing the PowerPoint presentation for this book, and to John and Rhonda Wincek, who designed and typeset the book.

Finally, from Nancy and Joan: High-fives to our husbands, Gary and Charlie, who were ever patient and supportive as we took precious time away from family life to bring this book to fruition. Heartfelt thanks to you both. And from Marcy: Thank you to Nancy and Joan for inviting me to contribute to this edition, and to Miriam and Natalie for being so patient as I worked on the book.

DR. NANCY LEE CECIL has had a rich and varied background in education, as an elementary school teacher and a literacy specialist in New York, urban Savannah, Georgia, and in the public schools in the U.S. Virgin Islands. She is especially attuned to the needs of linguistically and culturally diverse children.

Dr. Cecil received her doctorate from the University of Buffalo and currently teaches in the Department of Teacher Education at California State University in Sacramento, where she won the prestigious Outstanding Educator Award. She has written nineteen books on literacy, most recently *Striking a Balance: A Comprehensive Approach to Early Literacy,* 4th ed., and received the Teacher's Choice award for an earlier book, *For the Love of Language: Poetry for All Learners.* Dr. Cecil has published articles in many literacy journals, including *The Reading Teacher.* She often speaks about literacy to groups of educators on the local, national, and international levels. She lives with her husband, Gary, in Carmichael, California with two cats and a dog, where she enjoys reading, traveling, and hiking, and is involved in the issues of foster care youth.

DR. JOAN P. GIPE has spent many years working with learners of all ages, as a reading specialist in Kentucky, a grade 5 teacher in Indiana, a supervisor in a university reading clinic, and instructor for undergraduate, graduate, and doctoral students in several university contexts. She also has been a supervisor of student teachers, coordinator for teaching enhancement, university liaison for professional development schools, and department chairperson of Curriculum and Instruction.

Dr. Gipe received her doctorate from Purdue University in West Lafayette, Indiana, where she also earned a Distinguished Education Alumna Award. She is Research Professor Emeritus from the University of New Orleans, Department of Curriculum and Instruction, where she was a recipient of several teaching awards and a Career Service Award. She is also Lecturer Emeritus from the Department of Teacher Education at California State University in Sacramento, and is currently engaged in online mentoring of doctoral students for Walden University's Ed.D. Program in Teacher Leadership. Her textbook, *Multiple Paths to Literacy: Assessment and Differentiated Instruction for Diverse Learners, K–12,* is in its eighth edition. Dr. Gipe has published articles in many literacy journals, including *Reading Research Quarterly* and *Journal of Adolescent and Adult Literacy.* She lives in Healdsburg, California with her husband, Charlie, where she enjoys romping with her dog, Cocoa.

DR. MARCY E. MERRILL, before becoming a literacy professor at California State University, Sacramento, was a teacher and reading specialist in Charlottesville, Virginia, city schools, and taught public school in both Georgia and Vermont before that. She has taught students in many grades and at many instructional levels.

Dr. Merrill received her doctorate in reading from the University of Virginia, Charlottesville, following her undergraduate work in English and education at the University of Wisconsin, Madison. Currently, Dr. Merrill works with pre-service teachers in the areas of English methods and academic language or reading across content areas, and with masters students in language and literacy. She has written several publications, and contributed to the Expository Reading and Writing Course curriculum used by California teachers statewide, and has presented at literacy conferences at state, national, and international levels. Dr. Merrill received the Community Service Award and the University Service Award from CSUS. Her research interests include content literacy, writing assessment, expository reading and writing, writing and technology, and digital literacy. She has two wonderful daughters who currently are in middle school.

ONE

A Comprehensive Literacy Program for Grades 4-8

CHAPTER

FOCUS QUESTIONS

- What is literacy?
- What are the major characteristics of the reading process?
- What are the major building blocks for development of literacy knowledge and enjoyment in grades 4–8?
- How does a balanced and comprehensive literacy program for grades 4–8 differ from a more traditional program?
- What are some of the characteristics of learners in grades 4–8?

Mr. Piper's fifth-grade class is learning about the desert. He uses Google Earth to show his students the many deserts that exist around the world. He then asks them to share what they already know about deserts. He writes their answers on the whiteboard under a heading labeled "What We Know." Next, Mr. Piper asks them to think about what they would like to know about deserts and desert life. Students respond enthusiastically, and he writes their questions—such as "Does it ever get cold there?" and "Do they ever run out of water?"—on the whiteboard under a heading labeled "What We Want to Know."

Mr. Piper then invites his students to close their eyes as he takes them on a guided imagery of a trek across the arid desert of Israel's Negev region in the blazing noonday heat. They ride camels for several long, uncomfortable miles and finally stop to rest when the stubborn animals will go no farther. They encounter an angry scorpion behind a bush and, as the sun is at its brightest in the cloudless blue sky, they realize (oh no!) that their water canteens... are empty.

As the students open their eyes, Mr. Piper tells them they will be reading a true story about a 10-year-old boy who gets lost in the harsh desert and must save himself from dehydration by drinking the juice of a giant cactus. He asks them to read silently while thinking about what they would do in the same situation. After everyone has finished reading, a lively discussion ensues, inspired by Mr. Piper's provocative question, "What would you do to survive if you were lost in the desert?" Mr. Piper waits until all the students have had a chance to respond to this question in their journals; then he calls on them, one at a time, until everyone has had a chance to respond. All answers are validated and written on the whiteboard. Later, in writing workshop, the students are divided into small groups to create their own desert survivor manuals using information gleaned from the Internet. Finally, the students revisit their lists and share all that they have learned about desert life, while Mr. Piper records their responses under a heading labeled "What We Learned." Any questions not answered by the reading of the passage lead to a discussion of where answers can be found and, ultimately, self-directed research using the Internet and media center resources.

What Is Literacy?

Literacy is not something we do in school during English, reading, or language arts class. The term *literacy* has come to describe competence in a special field, such as computer or math literacy, and includes many types or multiple literacies, such as visual, media, cultural, and workplace, to name a few.

Today's broader definitions of literacy also include a sociocultural perspective, studying the ways people communicate in various settings and exploring how communication can mediate issues of power and privilege (Gee, 2001; Moje & Lewis, 2007). Academic literacy, or the language of instruction, is taught to help ensure that all students can access the language of school and texts. Disciplinary literacy focuses on the ability to communicate in a specific discipline, such as science. Content literacy refers to skills and strategies used to best understand content information about that discipline. Teachers also need to recognize the importance of visual literacy for today's digital natives. **Visual literacy** refers to the ability to interpret the meaning of visual images as well as being able to construct effective visuals to convey one's ideas to others.

● visual literacy

The union of reading and technology has caused educators to reconsider what it means to be literate in today's world (Leu, 2002; Leu & Kinzer, 2000). Students are now called on to know how to read, write, and comprehend in both the print and digital worlds (Schmar-Dobler, 2003). For example, a student may read a print version of a poem and also listen to an audio version and/or view an illustrated version online. The New Literacies Research Lab at the University of Connecticut studies new literacies and the connection between reading comprehension and technology.

Literacy also involves how new technologies change the ways we think, read, write, speak, visually represent, and so forth. Today's students, for the most part, are learning and growing in a technological environment with access to resources beyond the classroom and school. Technology can enhance the literacy development of students and help to foster relevance and creativity. It is important that we as teachers learn to use these tools effectively. In the United States, most grade 4–8 schools have access to various technological tools and resources, but in some cases only a few teachers are trained to use these tools and integrate them in the classroom to enhance student learning.

Historically, readers who wanted more information would look for it in supplemental readings—either other printed texts or in a different part of the same text. Today, readers using digital technology no longer read linearly. They read in layers or in a recursive way; from a typical starting point, they may explore and follow a number of paths to various interesting places. With the ability to hyperlink, they can make relevant connections with little effort. With nonlinear reading, readers select which links to follow and thus influence their own learning and their interpretations of the text and other resources they encounter. Ideally, all students will know how to navigate online and be able to perform technologically literate tasks such as linking to supporting articles, graphics, videos, audio, and so forth. Today's young people are digital natives, and they prefer to learn this way, negotiating the additional layers of meaning available to them.

Classrooms today must embrace new technologies and the continuously evolving means of acquiring and communicating information (Leu, 2000). Because technological innovations allow us to meet and learn from others around the world, our ability to seek and find information is greater than ever and our global awareness has increased. Our students were once bound by the walls of their school but now are able to become literate members of the worldwide community. As teachers, we need to impart the skills needed to participate in global conversations, but we also need to be mindful of and promote safe uses of this new technology.

From the above discussion, it should be apparent that one definition of literacy cannot encompass all the meanings the term has acquired. For the purpose of this book, however, the following description is useful to consider: **Literacy** is a continuum of skills, including reading, writing, speaking, listening, viewing, visually representing, and critical thinking, applied in a social context to enable a person to function effectively in his or her group and community (Harris & Hodges, 1995).

WWW●●●

**New Literacies
Research Lab**
www.newliteracies.uconn.edu

● literacy

Literacy Instruction and the Constructivist Model

The definition of literacy instruction we use in this book draws on research on the nature of literacy and literacy learning best understood through the ideas of Lev Vygotsky. This forerunner of current understandings of how students learn to read and write defined *instruction* as "helping the student to become interested and involved in a meaningful activity, then providing the student with the support needed to complete the activity successfully" (Vygotsky, 1978, p. 68).

At the heart of the **constructivist model of learning** is the belief that students must actively build their own understandings of all literacy activities. Vygotsky further asserted that all learning is basically a social and psychological process that takes place through interactions between students and others in their environment. Over time, students begin to internalize the skills and knowledge acquired through these social interactions. Bauer (2003) underscores the complexity of this task: "To tackle a course of reading successfully, we have to retrain our minds to grasp new ideas by first understanding them, then evaluating them, and finally forming our own opinions" (p. 19).

● constructivist model of
learning

Teachers whose instruction proceeds from a constructivist model generally include many discussions of literature in their classes, in small, teacher-led groups or in literature circles (see Chapter 5). While teachers may help students get started and then influence the course of the discussions, students are encouraged to share their own responses to what they've read. They keep journals in which they write their reactions and responses to what they have read, or they may decide to create a multimedia project—such as a Prezi or a PowerPoint presentation, a book poster, or a skit based on a scene from the story—to share their responses with their teacher and classmates.

What Is Reading?

reading ●

R eading is the mechanical skill of turning printed symbols into the sounds of our language. Of course, the reason we turn print into sound—in other words, why we read—is to get at the meaning. A major purpose of our reading is to acquire information or enjoyment of some sort from the text, be it printed or digital. We decode printed symbols to discover the author's message and then, more important, we make some meaningful connection to our world (Pearson, 1993). In addition to reading words, new literacies encourage us to read symbols and cues, body language and tone, art, and music—all with the same end goal of comprehension.

Considering that we get information in the same way from spoken language, with meaning residing in the relationship between language and the receiver, we might then ask how writing (which we read) is related to language (which we hear). If language, which is composed of sounds, carries the meaning, what is writing? Writing is a device or a code for representing the sounds of a language in visual form. The written words of a language are just symbols of the spoken words. Reading, then, is the process of turning these printed symbols back into sounds.

But there is more to it. Reading entails both reconstructing an author's message and constructing one's own meaning from the print on the page. We can think of it as a transaction, or an exchange, among the reader, the text, and the purposes and context of the reading situation. A reader's reconstruction of the author's intended ideas and information is somewhat like a listener's reconstruction of ideas from the combination of sounds a speaker makes. Put another way, an artist creates a masterpiece that means one thing to her but has a host of different meanings to admirers of her work. Likewise, the reader may create meanings that are different from those intended by the author. What readers understand from the reconstructed and constructed meanings depends on their prior knowledge, prior experiences, and proficiency in using language in differing social contexts.

Characteristics of the Reading Process

A comprehensive approach to literacy instruction starts with the assumption that the purpose of reading is to create meaning from print. Early readers focus their attention on acquiring fluency as they learn to decode print; more proficient decoders are better able to address the subtle facets of critical reading and responding. In either case, the reading process consists of similar fundamental characteristics—whether the reader in question has recently learned to "crack the code" or is decoding fluently and "reading to learn."

Four essential underlying characteristics comprising the meaning-making process are the assumptions that

① reading is a *holistic* process,

② reading is a *constructive* process,

③ reading is a *strategic* process, and

④ reading is an *interactive* process.

The students in the classroom scenario at the beginning of this chapter were engaged in a literacy lesson that incorporated all of these underlying characteristics.

In the following sections, we will explore these characteristics to provide a better understanding of the complex nature of the reading process.

① Reading Is a Holistic Process

The students in Mr. Piper's class used reading as a *holistic* process: they pieced together all of their decoding and comprehension skills to think about the story. Observing such advanced readers shows us that reading is not simply the sum total of the discrete skills that we have students practice; rather, reading is a holistic process whereby the various subskills—such as decoding, finding the main idea, and using imagery—must be integrated to form a smooth, coherent whole (Baumann, Hoffman, Moon, & Duffy-Hester, 1998). The subskills, though crucial, must be applied to the act of reading by a competent reader who puts all the pieces together through constant practice. These subskills, and how they relate to each other, are outlined in Figure 1.1. As you can see, the subskills lead to recognizing and understanding words and ideas.

② Reading Is a Constructive Process

The students in Mr. Piper's class saw reading as a *constructive* process: they read to discover how the boy survived in the desert and thought about what they might do under the same circumstances. As proficient readers engage in reading text and predicting what may happen next, they construct meaning in their minds (Rumelhart, 1977; Stanovich, 1980). That meaning is not only found in the words of the text but is also negotiated with the reader's imagination and experience. Readers need to use what is already in their minds and combine it with what they find on the page (or on screen) in order to construct a meaning based on a reconciliation of these two sets of input.

Construct meaning by Predicting

③ Reading Is a Strategic Process

The students in Mr. Piper's class used reading as a *strategic* process: they used mental imagery to "see" the desert in their mind's eye. Proficient readers use different strategies depending on the purpose for reading and the difficulty and genre of the material. The purpose for reading may be to determine who stole the wallet, to learn more about the beauty of faraway places, to memorize a poem, or to put together a model airplane. Having in mind the exact purpose for which they are reading helps students use appropriate strategies for the nature of the literacy task at hand.

Tell students the Purpose

④ Reading Is an Interactive Process

Finally, the students in Mr. Piper's class used reading as an *interactive* process: they compared their own knowledge of the desert with the information the

I. EMERGENT LITERACY FACTORS

Concepts about print (orthographic knowledge)

Experiential background

Language development

Visual acuity and discrimination

Auditory acuity and discrimination

Phonemic awareness

II. RECOGNIZING AND UNDERSTANDING WORDS

Sight Words

Word Study Skills

- Context clues
- Phonic analysis (single consonants, blends, vowels, digraphs, diphthongs, accents)
- Structural analysis (root words, inflectional endings, compound words, contractions, prefixes, suffixes, syllables, morphemes)
- Orthography

Vocabulary Development

- Context clues
- Multiple meanings
- Synonyms and antonyms
- Shades of meaning
- Word origins (etymology)

Dictionary Skills

- Locating words
- Using pronunciation key
- Finding appropriate definition
- History of words

Oral Reading Skills

- Phrasing and punctuation
- Fluency (accuracy, rate, prosody, and expression)
- Pronunciation and enunciation
- Eye–voice span

III. RECOGNIZING AND UNDERSTANDING IDEAS

Comprehension Skills

- Receptive (non-oral) reading
  - Literal meanings (details, main ideas, sequence, directions)
  - Implied meanings (genre-specific knowledge, fact or fiction, characterization and setting, relationships, predicting outcomes, author's tone, mood, intent, comparisons and contrasts, conclusions and generalizations)
  - Background knowledge required (amount, kinds, accessing background knowledge, integrating text information with knowledge of other texts and experiences)
- Critical reading
  - Fact or opinion
  - Appraisal of author
  - Biased statements
  - Propaganda techniques
  - Cause and effect
  - Comparison and contrast
  - Figures of speech
  - Drawing conclusions
  - Locating information
  - Selecting and evaluating sources
  - Organizing
  - Interpreting maps, graphs, etc.
  - Using SQ3R procedure
- Creative reading
  - Convergent (read to solve a problem)
  - Divergent (go beyond author to new ideas)
- Ability to use complex reading skills to comprehend information
  - Implied textual information
  - Metacognition to acknowledge and revise meaning when text does not make sense
  - Integration of new information
  - Use of ideas and information from text to meet specific purpose set as reader
  - Ability to respond to multiple levels of rigor to answer questions about a text
- Rate of Comprehension Skills
  - Flexibility
  - Skimming
  - Silent reading habits

author provided. Reading is a process in which the reader must actually interact, or negotiate meaning, with the author and text in order for true comprehension to occur (Buehl, 2001; Rosenblatt, 1983). What the reader brings to the text in terms of prior knowledge of content, writing style, and vocabulary determines how well he will be able to derive a rich meaning from the text. We have all had the experience of reading something about which we had little or no background knowledge, or **schema**. When this happens, we soon realize that although we may know many of the words, we cannot make sense of the material. We do not have the background needed to construct meaning.

● schema

The Relationship of Reading to the Other Language Arts

Literacy is more than just reading, for it encompasses all the various ways in which we can communicate. Learning to communicate through language is at the heart of how we relate to others and, therefore, who we are. We learn language naturally by listening to and imitating the language of others and then, gradually, by using that language to express our needs and wants. Constant modeling and feedback from family members, teachers, and caretakers help us understand how to interpret and construct language for our own purposes.

We call the set of language processes that form literacy the *language arts*. The six language arts, as designated by the National Council of Teachers of English (NCTE) and the International Reading Association (IRA), are listening, speaking, reading, writing, viewing, and visually representing (*Standards for the English Language Arts*, 1996). The first four have historically been considered the language arts, but the Internet and other visual media have changed the way we obtain our information; hence, viewing and visually representing have come to be accepted as valid means of communication and comprise the last two entries in the list (Eagleton & Dobler, 2006). Three of the processes—speaking, writing, and visually representing—are ways of actively expressing information; reading, listening, and viewing, by contrast, are ways of receiving information (Roe & Ross, 2006).

Both reading and writing require interpretation of meaning.

Students do not gain reading proficiency in isolation; they develop, simultaneously, all of the language skills they need to communicate. Research and practical classroom experience clearly indicate how each of the language arts depends on the others for successful communication. Let us now look at the importance of the other five language arts, which are reciprocal and supportive processes for reading development.

● *Listening.* Listening has been called the "neglected" language art because it is so seldom taught in the literacy curriculum (Pinnell & Jaggar, 2003). Good listening consists of the ability to understand what is said: that is, to interpret the use of words, phrases, and intonation so that the content and intent of what is communicated are appreciated. Listening ability is also important in learning to differentiate various speech sounds and to associate sounds and meaning with particular letter shapes and word forms. Listening is, therefore, an aid to word recognition. It directs attention to words that have common sounds and helps students, especially those for whom English is a second language, to appreciate the unique cadences of the English language. Moreover, highly developed listening comprehension skills, not surprisingly, are strongly correlated with increased reading comprehension skills (Pinnell & Jaggar, 2003).

- *Speaking.* Speaking, or oral language facility, is directly related to the ability to read; in oral language the symbols are spoken, whereas in reading the same symbols have been written. Reading instruction builds especially on oral language. If this foundation is weak, progress in reading can be slow and uncertain (Pinnell & Jaggar, 2003). Readers must have at least a basic store of words, a reasonable knowledge about the world around them, and the ability to talk about their knowledge. These abilities form the basis for comprehending text.

- *Writing.* Reading involves learning to communicate through written symbols using a background of experiences. Writing involves encoding those symbols in order to communicate ideas—based on experience, imagination, or research—to others. Additionally, both reading and writing require interpretation of meaning. With writing, the writer interprets a message for or conveys the meaning to readers through the creation of text, whereas with reading the reader interprets the meaning of text already formulated. There are practical benefits to connecting reading and writing. Reading contributes to students' writing development, and writing contributes to students' reading development. Reading influences writing skills because readers unconsciously begin to "read like writers" (Gambrell, 2005). To read like a writer, a student must engage with the author and what that author is thinking and feeling. Over time, that student learns to write like a writer.

viewing ●

- *Viewing.* **Viewing** refers to the interpretation and analysis of visual media. These media include photographs, illustrations, graphs, maps, and diagrams found in books, as well as videos viewed on television, in movies and on DVDs, or online. Until recently, this skill was largely ignored. Today's students are inundated with visual media that attempt to convey information, persuade them to believe something or take a particular action, or entertain them. Messages received from visual media must be understood using the same thinking processes used for understanding printed material.

visually representing ●

- *Visually representing.* Visual representing has become more prominent as technological media have become more available. **Visually representing** refers to communicating through visual images, which can be as varied as photographs, cartoons, drawings, video presentations, and other image types. Much as students become readers by writing, they become more astute at, and open to, viewing media critically if they have been given plenty of opportunities to enhance written reports and narratives by creating their own multimedia presentations.

What Is a Balanced and Comprehensive Approach to Literacy in Grades 4–8?

In recent years, teachers of grades 4–8 have worked to reconcile differences in perspectives on literacy. Most teachers now agree that reading is a complex process incorporating the four characteristics (holistic, constructive, strategic, and interactive) discussed previously and evident in the chapter-opening scenario. Moreover, research has provided abundant support for the notion that a committed teacher who can integrate a program of explicit, systematic phonics instruction into a curriculum rich with quality literature, easily decodable text, and a variety of meaningful writing experiences will have the best chance of teaching students who will learn how to read and do so willingly—far beyond the classroom door (Larsen-Blair & Williams, 1999; Stahl, 1992).

Most reading educators have long agreed that a certain amount of direct instruction in phonics is vital for learning how to decode automatically, but most have also maintained a belief that incorporating the basic elements of a holistic, meaning-based program into such instruction will increase the instruction's positive influence on students' later attitudes toward reading as a chosen activity (Wink, 1996). To one degree or another, most literacy teachers now try to incorporate the best of both perspectives in a balanced and comprehensive approach to teaching literacy. They are seeing results, too, measured by their own observations and rising test scores; these results have come about by infusing many meaning-based strategies with a structured, skills-based program, or by supplementing a holistic, literature-based program with a systematic phonics program (Cecil, 2011).

Attention has focused not only on early reading instruction, with its emphasis on teaching students *how to read,* but on another, equally important phase: when readers have mastered the basic foundational skills of reading, they then need help learning *how to read to learn.* As students move through grades 4–8, when most are well supplied with a compendium of automatic decoding skills, they require a program of literacy that is both balanced in instruction and comprehensive in breadth.

Unfortunately, such a rich, comprehensive program often proves elusive. Dillon (2006) reports on a survey conducted by the Center on Education Policy that shows a majority of the nation's school districts have reduced the amount of time spent on the content areas to allow more time for basic reading and math, thus narrowing the curriculum. Pearson (2006) expresses concern that reducing the amount of time spent reading in the content areas is harmful for reading proficiency. In his opinion, "Reading and writing must always be about something, and the something comes from subject matter pedagogy—not from more practice of reading skills. Reading skills are important, but without knowledge, they are pretty useless" (p. 22).

The Alliance for Excellent Education agrees, reporting in *Reading Today* (2005) that middle school youngsters need a "more balanced approach to literacy education that builds on what was taught in the earlier grades" (p. 23). Their report lays out the elements that must be contained in a comprehensive and exemplary literacy curriculum:

- direct, explicit comprehension instruction
- instructional principles embedded in content reading
- self-directed learning
- collaborative learning
- tutoring
- a rich diversity of texts
- much writing
- instruction in technology
- ongoing assessment
- a large block of time for reading

We would enlarge this list somewhat and suggest that a comprehensive program also include:

- quality literature with personal response and analysis
- the use of multiple measures for assessment
- instruction in word identification and vocabulary strategies, such as the morphology and etymology of words
- instruction in reading comprehension strategies
- fostering of independent reading
- development of oral and written language and visual learning

Teacher and Student Roles

One basic difference between a balanced and comprehensive literacy program and a more traditional/skills-based view can be seen in the relative roles of the teacher and students in such classrooms. In a balanced and comprehensive program, the teacher's role is one of facilitator, offering students prompts and questions to focus their attention on strategies that will help them independently overcome challenges in present and future texts; in more traditional approaches, the teacher's role is directive, supplying short-term help by telling students exactly what to do when they encounter difficulties. The aim of a balanced and comprehensive literacy program is to develop enthusiastic readers and writers who question, consider alternatives, and make informed choices as they seek meaning or express meaning; the aim of the more traditional approach to literacy is often to lead students through a predetermined teaching sequence to ensure that all the basic skills of literacy are covered. Finally, as Figure 1.2 shows, a balanced, comprehensive literacy program is based on the understanding that it is students themselves who are readers and, as such, they must bring meaning to and gain meaning from text as they read.

Affective and Cognitive Components

A balanced and comprehensive literacy program in grades 4–8 also consists of five major affective and cognitive components. When offered separately, these components are crucial building blocks for literacy knowledge and enjoyment; when they come together as a whole entity, they are the essence of a strong literacy program. These five components are:

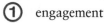

① engagement

② transmission and transaction

③ explanations and examples

④ application, guided practice, and personal response

⑤ respect for each student's culture and background

① Engagement

That a student must be engaged in a subject to learn most effectively is not a new concept, nor one espoused only by literacy experts. Many years ago Jerome Bruner (1966) expounded on the importance of getting students interested and involved in learning, and a plethora of motivational educational programs and learning theories have emanated from his hypotheses. Educators are now convinced that when students are highly engaged in what they are doing and their

Comparison of two approaches to teaching reading/literacy.   *figure* **1.2**

BALANCED AND COMPREHENSIVE LITERACY PROGRAM	TRADITIONAL/SKILLS-BASED LITERACY PROGRAM
The teacher's role is to empower by providing instruction and questions that focus students' attention on: • strategies that will help them to decode and understand text; • becoming aware of textual cues that help students decode and comprehend. Readers are taught directly how to overcome challenges in present and future text.	The teacher's role is to supply short-term help by: • focusing students' attention on specific textual details; • explaining the meaning of a word if they don't know it; • explaining the meaning of text. Readers become dependent upon the teacher to tell them exactly what to do in each reading situation.
The goals of a balanced and comprehensive literacy program are to: • create independent readers who question, consider alternatives, and make informed inferences as they search for meaning; • entitle students to become independent problem solvers who can become long-term learners; • show students how and why to choose and employ strategies to ensure that meaning is gained and maintained; • use assessment to inform instruction.	The goals of a traditional, skills-based literacy program are to: • lead students through a predetermined teaching sequence using a specific book to teach a particular skill; • see that every student receives all the skills in a predetermined hierarchy, whether they are needed or not; • frequently administer formalized assessment devices that provide information about progress in the specific program.
A balanced and comprehensive literacy program is based upon the understanding that: • students are the readers; • students are the ones who must bring meaning to, and gain meaning from, the text they read. The teacher is aware of the constant need for comprehension to be considered as the act of the reader engaging with, and responding to, the text during reading.	A traditional, skills-based literacy program is based upon the understanding that: • connections between the reader and the author depend upon the teacher as interpreter; • the teacher is responsible for determining whether students understand. The teacher oversees comprehension for students and alerts them to mismatches between the errors and the text, hoping the students will use this behavior in the future.

experiences are meaningful and purposeful to them, learning is optimal (Guthrie & Wigfield, 1997).

Engagement with reading material may be considered the key to learning in a balanced and comprehensive literacy program; however, it often seems that, as students go through school, their motivation for school—and for reading— too often decreases. The less they enjoy reading, the less they will read, and a downward cycle is set in motion. Practice in literacy, as in anything else, results in greater proficiency. Indeed, how much students read is one of the best predictors of how well they read and write. Therefore, if we want all students to read and write as well as they possibly can, we must find ways to combat the problem of decreasing motivation leading to *aliteracy*—a state of being able to read but choosing not to—especially as students move into the middle grades (Cunningham & Allington, 2010).

engagement ●

The answer to the question of how to engage students lies not only in the method used, but also in the effectiveness and enthusiasm of the teacher. **Engagement** involves a complex set of ongoing attitudes and activities that occur in the classroom and that lead to the creation of a community of learners (including the teacher) finding excitement and pleasure in all aspects of the literacy process. Such a teacher is thoughtfully eclectic, modifying methods and programs to fit students' needs. Teachers with the ability to engage learners do not rely on a single method or program for all students in their charge, because they know that good teaching requires "doing the right thing the right way and at the right time in response to problems posed by particular [students] on particular occasions" (Garrison, 1997, p. 132; see also Nelson-Levitt, 2000).

② Transmission and Transaction

transmission model ●

transactional model ●

In grades 4–8, a balance must exist between directly conveying information to students through explicit instruction and systematic teaching—the **transmission model**—and negotiating with them about their individual thoughts and ideas about what they are reading and writing—the **transactional model** (Rosenblatt, 1978). A balanced and comprehensive approach to literacy uses both a transmission model and a transactional model, but at different times and for different purposes.

③ Explanations and Examples

In a balanced and comprehensive literacy program, students need to be explicitly taught how proficient readers construct text in order to comprehend written material. Explicit teaching involves making clear to students the particular skill they are learning, how they can best learn it, when and under what conditions to use the skill, and how they will know when they have been successful. They must be shown how effective comprehension strategies work, and then they must be given examples of how each strategy can help them as they read to create meaning from the written page. Although this may appear to be a basic truth, such explicit teaching has not always occurred in U.S. schools.

Dolores Durkin, in a landmark study of comprehension instruction in American schools (1990), found that little, if any, explanation of how to use comprehension strategies was offered in elementary schools. Instead, much time was devoted to assessing how well students comprehended, using reams of basal workbook pages to do so. In other words, students were expected to "intuit" comprehension strategies without anyone ever having taught them, directly, how to use them! The results of this study caused a flurry of reform, dedicated to teaching comprehension strategies to students directly in a systematic fashion.

Explanations and examples are necessary in a balanced and comprehensive literacy program and are useful for fostering construction of text; most teachers are now aware of the need to teach strategies directly to students. Teaching suggestions come from well-regarded researchers; for example, Nell Duke and her colleagues determined from their research that teachers must provide the following essential elements of effective reading comprehension instruction (Duke, Pearson, Strachan, & Billman, 2011, p. 52):

1. Build disciplinary and world knowledge.
2. Provide exposure to a volume and range of texts.
3. Provide motivating texts and contexts for reading.
4. Teach strategies for comprehending.

5. Teach text structures.
6. Engage students in discussion.
7. Build vocabulary and language knowledge.
8. Integrate reading and writing.
9. Observe and assess.
10. Differentiate instruction.

As teachers embrace the strategies that will provide opportunities for more critical thinking and deeper understanding of text, their students will become more strategic, independent readers who are better prepared to encounter new ideas and text.

④ Application, Guided Practice, and Personal Response

A review of important research on successful literacy programs offers teachers surprisingly consistent findings about what factors are critical in setting the stage for a successful balanced and comprehensive literacy program that enables students to construct meaning. Fielding and Pearson (1994), synthesizing the findings of research on reading comprehension, offer three critical findings to teachers:

- **Provide a large block of time for application of newly acquired literacy skills.** The amount of time devoted to actual reading and writing practice should be greater than the sum total of all specific skill instruction. In other words, after a skill or comprehension strategy has been introduced, students should have ample time immediately following these instructional sessions to internalize their new understandings; students should be actively adding them to their increased literacy knowledge through extensive teacher-guided practice.

- **Provide opportunities for students to practice literacy skills in a social setting.** Students, especially English learners, learn best when they are able to talk about what they are reading and writing. When reading becomes a social activity, it enhances student learning by adding sensory input and vocabulary development afforded by oral discussion; it is also more enjoyable for most students. Therefore, in a balanced and comprehensive literacy program, a continuum of literacy instructional configurations should be offered in most classrooms.

- **Ensure that students are given myriad opportunities to respond personally to text.** To act on this suggestion, teachers must allow time for the type of critical and creative questions for which there is no one "correct" answer and to which every student has an opportunity to voice an opinion (e.g., "What would *you* have done if the bully had treated you that way?"). It is also helpful for teachers to pose provocative questions for which they themselves do not have an answer, not seeking a specific response or one provided by the teacher's manual. Moreover, in a truly balanced and comprehensive program for grades 4–8, adequate time should be set aside for sharing reactions to literature, or for original writing—in small groups or in email, wikis, or blogs—where the climate is risk free and conducive to personal conversations about text.

⑤ Respect for Each Student's Culture and Background

Finally, perhaps the most pressing issue in a balanced and comprehensive classroom is for teachers to possess a deep sensitivity and appreciation for learners of all backgrounds. Diversity must never be merely tolerated but must be actively celebrated by the teacher as well as by students. We cannot hope to be successful with all learners in today's heterogeneous classrooms without first understanding our students' reasons for becoming literate. Without that knowledge, we may fail in our attempts to fully engage learners as equal partners in their pursuit of knowledge. As teachers, we must lead students to fall in love with reading and writing and, as Lucy Calkins (1994, p. 111) suggests, we must get them to "write from the heart about their own unique experiences with the world." Then they will be able to see the purpose of learning and, consequently, become actual co-conspirators in their quest for literacy.

Instruction in literacy, to be successful, must take into account each student's culture and understand each student's particular way of learning. All human beings learn according to their existing understandings and cultural backgrounds in socially constructed settings, particularly through conversations with family and loved ones. Therefore, any instructional plans in literacy must be developed with great care, using observation, home visits, and formal and informal assessment, along with all other available background information about students' language, culture, values, knowledge, and interests.

A National Focus on Literacy

This is an exciting time to be a literacy teacher. We have more conclusive evidence about what can be considered "effective literacy instruction" now than at any other time in history (Block, 2004); this evidence is supported by a number of reports from national advocacy groups about best practices in reading (National Institute of Child Health and Human Development, 2000a, 2000b; Sweet & Snow, 2002).

Educators have long known that the teaching of literacy is one of the most important tasks—if not *the* most important task—that every teacher faces. For years teachers may have taught literacy using the instructor's manual of the basal reader, but they always sought additional ways to reach every student, to find out what would work best. They often supplemented the literacy curriculum with activities taken from *Instructor* magazine or from an educational website or blog, or they may have borrowed ideas from other teachers or a summer workshop, trying every new commercial program that promised to make all students successful readers (Kronowitz, 2011). Some have even tried to implement quick-fix programs that promote "the best way" to help students learn to read and write. We know these programs can be problematic, because every student is different and every class has different needs; thus, there can be no one perfect program or one identified remedy to fit all students. Instead, literacy learning needs teachers who assess the needs of their classrooms, identify patterns of strengths and weaknesses in their students, and teach students what they need to know using a comprehensive approach to learning that best fits all learners. As instructional leaders, it is imperative that teachers select appropriate materials that provide instruction for students (not merely assign them work to do), facilitate practice time, and assess the learning process. When these necessary steps happen, learning takes place.

The teaching of literacy is one of the most important tasks that every teacher faces.

Literacy is very much on the minds of politicians, the media, and the public. Teachers in the United States have witnessed unprecedented political insistence on the use of research-based, scientifically proven assessments and instructional techniques (Invernezzi, Landrum, Howell, & Warley, 2005). Research offers compelling reasons to explain why so many students have failed to read using traditional reading methods. The Eunice Kennedy Shriver National Institute of Child Health and Development (NICHD), for example, conducts and supports a variety of research aimed at understanding the process of reading and identifying the best ways to help people who struggle with reading; it also aims to understand the mechanisms of reading disorders and the best interventions for improving reading skills. Their website, at www.nichd.nih.gov, offers more information on their research goals, activities, advances, and myriad scientific articles.

In 2000, the National Reading Panel (NRP) added another voice to the discussion. They issued a report in response to a congressional mandate to help parents, teachers, and policymakers identify key skills and methods crucial for reading achievement. In addition to discussing effective practices, the panel identified five areas that are essential to reading success: phonemic awareness, phonics, fluency, vocabulary, and comprehension.

Influenced by the NRP's report, the No Child Left Behind (NCLB) Act of 2001 mandated higher standards and greater accountability throughout the nation's school systems. A decade later, in 2010, the National Governors Association Council for Best Practices (NGACBP) and the Council of Chief State School Officers (CCSSO) led the development of the Common Core State Standards (CCSS). These are a set of English language arts and math standards voluntarily adopted across states to ensure that students are prepared to succeed in college and in their careers. Currently, almost all states have adopted the CCSS. Although some states have minimally modified them to adjust to their specific needs, the standards all remain rigorous. The mission of the CCSS is to

> Provide a consistent, clear understanding of what students are expected to learn, so teachers and parents know what they need to do to help them. The standards are designed to be robust and relevant to the real world, reflecting the knowledge and skills that our young people need for success in college and careers. With American students fully prepared for the future, our communities will be best positioned to compete successfully in the global economy. (NGACBP & CCSO, 2010)

Even in grades 4–8, teachers are being asked to prepare students for college and the workplace. What is most promising about these standards is that English language arts are woven throughout the content areas, offering literacy in history/ social studies, science, and technical subjects, and they "insist that instruction in reading, writing, speaking, listening, and language be a shared responsibility within in the school" (NGACBP & CCSO, 2010, p. 4). Since we know that each subject area contributes to students' literacy learning, the standards highlight particular skills and strategies to emphasize in content area classes. Therefore, when we discuss standards in this book, it is content standards that are our focus.

WWW○○○

Common Core State Standards

www.corestandards.org

The report of the National Reading Panel, NCLB, resultant legislation, and the CCSS have all changed the way teachers regard instruction. A more informed profession now demands materials that are based on sound scientific evidence. This can only be good; however, other aspects of literacy besides the five areas specifically identified by the NRP are also important. These aspects provide richness and motivation for students and create a broad-based literacy program that ensures that students learn to read, read to learn, and enjoy the process. This text takes a wider focus, providing the reader with the tools for what can be called a balanced, comprehensive approach to literacy.

Characteristics of Learners in Grades 4–8

Teaching literacy in grades 4–8 offers a wide range of exciting instructional possibilities, as well as the satisfaction that comes from sharing the spectrum of literacy activities with a community of young learners who have curious, challenging, and highly creative minds. Students in this age group also often possess a fascinating combination of tremendous enthusiasm and an increased ability to examine ideas critically. The challenges and the rewards of teaching students in this age group are, arguably, greater than for any other (Atwell, 1998).

Ages 9 to 14, the traditional age span of students in these grades, are times of major transitions. Students in the turbulent period of pre- and early adolescence universally experience challenging physical, intellectual, and emotional characteristics. It is essential that we as teachers consider these characteristics, as they have a direct bearing on student responses to the literacy curriculum.

Students in this age group can manifest pronounced behavior that often baffles new teachers. Student attitudes and behavior can change from one moment to the next, seemingly for no reason. The unexpected becomes the norm. A student who one day exhibits all the traits of an extremely engaged reader and writer may, the next day, be difficult and unresponsive. This inconsistent behavior in pre- and early adolescence is due in part to the tremendous physical changes taking place at a rapid and irregular pace as youngsters reach physical maturity.

Any successful intermediate or middle school literacy curriculum must consider the unique attributes of students at this age. Teachers learn to build a degree of flexibility into their lessons to capitalize on students' boundless energy and to accommodate the shifting patterns of their behavior. Goals and objectives may be accomplished through a variety of literacy activities and experiences that can become helpful outlets for the students' volatile—and confusing—feelings. Writing, speaking, creating multimedia presentations, reading (whether it is informational texts or fiction about matters that interest them), and researching and learning interactively online, among other literacy forums, can provide outlets for students' energies, as long as they are given choices and opportunities to use their increasing social skills to collaborate with their peers.

Finally, although students of all ages need verbal reinforcement and praise to develop positive self-perceptions and the confidence to attempt new challenges, this is especially true for students in grades 4–8. The ultimate goal for literacy teachers is to help these students become consumers and producers of all facets of literacy.

Summary

The past decade has seen a major emphasis on creating a balanced and comprehensive literacy program not only with young children learning how to read but also with older students, most of whom have mastered early skills and are now ready to turn their attention to reading to learn. For either developmental level, the fundamental characteristics of the process are essentially the same. Reading is a holistic process, not just a sum of all of its parts. It is a constructive process whereby readers predict the meaning of the text. It is also a strategic process in which readers must choose which strategies in their repertoire are appropriate to the task. Additionally, reading is an interactive process, with readers and authors together negotiating the meaning of the text.

A balanced and comprehensive approach to literacy differs from a more traditional approach mainly in its view of who holds responsibility for meaning-making from text. In a balanced and comprehensive approach, the teacher accepts the role of facilitator—prompting, advising, questioning, and providing direct instruction about reading strategies, yet allowing students the freedom to interpret text according to their own experiences.

A balanced and comprehensive approach to literacy for students in grades 4–8 differs from a similar approach used for early readers in that the focus is less on decoding and more on making sense of the world through print. Many of the underlying beliefs remain the same, but the focus shifts slightly in subtle ways. While there must continue to be a transmission of strategies—in this case related more to comprehension than to decoding—there must also be an emphasis on transaction, or a personal meaning-making with text. In addition, engagement is crucial to ensure that students, now able to read, do so willingly as a chosen recreational activity. Clear explanations and examples are critical to make sure students know exactly how to apply the comprehension strategies that proficient readers use. In addition to providing examples, teachers regularly assess students to be sure they can apply these lifelong reading strategies, providing more practice time as needed. Abundant guided practice and opportunities to apply the skills that have been taught will help to solidify understandings and increase students' confidence and enjoyment. Whole texts and authentic literature, both fiction and nonfiction, can be used for these purposes. Finally, a clear respect and appreciation for the culture and background of all learners will enable the teacher to understand what each learner needs to become a literate individual.

Our definition of literacy has expanded. New technologies bring great promise to classrooms as we explore multimedia/hypermedia resources, digital storytelling, handheld personal communication devices, and much more. Will we devote the needed time and resources to professional development to learn what technology can do to support young learners? What research is being done to support this effort? Our students are motivated and engaged with technology, new literacies help to promote critical thinking by way of technology, and the majority of our schools have technological tools to use with our students. Even though technology continually changes, we must integrate new ways of thinking and engaging students with text through the use of new tools.

In the following chapters we explore the specific components needed in a balanced and comprehensive literacy program for grades 4–8 that will help to develop readers and writers who have the tools to read, write, and incorporate technology—and do so joyfully—to explore their worlds.

Questions FOR JOURNAL WRITING AND DISCUSSION

1. Reflect on your own experiences with reading and writing when you were in grades 4 through 8. What kind of model of instruction did you receive? Do you believe it was balanced and comprehensive, or was it a more traditional method of instruction? Give examples. In retrospect, can you think of any measures your teachers might have employed to make your literacy instruction more meaningful?

2. Think about your own definition of what it means to be a literate person. How do you think your definition will influence how you teach reading, writing, listening, speaking, viewing, and visually representing?

3. Discuss with a classmate what you consider to be the three most striking differences between literacy instruction today and in the recent past. What do you think caused these differences?

ⓢuggestions FOR PROJECTS AND FIELD ACTIVITIES

1. Make notes while observing a literacy lesson in a grade 4–8 classroom. Analyze the lesson in terms of the components of a balanced and comprehensive literacy program proposed in this chapter.

2. Ask a group of intermediate or middle-school students to discuss the characteristics they feel a good literacy teacher should possess. Then ask them how they feel when they are allowed to select their own materials to read, write about, discuss, or analyze. Is it easier or more difficult for them to create without first being given an idea and/or a direction?

3. Consider the ways you will provide instruction in literacy development. What kinds of activities would you have liked to experience in these grades? How will you model these learning activities? How will you practice facilitating them? How will you assess your students' learning and understanding? With your instructor or a classmate, plan a lesson, including these learning activities, that you might teach to a small group of intermediate or middle-school students.

4. List the six components of the language arts outlined in this chapter. Ask some middle-school teachers to describe how they address each of them when planning the year's literacy curriculum.

REFERENCES

Alliance for Excellent Education (2005). Report targets reading in middle school and high school. *Reading Today* (February–March), 22, 23.

Atwell, N. (1998). *In the middle: New understandings about writing, reading, and learning* (2nd ed.). Portsmouth, NH: Boynton/Cook.

Bauer, S. W. (2003). *The well-educated mind: A guide to the classical education you never had.* New York: W.W. Norton.

Baumann, J. F., Hoffman, J. V., Moon, J., & Duffy-Hester, A. M. (1998). Where are the teachers' voices in the phonics/whole language debate? Results from a survey of U.S. elementary teachers. *The Reading Teacher, 51,* 636–650.

Block, C. C. (2004). *Teaching comprehension: The comprehension process approach.* Boston: Allyn & Bacon.

Bruner, J. (1966). *Toward a theory of instruction.* Cambridge, MA: Harvard University Press.

Buehl, D. (2001). *Literacy-building strategies for content teachers.* Newark, DE: International Reading Association.

Calkins, L. M. (1994). *The art of teaching writing.* Portsmouth, NH: Heinemann.

Cecil, N. L. (2011). *Striking a balance: A comprehensive approach to early literacy* (4th ed.). Scottsdale, AZ: Holcomb Hathaway.

Cooper, J. D., Kiger, N. D, Robinson, M. D., & Slansky, J. A. (2012). *Literacy: Helping students construct meaning* (8th ed.). Independence, KY: Wadsworth Cengage Learning.

Cunningham, P. M., & Allington, R. L. (2010). *Classrooms that work: They can all read and write* (5th ed.). New York: Pearson.

Dillon, S. (2006). Schools cut back subjects to push math and reading. *New York Times* (March 26): 1, 16.

Duke, N. K., & Carlisle, J. F. (2011). The development of comprehension. In M. L. Kamil, P. D. Pearson, E. B. Moje, & P. Afflerbach (Eds.), *Handbook of reading research* (Vol. IV), pp. 199–228. London: Routledge.

Duke, N. K., Pearson, P. D., Strachan, S. L., & Billman, A. K. (2011). Essential elements of fostering and teaching reading comprehension. In S.J. Samuels & A.E. Farstrup (Eds.), *What research has to say about reading instruction* (4th ed.), pp. 51–93. Newark, DE: International Reading Association.

Durkin, D. (1990). Delores Durkin speaks on instruction. *The Reading Teacher, 43,* 472–476.

Eagleton, M. B., & Dobler, E. (2006). *Reading the web: Strategies for Internet inquiry.* New York: Guilford Press.

Fielding, L. G., & Pearson, P. D. (1994). Reading comprehension: What works. *Educational Leadership, 51* (5), 62–68.

Gambrell, L. B. (2005). Reading literature, reading text, reading the Internet: The times they are a' changing. *The Reading Teacher, 58,* 588–591.

Garrison, J. (1997). *Dewey and Eros: Wisdom and desire in the art of teaching.* New York: Teachers College Press.

Gee, J. P. (2001). "Literacy, discourse, and linguistics: Introduction and what is literacy?" In E. Cushman, E. R. Kintgen, B. M. Kroll, & M. Rose (Eds.), *Literacy: A critical sourcebook* (pp. 525–544). Boston: Bedford/St. Martin's.

Guthrie, J. T., & Wigfield, A. (Eds.). (1997). *Reading engagement: Motivating readers through integrated instruction.* Newark, DE: International Reading Association.

Harris, T. L., & Hodges, R. E. (Eds.). (1995). *The literacy dictionary: The vocabulary of reading and writing.* Newark, DE: International Reading Association.

Invernezzi, M. A., Landrum, T. J., Howell, J. L., & Warley, H. P. (2005). Toward the peaceful coexistence of test developers, policy-makers, and teachers in an era of accountability. *The Reading Teacher, 58,* 610–618.

Kress, G. (2003). *Literacy in the new media age.* London: Routledge.

Kronowitz, E. L. (2011). *The teacher's guide to success* (2nd ed.) Boston: Pearson Education.

Larsen-Blair, S. M., & Williams, K. A. (1999). *The balanced reading program: Helping all students achieve success.* Newark, DE: International Reading Association.

Leu, D. J., Jr. (2000). Literacy and technology: Deictic consequences for literacy education in an information age. In M. L. Kamil, P. B. Mosenthal, P. D. Pearson, & R. Barr (Eds.), *Handbook of reading research* (Vol. III), pp. 743–770. Mahwah, NJ: Erlbaum.

Leu, D. J. (2002). The new literacies: Research on reading instruction with the Internet. In A. E. Farstrup & S. J. Samuels (Eds.), *What research has to say about reading instruction* (3rd ed.), pp. 310–336. Newark, DE: International Reading Association.

Leu, D. J., & Kinzer, C. K. (2000). The convergence of literacy instruction with networked technologies for information and communication. *Reading Research Quarterly, 35,* 108–127.

Moje, E. B., & Lewis, C. (2007). Examining opportunities to learn literacy: The role of critical sociocultural literacy research. In C. Lewis, P. Enciso, & E. B. Moje (Eds.), *Identity, agency, and power: Reframing sociocultural research in literacy* (pp. 15–48). Mahwah, NJ: Erlbaum.

National Governors Association Center for Best Practices (NGACBP) & Council of Chief State School Officers (CCSSO) (2010). Common Core State Standards: English Language Arts. Washington, DC: Author.

National Institute of Child Health and Human Development (2000a). *Report of the National Reading Panel. Teaching children to read: An evidence-based assessment of the scientific literature on reading and its implications for reading instruction.* (NICHD Publication no. 00-4769). Washington, DC: U.S. Government Printing Office.

National Institute of Child Health and Human Development (2000b). *Teaching children to read—Summary report of the National Reading Panel.* Washington, DC: U.S. Government Printing Office.

Nelson-Levitt, J. (2000). *Why Jeannie can't teach: Reflections of a first-grade mentor teacher.* Unpublished master's thesis, California State University, Sacramento.

Pearson, P. D. (1993). Teaching and learning reading: A research perspective. *Language Arts, 70,* 502–511.

Pearson, J. D. (2006). Reading, rehashing, 'rithmatic: To the editor. *New York Times* (March 28): A22.

Pinnell, G. S., & Jaggar, A. M. (2003). Oral language: Speaking and listening in the classroom. In J. Flood, D. Lapp, J. R. Squire, & J. M. Jensen (Eds.), *Handbook of research on the teaching of the English language arts* (2nd ed.), pp. 881–913. Mahwah, NJ: Erlbaum.

Roe, B. D., & Ross, E. P. (2006). *Integrating language arts through literature & thematic units.* Boston: Pearson.

Rosenblatt, L. (1978). *The reader, the text, the poem: The transactional theory of the literary work.* Carbondale: Southern Illinois University Press.

Rosenblatt, L. (1983). *Literature as exploration* (4th ed.). New York: Modern Language Association.

Rumelhart, D. E. (1977). Toward an interactive model of reading. In S. Dornic (Ed.), *Attention and performance* (Vol. 6). Hillsdale, NJ: Erlbaum.

Schmar-Dobler, E. (2003). Reading on the Internet: The link between literacy and technology. *Journal of Adolescent & Adult Literacy, 47,* 80–85.

Stahl, S. A. (1992). Saying the "P" word: Nine guidelines for exemplary phonics instruction. *The Reading Teacher, 15,* 33–50.

Standards for the English Language Arts (1996). Urbana, IL: National Council of Teachers of English and the International Reading Association.

Stanovich, K. (1980). Toward an interactive-compensatory model of individual differences in the development of reading fluency. *Reading Research Quarterly, 16,* 22–71.

Sweet, A., & Snow, C. (2002). *Understanding comprehension: RAND report on comprehension.* Washington, DC: RAND.

U.S. Congress (2001). No Child Left Behind Act. Retrieved October 5, 2006, from http://www.ed.gov/policy/elsec/leg/esea02/index.html.

Vygotsky, L. S. (1978). *Mind in society.* In M. Cole, V. John-Steiner, S. Scribner, & E. Souberman (Eds.), pp. 128–173. Cambridge, MA: Harvard University Press.

Wink, J. (1996). Jonathan: Linking critical pedagogy and literacy. *Clip: A Journal of the California Literacy Project, 2* (4), 27–30.

TWO

Assessment of Progress in Literacy

CHAPTER

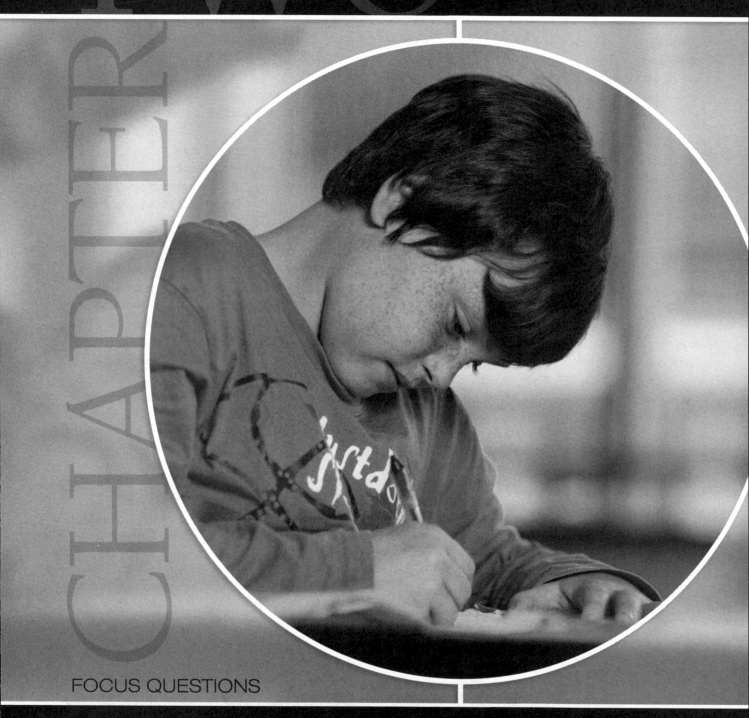

FOCUS QUESTIONS

- How is assessment different from evaluation?
- What types of literacy assessment can be used in grades 4–8?
- In what ways can literacy assessment inform instruction?

Small groups of four or five students each arrange their desks in clusters around Ms. West's fourth-grade classroom. Within each group, one student will present a language arts portfolio to the others. Ms. West scheduled this sharing of portfolios as a kind of dress rehearsal in preparation for student-led conferences with parents later in the week. Let's eavesdrop on one student, Artis, and listen to his portfolio introduction.

My name is Artis. I hope I will be going to the fifth grade next year. I created this language arts portfolio during fourth grade. My teacher's name is Ms. West.

I began working on projects and saving them for my portfolio on September 15 and put my portfolio together on May 20. I began deciding what to include in my portfolio in April and May.

I picked items that were important to me to include in this portfolio. I wanted to show what I had learned, and I put all of my favorite projects in the portfolio. I also wanted to show that I am a hard worker.

The way I decided which things would go first in my portfolio was easy—I picked my favorite thing first. I had a list of everything I wanted in my portfolio, and I just put it in order starting with my favorite item.

This portfolio shows that I kept a book list for my readings. It also shows that I have a prediction log that I use when I am reading stories. My portfolio shows what I learned through read-

ing. I learned about hurricanes and sand dollars. It also shows that there are some things about my reading that I still have to work on.

My portfolio shows the different types of writing I can do. I included a book that I wrote and illustrated. I also included some comic strips that I wrote the story for, as well as a story that uses new vocabulary. I also reviewed a movie I really enjoyed.

I think that my best items are the comic strips, my hurricane book, and my movie review. These activities were all fun, and I learned a lot from completing them.

My portfolio shows the improvements I have made this year. It shows what I can do. I can write a book if I use my imagination! It shows I can improve with practice, and it shows that I am a hard worker.

Artis proceeds to share individual items from his portfolio with his group members. He explains why each item is special to him and what he has learned from that item. Later, he will also be asked to share with his parents those areas where he feels he needs to learn more. By the end of this day, all of Ms. West's students will have an idea of what their classmates have accomplished and will see everyone at their best. The students are proud of their efforts, and it is truly a literacy celebration. Following the sharing, students are invited to have pizza and cold drinks in the cafeteria, compliments of Ms. West.

Current Views of Assessment

Many in the field of education are dismayed by what appears to be a testing frenzy in our school systems (O'Sullivan & Jiang, 2002). Each day it seems students at all levels face more and more testing.

The common belief is that if we want our students to perform better, we need to test them more. Everyone wants students to perform at their best, but is testing

evaluation ● the way to achieve this? Testing is about **evaluation,** or placing a value on a performance. "Evaluation" is not synonymous with "assessment," however.

Defining Assessment

assessment ● **Assessment** is the process of gathering information (data) about students' abilities that will help teachers, parents, and other caregivers know more about a learner's strengths and weaknesses so they may provide appropriate instruction or assistance for the learner. As such, assessment certainly can include tests, since they provide one piece of data, but assessment is about more than just testing. It is about looking at instruction in terms of how it impacts student learning. It is about self-evaluation, much like what Artis (in the chapter-opening vignette) did when he prepared his portfolio. It is about performing to a set of identified criteria. Thus, assessment is a much broader and richer concept than testing.

Ongoing assessment of literacy development refers to the use of multiple instruments, daily observation, and many work samples to measure progress. It also refers to the ongoing analysis of the data from these instruments—as well as observations concerning individuals, small groups, and the entire class—so that the teacher can customize instruction and plan appropriate interventions when necessary. This type of ongoing assessment is also referred to as *formative assessment*; it helps us know how students are progressing. *Summative assessment* is a compilation of formative assessment data, or summary data provided at the conclusion of a program or study unit or at other intervals (e.g., midterm, final, every eight weeks), to report progress (report cards are one example).

The assessment in Ms. West's classroom is ongoing and dynamic; it is the basis on which she makes all of her instructional decisions. In effective classrooms, instruction is based on information acquired through valid and authentic assessment procedures; for example, looking at students' writing growth over time. Moreover, students in the class are also involved in their own assessment and, like Artis, are able to develop metacognition and recognize their own strengths and limitations; they are encouraged to use strategies designed to increase their literacy competence. Finally, in a classroom like Ms. West's, the teacher is able to use and interpret the results from a variety of curriculum-based and standardized assessment tools and effectively communicate those results to students, their parents or caretakers, and relevant school personnel. Artis knows how well he is doing, and so does everyone who cares about his learning process.

Standards and Assessment

Teachers today are held accountable for meeting a wide array of standards. These standards are of two basic types: **professional teaching standards** (i.e., related to how well the teacher performs) and curriculum or content standards (i.e., related to what the teacher must teach). As discussed in Chapter 1, many states have adopted the Common Core State Standards; various assessments, referred to as Next Generation Assessments, have been developed to measure how states and school districts are meeting the new and more rigorous standards. Some states have chosen to be part of the Partnership for Assessment of Readiness for College and Careers (PARCC) assessments, while others have opted to be part of the Smarter Balanced Assessment Consortium. In either case, students are required to apply their knowledge in real-world situations as they are evaluated with performance events that reflect students' ability to navigate text complexity.

The assessment tools discussed in this chapter can coordinate easily with national and state-mandated content standards. English language arts standards need not be viewed as something above and apart from the practices of actual classroom teachers. Rather, well-designed standards represent what "teachers and the many others involved in English language arts education agree is the best and most productive current thinking about teaching and learning" (Smith, 1996, p. v). Hill, Ruptic, and Norwick (1998) provide an appropriate analogy: "Classroom based assessments provide sign posts to document growth. The [standards] provide the roadmap to show where we are going" (p. 175). Teachers across the content areas, however, may need continuing professional development to guide their practice and to best employ literacy strategies in their classrooms. Collaboration among teachers and administrators enhances teaching across the content areas, provides professional opportunities for developing curriculum to best meet learners' needs, and allows time to assess students' learning.

Standards provide performance goals to students and motivation to teachers; they also offer guidance for how to give feedback to students (Guskey, 2005).

● professional teaching standards

WWW●●●

Next Generation Assessments

PARCC

www.parcconline.org/

Smarter Balanced Assessment Consortium

www.smarterbalanced.org/

Wiggins (as cited in Wilcox, 2006) argues that providing helpful feedback, not just praise or advice, is perhaps the most important skill a teacher should have—and is one that is often neglected. Wiggins states, "We get fixated on the inputs, the content, and not enough on the desired output: resultant quality performance. The result is superficial. To get quality performance, you need feedback. . . . Feedback tells you what you just did. Feedback is information you can use. It's descriptive and useful information about what you did and didn't do in light of a goal" (pp. 2, 6). In order for teachers to know what feedback to provide students, they need to do more *assessing*; that is, rather than testing, they should be gathering information about student learning while the learning is still happening.

Principles of Assessment

As a result of reflective practice, lesson observations, checklists, and other measures, teachers perform assessments; in turn, these assessments inform teachers as to what needs to be taught, or retaught, and the kinds of feedback to provide students. The six principles of assessment discussed in the following sections reveal this reciprocal, synergistic relationship between assessment and teaching. Careful study of these assessment principles can help teachers determine whether their assessment plan will be complementary to instruction (adapted from Cooper, Kiger, Robinson, & Slansky, 2012).

1. The core of assessment is daily observation. Teachers—through frequent observations and note-taking on each aspect of literacy development—know much more about the status of their students than can be obtained from any standardized testing, no matter how reliable the testing is purported to be. It is imperative that assessment be a daily event, occurring as the students read and write. By observing patterns of growth over time, the teacher is in the ideal position to get a clear picture of how students are progressing. By paying close attention to several students each day, the teacher should be able to observe all students at least once each week.

2. Assessment takes many different forms. The various types of assessment tools should be used for specific purposes to ensure that the most accurate measure of each learner's literacy progress is obtained. For example, comments on writing samples, teacher-developed checklists, and anecdotal notes give insights that are not scientific but based solely on the teacher's judgment. Although these data are critical to effective planning and decision making, the teacher also needs standardized test results that have accepted statistical *reliability* (i.e., dependability and consistency) and *validity* (i.e., soundness); in other words, when tests are given to students, results will reflect reliability of scores or consistency over time. Validity means that the test does indeed measure what it should measure. To get a truly multidimensional overview of a student's performance in any aspect of literacy, teachers need to look at the data from all available sources.

3. Assessment must avoid cultural bias. Learners from different cultures, linguistic groups, and backgrounds may have various language issues as well as varied experiences and styles of learning. When planning assessment procedures, and particularly when interpreting and reporting them to others, teachers should consider these factors judiciously (Schellenberg, 2004).

As we would anticipate, the traditional summative biannual reading achievement tests, conducted in whole class settings, are not ideal for assessing the literacy skills of students for whom English is a second language. Even the academic language used in the instructions may cause confusion and render the test results invalid. To remedy this problem, some researchers suggest that either the test or the test procedures be modified to provide clarity as to what the instrument is actually testing (Lindholm-Leary & Borsato, 2006). Such modifications could include simplified instructional language or easier syntax, possibly with shorter sentences and fewer clauses. Other strategies include translating the assessment into the student's home language or giving the student more time to complete the test. As such accommodations may not always be possible, teachers should balance the (potentially questionable) test scores with additional classroom observations and work samples to provide more accurate conclusions about the student's literacy.

The importance of considering cultural bias can be illustrated by a situation encountered by a student from the Virgin Islands. After she took a standardized test, it was determined that she had a severe reading disability. Upon examining the test questions and the results, however, her teacher realized the student was certainly not reading disabled; she had scored poorly because she had not known many vocabulary words, such as *chimney* and *caboose*—words that have little meaning for residents of a tiny tropical island!

4. Students should be actively engaged in the assessment process. Although students cannot be involved in every aspect of literacy assessment, asking for their input when evaluating their work can be a key factor in encouraging them to take charge of their own learning, and it invites ownership of their successes. Since teaching and learning are ideally collaborative processes, we do not want students to view assessment as an uncomfortable practice that the teacher does *to* them. Therefore, when students and teachers are allowed to work and think together, assessment becomes a shared responsibility, with students participating enthusiastically as team players in their own learning (Stiggins et al., 2004).

5. Assessment should focus on students' abilities. Assessment should focus on determining what learners *can* do, not what they *cannot* do. When teachers really understand their students' reading and writing abilities, it becomes much easier to decide which new literacy experiences should be offered to help them develop further and to provide them with useful feedback. Not only is this a more constructive way of looking at learning, but students benefit in other crucial ways. They are able to progress more readily when the atmosphere is one in which mistakes are viewed as building blocks rather than failures that must be avoided (Cousin, Weekly, & Gerard, 1993).

6. Teachers use assessment to inform instruction. The principles of assessment discussed here suggest that there must be a reciprocal, synergistic relationship between assessment and teaching; in other words, teaching and assessing must continually inform one another. Putting this into practice, however, takes skill and shrewd observation on the part of the teacher. Assessments should be performed with a purpose; assessing students with no clear plan as to what will be done with the results wastes valuable instruction time. A teacher may use a specific diagnostic assessment to find out why a student is not progressing as well as expected in a certain area, for example. End-of-chapter and unit tests are examples of assessments that would be used to determine if all students have attained specified learning objectives. Other classroom assessments, such as quick-writes and random quizzes, are administered to measure student progress. Such assessments offer feedback about students and provide material for reflection about areas that might require alternative teaching strategies or modified pacing.

Sometimes an assessment tool tells the teacher what *not* to teach; that is, it reveals that the teacher does *not* need to teach a specific concept or skill. For example, a quick write at the beginning of a science unit might reveal that the students already know a great deal about animal habitats, requiring the teacher to revise and enhance his or her unit plans.

Assessment Options

Teachers have at their disposal an almost overwhelming array of instruments to use as part of the assessment process. Many of these instruments blend naturally into instruction; others provide a separate means to assess literacy progress using methods that vary in how direct or formal they are. At various times, we may assess process—the steps or procedures underlying a particular ability or task—or product—the result or outcome of a process (Anthony, Johnson, Mickelson, & Preece, 1991).

Think of assessment as a continuum. As shown in Figure 2.1, teacher observation is the most direct method of assessment (in terms of actual classroom instruction), and standardized tests are the least direct method (Johnston, 1992). Traditionally, these distinctions in assessment have been referred to as informal and formal, respectively.

Distinctions in assessment can also be thought of as formative and summative. As briefly described earlier, **formative assessment** refers to the process of ongoing data gathering during instruction that both informs and guides teachers as they make instructional decisions. It also guides students as they recognize gaps in their learning and then proceed to fill those gaps. Formative assessment is closely related to the ongoing direct assessment measures used by teachers; it is also referred to as classroom assessment (although not all forms of classroom assessment are formative). Information gained from formative assessments helps teachers provide the level of quality feedback students need about their learning.

Summative assessment refers to evaluative assessments, or tests, resulting in a grade or a ranking; these might include a final unit test, end of chapter test, weekly spelling test, or standardized achievement test. Large-scale, high-stakes testing is an example of summative assessment. Summative assessments are more comprehensive in nature than formative assessments and provide for some degree of accountability. Because so many assessment tools are available, it is impossible to discuss each one in this chapter. Therefore, we explore a sampling of some of the most common assessment devices that are compatible with a balanced and comprehensive literacy program. Figure 2.2 is an example of a balanced and comprehensive framework for guiding the assessment process. Here, the assessment process is guided by two questions: What kind of information do I need? How am I going to gather this infor-

formative assessment ●

summative assessment ●

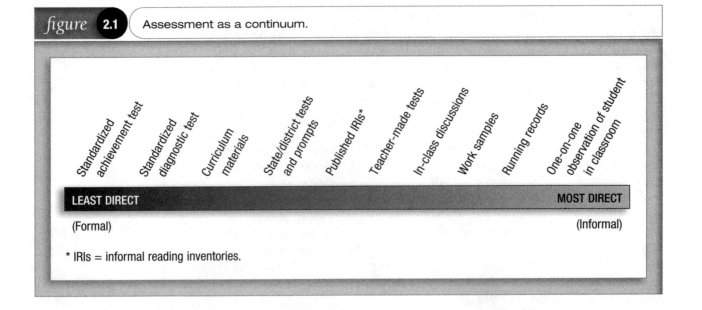

figure **2.1** Assessment as a continuum.

Standardized achievement test · Standardized diagnostic test · Curriculum materials · State/district tests and prompts · Published IRIs* · Teacher-made tests · In-class discussions · Work samples · Running records · One-on-one observation of student in classroom

LEAST DIRECT   MOST DIRECT

(Formal)   (Informal)

* IRIs = informal reading inventories.

A framework for guiding the literacy assessment process.   *figure* **2.2**

What kind of information do I need?   How am I going to gather this information?

	DIRECT	ONGOING	INDIRECT
Structural analysis/ word analysis	One-on-one observation Word games	Anecdotal notes Running records	Stanford Diagnostic Subtest Woodcock Reading Mastery Test
Vocabulary	Observation Pretest Free writing Class presentations Vocabulary self-assessment charts Cubing activity	Daily discussions Anecdotal notes Weekly tests Writing samples	Stanford Achievement Test Language Assessment Scales Carver Vocabulary Test Peabody Picture Vocabulary Test
Fluency	One-on-one observation Paired reading	Anecdotal notes Running records Tape recordings IRI/miscue analysis	State/district-developed instruments
Spelling	Free writing Pretests Dictations	Writing samples Journals Weekly tests	Standardized tests
Reading comprehension	Retellings QARs Discussions Cloze tests	Paraphrases Summaries Class contributions Sketchings IRIs	Standardized tests (Stanford Achievement, Metropolitan Achievement, California Achievement)
Writing	Free writing Journals Quick writes Editing checklist	Writing samples Daily work Norming/scoring writing collectively	Rubrics that accompany curriculum materials (scaled scores) Language Assessment Scales
Reading/writing attitudes	Reading logs Number of books read/written Teacher interviews	Conferences Reading response journals	Questionnaires Attitude surveys Interest inventories (published versions)
Student views of own literacy	Books chosen Self-evaluations Response journals Teacher interviews	Portfolio choices Dialogue journals Reflection log	Attitude surveys Reading surveys Questionnaires (published versions)

IRI = informal reading inventory; QARs = question-answer relationships

Various assessment tools should be used to ensure the most accurate measure of each learner's literacy progress.

mation? From there, teachers make instructional decisions based on the assessment results. The options for gathering information are (1) *direct,* which refers to teacher-developed or one-on-one observations of what the student can do; (2) *ongoing,* which refers to a set of direct data collected over time; and (3) *indirect,* which refers to data that come from standardized instruments or instruments devised by someone outside the classroom setting. Once teachers have determined the areas for which they need information, the framework provides several alternatives for obtaining that assessment data.

Most of the techniques discussed in the remainder of this chapter can be used easily on the basis of the information given; others require reviewing an examiner's handbook. Appropriate references are given for those that require more detailed study.

Common classifications for the assessments used in grades 4–8 are: standardized testing, curriculum-based assessment, standards-based performance assessment, and process-oriented assessment. These classifications are not always mutually exclusive. For example, criterion-referenced tests (often curriculum-based) can also be standardized, and checklists can be used across classifications. It may be helpful to think of these classifications as related to the purpose for assessment. In other words, is an assessment needed to screen, diagnose, or monitor progress? Or is the purpose to measure the outcome of instruction? As discussed in the following sections, each classification offers a unique perspective for a balanced and comprehensive literacy program, providing information for both formative and summative purposes.

Standardized Testing

standardized testing ● **Standardized testing** focuses on the use of norm-referenced tests to measure reading and writing skills as well as the subskills of these areas. (See the section on "Standardized, or Indirect, Assessment Procedures" later in this chapter for specific, technical information about tests that fall under this category.) Because

norm-referenced tests ● they are **norm-referenced tests**—that is, administered to a large group of students to establish the reference scores to which subsequent scores are compared (see Figure 2.3)—they have not been developed to assess a specific curriculum. These tests are administered by the teacher or reading specialist and usually provide numerical scores that represent a student's rank compared to the performance of others at the same age or grade. The data obtained from these tests can be, but are not always, related to the content of instruction. Therefore, some questions may address material a teacher has taught, but the test might also include questions about topics that have not been taught. Or, the test might measure the content of the curriculum, but in ways that differ from the instructional format used by the teacher. For instance, a teacher might discuss synonyms within the context of sentences, whereas the standardized test might assess knowledge of synonyms through word matching.

As discussed earlier, many states are adopting tests that measure progress toward the CCSS. For a closer look at what your state is doing, visit your state's

Comparison of norm- and criterion-referenced assessments.   *figure* **2.3**

NORM-REFERENCED ASSESSMENTS

1. Assess student's knowledge of particular subject matter.
2. Compare performance with that of a norm group (large number of students representative of the students for whom the test was designed in order to establish scoring values for the test).
3. Are used annually as pretests/posttests to determine student gain and compare gains with those of the norm group.
4. Contain items considered to be precise, valid, and reliable for the purpose of identifying low-achieving and high-achieving students.
5. Have high **construct validity** (items assess the skills, knowledge, and understandings that most experts agree comprise the area being tested).
6. Have high **reliability** (consistently measure the same behavior with each administration of the test).
7. Are interpreted by comparing student's scores with those obtained by the norm group.
8. Yield global measurements of general abilities.
9. Provide scores that are statistically compared with those of a norm group (e.g., percentiles).
10. Are written to create variability among individual scores in a group for the purpose of sorting students.

CRITERION-REFERENCED ASSESSMENTS

1. Assess student's ability to perform a specific task.
2. Determine whether the student has the skill needed to progress to the next level of learning.
3. Are used as often as needed to determine skills to be taught and skills that have been mastered.
4. Contain items that determine whether the student is able to use a learned skill in a variety of situations.
5. Have high **content validity** (items assess the ability needed to perform the behaviors expected in the course or in the curriculum).
6. Are not concerned with reliability; students are not expected to show the *same* behavior, but *improved* behavior.
7. Are interpreted by noting whether the student is able to perform a specific task, and to what degree.
8. Yield analytical data regarding specific objectives.
9. Provide a score that is considered acceptable by the teacher (e.g., 80 percent accuracy); incorrect items can be further examined.
10. Are designed to assess ability to perform a specific task as stated by a specific objective or curriculum content standard.

Source: Adapted from Eddie Kennedy, *Classroom Approaches to Remedial Reading,* 1977. Itaska, FL: F.E. Peacock Publishers.

Department of Education website. While most teachers are familiar with administering standardized achievement tests, including the Stanford Achievement Test (SAT) and Iowa Test of Basic Skills (ITBS), standardized tests are also available for diagnostic purposes. Examples include the Woodcock Reading Mastery Test, Pearson Assessments, and Stanford Diagnostic Reading Test (SDRT). The versions of these instruments that are appropriate for grades 4–8 offer subtests that provide a systematic appraisal of a student's ability to recognize meaningful word parts (roots, affixes, and compounds), to determine main ideas and supporting details, and to correct sentences that are poorly written, as well as an accounting of vocabulary words the student knows compared with age-matched peers. For instance, the Green (grades 3.5–4.5), Purple (grades 4.5–6.5), and Brown (grades 6.5–8.9) levels of the SDRT cover the range of intermediate and middle grades.

The results of standardized tests are most appropriately used to get an overall sense of how well a group (school, class) is performing and what general academic areas might need more focus in the classroom. Teachers often view these indirect assessments before they have had an opportunity to get to know their students' strengths and needs better, and they may then use these tests to place students in instructional groups *before more direct information can be obtained with the actual materials the students will be using in the classroom.* It would be unfortunate if these initial placements were left unexamined once teachers have learned more about their students!

Curriculum-Based Assessment

curriculum-based assessment ●

criterion-referenced tests ●

Curriculum-based assessment uses school district–adopted curriculum materials to provide information about students' abilities. This category of assessment relates directly to the teacher's literacy curriculum to identify instructional needs and to determine what is required for learners to "master" a concept. Such assessment may also include **criterion-referenced tests**—tests that compare a student's performance to standards (the criteria) deemed appropriate for mastery in a particular area. Scores from such tools typically offer a number, or percentage, for the amount of material each student has mastered. These scores are then compared with the criterion score required; usually 80 percent accuracy determines "mastery." Refer back to Figure 2.3 for a comparison of norm- and criterion-referenced assessments.

Curriculum-based assessments are usually administered in the classroom using items and materials derived from the curriculum. Examples of curriculum-based assessments include asking a student to read a passage aloud from a text and counting the number of words read correctly per minute, or wrapping up a thematic unit on exploration by asking students to write down as many exploration-related words as they can in a limited time. The first example represents a criterion-referenced test in that students are expected to be able to read a certain number of words correctly per minute at particular grade levels (see Figure 8.1, later in this book). The teacher is evaluating whether this criterion has been met. The second example is more direct, as the results will inform the teacher how effectively the thematic unit increased students' vocabulary for a particular area of instruction. The teacher might have certain expectations about the number of words that each student should be able to list, but these expectations can vary according to the student. An English learner might be expected to list at least 5 words, whereas a native English speaker might be expected to list 10.

Standards-Based Performance Assessment

standards-based performance assessment ●

Performance Assessment
www.performanceassessment.org

Standards-based performance assessment, a type of criterion-referenced assessment, describes assessment that views standards—for example the Common Core State Standards or a state's adaptation of the CCSS—as the criteria on which performance is evaluated. Students and their teachers can use a variety of methods to meet standards (e.g., essays, exhibitions, performance by a group, short story writing); students can reflect on their progress as they work toward achieving the standards (Wilhelm, 1996). In other words, *using standards-based performance assessment does not dictate the type of tools that might be used for assessment.* Any of the tools found in Figure 2.2 could be used; each standard provides only the criterion for the assessment. Rather than ask what students know and can do in relation to other students (norm-referencing), standards-based performance assessment asks what students know and can do in relation to a set of standards. For example, Figure 2.4 (see pp. 32–34) offers three separate sets of activities based on the College and Career Readiness Anchor Standards for Reading; the three "Context" columns are based on three different genres and three different audiences. The checklist can be made grade-level specific using state standards or the grade-level specific CCSS.

Beverly Falk (2000) provides a clear statement of the purposes and benefits of standards-based performance assessments:

Standards-based performance assessments support teaching by providing teachers with a guide for their teaching and with information about *what* students can do as well as *how* they do it. They support student learning by offering students opportunities to demonstrate their understandings in a variety of ways and, because of their open and clear expectations, by giving students a fair shot at demonstrating what they know. At the same time, standards-based performance assessments are useful accountability measures because they allow the public to see student and school progress in relation to valued goals. (p. 83)

Teachers using standards-based performance assessment are always thinking of how they can organize a set of experiences that will help their students meet the standards. They try to use what they know about their students' interests, abilities, and competencies. The term *authentic assessment* has some relevance here.

WWW ● ● ●

Designing Assessments

http://edrev.asu.edu/reviews/rev50.htm

Observation Tools

www.colorincolorado.org/webcasts/middleWebcast%201003%20-%20Teacher%20checklist.pdf

---

 An Assessment Program

Ms. West, the teacher we met at the beginning of this chapter, has created an assessment program that incorporates data from a wide variety of assessment tools to evaluate the literacy growth of Artis and the other students in her class. The tools listed here are discussed throughout this chapter.

- Once a year, usually during the spring, the students take a norm-referenced *achievement test* called The Stanford Achievement Test (The Psychological Corporation). Reviewing these results at the beginning of the following school year allows Ms. West to obtain general literacy information about her new class and an indication of how well the students in her school are doing compared to other students of the same age and grade across the nation (standardized testing).

- At the beginning of the year, Ms. West gives students a *group cloze test,* developed from the material they will be expected to read, to evaluate their ability to handle the content area texts (curriculum-based).

- For students who score below 30 percent accuracy on the group cloze test, Ms. West administers an *informal reading inventory* to more carefully evaluate their reading strategies, determine their reading levels, and identify specific strengths and needs in comprehension and word analysis. Eventually, Ms. West will administer an informal reading inventory to all her students (process-oriented).

- Twice a month Ms. West listens to each student read from either narrative or expository material (alternating each time) and takes *running records* to check their comparative reading fluency (curriculum-based, standards-based).

- Every day Ms. West observes her students and takes *anecdotal notes* monitoring anything she considers significant in their struggles, their successes, and their attitudes; she sometimes uses *checklists* to make these observations more structured when determining students' knowledge of multisyllabic words, ability to answer a range of comprehension questions, or progress toward state standards (process-oriented, standards-based).

- At the end of each content area unit, Ms. West gives students an oral or a written *cloze test* to determine their comprehension and their understanding of grammatical structures and content vocabulary (curriculum-based, standards-based).

- Once a week Ms. West listens as students *summarize* and *paraphrase* both narrative and expository material to evaluate their English language fluency, knowledge of story structure and expository organizational patterns, and comprehension skills (process-oriented, standards-based).

- Once or twice a week Ms. West and her students examine and briefly discuss the work in their *writing portfolios* (process-oriented, standards-based).

- Every six to eight weeks Ms. West administers a *structural analysis word list test* to those students who need it to measure growth in structural elements; she also conducts a quick survey of specialized vocabulary words to determine which words students still need to master (standards-based, curriculum-based).

figure 2.4 Checklist for observations of progress toward standards.*

NAME: _____

GRADE: _____

STANDARDS	CONTEXT: Informational passage on Mt. Vesuvius[1]	DATE OBSERVED	CONTEXT: Informational passage on cloning[2]	DATE OBSERVED	CONTEXT: Fictional passage on bullying[3]	DATE OBSERVED
CCSS.ELA-Literacy. CCRA.R.1 Read closely to determine what the text says explicitly and to make logical inferences from it; cite specific textual evidence when writing or speaking to support conclusions drawn from the text.	Students read a passage about the eruption of Mount Vesuvius that destroyed the Roman city of Pompeii. They write a newspaper article from the time about the event. They must include an interview with a survivor of the event. Using the facts from the passage, they must properly use direct quotations from the passage in the article.		Students read an article about cloning cats. They use the margins to annotate the first paragraph, noting the meaning or summary in the right margin, and the purpose or function it serves in the left margin. Then, students revisit these margin notes to support their claims as they write an essay to support or not support cloning.		From this collection of stories, students read the story "Priscilla and the Wimps" by Richard Peck. Students discuss what happens to the antagonist at the end of the story and indicate what textual evidence they have to back up their idea(s).	
CCSS.ELA-Literacy. CCRA.R.2 Determine central ideas or themes of a text and analyze their development; summarize the key supporting details and ideas.	Students identify and list facts leading up to the volcanic eruption and the consequences of the event.		Students examine the relevant anecdotes and details, which enrich the central theme. Students attend to the emotions expressed by the pet owners as they state their reasons for cloning their cats. Students act out or role play one person's reason(s) for wanting a clone of a beloved pet, or they develop their own reasons and act that out.		Students discuss bullying and identify examples of bullying in the text. Using these events, students discuss whether a solution to the school's bullying problem existed, and what might change as a result of the events at the end of the book.	
CCSS.ELA-Literacy. CCRA.R.3 Analyze how and why individuals, events, or ideas develop and interact over the course of a text.	Students make a graphic organizer of events that occurred around the volcanic eruption. Then, using the graphic organizer, they write a paragraph to explain why the town was destroyed.		Using the pet owners who were interviewed in the article, students explain the pros and cons of cloning, and discuss to what extent each side's argument is appealing. Students create a T chart.		Students select a character to examine and write about. They examine descriptions of the character (what the character says, does, thinks; what others say about that character) and discuss how he or she contributes to or impacts the bullying at the school.	
CCSS.ELA-Literacy. CCRA.R.4 Interpret words and phrases as they are used in a text, including determining technical, connotative, and figurative meanings, and analyze how specific word choices shape meaning or tone.	Students keep a vocabulary log of volcano terms, terms related to destruction, and terms for specific tools or artifacts from Pompeii during that time period. Students share these lists with each other, build their lists, and use the vocabulary in their writing assignments to demonstrate precision and specificity in their writing.		By pointing out some of the article's stylistic choices and the effect they have on the text at large, teachers can improve students' recognition and understanding of these expressions—and thus of the larger text. Teachers can walk through some expressions from the text to determine meaning. Some examples are "The proof is in the Puddy-cat" and "Pandora's box." Students return to the text to find some expressions or new words or terms to interpret. Class discussion will revolve around the meaning of the expression, choice in using a word or expression, and what it does to the writing as a whole and for the reader. Students keep a log of these expressions or annotate them in the text.		Ask students to restate this quotation and explain its purpose and the extent to which it is effective: "Monk ran a tight ship." Ask students to identify other quotations from the book that describe a bully.	

figure 2.4 Checklist for observations of progress toward standards*, continued.

STANDARDS	CONTEXT: Informational passage on Mt. Vesuvius[1]	DATE OBSERVED	CONTEXT: Informational passage on cloning[2]	DATE OBSERVED	CONTEXT: Fictional passage on bullying[3]	DATE OBSERVED
CCSS.ELA-Literacy. CCRA.R.5 Analyze the structure of texts, including how specific sentences, paragraphs, and larger portions of the text (e.g., a section, chapter, scene, or stanza) relate to each other and the whole.	Because this text is divided into chapters, students will provide a title to each chapter that describes its point and purpose. Also, ask students to use the topic sentences and concluding sentences of the chapters to help determine effectiveness of the titles.		As you review the cloning article, note on your text: • Where you think the introduction ends • Where the author notes the main idea • Where the author shares the researcher's findings/conclusions • EVIDENCE INCLUDED • The article's conclusion Then, as you work with students, make sure they have noted these same parts in the article and in their own writing.		Ask students to highlight sections of the story that pertain to bullying. Or ask students to highlight sections of the text that use symbolism relating to biblical allusions. Have students discuss and share highlights to determine the author's intent.	
CCSS.ELA-Literacy. CCRA.R.6 Assess how point of view or purpose shapes the content and style of a text.	This text provides a great deal of information about Pompeii and the eruption of Mount Vesuvius, but the story is told in a way that is easy to read and understand. Have students explain in list form the ways the author accomplishes this.		Students identify the author's intentions by examining the use of pet names, such as "Fluffy" or "Frisky." Students reflect on the author's purpose for using these names and what the effect is on the readers. Students use these examples to get at the author's bias.		This story is told from the point of view of a student at the school, who seems to be an outside observer. Have students explain in what ways this narrator helps the reader understand and believe the story. Does the narrator seem more reliable than if a main character had told the story?	
CCSS.ELA-Literacy. CCRA.R.7 Integrate and evaluate content presented in diverse media and formats, including visually and quantitatively, as well as in words.	Students will create a multimodal presentation about the damaging effects of volcanos, citing evidence from their text and including audio, video, and images to show their destructive nature.		To apply their new knowledge, have students use the following website to create their own genetically engineered clone; then, have them determine if cloning is a good idea. *Click and clone animation,* from Genetic Science Learning Center, University of Utah: http://learn.genetics.utah.edu/content/cloning/clickandclone		Students will create their own interactive story using the idea of bullying to share with the class. Students will work through the writing process and be trained to use a presentation tool such as Prezi or PowerPoint to create their interactive stories.	
CCSS.ELA-Literacy. CCRA.R.8 Delineate and evaluate the argument and specific claims in a text, including the validity of the reasoning as well as the relevance and sufficiency of the evidence.	Students are asked to write an essay about the extent of the eruption of Mount Vesuvius and whether it could have been less deadly. Students must cite evidence from the text that offers support to their claims.		Students will look at the evidence, cite it, and judge evidence about cloning to determine to what extent they agree or disagree with the practice. Specifically, students could examine • differences between the clone and the original • arguments in favor of cloning • arguments not in favor of cloning • personal reactions to the claims		The teacher models finding one instance of Monk exhibiting power, cites page and paragraph, and models proper citation technique (quotation marks, page number, proper length). Start with an example from Standard 4 above ("Monk ran a tight ship"). Students can then work independently to find examples of Monk exhibiting power.	

figure **2.4** Checklist for observations of progress toward standards*, *continued*.

STANDARDS	CONTEXT: Informational passage on Mt. Vesuvius[1]	DATE OBSERVED	CONTEXT: Informational passage on cloning[2]	DATE OBSERVED	CONTEXT: Fictional passage on bullying[3]	DATE OBSERVED
CCSS.ELA-Literacy. CCRA.R.9 Analyze how two or more texts address similar themes or topics in order to build knowledge or to compare the approaches the authors take.	Students compare this text about Mount Vesuvius with an online source of the events (see CCRA.R.10, below); discuss the author's opinion about the events that took place. Students examine particular events or topics the author chose to leave out, exaggerate, or develop more fully.		Using the other articles on cloning presented to the class (see CCRA.R.10, below), students examine the bias in the original article, determine if any information was left out or further developed as compared with the others, and write a paragraph that discusses how this article influences or persuades the reader more or less than the others. Students identify articles that are more recent and offer more current information.		Students compare and contrast other works of literature on the topic of bullying and describe the authors' craft. Students identify the solutions to bullying as noted in the other works.	
CCSS.ELA-Literacy. CCRA.R.10 Read and comprehend complex literary and informational texts independently and proficiently.	Students use online sources to learn more about the history of Pompeii and current information about Mount Vesuvius and the volcanos of the area. Students develop questions ahead of time that they then answer as they read the online materials. Students compare questions and their answers.		Students are presented with other article(s) on cloning and asked multi-leveled questions to check their comprehension of the text. Using the new articles' information, students compare and contrast ideas about cloning.		Ask students to read this chunk of the text before reading the story or hearing the title: "Monk's not happy with this answer, but by now he's spotted Melvin, who's grown smaller in spite of himself. Monk breaks his own rule by reaching for Melvin with his own hand. 'Kid,' he says, 'you're going to have to educate your girl friend'" (page 45). Ask them to select key ideas that this excerpt from the story contains. Students should be able to identify such ideas as aggression, bullying, and sexism. Students can learn more about these issues through other texts.	

*The standards used in this checklist are the English Language Arts Standards, College and Career Readiness Anchor Standards for Reading. Any state standards could be used, and the checklist can be made grade-level specific using state standards or the grade-level specific CCSS.

Sources:

(1) Kunhardt, E. & Eagle, M. (2003). *Pompeii—Buried Alive!* New York: Random House.

(2) Said, C. (2004, April 15). Here, kitty-kitty-kitty: Sausalito firm offers clones for $50,000, signs up 5 cat owners. *San Francisco Chronicle*, p. A1.

(3) Peck, R. (1984). "Priscilla and the Wimps." *Sixteen: Short Stories by Outstanding Writers for Young Adults.* Ed. D. R. Gallo. New York: Dell.

Authentic assessment is often understood to mean assessment that represents literacy behavior found in the community and in the workplace. Instruction focuses on learning that has direct application in the real world. For example, students interested in environmental concerns may engage in service-learning projects centered around recycling. (See Chapter 10 for more about service learning.) In this example, authentic assessment would focus on how successful their recycling projects were in the eyes of the community. Teachers involved in such projects, just as those using standards-based performance assessment, often rely on anecdotal records, checklists, and scoring rubrics to help them determine how well their students have met the standards. The checklist in Figure 2.4 is one way a teacher can record evidence that students are working toward each of the standards.

● authentic assessment

Process-Oriented Assessment

Process-oriented assessment refers to a teacher's direct observations of students' actual reading and writing abilities for the purpose of noting which specific behaviors or strategies students use. In process-oriented assessment, the literacy behavior being examined is documented in the learning context in which it normally occurs. For example, a process-oriented assessment could consist of anecdotal notes or a checklist that asks such questions as, "Is the learner able to separate affixes from root words to assist decoding?" or "Is the learner able to use word parts to determine word meaning?" The assessment might take place when the student reads one-on-one with the teacher from a content area text, such as a social studies text. The key to making observation systematic lies in creating a tool for note taking and record keeping that reduces the amount of writing required. You will find examples of such tools throughout this chapter. Computer-based systems are also available for teachers to maintain observational records. In addition to anecdotal notes and checklists, *running records* and *informal reading inventories* (IRI) (both discussed later in this chapter), with follow-up miscue analyses, also fall under this category. Such assessments are quite compatible with standards-based performance assessment.

● process-oriented assessment

Standardized, or Indirect, Assessment Procedures

Using standardized assessment devices in the classroom has both advantages and disadvantages. Although standardized group tests can be used, in a very broad way, to compare student performance with that of a cross-section of students in other areas of the country, such tests provide little or no usable information about the specific needs of individual students in a particular classroom context. As with any assessment device, teachers must first determine what information they are seeking and then decide whether the standardized instrument is appropriate for discovering that information. As Cunningham and Allington (2010) so wisely remind us, "Tests that do not help us teach better are generally a waste of time and resources" (p. 263).

Achievement Tests and Their Application by Teachers

Most schools use a standardized, or norm-referenced, test to evaluate reading achievement. These tests have been administered to a large group of students, representative of those for whom the test is intended, in order to establish the norm, or reference, group. This, then, is the group to which the scores of other students taking the test are compared. Standardized tests also have a standardized set of directions that must be followed for valid comparisons to be made.

Achievement tests are generally administered in a group and offer the teacher a "ballpark" estimate of the students' reading performance. The results are more helpful for comparing groups than for making judgments about how to meet the specific needs of individual students. As mentioned earlier, teachers often use the results of these tests to help with *initial* placement of students into instructional groups. Scores can be charted, and decisions for planning general areas for instructional focus can be made (see Figure 2.5). A diagnostic test such as the SDRT, however, would also need to be administered in order to obtain more specific information from a standardized test. Teachers also use standardized test scores as confirmation of the results from their own direct assessments. Nevertheless, standardized tests present the teacher with a variety of types of scores that must be interpreted cautiously.

Interpretation of Standardized Test Scores

percentile scores ●

The most commonly reported score from a standardized test is the percentile score. **Percentile scores** range from 1 to 99, with an average score of 50, but they do *not* represent the percentage of items answered correctly on the test. They are scores that have been converted from the raw scores to allow comparisons among students of the same age or grade in the norm group, or in the same classroom or school. Each test's technical manual explains the manner in which this conversion was done. For example, students receiving a percentile score of 76 did not answer 76 percent of the items correctly; instead, this score means that these students have done as well as or better than 76 percent of students in the norm group and in their own classroom on this test. An individual's subtest scores can be compared, but not averaged. In other words, a comprehension subtest score of 65 and a vocabulary subtest score of 43 mean the student performed better in comprehension than in vocabulary and may benefit from enhanced instruction in vocabulary, which, in turn, might help both scores. However, we *cannot* say the student's average reading score is the 54th percentile (the average of 65 and 43).

stanine scores ●

Another type of reported standardized test score is **stanine scores.** These are scores that have been converted into nine equally spaced units, with 1 being the lowest and 9 the highest. A stanine of 5 is considered the mean (average) score, so stanines 1, 2, and 3 represent below-average performance; 4, 5, and 6 represent average performance; and 7, 8, and 9 represent above-average performance (see Figure 2.6).

standard deviation ●

When interpreting test scores, it is important to know the reported standard deviation for the test. The **standard deviation** (SD) is the number used to describe the variability in a set of scores as indicated by their distance—plus or minus 1, 2, or 3—from the mean (average) score. Think of the mean as the center of the distribution of scores. The higher the SD, the more spread out the scores are in a distribution. For example, consider means and standard deviations for scores on intelligence tests. The Wechsler Intelligence Scale has a mean (average) score of 100 and an SD of 15; thus, an IQ score of 100 is average. A score of 115 is one standard deviation above the average, or +1 SD; a score of 85 is –1 SD below the mean. Approximately 70 percent of all the scores in a normal distribution fall between +1 SD and –1 SD from the mean, or between 85 and 115 in the case of the Wechsler (Figure 2.6 shows cumulative percentages within a normal curve). Therefore, any score between 85 and 115 would not be considered exceptional but is within the average range. Similarly, about 95 percent of all scores are within two standard deviations; a score of 130 is 2 SD above the average (+2 SD), and a score of 70 is 2 SD below the average (–2 SD). However, a score of 145 (the criterion score for joining Mensa) is 3 SDs above the average—an extremely high score; a score falling 3 SDs or more below the mean would be exceptionally low. If we consider the distribution of percentile scores, those that are between approximately the 30th and 70th

Graphic profile for examining class standardized test scores.*

figure **2.5**

TEACHER: Ms. G		GRADE LEVEL: 4		DATE: September	
NAME OF TEST: CAT/6		DATE TEST ADMINISTERED: April			

Pupil's Name	Word Analysis		Vocabulary		Comprehension		Comments
Carolyn B.	39	4	37	4	35	4	steady progress
Artis C.	34	4	53	5	36	4	good progress
Mary D.	49	5	23	③	23	③	vocabulary & comprehension
Isaac D.	63	6	83	8	74	7	could peer tutor?
Doug F.	18	②	29	③	18	②	use vocab. to build skills
Raul H.	38	4	38	4	6	①	focus on comprehension
Brandon L.	53	5	18	②	40	4	verify vocabulary
Cory M.	56	5	39	4	9	①	twins—but very different
Kerri M.	29	③	56	5	54	5	could Cory lean too much on Kerri?
Kalisha P.	36	4	26	③	3	①	focus on comprehension
Darlene P.	30	4	24	③	27	③	some comp. & vocab. work
Marcus R.	10	②	57	5	58	5	verify word analysis skills
Brenda R.	99	9	98	9	85	8	could peer tutor?
Sara R.	6	①	8	①	5	①	English learner: vocab work
Carmen T.	12	②	14	②	11	②	English learner: polysemantic words
Luis T.	37	4	31	4	14	②	comprehension strategies
Patricia W.	8	①	34	4	25	③	verify with an IRI
Mark W.	38	4	26	③	21	③	some comp. & vocab. help
Greg W.	57	5	38	4	37	4	good, steady progress
Linda Y.	36	4	35	4	16	②	comprehension strategies

percentile   stanine   percentile   stanine   percentile   stanine

*Below-average stanine scores are circled. Twelve of 20 students, more than half, are below average in comprehension. The instructional focus needs to be on comprehension.

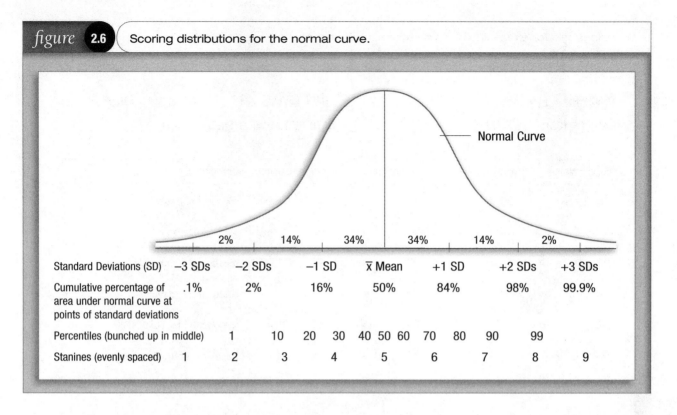

figure **2.6** | Scoring distributions for the normal curve.

Standard Deviations (SD)	−3 SDs	−2 SDs	−1 SD	x̄ Mean	+1 SD	+2 SDs	+3 SDs
Cumulative percentage of area under normal curve at points of standard deviations	.1%	2%	16%	50%	84%	98%	99.9%
Percentiles (bunched up in middle)	1	10	20 30	40 50 60	70 80	90	99
Stanines (evenly spaced)	1	2	3	4	5	6	7	8	9

(Normal curve percentages shown above axis: 2%   14%   34%   34%   14%   2%)

percentiles fall within an average range, as shown in Figure 2.6. Likewise, stanine scores of 4, 5, and 6, also shown in Figure 2.6, are considered average scores.

When interpreting test results, it is important to know not only the mean and SD, but also to know how much error is associated with the test. All tests have some error, and that error is represented by a number known as the **standard error of measurement** (SEM). Using this number provides a range of scores that a student's "true" score will likely fall within. For example, let's say the standardized test score for a student is the 77th percentile, but the SEM for this test is 12. This means that the student's "true" score falls somewhere between the 65th (77 − 12) and the 89th (77 + 12) percentile. This is quite a range. With so much room for error, we might wonder why so much emphasis is placed on standardized test scores. Of course, the SEM may be lower, but this example indicates why it is important for those reporting test results to provide this information; it all helps with interpretation. Information about the mean, SD, and SEM is available in the test's technical manual.

standard error of measurement ●

Informal, or Direct, Assessment Procedures

Numerous literacy assessment devices provide a teacher with information *directly* applicable to instructional planning. They include IRIs; running records; interest and attitude surveys; interviews; teacher-made activities such as cloze tests; curriculum material placement tests; retelling tasks; word list and spelling tests; and written teacher observation procedures such as checklists, anecdotal notes, and scoring rubrics. Instructional lessons themselves are inextricably intertwined with direct assessment, as teaching and assessing continually inform one another. A discussion of all available assessment devices is beyond the scope of this chapter, and it is not necessary or possible for a teacher to use every device discussed here. Because a teacher has limited instructional time, the choice of which tools to use should be based on the specific literacy needs of the class and the type of information the assessment tool provides. For example, teachers who wish to use interest groups when studying particular content area units would administer an interest inventory developed to help identify potential groupings (see Appendix C). The descriptions that follow should help teachers decide what tools would be best to use for their particular purposes.

Informal Reading Inventory

An **informal reading inventory,** or IRI, is one of the most valuable diagnostic tools for assessing the reading progress of each student as well as diagnosing specific reading strengths and needs. These inventories are referred to as "informal" because they are not norm-referenced. The IRI is an individual diagnostic reading test composed of lists of leveled sight words or sentences and a set of graded reading passages (both narrative and expository) from preprimer through grade 8 or even grade 12, with accompanying comprehension questions for each passage. Most basal reader series include their own IRI (sometimes called a *student placement test*) as part of their evaluation program, but devices such as the *Analytical Reading Inventory* (Pearson), the *Basic Reading Inventory, Pre-Primer through Grade Twelve* (Kendall/Hunt), the *Flynt–Cooter Comprehensive Reading Inventory* (Pearson), and the *Qualitative Reading Inventory* (HarperCollins) are also available. Teachers can also design their own IRI by compiling a series of graded passages from their own curriculum materials, using readability formulas and taxonomies (tools that provide a classification of types of knowledge, such as Bloom's Taxonomy) to develop appropriate questions. Because they actually listen to the student reading aloud, observant teachers are offered a kind of "window into the learner's brain" to see what strategies for word analysis and construction of meaning the student uses. The IRI is an invaluable tool because it enables the teacher to:

- estimate a student's independent, instructional, frustration, and listening comprehension levels;
- determine strengths and needs in word analysis and comprehension abilities;
- understand how a student is using syntactic (structure), graphophonic (visual–sound), and semantic (meaning) cues to make sense of reading;
- compare how a student decodes words in isolation with how that student decodes words in the context of meaningful sentences; and
- assess oral reading fluency if the oral reading is timed. The reading rate in words per minute can then be computed, and a determination can be made about fluency as related to reading rate (see Figure 8.1, later in the book).

Procedures for administering published IRIs vary, so teachers should follow the instructions for the particular IRI chosen. In general, the following guidelines, while not universal, are representative of the recommended procedures for administering IRIs.

The IRI takes about 20 to 30 minutes to administer and is often recorded; the student reads aloud while the teacher records **miscues**—deviations from the actual text—by using a kind of shorthand. After the oral reading, the teacher asks for a retelling and then poses a series of comprehension questions. The **retelling,** which asks the student to describe what she just read, gives insight into the reader's general ability to recall, interpret, and draw conclusions from the text. The follow-up comprehension questions assess specific aspects of the reader's understanding of the material read. Because comprehension of text is a critical issue beyond the early grades, it is helpful for teachers to ask for retellings and follow-up questions after students have also read passages silently. These results can then be compared with results following

● informal reading inventory

● miscues

● retelling

an oral reading, especially when the oral reading reveals a low comprehension score. Oral performance can interrupt students' comprehension as they focus on a flawless performance. Additionally, since most reading in grades 4–8 and beyond is done silently, the results are important for the classroom teacher. In addition to providing both narrative (stories) and expository (informational) passages, published IRIs provide several forms, so the teacher can use one form for oral reading and another for silent reading. The following questions, modified as appropriate, can be asked to elicit a thorough retelling for both narrative and expository material:

- What can you tell me about [topic of passage or story]?
- What else was this passage/story about besides [the topic that the student has mentioned already]?
- What happened after [event mentioned in retelling]?
- What do you think the author(s) is (are) trying to tell us [in the part mentioned in retelling]?
- How was [event or fact mentioned in retelling] important to this passage/story?
- How do you think you might use this information?
- How is this reading like other material you have read before?

Retellings should be done prior to asking the comprehension questions provided in a published inventory. If a retelling is complete enough and time constraints are an issue, very few comprehension questions may need to be asked because they would essentially have been answered already. Whenever possible, however, all the comprehension questions should be asked directly. In reviewing and selecting published IRIs, it is important to look for 8 to 10 questions per passage and a balance of the following question types:

- *Literal*—The student recalls or recognizes information directly stated in the text.
- *Inferential*—The student recognizes or discovers relationships in the text that are not directly stated.
- *Critical/evaluative*—The student uses original and logical thought and previous knowledge or experiences to solve a problem or make a value judgment.

Analysis of results might indicate strengths in literal comprehension but weaknesses in inferential or critical/evaluative thinking. Such information certainly helps a teacher plan appropriate instruction.

After beginning the IRI with an easy passage, the student continues to read progressively more difficult passages. When the student falls below about 90 percent in word recognition accuracy for oral reading, achieves less than 60 percent accuracy in comprehension, or appears frustrated, the test is terminated; the passage level at which this occurs is called the **frustration level**. After the student reaches the frustration level, the teacher reads aloud passages at successively higher grade levels until the student is unable to answer correctly at least 75 percent of the comprehension questions. This percentage may vary depending on the IRI being used. The purpose of this last step is to determine the learner's reading capacity level, also called *listening comprehension level*. A **reading capacity level** is the highest level of material a student can understand when the passage is read to him.

Material is at the student's **independent level**—appropriate for recreational reading—when that student can read the passage without stress, correctly pronounce 97 percent of the words, and correctly answer at least 90 percent of the comprehension questions. The passage at which the student can correctly pronounce between 91 and 96 percent of the words and correctly answer at least 60 percent of the comprehension questions is the student's **instructional level**, the appropriate level of difficulty for classroom instruction in reading (see Figure 2.7).

frustration level ●

reading capacity level ●

independent level ●

instructional level ●

	WORD RECOGNITION	COMPREHENSION
Summary of informal reading inventory percentages.*		*figure* **2.7**
Independent level	97% or above	90% or above
Instructional level	91–96%	60–89%
Frustration level	90% or below	Below 60%
Listening comprehension level		75% or above

*Percentages may vary among inventories and for grade levels. These percentages of accuracy are suggested for grades 4–8 (Cooper, 1952; Klesius & Homan, 1985; Powell & Dunkeld, 1971).

After analyzing decoding and comprehension errors to establish what instruction is needed in these skill areas, the teacher conducts a *miscue analysis* to determine how the student is using language clues (i.e., syntactic, semantic, graphophonic) to think about reading. The teacher looks for patterns of miscues, such as those that retain the meaning (e.g., *Dad* for *father*), those that retain the syntactic pattern (e.g., *being* for *begging*), or those that simply retain the visual/sound similarities (e.g., *father* for *feather*). Miscues such as repetitions of words or phrases usually do not signify errors but indicate that the student may be rereading to try to rework a word or passage that did not seem to make sense.

Teachers should choose a commercial IRI that corresponds as closely as possible to the instructional materials used in the classroom and should agree with what the inventory considers a text deviation (e.g., a *repetition* is usually considered a positive second search for meaning). Additionally, by noting the types of comprehension questions, the number asked, and how scoring is handled, teachers can examine how the inventory evaluates comprehension. Teachers should also look at the clarity of instructions for administration, scoring, and interpretation and select an IRI with which they feel comfortable. See Figure 2.8 for an example of a completed IRI protocol demonstrating coding, scoring, retelling, comprehension, and miscue analysis for one student (Woods & Moe, 2011).

Running Records

Another method for analyzing a reader's miscues is a **running record** (Clay, 1985, 2000). Running record assessments use a system of checks and other marking conventions to represent what a reader says and does while reading text aloud. Analysis of running records reveals whether the reader uses the language cue systems (V = visual, or graphophonic; S = syntactic; M = meaning, or semantic) and engages in self-correction of errors. Running records may appear easier to administer than IRIs and more expedient because no special materials are needed other than paper and pencil. The IRI, however, is a more thorough assessment, because it generally requires the student to read more than one passage and allows for comparisons of the student's oral reading with the silent reading. It is important to keep in mind that multiple samples will always offer a clearer picture of any stu-

● running record

figure **2.8** Example of a completed IRI protocol.

FORM C, LEVEL 4	READER'S PASSAGES PAGE 31

Prior Knowledge/Prediction

☐ Read the title and predict what the story is about. A sick pony.
  Q: What do you know about a sick pony?
  SR: I don't know. I've never been on a pony.

☐ Read the first two sentences and add more to your prediction.

  A boy is really worried about his pony. The pony's sick.

Prior Knowledge
☐ a lot
☐ some
☑ none

A Sick Pony*	O	I	S	A	Rp	Rv
1 Jody was so/worried that he didn't even want to eat. He had stayed						
2 in the barn all day/to take care of his sick pony, <u>Gabilan</u> (Gab/Gabil). The pony's/condition (cold)			/	/	/	
3 was growing worse as/his/breathing (breath) grew louder and harder.			/		/	
4 At nightfall (night), Jody/<u>brought a blanket</u> from the house so he could sleep/ (horse SC)			/		/	
5 near/Gabilan. In the middle of the night/the wind whipped around the barn (wind SC)					/	
6 and blew the door open.						
7 At dawn Jody awakened to the banging of the barn door. Gabilan						
8 was gone! In (alarm) he ran from the barn following the pony's tracks. (follow)	/		/			
9 Looking upward (up) he saw buzzards, the birds of/death, flying overhead. (buzz SC)			/			
10 Jody stood still, then ran to the top of a small hill. In a clearing (clear) below, he			/			
11 saw something that filled his heart with anger and hate. A/buzzard/was (anjer)			/		/	
12 <u>perched</u> (pointed) on his (dying) pony's head.	/		/			
TOTALS Number of miscues __16__ Number of self-corrections __3__						

O = omission   S = substitution   Rp = repetition
I = insertion   A = aided by teacher   Rv = reversal

Source: Analytical Reading Inventory by Woods & Moe, © 2011. Reprinted by permission of Pearson Education, Inc., Upper Saddle River, NJ.

Example of a completed IRI protocol, *continued.*

figure **2.8**

FLUENCY: Does the reader . . .

- ☐ read smoothly?   ☑ word-by-word?   ☐ read words in meaningful phrases?
- ☐ use pitch, stress, and intonation to convey the meaning of a text?
- ☑ repeat words and phrases because he or she is monitoring the meaning (self-correcting)?   *some*
- ☑ repeat words and phrases because he or she is just trying to sound out the words?
- ☑ use punctuation to divide the text into units of meaning?   *Some WR difficulties are beginning to interfere.*
- ☐ ignore the punctuation?

RATING SCALE

1 = clearly labored, disfluent reading, very slow pace ⟶ 3 = poor phrasing/intonation/reasonable pace
2 = slow and choppy reading/slow pace ⟵ *2.5*   4 = fairly fluent reading/good pace

Cueing Systems				
LINE #	Miscue	Graphophonically Similar Initial Medial Final (word level)	Syntactically Acceptable Unacceptable (sentence level)	Semantic Change in Meaning (CM) No Change in Meaning (NCM) (sentence level)
2	cold	I	A	CM
3	breath*	IM	A	*slight* CM
4	night*	IM	A	*slight* CM
8	follow*	IM	A	*slight* CM
9	up*	I	A	NCM
10	clear*	IM	U	CM
11	anjer	IF	U	CM
12	pointed	IF	A	CM
	* Note the omissions of word endings.			

SUMMARY

- ☑ Most, ☐ few, ☐ no   *some*   miscues were graphophonically similar to the word in the passage.
- ☑ Most, ☐ few, ☐ no   miscues were syntactically matched.
- ☐ Most, ☑ few, ☐ no   miscues maintained the author's meaning.
- ☑ The self-corrections demonstrate that the reader monitors the meaning.

figure **2.8** Example of a completed IRI protocol, *continued.*

RETELLING

It's about a pony. Jody is really worried about the pony. It's sick. And the barn door started banging.

Q: Can you tell any more?

SR: That night Jody stayed with the horse. He saw something buzz around. The pony was gone.

Q: Can you tell more?

SR: No

RETELLING SUMMARY: ☐ many details, logical order ☐ some details, some order ☑ few details, disorder

Note: Indicate any probing with a "P"

Story Elements	All	Some	None
Main Character(s)	✓		
Time and Place		✓	
Problem		✓	
Plot Details in Sequence			✓
Turning Point			✓
Resolution			✓
Reader's Thumbnail Summary:	A pony is sick.		

COMPREHENSION QUESTIONS AND POSSIBLE ANSWERS

(RIF = Retells in fact; PIT = Puts information together; CAR = Combines author and reader; EAS = Evaluates and substantiates)

_+_ (RIF) 1. Who are the two main characters in this story? (Jody and his sick pony, Gabilan)

_+_ (RIF) 2. Where does this story take place? (in a barn, in the country)

_1/2_ (PIT) 3. What is the problem in this story? (the pony is sick and getting worse)

_−_ (CAR) 4. What do you know about the phrase the ***pony's condition***? (state of health, Gabilan is sick, his health was poor) He has a cold.

What does the phrase ***pony's condition*** have to do with this story? (the pony's condition was growing worse as his breathing grew louder and harder) He's sick.

_+_ (RIF) 5. Why did Jody take a blanket from the house? (so he could sleep near Gabilan) with his pony

_−_ (CAR) 6. What do you know about the word ***dawn***? (sunrise, the start of the day)

What does the word ***dawn*** have to do with this story? (Jody woke up at dawn) I don't know.

_−_ (PIT) 7. Why was the barn door banging? (in the middle of the night a wind whipped around the barn and blew the door open; at dawn some wind was still blowing) It's loose.

_−_ (EAS) 8. Do you think Jody's pony was dying? You think this because . . . (yes, he was really sick; it didn't say that the veterinarian had been to treat the pony; his breathing was loud; when Jody found Gabilan he saw a buzzard perched on his head) No. It ran out of the barn.

READER TEXT RELATIONSHIP (RTR): From the Text ☐ adequate ☑ not adequate

From Head to Text ☐ adequate ☑ not adequate

Scoring Guide Summary		
Word Recognition Independent 2 Instructional 7 −16 Frustration 14+	Comprehension Independent 0–1 Instructional 2 −4½ Frustration 4+	Emotional Status: Uncertain, signs of stress and tension

dent's "true" reading ability; at times, the expediency of the running record makes it more appealing, especially as a means of tracking reading fluency or measuring reading rate if the reading of the passage is timed. The number of words read correctly per minute has been shown to be an accurate indicator of overall reading performance (Fuchs et al., 2001). National performance norms for oral reading fluency are available and can be found in Hasbrouck and Tindal (2006) or at the website provided here.

WWW○○●

Norms for Oral Reading Fluency
www.readnaturally.com/pdf/oralreadingfluency.pdf

With the running record, students orally read text passages ranging from easy to difficult. Running records can be taken during small group and one-on-one conferences with a text, either narrative or expository, that the student is currently reading. The teacher sits beside the student and, using a running record form (see Appendix C.6) or a blank sheet of paper and the coding system shown in Figure 2.9, records the student's reading of approximately 100 words from any point in the text. Because the focus of running records is the word level, they may be more appropriate for use with struggling students in grades 4–8. Although understanding is not assessed with comprehension questions, teachers often ask readers to do a retelling after the passage is read to check for understanding. Teachers are able to examine students' strengths and limitations in their use of various decoding strategies by making a check mark on a piece of paper as the student reads each word correctly, and by writing the word diacritically to denote substitutions, repetitions, mispronunciations, or unknown words.

Refer to Figure 2.9 for an illustrative example of the coding conventions used for running records. A check mark indicates the word was read correctly; *R* indicates repetition, and the arrow shows what was repeated. Words in the original text are written below the horizontal lines, and what the reader said is written above the lines. *SC* means self-correct; these miscues are analyzed in a separate column because they give important information, but they do not count as words read incorrectly for scoring purposes. *E* means error. Alternatively, teachers can duplicate the pages the student will read and record errors next to or on top of the text copy.

After identifying the words that the student has read incorrectly, the teacher calculates the percentage of words read correctly. For the example in Figure 2.9, this would be 92/96, or 96 percent accuracy. Teachers use the percentage of words read correctly to determine whether the material is too easy, too difficult, or at the appropriate instructional level for the student using the same percentages discussed for the IRI estimation of reading levels.

As with the IRI, the teacher can then do a miscue analysis—categorizing the student's miscues according to the semantic, syntactic, and graphophonic cueing systems—in order to examine what word identification strategies are being used. The letters *M* (for meaning cues), *S* (for syntactic cues), and *V* (for visual cues) are used. Errors can then be classified and charted, and instructional decisions can be made accordingly.

Anecdotal Notes

Many teachers incorrectly assume that their own observations about a student's literacy status are not as important as the results of standardized tests. Researchers strongly dispute this belief (Cambourne & Turbill, 1990). One of the most powerful and reliable parts of any teacher's assessment and evaluation process, researchers claim, is teachers' daily, systematic observation of their students, documented in writing or audio or visual format. Ideally, teachers should schedule some observation time every day to focus on particular students and take brief logs, or **anecdotal notes,** about the students' involvement in literacy events (Rhodes & Nathenson-Mejia, 1992). Teachers should observe students in every possible

● anecdotal notes

figure 2.9 Example of a coded and analyzed running record.

CLAIRE'S READING

Claire made a number of errors on this text but she often self-corrected without any assistance. (Only a portion of the record is shown.)

Analysis of errors and self-corrections

CLAIRE'S RECORD

Information used

Page of Text	Running Record	E M S V	SC M S V
"Because I'm years older," Hannah smirked.	✓ ✓ ✓ ✓ R ✓ ✓.		
He gave up arguing and stomped off towards his	✓ ✓ ✓ ✓ ✓ ✓ ✓ ✓ ✓		
room. "See you in the morning," he said to	bedroom. She |SC / room. See ✓ ✓ ✓ ✓ ✓ ✓	Ⓜ Ⓢ Ⓥ / Ⓜ Ⓢ Ⓥ	M S Ⓥ
his mother to emphasize that he was ignoring	✓ ✓ and|SC emphases / to | emphasize ✓ R ✓ ✓ ✓	Ⓜ Ⓢ V / M S Ⓥ	M S Ⓥ
Hannah.	Anna |SC / Hannah |	Ⓜ Ⓢ Ⓥ	M S Ⓥ
He posed in front of his bedroom mirror. If	✓ possed / posed ✓ ✓ ✓ ✓ ✓ ✓. ✓	M S Ⓥ	
Hannah was a damsel in distress, she couldn't	✓ ✓ ✓ ✓ ✓ district | SC / distress | ✓ ✓	M S Ⓥ	Ⓜ Ⓢ Ⓥ
expect him to come galloping to her rescue.	✓ ✓ ✓ ✓ ✓ ✓ ✓ ✓.		
She could stay tied to the stake. He would	✓ ✓ ✓ died | SC / tied ✓ ✓ ✓. ✓ ✓	M S Ⓥ	Ⓜ Ⓢ Ⓥ
charge in cutting this way and that with his	✓ ✓ ✓ the / this ✓ ✓ ✓ ✓	M Ⓢ Ⓥ	
fearsome sword. All would fall before him and	✓ sword|SC / sword. | ✓ ✓ ✓ ✓ ✓ ✓	M S Ⓥ	Ⓜ Ⓢ V
he would fight his way to where she was tied	✓ ✓ ✓ ✓ ✓ ✓ ✓ ✓ ✓		
and then . . .	✓ ✓ . . .		

Her teacher summarized the analysis of the reading like this:

Claire uses meaning, structure, and visual information, repeats words occasionally, self-corrects most of her errors, picking up more visual information, and attempts all words.

Claire needs to take more responsibility for making all the information match. She needs to be encouraged to recognize when meaning is lost, and self-correct.

language context: one-on-one interactions, small group discussions, and large class settings. The focus should always be on what learners *do* as they read and write. The most useful notes are those that

- describe specific events.
- report rather than evaluate.
- relate the events to other information about the student.

Teachers can make observations about learners' attempts to use word parts, their success with daily reading and writing activities, the questions they ask, the books and online materials they are reading, what they seem to like and dislike in reading, and whether they use strategies and skills fluently or indicate some level of confusion.

These anecdotal records provide truly dynamic documentation of students' growth over time while also directing the teacher's attention to problem areas needing direct instruction for individuals and possible minilesson topics for small groups. Based on the anecdotal notes provided in Figure 2.10, Luke's teacher concluded that he

- is learning to use his prior knowledge and the context of the passage to determine the meanings of new words.
- is developing positive reading habits.
- still needs to expand his vocabulary but is developing more confidence in using background knowledge, context, and word parts.
- has an interest in the topic of planets.
- has a well-developed spatial intelligence.

This information helps Luke's teacher provide appropriate instruction for him that might include the use of literature circles, which allow students to choose the books they wish to read and discuss with their peers (see Chapter 5) and provide opportunities to create artistic responses to what they have read.

Example of anecdotal notes for Luke.   *figure* **2.10**

DATE	NOTES
12/4	During independent reading, Luke attempted a guess at a new word's meaning, spectacles. He said he remembered his brother talking about his glasses as his "specs."
1/6	Luke asked to return to the library to find a different book after starting one that he said was not interesting.
1/14	During guided reading, Luke came across the word tireless. He immediately recognized the -less ending and said "without tire." After a brief time, he said, "Oh, they wanted to make enough money to get a gift for their mother and they were working as if they were not tired."
1/27	Luke assembled a set of nonfiction literature and located several websites on the topic of planets. He has chosen drawings, charts, and diagrams as the activities he will use to show what he has learned.
2/17	Luke created an attractive and accurate mobile of the sun and the planets to share with the class as a visual for his oral report.

Checklists

Teachers often use checklists as a starting point for documenting their observations. These checklists can be developed by school districts to reflect district criteria, developed by the teacher, or located in other print or online professional references. A checklist is especially helpful in providing guidance to novices for what they should observe. Checklists should provide for multiple observations and should be used in various contexts so that conclusions are more accurate. They can be used quite effectively to gather large amounts of data that are easily compiled and reviewed. For example, a teacher can use school district content standards to develop a checklist of strategies that students are being taught. The checklist includes columns for marks (e.g., checks, plus signs, minus signs) and space for comments. Checklists can be used while observing individuals or groups, with dates or students' names inserted as column headings. Such checklists can be used and revisited periodically to monitor students' progress. Figure 2.11 is an example of a checklist for observing reading behaviors in grades 4–8 for individuals over time as well as groups of students; Mrs. B looked at how a group of six students made predictions; she also observed a number of reading behaviors exhibited by students Jen and Mark.

Checklists can also be constructed for students to use for self-assessment. Such checklists help students recognize the specific elements of performance that are expected of them. The checklists also provide a kind of road map as students complete their work. Figure 2.12 is an example of a checklist used for effective writing with students in grades 4–8.

Scoring Rubrics

scoring rubric ●

performance
descriptors ●

A **scoring rubric** describes the levels of performance that a student must demonstrate related to a particular achievement goal, whether it be written, oral, or multimedia. These criteria, or **performance descriptors,** help communicate—to both teachers and students—the standards that will be used to evaluate students' work. Scoring rubrics help provide consistency in evaluating student work. Appendix C offers examples for evaluating written work, oral performance, and multimedia presentations. Scoring rubrics represent a more analytical assessment of student work in that specific areas of strength and weakness can be readily identified.

The use of scoring rubrics also provides opportunities for involving students in self-assessment and in the formative assessment process. Effective rubrics help provide descriptive feedback to students, and as such model the kind of metacognitive thinking we want students to do as self-assessors. For example, using a rubric like the one in Figure 2.13 engages learners in reflecting on their own learning and in setting goals for meeting a specific learning target. As students engage in self-assessments, they become capable of designing their own rubrics. The results of including students in self-assessment and goal setting may be more purposeful learning and more motivated students (Locke & Latham, 2002; Shepard, 2005). Many effective rubrics can be found online. Various websites also describe the process of designing, refining, and implementing rubrics in a variety of subject areas, for both teacher- and student-generated rubrics.

Some questions to consider when constructing rubrics are as follows:

- Do the degrees of quality for the various levels change with specific detail so students know how to achieve growth?
- Will the rubric use language or numbers as scoring indicators?
- How will items be weighted—equally or uniquely?
- Does it include examples for learners?
- Is it clear and relevant to the learner?

WWW●●●

Effective Rubrics

www.rubrician.com

www.schrockguide.net/
assessment-and-rubrics.html

http://eduscapes.com/tap/
topic53.htm

Ideas for Teachers

www.readwritethink.org/lessons/
lesson_view.asp?id=101

www.readwritethink.org/lesson_
images/lesson116/Narrative
Rubric.pdf

**Teacher/Student
Rubric Design**

www.teachervision.fen.com/
teaching_methods/rubrics/
4521.html

Reading observation checklist for grades 4–8.

figure **2.11**

GRADE LEVEL: 4   **TEACHER:** Mrs. B

CONTENT STANDARDS	Brad	Sasha	Jen	Mark	Raul	Jack	COMMENTS
Reads narrative text with fluency		9/8	9/8	9/11	9/11		partner Jack & Raul
Reads expository text with fluency			9/20		9/20		
Identifies main events of the plot		9/8	9/8	9/11	9/11	9/11	
Makes inferences using text		9/8		9/11			
Makes inferences using illustrations			9/8			9/11	work with Brad 1-on-1
Identifies structural patterns in expository text:							Do more in next grading period
—compare and contrast							
—cause and effect							
—order (enumeration or sequential)			10/4	10/4			
Asks questions				9/16			
Makes predictions	9/16	9/16	9/16	9/16	9/16	9/16	
Monitors own understanding			9/20				
Applies appropriate fix-up strategies			9/20				
Creates mental images while reading							
Retells to include salient points		10/12	10/12	10/12	10/12		focus more on this
Makes text-to-self connections	10/4						
Uses clues to determine word meanings:							
—word clues							work on affixes
—sentence or paragraph clues			9/16	9/16			
—background knowledge				9/16			

figure **2.12** Student self-assessment checklist for effective writing.

NAME: Mark

TITLE(S) OF WORK ASSESSED: The Solar System

Did I . . . ?

☑ have a plan before I started writing?

☑ write complete sentences that are not run-on sentences?

☑ write some compound sentences that are connected with *and, or, but?*

☑ write a good topic sentence for each paragraph?

☑ write supporting sentences that help support the topic sentence in each paragraph?

☑ write accurate nonfiction that is also interesting?

☑ provide good transitions between paragraphs?

N/A write a story that has a beginning, a middle, and an end?

N/A write a story with a problem and a solution?

N/A describe the main character well?

N/A include dialogue in my story?

N/A use correct punctuation in any dialogue?

☑ use interesting and vivid words?

☑ confer with others to revise?

☑ edit my drafts?

- What are the focus area(s) for instruction and assessment?
- Is it developmentally appropriate for the age and grade?
- Are form and function represented? (That is, does the rubric assess both the form produced as well as the functions used?)
- Does it use clear, positive, specific, observable language?
- Are there no zero scores? (Students cannot get a score for not doing something, so there can be no zero. A 1 means they are still doing something, even if it is minimal.)

Cloze Tests

cloze test • A **cloze test** is an easy-to-use assessment device that consists of a representative 250–300 word passage from any relevant reading material, making it a useful tool across the curriculum, as Figure 2.14 illustrates. To construct a cloze passage, the first sentence is left intact, followed by an every-*n*th-word (*n* = 5, 7, or 10) deletion pattern to achieve 25–50 blanks to be filled in. Cloze tests are used to determine

Example of a self-assessment scoring rubric for a specific learning target.

figure 2.13

RUBRIC: Creatures of the Sea From A to Z   STUDENT: Luke

Requirements	FANTASTIC 4	NICE JOB! 3	OKAY 2	NEEDS IMPROVEMENT 1	SELF-ASSESSMENT	TEACHER'S ASSESSMENT
Cover Page	Includes title, author, and an appropriate illustration.	Includes two of the three required elements.	Includes one of the three required elements.	Does not include any of the three required elements, or is missing.	3 I forgot to put my name on the cover page.	3 No name on cover page
Alphabet Pages	Each of the 26 pages includes all required elements: (1) target word (2) word used in context (3) three facts about word (4) illustration for the word	Most pages include at least three required elements, and frequently four elements.	Many pages include two required elements, with several including three or four elements.	Many pages include only one or two required elements, or some pages are missing.	4 I did pages for all the letters.	3 Sometimes the three required facts were left out.
Author Page	Includes author name, background information, an illustration or photo.	Includes two of the three required elements.	Includes one of the three required elements.	Does not include any of the three elements, or is missing.	1 I forgot to do the author page.	1 The author page is missing.

My strengths are: My illustrations are really first-rate. I am skilled at drawing.

What I need to work on: I need to read the directions for my assignments carefully.

figure **2.14** (Example of group cloze test for eighth-grade social studies material about Joseph Cinque.*

Directions: In the numbered space preceding each line of text, write one word that you think best fits the blank. Read through the entire selection before you begin. This will give you clues for filling in the missing words.

MISSING WORDS	TEXT
	Human bondage has always been part of civilization.
1. _____	The ancient Egyptians enslaved the people _____
2. _____	conquered. So did the ancient Romans _____ Greeks.
3. _____	Moslem traders of the eleventh _____ exported
4. _____	their North African captives to _____ Moslem
5. _____	countries. Long before Europeans came _____ the
6. _____	scene, a small percentage of _____ Africans
7. _____	enslaved fellow black Africans. But _____
8. _____	was a difference between ancient and _____
9. _____	slavery. In ancient times, slavery was _____
10. _____	about race. Most victims were convicted _____
11. _____	or captives in wars and religious _____. They
12. _____	usually remained in the same _____ area or at
13. _____	least on the _____ continent.
14. _____	The global economy did not _____ the
15. _____	African slave trade until Spain _____ Portugal
16. _____	discovered the New World. Even _____, the
17. _____	Spanish first tried to enslave _____. They failed
18. _____	because Indians were nomadic _____, not laborers or
19. _____	farmers, and fiercely _____. As forced laborers, they
20. _____	tended to _____ and die. In fact, so many
21. _____	_____ that in 1517 a missionary named

*To be used to determine the suitability of the text for the students. *Source:* Adapted from K. Abdul-Jabbar and A. Steinberg, "Resistance," in *Black Profiles in Courage*, pp. 40–45. Copyright © 1996 by William Morrow & Co.

Continued.

figure **2.14**

22. _____   _____ Bartolome de las Casas suggested substituting

23. _____   _____ blacks instead. And that's what happened.

24. _____   _____ blacks were better suited. Most lived

25. _____   _____ settled villages, towns, and cities. They

26. _____   _____ expert farmers who grew permanent crops,

27. _____   _____ the men were used to laboring

28. _____   _____ the fields. Also, Africans understood that

29. _____   _____ could become a slave at any

30. _____   _____. And once enslaved, especially in a

31. _____   _____ culture, they knew they could not

32. _____   _____ and hide in the crowd. In

33. _____   _____ Caucasian society, where could a black

34. _____   _____ hide? . . . So African blacks quickly became the

slaves of choice. (A minimum of 25 blanks are scored.)

ANSWER KEY:

1. they	13. same	25. in
2. and	14. impact	26. were
3. century	15. and	27. and
4. other	16. then	28. in
5. on	17. Indians	29. anyone
6. black	18. hunters	30. time
7. there	19. independent	31. different
8. modern	20. sicken	32. escape
9. not	21. died	33. a
10. criminals	22. Bishop	34. person
11. feuds	23. African	
12. geographic	24. African	

a student's ability to comprehend the ideas in the sentences as well as in the entire passage (Taylor, 1953). Students must read the passage and supply the missing words. Besides establishing whether or not the text is at the appropriate instructional level (or *suitability*) for a student, this procedure may be used to assess the student's ability to use context clues in reading (see Chapter 4). By examining each incorrect response the student has made, the teacher can determine whether the response makes sense syntactically or semantically. Often, a response may be both semantically and syntactically correct without being the exact keyed response (e.g., for "The boy *stroked* the dog" the reader substitutes "The boy *petted* the dog"), which would be considered acceptable as evidence of using these two cueing systems. However, for determining appropriateness of the material in terms of reading level, only the exact keyed response can be accepted as correct. A score of 30 to 50 percent accuracy is considered instructional level, quite a lenient score as a result of only accepting exact keyed responses. A score above 50 percent is considered independent level, and a score below 30 percent is considered frustration level. The cloze material can be designed in written form or orally (recorded) for struggling readers. A variation on cloze, called *maze,* provides three word choices for deleted words instead of a blank. Students must choose the best word that fits the passage. The same deletion patterns that are used with cloze can be used with maze; however, word choices are very specific (the correct word, a word of the same part of speech, a word of a different part of speech), and the scoring changes to 85 percent for independent level, 60 to 75 percent for instructional level, and below 50 percent for frustration level (Guthrie, Siefert, Burnham, et al., 1974).

Writing Folders

writing folder ●

The **writing folder**, whether electronic or paper, is a folder where students keep all their rough drafts in various stages of the writing process and other daily compositions or reports, topics for future pieces they might like to write, and notes from minilessons. Students also include their own assessments and reflections about any piece they have completed. Pieces can be assessed using an analytic approach (see the earlier section on "Scoring Rubrics") or a holistic approach. In a *holistic approach* to writing assessment the whole piece is judged, whereas in an *analytic approach* the individual parts are assessed. Important characteristics of good writing are considered, such as the impact of the piece (does the paper engage the reader in a clear, imaginative, convincing way?), its inventiveness (does it surprise or is it clever?), and its individuality (does it have a voice?) (Kirby, Liner, & Crovitz, 2012). Material from writing folders is the basis for teacher–student conferences on individual instructional needs, and minilesson topics are chosen from observations during these sessions.

For special displays, publications, or parent–teacher meetings, the teacher often meets with each student to make collaborative decisions on what piece(s) should be selected to put in a special "showcase portfolio" that will be shown to parents (see the section on "Using Portfolios for Managing Assessment Data" later in this chapter). Writing folders are often proudly decorated and personalized by students and kept in a special place in the classroom where they are easily accessible. Anecdotal notes, checklists, or scoring rubrics regarding the contents of these folders provide important assessment data on students' writing progress.

Word Lists

Periodically, teachers in grades 4–8 may wish to conduct an informal assessment of their students' recognition of particular words, and especially of students' use of structural elements often found in multisyllabic words. To keep an account of known structural elements for each student, 3 x 5 index cards can be numbered and arranged in the same order as the words on a list of polysyllabic words such as *The Nifty-Thrifty-Fifty* (Cunningham & Hall, 1998). While holding the cards for a student to respond to, the teacher uses an accompanying checklist to note which words the student recognizes and reads successfully. (Appendix D lists the Nifty-Thrifty-Fifty; Figure 2.15 shows a partial checklist; Appendix C.12 includes the full checklist.) The student must say the entire word quickly, with no hesitation or sounding out, in order to receive credit for knowing that particular word. For each correct response, the teacher makes a check mark next to the corresponding word on the list. If the student cannot say the entire word correctly but does pronounce some of the transferable chunks, these recognized parts should be checked, but the word will not be considered correct in the final scoring. The teacher can also write above the word any attempts, parts recognized, mispronunciations, or substitutions for later analysis. The student's score is the total number of words, not chunks, checked. This raw score can then be converted easily to a percentage since the list contains 50 words. Lists of academic words (see Chapter 4) can also be used for this purpose.

Interest and Attitude Inventories

Students' interests and attitudes about reading, writing, and school in general have been found to be highly correlated with success in literacy. **Interest and attitude inventories** provide information about these factors and should therefore be included in any comprehensive assessment program. Given the importance of these factors, they should be monitored incidentally, using anecdotal notes, and deliberately through an interview or questionnaire (which can be administered orally, in writing, or online) to the whole class or to individuals. A sample reading interest inventory and an attitude survey are found in Appendix C. Teachers can design their own inventories that are appropriate to the age and developmental level of their learners, but the questions should be designed to solicit at least the following critical information:

● interest and attitude inventories

- the subject areas that the student finds motivating
- the student's favorite book
- what the student does in his or her spare time, including sports and hobbies
- the student's favorite television program
- the student's preferred instructional arrangements (e.g., teacher directed or working alone, with a small group, or with one other student)
- the student's attitudes toward reading and writing
- reading materials, websites, and experiences the student has been exposed to

Teachers can then use these data to form interest groups or to establish "partners" for reading, or to provide appropriate book selections for students to choose from for participation in book clubs (see Chapter 5).

Using Portfolios for Managing Assessment Data

Teachers and students work together toward literacy development, so they each have responsibilities for managing assessment data that document that development. Teachers engaged in data-driven decision making welcome suggestions for organizing and managing assessment data (Harp, 2006). In Ms. West's classroom, portfolios offer a management system for classroom work. They also

figure **2.15**   Cards and partial checklist for assessing the Nifty-Thrifty-Fifty.

NIFTY-THRIFTY-FIFTY*		TRANSFERABLE CHUNKS

1. ✔ antifreeze
   beauty-ful
2. ____ beautiful
   class - class - classy
3. ____ classify
   com - tees
4. ____ communities
   com - ty
5. ____ community
   composition
6. ____ composer
   continent
7. ____ continuous
8. ✔ conversation
   deodorant
9. ____ deodorize
10. ✔ different
11. ✔ discovery
12. ✔ dishonest
13. ✔ electricity
14. ✔ employee
   encourage
15. ____ encouragement
   expense
16. ____ expensive
17. ✔ forecast
18. ✔ forgotten
   government
19. ____ governor
20. ✔ happiness

1. ✔ anti

4. ✔ com
5. ✔ com
6. ✔ com
7. ✔ con
8. ✔ con
9. ✔ de

11. ✔ dis
12. ✔ dis
13. ✔ e
14. ✔ em
15. ✔ en
16. ✔ ex
17. ✔ fore

2. ✔ ful (y - i)
3. ____ ify
4. ✔ es (y - i)
5. ✔ y
6. ____ er
7. ____ ous (drop e)
8. ✔ tion
9. ____ ize
10. ✔ ent
11. ✔ y

13. ✔ ity
14. ✔ ee
15. ____ ment
16. ____ ive

18. ✔ en (double t)
19. ____ or
20. ✔ ness (y - i)

[Cards:] 1. antifreeze   2. beautiful   3. classify   4. communities

provide a way for students to take on some responsibility for organizing and self-evaluating their work. Students have the opportunity to collect, select, and value their own writing; reflect on the items chosen; and then share them publically. Teachers find portfolios helpful because they

- allow students to self-assess
- provide time for collaborative assessment
- have a recursive structure
- offer additional opportunities for feedback
- involve non-competitive learning
- accommodate individualized learning
- maintain accessible writing
- motivate students to revise, edit, share, and revisit their own writing
- offer flexibility for students who are not done after writing draft(s)

Portfolios are defined here as a collection of selected products accompanied by evidence of reflection and self-evaluation. Each artifact, or selected product, within the portfolio is accompanied by a caption, which provides a brief description of the artifact and explains why it has been included. This latter part of the caption is referred to as a *reflective statement* because it requires the portfolio-maker to reflect on why it is important to include this artifact, and to self-evaluate his or her growth in the area it represents. The teacher may decide to further discuss these reflections on the submitted product.

● portfolios

In some cases, the teacher and the student may select a piece together and then both reflect on it, stating why it was selected. In other cases, the teacher may select the piece because it demonstrates a skill that has been attained or highlights growth in a specific area. Finally, the student may select a piece just because he or she likes it and wants to show it off. In any portfolio, the teacher must design the system or process by which artifacts are chosen and decide who will reflect on them and with whom the writing and reflections will be shared.

Use of self-assessment checklists, such as the one shown in Figure 2.12, will help students prepare their reflective statements. The process of constructing a portfolio helps students understand what they know and what they still need to learn; the process of explaining what they have learned and still need to learn, as Artis did in the opening scenario, helps students gain insight into themselves as learners (Chappuis, 2005).

A portfolio with defined categories can keep products systematically sorted. For example, one portfolio system could define categories that match the curriculum framework or state standards. Thus, portfolios from students in grades 4–8 might use "comprehension," "composition," "vocabulary and word study," and "independence" as defined categories (Glazer, 1998). This kind of system enables both the teacher and students to stay organized, and it provides a point of entry for regular student–teacher conferencing. Selected artifacts are generally items the teacher designates for the portfolio (e.g., an attitude survey administered at the beginning of a school year to be compared with end-of-school-year attitudes) and those the student self-selects for particular reasons that are explained by the student. Figure 2.16 provides an example of the table of contents for a seventh-grade student's portfolio.

Electronic portfolios provide an effective assessment option for today's students, who have grown up with computers, digital cameras, smartphones, and other technologies; they may find it quite easy to use such programs as Power-Point, Prezi, and HyperStudio to create their portfolios. Electronic portfolios give students the option of storing a great deal of information on a hard drive, jump/flash drive, CD, DVD, or the Cloud. Items such as work samples, photos, art-

● electronic portfolios

---

figure **2.16** Table of contents for a seventh-grade student's portfolio.

TABLE OF CONTENTS

Introduction to the Portfolio

Comprehension

- Written analysis for *Long Gone Daddy*
- Science project drawing of the plant cells compared to animal cells and summary report
- Audio recording of Book Club discussion

Composition

- Original story: "How the Red Cabbage Became Red"
- Persuasive letter to school principal for change in PE time
- Research report
- PowerPoint presentation

Vocabulary and Word Study

- Word sort sheets for contractions, prefixes, and suffixes
- Idiomatic expressions and what they really mean
- Roots and branches (Greek and Latin roots)
- New terms for math
- New terms for social studies
- New terms for science

Independence

- Self-assessment of writing checklist
- List of books read and time sheet initialed by parent

---

work, and even oral reading samples that would be cumbersome to store and difficult to present to others using binders or files are easily stored, accessed, and presented through digital technology. The ability to connect sections of a portfolio through hyperlinks, allowing access to a variety of artifacts that might show how specific goals have been met, is another benefit of the electronic portfolio. Sound, music, and video clips can also be included to enhance the portfolio. Usually, students develop and maintain two types of portfolios: working and showcase. The **working portfolio** contains completed work samples or works in progress. It is the holding place for artifacts that may eventually be selected for placement in a showcase portfolio. The **showcase portfolio** is a collection of artifacts chosen to demonstrate excellence in achievement. Selected from the working portfolio, these artifacts are few but represent a student's best efforts. Both types can also be developed as electronic portfolios.

The portfolios that Ms. West's students shared, described at the beginning of this chapter, are examples of showcase portfolios. These portfolios were prepared and finalized for presentation to parents and other caretakers as a way of demonstrating each student's achievements for the school year.

working portfolio

showcase portfolio

Summary

Literacy assessment has two major goals: to determine how each student is progressing in a particular area at a given time, and to make instructional adjustments that are focused on students' needs. The best way to achieve these assessment goals is to use a variety of direct and indirect assessment tools; that is, to take a multidimensional approach for examining students' strengths and needs.

Indirect measures, or standardized instruments, provide important comparative data that have been proven to be valid and reliable but do not always provide accurate and specific information for individual students. Data from such measures should, therefore, be interpreted cautiously, especially when the test-takers are culturally or linguistically diverse learners.

Direct assessments—such as observations, anecdotal notes, and checklist data—can support or refute standardized test data. Data compiled frequently and interpreted carefully by means of direct assessments are excellent for continually informing instruction.

The value of the assessment tools presented in this chapter depends largely on reflective analysis and how the devices are used for communicating literacy progress and resultant instructional plans with students and their caregivers. By recognizing the strengths and limitations of different types of assessment tools, teachers can maximize their value within a balanced and comprehensive literacy program.

Questions FOR JOURNAL WRITING AND DISCUSSION

1. Interview some local teachers in grades 4–8 to determine what assessment strategies they use. What components of literacy do they assess? How are these areas assessed? Do the teachers rely more on direct or indirect assessment, or is there a balance? Discuss your findings with your classmates to compare your findings to theirs.

2. Daniels and Bizar (1998, pp. 207–209) offer 12 ideas to keep in mind for making sure assessment methods enact the ideals of best practice. Using the content of this chapter and other readings or information you have, consider these ideas. In your journal, choose two or three of the statements shown below and indicate whether you agree with the statement and why (or, if not, why not). Then, in class with a partner or small group, discuss the statements you chose.

   a. Assessment should reflect, encourage, and become an integral part of good instruction.

   b. Powerful evaluation efforts focus on the major, whole outcomes valued in the curriculum (real things such as writing, researching, reading, experimenting, problem solving, creating, speaking).

   c. Most school assessment activities should be formative (to ensure students learn better and teachers teach more effectively).

   d. Traditional norm-referenced, competitive measures that rank students against each other provide little helpful formative assessment and tend to undermine progressive instruction (constructive programs rely more on self-referenced growth measures).

   e. A key trait of effective thinkers, writers, problem solvers, readers, researchers, and other learners is that they continually self-monitor and self-evaluate (self-assessment).

   f. Skillful and experienced evaluators take a developmental perspective (stages).

g. Teachers need a rich repertoire of assessment techniques.

h. It is never enough to look at learning events from only one angle; rather, we now use multiple measures, examining students' growth from several different perspectives (for a "thick" picture of students' learning).

i. Teachers need to reallocate the considerable time that they already spend on assessment, evaluation, record keeping, testing, and grading activities (less time scoring, more time saving and documenting—new assessment procedures do not require any more time, nor any less).

j. Sound evaluation programs provide, where necessary, a database for deriving legitimate, defensible student grades (however, norm-referenced grading should be deemphasized).

k. It takes many different people working cooperatively to effectively evaluate student growth and learning (external test-makers, teachers, students, parents or guardians, school support personnel).

l. The currently available state and national standardized tests yield an exceedingly narrow and unreliable picture of student achievement, are poor indicators of school performance, and encourage archaic instructional practices (professional teachers avoid teaching to standardized tests).

3. It is no longer enough to provide students with opportunities to learn and develop their literacy skills; schools must now provide proof—in the form of standardized test scores—that learning has actually taken place. Discuss this pervasive approach to measuring learning. What implications does it have for other forms of literacy assessment?

ⓢuggestions FOR PROJECTS AND FIELD ACTIVITIES

1. Arrange to meet with a teacher and examine the report for one student's achievement test results (no need to see the student's name). With the teacher, analyze the report as though you were trying to use the data for planning instruction. What additional information do you feel might be helpful?

2. Administer a reading or writing attitude survey to a student from grades 4–8. Tabulate and analyze the responses. The following questions are provided to help you analyze the information. What are the implications for instruction?

   a. What are the student's perceptions about reading/writing?

   b. What does the student feel are important characteristics of good reading/writing?

   c. How insightful is this student in terms of how he or she perceives reading/writing?

   d. What other relevant information did you discover about the student?

   e. Do your data indicate that the student has a healthy attitude toward reading/writing?

3. Observe classroom teachers as they administer a specific literacy assessment tool (e.g., running records, cloze test, word lists, spelling test, district writing prompts). Discuss the interpretation of the results with the teachers. Why was the assessment given? What was learned? How will they adapt instruction as a result of the information gained?

REFERENCES

Anthony, R., Johnson, T., Mickelson, N., & Preece, A. (1991). *Evaluating literacy: A perspective for change.* Portsmouth, NH: Heinemann.

Barr, R., Blachowicz, C., Bates, A., Katz, C., & Kaufman, B. (2013). *Reading diagnosis for teachers: An instructional approach* (6th ed.). Boston: Allyn & Bacon.

Bishop, R. S. (1992). Multicultural literature for children: Making informed choices. In V. J. Harris (Ed.), *Teaching multicultural literature in grades K–8.* Norwood, MA: Christopher-Gordon.

Cambourne, B., & Turbill, J. (1990). Assessment in whole language classrooms: Theory into practice. *Elementary School Journal, 90,* 337–349.

Chappuis, J. (2005). Helping students understand assessment. *Educational Leadership, 63*(3), 39–43.

Clay, M. (1985). *The early detection of reading difficulties* (3rd ed.). Auckland, New Zealand: Heinemann.

Clay, M. (2000). *Running records for classroom teachers.* Portsmouth, NH: Heinemann.

Cooper, J. D., Kiger, N. D., Robinson, M. D., & Slansky, J. A. (2012). *Literacy: Helping children construct meaning* (8th ed.). Belmont, CA: Wadsworth, Cengage Learning.

Cooper, L. J. (1952). *The effect of adjustment of basal reading materials on achievement.* Unpublished doctoral dissertation, Boston University.

Cousin, P. T., Weekly, T., & Gerard, J. (1993). The functional uses of language and literacy by students with severe language and learning problems. *Language Arts, 70,* 548–556.

Cunningham, P. M., & Allington, R. L. (2010). *Classrooms that work: They can all read and write* (5th ed.). Upper Saddle River, NJ: Pearson.

Cunningham, P. M., & Hall, D. P. (1998). *Month-by-month phonics for upper grades: A second chance for struggling readers and students learning English.* Greensboro, NC: Carson-DeLosa.

Daniels, H., & Bizar, M. (1998). *Methods that matter: Six structures for best practice classrooms.* York, ME: Stenhouse.

Falk, B. (2000). *The heart of the matter: Using standards and assessment to learn.* Portsmouth, NH: Heinemann.

Fuchs, L. S., Fuchs, D., Hosp, M. K., & Jenkins, J. R. (2001). Oral reading fluency as an indicator of reading competence: A theoretical, empirical, and historical analysis. *Scientific Studies in Reading, 5,* 239–256.

Glazer, S. M. (1998). *Assessment IS instruction: Reading, writing, spelling, and phonics for ALL learners.* Norwood, MA: Christopher Gordon.

Guskey, T. R. (2005). Mapping the road to proficiency. *Educational Leadership, 63*(3), 32–38.

Guthrie, J. T., Siefert, M., Burnham, N. A., & Caplan, R. I. (1974). The maze technique to assess, monitor reading comprehension. *The Reading Teacher, 28,* 161–168.

Harp, B. (2006). *The handbook of literacy assessment and evaluation* (3rd ed.). Norwood, MA: Christopher-Gordon.

Hasbrouck, J., & Tindal, G. A. (2006). Oral reading fluency norms: A valuable assessment tool for reading teachers. *The Reading Teacher, 59,* 636–644.

Hill, B. C., Ruptic, C., & Norwick, L. (1998). *Classroom based assessment.* Norwood, MA: Christopher-Gordon.

Johnston, P. (1992). Nontechnical assessment. *The Reading Teacher, 46,* 60–62.

Kirby, D. L., Liner, T., & Crovitz, D. (2012). *Inside out: Developmental strategies for teaching writing* (4th ed.). Portsmouth, NH: Heinemann.

Klesius, J. P., & Homan, S. P. (1985). A validity and reliability update on the informal reading inventory with suggestions for improvements. *Journal of Learning Disabilities, 18*(2), 71–76.

Lindholm-Leary, K., & Borsato, G. (2006). Academic achievement. In F. Genesee, K. Lindholm-Leary, W. M. Saunders, & D. Christian (Eds.), *Educating English language learners: A synthesis of research evidence* (pp. 176–222). New York: Cambridge University Press.

Locke, E. A., & Latham, G. P. (2002). Building a practically useful theory of goal setting and task motivation: A 35-year odyssey. *American Psychologist, 57*(9), 705–717.

O'Sullivan, S., & Jiang, Y. H. (2002, Summer). Determining the efficacy of the California reading instruction competence assessment (RICA). *Teacher Education Quarterly, 29*(3), 61–72.

Powell, W., & Dunkeld, C. (1971). Validity of the IRI reading levels. *Elementary English, 48,* 637–642.

Rhodes, L. K., & Nathenson-Mejia, S. (1992). Anecdotal records: A powerful tool for ongoing literacy assessment. *The Reading Teacher, 45,* 502–511.

Schellenberg, S. J. (2004, April). Test bias or cultural bias: Have we really learned anything? Paper presented at the Annual Meeting of the National Council for Measurement in Education. San Diego, CA.

Shepard, L. A. (2005). Linking formative assessment to scaffolding. *Educational Leadership, 63*(3), 66–70.

Smith, K. (1996). Foreword. In M. Sierra-Perry (Ed.), *NCTE standards in practice: Grades 3–5* (p. v). Urbana, IL: National Council of Teachers of English.

Stiggins, R. J., Arter, S., Chappuis, J., & Chappuis, S. (2004). *Classroom assessment for student learning: Doing it right—using it well.* Portland, OR: Assessment Training Institute.

Taylor, W. L. (1953). Cloze procedure: A new tool for measuring readability. *Journalism Quarterly, 30,* 415–433.

Wilcox, J. (2006, February). Less teaching, more assessing: Teacher feedback is key to student performance. *Education Update, 48*(2), 1–2, 6, 8.

Wilhelm, J. D. (1996). *Standards in practice: Grades 6–8.* Urbana, IL: National Council of Teachers of English.

Woods, M. L., & Moe, A. J. (2011). *Analytical Reading Inventory: Comprehensive standards-based assessment for all students including gifted and remedial* (9th ed.). Boston: Pearson.

FOCUS QUESTIONS

- What should be the major objectives of an oral language program in grades 4–8?
- What are some evidence-based strategies to foster the development of both informal and formal oral language?
- How can drama be used to make language accessible for English learners?
- How can students become better listeners?

Mr. Pollard is preparing for a guided reading selection about tornadoes with his fourth-grade class. The school in which Mr. Pollard teaches is on the coast of North Carolina and, although most of the students have had firsthand experience with hurricanes, he wonders how much they know about another severe natural disaster—tornadoes. To prepare the students for the selection, Mr. Pollard leads a discussion:

Mr. Pollard: Many of our families have been affected by hurricanes, such as Katrina, Irene, and Sandy, but how many of you have ever known anyone who was in a tornado? (Several students raise their hands.) So what do you know about tornadoes, Josh?

Joshua: We lived in Kansas when I was a baby. My mother told me there was a special kind of cellar you go into when a tornado is supposed to come. A tornado can pick a house right up in the air—or even a car—but a cellar is under ground, so you're safe there.

Mr. Pollard: Yes, tornadoes are very strong and can do a lot of damage.

Patricia: Did you guys see the movie *Twister?* A huge tornado threw a cow way up in the air and even a semi! Do you think that could really happen, Mr. Pollard?

Mr. Pollard: Well, it was certainly sensational, but if you recall from the movie, there are several degrees of severity for tornadoes, and that may have been an especially fierce one.

Kendra: There was a fierce tornado in *The Wizard of Oz* that picked up their house.

Hoa: Oh, yeah, I saw that, and my little sister has the book!

Mr. Pollard: You are exactly right, Kendra and Hoa; a tornado was an important part of the book. Can anyone tell me how a tornado is different from a hurricane?

Joshua: From what I have seen on the news, it seems like you don't get much warning for a tornado. Like, there's this funnel cloud that rips through the town really quickly, smashing everything in its path. But when we had the hurricane here, they were telling us on the news to evacuate for a whole day.

Mandy: Yeah, the movie showed the tornado happening really fast, before the guys who were studying it had time to get out of the way! And they were in a car!

Mr. Pollard: So, you think the tornado comes on more suddenly?

Joshua: Oh, yeah—way more suddenly. I guess that would make 'em even scarier than a hurricane, and that was for sure the most scared that I have ever been! (Others murmur in agreement.)

Raul: They're bigger and black, too. And I don't think you have to have any rain with them. At least from what I've seen on the news.

Kendra: And is there an eye with them, the part that is the worst, like with a hurricane? I don't ever remember hearing about it if there is.

Hoa: Do we have tornadoes in North Carolina? I hope not!

Crystal: I'm pretty sure we do! My aunt lives in Greenville, and there was one there a long time ago. My cousin told me about it. The roof of their trailer was torn off, and a telephone line came down on it. But it was weird because it was just in some parts of the town and not in others. My aunt was shopping when it happened, so she didn't get hurt.

Mr. Pollard: I am glad to hear your relatives weren't hurt! You all seem to know quite a bit about tornadoes. From your comments, it seems that tornadoes are similar to but also different from a hurricane. Let's find out more. I brought in some photographs that I got from the Internet showing a recent tornado in Oklahoma. (He passes these around.)

Mr. Pollard explains that tornadoes are often called "twisters" because of their funnel shape. He adds that tornadoes usually occur in flat prairie land, so the chances of having one on the North Carolina coast, while not impossible, are not likely. He then asks students if they have any questions about tornadoes. Several students respond, and he writes their questions on the whiteboard:

> What causes tornadoes? What kind of weather makes them happen?
>
> Why do they twist and have a funnel shape?
>
> Why are they generally found in flat prairie land but not on the coast?
>
> How are they different from hurricanes?

Throughout the discussion, Mr. Pollard has not only assessed the prior knowledge of the students in his class about the upcoming science selection, but he has allowed them to share their experience and knowledge with each other. While doing so, they have set purposes for their subsequent reading and will have a more personal involvement with it.

After the reading, Mr. Pollard leads a discussion based on the students' questions. They talk about the new information they have learned and compare the data from the selection with what they remembered from *Twister,* the movie many of them had seen, as well as their other previous associations with the topic. From their comments and questions, Mr. Pollard can evaluate how well the children read and understood the reading selection, and how they are able to synthesize the new information with their prior knowledge. The last question—about how tornadoes are different from hurricanes—was not addressed in the text, so Mr. Pollard breaks the class into discussion groups consisting of three or four members each and invites them to use a Venn diagram to come up with lists of similarities and differences between tornadoes and hurricanes using information they find online and in trade and reference books (see Figure 3.1). Finally, Mr. Pollard helps the groups to consolidate their lists into one set, thus deepening their understanding of the two types of storms through reading and much rich oral discussion.

The Venn diagram used in Mr. Pollard's class to compare tornadoes and hurricanes. *figure* **3.1**

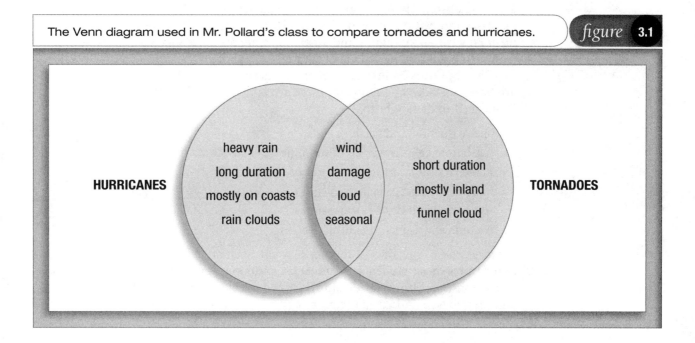

Introduction

The importance—academically, socially, and vocationally—of the ability to speak and listen with ease in contemporary society cannot be emphasized enough. Although it seems that speaking and listening are learned automatically simply through contact with other people, we do need to reserve considerable classroom time for work with many forms of speaking and listening. Better still, we need to find ways to integrate the language arts of listening and speaking (as well as the other language arts) with other content areas. Additionally, with the arrival of non–native English speakers in our schools, it becomes even more critical to create classrooms that are rich with the spoken word.

It is important to foster communication in the classroom, but teachers should consider much more than just talking. It is essential that teachers attend to discourse patterns, or the language used to communicate naturally and with expertise within a certain population (Hicks, 1995). Because discourse is social, and the communication between speaker and listener or between author and reader inherently requires positioning of power (Gee, 1996), some students are more apt to lead conversations in class, influence the opinions of others, and make sure their cultural bias or social understanding is dominant. Students, as part of the discourse community that is their classroom, need to know how to navigate and practice using the academic language of the school.

All students need a strong oral language base not only to participate in classroom discourse but also to use in developing other literacy skills. Through speaking and listening, students improve vocabulary, acquire new concepts, and become familiar with the structure of the English language—the essential building blocks of all learning (Smith, 2001). If students are going to learn speaking skills, it seems axiomatic that they must have many opportunities to practice different types of speaking (Pinnell & Jaggar, 2003). Students who possess strong oral language skills have a better chance of becoming proficient readers and have greater potential for writing well than do students who lack such skills (Heath, 1983; Loban, 1976; Sampson, 1986). Moreover, some educators have discovered that peer talk increases motivation to read (Griffin, 2001); as a result, there has been a movement toward encouraging and fostering students' listening and speaking, away from perpetual teacher-led classroom talk.

The objectives of an oral language program around which most state standards are based include the following; these are addressed at length in this chapter. Students need to be taught to

- speak fluently and easily.
- use language as a way to communicate their ideas.
- perceive oral language as a way of learning.
- be familiar with specific skills of effective speaking.
- use various modes of expression.
- become strategic and skillful listeners.

To reach these objectives, a teacher in a balanced and comprehensive literacy program can expose students to informal speaking (e.g., conversations, classroom discussions, and informal debates); formal speaking (e.g., speeches, oral reports, and interviews); and drama (e.g., role playing, readers theatre, and simulations).

Informal Speaking

informal speaking ●

Informal speaking, such as that contained in conversation and spontaneous or directed discussions, is the most frequently used expressive language mode. Most native English–speaking students are fluent users of oral language in English by the time they start school. (English learners are likely fluent in their own native languages but non-fluent in English.) Because most students have already acquired considerable competence using oral language, teachers often assume that they don't need to emphasize oral language in their classrooms, especially as students enter middle school. (In fact, some teachers expend considerable energy trying to *prevent* students from talking in class!) A significant body of research has shown, however, that students benefit greatly from participation in both formal and informal oral language activities (Strickland & Feeley, 2003). Moreover, it has become increasingly important for all students to have a language-rich environment, and such a classroom is the best source of language learning for students who do not speak English or who are in the process of acquiring it (Peregoy & Boyle, 2013).

Conversations

Oral language can and should be a natural, essential part of a balanced and comprehensive literacy program. Students must be taught how, and given the opportunity, to have productive academic conversations. For example, have students converse with their peers as they plan and carry out collaborative projects or conduct writing conferences. Teachers, the primary models of standard English in any classroom, can also conduct informal conversations with students at various times during the day. Special time can be set aside for teachers to communicate with shy students, students who are experiencing difficulties in their lives, or those who need extra attention.

The rich context of a personally relevant conversation creates the *schema,* or background, necessary to store new word meanings. Moreover, the definitions students learn through conversations will probably be in terms they are developmentally able to understand. Then, in the context of that same conversation, students will often use the new word or words they have just learned. This immediate application further ensures that these terms will become part of students' permanent speaking, reading, and writing vocabularies.

Besides increasing vocabulary and helping students crystallize their thoughts on a variety of subjects, conversations provide a way for teachers to make their students feel important and show respect for their ideas. Conversations can also provide teachers with important insights into the possible reading interests of their students as they discuss their likes and dislikes in the context of everyday discourse.

Students with similar interests can form self-initiated **conversation clubs,** to chat about an event, an idea, or an experience they have in common. During these sessions, teachers can learn much about students' oral language prowess by taking anecdotal notes about whether students

Conversations can provide teachers with important insights into the possible reading interests of their students as they discuss their likes and dislikes in the context of everyday discourse.

- extend the conversation without coaxing.
- hold listeners' attention.
- check for accuracy without being told to do so.
- ask questions for clarification.
- add interesting information.
- have adequate grammar and vocal habits.

● conversation clubs

Based on their findings, teachers can group students for minilessons on informative and interpersonal language uses.

Teachers may find it helpful to have at their command a list of provocative topics to which they can refer when they wish to plan a special conversation time (see Figure 3.2). Additionally, the following activities are sure to provoke even the quietest student to contribute an oral response.

Topics for informal conversations.   *figure* **3.2**

What movies have you seen that you liked? Why?	What things make you happy or sad?
What do you do on weekends?	What is your favorite website? Why?
What qualities do you value in a friend? Why?	Do you have any pets? Describe your pet(s).
What music groups do you enjoy? What do you like about them?	What is your favorite holiday? Why?
What is your favorite place to be? Why?	If you could go anywhere in the world, where would you go? Why?
What is your favorite TV show? Why?	Who is your favorite relative? Why?
What is your favorite video game? Why?	What do you do to be kind to your friends or brothers and sisters? How do they respond?
What would you do if you had a million dollars?	

activity Just Suppose . . .

1. Develop a set of cards containing interesting suppositions (see suggestions below).
2. Pair up students.
3. Give each pair a card with a printed Just Suppose . . . idea.
4. Allow students to discuss their supposition for five minutes, weighing positives and negatives.
5. Encourage each pair to arrive at a consensus.
6. Invite pairs to share their responses with the rest of the class.

SUGGESTIONS FOR "JUST SUPPOSE . . ." CARDS
. . . everyone looked exactly alike.
. . . you could talk to animals.
. . . you could become invisible.
. . . you could fly.
. . . you could travel by "transporter"
. . . you were President of the United States.
. . . you could read people's minds.
. . . there was no money.
. . . you could "rewind" your life.
. . . there was only one kind of food.

activity Campfire

1. For this activity, change the classroom seating arrangement to make it enjoyable and relaxing. For example, have students sit in a circle and pretend they are around a campfire. Be sure to video- or audiorecord the sharing period so that a recording will be available in a media center designated for this purpose.
2. Select a topic (see Figure 3.2) or allow students to talk about a favorite object. Ask them to speak loudly enough so everyone can hear.
3. Instruct the class to listen politely as each student takes a turn speaking. As each speaker finishes, invite students to ask follow-up questions. Questions must begin with one of the five Ws: Who, why, what, where, when. For example: "Where did you get that skateboard? Why is it so important to you?"
4. Correlate other subjects with this oral-sharing time. For example, it might be combined with a current events lesson, where students can share something they have read online or heard on the news.

To provide opportunities for students to have unrestricted conversations about a text or other classroom information, ask open-ended questions. To stimulate an open-ended conversation, ask your students to choose one of the following prompts and jot down ideas to finish the sentence. Then have them share their thoughts with a partner. Prompts can include:

- One thing that interested me about today's reading was . . .
- While reading, I realized . . .
- I didn't understand the text's discussion about . . .
- Why does the author or character . . .

- The most important or interesting event was . . .
- I was especially taken with this line _____ on page ___ because . . .
- I can relate to this story or event because . . .
- I wish I could ask the character or author . . .
- One strategy I used when I did not understand _____ from the reading was I . . .
- A good discussion question for this reading is . . .

Directed Group Discussions

Discussions are similar to conversations in several ways. Both involve the use of oral language in an informal setting. Both involve an exploration of an issue or a topic and offer students the opportunity to use a variety of speaking skills. A discussion can be defined as "problem-solving by cooperative thinking." The goal of any discussion or problem resolution should be to consider a question from many angles, allowing all participants a voice.

• discussion

As students advance through school, teachers focus less on informal discussions and more on teacher-directed discussions, with a specific learning goal that the teacher has identified. Discussions are the principal means through which the conversational skills related to thinking patterns and interpersonal functioning are developed. In the primary and on into the middle grades, these skills are taught largely through teacher modeling. The teacher contributes as well as solicits comments related to the topic under discussion; points out the connections among ideas being discussed; and demonstrates the processes of hypothesizing, summarizing, generalizing, and relating new information to one's own experience.

Asking provocative questions that probe students' imaginations helps large- or small-group discussions become one of the richest sources of learning and processing information. Question depth varies, depending on the skills needed to respond to the questions. For example, asking students to recall information is a low-level skill, but combining that with an inference question—a question that asks students to draw a conclusion based on evidence—brings it to a higher level. Multi-level questions require students to use many different skills when responding and can foster meaningful discussions.

Gradually, as students progress through grades 4–8, they begin to incorporate these conversational skills into their own discussions. For example, in the discussion opening this chapter, the students in Mr. Pollard's class were able to relate a new concept to their own experiences, make generalizations about hurricanes, and hypothesize about how they differ from tornadoes.

Inquiry teaching, which is often used in social studies and science units, involves generating questions to be discussed with students. With inquiry teaching, learners are actively involved in deciding on topics to explore and directing their own discussions. This technique fosters rich oral language production for *all* students (Strickland & Feeley, 2003).

With inquiry learning, it is helpful to precede discussion periods with time during which students can explore a specific content area topic, such as "Why are the rain forests diminishing and what can we do about it?" Establishing this exploratory time helps students attain a depth of information as background for the subsequent discussion. One of the benefits of creating such informative and interactive discussions is that—provided the teacher has set up a safe, nonthreatening classroom environment where no put-downs are allowed—students will appreciate their classmates' oral exchanges even more. They will actually learn from each other in a powerful way that is not always possible from a conversation with an adult.

Suggestions for Teacher-Guided Discussions

Plan for the discussion by

- defining the issue to be discussed.
- preparing some leading questions.
- allowing students to research the topic.

Initiate the discussion by

- making a brief statement or offering a pertinent quotation.
- providing a handout with a summary of information about the topic.
- reminding students of guidelines for courteous behavior.

Keep the discussion running smoothly by

- having a recorder write responses on the whiteboard.
- discouraging domination of discussion by a vociferous few.
- inviting shy students to contribute.
- allowing English learners to use gestures and their home language.

Bring out all sides of the topic by

- providing informative data from all sides of the issue.
- asking students to consider the opposing viewpoint.
- playing the role of "devil's advocate."

Help students to reach a consensus by

- summarizing points made by students on all sides.
- clarifying problematic issues as they arise.
- offering topics for subsequent discussion.

For more formal discussions and to foster a more student-centered classroom, it is sometimes helpful to appoint a discussion leader. The discussion leader has specific responsibilities. The leader opens the discussion and establishes its goals; the leader may also find it necessary to clarify participants' statements and summarize progress as a basis for continuing productive discussion. Occasionally, the discussion leader will have to handle differences of opinion among participants. The leader also may need to learn to approach, diplomatically, a talkative student who attempts to dominate the discussion, and to draw in a shy student who needs to be invited to participate. Teachers will find it necessary to model discussion-leader behavior for students initially; then all students should have an opportunity to perform this role, which is so pivotal in developing leadership qualities.

The following guidelines may be helpful to share with students when initiating formal classroom discussions:

- Find out as much as you can about the topic ahead of time.
- Support your opinions with facts.
- Stay on topic.

- Listen carefully to other speakers.
- Do not repeat what has already been said.
- Ask for clarification when you don't understand what has been said.
- At the end, help the leader summarize the most important points.

Discussions About Text

Teachers continually assess whether students have understood the information in reading material; they then make instructional decisions, providing modeling and support to help students better understand what they have just read. One way to check for understanding is to attend to interactions as students respond to text, before, during, or after reading. Specifically, teachers observe students' discussions, responses to questions or prompts, or any classroom activity that promotes small or large group sharing. Once teachers have made these informal assessments, they may opt to use various discussion "moves" to assist students as they explore texts and ideas. Adapted from recommendations by Beck, McKeown, Hamilton, & Kucan (1997), the following discussion techniques will help students become more strategic readers:

- *Marking:* The teacher or facilitator points out particular ideas to stress their importance or their noteworthiness in the context of the conversation or text.
- *Turning it back to students:* Instead of answering students' questions or offering suggestions to problems, turn the responsibility back to the students; have them problem-solve or come up with creative answers to their questions or the problem at hand.
- *Turning it back to text:* The teacher or facilitator turns students' attention back to the text to answer a question, to clarify their thinking, or to find answers.
- *Revoicing:* In this instructional move, the teacher first interprets what the student is trying to say, rephrases her ideas, and then helps her to feel included in the class discussion. The teacher must make sure the student agrees with the teacher's interpretation. This move allows the teacher to increase the academic language in the classroom, as the comment is rephrased and clarified with specific and perhaps more sophisticated language related to the topic.
- *Modeling effective responses to text:* In a think-aloud fashion, the teacher models how a reader interprets a part of the text. The teacher reads aloud the chunk that may be confusing and shares how he understands the text as it is read. The teacher may say, "I am confused now, because in the last paragraph, the dog came home, but now he has returned. I wonder what the author meant by 'returned.'"
- *Annotating:* The teacher asks the students to mark their texts. The teacher can provide particular focus points or prompted spots, or the teacher can ask students to select particularly interesting or confusing parts to summarize or discuss. Then, students can share these in small groups or with the class as a whole. The teacher, through this annotation activity, allows students to be prepared ahead of time for text conversation and for future writing by responding and reacting to text, he allots time for students to consider the text and clarify their ideas about it before hearing the opinion of others.
- *Recapping:* The teacher shows students how to highlight the major ideas discussed in a given portion, rather than highlighting each idea or event. The ability to recap provides students with the skills to summarize and gather evidence; it also enables them to present this information in a concise manner aloud or in writing.

As part of direct instruction, teachers model these techniques for students so they can use them in small groups or independently as they read.

Students need many opportunities to discuss books they have read or to hear discussions about books they may not yet have read. Smith (1998) cautions that simply asking students a list of questions about text to probe their thinking is rarely productive. Literature circles (see Chapter 5) are a wonderful means for encouraging intensive discussion and reflection about the books students are reading. When students share their personal responses and interpretations of a book with their peers, they are able to gain a deeper understanding of themselves and their world. Moreover, the discussions can lead to enhanced enjoyment of both literature and informational text (Straits & Nichols, 2006).

The most common approach to literature circles is for partners or small groups simply to sit together following the reading of a book or a portion of a book to talk about what they have read. They may share their responses to the same title; alternatively, they may discuss different books all on a similar theme or topic, perhaps by the same author or illustrator, or from a particular literary genre. The teacher sets up a system that allows students to select their own books and then schedules class time for students to meet. The partners or groups may have rotating, assigned roles, such as "discussion director" or "illustrator" or "vocabulary enhancer," or—in the case of expository text—"fact finder" or "science sleuth" (Straits & Nichols, 2006) to give individuals accountability for the reading and ensure that each student has a voice in the group discussion (refer to Figure 5.6, in Chapter 5). This kind of rich, open-ended literature discussion offers literature experiences to all students regardless of current reading level.

grand conversations ●   **Grand conversations,** as they are sometimes called (Eeds & Wells, 1989), provide another opportunity for students to discuss reading materials. Grand conversations follow a read-aloud or the independent reading of chapters in a novel. In small groups or in pairs, students can respond to story elements such as plot, illustrations, imagery, or specific characters. They can make connections between books, compare works by the same author (or compare this one to those of another author), contrast other versions of the story, or compare some facet of the story to their own lives. These same discussions about a text can follow the reading of a poem, listening to a story at a listening center, or watching a video of an author reading on YouTube, or after a guided reading of a difficult piece of literature with finely shaded meaning. Much as adults often wish to share their feelings about a book that has touched them in some way, students' oral response to literature can deepen their appreciation for literature. Hearing their peers' perspectives on what they have read increases their critical and evaluative thinking about text (Gambrell & Almasi, 1996; Paratore & McCormack, 1998; Roser & Martinez, 1995). A *paideia seminar*—a collaborative, intellectual dialogue about a text inspired by open-ended questions—is a similar method of promoting classroom interaction (Billings & Roberts, 2006). Students engage in conversations and stress higher level thinking as they debate topics and discuss text. (Another, less structured, form of literature discussion uses double-entry journals, as discussed in Chapter 5.)

All of these text-based activities promote reading, speaking, and listening. With the right facilitation, prompting, and selections, students become engaged and excited to share the books they have read.

Informal Debates

When a whole-class discussion has revolved around a controversial issue and the class has seemingly taken sides, an informal debate can be a perfect avenue for combining critical thinking with informal speaking. First, the teacher helps students to clarify the issue and the opposing positions. Then students are asked to move to opposite sides of the room, designated "supporters" and "opposers," depending on the position they have taken, and to appoint a spokesperson. If certain students have not made up their minds, they are asked to take a seat in the middle of the classroom. The opposing sides are then given 10 to 15 minutes to draw up several arguments in support of their position. Next the teacher starts the debate by asking the spokesperson of the supporting group to make an opening statement. The opposition is then allowed to make a statement. After each statement, both the neutral students and those on the opposing side may ask questions. After the debate, participants render an evaluation of the points made on both sides. No vote is required, but some kind of consensus may emerge.

Some possible topics for informal debate include:

- Should we have homework on weekends?
- Should we explore outer space?
- Should scientists be allowed to clone human beings?
- Should animals be allowed in restaurants?
- Should 12-year-olds be allowed to drive? Vote?

Formal Speaking

rom their experiences with extensive classroom conversations and discussions, students gain confidence speaking in groups, where the responsibility for communication is shared with others. As students gain experience and confidence, they should be introduced to more formal oral language experiences that require more preparation. Oral reports, interviews, panel discussions, announcements, and impromptu speeches are some of the formal ways students can organize information and fluently express their ideas and information.

Oral Reports

Oral reports are a way of sharing information and ideas before a group of people. Learning to prepare and deliver oral reports is an important part of the curriculum. It can be a positive, confidence-building event if authentic purposes are honored and adequate guidance in the process is provided. Teachers must remember (and convey to students) that research reports serve genuine language functions—to inform or persuade. When students give reports, they are also learning a great deal about their chosen topic and developing their communication abilities. Teachers will need to guide learners through the four steps of preparing a report:

● oral reports

1. choosing a topic
2. gathering information
3. organizing the information
4. making the presentation

Choosing a topic. Oral reports are most successful when students are involved in choosing their own topic. Choice allows them to take ownership of the project, which will often motivate them to invest more time and energy in the preparation. In some cases students may choose any topic that interests them, but in other cases the teacher may need to limit students to a broad topic within an area of class study. Within this broad area, they are then free to choose their specific topics. For example, the class may be studying the California Gold Rush of the mid-nineteenth century. From that broad area, students could choose a variety of topics such as the cultural groups involved, how to pan for gold, people's reasons for heading out West, or the hardships encountered there.

Gathering information. Students should be directed to gather information from a variety of sources, including the Internet, academic software, encyclopedias, almanacs, reference and trade books, magazines, and primary sources such as interviews (discussed later). In addition to these sources, students should learn to use video and podcast excerpts and to talk with experts in the area they are studying. Chapter 7 offers more information on researching. Notes in the form of key words or phrases may be recorded on index cards, outlines, mapping, or other types of diagrams; students might also use note-taking software.

Organizing the information. After gathering information, students need to sort through it and decide in what sequence to present it. They should be encouraged and shown how to create visual aids such as posters, graphs/infographics, pictures, models, Prezi or PowerPoint presentations, or video, all of which serve to enhance audience interest and understanding. They may also choose an unusual format for presentation if it lends itself to the specific topic. For example, a short skit or video clip might help an audience gain insight into the decision-making process a family had to go through in order to make the westward journey in the 1840s in their quest for gold.

Making the presentation. The final step in the oral report is the actual presentation. Students should rehearse the presentation several times by reviewing key points and reading over their note cards or diagrams. Before the presentations begin, the teacher should discuss the critical points that students need to remember. For example, speakers should speak slowly and loudly enough for all to hear, keep to the main points, refer to their note cards only when needing a prompt—rather than reading from them—and weave in the visuals they have prepared. They should also make eye contact with the audience and speak with expression as opposed to speaking in a monotone voice.

Students may present their oral reports to the whole class or to small groups of fellow students. For example, have students studying the Gold Rush give their reports to groups of five or six students at a time. Groups may be spread around the room; members of the group listen to each report, ask questions, and offer constructive feedback on the content and effectiveness of delivery. Speakers then rotate to a different group. In this way, students will give their first formal report to a small group, which is less intimidating than a large one, and they will each get a chance to give their report multiple times, affording practice and refinement. When students are more experienced, they can deliver their oral reports in front of the whole class and perhaps be video recorded.

For information about assessing oral reports, see Chapter 2 and the scoring rubric for oral presentations in Appendix C.13.

Interviews

interview ● An **interview** is a form of oral information gathering. Interviewing is an important language tool that can be integrated effectively with almost any area of the curriculum. The interviewer may speak with one or two individuals or with a small group. The interviewer may gather information regarding an individual's life history, a group he is involved with (e.g., sports, musical, political, or humanitarian), or a situation that concerns him (e.g., recycling, crime, terrorism, or climate change). Students may choose to interview people living nearby, such as a teacher, the principal, a local artist, the winner of a spelling bee, or a person from a culture that is different from theirs. Students can also interview longtime area residents about local history, or even people who live far away—such as a favorite author or a professional athlete—using Skype or some other form of online conversation.

The interviewer prepares a set of questions designed to obtain the desired information. The questions should be written on note cards, one per question, and consist of open-ended queries as opposed to questions that could be answered "yes" or "no." An example of an open-ended question might be "Why did your family emigrate from Russia?" The questions should be organized according to related topics; the teacher should then review them to ensure that they will elicit the information the interviewer is seeking. As they become more experienced, students can ask follow-up questions, such as, "Could you tell me a little bit more about that?"

Students should contact the person or persons being interviewed in advance to set up an appointment. They should also learn as much as they can about the person prior to the interview. Interviewers often record interviews (video or audio), but they need to obtain permission ahead of time. Many computers, smartphones, and other mobile devices have built-in cameras, and students may be able to videocast their interviews. If, however, the interviewee does not want to be recorded, then the interviewer should carefully write down all responses. When the interview is complete, the interviewer should thank the person for her time and follow up with a written note.

To share the results of an interview, the student should first carefully read over all notes, listen to, or watch the recording of the interview. Then organize the information and decide on a format for presenting it (see Figure 3.3).

Early in the school year, use the following informal interview activity to help the class become acquainted and feel comfortable asking questions, an important precursor to a more formal interview.

PERFORMANCE	GRAPHICS/VISUALS/AUDIO
report	poster
review	collage
panel	PowerPoint or Prezi presentation
debate	video
skit	time line
role play	map
simulation	mural
expert guest speaker	flow chart
	model
	overheads
	podcast

Project presentation options. *figure* 3.3

activity   Getting to Know You

1. Elicit a set of questions about things students may or may not have done. For example:

HAVE YOU EVER . . .	DO YOU . . .	WHO IS . . .
had something painful happen, like being stung by a bee or falling off your bicycle?	have a brother or a sister?	the person you admire most?
had a fight with a friend?	have a pet?	a teacher you remember well?
celebrated a birthday in an unexpected way?	like to read?	a relative with some unique qualities?
received money as a happy surprise or earned it?	have a hobby?	your favorite singing group?
taught someone something new?	have a birthmark or tattoo?	your favorite TV star?
appreciated something you did not think you would?	have a secret that you've kept with a family member or friend?	your favorite movie star?
	prefer being outdoors or indoors?	

2. Write these questions on the whiteboard and ask students to copy them on a sheet of paper.

3. Have students, with a partner, select a few questions to discuss. Each partner writes down his or her responses to the interview questions.

4. Designate which partner in each group is the interviewer and which is the interviewee.

5. For variety, allow each interviewer to ask a few "off-the-cuff" questions in addition to the listed ones. Instruct each interviewer to write down all responses.

6. After the interviews are completed, have students switch roles and repeat the process.

7. You may choose to have the whole class compile the results in tallies, maps, or graphs, or use the results in a bulletin board display entitled "Who Did What?"

Oral Histories

An interesting blend of oral reports and interviews is the *oral history,* a way to connect history to students' own lives. One seventh-grade teacher in Los Angeles made history come alive using this approach. James Green had his students discover their own histories (Cummins, Brown, & Sayers, 2007). He asked students to concentrate on two research questions: "Where does my family come from?" and "What history is contained in my family?" Then, Mr. Green introduced the approach that oral historians use to design interview questions, take notes, and organize information. He showed them how to use a tape recorder to record a conversation and later transcribe it. He also helped students prepare open-ended questions to invite conversation, such as "What was life like when . . . ?" and "What do you remember about . . . ?" Finally, he gave them time in the computer lab to look at other oral history projects online.

In addition to conducting interviews, students used a number of primary sources and other research tools. Mr. Green showed them how to locate primary source material and historical documents on the Internet, explaining that all information viewed there must be evaluated critically for its accuracy and completeness, and reinforcing visual and media literacy (see Chapter 10). He also asked students to consider the effectiveness of each tool for the task for which it would be used; for example, some students found that making a recording hampered spontaneity when family members were sharing personal recollections; others found that a family-tree template they discovered on the Internet did not readily accommodate their nontraditional family. Additionally, some students were able to use a genealogical website that revealed much about previous generations, while other students found nothing and had to rely on interviews.

Using these techniques, students conducted individual investigations of their own families, wrote reports, and then presented their findings in oral presentations. After initially balking at the assignment, students became excited as they discovered many fascinating details about the former lives of close and distant relatives. They were eager to share their new insights. Their newfound knowledge resulted, suddenly, in many student-generated history questions in class: "What was D-Day, Mr. Green?" from a student whose great-grandfather had been a soldier in World War II, or "Why were so many people against the Vietnam War?" from a student whose great-uncle had fled to Canada rather than be drafted.

Mr. Green taught the students to use a digital video recorder to create an iMovie to capture the class's entire experience of researching and presenting their families' oral histories. The class iMovie was shown at an open house to a record number of eager parents and other family members, who had enjoyed participating in the oral history project. Many parents exclaimed how their communication with their youngster had been enriched through the project, with the students demonstrating a deeper pride and respect for their heritage. The project, while meeting many literacy and social studies goals, went far beyond the state standards as students were given the opportunity to connect with history in a deeply personal way.

Panel Discussions

A panel discussion is a favorite activity for formally sharing different kinds of information. The panel, usually consisting of three to eight members, conducts a discussion in front of the rest of the class. The topic, issue, or question is predetermined. The panel format is most effective when the presentation is thoughtful, informative, and researched ahead of time rather than argumentative or spontaneous. After panelists conclude their presentations, class members are invited to ask them questions regarding a specific point.

 Online Resources for Oral Histories

Making Sense of Oral History, http://historymatters.gmu.edu/mse/oral/

This website includes a guide to finding and using oral history online. It is a great first step for teachers and students to start using oral history interviews as historical evidence.

Step-by-Step Guide to Oral History, www.dohistory.org/on_your_own/toolkit/oralHistory.html

This handy guide offers suggestions for collecting and organizing oral history. The website also discusses many issues that students should keep in mind when conducting and using oral histories.

Oral History Society, www.ohs.org.uk/

This comprehensive website explains what oral history is and how it can be used to bring a new dimension to the study of local and family history.

It is suggested that the teacher or panel members select a moderator; this person is responsible for organizing the panel to ensure that various points of view are represented and for monitoring the discussion to ensure that all participants have an opportunity to speak. A time limit should be placed on individual participation as well as the posing of questions by classmates. With practice, students will gain confidence in presenting information to their peers. Teachers are often surprised at how deeply student panelists will research a topic, especially when it is a provocative subject.

The following is a variation on a panel discussion known as controlled participation, or CONPAR. The process was developed by General Motors for use with sales personnel in training sessions, but it is adapted here for use in grades 4–8. CONPAR is one of the best methods to guarantee the participation and involvement of all members of a group, regardless of group size or the age of the participants.

◎ activity ◎   Controlled Participation (CONPAR)

1. Decide on a problem to be solved or a topic to be discussed (e.g., the diminishing rain forest).

2. Select three to eight panel members.

3. Have the panel members and other class members learn everything they can about the topic or problem.

4. Divide the other class members into groups and seat group members together.

5. Select a chairperson whose job is to keep the discussion going; then, for each group, select a recorder.

6. Allow 10 minutes for discussion about the problem or topic. Instruct students in each group to come up with three questions, and have the recorder write these on note cards.

7. After the groups turn in the cards, shuffle them and read the first question aloud.

8. Invite one or more panel members to respond to the question. Limit each response to two minutes.

9. Read the second card aloud and ask different panel members to respond. Continue in this manner until all the questions have been answered.

10. At the end of the session, take a few minutes to summarize key points that have been made.

Impromptu Speeches

An **impromptu speech** can be defined as a talk that is prepared without extensive planning, thus requiring a modicum of creativity and "thinking on one's feet." The ability to give an impromptu speech is a very important formal oral language skill to develop because it is perhaps the one that people will use most frequently in later life.

To stimulate this type of formal speaking, prepare several 3 x 5 cards with thought-provoking topics, such as "The strangest dream I ever had." Have each student select a card and then allow a few moments for them to think about their responses to these topics. In a comfortable and safe small-group setting, invite each student to speak for three minutes on their topic. Evaluations of this type of speaking should be supportive and positive. The following are additional examples of topics to use for impromptu speeches:

> My favorite thing to do
> If I were stranded on a desert island
> Why conservation is important
> The best movie I have ever seen
> The person I most admire
> Things that make me happy
> How I would like to change the world
> What I do on weekends
> A place I have been
> If I were an animal

Drama

Drama is an integral part of a balanced and comprehensive literacy program. Participating in classroom drama is an incomparable forum for language enjoyment, enriched comprehension, and community building. Additionally, drama can be a powerful way of learning and an alternative way of knowing—the actors become participants in the learning process and not merely passive bystanders (Wagner, 2003). Drama makes especially strong contributions to the growth of English learners' speaking ability, because it provides natural comprehensible input: the actions accompanying the spoken words give them an immediate context. Furthermore, drama gives students opportunities to experiment with words, emotions, and social roles and encourages them to make sense of their world in a multisensory way. Above all, through drama, students become more sensitive, confident communicators.

In this section, we explore three types of drama well suited to students in grades 4–8: role plays, simulations, and dramatic productions.

Role Plays

The term *role playing* refers to a type of play-acting in the classroom. By definition, **role playing** is a dramatic oral language activity in which students explore, in the most intimate way, the relationships of human living for the purpose of acquiring needed understandings and interpersonal communication skills. But unlike the dramatic play common to most primary classrooms, role playing can be structured for older students with clear goals and desired outcomes. And unlike more formally structured theatrical presentations, in which set lines are read from a script or memorized, role playing unfolds rather spontaneously, without a predetermined script. It uses the dramatic elements of characterization and dialogue. Empathy for another point of view is usually heightened because the actor is attempting to take on the internal characteristics of the person being emulated.

role playing

Role plays can grow out of current daily situations, problems, previous role plays, or dilemmas students may soon face, such as moving to a new grade. At times, the current daily situation may be the point of departure; at other times, the teacher may set the scene for the role play. Still another approach to role playing is to bring to life a story or scene from young adult literature in which there are complex relationships to be understood and rich opportunities for characterization, as will be discussed later. Lee Galda (1982) conducted a study in which a teacher read a familiar folktale to the class and then divided the students into three groups. The first group drew a picture about the story, the second group discussed the story, and the third group acted out a role play of the story. According to scores on a subsequent comprehension test and a retelling of the story, the dramatic activity was significantly more beneficial in deepening the students' understanding of the text.

Problem solving/conflict management through role plays

Role playing is the vehicle through which conflicts and arguments might be transformed into a dynamic oral language/social studies lesson, not only for the students directly involved but for the rest of the class as well. Because a variety of solutions are available for dealing with any conflict, role playing the various options and then discussing them can provide insights into what causes conflicts and what effects can be expected from the different solutions.

activity | Role Play

To help students gain insight from a scenario that actually occurred or from one that you create, guide students through the following activity:

1. Have a neutral observer from the class give his version of what took place—in either the actual classroom scenario or the one that's been created for this activity.
2. Select students to play the roles of each person involved.
3. Ask the actors to take a few moments to prepare two role plays: the first a reenactment of the situation as it actually occurred, and a second that changes the outcome to a more positive solution to the conflict.
4. As the actors are preparing their role plays, instruct the other students: "Watch what the actors do and say. Try to put yourself in their shoes and feel what they must be feeling. As you watch, be thinking of other ways the conflict could have been resolved."
5. Have the actors present their two role plays in the center of the classroom, surrounded by the other class members.
6. Discuss the differences in the outcomes of the two role plays. Invite other class members to contribute their alternative solutions to the problem. Write these on the whiteboard without evaluation.
7. Discuss the "cause" and "effect" patterns in the two role plays in terms of words or actions and resultant feelings and events.

For an actual scenario that occurred with the class, students might be asked to play themselves in the reenactment; or, to develop more insight into each other's point of view, they could be asked to switch roles. Other class members then watch both the reenactment and the alternative-outcome role plays, providing some resolutions to the conflict. For example, if the conflict was about bullying that occurred on school grounds, through role plays students can explore different ways to handle, diffuse, or avoid the situation.

Subsequently, through a teacher-guided reflective discussion, all students can begin to see exactly which turn of events caused the buildup of bad feelings that resulted in an argument instead of effective communication to solve a conflict. Moreover, the entire class has orally problem-solved ways to avoid the repetition of such an unfortunate event, while English learners have been provided with a rich context—the role play—for the ensuing discussion. To reinforce the concept of role play, a relevant literature selection could be read and discussed as a follow-up activity.

Role playing characters in literature

When students are reading a book that has many complex characters, role playing can help make those characters come alive; it also enables students to discover the relationship between what they are reading and their own lives.

Role playing of literature can be used with many favorite children's and young adult books, but those with many characters are best suited. For this activity, students can be assigned partners, with shy students paired with more outgoing ones. The names of all the characters in the book or in a scene are written on the whiteboard, and then each pair is assigned to one character, or to the author or illustrator of the book. The characters assigned for a Harry Potter novel, for example, might be these:

J. K. Rowling	Harry Potter	Ron Weasley
Hermione Granger	Professor Dumbledore	Lord Voldemort
Draco Malfoy	Hagrid	Uncle Vernon
Neville Longbottom	Crookshanks	Nearly Headless Nick

After reading the book, students are asked to reread it in order to study their own character's contribution. Each pair discusses their character's personality, behaviors, and motivation. Then they create a list of at least three questions that their character might wish to ask another character, including questions that go beyond its scope. For example, Hagrid might ask: "Draco, what happened in your early childhood that made you such an awful boy?" Similarly, Neville Longbottom might ask Harry, "How do you steer and control the speed of your broomstick during a Quidditch match?" Or Hermione Granger might ask, "Lord Voldemort, what would you do to defeat Professor Dumbledore in a duel?"

After the preparation phase is completed, students are ready for the role play. Students should be seated in a circle. Simple costumes can add to the characterization, or character name tags may be used so other class members can recognize the characters they wish to question. Members of each pair take turns answering the questions, although they are free to consult with each other.

The teacher opens the session by asking the character on her left the first question. For example, "Professor Dumbledore, are there any Muggles who can perform real magic?" Then, pair by pair, students ask a question of a different character until each pair gets a turn to role play. Students should be encouraged to ask follow-up questions related to previous role plays, as well.

Similar role plays can be created with any number of books that contain a large cast of three-dimensional characters that in some way reflect real life or real situations. Students gain a deeper appreciation for the characters and new insights into themselves; they can actually bring the characters—who have become infinitely more memorable—to life, while investigating another person's feelings and motives.

Mock interviews

Some years ago, the late Steve Allen hosted a program called *Meeting of the Minds* during which he would question, or conduct a "mock interview" of, noted historical figures who were played by actors. A fascinating discussion would ensue as Mr. Allen asked his pretend guests—which could be the interesting pairing of Cleopatra and Marie Antoinette—probing questions relating to their thoughts on current problems in the world.

Students will thoroughly enjoy similar role plays in the classroom. This type of oral language activity becomes a self-motivating reason to do historical research, because such activity will, in this situation, lead to a chance to become, for a short while, a famous person.

To prepare for the mock interview, a pair of students must decide on a historical figure, preferably one who has been studied in class or is familiar to the rest of the class. The pair must then research the person thoroughly—using the Internet, videos, books, magazine articles, and other resources—so that they can become intimately acquainted with the significant events of the person's life, personality, style of dress, opinions or political stances, mannerisms, and style of speech, and perhaps even memorize some of the particular quotations for which the person is best known. Among the historical figures who will work well are the following:

Nelson Mandela	Will Rogers	Mahatma Gandhi
Golda Meir	Jesse Owens	Albert Schweitzer
Jackie Robinson	John F. Kennedy	Abraham Lincoln
Martin Luther King, Jr	Clara Barton	Amelia Earhart
Rosa Parks	Arthur Ashe	Ludwig van Beethoven
Mother Teresa	Jacques Cousteau	Helen Keller

Next, from their research the pair draws up a list of questions they would ask their historical figure to learn how she would respond to current world issues or events. For example, Abraham Lincoln might be asked, "What are your thoughts on apartheid in South Africa?" or "How do you feel about the current state of civil rights in this country?" The actor's response would be largely based on what the two researchers have discovered about Lincoln's contributions to the abolition of slavery, as well as their general understanding of the man's core values.

For the presentation, the pair decides who will play the part of the historical figure and who will be the interviewer and ask the prearranged questions. After the interview session, the rest of the class, who have been taking notes, are encouraged to ask their own questions of the historical figure, while the actor playing that part tries to "think in character" and respond appropriately.

The follow-up discussion is a time for the teacher and the students to try to clear up any inconsistencies between what they know about the figure and the actor's responses, providing documented reasons for their objections to what the actor had said. For example, if a student playing the role of Mahatma Gandhi stated that he would support a war in the Middle East, an audience member could remind the actor about the implications of Gandhi's credo of passive resistance. Most important, during the reflective discussion there must be ample time to share new insights and appreciation for the historical figure in a now vibrant, multidimensional form and to explore any questions or concerns that were raised.

In order to practice using academic language in a certain discipline, students may choose to be an expert in an area they are interested in; for example, a student might choose Jacques Cousteau if he knows something about marine biology, or Amelia Earhart if she is interested in flying and history, or Shel Silverstein if the student wants to be a poet.

Simulations

Sometimes, in the course of working with students, it becomes clear that all the verbalization in the world is unable to impart an important concept or idea.

In such a situation, it may be advisable to preplan an experience where students can actually simulate—or vicariously play out—the concept. Acting out an idea brings about a sense of discovery of the concept being introduced and also offers, in many cases, a visceral response that is not soon forgotten. Setting the stage for such discovery through simulation can be time consuming and is therefore not feasible for every concept that is addressed. Some concepts, however, such as the activity described next, are worth the time and effort involved.

Prejudice   ⊙ **activity** ⊙

The following simulation can enhance a multicultural unit in social studies. Because of the anger and frustration that this simulation quite naturally can produce, the activity should not continue for more than a morning or afternoon, at most; of course, parents should be advised of the intentions of the simulation in advance.

1. Categorize students, artificially, as "good" or "bad" according to some trait over which they have no control, such as the color of their eyes or their gender. If eye color is chosen, for example, tell students that those with brown eyes will now have special privileges, such as being the first to go to lunch and extra computer time. Throughout the simulation period, they will receive many other special privileges, simply because of the color of their eyes.

2. When students question this favoritism, tell them that brown-eyed students are receiving special privileges because some people might believe that brown-eyed students are superior to students with blue or hazel eyes.

3. When the simulation is over, conduct an oral debriefing. Draw two columns on the whiteboard—one for brown eyes and one for other eye colors. Have the brown-eyed students share their feelings and reactions to the special treatment; then ask the students with other eye colors to share their feelings. Summarize the students' contributions on the board.

4. Explain that, although this was a rather unfair exercise, many people really do judge people merely on the basis of the color of their skin, their gender, or other traits they can do nothing about.

5. Lead a reflective discussion on how this activity might change the way participants behave toward others in the future.

Creating Original Drama

The ultimate goal of the drama component in a balanced and comprehensive literacy program is to have students eventually create and put on their own plays, thus bringing to life words, feelings, and ideas that have personal significance. Writing plays, however, demands some experience with the play as a unique form of expression; many teachers often feel pressured to teach skills that will be measured in annual testing, so they tend to devalue this critical oral language activity—even though such language activities can actually help prepare students to do well on standardized tests.

Many students enjoy writing their own original scripts for puppet shows, skits, and formal productions. Such activities offer teachers an excellent opportunity to integrate the language arts into the coursework because students will be discussing, writing, and then producing their work. Frequently, students enjoy working together to write the scripts, providing a remarkably natural vehicle for focused conversations.

It is often advisable to help students "work up" to the goal of writing their own plays, especially if they have had little or no previous experience with formal drama. To minimize frustration, dramatic productions can be introduced in phases: First, stories and books shared in literature circles or through guided reading in readers theatre (see Chapter 8) can be read dramatically, or students can recall, block, and turn them into plays. Particular script conventions are pointed out to students through minilessons. Students can study existing play scripts to learn the layout and specific conventions used in preparing scripts. With this background of script reading and the creating of characters, settings, and actions, students are ready to write and take part in their own original plays. As students go from reading and acting out the words of others—memorizing or paraphrasing their lines, speaking them on cue, and creating appropriate characterizations—to bringing their own words to life, they gain an enormous sense of pride and ownership from the cooperative undertaking. Figure 3.4 identifies a structure that students can follow to create their own scripts.

To ensure successful play writing, the following suggestions may be helpful:

- Begin with simple one-act skits.
- Divide students into small, cooperative groups.
- Provide each group with a "plot" or structure from which to build.
- Eliminate makeup, which is distracting.
- Do not use prompters, thus encouraging students to learn each other's lines.
- Allow "spontaneous paraphrasing" of the script.

Although all dramatic enterprises fare best with an audience, the first skits do not necessarily require a stage or extensive props and scenery; in fact, a "propless playlet" has the advantages of increasing students' ability to imagine and being easily moved from classroom to classroom. This way, students are not overwhelmed by large crowds, nor must they shout to be heard during their first efforts.

---

figure **3.4** Structure for creating original drama (adapted from Block, 2000).

To help students create an original script, ask them to consider the following four strands that constitute a complete drama:

(1) ROLES (OR IDENTITY)	(2) PLACE (OR SITUATION)	(3) FOCUS (OR ISSUE)	(4) CONFLICT (OR PROBLEM)
Who are you?	Where are you?	What is the play about?	What is the problem that needs solving?
Examples:	**Examples:**	**Examples:**	**Examples:**
a compassionate nurse	a hospital	saving lives and caring	nurse gets a disease
a sad soldier	a barracks	missing loved ones	soldier can't kill
a benevolent alien	a corn field	accepting differences	alien is feared

Listening Instruction

Research suggests that students who receive direct practice in listening comprehend better than students who have not received this instruction; listening plays a crucial, although often ignored, role in the literacy development of students, especially English learners (Opitz & Zbaracki, 2004). Research conducted with students in the intermediate and middle grades (Pearson, 1985) produced especially positive results. Pearson reached the following conclusions based on his synthesis of research on comprehension and listening instruction:

1. Listening practice in the same skills typically taught in reading instruction (i.e., getting the main idea, comparing and contrasting) tends to improve comprehension in both listening and reading.
2. Listening comprehension is enhanced when students offer personal verbal reactions during and after listening.
3. Reading literature aloud to students tends to improve listening comprehension.
4. All the language arts tend to reinforce one another; in other words, instruction in one of the arts of reading, writing, listening, speaking, viewing, and visually representing is correlated with gains in the other language arts.
5. Direct teaching of listening strategies seems to help students become conscious of their listening habits better than less explicit approaches do.

Designing Listening Instruction

Listening instruction must be a major part of the curriculum if it is to improve students' listening ability. To increase listening comprehension, strive to integrate it into daily lesson plans rather than providing a "one-shot," infrequent activity. Five to 10 minutes a day of listening instruction or practice is generally more effective than longer, less frequent lessons.

Listening comprehension should focus on teaching students strategies they can use to listen, while listening activities can be included to give students an opportunity to practice these skills in various settings. Above all, listening instruction should provide for transfer of listening skills from practice situations to actual use in the classroom and beyond. Ideally, listening comprehension—through reading to students, modeling one's thinking, and asking thought-provoking questions—should be an integral piece of content area instruction; listening for the main idea in practice material should be quickly transferred to social studies or science content material.

Why should listening be taught?

Listening stimulates language learning.

Listening maximizes learning.

Listening enhances reading, writing, and speaking abilities.

Effective listening skills do not always develop naturally.

Listening is a life-skill.

Source: E. Dobler, D. Johnson, & T. D. Wolsey, *Teaching the Language Arts: Forward Thinking in Today's Classrooms.* Copyright © 2013 by Holcomb Hathaway, Publishers. Used with permission.

Successful listening instruction encourages students to listen to meet their own needs, interests, and desires. For instance, students who are listening in order to complete an assignment, create an argument for escaping punishment, or find out how to build a robot, or who are simply listening to a story for pleasure, have differing purposes for attending, yet each situation is authentic and very important to them. The suggested teaching guidelines that follow develop both active listening and oral responses, because research shows that such responses result in optimal listening skill development:

1. Always set a purpose for listening by asking questions that will focus thought and encourage students to predict what will be included in the content.

2. Look for the structure of the content of informational material. Has the author organized the passage through comparison, contrast, sequential order, or simple enumeration? Brain researchers tell us that human beings naturally seek patterns in their experience. Use this tendency to point out to students the patterns in the text they are listening to.

3. When reading to students, categorize, relate, and associate new ideas with those that are already familiar to them. Give students guided practice, encouraging them to ask questions such as: How does this concern me? How does this relate to what I already know? What does this remind me of in my own life? How can I apply this information?

4. Summarize periodically as you read to students. In summarizing, the main ideas are identified and related briefly. Stop occasionally and encourage students to summarize also, in their minds, orally, or on paper.

5. Make oral or written responses to content and invite students to add their ideas to yours. This, as much as any other strategy, helps students to become active listeners and thinkers. Moreover, encourage students to listen with pencil or pen in hand. This offers them a minimal structure for response, allows for physical involvement, and is a link to note taking.

6. Provide a structure for responding to a presentation, such as the following:
   - What was the speaker's purpose (persuading, informing, sharing, etc.)?
   - List five ideas the speaker had.
   - Write a three-sentence summary of the presentation.
   - Write down two things that you would now like to know more about.

◉ activity ◉ | Listening Comprehension | (ADAPTED FROM BLOCK, 2000)

This activity can be used to help students practice the skills of listening comprehension. It can also be used to help teachers diagnose problems that individual students may have with listening comprehension.

1. Pair up students and provide each pair with an unfamiliar short story on their instructional level.

2. For each pair, select one student to be the reader and the other to be the listener.

3. Have the reader read two pages silently and then "tell" the two pages to the listener.

4. Once the story has been read and retold in these segments, have the listener summarize the entire story to the reader.

5. Have the reader write down everything the listener has said.

6. Have the pair look at the book together and compare it to the written retelling.

7. Have the pair discuss why certain parts were not included in the original retellings or the final summary (e.g., "not important," "didn't hear it," "didn't remember that part").

8. Have the pair note the omissions on the back of the story summary sheet, along with the listener's explanation for each absence.

9. Have partners switch roles and repeat the process.

10. Analyze each student's listening comprehension strengths and needs. Students can also be encouraged to assess their own listening skills by using the checklist provided in Appendix C.15.

Troubleshooting

The oral language skills—and confidence—of every learner can be enhanced through ample practice speaking and performing before a group of caring and supportive peers. However, several universal oral language concerns may need to be addressed when they occur.

Dominating a Discussion

Students who tend to dominate conversations and discussions and who do not listen to others can cause other students to withdraw entirely in any oral language situation. Teachers can help such dominating students by providing them with specific listening purposes and then discussing these purposes with students after the oral language event. Another alternative is to advise everyone that students will have *one* turn to share ideas in the particular oral language event to ensure that everyone gets a chance to speak. Finally, a successful concentration strategy that some teachers use is to teach all students to stop, listen, and think before they raise their hand. Making individual stop signs also helps them to remember the three steps of stop, listen, and think before participating in any discussion. After everyone is cognizant of this strategy, students begin to monitor each other to be sure that everyone listens and thinks before speaking.

Teachers can help students who tend to dominate discussions by providing them with specific listening purposes.

Lack of Verbal Skills in English

If students are in the initial stages of learning to speak English, the best course of action is to allow them the time they need to emerge from their "silent period" before they say their first words in the new language. Concentrate on building students' receptive language, and allow gestures and other nonverbal cues when communicating with them. Make certain the classroom environment is supportive and safe to the degree that other classmates are rooting for these students to say their first English words. Additionally, in any oral or written language venture, encourage **code switching,** or having students speak some words in English and words they do not know in their home language. Finally, totally disregard grammar and accent concerns whenever these students do speak. Concentrate only on understanding what they are trying to communicate. Then, paraphrase their contribution in standard English while expressing appreciation for their participation.

● code switching

Lack of Participation

In some classrooms, a student who rarely speaks may seem a blessing; at the same time, however, students must be allowed many opportunities to talk in order to process their ideas and learn on a deeper level; moreover, in our society the ability to speak fluently is arguably even more of an asset than the ability to read and write.

Some students who will not participate in large- or even small-group oral language events can practice speaking and become more comfortable doing so by conducting a series of speaking activities using a recording device. This allows the teacher to assess oral language development to determine if there is an underlying language problem that prevents the student from speaking out, or if the student is simply shy. Additionally, some shy students will speak fluently with the aid of a prop, such as a puppet or a model, that turns attention away from them; similarly, shy students can often be coaxed to take part in a dramatic activity, and many seem to "bloom" when they are able to don a different persona. In addition to shyness, some students may experience higher levels of nervousness and anxiety than their peers when speaking in front of others. These students will benefit from the same type of oral activities as shy students and should be encouraged to speak publically as often as possible to reduce their fears.

Limited Voice Projection

A commonly reported problem with oral language activities is that many students speak so softly that they cannot be heard. This becomes a distinct problem when other classmates have been urged to listen politely. After a few minutes of straining their ears, even the most courteous students will begin to turn their attention elsewhere. Students who speak softly must learn to lift their heads up and project their voice. One way to achieve this is to have them stand at their desks and project (not shout) the phrase, "How now, brown cow!"; tell them to "throw their words across the room and make them bounce off the opposite wall of the classroom." Additionally, choral reading, singing, and readers theatre provide opportunities to practice projecting one's voice.

Summary

It is easy, but untrue, to assume that students have already developed their oral language abilities, especially if they are native English speakers. With such an assumption, we often overlook the importance of helping students further their ability to speak confidently in many different situations. The basic curriculum cornerstones of reading and math take precedence over most other parts of the curriculum, and speaking is not often interwoven effectively into content areas. However, oral language must be continually nurtured in a balanced and comprehensive literacy program, for speech is the most widely used of the expressive forms of discourse. Moreover, proficiency in speaking enhances ability in all the other language arts.

The foundation for a sound oral language program is the variety of spontaneous and planned speaking situations that occur every day in most classrooms. Opportunities for instruction in oral language include informal speaking, as in casual conversations and discussions, and more formal speaking, as in oral reports, interviews, and panel discussions.

Finally, there is no better avenue than drama for channeling the boundless energy and emotions of students. Drama is a way of learning as well as a communication mode. Students thrive on a medium that allows them to create with their minds and bodies using expressive movements as well as words. In addition, drama may be the prime vehicle to attach words with concepts in authentic context for the benefit of English learners. Used on a routine basis, the recognition and community building afforded by drama can enhance the self-esteem of all learners. One budding sixth-grade actor summed it up this way: "I helped to write this play and put it on with my class. I got to be the biker dude and I also sang a song that had 'em rolling in the aisles. I also helped everybody else remember their lines. I usually hate writing and talking in front of the class, but this was more fun than summer camp!"

Questions FOR JOURNAL WRITING AND DISCUSSION

1. Of the four interrelated literacy skills of reading, writing, listening, and speaking, which, if any, do you believe to be the most important? Why? Defend your answer.
2. Recall a time, in grades 4–8, when you were in a skit or a play. What was your role, and how did you prepare for it? What else do you remember about this event? How can such classroom activities be conducive for confident oral speaking by native English speakers? By English learners?
3. Respond to the following statement that an uninformed parent might make: "An oral language program in the intermediate grades is a waste of time, because kids spend plenty of time talking on the playground and at home." How would your argument change if there were several English learners in your classroom?

Suggestions FOR PROJECTS AND FIELD ACTIVITIES

1. Find a teacher in grades 4–8 who is currently preparing a dramatic production with students. Discuss with the teacher her reasons for using this instructional activity. Observe the students as they practice their roles. Are all students involved? In what capacities? What major oral language goals are being achieved through this activity?
2. Observe a class giving oral reports. In what ways, if any, are students encouraged to use technology and multimedia to enhance their presentations? How has the delivery of oral presentations changed since you were in school?
3. After carefully reviewing the guidelines in "Suggestions for Teacher-Guided Discussions," earlier in this chapter, lead a discussion with a small group of students on a controversial topic such as "Is homework a necessary evil?" Reflect afterward and share your reflections with the rest of the class. What went well? What was difficult? What would you do differently next time?
4. With another small group of students, examine several curriculum guides to determine what provisions are made for the development of oral language from grades 4 through grade 8. Categorize your findings according to the types of purposeful speech activities presented in this chapter.

REFERENCES

Beck, I. L., McKeown, M.G., Hamilton, R.L. & Kucan, L. (1997). Questioning the Author, An approach for enhancing student engagement with text, Newark, DE: International Reading Association.

Billings, L., & Roberts, T. (2006). Planning, practice, and assessment in the paideia classroom. *High School Journal, 90*(1), 1–8.

Block, C. C. (2000). *Teaching the language arts: Expanding thinking through student-centered instruction* (3rd ed.). Needham Heights, MA: Allyn & Bacon.

Cummins, J., Brown, K., & Sayers, D. (2007). The oral history project: From a shrug to 'How much time do I have, Mr. Green?' In J. Cummins, K. Brown, & P. Sayers (Eds.), *Literacy, technology, and diversity: Teaching for success in changing times.* Boston: Allyn & Bacon.

Dobler, E., Johnson, D., & Wolsey, T. D. (2013). *Teaching the language arts: Forward thinking in today's classrooms.* Scottsdale, AZ: Holcomb Hathaway.

Eeds, M., & Wells, D. (1989). Grand conversations: An exploration of meaning construction in literature study groups. *Research in the Teaching of English, 23*(1), 4–29.

Galda, L. (1982). Playing about a story: Its impact on comprehension. *The Reading Teacher, 36,* 52–56.

Gambrell, L.B., &Almasi, J.F. (1996).*Lively discussions! Fostering engaged reading.* Newark, DE: International Reading Association.

Gee, J. P. (1996). *Social linguistics and literacies: Ideology in discourses* (2nd ed.). London: Taylor & Francis.

Griffin, M.L. (2001). Social contexts of beginning reading. *Language Arts, 78,* 371–378.

Heath, S. (1983). *Ways with words.* London: Cambridge University Press.

Hicks, D. (1995). Discourse, learning, and teaching. In M. W. Apple (Ed.), *Review of research in education* (Vol. 21, pp. 49–95). Washington, DC: American Educational Research Association.

Loban, W. (1976). *The complete book of language development: Kindergarten through grade twelve.* Urbana, IL: National Council of Teachers of English.

Opitz, M. F., & Zbaracki, M. D. (2004). *Listen hear! 25 effective comprehension strategies.* Portsmouth, NH: Heinemann.

Paratore, J. R., & McCormack, R. L. (1998). *Peer talk in the classroom: Learning from research.* Newark, DE: International Reading Association.

Pearson, P. D. (1985). Changing the face of reading comprehension instruction. *The Reading Teacher, 38*(8), 724–738.

Peregoy, S. F., & Boyle, O. F. (2013). *Reading, writing, and learning in ESL: A resource book for teaching K–12 English learners* (6th ed.). Upper Saddle River, NJ: Pearson.

Pinnell, G. S., & Jaggar, A. M. (2003). Oral language: Speaking and listening in elementary classrooms. In J. Flood, D. Lapp, J. R. Squire, & J. M. Jensen (Eds.), *Handbook on teaching the English language arts* (2nd ed., pp. 881–913). Mahwah, NJ: Erlbaum.

Roser, N. L., & Martinez, M. G. (Eds.). (1995). *Book talk and beyond: Children and teachers respond to literature.* Newark, DE: International Reading Association.

Sampson, M. R. (1986). *The pursuit of literacy: Early reading and writing.* Dubuque, IA: Kendall/Hunt.

Smith, K. (1998). Entertaining a text: A reciprocal process. In K. G. Short & K. M. Pierce (Eds.), *Talking about books: Literature discussion groups in K–8 classrooms* (pp. 17–31). Portsmouth, NH: Heinemann.

Smith, P. G. (2001). *Talking classrooms: Shaping children's learning through oral language instruction.* Newark, DE: International Reading Association.

Straits, W., & Nichols, S. (2006). Literature circles for science. *Science & Children, 44,* 52–55.

Strickland, D. S., & Feeley, J. T. (2003). Development in the elementary school years. In J. Flood, D. Lapp, J. R. Squire, & J. M. Jensen (Eds.), *Handbook of research on teaching the English language arts* (2nd ed., pp. 339–356). Mahwah, NJ: Erlbaum.

Wagner, B. J. (2003). Imaginative expression. In J. Flood, D. Lapp, J. R. Squire, & J. M. Jensen (Eds.), *Handbook of research on teaching the English language arts* (2nd ed., pp. 1008–1025). Mahwah, NJ: Erlbaum.

FOCUS QUESTIONS

- What factors are important to keep in mind when teaching vocabulary?
- What are the key components of word study at these grade levels?
- In what ways do elements of word study for the middle grades differ from the elements of primary-grade word study?
- What are some research-based instructional strategies to teach vocabulary directly to students?
- How can teachers help students figure out the meanings of new words on their own?

Mrs. Chase briefly explains the term *eternal life* to her sixth-grade students and gives them a minute to imagine what it would be like to live forever. She then leads a lively discussion about the possible advantages and disadvantages of living forever, writing the students' comments on the whiteboard. Jennifer believes that living forever would be a wonderful thing because "you wouldn't have to die and make people sad"; Ethan counters that all his friends would be gone and he might become "lonely and bored."

Following the discussion, Mrs. Chase's students begin reading Natalie Babbitt's *Tuck Everlasting* (1975) in heterogeneous literature groups. During this time, Mrs. Chase uses a *clarifying table* to anchor the meaning of the term *eternity* within the context of the book. She writes the word "eternity" under the heading "Core Idea" and then notes below it that this term means "an endless period of time." She asks if someone can give an example of what eternity means from his or her own life experience. "When you're waiting for the mail to arrive because you are expecting a special birthday present from your aunt. It seems like an eternity! But it's not really," exclaims Raul.

Next, Mrs. Chase asks the students for examples of another word with which the term might be easily confused. Tam suggests, "Anything that has a life span that you can predict would not be a good example of eternity. Recess lasts for about 15 minutes, which is a fixed amount of time—not an eternity." After this, the teacher asks for "clarifiers," or phrases that will help the students to think more clearly about what the term does and does not mean. After the students brainstorm in small groups, the teacher writes down their responses:

- You don't know the beginning and you don't know the end.
- Some religions believe that we live on for an eternity after we die.
- Always and forever.
- Events that go on longer than you want them to seem to take an eternity, but that's an exaggeration.

At this point, Mrs. Chase asks the students to think about how the concept of *eternity* was used in the book. They mention that the Tuck family drank from a spring that gave them everlasting life so they would never grow older and would exist for "all the time that will ever exist in the world." Finally, the teacher asks the students to create a sentence using the term *eternity*. After thinking about the meaning of the word, all the students are able to complete the task quickly, providing sentences that reflect their own lives or the book they have just read.

Andy's contribution is typical: "An eternity is an amount of time that has no end, or just feels like it will never end."

Mrs. Chase's use of the clarifying table has solidified the students' understanding of the most critical concept discussed in the book they are reading and discussing. (See the activity "Constructing and Using a Clarifying Table," later in this chapter.)

Introduction

vocabulary

Our knowledge of words—our **vocabulary**—is an often overlooked, yet critical factor in the mosaic of our entire personalities. Indeed, the word knowledge we have stored in our minds determines how well we are able to take part in discussions; comprehend the books, websites, and other materials we read; share our most intimate thoughts; explain our ideas for others; and, in sum, form a cohesive worldview. A larger vocabulary means not only that we know more words but, more important, that we are able to express our thoughts and feelings in a more complex and satisfying way. We use our storehouse of words to think and even to dream; therefore, it follows that the richer our vocabulary, the more potentially productive our inner life can be.

In a more specifically educational setting, vocabulary is absolutely integral to proficient reading. If students do not understand the meaning of the words in the text, the process of reading is reduced to meaningless word calling, or "barking at print." No student should ever have to struggle along producing only a series of verbal nonsense. As teachers, we want students to understand a wide range of words. A fundamental part of critical thinking necessary for adequate reading comprehension is rapid access to the necessary word meanings (Baumann & Kame'enui, 2012; Baumann, Kame'enui, & Ash, 2003; Graves, 1986).

The College and Career Readiness Anchor Standards for Reading, which are part of the Common Core State Standards, state that students should be able to "interpret words and phrases as they are used in a text, including determining technical, connotative, and figurative meanings, and analyze how specific word choices shape meaning or tone" (NGACBP & CCSSO, 2010, p. 10). Proficient readers are able to connect new words with other words they know, and they understand the connotations attached to them by virtue of their various uses. Because each proficient reader's particular background varies, for every passage a social history and context are created that continually attach personal meaning to it. Encountering words repeatedly, both through text and in conversation, builds a fabric of understanding that clarifies the meaning of familiar words and then makes it even easier to determine the meaning of new words, creating a snowballing spiral of vocabulary acquisition. Good readers read more and learn more new words. As a result, by merely encountering more words, good readers learn much more about language (Beck, McKeown, & Kucan, 2013; Graves & Watts-Taffe, 2008).

Types of Vocabulary

Two major types of vocabulary are relevant in grade 4–8 classrooms: meaning vocabulary and reading vocabulary. **Meaning vocabulary,** as the name implies, is the sum total of a person's understanding of the meaning of words. Some words are understood when spoken or written by others (*receptive vocabulary*), and other words are those we are able to use in our own speech or writing (*productive or expressive vocabulary*) (Graves, 2006). Meaning vocabulary is extremely important because readers need to draw from this store as they emerge into reading to learn. Meaning vocabulary can therefore be likened to a vast reservoir from which readers draw known meanings when figuring out new meanings as they read. **Reading vocabulary** refers to words that are both recognized and understood when reading (Harris & Hodges, 1995, p. 213). Reading vocabulary uses receptive vocabulary.

● meaning vocabulary

● reading vocabulary

Vocabulary can be further broken down into three subcategories (or tiers) that have major implications as to how various words, once encountered, could most effectively be introduced to students in grades 4–8 (Beck et al., 2013). These subcategories are

1. basic words
2. general-utility words
3. low-utility words

Our decision about which words to teach students directly is influenced by how frequently students will see the words in text. The number of opportunities that students have to practice a word should be in direct proportion to the time we spend introducing the word (Beck, McKeown, & Omanson, 1987). Once we are aware of which words are the most instructionally significant, then we can consider various methods for teaching those words, either directly or by assisting students in using strategies that aid in new vocabulary acquisition.

Basic words are the building blocks of everyday language. They are so commonplace and are used so often that their meanings do not require specific instruction except in the case of English learners, who usually will understand the concept but will require an English label for the word. Often referred to as "sight words," examples include *am, dog, said,* and *from.*

● basic words

general-utility words ●

academic language ●

WWW●●●

Academic Word List

www.victoria.ac.nz/lals/
resources/academicwordlist/

**Self-Checking
Vocabulary Exercises**

www.englishvocabulary
exercises.com/

low-utility words ●

General-utility words are more complex terms that proficient readers and speakers use often in speech, but they are not specific to any one subject area and include words considered part of **academic language.** Thus, the words on the Academic Word List (AWL; Coxhead, 2000) are considered general-utility words. This list consists of 570 word families that are divided into 10 sublists. When studying the sublists, students should also study the derivations for the word families (i.e., the verb, noun, adjective, and adverb forms, plus variants). The AWL represents Tier Two words (Beck, McKeown, & Kucan, 2013) because they appear with great frequency in a broad range of academic texts. Although intended for older students, teachers in grades 4–8 can readily identify words from the AWL that are appropriate and necessary for their students to learn. These words are best learned in context. Exercises such as fill-in-the-blank or matching are appropriate ways to practice using these words; some sample fill-in-the-blank, self-checking exercises are available online at www.englishvocabularyexercises.com/. Instruction in common root words, prefixes, and suffixes can also help students to discover the meaning of words in this category. The majority of vocabulary study during a reading lesson would be directed at this second tier of words. Words such as *create, combine, examine,* and *transfer* are examples of general-utility words.

Low-utility words, the third tier of vocabulary, are the words that are encountered less frequently, and they are usually found in particular content areas. Such words should be introduced before students engage in their content area texts and tasks, and they should be grouped according to the particular concept with which they are identified. Examples of such words include *tropism, solar, biped,* and *crater.*

Selecting Vocabulary Words to Teach

Choosing which words to teach is a more complicated task than one might think. Graves (2006) estimates that the reading materials students will encounter during their school years include more than 180,000 different words. Because students need to learn so many words each year, it is critical that teachers select "words that are most important for understanding a specific reading selection or [content area] concept, [and] words that are generally useful for students to know and are likely to encounter" frequently in their reading (Hiebert, Lehr, & Osborn, 2004, p. 10). Ellis and Farmer (2000) offer the following suggestions for selecting vocabulary:

- *Teach only key concepts—those words that are essential to the unit or theme of study.* Instead of teaching all words that appear in a list at the end of a chapter, teach the ones that are so critical that it would be impossible to understand the chapter without knowing them. These words provide precision and specificity; they have many purposes and can be worked with in a variety of ways so that students can build rich representations of them and their connections to other words and concepts (Beck et al., 2013).
- *Go for depth and connections, and reinforce words that will be used often during the school year.* Do not try to teach a large quantity of words that students may never encounter again; instead, teach a few words in a manner that results in deep understandings by connecting them to concepts with which students are already familiar. These words are typically characteristic of mature language users and appear frequently across various domains.
- *Reinforce general-utility words.* They provide a foundation upon which much information will be built over time.

While these criteria for selecting words to teach can be useful, teachers still need to apply these guidelines with the specific needs of their students in mind. Each teacher should use careful thought and good judgment when deciding which words to teach.

Levels of Word Knowledge

Knowing a word is *not* an all-or-nothing proposition. Words often have both a denotation and a connotation and can evoke a constellation of meanings and ideas to different people depending on their experiences and cultural settings. Moreover, knowing a word in context is different from knowing a word in isolation, and being able to use a word in daily conversation is different from merely being able to understand the word when seeing it written (see Figure 4.1).

Knowledge of a word, then, can best be viewed in terms of the extent or degree of understanding that a person has about it. Students can engage in self-assessment by rating their knowledge of a word using the four levels seen in Figure 4.1. Pointing out to students that they can be familiar with a word in a number of ways helps them begin to experience how working with words and reading widely support growth in meaning vocabulary. For example, a reader may come across an unfamiliar word (*extinction*); using the context of the material, however, she can associate it with something with which she is familiar (preservation of animals). This partial recognition, supported by context, may let her continue to read without interrupting the "flow" of her understanding. In fact, encountering a partially known word in context and relating it to the meaning of a whole text is the kind of literacy event that will gradually enhance her knowledge of that word and help her to move it along the continuum toward a richly known word. As the student encounters the word again and again, her recognition of its meaning will grow at a relatively constant rate, depending on the helpfulness of the context (Schwanenflugel, Stahl, & McFalls, 1997). Finally, Beck, McKeown, and Kucan (2013) have suggested that when readers reach the stage where they feel they truly "know" a word, they are able to provide an original sentence containing the word, or a restatement of its definition in their own words.

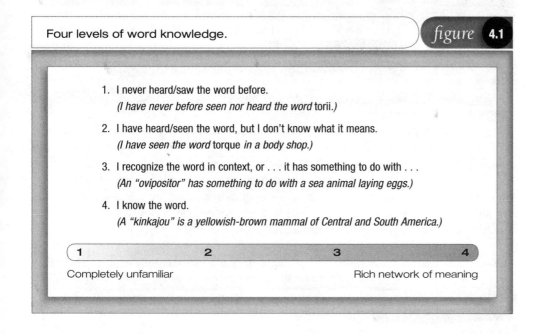

Four levels of word knowledge.   *figure* **4.1**

1. I never heard/saw the word before.
    (I have never before seen nor heard the word torii.*)*

2. I have heard/seen the word, but I don't know what it means.
    (I have seen the word torque *in a body shop.)*

3. I recognize the word in context, or . . . it has something to do with . . .
    (An "ovipositor" has something to do with a sea animal laying eggs.)

4. I know the word.
    (A "kinkajou" is a yellowish-brown mammal of Central and South America.)

| 1 | 2 | 3 | 4 |

Completely unfamiliar   Rich network of meaning

Principles of Vocabulary Instruction

E ffective vocabulary instruction for students in grades 4–8 begins with *explanations* as opposed to definitions (Feldman & Kinsella, 2003). These "explanations" should use (1) language that is familiar to students; (2) examples that exist in students' background knowledge or worldviews; and (3) known images or metaphors.

Such instruction is not accomplished through traditional vocabulary acquisition methods of having students copy the words, look them up in a dictionary, memorize definitions, and then use the words in contrived sentences. Rather, some guiding principles for effective vocabulary instruction, with examples, include the following (Blachowicz, Fisher, Ogle, et al., 2006; Graves, 2006; NICHD, 2000):

New words should be integrated with familiar words and concepts. A major task in vocabulary instruction is to choose words that include known as well as unfamiliar words so that students can make personal connections. Students can create knowledge connections between new words and their own background knowledge in a variety of ways. For example, teachers can help them to identify how the new words are related to previous subject matter they have learned (e.g., "a novel is like a long story"), to identify something from their personal life experiences that reminds them of a particular word (e.g., "filibuster reminds me of my talkative Uncle Buster"), to create metaphors or similes for a term (e.g., "a chrysanthemum is like a yellow mum"), or to discuss how some of the words might relate to solving a real-life problem they have had (e.g., "because I always procrastinated about feeding my hamster, I taped a sign on his cage to help me remember").

Students should experience multiple exposures to words in meaningful and varied contexts. Comprehension is greatly enhanced when students can quickly identify examples of words or ways in which new words can be appropriately applied in the context of a discussion of an already familiar concept. When choosing words to be taught directly, teachers should focus not only on words that are important for understanding the material, but also on words their students will encounter often in their reading (Beck et al., 2013). These new words should be taught in the context of a meaningful subject-matter lesson, and discussion with students should then center on the use of the new words. For example, the word *phototropism* could best be taught after a science experiment in which plants are observed growing toward the sun. Students should then be encouraged to use the new terms in multiple contexts—through reading, writing, listening, and speaking. In short, they should frequently use newly learned words in a variety of language experiences.

Increasing the amount of reading that students complete will also increase vocabulary. Beginning in the intermediate grades, widespread "reading becomes the principal language experience for enlarging students' vocabularies" (Cunningham & Stanovich, as cited in Graves, 2006, p. 5). Wide reading can provide the multiple encounters necessary for learning new vocabulary (Beck et al., 2013; Taylor, 2007); however, students must be taught word knowledge and strategies so they can learn new words as they read independently. As previously stated, teachers should select which words to teach purposefully and develop methods for teaching the words sensibly (Biemiller, 2005).

Students should be taught word-learning strategies they can independently apply to words they meet in other contexts. *Independent word-learning strategies* are procedures teachers can model and teach explicitly to show students how to determine the meanings of unknown words (Baker, Simmons, & Kame'enui, 1998). "While teaching word

Teacher Behaviors That Enhance Vocabulary Learning

LINK	Relate students' past experiences with present ones.
ELABORATE	Add more information about familiar content, or suggest a rewording of the content.
REINFORCE	Introduce new vocabulary and reinforce through constant use.
CONNECT	Tie new words to the activity or the activity to the new words.
CLARIFY	Add examples, illustrations, or descriptions.
QUESTION	Stimulate thinking about terms through questioning.
RELATE	Show how new words compare with those that students already know.
CATEGORIZE	Group new words, ideas, and concepts.
LABEL	Provide names for concepts, ideas, and objects.

meanings is a major goal of vocabulary programs, helping students become independent word learners is another aspect of vocabulary development that cannot be ignored, especially for students who have developed meager strategies and weak views of themselves as word learners" (Harmon, 2000, p. 526). Three important word-learning strategies are (1) using context clues to infer word meanings; (2) using morphemic analysis (word parts) to decipher word meanings; and (3) using the dictionary (Baumann et al., 2003; National Reading Panel, 2000). These are discussed in more detail later in this chapter.

Vocabulary instruction should engage students in active processing of word meanings and in developing an interest in learning new words. Whereas some students can acquire new vocabulary through listening and discussion, many others, including English learners, need more active engagement in order to process new words (Carlo, August, McGlaughlin, et al., 2004). For example, the teacher could relate the word *propaganda* to a sales pitch with which students may be familiar (for example, well-known athletes promoting sneakers not by virtue of their knowledge of the product but merely on their fame alone, or a "doctor" who is an actor and not really a doctor selling a medication) and then lead a discussion of other high-pressure, and often misleading, advertisements they have seen on television. Ask students to take notes on some of the most misleading commercials they encounter. End the discussion with an informal survey about which propaganda techniques the students like the least and why.

The impact of electronic text on vocabulary learning has also been explored (Blachowicz et al., 2006). These authors conclude that "electronic texts can be both motivating and effective for word learning when they provide or couple their presentations with facilitation that calls on the students to actively engage with the words" (p. 533). The term *facilitation* in this context refers to some form of mediated instruction that emulates what a supportive adult might provide if the reading were not occurring through electronic text. For example, to facilitate vocabulary learning, illustrative sentences or pictures rich with information could be linked to difficult concepts to enhance their meaning. Using new terms in essays or creative writing offers students an even greater opportunity for reflection and thinking about how words are used. Other forms of active engagement include acting out the words, creating mnemonic devices, or drawing pictures that capture the essence of the word's meaning.

Developing a curiosity and interest in learning new words is also critical to vocabulary instruction. Researchers have referred to students' awareness of new words and their desire to learn and use them when speaking and writing as **word consciousness** (Graves & Watts-Taffe, 2002). Activities focused on raising the level of curiosity and interest in learning word meanings include (1) learning the history and derivation of some English words (e.g., *bayou, pecan, toboggan* from the American Indian tribes Choctaw, Illinois, and Micmac, respectively; *renegade, mosquito, tuna* from the Spanish language; and *gingham, ketchup* from Malay); (2) learning figurative uses of words (e.g., idioms, puns, tongue twisters); (3) engaging in word play (e.g., Hinky Pinky and word riddles such as, Riddle: How do you take a pig to a hospital? Answer: In a hambulance!; Blachowicz & Fisher, 2004, p. 229); and (4) participating in word contests. Similarly, Marzano (2009) offers these concise and helpful recommendations for word teaching:

> word consciousness

1. The teacher provides a description, explanation, or example of the new term or word.

2. Students restate the definition of the new term in their own words.

3. Students create a nonlinguistic representation of the word (e.g., picture or other symbolic representation).

4. Students periodically engage in activities that help them add to their knowledge of vocabulary terms.

5. The teacher asks students to discuss the new words with one another.

6. The teacher involves students in games that allow them to play with the words.

Word Study

> word study

Word study is a systematic, conceptual learner-centered approach to instruction in spelling, word analysis (to include phonics), and vocabulary (Bear, Invernizzi, Templeton, et al., 2012). Essentially, word study is the interplay among reading, writing, and spelling instruction. Students learn sounds that correspond to letters, and they form words that have patterns of meaning and connections to derivations and histories of words. The developmental process allows students to increase their word knowledge as they apply their spelling patterns to their reading, writing, and vocabulary. This process is developmental in approach, aligned with Vygotsky's zone of proximal development, because students need to master the stage of reading/spelling development before they move on to new or more difficult words or patterns, thus solidifying their transition from alphabetics, to patterns, to meaning making (Bear et al., 2012). Students study words to identify irregularities in the English language, to be able to recognize words quickly and automatically, and to understand their meanings.

Instruction of approximately 10 to 15 minutes each day links directly to the texts and other materials being used in the classroom and provides many opportunities for students to manipulate word parts. Word study teaches students how to look at words and, as stated above, should be approached developmentally. At the primary-grade level, word study is mainly about

> alphabetic principle

1. developing an understanding of the **alphabetic principle** (knowing that each speech sound has a distinctive graphic representation).

2. helping students learn about and use phonics to decode unknown words in print.

At the intermediate level, word study is primarily about

1. developing spelling at the **syllables and affixes stage** and the **derivational relations stage** (stages of spelling development characterized by polysyllabic words that often contain **affixes** [prefixes and suffixes], and derive from Greek or Latin roots, respectively).
2. helping students determine word meanings using the meaningful parts of words (Henderson, 1990; Kemper & Brody, 2001).

- syllables and affixes stage
- derivational relations stage
- affixes

Although word study is developmental, and we hope that students will be ready to study words at the syllables and affixes stage, this might not be the case. A teacher may want to assess students directly using a spelling inventory (see Appendix C.10) to look at the ways in which they spell words. By analyzing what learners do when they spell, the teacher can determine learners' conceptual understandings of the English word system and the level at which students are able to study words. Rather than causing a learner to become frustrated, it is a better idea to turn back to where the learner was confused and work on that section before introducing more complicated word study.

Following is a brief review of reading and spelling stages. This information is provided to help teachers determine students' readiness for word study based on their individual spelling/reading stage.

A Review of Reading and Spelling Stages

Briefly, emergent readers demonstrate a lack of understanding of the alphabetic principle, and they do not have a concept of letter–sound correspondences (see Figure 4.2). Their "spelling" consists of scribbles, random marks, drawings, or mock letters.

Stages of reading/spelling development.

figure **4.2**

READING/SPELLING STAGE	APPROXIMATE AGES	GRADES	CHARACTERISTICS
Emergent	1–7	pre-K to mid-1	scribbles, random marks, drawings, mock letters
Beginning/Letter name	4–9	K to early 3	M or MN for *man*; L or LD or LED for *land*; B or BP or BOP or BUP or BOMP for *bump*
Transitional	6–12	1 to mid-4	MEET or METE for *meat*; NALE for *nail*; SOKE for *soak*; SMOAK for *smoke*; FOWT for *fought*; FODE for *food*; CAFE for *cough*; CLOKE for *clock*
Intermediate/Syllables and affixes	8–18	3 to 8	GRIPING for *gripping*; MIDLE for *middle*; CONFUSSHUN for *confusion*; PLESURE for *pleasure*; RUPSHUR for *rupture*; MONKY for *monkey*; BARBAR for *barber*; DISPOSUL for *disposal*
Advanced/Derivational relations	10+	5 to 12	SOLEM for *solemn*; ANAMAL for *animal*; OPISITION for *opposition*; CRITASIZE for *criticize*; BENAFIT for *benefit*; TELAGRAM for *telegram*; APPEARENCE for *appearance*; AMMUSEMENT for *amusement*

Word study instruction in the primary grades focuses on helping students learn phonics and apply it most often to single syllables or to one-syllable, decodable words.

letter name/alphabetic
stage •
transitional reader •
rimes •
phonemic awareness •
phonics •
onset •

roots (base words) •

etymology •

As learners develop an understanding of the alphabetic principle and become beginning readers, they demonstrate the **letter name/alphabetic stage.** They spell by using letters they hear in words, usually consonants, even if it might be only one letter per word. Further development produces the **transitional reader,** who understands there are letter pattern units, also called word families, and frequently occurring **rimes** (vowel[s] with any of the following consonants in a single syllable) such as *-at, -in, -and,* and *-ot;* this reader spells words using these patterns, but not always correctly. For example, the beginning speller might spell boat as BOT, but the transitional speller will try to use a long *o* pattern and might produce BOTE, BOWT, BOOT, or BOAT. At the intermediate and advanced stages of reading development, students recognize single syllable patterns automatically and have already been reading and writing polysyllabic words, so they begin to apply this knowledge to spelling words containing syllables and affixes and word derivations—thus, the respective spelling stages.

In addition to this review of reading/spelling stages, a brief overview of primary-grade–level word study elements is in order because not all intermediate-grade students will have reached an advanced word study stage.

Early Word Study Instruction

Instruction in word study begins in the primary grades with activities that develop **phonemic awareness,** that is, the ability to attend to sounds in the context of the spoken word independent of the visual representation or meaning of the word. These activities usually focus on rhyming, blending, segmenting, and manipulating sounds in spoken language. From there, students learn to recognize the relationships between the 44 sounds in the English language and the 26 graphic symbols (the letters of the alphabet) used to represent those sounds. This focus on learning letter–sound correspondences is called **phonics.**

Word study instruction in the primary grades focuses on helping students learn phonics and apply it most often to single syllables or to one-syllable, decodable words. For example, students are directed to remove the beginning consonant(s) (the **onset**) from the rest of a one-syllable word (e.g., h—at). They then say the sounds indicated by the rime, or /at/. They are directed to say, and finally add to the rime, the sound for the beginning consonant(s) (/h/ + /at/ = hat). At this point, they have pronounced the word and must cross-check it within the context of what they are reading to be sure it makes sense: *He wore a hat on his head.*

Advanced Word Study Instruction

Students in grades 4–8 must continue to learn to recognize increasingly complex words quickly and accurately. While some students still need instruction with phonics, or decoding (see "Troubleshooting," later in this chapter), a major focus of word study instruction in grades 4–8 is having students

1. learn to syllabicate, or "chunk," multisyllable words.
2. study the internal structure of words, including (a) affixes and **roots (base words)** and the forms of various parts of speech (morphology; also structural analysis), and (b) the origins and derivations of words (**etymology**).

Focusing on the internal structure of words will also enhance spelling development because these word parts will be learned and spelled as whole units. Additionally, much of this work will be helpful for learning new word meanings, so it can also be intertwined with vocabulary instruction.

Syllabication

The process of analyzing a polysyllabic word is the same as that for one-syllable words, except the process is applied more than once. Multiple applications are based on the total number of syllables in the word; that is, the process will be applied twice for a two-syllable word, three times for a three-syllable word, and so forth (Gipe, 2014). Essentially, the learner must first divide the unknown word into individual syllables, then pronounce each syllable, and finally put the syllables back together. The steps are as follows:

1. To begin to locate syllables in a polysyllabic word, locate the vowels.
2. Try to make syllables by using the consonants just before and after the vowels.
3. Attempt to pronounce these trial syllables.
4. Try to blend the trial syllables together.
5. Cross-check the pronounced word within the context of what is being read to see whether it makes sense. If the resulting pronounced word does not seem right, try segmenting the syllables in another way (see Figure 4.3).

This strategy is not always precise; if the word is part of the student's **listening vocabulary** (words understood in speech, but not recognized in print), however, it may provide a close enough approximation that the context will help identify the word. In the case of a totally new word, students will need to be told what the word is. That word then becomes part of a personal dictionary for further vocabulary study and assistance with spelling if the word is later needed for writing purposes.

● listening vocabulary

Analyzing a multisyllabic word.

figure **4.3**

STEP	WORD: HOSPITAL
1. Find the vowel(s).	o i a
2. Make syllables with the consonants just before and after the vowels.	"hos" "pit" "tal"
3. Try to say these syllables.	"hos" "pit" "tall"
4. Blend the syllables together.	"hospit" "tall" . . . "hospital"
5. Cross-check with the context.	"Oh yes, it makes sense. His father was sick so he went to the hospital."

Morphology

morphology ●

In addition to syllabication, students need instruction on morphology to help them recognize words (Carlisle & Stone, 2005). **Morphology** refers to the internal structure and forms of words. The structural features of words that need to be taught are

- *roots* (base words),
- *prefixes* (affixes that precede the root),
- *suffixes* (affixes that follow the root), and
- *inflections* (plurals, past tense endings, possessive form).

compound words ●

Another structural form is **compound words** (two base words together, e.g., *doghouse*). Roots, prefixes, and compound words are most directly tied to meaning, so they provide the most helpful information related to vocabulary. Suffixes and inflections also carry meaning, but it is more general in nature (Ruddell, 2008). Consider the differences by examining the word *dentist*. If the reader recognizes the "ist" suffix and knows "ist" means "one who," but she does not know that the root "dent" means "tooth," then recognizing "ist" is not much help other than to know the word is a noun.

Students should be shown how to figure out the meaning of unknown multisyllabic words by recognizing the many meaning-bearing affixes that are added to the base, or root, of other words. Figure 4.4 presents some common meaning-bearing prefixes, roots, and suffixes that, if memorized, will go a long way toward helping students discover the meaning of hundreds of words (Bear et al., 2012). Activities that require students to use these word parts will assist in their memorization.

structural analysis ●

A direct approach for teaching **structural analysis** (identification of meaningful word parts) is to identify a structural element found in a critical word from stu-

---

figure **4.4**   Meaning-bearing affixes and roots.*

auto (self)	graph (writing)	phobia (fear of)
anti (against; opposite)	phon (sound)	ist (one who)
tele (far)	hydr (water)	ic (pertaining to)
bi (two; twice)	therm (heat)	ism (condition of)
dia (through)	meter (measure)	able, ible (able to)
con (together)	dic (say)	ment (state of)
trans (across)	post (carry)	er (one who)
re (back; again)	vit, viv (life)	tion, ion (act of)
in, im, in (not; within)	vert (turn)	less (opposite of)
pre (before)	sol (sun)	
circum (around)	mania (fondness for)	

* A more detailed list of such word parts can be found in *The Reading Teacher's Book of Lists: Grades K–12,* 5th ed. (Fry & Kress, 2006).

dents' reading assignments. For example, in a social studies unit dealing with forms of government, the element "cracy" in the words *aristocracy* and *autocracy* might be chosen. Instruction proceeds by examining the more familiar word *democracy*. The important element "cracy" should be highlighted; students are then invited to provide a meaning for that part based on their understanding of the word *democracy*. Most students can define a democracy as majority rules, or a government of the people, by the people, and for the people; in short, rule by the people. Then students are told that "cracy" comes from the Greek *kratia* and means strength or power; in other words, who rules. Whatever is attached to "cracy" describes who does the ruling. The word "democracy" contains the roots "demo" and "cracy," so students can deduce that "demo" means people, and, in fact, "demo" is from the Greek *demos*, meaning "people."

Other forms of government can now be examined in the same way (e.g., aristocracy, autocracy, theocracy, bureaucracy). Additionally, for this example it would be useful to introduce and discuss the membership structure for each of these forms of government, that is, aristocrat, autocrat, theocrat, and bureaucrat, respectively.

Related words should be introduced and discussed at this time. These might be posted on a word wall, or they could become part of a word study notebook or folder online that students maintain. Both of these methods will assist with spelling development because the words are written and a visual representation is also readily available. Some examples are *demography, demagogy, epidemic, aristocratic, autobiography, autonomy, automatic, bureau, bureaucratic, theology, theocentric,* and *atheism*.

Learning the words on a word list such as the Nifty-Thrifty-Fifty (Cunningham & Hall, 1998, discussed in Chapter 2 and Appendix C.12 and Appendix D) will provide students with morphological patterns for figuring out many other words. These 50 words include common affixes (see Figure 4.4 for others) as well as reveal common spelling changes that occur when suffixes are added to root words. These words can be introduced in groups of five each week using daily activities (see Appendix E for a typical week's study plan). After 10 weeks, all of the words will have been learned. Because these 50 words contain morphological patterns for so many other words, they should be overlearned. The various elements will then be recognized and recalled automatically when needed during reading and writing. The **transfer words**—words containing elements that are also found in many other words—in Appendix D contain parts of the Nifty-Thrifty-Fifty words. Many other words can also be used as transfer words.

● transfer words

Teachers can use this general pattern when teaching the morphology and etymology (see below) of words:

1. Begin with the known and move to the unknown.

2. Provide a means for making the transfer. Talk through the process. With practice and repetition, the process becomes internalized.

3. Discuss related words so that knowledge increases in an exponential way as opposed to just one word being studied at a time.

4. Value the content of particular disciplines by using the critical language in that discipline as a means of teaching a functional skill—word analysis.

Chosen words should be taught within their authentic contexts; then, students will recognize them and also know how they are used.

Bloodgood and Pacifici (2004) use a strategy for word study that focuses on Greek and Latin roots—from which a majority of English words derive—to discover within-word patterns that will help with word recognition and meaning, as well as spelling.

activity   Roots and Branches   (BLOODGOOD & PACIFICI, 2004)

1. On a whiteboard or a large piece of poster paper, present a root written within a circle (e.g., *graph*). Don't reveal its meaning.

2. Ask students to provide words they already know that contain that word part. Record these as branches off the central root (see Figure 4.5). The web in this figure uses the roots *tract, graph, dic/dict, spect,* and *ortho.*

3. As students discuss these words, they can infer the meaning of the root (e.g., "graph means to write"); write that meaning in the circle.

Additional posters can be created as students encounter new words during the course of the school year. Several "Roots and Branches" posters can be prepared and hung around the classroom for students to add to as they finish other assignments. As posters are added, students discuss the meaning of the root written within a circle; as new words are added to the branches, they are discussed as to their relationship to the central root.

figure **4.5**   Roots and branches.

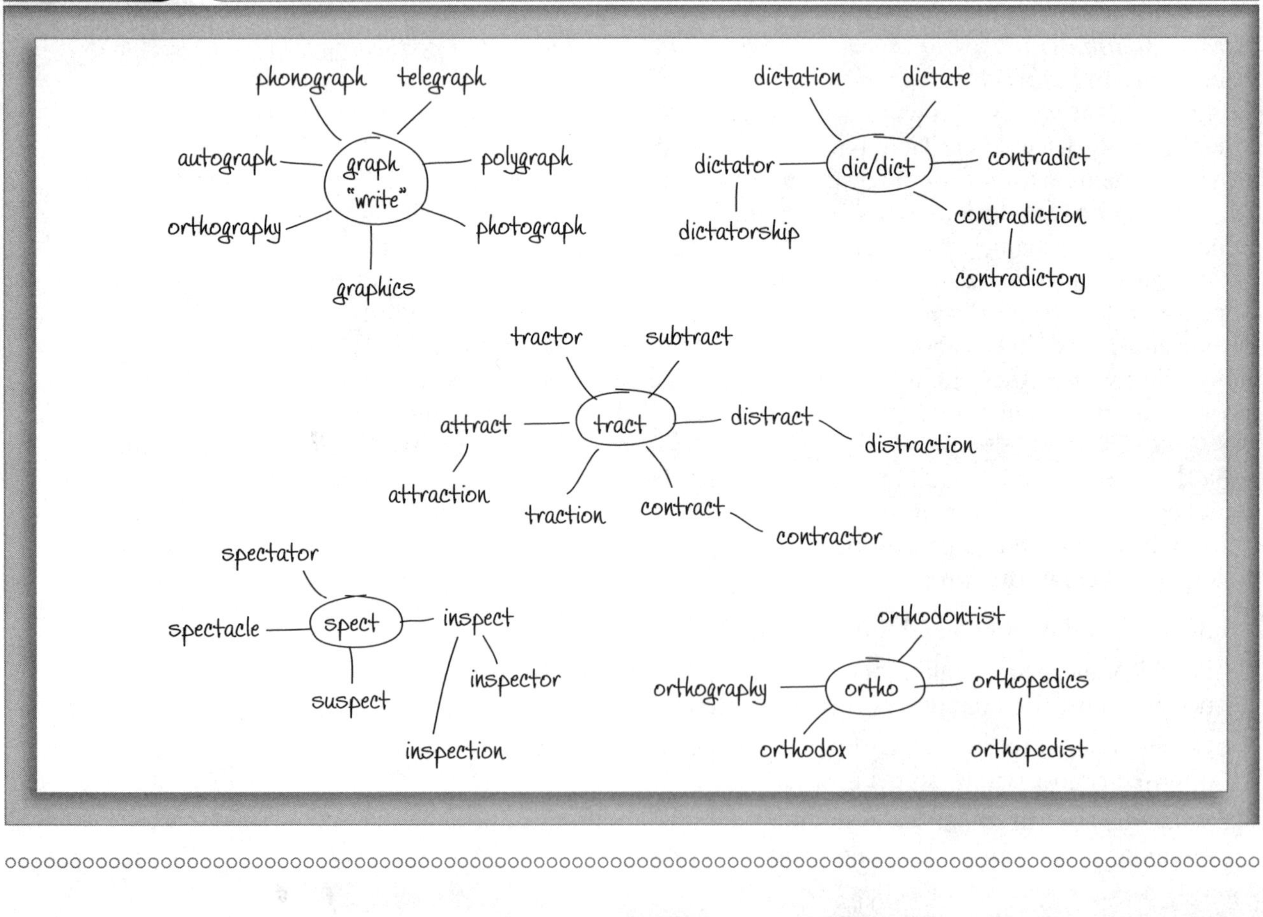

Etymology

Exploring the histories or derivations of words (etymology) with students helps them with spelling (e.g., knowing that *ballet* and *buffet* are both French words helps them to understand that the "et" has a long /a/ sound), and it also provides interesting multicultural word walls and lessons. Many dictionaries, in print or online, offer information about the language from which each word derives. Additionally, books on the history of words—found in any school library—can provide entertaining stories of words' origins. For example, the word *tank,* which is defined as a heavily armored vehicle, was originally used as a code word to keep the vehicle's existence a secret during World War I. The sharing of such information adds a spark to the study of history, and it can also help students remember the concept and meaning of the word (Rasinski, Padak, & Fawcett, 2010). Other examples include *lagoon,* which derives from French (*lagun*) and Italian (*laguna*) and means a shallow lake or pond, and *lagniappe,* whose origins are in Creole French (*la*) and Spanish (*napa,* meaning "gift"). This combination of languages results in a word that means a small present given to a customer with a purchase, or, as the store owners would say, "a little something extra." English learners may be interested in identifying English words that originate from their native language. Many prefixes and suffixes in the English language are also derived from other languages, and understanding these word parts will often give students an idea as to their meaning in new words.

Books on the histories of words, found in any school library, can provide entertaining stories of words' origins.

Word play/word formation

Students need to realize that English is a living, growing language, with new words being continually added. Dictionaries today contain words that were not there a few short years ago. And using word parts is generally how new words come into existence. Prefixes and suffixes are added to existing root words to form new words (e.g., *preview, Americanism*). Sometimes two words are combined to create a new word. These are called **portmanteau words,** or words that are blended together (e.g., *phablet* from *phone + tablet, motel* from *motor + hotel,* or *smog* from *smoke + fog*). Students get excited about creating potential new words, and they enjoy sharing them and their definitions with classmates.

portmanteau words

The following examples of "created" words were found, unclaimed, online (modified from Johnson, 2001, p. 162). They could be used as examples for challenging students to create their own words:

Aquadextrous (akwa DEKS trus) adj. Having the ability to turn the bathtub faucet on and off with your toes. Rosa was able to relax in her reclined position as she used her *aquadextrous* ability to warm up her cooling bathtub water.

Elevacelleration (el a VA celer AY schun) n. The mistaken idea that the more you press the elevator button, the faster it will arrive. The businessman, anxious to get to his meeting on the fifteenth floor, tapped his foot impatiently as he demonstrated *elevacelleration*.

Elboatics (el bo AT iks) n. The physical maneuvering two people engage in while trying to use the one armrest between them at the movie theater. While they were engaged in *elboatics,* the couple missed a key line of dialogue between the hero and villain.

Students can work in teams or alone to create new words. Each new word should be presented like a dictionary entry with the pronunciation key, part of

Word Walls

One way to emphasize new, essential, or troublesome words is to post them on word walls, so students will have ready access to these words. Prior to fourth grade, word walls typically are filled with sight words. And for high school students, word walls are used for common content area terms. But for middle level students, word walls are best used to house words connected by derivation, affix, history of the word and similar words, or connected by concept. For students this age, it is especially helpful for word walls to focus on particular syllabic elements. Word walls can be organized into the prefixes, suffixes, and roots most appropriate for a particular topic of study, by meaning, or as identified by grade-level curriculum groups.

Another way to organize word walls is to introduce a word part that has a large family of words associated with it and encourage students to add words to this group as they find them in their reading. They can place the word on a word card, share it with the class along with its meaning and where they found the word, and then place the card on the word wall. These word groupings can also become the spelling words to be studied. For instance, "ology" is a good example of one such family. Many content areas use words that have "ology" in them (see Figure 4.6).

figure **4.6** Example word wall.

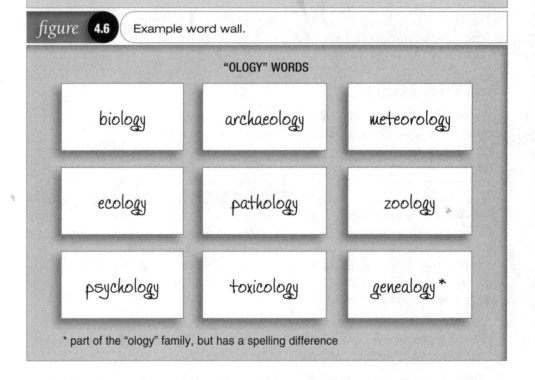

"OLOGY" WORDS

biology	archaeology	meteorology
ecology	pathology	zoology
psychology	toxicology	genealogy*

* part of the "ology" family, but has a spelling difference

speech, a definition, and a sample sentence, as seen in the examples above. If an illustration is appropriate, they should be encouraged to provide one.

Students also can play with words to come to their own understandings of the terms they need to learn. One such game involves helping students remember and understand a word they are learning and studying by answering some questions, clues, or prompts that the teacher (or another student) offers the class. For example, using the word "relative," the teacher may offer the prompts seen in Figure 4.7 and have the class come up with the answers (also shown in the figure).

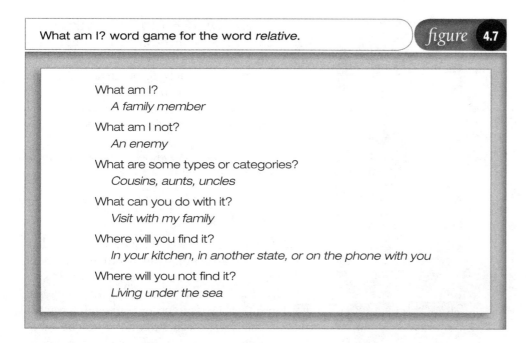

What am I? word game for the word *relative*.　　*figure* 4.7

> **What am I?**
>   *A family member*
>
> **What am I not?**
>   *An enemy*
>
> **What are some types or categories?**
>   *Cousins, aunts, uncles*
>
> **What can you do with it?**
>   *Visit with my family*
>
> **Where will you find it?**
>   *In your kitchen, in another state, or on the phone with you*
>
> **Where will you not find it?**
>   *Living under the sea*

Teaching Individual Word Meanings

Teachers are always looking for better ways to increase their students' vocabularies because they are aware that the traditional methods, for the most part, did not result in long-term retention of new words. In the past, students copied a list of words from the chalkboard, looked up their meaning in the dictionary, memorized a definition (usually a simple synonym), and then wrote sentences that were supposed to demonstrate an understanding of the word's essence. Here is an example of a product from such a method: "I was exhausted." This method of memorizing isolated vocabulary words one word at a time is not only ineffective, as the example suggests, but it is also impractical. While students may remember approximately 200 words a year through this rote method, Anderson and Nagy (1992) advise that students must acquire more than 3,000 words a year to keep up with the demands of content area material! However, results of vocabulary intervention studies suggest that only about 8–10 words can be taught effectively each week, so only about 360 words (180 school days/5 = 36 weeks; 10 words (36 weeks = 360 words) can reasonably be learned through direct instruction (Stahl & Fairbanks, 1986). Clearly, teachers must offer a variety of approaches to vocabulary instruction—beyond the traditional methods—to assist students with their substantial vocabulary needs and to enable them to acquire new vocabulary through incidental learning and from explicit instruction.

Incidental Learning

Although how it happens is not clear, most people learn new word meanings through incidental learning: listening and discussing, writing, and the act of reading widely (Graves, 2006; NICHD, 2000). Teachers who want to enhance their students' vocabularies make conscious decisions to include new and sometimes challenging words in their verbal interactions with the class, sometimes stopping to explain the word's meaning but more often just using the words in appropriate contexts. For example, "Today we will *commence* our lesson by sharing what we know about whales."

Teachers can encourage wide reading not only by building a well-stocked classroom library, but also by providing time for students to read the books in that library. Scheduling in-class independent reading using a structured silent reading

Estimates indicate that students must learn more than 3,000 words a year to keep up with the demands of content area reading.

program (e.g., DEAR, or Drop Everything and Read; SSR, or Sustained Silent Reading) with some sort of written follow-up in a vocabulary log or journal is strongly recommended (see the activity: "Very Important Term Word Book" later in this chapter). Teachers can also encourage independent reading through **book talks** (reading aloud a brief, enticing selection from and/or sharing positive impressions about a book to arouse interest in it.

Explicit Instruction

Even if students are reading independently, they will still need to learn many word meanings in order to comprehend content area materials successfully. Explicit instruction for such individual word meanings needs to occur. Although a teacher can take many approaches to directly teaching students the meaning of a word, which approach to use depends on three discrete factors (Stahl, 1999):

1. the nature of the word—concrete or abstract?
2. the possibility for grouping the word with others
3. the possibility for graphically illustrating the word

book talks ●

Is the word concrete or abstract? First, the word itself should be considered. If the word requires little explanation (e.g., *mountainside*), or it can be easily shown to students (e.g., *rutabaga*), then little extended elaboration is required. However, if the word is more abstract and difficult, such as *propaganda,* a lengthier explanation might be more appropriate. Additionally, an instructional strategy designed to help students focus on what the word *is* as well as what it is not, in relationship to words they already know, is often illuminating.

Can the word be grouped with others? Second, since teaching word meanings solely, as single units, is decidedly inefficient, teachers should look for ways to link words and ideas together so that students encounter a group of similar, or related, words together. For example, if students are studying newspapers, it would make sense to introduce all parts of the paper—headlines, editorials, classified advertisements, business pages, obituaries, and so forth—because these elements are all related to the same concept, or belong to the same "semantic field." Similarly, as mentioned earlier, skill in morphemic analysis makes it possible for students to determine the meanings of many words that share the same root. As Carlisle and Stone (2005) state, "Combining instruction in morphemic units for purposes of both reading and vocabulary development inherently makes sense, as such instruction might provide the essential links between form and meaning that are the potential benefit of morphemic processing in the natural act of reading [i.e., incidental learning]" (p. 446). For example, a student reading a selection on medical professions might encounter *ophthalmologist* and mentally associate it with *cardiologist, psychologist,* and *optometrist* at the same time.

Can the word be graphically illustrated? Finally, a word should be acted out or in some other way made graphic to students when the word in question lends itself to such treatment. Such words as *meandered* or *exhausted* can be immediately made clear through pantomime or drawings; likewise, the word *chrysanthemum* is instantly accessible by looking at a photograph or by examining the live flower. Moreover, such multisensory approaches to vocabulary development, with their reduced emphasis on oral language, help encourage English learners to be active participants in the learning and comprehension process.

Alber and Foil (2003) describe a procedure for introducing new vocabulary that includes physical action or dramatic movement to represent a word's meaning. Some examples of words with their corresponding actions include:

Exalted: start at floor level and lift an imaginary object high into the air
Lugubrious: make a sad face and pretend to cry uncontrollably
Pirouette: spin around on the ball of one foot
Studious: pretend to read a textbook with a serious expression on face

Effective Strategies for a Comprehensive Vocabulary Program

Through a well-planned vocabulary instructional program, students will add new words to their meaning vocabulary; in addition, the stress of learning an overwhelming number of new words and concepts encountered in instructional reading material will diminish. The end result is that by reducing the number of unfamiliar words with which readers must struggle, the teacher increases the chances of creating a positive literacy experience. In this section, we explore six student goals for an effective program in vocabulary instruction that ensures the maximum acquisition of new words. Students should strive to:

1. relate new words to what they already know.
2. use context to figure out partially known words.
3. consult a resource (e.g., a dictionary) when necessary.
4. learn to determine the meanings of polysemantic words.
5. infuse new vocabulary words into their writing and speaking.
6. commit to learning new words.

In the remainder of this chapter, we also consider the assumptions about vocabulary knowledge that underlie practice. Through an understanding of the options involved in teaching vocabulary, preservice and practicing teachers will be able to make informed instructional choices in this critical area.

① Relate New Words to Known Words

Two primary methods for clarifying and enriching the meanings of known words as related to new ones are (1) graphic organizers, such as semantic maps, and (2) semantic feature analysis.

Graphic organizers

Graphic organizers, also referred to as visual organizers, graphic representations, and structural overviews, work well for meaning-related concepts. A graphic organizer visually represents a body of knowledge that includes the critical concepts, ideas, events, generalizations, and/or facts pertaining to the word, using a diagram, cluster, or other type of visual display. Examples of graphic organizers include semantic maps and clarifying tables.

Semantic maps (Johnson & Pearson, 1986) help students visualize related information and develop new words for the same concept (see the following activity and Figure 4.8). Semantic mapping can also be used as a valuable prewriting strategy. The steps outlined in the activity can be adapted for individual purposes.

activity | Semantic Map

Using the following instructions, help students create a semantic map:

1. Choose a key word or concept from a book, story, or passage that students will be reading soon.
2. At the beginning of the lesson, write the core idea at the center of a whiteboard or large sheet of paper.
3. Ask students to think of as many words as they can that are related to the word or concept. As you list them, place them in broad categories (see Figure 4.8). You may wish to add related categories that students overlooked.
4. Lead students in a discussion of the broad categories and invite them to help you label these. Some words may fit into more than one category.
5. When the map is completed, discuss the categories and focus attention on those that will be highlighted in the passage to be read (e.g., students will be reading material about minting currency after completing the semantic map in Figure 4.8).
6. After reading the passage, revisit the map and augment it with new categories and words that were not mentioned in the original map-creating discussion.

figure **4.8** A semantic map for "money."

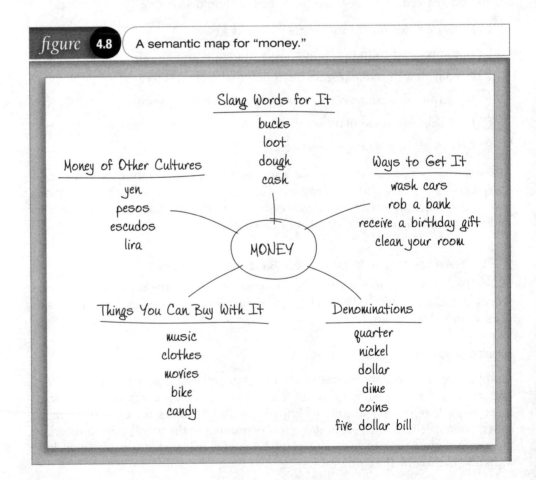

Slang Words for It
bucks
loot
dough
cash

Money of Other Cultures
yen
pesos
escudos
lira

Ways to Get It
wash cars
rob a bank
receive a birthday gift
clean your room

MONEY

Things You Can Buy With It
music
clothes
movies
bike
candy

Denominations
quarter
nickel
dollar
dime
coins
five dollar bill

A **clarifying table** is a graphic-organizing strategy that teachers may use to pre- clarifying table
teach, or "clarify," vocabulary terms—usually low-utility words—students will
encounter in an upcoming lesson, or to anchor the meanings of terms that have
already been explored through content area lessons. As a rule, clarifying tables
work best when the meanings of the new words are introduced at the beginning of
the content area lesson and then explored more thoroughly during the lesson; the
terms that are most critical to the lesson are solidified using the clarifying table (see
Figure 4.9). The following activity illustrates how to construct a clarifying table
and the steps used to employ it.

Constructing and Using a Clarifying Table   (ELLIS & FARMER, 2000)   **activity**

1. From the content area selection, identify several low-utility words that are
   particularly critical to its understanding.
2. Write one of those words on the whiteboard or poster paper, together with
   its core idea or simple definition. For example, the core idea of "propaganda"
   would be "a plan to spread opinions or beliefs."
3. Under the core idea, label a row "Clarifiers." With students, brainstorm some
   descriptions of propaganda, such as "it's used by people who want you to
   think the way they do for some reason."
4. After discussing the word with students, brainstorm some examples of propaganda and write on the chart one or more that clearly epitomize the essence
   of the concept. List these under the heading "Examples": "Political candidates give lots of facts and figures of why you should vote for them."
5. With students, brainstorm some instances that might easily be confused with
   the term but are substantively different; propaganda is not the same as some-

A clarifying table.   *figure* **4.9**

TERM:	Propaganda
CORE IDEA:	"A plan to spread opinions or beliefs"
CLARIFIERS:	It's used by people who want you to think the way they do for some reason.
EXAMPLES:	Political candidates give lots of facts and figures of why you should vote for them. Advertisements tell you why you should buy their product.
CONFUSED WITH:	An opinion. Jennifer believes cats make better pets than dogs. However, she is not trying to make others believe this.
KNOWLEDGE CONNECTIONS:	Door-to-door salespeople offer propaganda. Salespeople on the telephone. Activists. Lobbyists.
EXAMPLE SENTENCE:	The senator used lots of propaganda—like telling us he had reduced crime in the state by 18 percent—to convince us we should reelect him.

Source: Adapted from Ellis & Farmer, 2000.

one's opinion. Discuss how the instances differ. Example: "An opinion. Jennifer believes cats make better pets than dogs. However, she is not trying to make others believe this." Use the heading "Confused with:" for these entries.

6. Brainstorm some everyday examples of how propaganda is used and list these under the heading "Knowledge connections." Examples that students may be familiar with might include certain types of spam email or members of an activist group.

7. Place students in small groups and have them create a sentence for the term *propaganda,* illustrating that they understand its meaning. Using a group consensus, select a sentence that captures the sense of the word to complete the clarifying table. Example: "The senator used lots of propaganda—like telling us he had reduced crime in the state by 18 percent—to convince us we should reelect him."

Semantic feature analysis

semantic feature ● analysis

Semantic feature analysis works best for words that form a group and are similar in meaning; it can also be used when the concepts fall into one category (e.g., kinds of trees, breeds of dogs, past presidents). The procedure can also compare two versions of the same story or compare a movie with its source novel (Pittelman, Heimlich, Berglund, et al., 1991). The following activity outlines steps for creating a semantic feature analysis (Nagy, 1988).

◎ **activity** ◎   Creating a Semantic Feature Analysis

1. Select words that form a semantically close group (e.g., words that represent or are related to precipitation: *rain, snow, sleet, hail, slush, fog*). At least some of the distinctions in meaning should be immediately understandable to students.

2. On the whiteboard, use the selected words as column heads in a two-dimensional matrix (see Figure 4.10).

3. For the horizontal rows, decide on a number of words or phrases describing components of meaning shared by some of the words, or phrases that distinguish some words from others, such as *solid, liquid, cold, frozen,* and *white*.

4. One square, or cell, will represent the intersection of a given word and a semantic feature. One by one, ask students if the feature is shared by the given word. Discuss why or why not.

5. Record in the square whether or not, or to what extent, the feature applies to each word. Students may also suggest words to be added (e.g., mist), as well as descriptive terms (e.g., clear, wet).

② Use Context

Proficient readers use many strategies to identify and pronounce words that might be unfamiliar to them in print. Often, such words are in a reader's speaking and listening vocabularies, but the student may not have encountered these words in written material before. In such cases, readers try to use context clues to identify and pronounce the words. The syntactic (grammar) and semantic (meaning) information provided in the words, phrases, sentences, and paragraphs in a text are called *context clues*. Context clues occur in the sur-

| Semantic feature analysis. | *figure* **4.10** |

Precipitation

	rain	sleet	hail	fog	snow	slush	mist
solid	no	yes	yes	no	yes	sort of	no
liquid	yes	no	no	no	no	sort of	sort of
cold	sometimes	yes	sometimes	no	yes	yes	no
frozen	no	yes	yes	no	yes	yes	no
white	no	yes	sort of	sort of	yes	yes	sort of
clear	yes	no	yes	no	no	no	yes
wet	yes	yes	yes	yes	yes	yes	yes

rounding information, including pictures, to help identify a word. They are very important to word analysis and, ultimately, comprehension. *Context clues can be tools to help readers develop word-learning strategies they can use independently during incidental learning opportunities* (Nagy, 1988).

Contexts that provide helpful clues for figuring out a word's meaning are referred to as **directive contexts,** while those that are less helpful are referred to as **nondirective contexts** (Beck et al., 2013). Directive context clues can sometimes help students find the meaning of an unfamiliar word in the following ways:

- directive contexts
- nondirective contexts

- by directly defining the word
- by providing an appositive or comparison of the word
- by contrasting the word with a known word

Readers are also using context clues when they:

- think logically through the rest of the sentence
- consider examples provided in the sentence

Sentences with one or more of these features should be used to show students how word meaning can be gleaned through context. Examples of each of these context clues are as follows:

A <u>gendarme</u> is a police officer in France and several other European countries who has had military training. (definition)

She was <u>exhausted,</u> or extremely tired, after being up half the night. (appositive)

Rather than being famous in his homeland for defeating the enemy in the war, the man learned he was <u>notorious.</u> (contrast)

Sandra said <u>morosely,</u> "This town will be the death of us." (logic)

Cats, dogs, and hamsters are all examples of <u>domestic</u> animals. (illustration or description)

Context clues can also be found in sentences other than the one in which the new word appears, so students should be encouraged to read surrounding sentences for clues to meaning. Sometimes an entire paragraph embodies the explanation of a word, as in the following example: "The climb took far longer than Sara and Michelle had expected. But when they arrived at the top, they were greeted by the most spectacular sight of the valley below. Their whole five-mile hike had been worth it. They were exhilarated!" Research in using context clues to infer word meanings reveals that effective instruction takes time and must be well planned. Graves (2006) recommends ten 30- to 45-minute sessions devoted to teaching students to use context clues.

◎ **activity** ◎	C(2)QU	(BLACHOWICZ, 1993)

C(2)QU stands for "context and two questions." This instructional activity can help teachers show students how to work through the use of context clues to discover the meaning of an unfamiliar word.

1. Provide a broad, meaningful context for an unfamiliar word using one of the five context types: definition, appositive, contrast, logic, illustration. Example: "When it was time to help clean up the house, the little girl <u>vanished</u>." Invite students to offer suggestions about the meaning of the word using the hints provided by the context of the sentence(s)—that is, how the word was used.

2. Provide one or two sentences that offer more explicit contextual information for the word. Example: "Ramon watched as the horse grew smaller and smaller and finally <u>vanished</u> from sight. Now it was really gone." Now ask students to reconsider their original hypotheses about the word's meaning.

3. Ask students direct questions that involve the meaning of the word. Example: "When something vanishes, do you expect to see it again? What kinds of things might vanish?"

4. Invite students to use the word appropriately in oral or written form. Example: "The puppy was so hungry that the food we put out for her <u>vanished</u> in an instant."

When working with English learners, teachers can suggest that students draw or identify pictures representing the word's meaning rather than attempt an oral or written. For example, Morgan and Odom (2006) had their fourth- and sixth-graders draw cartoons for clarifying word meanings, increasing both vocabulary knowledge and motivation for learning new words. Some examples follow:

To illustrate *fortune,* Alison drew a Magic 8 Ball showing the words "Better not tell you now."

Jack drew an *echo* powerful enough to knock a man off the rim of the Grand Canyon. As the man fell—portrayed by a series of tumbling stick figures—he repeatedly bounced off ledges and rocks, shouting "Ouch!" each time.

Meg's idea of a *labyrinth* was a hungry girl wandering through an endless maze, trying to reach the Pizza Palace.

In Alexa's cartoon, *hypnosis* was the only way a frustrated mom could get her daughter to clean her room. (p. 41)

In addition to context clues, Graves (2006) suggests that students also use word parts (structural analysis, as discussed earlier) to infer the meaning. Research conducted by Baumann, Edwards, and colleagues (2003) with fifth-graders in the context of learning social studies content supports this suggestion. They found that combining context and morphological, or structural, analysis led to success at inferring the meanings of affixed words and contextually decipherable words on a delayed test.

To summarize what we know about using the context, keep four key points in mind when teaching students to use this important skill:

1. Acknowledge that context may not always be enough.
2. Select only those examples of text that allow students to discover the word.
3. Model for students a strategy for thinking through how to get the meaning from context, using a "Think Aloud" (see Chapter 5).
4. Encourage students to immediately apply the new word to their own experience in written form (e.g., have them write about a time they felt "rejected").

③ Consult Resources to Discover the Meanings of Words

Proficient readers use various strategies to discover the meanings of unknown words. For example, they might ask someone, read around the word, use the context, or look up the word in a dictionary (in print or online) or the book's glossary. The last option is one that directly leads to autonomy in acquiring vocabulary, but if we ask students to look up every unknown word they may lose the continuity of what they are reading and, eventually, lose interest in reading.

Allen (1999) offers 12 options students can consider as resources to figure out the meaning of unfamiliar words:

1. See how the word fits into the sentence (i.e., part of speech).
2. Use the dictionary to find the meaning of the word.
3. Say the word out loud to see if it can be recognized.
4. Read the sentence again to see if the meaning of the word becomes clearer.
5. Look at the beginning of the sentence again.
6. Think about what other word would make sense in the sentence.
7. Look for other words in the sentence that give clues.
8. Ask someone else to read the sentence out loud.
9. Look at the picture, if there is one.
10. Read around the word and then go back to it.
11. Skip the word if it is not needed.
12. Ask the teacher, another adult, or a classmate.

Online Resources

www.Factmonster.com

www.ldoceonline.com

http://nhd.heinle.com/home.aspx

www.mycobuild.com/free-search.aspx

Dictionaries can be valuable resources for learning word meanings, but instruction using dictionaries is seldom helpful if students are asked only to look up definitions and then use the word in a sentence (Gipe, 1978/1979; Scott & Nagy, 1997). Effective dictionary instruction includes teacher modeling of how to use a dictionary and how to select the most appropriate meaning for a word. Students should also have access to learner-friendly dictionaries, such as *Collins COBUILD Learner's Illustrated Dictionary* (2012), that provide age-appropriate definitions and example sentences (Feldman & Kinsella, 2003). Collegiate dictionaries may not be the most appropriate for students in grades 4–8 or for English learners. Students also need instruction in using online versions of resources, such as dictionary. com and thesaurus.com.

Students tend to use dictionary resources without giving much thought to the best definition for the word as it appears. They must be aware of the context in which it is used, they must understand the part of speech so they know which use of the word is best in the situation, and they must be able to understand the word and be able to define it in their own words. Since students most likely already use an online dictionary to find definitions, teach students to carefully assess which site provides the best information. Give students a word or two and have them compare definitions from at least three online dictionaries. Ask them to identify the *best* definition, the one that supports their understanding the most, and the one that works best in the context of the text. Teach them to ask questions as they compare the definitions they find online. Students often believe everything they read on the Internet, and they will benefit from this exercise.

Whether the resources are online or in print, we still need to teach students the value of using the dictionary to learn about the meanings of words and the thesaurus to learn how to locate synonyms and antonyms. Teachers can provide structured opportunities for students to use these important tools during minilessons and other word study activities. Additionally, students can be encouraged to use dictionary resources through ongoing practice of the Very Important Term Word Book activity.

◉ activity ◉ — Very Important Term Word Book

1. Ask students to designate a binder or special folder (an actual folder or online) as their Very Important Term (VIT) Word Book.

2. Select words from any number of sources that are appropriate for the grade level, and divide the total number of words into lists of ten words each. The words might come from the Academic Word List mentioned earlier, or from the curriculum materials used for a specific subject area.

3. Each week, introduce ten words—five words on Day 1 and five words on Day 2—by pronouncing each word, showing the syllabic breakdown or pronounce-able parts, and having students guess at their meanings (see Part A, Figure 4.11).

4. Develop and read aloud sentences for each word to provide a meaningful context, and ask students to make additional predictions about the meaning of the words (see Part B, Figure 4.11).

5. Solicit student volunteers to offer their definitions, and write them on the whiteboard. Circle those that are accurate or partially accurate.

6. Have students go to their dictionaries, find the words, and write the page number on which the word is found, the part of speech, and the definition(s) (see Part C, Figure 4.11). Alternatively, have students search for words online, write the source where they found their definition, the part of speech, and the definition(s).

7. Direct students to use the words in their own sentences, including different forms of the word (e.g., different part of speech, past tense, plural) (see Part D, Figure 4.11).

8. On Day 3, go back to step 6 (Part C, Figure 4.11) and give the correct definition for each word. Students self-correct their work or confirm that a meaning they have predicted is acceptable. Then start again at step 3 with five new words.

9. On Day 4, ask students to write a paragraph using five of the new words and indicate the part of speech for each word. In order for students to check the appropriate use of the word, have them rewrite the same paragraph; instead of the new words, however, students should write in the definition of that word where it would occur to see if the sentence/paragraph makes sense.

10. On Day 5, administer a vocabulary test. For example, choose 8 of the 15 words for students to use in sentences. Then ask them to write three more sentences using any additional three words of their choice.

Sample Very Important Term Word Book, grade 7. **figure 4.11**

Name: Sam Walker Period: 7

Date: 2-20 Vocabulary List # 21 Total Points Earned:

PART A Day 2 Words: Copy each word from the board. Write what you think is the meaning of each.

1. Digit (dig-it) A single form in a number
2. Dismal (dis-mal) To become mad or bad
3. Enclose (en-close) To be put in an object
4. Garb (garb) Like a dog's bark
5. Portion (port-ion) An amount of something

PART B The teacher will read a sentence using each word; thereafter, the class will discuss the word and possible definitions. Write the word again & write what you now think the word means.

1. Fingers or toes
2. Bad or dreary
3. To be sealed in an object
4. Clothing
5. An amount of something

PART C Go to the dictionary. Look up each word and write its dictionary definition.

1. (p184)(n) A finger or toe
2. (p189)(adj) ~~Dark & gloomy~~ Dreary
3. (p215)(v,n) To shut in all around
4. (p268)(n) Clothing
5. (p512)(n) ~~Helping of food~~ Part of

Reprinted with permission.

(continued)

figure **4.11**   Sample Very Important Term Word Book, grade 7, *continued.*

PART D   For this section you need to work with one other person.

1. Write three different sentences (at least six words in length) for each of the five vocabulary words.

2. Each sentence must (if possible) be a different form of the word (plural, past tense, different part of speech, etc).

3. Identify the part of speech of each vocabulary word as it is being used in that sentence.

4. Underline each vocabulary word.

1a. One of my digits(pln) are shorter than the other.

1b. Barney picks his nose with his digitas.

1c. The digits(possn) length was truly unbelievable.

2a. It was a dismal(adj) day from the fog.

2b. His dismalness(n) made him look part Emo.

2c. This day is more dismal.(comadj) than the other day.

3a. The toy was enclosed(ptv) in a very small box.

3b. I was born while enclosing(v) my brain in my head.

3c. She will enclose(ftv) a shell in her hands.

4a. My garb(n) costs way more than your's does.

4b. The garb's(possn) beauty was barely stunning.

4c. All the garbs(pln) added up to 100 pounds of cloth.

5a. My portion(n) of food wasn't enough for me.

5b. The portions(pln) of crumbs filled the rat's stomach.

5c. The portion's(possn) taste was like eating an eraser.

④ Learn to Determine the Meanings of Polysemantic Words

polysemantic •   Many words in the English language are **polysemantic:** that is, they have multiple meanings. If we include shades of meaning or related meanings as multiple meanings, then nearly every word in the English language in some way has more than one meaning associated with it. Readers are often perplexed to find a word they thought they knew used in a context that is unfamiliar to them. In some cases, the student may be familiar with a word's common definitions but not with the specialized meaning found in content area subjects such as science, social studies, and mathematics.

Because polysemantic words can have different meanings depending on the context in which they are used, such words can be extremely confusing. The following activity can help show students, especially English learners, how to determine the appropriate definition for a polysemantic word.

How Is It Used?

1. Write the following sentences on the whiteboard:
   The man had to pay room and board at the country inn.
   She was on the Board of Education in her city.
   The board was made of the finest redwood.
   We got on board just as the train was departing.
   The board member offered advice on the proposed idea.
2. Pair up students and give them dictionaries (or provide them with access to online dictionaries).
3. Ask each pair of students to look up the word *board* and find the specific definition to fit each sentence.
4. With the whole class, discuss each meaning as it is located.
5. Ask students to create new sentences of their own that fit each definition.
6. Have students read other dictionary definitions for the word *board*—beyond the five they have already read—and compose sentences for these meanings.
7. Use the same procedure for other multiple-meaning words as they are encountered.

If a variant meaning for a word does not represent a difficult concept, it can be taught simply by discussing with students their current understanding of the word's meaning, presenting the word's new meaning, and then noting the similarities and differences when the word is used in the alternative way. If the new meaning is more complex, then the method outlined in the following activity, ideal for expository text, may be more helpful.

Possible Sentences   (STAHL & KAPINUS, 1991)

1. From an upcoming reading assignment, choose several key terms that might be difficult for students because they are being used in unfamiliar ways (for example, *base, run, board*).
2. Provide short explanations for the words as they will be used in the upcoming assignment. For example:

   A character in literature can have *base*, or evil, motives for doing seemingly good deeds.
   A person decides to *run* for, or pursue, a political position, such as mayor.
   A *board* of directors is a group of people who get together to oversee a project.

3. Have the students form small groups and ask them to create *possible sentences,* using the words as they believe the words might be used in the passage they are about to read.

4. Write the possible sentences on the whiteboard. Read and discuss them together.

5. After reading the assignment, revisit the possible sentences and discuss whether they reflect the appropriate meaning of the specified word, based on the new information gleaned from the passage.

6. If students decide one or more sentences do not reflect the appropriate meaning of the word, help students revise them to make the meanings match. For example:

The men will <u>run</u> for their life when they are chased by the lion. (would not be a meaning match)

She was the first woman to <u>run</u> for governor of Kentucky. (revised)

⑤ Infuse New Vocabulary into Writing and Speaking

Teachers can encourage students to expand their speaking vocabularies, or the words they use in oral language, by actively recognizing and praising appropriate word usage in the classroom; they should also allow ample time for spontaneous word play, in which students experiment with words they discover and choose to share. Students often have words in their reading and listening vocabularies they have never used in speaking or writing. "Rich" instruction (i.e., "instruction that goes beyond definitional information to get students actively involved in using and thinking about word meanings and creating lots of associations among words" (Beck et al., 2002/2013, p. 73) is important in getting students to use new words. For example, semantic gradients, used with a dictionary or thesaurus, can help older students think about and discuss relationships among similar and different words (synonyms and antonyms) as well as discern slight shades of meaning between words.

◎ activity ◎ Semantic Gradient

1. Have students form small groups and ask them to choose two known words with opposite meanings, such as *race/crawl, gigantic/minuscule,* and *frigid/scorching.* (An easier version would be to supply a list of words for the students.)

2. Have students write one of the words toward the top of a sheet of paper and the opposite word toward the bottom. The space in the middle will be used for the placement of other words according to how closely they fit in terms of meaning.

3. With the help of a dictionary and/or thesaurus, invite students to discuss the meanings of the two words and then list other words in the continuum according to how closely they match the meaning of the first two words. Explain that each word they add to their paper must be the same part of speech as the original two words. Also, stress that there are no right or wrong answers but remind them that they should be able to defend their placement of words. For example (for fifth-graders):

fly

race

skedaddle

run

jog

power walk

trot

walk

stroll

saunter

meander

shuffle

crawl

stand still

4. Invite students to share their lists and explain why they placed the words where they did by giving examples of how such words could be used in sentences. Greenwood and Flanigan (2007) provide examples of sentences for use with semantic gradients.

5. Use lists to create linear charts (see Figure 4.12) and place them around the classroom so that they can be added to as students encounter other words that are related to the original two words.

6. Optional: Have students act out words.

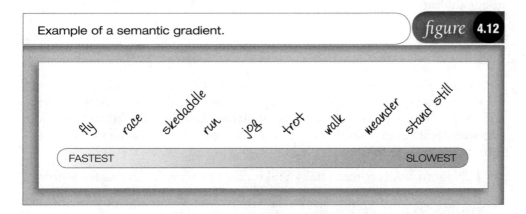

Example of a semantic gradient. *figure* **4.12**

⑥ **Commit to Learning New Words**

Because of the sheer number of words that students must learn every year, as noted earlier, perhaps the most proactive instructional approach teachers can take with vocabulary is to encourage students to commit themselves individually to building their word knowledge. Having such a personal commitment is, of course, especially critical for students who face the task of learning English as a second language.

One way in which teachers can have students commit to building their word knowledge is to discuss, with the whole class, a number of ways to learn new words. During this discussion, teachers should offer their own ideas while also incorporating those that the students suggest. Some ideas to consider are the following:

• Learn one new word a day, from any source.

- Look up—online or in the dictionary—one word each day that has been heard in conversation or on the news.
- "Adopt" a certain prefix or suffix, or Greek or Latin root, and learn and use words containing these elements over a few weeks' duration.
- Agree to acquire at least two or three new words from their context each week and then record both the words and the context from which they were derived in a vocabulary notebook (e.g., VIT Word Book).
- Make a list of "tired" words, or words that are used too often in one's own writing and speaking (e.g., *nice*). Look up the words in a thesaurus and commit to using newly discovered synonyms for these tired words, one a week.
- Find one word that will "stump the teacher." Allow a different student each day to write his or her word on the whiteboard for you to try to define. Keep a running list of the new words—and how often you've been stumped.

Finally, we believe it is the teacher's own enthusiasm, creative word play, fascination with words—their history, sound, origin, and so forth—that can make all the difference in students' curiosity about and interest in acquiring them. Ultimately, a love for language is "caught" rather than "taught." Consequently, a teacher who frequently stops reading a passage to dramatically repeat a phrase filled with imagery, or one who often shares favorite words, puns, riddles, and other word play with students, will help to create learners who notice words and remember them. Word play can be done incidentally during any literacy activity, or it can consist of structured word games such as crossword puzzles, Scrabble, Balderdash, or Password. The following activities are prototypical of the kind that help instill in our students a love of language.

◎ activity ◎ Hinky Pinkies

Hinky Pinkies is an activity that fosters appreciation of rhyme, requires students to use the dictionary or thesaurus to look up unknown words, and motivates them to add the new words to their speaking vocabularies. Additionally, the game provides important practice in determining what is and is not an appropriate synonym. The activity proceeds as follows:

1. Explain to students that Hinky Pinkies are rhyming definitions for words with either one syllable (*hink pinks*), two syllables (*hinky pinkies*), or three syllables (*hinkety pinketies*).
2. Have students form pairs and provide access to a dictionary and a thesaurus to each pair.
3. Show the following example to students:

   a thicker arachnid

4. Explain to students that in order to find the answer, they must find synonyms for both the word *thicker* and the word *arachnid*. Advise them that they may use the dictionary or thesaurus if they do not know the meaning of a word and for help finding appropriate synonyms. Further, explain that the synonyms for the original words must rhyme and be the same number of syllables. In this example, each word consists of two syllables—a hinky pinky.
5. Ask students to look up the word *arachnid* in the dictionary or thesaurus. Write the words they discover on the whiteboard (the most prominent definition will be *spider*).

6. Ask students to think of a two-syllable word that rhymes with "spider" and means the same thing, or is a synonym for, the word *thicker*. Write the answer on the board:

> a thicker arachnid = a wider spider

7. Complete this exercise for several other examples, making sure to use one word that is unfamiliar to students in each definition:

> an evil pastor (sinister minister)
> an ebony slit (black crack)
> a mean gem (cruel jewel)

8. Create 20 of these word plays for students to do in pairs. Then ask each pair of students to create their own hink pinks, hinky pinkies, or hinkety pinketies with the help of the dictionary or thesaurus.

9. Have each pair of students read their examples to the class so that the other students can guess the answers. Make a class book of their contributions.

Paraphrastics

Learners are intrigued by adages in which synonyms have replaced the original words and phrases, although the original meaning has been kept intact. Additionally, understanding such adages often requires a dictionary and a thesaurus, thus making them excellent activities for increasing vocabulary and awareness of appropriate synonyms.

1. Place students into small groups and provide each group with access to a dictionary and a thesaurus.

2. Using the whiteboard, show students several adages that they are likely to know but that have been modified by different words and phrases so that it now sounds entirely different. For example:

> Members of an avian species of identical plumage congregate. (Birds of a feather flock together.)
> All articles that coruscate with resplendence are not necessarily auriferous. (All that glitters is not gold.)
> The stylus is more potent than the claymore. (The pen is mightier than the sword.)
> Male cadavers are incapable of yielding any falsehoods. (Dead men tell no lies.)

3. Ask students to try to figure out the original adage by looking up unfamiliar words in the dictionary. After they have come up with the solution, write the original adage on the board, under the paraphrased one.

4. Brainstorm some other adages that students have heard. Invite them, in their small groups, to paraphrase these adages using the thesaurus for synonyms.

5. When all groups have finished this exercise, have them read their revised adages to the rest of the class so that the other students can try to guess the original. Create a class book with the paraphrased adages. Encourage students to try to stump their parents, caregivers, and other family members with the paraphrased adages.

6. For an added challenge, encourage students to take the original adages and design new phrases that mean just the opposite of the originals. For example, "All that glitters is not gold" would become "None that tarnishes is silver."

Troubleshooting

Inadequate vocabulary is often the result of limited experiences and intellectual stimulation, as well as a lack of habitual reading. Lack of oral stimulation, limited contact with print materials, few books in the home for recreational reading, and an aversion to reading can all contribute to a vocabulary deficit. Speech defects or hearing difficulties may also be factors in slow or weak language development (Crawley & Merritt, 2011). The following suggestions will be helpful for learners with inadequate vocabularies while also enriching the vocabularies and intellectual lives of all students in a class. These suggestions will be especially valuable for English learners.

Limited Interest/Experience in Independent Reading

The importance of wide reading for its impact on vocabulary development cannot be overemphasized. Just reading a few minutes each day will make staggering differences in the number of words that students encounter in the course of a school year. Therefore, students who read widely will come across a plethora of new words and, with every subsequent encounter with each word, will begin to move the words through the four levels of word knowledge (refer back to Figure 4.1), from never having heard it before to knowing it well. Teachers can encourage students to read widely by continuing to read aloud to them, from books selected from a variety of genres and representing diverse ethnic groups.

The positive impact that reading aloud to students has on their vocabulary development is well documented (National Reading Panel, 2000; Serafini & Giorgis, 2003). Jim Trelease (2013) had it right when he began writing popular books such as the *Read Aloud Handbook,* which provides practical information about reading aloud to students of all ages. Reading aloud benefits students by helping them build vocabulary—gained by listening to the text and learning and hearing new words—creating background knowledge, offering a prosodic reading from an adult role model, and motivating them to read.

interactive oral reading ● Using an **interactive oral reading** technique, in which the teacher reads aloud, stopping periodically to focus on and discuss individual words, as well as other aspects of what is being read, is highly recommended for developing the vocabulary of students who are linguistically disadvantaged and English learners (Carlo et al., 2004; Carlo, August, & Snow, 2005). In their research with young students, Coyne, Simmons, and Kame'enui (2004) found that "explicitly teaching word meanings within the context of shared storybook reading" is especially helpful to learners at risk of experiencing reading difficulties (pp. 49–50). Hickman, Pollard-Durodola, and Vaughn (2004) found read-alouds to be central to developing the academic language of English learners. Read-alouds also provide access to books that these learners may not be able to experience on their own. In this way, students are introduced to a wide variety of genres and text structures, as well as vocabulary.

The following are guidelines for using read-alouds with English learners and students who are linguistically disadvantaged (Carlo et al., 2004; Carlo et al., 2005; Harmon, 2002; Hickman et al., 2004; Ulanoff & Pucci, 1999):

1. Provide 20–30 minutes of read-aloud time daily.
2. Choose books thematically—e.g., for an immigration theme, have students read three of the following: *Farewell to Manzanar* (2012) by Jeanne and James Houston, *Crossing the Wire* (2006) by Will Hobbs, *The Good Braider* (2012) by Terry Farish, *Illegal* (2011) by Bettina Restrepo, and *Heat* (2006) by Mike Lupica—and read each book over a period of five days; focus on

three or four new words each day. An academic word list, such as the one mentioned earlier, may help in choosing words (Coxhead, 2000).

3. Separate the text to be read into passages that fit the natural flow of the story.

4. Stop during each day's reading to check for understanding and to review the vocabulary words.

5. In addition to choosing three or four words to discuss, invite students to identify words for which they do not know the meanings.

6. At the end of each day's reading, and again at the end of the book, provide opportunities to discuss the words further, reread certain passages for clarification, and engage students in "facilitated peer dialogue"—an activity for readers who struggle to focus on vocabulary and word-learning strategies (Harmon, 2002, p. 606).

Providing a good selection of literature in the classroom (see Appendix A and Table 5.2 in Chapter 5) and allowing ample time during the school day for students to read self-selected material (e.g., DEAR, SSR) help foster an interest in reading. Finally, students tend to encourage each other to read when time is set aside for them to share and respond to what they are reading in meaningful ways (e.g., literature circles, book clubs).

Students who read widely come across a plethora of new words and, with every subsequent encounter with each word, begin to move the words through the four levels of word knowledge.

Limited Schema for Remembering New Vocabulary

The term *schema* refers to a person's organized knowledge of the world. This knowledge provides the basis for understanding and remembering new vocabulary words. If the learner already has some relevant background or word knowledge, or both, about the topic being introduced, new vocabulary can be enhanced by activating the existing schema or bringing it to the surface. The more actual, concrete experiences teachers provide for their students, especially those for whom English is a second language, the more teachers will be adding to a schema on which students can attach new words and concepts. Words seldom exist in a vacuum, and offering such experiences helps students greatly expand their knowledge of the words associated with the topic under consideration in a relatively short amount of time. Book talks, art in all its forms, cooking, experiments, and objects associated with reading and discussion are forms of realia that engage learners in questioning, discussing, and thinking about new words and incorporating them into their meaning vocabularies.

Sometimes a student has limited knowledge of or background about a certain subject being discussed. In that case, the teacher must construct a schema for that student. Since it is not always possible to offer either virtual reality or an opportunity to experience an event directly, sometimes vicarious (or "simulated") experiences can provide a context for new vocabulary. For example, a chapter on the Amazon rainforest would clearly be best enhanced by a field trip to show students the forest, the canopy, and the different flora and fauna; however, because such a journey is not generally feasible, activities involving video clips, television documentary excerpts, websites, or photographs are usually more practical. With appropriate explanation and description, these activities can result in almost as much new vocabulary acquisition as an actual field trip would provide.

◉ activity ◉ | Virtual Field Trip (ADAPTED FROM KANE, 2011)

Although field trips to actual places are not always possible, virtual field trips can often provide students with a simulated experience to help them learn new vocabulary associated with a particular place or time.

1. Choose a place or location relevant to a content area lesson you are preparing, such as the Gobi Desert or the Amazon rainforest.
2. Select book(s), websites, photographs, videos, artifacts, or other materials relevant to the lesson.
3. Brainstorm what a student might expect to find at the chosen location.
4. Divide students into groups and have them prepare questions for their "tour guide."
5. Have the groups "tour" the location by reading and viewing.
6. Ask students to prepare a summary of the highlights of their tour, describing what they learned about the location and its related content area subject.
7. Have students plot their journeys on a map or timeline, or both.
8. Discuss where the students' inquiry can go from here and what other resources they might "tour" next to learn about the topic in more depth; answer any remaining or new questions.

Picture books can also be used to enhance schema and provide visual clues to the meanings of new words. For example, in *The Shell Book*, Lember (1997) presents stunning photographs of seashells commonly found along the shore and provides brief descriptions of the seashells. After sharing this picture book, a teacher could invite students to generate seashore murals depicting the variety of shells associated with a particular coastline (e.g., limpets along the Pacific coast; cockles on the Atlantic coast). Not only will students learn many new shells, they will also learn the academic vocabulary associated with geography and the coastal United States. See the website cited in the margin for a database of similar picture books.

WWW●●●

Picture Book Abstracts
www.lib.muohio.edu/pictbks

Professor Garfield
http://www.professorgarfield.
org/parents_teachers/links/
vocabulary_links.html

Similarly, well-chosen comic strips can provide visual representations for help in learning word meanings (McVicker, 2007). For instance, the *Family Circus* cartoon often embeds visual clues to the meanings for words. One example shows the oldest child Billy asking, "What does meandering mean?" as he winds through his neighborhood and a dotted line connects all the places he visits. Also, *Garfield* cartoonist Jim Davis hosts a website useful for vocabulary building; see the website mentioned in the margin.

Summary

A cquiring the meaning of many new words is not all there is to reading; because words can be considered the building blocks that comprise all written and spoken text, however, their importance in a balanced and comprehensive literacy program must not be underestimated. Students need to learn the meanings of approximately 3,000 new words a year—and more if those students are learning English as a second language—so a teacher needs to do more than simply have students memorize a list of vocabulary words and their meanings.

Word study is presented as a continuum of development in spelling, word analysis, and vocabulary abilities. In grades 4–8 the focus changes from attention to mapping sounds onto letters to recognizing the units that make up whole words.

Most important are units that hold meaning, such as prefixes, suffixes, roots, and endings. These units are also consistent in their pronunciation and meaning, thus aiding both decoding and spelling. Because the nature of word study in grades 4–8 involves word parts that hold meaning, instruction is also closely tied to meaning vocabulary. It would be extremely difficult to avoid talking about the meanings of words when providing instruction in roots, prefixes, suffixes, compound words, and derivational words. While students in the primary grades learn to decode words that are for the most part in their speaking and listening vocabularies, older students are learning to decode many words for which they have no conceptual knowledge. Instruction in word recognition, then, must be closely related to instruction in meaning vocabulary to be most effective and efficient.

Strive to provide effective meaning-vocabulary development strategies, such as helping students appreciate words and their origins and urging them to make a personal commitment to find out about them. Furthermore, encourage wide reading and provide strategies for independently figuring out the meaning of unknown words. Above all, share your fascination with and curiosity about words. Ultimately, the goal of all vocabulary instruction should be to inspire students to become independent word collectors who actively enjoy learning new words. Such learners become the students who comprehend best and thus read the most, entering into a self-perpetuating cycle of success.

Actively learning the meanings of many new words, through a wide variety of means, is unquestionably an integral part of a balanced and comprehensive literacy program. The more numerous the reading, writing, listening, and speaking experiences students are offered, the more they will come into contact with intriguing new words. And it is through just such experiences that students' stores of vocabulary steadily grow, just as it is through the excitement of abundant reading and writing that they become proficient readers and writers.

Ⓠuestions FOR JOURNAL WRITING AND DISCUSSION

1. Using a page in this chapter, create three columns of words: title the first column "Basic Words," the second "General-Utility Words," and the third "Low-Utility Words." With a partner, arrange the words from this page in the three different categories. Discuss your decisions with your classmates, and defend your choices. Why do you think it is important to classify the words you would teach to your students in this manner?

2. Consider the following selection from *Venus Among the Fishes* (Hall & O'Dell, 1996). The underlined words are those chosen for direct instruction with students in grades 4–8. In this work of fiction, the narrator is Coral, a young female dolphin. Her story captures the drama of underwater life. Referring to the criteria for selecting words to teach (Beck et al., 2013; Ellis & Farmer, 2000), decide which underlined words you agree are important and useful words to teach and which are not.

   My father was the largest male in our <u>herd</u> of white-sided <u>dolphins.</u> From his white face, a light <u>stripe</u> <u>curved</u> up over his head and along his <u>gleaming</u> black back to his white and black <u>dorsal fin.</u> His belly was a <u>pearly</u> white. Father was such a <u>skillful</u> swimmer that his skin had never been <u>scraped</u> or <u>scarred,</u> <u>despite</u> his many <u>encounters</u> with sharks, orcas, or angry dolphins.

   As I watched for orcas now, my father and the older males swam on the sides of the herd, looking for squid and herring. Our <u>pod</u> swam with other pods in the <u>center,</u> where it was safe.

   I could hear the herd call as it moved through the water. Again and again each dolphin <u>whistled</u> its name and <u>announced</u> that all was well. The <u>messages</u> told the rest of the herd that it was safe to <u>continue</u> the hunt. At the first <u>threatening</u> <u>echo</u> from behind, I would stop whistling my name and warn the herd with the loud crack of <u>sensor sound</u> that <u>signaled</u> danger. <u>Warnings</u> travel fast <u>beneath</u> the water. (pp. 2–3)

3. Describe in your own words the stages of reading/spelling development. What characteristics might a student demonstrate in each of the stages? Explain how being aware of these stages might help a teacher plan appropriate spelling instruction for each learner.

4. Discuss how word study may be of particular value to English learners.

5. What is the value in teaching morphology to students? Use examples to support your response.

6. As you are reading for work or pleasure, make note of several words that are unfamiliar to you. What strategies would you use to determine the meaning of these new words? Do you always use the same strategies? What factors determine when you would resort to looking up the words online or in a dictionary? How are your own habits relevant to your future classroom teaching?

Suggestions FOR PROJECTS AND FIELD ACTIVITIES

1. With the other members of your class, list 10 words from an article on an Internet news site. From this chapter, consider the different instructional strategies you might use to teach these words to students. In a classroom of students in grades 4–8, use one of the strategies to teach the selected words to a small group. How successful were you? Compare your experience with that of other classmates who chose to use a different instructional strategy.

2. Administer a spelling inventory (see Appendix C.10) to three students. Analyze their responses as to what reading/spelling stage is represented most often in their spelling. What instructional activities would benefit these students?

3. Develop a list of 15 words based on similar or related roots, affixes, or derivations. Invite a small group of students to sort the words as they think they should be sorted. Then have these students make statements about their findings. Present your list and your findings to your classmates. What were the students able to learn from the sorting activity?

4. Observe a word study lesson. Through discussion with the teacher and your direct observation, answer the following questions:
   a. What strategies are students being taught about how to spell new words?
   b. How are students being taught about syllables, affixes, and derivations?
   c. How is word study applied in reading and writing situations in the classroom?

5. Spend a day discovering the interesting words that students are naturally curious about. Can you categorize these words? How would you incorporate these concepts into the daily curriculum to encourage curiosity about words?

6. Prior to reading a short story to a group of students, ask them to guess the meaning of three or four words that you feel are especially difficult. While reading, ask them to determine the meaning of each word after it occurs. Are the responses enhanced with the additional contextual information? What does this experience teach you about the value of discussing words as they occur when reading aloud?

REFERENCES

Alber, S. R., & Foil, C. R. (2003). Drama activities that promote and extend your students' vocabulary proficiency. *Intervention in School & Clinic, 39*(1), 22–29.

Allen, J. (1999). *Words, words, words.* Portsmouth, NH: Heinemann.

Anderson, R. C., & Nagy, W. E. (1992).The vocabulary conundrum.*American Educator, 16*(4), 14–18, 44–47.

Baker, S. K., Simmons, D. C., & Kame'enui, E. J. (1998). Vocabulary acquisition: Research bases. In D. C. Simmons & E. J. Kame'enui (Eds.), *What reading research tells us about children with diverse learning needs: Bases and basics* (pp. 183–218). Mahwah, NJ: Erlbaum.

Baumann, J. F., Edwards, E. C., Boland, E., Olejnik, S., & Kame'enui, E. J. (2003). Vocabulary tricks: Effects of instruction in morphology and context on fifth-grade students' ability to derive and infer word meaning. *American Educational Research Journal, 40*, 447–494.

Baumann, J. F., & Kame'enui, E. J. (2012). *Vocabulary instruction: Research to practice* (2nd ed.). New York: Guilford.

Baumann, J. F., Kame'enui, E. J., & Ash, G. E. (2003). Research on vocabulary instructing: Voltaire redux. In J. Flood, D. Lapp, J. R. Squire, & J. M. Jensen (Eds.), *Handbook on research on teaching the English language arts* (2nd ed., pp. 752–785). Mahwah, NJ: Erlbaum.

Bear, D. R., Invernizzi, M. R., Templeton, S., & Johnston, F. R. (2012).*Words their way: Word study for phonics, vocabulary, and spelling instruction* (5th ed.). Columbus, Ohio. Pearson/Prentice Hall.

Beck, I., & McKeown, M. (1991). Conditions of vocabulary acquisition. In R. Barr, M. Kamil, P. Mosenthal, & P. D. Pearson (Eds.), *Handbook of reading research* (vol. 2, 789–814). New York: Longman.

Beck, I. L., McKeown, M. G., & Kucan, L. (2002). *Bringing words to life: Robust vocabulary instruction.* New York: Guilford .

Beck, I. L., McKeown, M. G., & Kucan, L. (2013). *Bringing words to life: Robust vocabulary instruction*(2nd ed.). New York: Guilford.

Beck, I. L., McKeown, M. G., & Omanson, R. C. (1987). The effects and uses of diverse vocabulary instructional techniques. In M. G. McKeown & M. E. Curtis (Eds.), *The nature of vocabulary acquisition.* Hillsdale, NJ: Erlbaum.

Berne, J., & Blachowicz, C. L. Z. (2008). What reading teachers say about vocabulary instruction: Voices from the classroom.The Reading Teacher, 62(4), 314-323.

Biemiller, A. (2005). Size and sequence in vocabulary development: Implications for choosing words for primary grade vocabulary instruction. In E. H. Hiebert & M. L. Kamil (Eds.), *Teaching and learning vocabulary: Bringing research to practice.* (pp. 223–242). Mahwah, NJ: Erlbaum.

Blachowicz, C. L. Z. (1993). C(2)QU: Modeling context use in the classroom. *The Reading Teacher, 47,* 268–269.

Blachowicz, C. L. Z., & Fisher, P. (2004). Keep the "fun" in fundamental. In J. F. Baumann & E. J. Kame'enui (Eds.), *Vocabulary instruction: Research to practice* (pp. 218–237). New York: Guilford.

Blachowicz, C. L. Z., Fisher, P. J. L., Ogle, D., & Watts-Taffe, S. (2006). Vocabulary: Questions from the classroom. *Reading Research Quarterly, 41*, 524–539.

Bloodgood, J. W., & Pacifici, L. C. (2004, November). Bringing word study to intermediate classrooms. *The Reading Teacher, 58*, 250–263.

Blewitt, P., Rump, K., Shealy, S., & Cook, S. (2009). Shared book reading: When and how questions affect young children's word learning. *Journal of Educational Psychology, 101*(2), 294–304.

Carlisle, J. F., & Stone, C. A. (2005). Exploring the role of morphemes in word reading. *Reading Research Quarterly, 40*, 428–449.

Carlo, M. S., August, D., McGlaughlin, B., Snow, C. E., Dressler, C., Lippman, D. N., Lively, T. J., & White, C. E. (2004). Closing the gap: Addressing vocabulary needs of English-language learners in bilingual and mainstreamed classes.*Reading Research Quarterly, 39*, 188–215.

Carlo, M. S., August, D., & Snow, C. E. (2005). Sustained vocabulary-learning strategies for English language learners. In E. Hiebert & M. Kamil (Eds.), *Teaching and learning vocabulary: Bringing research to practice* (pp. 137–153). Mahwah, NJ: Erlbaum.

Collins COBUILD Learner's Illustrated Dictionary of American English (2012). (2nd ed.). Glasgow, UK: HarperCollins.

Coxhead, A. (2000). A new academic word list. *TESOL Quarterly, 34*, 213–238.

Coyne, M. D., Simmons, D. C., & Kame'enui, E. J. (2004). Vocabulary instruction for young children at risk of experiencing reading difficulties: Teaching word meanings during shared storybook reading. In J. F. Baumann & E. J. Kame'enui (Eds.), *Vocabulary instruction: Research to practice* (pp. 41–58). New York: Guilford.

Crawley, S. J., & Merritt, K. (2011). *Remediating reading difficulties* (6thed.). Columbus, OH: McGraw-Hill.

Cunningham, A. E., & Stanovich, K. E. (1998, Spring/Summer). What reading does for the mind. *American Federation of Teachers.*

Cunningham, P. M., & Hall, D. P. (1998). *Month-by-month phonics for upper grades: A second chance for struggling readers and students learning English.* Greensboro, NC: Carson-DeLosa.

Ellis, E., & Farmer, T. (2000).*The clarifying routine: Elaborating vocabulary instruction.* Kansas City, MO: Edge Enterprises.

Feldman, K., & Kinsella, K. (2003).Narrowing the language gap: Strategies for vocabulary development. Available at http://ela.fcoe.org/sites/ela.fcoe.org/files/Narrowing%20Vocab%20Gap%20KK%20KF%201.pdf

Fry, E. B., & Kress, J. E. (2006). *The reading teacher's book of lists: Grades K–12* (5th ed.). San Francisco: Jossey-Bass.

Gipe, J. P. (1978/1979). Investigating techniques for teaching word meanings. *Reading Research Quarterly, 14,* 624–644.

Gipe, J. P. (2014). *Multiple paths to literacy: Assessment and differented instruction for diverse learners k–12* (8th ed.). Upper Saddle River, NJ: Merrill-Prentice Hall.

Graves, M. F. (1986). Vocabulary learning and instruction. In E. Z. Rothkopf (Ed.), *Review of research in education* (vol. 13). Washington, DC: American Educational Research Association.

Graves, M. F. (2006). *The vocabulary book: Learning and instruction.* Newark, DE: International Reading Association.

Graves, M. F., & Watts-Taffe, S. (2002). The place of word consciousness in a research-based vocabulary program. In A. Farstrup and S. Samuels (Eds.), *What research has to say about reading instruction* (3rd ed., pp. 140–165). Newark, DE: International Reading Association.

Graves, M. F., & Watts-Taffe, S. M. (2008). For the love of words: Fostering word consciousness in young readers. *The Reading Teacher, 62*(3), 185–193.

Greenwood, S. C., & Flanigan, K. (2007). Overlapping vocabulary and comprehension: Context clues complement semantic gradients. *The Reading Teacher, 61*(3), 249–254.

Hall, E., & O'Dell, S. (1996). *Venus among the fishes.* New York: Yearling Books.

Harris, T. L. & Hodges, R. E. (1995). *The literacy dictionary: The vocabulary of reading and writing.* Newark, DE: International Reading Association.

Harmon, J. M. (2000). Assessing and supporting independent word learning strategies of middle school students. *Journal of Adolescent and Adult Literacy, 43,* 518–528.

Harmon, J. M. (2002). Teaching independent word learning strategies to struggling readers.*Journal of Adolescent and Adult Literacy, 45,* 606–616.

Henderson, E. (1990). *Teaching spelling* (2nd ed.). Boston: Houghton Mifflin.

Hickman, P., Pollard-Durodola, S., & Vaughn, S. (2004). Storybook reading: Improving vocabulary and comprehension for English-language learners. *The Reading Teacher, 57,* 720–730.

Hiebert, E. H., Lehr, F., & Osborn, J. (2004). A focus on vocabulary. Second in the Research-Based Practices in Early Reading Series published by the Regional Educational Laboratory at Pacific Resources for Education and Learning. Available at http://vineproject.ucsc.edu/resources/A%20Focus%20on%20Vocabulary%20PREL.pdf

Johnson, D. D. (2001). *Vocabulary in the elementary and middle school.* Boston: Allyn & Bacon.

Johnson, D. D., & Pearson, P. D. (1986). *Teaching reading vocabulary* (3rd ed.). New York: Holt, Rinehart and Winston.

Kane, S. (2011).*Literacy and learning in the content areas* (3rd ed.). Scottsdale, AZ: Holcomb Hathaway.

Kemper, L. W., & Brody, S. (2001). Advanced decoding and fluency. In S. Brody (Ed.), *Teaching reading: Language, letters and thought* (2nd ed., pp. 144–167). Milford, NH: LARC.

Lember, B. H. (1997). *The shell book.* Boston: Houghton Mifflin.

Marzano, R. J. (2009). Six steps to better vocabulary instruction. *Teaching for the 21st Century, 67,* 1, 83–84.

McVicker, C. J. (2007). Comic strips as a text structure for learning to read. *The Reading Teacher, 61*(1), 85–88.

Morgan, B., & Odom, D. (2006). Stories from tween classrooms.*Educational Leadership, 63*(7), 38–41.

Nagy, W. E. (1988). *Teaching vocabulary to improve reading comprehension.* Newark, DE: International Reading Association.

National Governors Association Center for Best Practices (NGACBP) & Council of Chief State School Officers (CCSSO) (2010). *College and career readiness anchor standards for reading.*Washington D.C.: Author.

National Reading Panel (2000). Report of the National Reading Panel: Teaching children to read. Bethesda, MD: National Institute of Child Health and Human Development.

NICHD (2000). Report of the National Reading Panel: Reports of the subgroups. Washington, DC: U.S. Government Printing Office.

Pittelman, S. D., Heimlich, J. E., Berglund, R. L., & French, M. P. (1991). *Semantic feature analysis: Classroom applications.* Newark, DE: International Reading Association.

Rasinski, T., Padak, N., & Fawcett, G. V. (2010). *Effective reading strategies: Teaching children who find reading difficult* (4th ed.). Upper Saddle River, NJ: Merrill.

Ruddell, M. R. (2008). *Teaching content reading and writing* (5th ed.).Hoboken, NJ: Wiley.

Schwanenflugel, P. J., Stahl, S. A., &McFalls, E. I. (1997). *Partial word knowledge and vocabulary growth during reading comprehension* (Research Report No. 76). Athens,: University of Georgia, National Reading Research Center.

Scott, J. A., & Nagy, W. E. (1997). Understanding the definitions of unfamiliar verbs. *Reading Research Quarterly, 32,* 184–200.

Serafini, F., & Giorgis, C. (2003). Thirteen good reasons to read aloud with older students. In F. Serafini & C. Giorgis, *Reading aloud and beyond* (pp.6–12). Portsmouth, NH: Heinemann.

Stahl, S. A. (1999). Vocabulary development. *Reading research to practice: A series for teachers.* Cambridge, MA: Brookline.

Stahl, S. A., & Fairbanks, M. M. (1986). The effects of vocabulary instruction: A model-based meta-analysis. *Review of Educational Research, 56,* 72–110.

Stahl, S. A., & Kapinus, B. (1991). Possible sentences: Predicting word meanings to teach content area vocabulary. *The Reading Teacher, 45,* 36–43.

Taylor, B. (2007). *The what and the how of good classroom reading instruction in the elementary grades.* Minneapolis: University of Minnesota Center for Reading Research.

Trelease, J. (2013). *The Read-aloud handbook* (7th ed.). New York: Penguin.

Ulanoff, S. H., & Pucci, S. L. (1999). Learning words from books: The effects of read-aloud on second language vocabulary acquisition. *The Bilingual Research Journal, 23,* 400–422.

FIVE

CHAPTER

Reading Comprehension

- What are the key factors that affect reading comprehension?
- What are the five most effective reading comprehension strategies?
- How can teachers use guided reading to help students learn comprehension strategies?
- What is a novel study?
- What skill areas are important for online reading comprehension?
- What strategies are appropriate for teaching online reading comprehension?

Mr. Perez is preparing for Monday's science lesson and wants to use the technique of *questioning the author* (Beck, McKeown, Hamilton, et al., 1997) to better engage his fifth-grade students in their expository reading *while* they read material from a new unit on mammals. He believes that this technique will also help them focus on their understanding of the content. He reads the following paragraph from his science materials:

What are mammals?

The name "mammal" refers to the female's mammary glands, which provide milk for her young. This characteristic sets off mammals among the warm-blooded, back-boned animals. Mammals are hairy; young are born alive. Most have varied teeth, for cutting, tearing, or grinding. The mammal's skull is unique; the brain is more complex than in other animals.

Mr. Perez realizes that this paragraph contains the major characteristics of mammals. He decides he will first direct his students' attention to the essential characteristic of the mammary glands. Following this, he will focus their attention on the other features found in mammals.

Mr. Perez then plans a set of queries. To begin the discussion, he decides to ask, at the end of the first paragraph, "What has the author told us about mammals?" If students do not mention the main characteristic, his follow-up query will be, "What does the author mean by saying that the word *mammal* refers to the female's mammary glands, and that this characteristic *sets off* mammals?" Next, Mr. Perez will use the query, "What else does the author tell us about mammals?" to begin a discussion that compares mammals with other warm-blooded, back-boned animals, and with other animals in general. He will use a visual, a T-chart (see Figure 5.12 later in this chapter), to keep track of students' ideas for later use.

As Mr. Perez proceeds through his material, he anticipates where he will need to assist his students in constructing their understanding of this material. He is aware that he may need to interpret what his students try to say (revoice), model how to arrive at meaning, or provide additional information not available in the text (annotate). He may also need to draw attention to particular students' ideas (marking) or to turn students' focus back to the text for further thinking or clarifying. Once students indicate they have understood the essential meaning and are ready to move on, Mr. Perez will recap, or summarize, the major ideas; alternatively, he may ask another student to recap. With this lesson plan in mind, Mr. Perez now feels ready to begin the new science unit about mammals.

Defining Comprehension

The reading assessment portion of the 2011 National Assessment of Educational Progress (NAEP) provides a broad definition of reading that includes the ability to understand written texts, develop and interpret meaning, and critique and evaluate. Readers draw on the ideas and information they acquire from text to meet a particular purpose or situational need. Certainly, comprehension includes all of these skills. **Comprehension** is thought of as the construction of meaning, and it is the ultimate goal of exemplary reading instruction.

comprehension •

The theoretical framework for reading comprehension instruction that we support in this chapter views comprehension instruction as an active process; that is, it encourages students

- to relate text to their own prior experiences, or make predictions about what might happen.
- to construct mental images during their reading.
- to question themselves about text ideas while they read.
- to summarize the big ideas in what they read. (Pressley, 2002)

This framework also recognizes that meaning is socially constructed; in other words, students need to engage in conversations about what they read to help clarify and broaden their understandings of the text.

The NAEP recommends that teachers attend to the following three cognitive targets, which help students attain new levels of thinking that develop reading comprehension: locate/recall, integrate/interpret, and critique/evaluate. In the first of these targets, readers must be able to understand written text, decoding print and accessing their reading vocabulary. Further, readers must pay attention to the information being presented and then be able to locate and remember information from the text. These abilities help readers achieve literal comprehension.

The second target is for a reader to develop and interpret meaning from text. At this stage, readers make sense of the text by integrating their relevant prior knowledge. The more difficult the text, the more complex their inference making must be. Good readers can move from a literal understanding of the text to a more sophisticated one; specifically, readers draw deeper implications from a text and integrate and assimilate new information with what they already know.

The last of the three target areas relates to evaluation of text. To gain higher levels of meaning, readers must be able to view the text critically. They should be able to assess its quality and identify the author's particular stance or the multiple perspectives from which the text can be read. Readers who look at the stylistic and rhetorical choices an author makes and the impact those choices have on the reader are evaluating text.

As readers progress through these levels of reading, their ability to comprehend text increases. The Common Core State Standards for reading (NGACBP & CCSSO, 2010) have made the comprehension of complex texts a key requirement, stating that "all students must be able to comprehend texts of steadily increasing complexity as they progress through school. By the time they complete the core, students must be able to read and comprehend independently and proficiently the kinds of complex texts commonly found in college and careers" (p. 2). They further state that "current trends suggest that if students cannot read challenging texts with understanding—if they have not developed the skill, concentration, and stamina to read such texts—they will read less in general" (p. 4).

The authors of this book support a **strategic reader model** for comprehension instruction that implies teachers will demonstrate for students strategies that help them actively process text. A combination of direct explanation and modeling, or "thinking out loud," can work well as a form of explicit teaching for comprehension strategies (Duffy, 2002). In addition, reading comprehension strategies need to be modeled and practiced, one strategy at a time, using a variety of text, in order to teach and practice the strategy at a deep level, while you gradually allow the student to take over use of the strategy (Pearson & Gallagher, 1983). This type instruction follows a model of *gradual release of responsibility* (Duke & Pearson, 2002; Fielding & Pearson, 1984; Pearson & Gallagher, 1983) in which teachers and students progress through a sequence of "I do" (teacher models/explains), "we do" (teachers and students work together), and "you do" (students work independently).

● strategic reader model

Factors Affecting Reading Comprehension

Fortunately, quite a bit of research has been done on reading comprehension. This research finds that a number of factors affect comprehension, including factors external to the reader and the reader's internal characteristics.

Factors External to Readers

The factors external to readers that affect comprehension include (1) the reader-friendliness of the text and (2) the context in which the reading takes place.

Reader-friendliness of text. It seems logical to expect that clearly written text, with a minimum level of abstractness, would be easy to comprehend. In fact, research studies do support this notion. For example, a seminal study by Jorm (1977) demonstrated that texts using high-frequency and high-imagery words are easier for all students to comprehend. Englert and Thomas (1987) found that texts organized sequentially are easiest to comprehend, followed by those that are enumerated, descriptive, and comparative/contrasting, in that order (see Chapter 7 for descriptions of these text structures). We refer to text that is easy to comprehend as user- or reader-friendly.

Context. The context, or environment, in which reading takes place can also affect comprehension. Consider how your own reading differs when you read within a classroom setting compared with when you read at home or in a library. The classroom environment itself can affect comprehension (Gipe, 2013). Opportunities for reading practice, access to appropriate materials, availability of modeling and direct instruction, and a risk-free atmosphere are all factors that teachers can influence in a positive way.

Readers' Internal Characteristics

The internal characteristics that affect readers' comprehension include (1) ability to construct a mental representation, (2) ability to make connections, (3) ability to attend to information in the text, (4) amount of background knowledge, (5) engagement with text, (6) knowledge of basic skills, and (7) knowledge of reading strategies and metacognition.

Ability to construct a mental representation. It has become increasingly apparent that the reader's ability to construct a mental representation, or picture, of the information read and its interpretation is a major factor in comprehension. Research on mental representations of text indicates that such representations resemble a network of nodes (the individual text elements) and connections (the meaningful relations between the elements) (Van den Broek, 1990; Van den Broek, Risden, Fletcher, et al., 1996). Two important types of connections are referential (e.g., pronouns) and causal/logical (e.g., if . . . then; this . . . because) (Graesser, McNamara, & Louwerse, 2003). That is, when events or statements have clear connections to other events or statements in the text—generally in the form of pronouns, direct references, or cause/effect relationships—they are more easily recalled. Readers proceed through text attempting to make sense of it by connecting explicitly stated information to two main sources of information: related concepts in their background knowledge (or **schema**), and a subset of concepts from the preceding text. As noted in the section "Factors External to Readers" above, a coherent, well-written text is reader-friendly and easy to comprehend. A coherent, well-written text also helps the reader make the necessary referential and causal/logical connections and facilitates a clear mental representation of the text. Even with reader-friendly text, however, the reader still needs to develop the ability to actually make connections.

schema ●

www●●●

Making Text Connections

https://curriculumdepot.
wikispaces.com/file/view/
Making_Connections_Strateg.pdf

www.decd.sa.gov.au/
northernadelaide/files/links/
4_VisualisingBooklet.pdf

Ability to make connections. A reader who can make meaningful connections between information in the text and related background knowledge will better comprehend the text. Readers need to be able to relate what they read to their own lives (text-to-self connections). They also need to make connections between the text they are reading and other similar texts (text-to-text connections) or events and concerns that occur in the world at large (text-to-world connections) (Harvey & Goudvis, 2000; Keene, 2008). Online resources are available for helping to make text connections, including those listed in the margin (Draper, 2010a; Draper, 2010b).

Ability to attend to information in the text. The general ability to attend to the information in the text is influenced by short-term memory, concentration, and motivation. In addition, how the reader approaches the comprehension process will vary depending on level of attention the reader thinks is necessary. A reader might decide that he does not need to devote a high level of attention to a book he has chosen to read for pleasure, especially when he is already very familiar with the author's writing style. In contrast, a reader may decide, upon opening her statistics textbook the night before a test, that she needs to give it a high level of attention.

Amount of background knowledge. A reader who has background knowledge that is relevant to the text being read has a head start on understanding the text. Such background knowledge may include, but is not limited to, knowledge of the text structure the author has used, familiarity with the literary genre, recognition of the vocabulary, and possession of information about the topic. This prior knowledge constitutes a schema for the topic. Try reading a topic about which you know very little (quantum physics?), and see how much you understand!

Engagement with the text. It is quite likely that the major issue in comprehension for students is engagement with the text (Wilhelm, 1997). To construct meaning, the learner needs to be purposefully and actively involved with the text. The use of multicultural literature (see Appendix A for some suggestions) provides "the textual features (recurring themes, linguistic patterns, and ethnic group practices)" that you may use as points of engagement for students of all ethnicities (Brooks, 2006, p. 390). Active engagement is also necessary for **critical analysis,** which requires the reader to interpret text and produce a cultural understanding of the text (Harris & Hodges, 1995). Activating relevant background knowledge, making real-life connections, collaborating with other students, and realizing when comprehension has occurred (or has broken down) are all important aspects of being involved with the text.

● critical analysis

Knowledge of basic skills. Well-developed basic skills—such as letter/sound recognition, word decoding, and knowledge of grammar—will increase the amount of cognitive energy available for constructing coherent mental representations of the text. In general, for many grade 4–8 students, word-decoding abilities are sufficient (see Chapter 4 for advanced word analysis skills). Ongoing vocabulary instruction (see Chapter 4) will enhance comprehension, especially in content areas that have specialized vocabulary.

Knowledge of reading strategies and metacognition (or metacomprehension). Knowledge of reading comprehension strategies is crucial (discussed later in the chapter); however, readers also need **metacognition** (understanding how one knows, or thinking about thinking) and **metacomprehension** (realizing when one has or has not understood) abilities to ensure that they will recognize when and under what conditions a comprehension strategy needs to be used. Students who demonstrate good metacomprehension, or comprehension-monitoring ability, know when they do and do not understand what they have read. They use fix-up strategies to resolve their comprehension difficulties. They can identify where their difficulty lies—"I don't understand the last

Students who demonstrate good metacomprehension know when they do and do not understand what they have read.

section on page 45"—and what the difficulty is—"I am confused by the phrase *cornhusk mattresses*. What kind of mattress is that?" They may try to use their own words to restate a difficult sentence or passage: "So the author meant the quiet forest became noisy with the sounds of crickets and a howling wolf when he said the stillness of the forest was broken." Students who use fix-up strategies do not hesitate to look back through the text for clues that might help them understand: "I think I remember something about how old Abe Lincoln was when he went to school, but by the time he was 16 he only had one year of school? I need to look back to see how old he was when he first went to school." And they also look ahead in the text for information that might help them: "This sentence says Abe Lincoln's first home was a one-room log cabin and that he was born in Kentucky. I thought he lived in Illinois? He must have moved. . . . Oh, I see the next section is called 'The Lincolns Move to Indiana.' That will tell me more about his later life and where else Lincoln may have lived."

Assessing and Selecting Texts

Reading comprehension is also greatly affected by the degree to which texts are matched to student needs and abilities. In addition to assessing *students'* abilities, as discussed in Chapter 2, teachers need to evaluate the texts they give to students. Texts should be reader-friendly and appropriate, providing the right level of challenge. Language, writing structures and styles, and the complexity of ideas and concepts must all be evaluated with the reader in mind. Evaluating texts in this way can be time-consuming, but students benefit greatly when teachers identify stumbling blocks that might hinder comprehension.

Determining Text Demands

Figure 5.1 provides categories of text demands that can be used as a starting point for evaluating student texts. While not exhaustive, this list categorizes textual demands into five areas: reading comprehension, functional language, vocabulary, textual features/internal and external text structure, and grammar/conventions.

As mentioned earlier, the process of assessment, which starts by looking at the class and individual students, continues with the evaluation of materials that best meet the needs of those students. If students are to read independently, what texts are best for them? For those texts used in class, which ones will provide opportunity for instruction and connect to the topic at hand? An easy assumption to make is that students who are frustrated with reading are not motivated; however, they may be frustrated because the texts they have been given are too difficult. We can use these mechanisms to determine the best texts for our students:

1. Estimate text readability (discussed below)
2. Measure student reading ability
3. Determine the appropriate reading range for independent reading
4. Continuously monitor comprehension and adjust book levels and genre

Here are some other text considerations, with more specificity:

Relationship to the content students are studying in class. District, state, and national educational standards help to guide study content and goals. A text should help students learn the content to meet the standards; therefore, teachers should make a connection between the text and the knowledge and skills the standards have identified. Select texts and design instruction that will best guide and support student

Demands of text.

figure **5.1**

Reading Comprehension	Are explanations written in a hierarchical fashion so students can quickly recall information? (for example, in a time-ordered fashion)
	Are facts interspersed with opinions?
	Has the text provided examples?
	Does the text relate to content students are studying?
Functional Language	Are signal words used to help the reader see what's coming up? Are such signal words used frequently?
	Are sentences predominantly complex, with many clauses, modifiers, and appositives? Do the sentences have clear main ideas?
	Does the text contain paragraph-long sentences?
Vocabulary	Does the text use
	• General academic vocabulary as well as specialized/disciplinary academic vocabulary?
	• Slang, clichés, portmanteau words and polysemous terms, figurative language, idioms?
Textual Features/Internal and External Text Structure	What features does the text contain? (e.g., title, section headings, pictures or captions to support text information, definitions, boldfaced terms, underlined terms/phrases)
	Does the dialogue indicate who is speaking and how the speaker is being represented?
	Does the text contain parenthetical expressions and other features that are new to the reader?
Grammar/Conventions	Is the text written in one tense throughout? Does it use helping verbs?
	Does the text include indirect or reported speech as well as direct quotations?
	Does the point of view shift? If so, why?

learning. Just because you like a text does not mean it is suitable for all students learning particular content. The reading level and concept may be too hard or too easy. The chosen text must be conceptually challenging enough for students and matched to their maturity level. Other considerations—such as the credibility of the author, the audience for whom the text was written, and how the point of view affects the reader—must also be taken into account.

Text structure and format. Carefully consider the organization of the text. Use graphic organizers and other tools to help students understand how the text functions. For example, does the text present information in a particular sequence, or does it use a problem and solution format. Chapter 7 discusses ways to teach students about these text structures.

Look at the text's physical aspects—its formatting—to determine how much support the text gives. Does it use transitional words, boldface terms, definitions embedded in the text itself, and other similar structures to aid comprehension? Look at the section headings and subheadings, glossaries, and table of contents to assess what resources are available for students as they work through the text.

When built-in supports are lacking, it is up to the teacher to scaffold them for the students as needed.

Other items to look at—which students are always interested in—include cover design, font style and size, book shape and size, and the number of pages and chapters. Does the book contain graphics or other types of illustrations; if so, will they aid readers? Some visuals are text supportive and enhance the content, while others are merely aesthetically pleasing. Take note of all charts, graphs, and other visuals so they can be acknowledged and taught as needed.

Language. It is essential to evaluate the text for language complexity. Determine whether the language is formal or informal, and gauge whether student readers will be able to navigate the style. Is there any profanity and, if so, is it appropriate for the story and character? Determine if student readers are mature enough for this sort of language. Watch carefully for sexist, racist, and otherwise hurtful or stereotyping language. Look, also, for loaded language that reveals the author's bias, and carefully consider the author's credibility. If the story is a multicultural one, was it translated from another language? Was it written by a native of the culture?

Note when the book was published; if it's not a recent publication, consider what your students know about the language, historical events, and culture of the time when it was written, especially if the world no longer functions in a similar way. Examine the text for outdated language.

If a particular book offers some challenges but also is worthwhile in other ways, you might not want to it abandon it altogether; some challenges can be addressed when you teach, as we'll discuss in later chapters.

The process of text evaluation is a critical part of selecting motivating, engaging, and appropriate materials for your students. Choose carefully based on their reading ability, background knowledge and experience, and interest/motivation, as well as the text's context, content, structure, and fair treatment of the material.

Estimating Reading Difficulty

www●●●

Fry's Readability Graph

http://go.nationalpartnership.org/
site/DocServer/Fry_Readability_
Formula.pdf?docID=5626

Teachers should provide material at different readability levels to accommodate students' different reading abilities. Using Fry's Readability Graph can help to identify the grade-level readability of a specific text. Although multiple leveling guides exist (e.g., Fry's, Raygor's, Flesch-Kincaid), the most appropriate way to evaluate a text's reading level and suitability for students is to go through it oneself. As mentioned above, note the demands of the text such as sentence complexity and variety, which words are commonly used, and whether they will be easily decoded and readily pronounceable. (See Figure 5.1 for more.) Other reading level considerations include number of syllables; vocabulary; and language at the word, sentence, and discourse/text level. Finally, consider such critical information as conceptual sophistication of the material, reader's background knowledge, and other textual issues.

Students can also help to estimate a book's readability to determine if it is suitable for them. Using "leveled" materials consisting of a variety of genres, print or online media (e.g., articles, books, magazines, newspapers), and topics, teachers can model a process for locating material that is just right for reading. Known as the

Goldilocks strategy ●

Goldilocks strategy (Ohlhausen & Jepson, 1992), this strategy is based on group discussion about what makes a book too easy, too hard, or just right. When students can read every word and understand every idea, that is an easy book. Hard books are those that contain many words students are unable to read and many ideas they cannot understand. When using books that are just right, students can read most words and can understand most ideas independently. A book that is "just right" contains material that is at a student's instructional reading level, or 95 percent word recognition accuracy. Thus, out of approximately 100 words, no more than five words should be unknown.

To help students understand the processing of choosing a just right book, discuss actual books with them. Think out loud about a "too easy" book using phrases such as "there aren't many words on each page," "I know all the words on the page," or "there are lots of illustrations in this book." When discussing a "just right" book, a teacher might describe it using phrases such as "there are a few words on each page that seem new to me," "I don't think I will have trouble with the number of words on each page," "I can figure out the words myself," "I know something about this topic already, and that will help me read this," or "the pictures [or headings] look interesting." Describe a "too hard" book using phrases such as "there are too many words, and too many new words, on each page," "the print is too small," or "I would have to ask for lots of help reading this." Finally, remind students that sometimes it is necessary to work with difficult material in order to locate a particular piece of information; most of the time, though, when the material seems too hard, students and the teacher should look for something else—something that is "just right."

The school library can be a great place for students to practice locating material on a particular topic and then deciding whether the material is appropriate and interesting. Students also have access to a librarian who can assist them in finding something suitable. This step will show students that they can independently seek information if they know what they are looking for. If possible, arrange a field trip to the public library to further enhance students' ability to self-select appropriate reading material.

The school library is a great place for students to practice locating material on a particular topic and then decide whether the material interests them and is appropriate for their reading level.

Comprehension Strategies for Readers to Use

Comprehension rates for middle school students are poor. Less than half read at grade level. Regrettably, many schools place students into reading groups or tracks based on what they sound like when they read aloud or how fast they read rather than on how well they comprehend (Altwerger, Jordan, & Shelton, 2007). The Alliance for Excellent Education convened a panel to examine the research related to adolescent literacy. The resulting report, *Reading Next: A Vision for Action and Research in Middle and High School Literacy* (Biancarosa & Snow, 2006), identifies nine research-based instructional strategies and six structural supports for effective instruction in adolescent literacy. Comprehension instruction is one of the nine instructional areas of focus. Reviews of research in this area reveal a relatively small but powerful set of strategies that are recommended for comprehension instruction (Pressley, 2000):

① Predicting

② Generating questions

③ Checking back

④ Imagery/visualizing

⑤ Summarizing

WWW○○○

Alliance for Excellent Education
http://all4ed.org/

Reading Next
www.scobre.com/download/readingNext.pdf

WWW●●●

Children's and Young Adult Literature Resources

www.ala.org/yalsa/

www.reading.org/Resources/ ResourcesByTopic/ ChildrensYALiterature/ Overview.aspx

www.hhpcommunities.com/ youngadultlit

www.carolhurst.com/index.html

These five strategies should be taught directly through considerable teacher explanation and modeling as well as class discussions of their use (see the procedures described in the Think-Aloud and Reciprocal Teaching activities later in this chapter). Then, students need extensive, long-term practice within a print-rich context, across content areas, and with a variety of text types (see the websites listed here and in Appendix A for literature resources). Although teachers may introduce the strategies separately, they need to emphasize to students that good readers do not use one strategy in isolation from the others but use several simultaneously. Teachers also need to emphasize that the strategies should be internalized and used only when needed.

① Predicting

Proficient readers make mental predictions, or calculated hunches, about what might happen next in the text they are reading. Their hunches are based on what they already know about the topic, what they know about the literary structure the author is using (e.g., narrative, expository, fairy tale, historical fiction, or autobiographical), and what they have learned thus far in the text. As skilled readers continue to read, they tend to confirm or deny their previous hunches according to new understandings that occur. With expository text, they often preview it to get an overview of what information will be covered, and they look through the text to see if it matches their expectations. Skilled readers also ask themselves questions for which they hope to find answers as they read, thus setting their own purposes for reading the text. (See the DRTA and Jigsaw: Read a Book in an Hour activities later in this chapter for example lessons that encourage students to use predicting.)

② Generating Questions

One of the most valuable ways proficient readers construct text meanings is by asking and answering important questions as they read. They are aware of the difference between "thinking-type" questions and "locating information–type" questions, and they are able to reflect later on the caliber of the questions they have asked themselves.

Students do not generate important questions automatically but learn this skill when their teachers model questioning skills and use productive questioning as an instructional tool. **Productive questioning** focuses on the process of both thinking about and learning the content of the text (Dantonio & Beisenherz, 2001). Through carefully crafted questions that use open question stems, as well as thoughtful reactions (both verbal and nonverbal) to students' responses, teachers guide the way their students think about their texts as they read. Open question stems (e.g., *what are, in what way, how, why*) allow for meaningful instructional conversations as opposed to closed question stems (e.g., *can you, will you, do you, are you, do you know*) that imply there is a correct answer. For example, changing the question *Do you understand?* to *What do you understand?* gives students the opening they need to share their understandings. In the classroom vignette that opened this chapter, Mr. Perez prepared questions that invite students to engage in the instructional conversation. (See the Reciprocal Teaching, Dyad Reading, QAR, and Jigsaw: Read a Book in an Hour activities later in this chapter for example lessons that require students to recognize question types and generate questions.)

productive questioning ●

③ Checking Back

Proficient readers are continually checking their own understanding as they read, making sure what they are confronting conforms to what they already know, as well as ensuring that they have not missed something. It is, therefore, quite normal for skilled readers to make frequent regressions, or to go back and reread a sentence or passage, to check that they "got it right." Such monitoring of understanding is very similar to the rereading that takes place when someone reads an unstimulating text late at night and suddenly realizes that she had not understood a word—a phenomenon to which most readers can relate! (See the GIST and DRTA activities later in this chapter for examples that encourage the use of checking back.)

④ Imagery/Visualizing

Proficient readers tend to create pictures in their mind's eye as they read text, especially material containing elaborate descriptions or well-developed story characters. Placing themselves in the story's setting or time period and/or imagining themselves as the main character, facing the same trials and tribulations, helps them appreciate, remember, and internalize the story that is unfolding before them. The experience of mental vision is so personal and intense that readers skilled in this strategy are often disappointed when they see the movie version of a story they have read, because it frequently pales in comparison to what occurs in their rich imaginations. (See the Sketch to Stretch and Going Beyond Visualizing activities later in this chapter for example lessons that use imagery.)

⑤ Summarizing

Proficient readers tend to remember important ideas and information they discover throughout a text and formulate them into a "big picture" of the reading material. Such a strategy is the basis on which skilled readers are able to summarize what they have read, or to articulate the main idea in expository text and separate it from the supporting details. Summarizing also includes the ability to identify the particular underlying themes in the material. In addition, summarizing can reveal personal opinions about the text. Proficient readers internalize the meanings certain works have held for them, review ideas frequently, and evaluate what they have read compared with other texts and what they had hoped to gain from the text. Summarizing text can thus be influenced by these previously internalized views. (See the GIST, Reciprocal Teaching, and Dyad Reading activities below for example lessons that use summarizing.)

Effective Direct Instructional Practices

The activities and instructional frameworks offered in this section incorporate and support the five comprehension strategies just discussed. Where appropriate, specific aspects of an activity are designated as *before reading, during reading,* or *after reading.* Students preread in order to activate their prior knowledge about a subject, learn critical background information, prepare for the reading to come, and become motivated to read. At this time, teachers ask for predictions about the text and provide opportunities to explore the essential idea or key concept in the teaching unit; in addition, teachers identify what students know and do not know about the key concept and any misconceptions they may have. During the reading, teachers guide student reading with multi-level questions, and they provide activities to build students' reading skills and allow them to read more strategically. In post-reading activities, students recall what they learned and process the text in deeper ways. Post reading may involve guided practice—again, teachers may ask multi-leveled critical thinking questions—but it almost always also involves assessing the comprehension of the reader either informally or formally.

Through these reading processes, teachers help students recognize when they know something or when they are unsure of what they have read. The next section shares particular before, during, and after reading activities to help students use higher-order thinking in their reading processes and to offer them strategies to become stronger and lifelong readers. In addition, based on the work of Liang and Dole (2006), the activities described here are identified by the main focus of the comprehension instruction: that is, a focus on understanding the content of a text, on understanding the process of comprehending the text, or on understanding both the content and the process.

Collaborative Strategic Reading

www.ncset.org/publications/
researchtopractice/
NCSETResearchBrief_1.2.pdf

Collaborative Strategic Reading (CSR) (Focus on Process)

A framework for comprehension instruction that focuses on process is Collaborative Strategic Reading (CSR). Based on the work of Klingner and Vaughn (1996), CSR has been adapted to include the following four comprehension strategies that students apply in small cooperative groups: (1) preview (before reading), (2) click and clunk (during reading), (3) get the gist (during reading), and (4) wrap-up (after reading).

Preview (before reading). Preview activates students' prior knowledge, facilitates predictions about the text they will read, and generates interest. It includes two activities: brainstorming and making predictions. To teach the strategy, begin by asking students to think about movie previews they have seen. Ask what they learned from the previews; use questions such as *What did you learn about the characters in the movie?* or *What did you learn about where and when the movie takes place?* Then ask students to preview the text they will read by skimming headings, looking at pictures, and examining the boldface terms to determine (a) what they know about the topic and (b) what they think they will learn by reading the text.

Click and clunk (during reading). Click and clunk encourages students to monitor their understanding and to use fix-up strategies when they fail to understand the material. To introduce the concepts of click and clunk, describe a click as something that "you really get" as in "you know it just clicks"; describe a clunk as when you feel you have run into a brick wall and do not understand the word(s) the author is using. When students understand these concepts, read a short selection aloud and have them identify their clicks and clunks. Then, teach fix-up strategies for the clunks.

Get the gist (during reading). Get the gist helps students identify a text's main ideas by answering, in no more than 15 words (1) Who or what is it about? and (2) What is most important about the who or what? In addition, students learn to limit their response so that their gist conveys the most important idea(s) and not unnecessary details. When teaching students to get the gist, begin by having them read a single paragraph and asking them to identify the most important person, place, or thing and what is most important about that person, place, or thing. Teach the students to state the information in a sentence containing no more than 15 words. (See the section "GIST" on pp. 145–146 for a sample activity.)

Wrap-up (after reading). Wrap-up includes the following two activities: (1) generating questions and (2) reviewing. To teach wrap-up, ask students to put themselves in the role of teacher and think of questions they would ask on a test based on the following question starters: who, what, when, where, why, and how. You should also encourage students to formulate some questions that require higher-level thinking skills rather than literal-level skills. Next, have students write the text's most important ideas in the form of a review.

The activities can be used with students of all abilities with some appropriate modifications. For instance, if written responses are called for, they can be included as soon as students have the required writing proficiency; in the meantime, oral responses are acceptable. Encourage oral discussions during the activities, and use pictures, objects, or other visuals, to allow English learners to listen to the way others are thinking and participate as they feel comfortable.

Think-Aloud

Think-aloud—the oral verbalizing of one's thinking—is one of the most effective ways you can model the comprehension strategies a reader uses to gain meaning from the printed page (Davey, 1983). Think-aloud activities also help learners, especially intermediate English learners, develop their comprehension monitoring ability (McKeown & Gentilucci, 2007). **Comprehension monitoring** is the reader's awareness of whether what is being read makes sense and, when it does not, her ability to make adjustments to improve comprehension. The following activity provides suggested steps for a think-aloud.

● think-aloud

● comprehension monitoring

Think-Aloud (FOCUS ON PROCESS)   ◉ activity ◉

1. Ahead of time, make copies of the text passage that will be demonstrated or prepare the passage to be displayed on an interactive whiteboard.

BEFORE READING

2. After looking at the text title and any illustrations in the passage, ruminate aloud about the passage. (Figure 5.2 represents an example of a teacher using the think-aloud procedure to model the strategy of visualizing.)

DURING READING

3. Read the passage aloud as the students track. Continually organize images by explaining the passage after every sentence or paragraph.

4. Answer aloud such questions as:

   What am I reminded of here that I already know? (tapping prior knowledge)

   What are some ways I can get help in understanding unfamiliar words and/or ideas? (monitoring understanding)

   What does this remind me of in my own life? (making connections)

AFTER READING

5. After modeling the reading of several paragraphs in this fashion, invite students to add their own problem-solving tactics and personal impressions by reading successive passages in pairs.

Guided Reading

Students need to be directly shown how to process text so that they can become independent readers. **Guided reading** is an instructional framework that provides direct teacher support for developing effective strategies for comprehending text independently at increasingly difficult levels. Generally you will work with a small group of students who are reading at a similar level of difficulty. A guided reading lesson involves three stages: before reading, during reading, and after reading.

● guided reading

figure 5.2 Teacher modeling of the think-aloud procedure for the strategy of visualizing.

Note: Text material is in bold; teacher think-aloud comments are in italics.

The title of the story is "The Desert Man." . . . I have a pretty good picture in my mind of what the desert looks like. Miles and miles of sand, blazing hot, very little vegetation.

The old man was hot and tired. His long white robe billowed in the dry desert wind.

My picture in my head is of a very old man. . . . He is dressed in a long white robe, and the material must be light enough to be blown by the wind. I can see his robe blowing in the wind.

He wiped his brow as he started to trudge up yet another of the endless dunes of the desert. He saw only a sea of sand surrounding him.

I can see in my own mind what the old man sees . . . hills and hills of hot sand . . . he is wiping his forehead and is bent over because he is so tired and weary.

The sun beat down on him mercilessly. He would not give up. He knew the camp was near.

The look on the old man's face is very clear to me now. He has a look of determination. He is very determined to make it to the camp. . . .

The pictures I made in my head about this passage helped me understand the story, and they will help me remember what I have read. This is a comprehension strategy that good readers use to help them learn and remember. It is a strategy that you can use to improve your comprehension.

Source: Gambrell, L. B., & Bales, R. J. (1987). Visual imagery: A strategy for enhancing listening, reading and writing. *Australian Journal of Reading, 10*(3), 147–153.

Before reading deals with building schemata for the reading selection. During reading is the core of the lesson, in which important strategies are modeled and practiced. Students are encouraged to read silently during this stage and request help as needed. After reading is a time to check for understanding, invite personal response, check the accuracy of predictions, and generally interpret and clarify what was read. More information about guided reading can be found in *Guiding Readers and Writers in Grades 3–6* (Fountas & Pinnell, 2001).

Directed Reading–Thinking Activity

directed reading–
thinking activity (DRTA) •

As a type of guided reading (teacher-led, small-group reading instruction that focuses on questioning and predicting to aid comprehension), the **directed reading–thinking activity (DRTA)** is one of the most commonly used approaches for enhancing comprehension with both narrative and expository materials, and especially with literature-based instruction. The objective of the DRTA, developed by Stauffer (1975), is to improve comprehension by having students focus on a particular passage and make predictions about it based on its textual features.

DRTA (FOCUS ON CONTENT AND PROCESS)

Although a DRTA lesson can be conducted in various ways, the steps usually include the following:

BEFORE READING

1. Direct students' attention to the title of the selection and ask them to predict its content. After students have volunteered their predictions and the reasons for their responses, ask a preselected group whether they agree or disagree with their classmates' predictions and why.

DURING READING

2. Read aloud, or have students read silently, several sentences, and then ask students what they think the text is about based on this new information.

3. Direct students' attention to particular vocabulary or phrases that are pertinent to the meaning of the text. Ask them to use these words to hypothesize what the text is about.

4. Ask students to look at pictures, graphs, and figures and make more predictions based on this new information.

AFTER READING

5. Ask students to reread or review the text to confirm or negate their predictions and hypotheses. Discuss their findings. See Figure 5.3 for an example of a teacher–student discourse that occurred during a DRTA conducted with social studies material.

GIST

The GIST procedure (generating interactions between schemata and text) is intended to improve students' comprehension and provide a tool for guiding student summary writing (Cunningham, 1982). **GIST** is a teacher-directed, small-group strategy that   ● GIST
takes students from summarizing paragraphs in no more than 15 words to summarizing short passages in no more than 20 words. Beginning with the paragraph version, students are asked to compose a summary sentence (consisting of 15 or fewer words) following the reading of each sentence in the paragraph. That is, after reading the first sentence, they summarize what is said. Then, as they read each new sentence, students incorporate the additional information into a new summary statement of no more than 15 words. The paragraphs selected should contain three to five sentences.

GIST (FOCUS ON CONTENT)

Using a paragraph from the chapter section read for the DRTA lesson above, GIST might proceed as follows:

1. Choose an appropriate paragraph. For example,

   Abe's father, Thomas Lincoln, worked hard to raise crops in the stony soil of his little farm. His mother, Nancy Hanks Lincoln, was a good housekeeper. When hunting was good, Thomas Lincoln could shoot deer, bear, rabbits, and turkeys in the woods. The family also had corn bread, greens from the garden, and potatoes.

(Activity continued on p. 148)

figure **5.3**   Example discourse from a DRTA lesson for social studies.

Before Reading:

Ms. Clark: Based on the title of this chapter section, "Abe Lincoln Grows Up With America," what do you predict that you might learn in this section and why?

Brian: I predict this section will tell me where Abe Lincoln grew up because it says "grows up" in the title.

Lilia: I think it will tell me where he was born and where he lived because in the picture it shows him sitting inside a house.

Ms. Clark (to other students): Do you agree with these predictions? Why or why not?

Students: Yes, agree. The title talks about growing up, so this section will talk about Abraham Lincoln when he was a young boy.

During Reading:

Ms. Clark: After reading the first page in this section (four paragraphs), what would you change about any of your predictions, or what new ones would you make?

Brian: Well, we now know where Abe Lincoln was born—Kentucky.

Tam: And he lived in a one-room log cabin, so we know that is where he is sitting in the picture. Inside the log cabin.

Lilia: And we found out he was born on February 12, 1809.

Ms. Clark: So it sounds like we need to make some new predictions.

Brian: The book talks about his mother and father and uses the word *children,* so I think Abe Lincoln had a brother or sister. I think we will find that out in the next part.

Ms. Clark: Tam told us Abe Lincoln lived in a one-room log cabin. Look at that sentence in your text. It says, "His first home was a one-room log cabin." What does that tell you or make you think about?

Brian: It makes me think he moved into another home sometime. This was just his first home.

Lilia: I think Abe Lincoln moves to Washington, D.C., and then he became president since Kentucky was where his first home was.

Ms. Clark: Look at that picture again. Where is Abe sitting, and why is he sitting there?

Brian: He is sitting by the fireplace. He might be cold. It might be winter.

Tam: But he has a book in his hand. He looks like he is trying to use the glow of the fireplace to see the book.

Lilia: Maybe the electricity went out!

Ms. Clark: What is there about the text or the picture that makes you think there was electricity in Abe's first house?

(continued)

Brian: The book says the house had deerskin windows, a door with leather hinges, and the floor was hard-packed earth. I think Abe Lincoln's family was very poor.

Ms. Clark: What do you think we will learn on the next page?

Brian: If Abe Lincoln has a brother or sister.

Tam: Where the family moved to.

Lilia: How Abe Lincoln became president.

Ms. Clark: Let's read the next page.

After Reading:

Ms. Clark: Now that you have finished this section, were your predictions supported? What did you find out?

Brian: We learned more about Lincoln's family. His father's name was Thomas Lincoln, and his mother's name was Nancy Hanks Lincoln. His father was a farmer and they had a cow.

Tam: Abe Lincoln went to school when he was seven.

Lilia: The family was very poor.

Brian: It just kept saying "children." I still don't know if Abe Lincoln had a brother or sister!

Tam: But it did tell us that the family moved to Indiana when Abe was still seven. And two years after they moved his mother died. So he was nine when his mother died.

Lilia: His father married a woman who had three children, so we know Abe had either brothers or sisters, or both, but not what they were. His stepmother's name was Sarah Johnston Lincoln.

Brian: Abe Lincoln only had about one year of school! But the book said that many people never went to school at all! Wow!

Tam: Abe grew up tall in Indiana. He was six feet, four inches by the time he was 16.

Ms. Clark: You learned quite a bit about the young Abe Lincoln. How do you think his early life may have helped him to become president of the United States?

Brian: Since he was poor, he would know what poor people need.

Lilia: He had to work real hard when he was young, so he knew how to work hard to become a president.

Tam: He read books and wrote things, so he was smart enough to be president.

2. Present only the first sentence to the students. The sentence should have 15 blanks underneath it.

Abe's father, Thomas Lincoln, worked hard to raise crops in the stony soil of his little farm.

___	___	___	___	___
___	___	___	___	___
___	___	___	___	___

3. Cover or remove the displayed sentence from view and have students, as a group, generate a summary from memory using the blank rules. After the summary statement has been created, reveal and reread the sentence. Students can decide at that time to revise their statement. Do not evaluate the statement or interfere with the group decision. Once the students are satisfied with their statement, go on to step 4. One summary statement for the sentence in step 2 might appear as

Abe's	hard-working	father	raised	crops
on	his	farm.		

4. Ask students to read the first two sentences and retell them using the same 15-word limit as they had for just the first sentence.

5. Have students create a summary statement, from memory, for both sentences one and two; it should be no longer than 15 words. Again, have students revise until they are satisfied. Then allow them to look at the text before proceeding to the next step. The new summary statement might look like this:

Abe's	hard-working	father	raised	crops
on	his	farm	and	his
mother	kept	house.		

6. Continue in the same manner for the rest of the paragraph. Students will soon realize that they are using up their allotted 15 words too quickly and will need to think of new ways to combine information, as well as to decide what information is most important to keep. The summary statement for sentences three and four might become

Abe's	hard-working	parents	provided	a
well-kept	house	and	food	from
crops	raised	or	from	hunting.

7. Now that students are becoming adept at sentence-by-sentence summarizing, have them write paragraph summaries using short passages. Explain to students that the procedures are the same, except the total number of words they can use is now 20.

This technique can be motivating for students if not overly used. Pretending to write tweets is another way to create summary statements. When writers are restricted to an absolute maximum number of characters or words, focusing on and choosing only the most important ideas for a summary becomes that much more critical. (See also "Writing in the Content Areas" in Chapter 7 for more information on writing summaries.)

Reciprocal Teaching

Reciprocal teaching is an interactive procedure that fosters comprehension by helping students actively monitor their thinking (Rosenshine & Meister, 1994). Students are taught to summarize text, anticipate questions, clarify unclear text, and make predictions about upcoming text. During reciprocal teaching, teachers demonstrate how to monitor reading comprehension using these strategies, how to observe the thinking process while reading, and how to determine when reading is successful and when it is not (Palincsar, 1987; Palincsar & Herrenkohl, 2002). Then, have students attempt the same activities on their own, offering them feedback on their performance. A typical reciprocal teaching session includes:

1. A review of the previous lesson and making predictions about the new text.
2. Students reading a chunk of the text (i.e., paragraph, page, chapter) silently to themselves.
3. Assigning a student to act as teacher, modeling strategies by:
   a. asking questions about the text chunk
   b. summarizing the text chunk
   c. clarifying questions from the group
   d. predicting what might be in the next text chunk (Dobler, Johnson, & Wolsey, 2013, pp. 174–175)

Teacher involvement remains high until students can use these strategies on their own.

Handwritten margin note: Teach strategies & model them ↓ Students then do it on their own

● reciprocal teaching

WWW●●●

Reciprocal Teaching General Information
www.ncrel.org/sdrs/areas/issues/
students/atrisk/at6lk38.htm

Reciprocal Teaching (FOCUS ON CONTENT AND PROCESS) ◉ activity ◉

This activity requires extensive modeling and guidance from you and is initially conducted as follows:

DURING READING

1. Read a paragraph from a passage of text, usually expository, aloud. (*Note:* As students learn these procedures, they will work in small groups, with each student taking on the teacher role for each new paragraph; thus the term *reciprocal*. At that point, reading will be done silently, or with partners in the case of struggling readers.)

AFTER READING

2. Model how the paragraph might be summarized. Focus on the main ideas in the paragraph, include the topic sentence, and point out that a summary should be no more than one-third the length of the original paragraph.
3. Ask the group an important question about the paragraph; the question should focus on the key issue. Solicit other questions from the group.
4. Think aloud about any unclear concepts or new vocabulary. Attempt to determine meanings from context. Also think about the need for clarifying information that might help students understand the paragraph more completely. (*Note:* This step is not always necessary for well-written paragraphs that are appropriate for the reader's skill level.) Solicit other ideas about what information might be needed.
5. Predict aloud what might be expected to be in the next paragraph or in the remainder of the passage. Explain the reason for this prediction. Solicit other predictions from the group.

6. Proceed to the next paragraph. According to Palincsar and Brown (1984, 1986), these modeling sessions should last about 30 minutes.

Dyad Reading

dyad reading ●

Dyad reading is a form of paired oral reading (also called "buddy reading," "partner reading," or "say something") that has the added dimension of reinforcing the important comprehension strategies of summarizing and questioning (Cecil, 1995).

activity   Dyad Reading (FOCUS ON CONTENT)

This activity consists of the following format:

DURING READING

1. Select two students to demonstrate the activity. Have one read a sentence or a paragraph aloud.
2. As that student reads, have the other student listen carefully and then summarize (orally or in writing) what was in the sentence or paragraph. For variation, the second student may simply draw a response to or summary of what was read and then describe the picture.

AFTER READING

3. Have the reader ask the listener critical comprehension questions.
4. Encourage the students to discuss the answers and, where there is disagreement, have them refer to the text selection to support their answers.
5. Have the students change roles with succeeding material.

Question–Answer Relationships

question–answer
relationships ●

Question–answer relationships, or QARs (Raphael, 2005), help students enhance their comprehension by learning to answer a range of questions and understand each question's relationship to the text, to the author, and to themselves. With this strategy, students ask themselves, "Where would I find an answer to this question in the text?" (For example, in the book, in my head.) Use the following hierarchy of questions and answers to help them decide.

Literal question (right there). The answer is "right there." This tells the student that the answer to the question is easy to find in the text. In fact, the exact words in the question are contained within the text.

Inferential question (think and search). The answer can be found if you "think and search" or "put it together." This tells the student that the answer is in the text, but two ideas will have to be brought together; that is, the words used in the question may be a bit different from the words used in the text and may span several paragraphs or chapters, so the answer will be slightly harder to find.

Critical question (author and you). The answer is in the mind of "the author and me." The answer is not directly stated in the text; if students bring their own ideas to the text and combine them with the opinions the author seems to hold, they will be able to answer the question.

Creative question (on my own). The answer has to be determined "on my own." The student will not find a direct answer to the question in the text. The question may have a wide range of correct answers; the student must use his imagination or information he already has about the topic to arrive at his best answer.

Raphael and Au (2005) describe the potential for QARs as a framework for comprehension instruction and an aid for helping students with test preparation. By delineating the comprehension strategies associated with each of the four QAR types, Raphael and Au provide a guide for alerting students to the task demands of the questions they will face both in their daily work and in the high-stakes tests they must take.

QARs (FOCUS ON CONTENT AND PROCESS)   ⊚ **activity** ⊚

Following is an outline of how students can be guided to incorporate the use of these questions to boost their own comprehension:

BEFORE READING

1. Give students four passages with questions for which the question types have already been determined. (Figure 5.4 shows a sample QAR lesson using a passage from a well-known nursery rhyme to help students identify the question types.)
2. Using the first passage, model how the answers to each question might be found in the text by identifying the appropriate QAR.

DURING READING

3. Read the second passage aloud to students. Then ask the questions aloud and have volunteers explain which kind of question is being asked and how they would find the answer in the text.

DURING/AFTER READING

4. Divide the class into small cooperative groups. Ask students to read the third passage and answer the questions, identifying the appropriate QARs.
5. Using the fourth passage, have students follow the same procedure individually, while you go around the classroom offering assistance as needed.
6. Follow-up would consist of practicing with questions such as those found in Figure 5.4.

Novel Study

You can apply all of these previous strategies in the curricular framework of the novel study. **Novel study** refers to an in-depth reading and interpretation of a novel (or a group of stories by one author), addressing both efferent (reading for information) and aesthetic (reading for enjoyment) dimensions. Common goals of novel studies are (1) to introduce students to quality literature, (2) to teach students to interpret literature and see meaning and relevance in a variety of genres, and (3) to familiarize students with the various literary awards.   ⦁ novel study

For example, a middle school might base its reading instruction on novel studies, which teachers term "anchor units" because the content is anchored in the grade level standards, benchmarks, and indicators from their state curriculum. Each anchor unit is designed to take four to five weeks to complete. Novels or stories are specifically chosen for grade-appropriate reading levels, high inter-

figure **5.4**   QAR sample passage and question types.

An introductory QAR lesson must first define all the question types. Using the familiar nursery rhyme "Jack and Jill," examine the following questions to note the characteristics of each type.

> Jack and Jill went up the hill
> to fetch a pail of water.
> Jack fell down and broke his crown
> and Jill came tumbling after.

1. Where did Jack and Jill go?
   Response: Up the hill to get some water
   QAR: Right there

2. Did Jill get the pail of water?
   Response: No, she fell down the hill too.
   QAR: Putting it together (or think and search)

3. What could have caused Jack's crown to break in his fall down the hill?
   Response: I bet the pail full of water hit him in the head.
   QAR: Author and me

   Or

   What happened to Jill?
   Response: She fell down the hill after Jack did and hurt herself too because when she fell, she rolled right into Jack.
   QAR: Author and me

4. Do you think Jack and Jill ever got the pail of water they went up the hill to get?
   Response: I think they got the water but it all spilled out when they fell down the hill. Then they were too badly hurt to go back up to get more water.
   QAR: On my own

est for students, and experiences with multiple genres in grades 6–8. Using novel studies geared more to a connection with a benchmark or indicator skill, rather than a retelling of the book, also allows teachers to use additional texts, including informational books, on occasion to accommodate special needs students or those whose parents may object on personal grounds to a particular author or text. The texts listed in Table 5.1 are used in the anchor units.

One teacher may conduct a novel study after completing the Grade 8 unit on Edgar Allan Poe. The group reads "Annabel Lee," "The Raven," "The Tell-Tale Heart," "The Pit and the Pendulum," "The Fall of the House of Usher," "The Murders at the Rue Morgue," "The Purloined Letter," and "The Masque of the Red Death." In each story the emphasis is on the setting, the mood, and the symbolism found or inferred in the text. Context clues to help determine meanings of unknown words address the grade level word study emphasis, and practice work-

Texts used for anchor units in grades 4–8.

table 5.1

TEXT	AUTHOR	DATE	GENRE	THEME/TOPIC
Grade 4				
The Kid in the Red Jacket	Barbara Park	1987	Realistic Fiction	Moving/Household/Humor
Jackie Robinson Breaks the Color Line	Andrew Santella	1996	Nonfiction/ Biography	Discrimination in sports/Baseball
Sadako and the Thousand Paper Cranes	Eleanor Coerr	1977	Historical Fiction	Hiroshima/Atomic bomb/Bombardment 1945/Leukemia in children/Death/ Psychological effect
The Cricket in Times Square	George Selden	1960	Fiction/Fantasy	Times Square, New York/Friendship/ Adventure/Crickets
Grade 5				
Sign of the Beaver	Elizabeth George Speare	1983	Historical Fiction	Frontier/Pioneer life/Survival/North American Indians/Friendship
George Washington's Socks	Elvira Woodruff	1991	Historical Fiction	U.S. Revolution, 1775–1783/George Washington/Space and time
Endurance: Shackleton's Antarctic Expedition	Janice Marriott	1995	Nonfiction	Survival/Endurance/Discovery and exploration
Mrs. Frisby and the Rats of NIMH	Robert O'Brien	1971	Fiction/Fantasy	Heroism/Friendship/Mice/Rats
Grade 6				
Maniac Magee	Jerry Spinelli	1990	Realistic Fiction	Legends/Athletes/Orphans
The Acorn People	Ron Jones	1977	Nonfiction	Children with disabilities
Where the Red Fern Grows	Wilson Rawls	1998	Realistic Fiction	Dogs/Hunting/Ozark Mountains
The Devil's Arithmetic	Jane Yolen	1988	Fiction/Fantasy	Jews/Concentration camps/Time travel/ Poland–occupation 1939–1945
Grade 7				
House of Dies Drear	Virginia Hamilton	1968	Historical Fiction/ Mystery	Underground Railroad/African Americans/ Mystery
City of Light, City of Dark	Avi	1993	Science Fiction/ Fantasy	Graphic Novel
No Promises in the Wind	Irene Hunt	1970	Historical Fiction	Great Depression/Family life
The Titanic	Daniel Harmon/ Victoria Sherrow	2001/ 1999	Nonfiction	Shipwrecks/Disasters
Grade 8				
My Brother Sam Is Dead	James Lincoln Collier and Christopher Collier	1974	Historical Fiction	Revolutionary War, 1775–1783
Izzy Willy Nilly	Cynthia Voight	1986	Fiction	People with disabilities/Amputees
Tangerine	Edward Bloor	1997	Fiction	Physical handicaps/Brothers/Soccer
The Pigman and Me	Paul Zindel	1992	Fiction	Social life/Customs
Driver's Ed	Caroline Cooney	1994	Biography	Children and youth

sheets are given at seventh- and eighth-grade reading levels. The group also reads a nonfiction article that summarizes symptoms, causes, and treatments of clinical depression. Students might write reading responses to each Poe work they've read, watch a documentary on Poe's life while taking notes using different graphic organizers, and keep an ongoing chart that summarizes story information about the setting, mood, symbolism, and theme of each story. Depending on available technology and student experience, readers might collaborate to create a multimodal presentation of the story; for example, using music, text designed to fit the story's mood and content, images, and video or audio clips.

Following the text study, students apply their understanding of mood, symbolism, theme, and context clues to a final assessment on "Goodbye, Grandma," by Ray Bradbury. Questions are written in multiple choice, short answer, and extended response formats, which mirror the format of the state achievement test. Students also complete an individual project about Poe independently. Students choose one of five design options, which are offered to accommodate multiple intelligences. Students

1. create a poster on Poe's life and works,
2. write a horror story in the style of Poe,
3. write three poems in the style of Poe,
4. create four illustrations for one of Poe's stories (since the texts are not illustrated), or
5. find three poems not read in class and prepare to read them aloud to the class with musical accompaniment, using instrumental music appropriate for the mood of the poem.

The final assignment is the writing of a critical essay about Poe's life and works, using the graphic organizers and discussion from the previous four weeks. Projects and essays are graded using rubrics that students receive prior to the due date. (This example of novel study using the works of Poe is based on an actual study from one middle school; M. Daniels, personal communication, October 29, 2007.) For additional examples of novel studies, see the websites listed in the margin.

Implicit Instruction

In addition to direct instruction in comprehension strategies, students learn to comprehend through more implicit types of instruction. Implicit instruction includes independent reading and activities that are often called *reader response activities* (Beach, 1993). A great deal of overlap exists between independent reading and reader response activities, as you will see in the section on literature circles and book clubs.

Independent Reading

Students need to be given time to read if we expect them to be able to practice using comprehension strategies and simply enjoy reading. Independent reading is a central factor to developing lifelong enjoyment of reading. According to the landmark study *Becoming a Nation of Readers* (Anderson, Hiebert, Scott, et al., 1985), "Children should spend more time in independent reading. Independent reading, whether in school or out of school, is associated with gains in reading achievement. By the time they are in third or fourth grade, children should read independently a minimum of two hours per week. Children's reading should include classic and modern works of fiction and nonfiction" (p. 119). In addition, the National Reading Panel (2000) found ample evidence showing that one of the major differences

www●●●

Example for Grades 4–8 of *A Company of Fools*

www.fitzhenry.ca/Download/ guides/CompanyofFoolsTG.pdf

Rainbow Horizons Publishing

(for one free unit of choice) www.rainbowhorizons.com

Novel Studies Links

www.edselect.com/novel_ studies.htm

between good and poor readers is the difference in the total amount of time they spend reading. This time spent reading provides students with increased vocabulary (as discussed in Chapter 4), and also promotes learning more about the world in general. The use of graphic novels, digital texts, and book contracts may help students' commitment to and interest during independent reading.

Graphic novels

For students who are reluctant to read traditional works of fiction or nonfiction, graphic novels may hold some appeal. **Graphic novels** are book-length (130 to 150 pages) stories presented in comic-book format and usually published in softcover. The highly visual, action-oriented story lines of many graphic novels can serve to increase student interest. "A student *reads* the words, *sees* the action, *comprehends* the meaning, and is motivated to read more. It's an end that justifies the means" (McTaggert, 2006, p. 2). And as Kiefer (1995) states, "the visual art . . . can illuminate such devices as character development, elaboration, mood, point of view, irony, and satire" (p. 184). *Anime* and *manga* are words associated with the visual art of graphic novels. **Anime,** a Japanese word for animation, refers to an art form that makes inanimate objects look like they are moving (see Figure 5.5). **Manga** is a highly stylized and intricate Japanese art form that has become a label used

● graphic novels

Graphic Novel Resources

www.brodartbooks.com/library-collection-development/graphic-novels/page.aspx?id=370

www.noflyingnotights.com

● anime
● manga

Anime and manga series, available by the thousands online, may stimulate interest in reading for some students resistant to more traditional print formats.

figure **5.5**

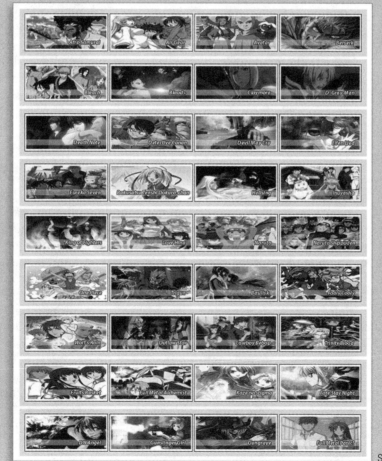

Source: www.animevenue.com

for Japanese print comics. These Japanese comics are read from back to front and from left to right. Graphic novels can be the start some students need to engage in other forms of reading and to avoid becoming aliterate. See suggested websites for more information about graphic novels and Appendix A for suggested titles.

Digital texts

Literacy in young adults has notably changed in the early years of the twenty-first century. Students live in a world of computers and other media devices, including smartphones. They text, tweet, and email to correspond with their friends and teachers, and they are likely to read or seek information online. They know how to navigate, and are indeed literate, in the world of multimedia text, which is layered with hyperlinks and thus is less linear than traditional texts. These books, printed on paper, meant to be read in a clear sequence, and with a singular authorial point-of-view, cannot be easily modified or enhanced. Traditional texts rely on the imagination and background knowledge of readers. Online digital texts, on the other hand, can be modified, updated, and enhanced. They do not have to be read sequentially; they provide opportunities for branching out when additional knowledge is needed for comprehension or when an image is needed for text support. Digital texts may also be interactive, allowing readers to respond to the text in some way. In other words, digital texts can be socially constructed. Importantly, they can also be shared among readers and classes—locally, nationally, and even globally. For all readers, including the young readers in our classrooms, *text* no longer refers exclusively to the printed word. It has evolved to include email, websites, text messaging, blogs, social networks, and even online gaming. One of the most important benefits of digital and interactive texts may be students' increased motivation to read them.

Ebooks are available in many forms and formats; they may be accessed online or via DVD, or downloaded. They may have fixed-page layout, or they may be reflowable. Ebooks may be interactive, and include multimedia elements such as music, dialogue, puzzles, games, maps, and all manner of visuals. Depending on an ebook's platform and format, it may be read on ereaders, desktop computers, laptops, tablets, and/or mobile devices.

Older students seem to prefer ereaders when reading texts for pleasure or gathering quick background information. According to a study done in 2010 by Scholastic, 57 percent of students ages 9 to 17 said they would read more books for fun if they had an ereader. Some ebooks and ereaders allow readers to respond to guiding questions, add virtual notes, and highlight passages. Ereaders also contain convenient tools such as interactive dictionaries, word search ability, and links to other resources. These tools may also help teachers to differentiate instruction according to students' reading needs, skill levels, and language development.

While students seem to enjoy ereaders, some critics say that they are less versatile than print books in meeting students' academic needs (Leu et al., 2007). Students who want to annotate, highlight key ideas in text, or quickly skim to locate information may feel that ebooks are less convenient than print texts.

When Ash (2010) explored using ereaders with students who are dyslexic or have other reading disabilities, she found that ereaders have drawbacks for these challenged readers: they don't allow students to easily skim over texts using headings and subheadings, to use the external text structure to orient them in the text, or to help them organize their thoughts about the text.

Teachers may be hesitant to use ebooks and ereaders if they lack the technical ability to do so; professional development may be needed to help them use ebooks as learning tools. Although ebooks offer many benefits, their use in the classroom may be limited until teachers have learned about the many tools and options these tools offer to enhance student learning. As they become more comfortable with the functions and capabilities of ebooks, teachers can set realistic expectations for their students who use them. Thus, while students may embrace technology, classroom teachers must understand not only how to use the technology but also how to use it to facilitate student learning.

Book contracts

Teachers who are held accountable for how students spend their independent reading time and for encouraging reader response may wish to consider the concept of a book contract. A **book contract** is a packet of required and alternative activities, such as the following: journal writing; cross-curricular activities that involve art, science, math, and/or social studies projects and that might involve multimedia, social media, or other technology; and author research, from which a student will choose in order to fulfill a contract with the teacher (see the Extension Activities in Figure 5.7 later in the chapter). The student may be expected to complete six of eight activities, but she will choose the six that she wishes to complete. The required activities usually consist of a chart for documenting the material read each day, a page for maintaining new vocabulary, and any other documentation that teachers may be responsible for collecting. The packet may include a cover page for the student to personalize; it may include a copy of the book's cover. Book contracts can be helpful to the teacher in individualizing instruction because, in one class, several different book contracts at different readability levels may be functioning at the same time.

● book contract

Literature circles and in-school book clubs

Daniels (2002) defines **literature circles** as "small, peer-led discussion groups whose members have chosen to read the same story, poem, article, or book. While reading each group-assigned portion, members make notes to help them contribute to the upcoming discussion, and everyone comes to the group with ideas to share" (p. 2). Similarly, **book clubs** are student-led groups whose members read literary selections, write reactions and questions in a reading response log, and engage in both small-group and whole-class discussions (McMahon & Raphael, 1997). (In-school book clubs may work differently than out-of-school book clubs; in Chapter 10, you will find more information on out-of-school book clubs.)

● literature circles

● book clubs

Literature circles and book clubs are similar in many ways. Both recognize the social nature of learning and the transactional nature of the reading process. Their success depends on students being given a choice of material to read and discuss with peers. In this way, the text being read is reconsidered and explored by a group of readers for a more thorough and complete understanding. The discussion group negotiates the meaning of the text, combines and connects ideas, and constructs meaning that one person reading alone might not ever achieve. In general, however, literature circles are more structured than book clubs and thus may be most appropriate for older grades. Literature circles may involve assigned roles, such as discussion facilitator and summarizer. Their intent is "to allow students to practice and develop the skills and strategies of good readers" (DaLie, 2001).

Literature circles and book clubs are especially beneficial for English learners, helping these students become part of a community and the school culture and encouraging them to engage in comfortable talk about books. English learners hear natural oral language when native English speakers talk about the books, and they pay closer attention to the way their English-speaking classmates use the language within the relaxed setting of the literature circle (Hadaway, Vardell, & Young, 2004). Feelings of anxiety about speaking before the whole class are diminished. Everyone in the literature circle has a turn to speak, so English learners gain much needed practice in using the language.

Literature circles and book clubs usually involve a written component—individual readers maintain written logs, also called reader response logs, that document special passages or issues, or they add notes with brief comments on particular pages and share those comments with group members. (The comments might be on actual sticky notes attached to a page, or they might be virtual notes in an ebook.) Readers also document interpretations of their reading with sketches, illustrations, and diagrams. Often teachers will initiate literature circles by using role sheets as a "getting started" tool for helping students understand how to participate in peer-led discussion groups (see Figure 5.6).

A book club can be more structured. For example, it may include the following components, which take place during a specific instructional time (Raphael & McMahon, 1994):

- *Community Share:* Time is set aside for whole group discussion or instruction.
- *Reading:* During this period, students are usually reading the text silently.

figure **5.6**   Role descriptions for literature circles.

DISCUSSION LEADER

Develop a set of questions that you will ask your group members to discuss in regard to the material you read for today. Think about what your own feelings are or areas that confused or concerned you. Ask questions about what was read, or try some general questions such as, How did you feel about what you read? Did it remind you of anything? Were you surprised by anything? What do you think were the most important ideas?

VOCABULARY MASTER

Choose three or four words from the reading that you find especially important, interesting, unusual, confusing, or totally new. Try to learn as much as you can about these words. Learn what they mean, and then help your group members learn these words also.

ARTIST

Draw a picture, sketch, diagram, or cartoon that is related to what you read. The drawing should be a representation of what the text was about. Show the drawing to your group members without telling them what it means to you. After they each have had a chance to say what they think it means, tell them what you intended.

Source: Adapted from Daniels (2002).

CONNECTOR

Make connections between what you read and your life experiences. You might make a connection to something you experienced as a student, or to something that has happened in the community, in another place or time, or to other people. You could also make a connection to something else that you have read. Sharing these connections with your group members may help to trigger other connections that they can share.

SUMMARIZER

In a one- or two-minute statement, summarize what today's reading was about. Focus only on the main points and give the essence of the reading assignment. You might wish to list the main points if there are several.

LITERARY LUMINARY

Locate one or two special sections of today's reading. There might be a part of the reading that is especially interesting, funny, sad, confusing, controversial, thought-provoking, or important. Decide which parts are worth rereading or revisiting. Then think about how to share them again with your group members. You might wish to read them aloud, or have group members reread them silently and follow up with a discussion.

- *Writing/Representing:* Students reflect on the reading and respond to it—aloud, in writing, or using a visual representation. Prompts may be used to elicit reflection.
- *Discussion:* Students, usually in small groups, share their responses and discuss the text and multi-level questions generated by both teacher and students. During this time, the teacher can model for, or explicitly teach, students how to lead and maintain good group discussions, as well as suggest ideas for what to write in a journal (Raphael, 2000).

Literature Circles/Book Clubs   activity

Literature circles and book clubs are powerful activities for readers in grades 4–8 because these "students find that peers provide important support for their comprehension and interpretation of text, and that the literate activities . . . help develop their ownership over literacy" (Raphael, 2000, p. 85). Steps for implementing literature circles and book clubs follow:

BEFORE READING

1. Provide students with a selection of books from which they can choose to read and discuss with classmates (see Table 5.2 for some recommended titles). This list can include informational books, young adult literature, or graphic novels, whether in digital or print format. Titles can be presented in the form of a book talk (reading aloud a brief selection and/or sharing positive impressions from a book to arouse interest in reading the book). Students can freely choose which book to read, but if no one else chooses the same book they may need to make a second choice. The optimum discussion group should have four or five members to ensure "a variety of perspectives on the text, a range of responses that enlivens discussion" (Daniels, 2002, p. 19).

Short list of books recommended by and for students in grades 4–8.   *table* **5.2**

TITLE/DATE	GENRE/THEME	AUTHOR/PUBLISHER	NOTES
Double Dutch (2002)	Realistic fiction/Social acceptance/Friendship/Dyslexia	Sharon M. Draper/Atheneum	Text-to-self connections are readily made with the focus on the fear of not fitting in. Delia, Randy, and YoYo reveal their secrets as they prepare for a jump rope competition.
The Slave Dancer (2001, revised format)	Historical fiction/Slavery	Paula Fox/Atheneum	This Newbery Medal book provides information about the history of slavery and what it was like to be a slave through the experiences of 13-year-old Jessie.
Travels of Thelonious: The Fog Mound (2006)	Fiction/Adventure	Susan Schade and Jon Buller/Simon & Schuster	Thelonious Chipmunk, along with a bear, a porcupine, and a lizard, sets out to prove that humans once inhabited the earth. Alternating chapters of prose and graphic novel appeal to reluctant readers.

(continued)

table **5.2**   Short list of books recommended by and for students in grades 4–8, *continued.*

TITLE/DATE	GENRE/THEME	AUTHOR/PUBLISHER	NOTES
Crossing the Wire (2006)	Realistic fiction/ Immigration/Survival/ Mexicans/Friendship	Will Hobbs/ HarperCollins	Fifteen-year-old Victor crosses the Arizona border to work in the United States in an effort to support his family.
Sand Dollar Summer (2006)	Realistic fiction/ Coming of age/Family	Kimberly K. Jones/ Simon & Schuster	Twelve-year-old Lise's formerly safe world becomes complicated after her mother's accident and by other personal and environmental obstacles.
Hana's Suitcase (2002)	Biography/Holocaust	Karen Levine/Albert Whitman & Co.	After Fumiko Ishioka, the curator of a children's Holocaust museum, receives the suitcase of a Czech girl, he researches the history of the suitcase and tells the story of Hana through alternating chapters.
Peter and the Star Catchers (2004)	Fantasy/Friendship/ Good versus evil	David Berry and Ridley Pearson/ Hyperion	This seafaring adventure serves as a prequel to J. M. Barrie's *Peter Pan,* revealing a secret about a chest full of a substance that can make people fly.
Locomotion (2003)	Juvenile poetry/ Self-discovery/African American boys/Orphans	Jacqueline Woodson/ G. P. Putnam's Sons	Lonnie discovers his own poetic voice when he has to adjust to the death of his parents and separation from his sister.
The Curious Incident of the Dog in the Night-Time (2004)	Realistic fiction/Autism/ Coping with loss	Mark Haddon/ Doubleday	Both a mystery and a comedy, this novel explores an autistic boy's reactions to emotional losses.
Al Capone Does My Shirts (2004)	Historical fiction/Family problems/Responsibility	Gennifer Choldenko/ G. P. Putnam's Sons	The story of 12-year-old Moose Flanagan and his life on Alcatraz Island during the 1930s.
The Time Hackers (2005)	Science fiction/Space and time/Computer games	Gary Paulsen/Wendy Lamb Books	Futuristic technology is used to play practical jokes on seventh grader Dorso Clayman. He and his good friend journey through space and time to stop the pranksters.
Hearts of Stone (2005)	Historical fiction/ U.S. Civil War/Family/ Personal cost of war/ Sacrifice	Kathleen Ernst/ Dutton Juvenile	Fourteen-year-old Hannah becomes head of her household when her mother dies in a raid and her father joins the Union forces. This is the story of Hannah and her siblings' 200-mile journey to a relative's house.
Something About America (2005)	Poetry/Immigrants/ National characteristics/ Children of immigrants	Maria Testa/ Candlewick	Told in simple verse, this is the tale of an eighth-grader who fled to the U.S. eight years earlier with her parents to escape Kosovo. It is a tale of fear, starting over again, hope, and challenge.

Book selection is critical for ensuring vibrant and meaningful discussions. It is important that the books relate to students' lives and interests, but the books offered for student choice must also encourage positive discussion strategies (Clarke & Holwadel, 2007). The sample of books included in Table 5.2 will inspire good conversations and debates. Text selection for the CCSS was governed by the further criteria of complexity, quality, and range (NGACBP & CCSSO, 2010). For help in choosing quality literature, and for a lesson example, visit the suggested websites. See also "Exemplars of Reading Text Complexity, Quality, and Range & Sample Performance Tasks Related to Core Standards" (www.corestandards.org/assets/Appendix_B.pdf) for additional suggestions. Finally, Appendix A of this book includes a list of quality literature recommendations.

2. Have students choose their books and meet with others who are reading the same book to determine how much they will read for their first discussion meeting. Meetings are regularly scheduled, daily or weekly, and should allow at least 30 to 45 minutes for group discussion.

DURING READING

3. Have students read the agreed-upon pages of the text. For the written preparation, have them record their comments about the text, listing important page numbers or sections, drawing pictures, noting difficult words or passages, making connections to their own lives, and developing questions to ask their group members. The nature of these comments is an individual one; however, they should help prepare the student for the upcoming group discussion.

AFTER READING

4. Have groups meet to discuss their reading. Students generally take turns leading the discussion, but all students must be involved. At the end of the discussion, have students decide on the amount of reading for the next period. At this point, it should be apparent how well the groups are functioning and whether each member is participating fully. The student-led discussions can indicate areas that need to be addressed during community share (book club) or whole-class sharing.

5. Have the whole class meet to listen to what the other groups have been talking about. This also provides an opportunity for you to offer explicit instruction or scaffolding.

6. If desired, ask students to complete self-assessments at the end of each discussion, or at the end of a complete book, to evaluate their own goals, roles, and performance as a group member.

WWW○○○

Overview Sites for Children's and Young Adult Lit

www.reading.org/Resources/ResourcesByTopic/Childrens YALiterature/Overview.aspx

www.ala.org/yalsa/

Annual IRA Children's Choices

http://www.reading.org/Libraries/choices/ira-cbc-childrens-choices-reading-list-2013.pdf

IRA Young Adults' Choices

http://www.reading.org/Libraries/choices/ira-young-adults-choices-reading-list-2013.pdf

ALA/YALSA Teens' Top Ten

http://www.ala.org/yalsa/teenstopten

Bookfinder (search by title, author, award winners, etc.)

www.literatureplace.com/awards/book_finder_by_subject.asp

Lesson example: "Give Them a Hand: Promoting Positive Interaction in Literature Circles"

www.readwritethink.org/lessons/lesson_view.asp?id=1078

Jigsaw: Read a Book in an Hour

Teachers in grades 4–8 find it especially difficult to provide the depth of coverage necessary to achieve thorough understanding for the breadth of content knowledge expected of their students. One approach that takes full advantage of collaborative working groups for the purpose of learning new material is jigsawing (Aronson & Patnoe, 2011). A specific jigsaw activity called Read a Book in an Hour (Cecil, 1990; Childrey, 1980) allows students to share responsibility for reading specific material. The material is divided into small portions and assigned to members of the class to read. Later, class members share the information to achieve the whole of the material. In other words, an individual student, or partnership, is responsible for reading and learning a small amount of material well enough to summarize it for others. As this information is shared, all members of the class learn the required material.

BEFORE READING

1. Identify a topic of study and its components along with books that correspond to the topic (see the earlier discussion of novel studies for an example). Then create a sign-up list that identifies enough "portions" for all members of the class to be involved.
2. Have students sign up for, or assign them, one portion of the topic/material/ novel.

DURING READING

3. Allow students ample time to read the material.
4. Students are responsible for understanding the material for which they are accountable. Instruct them to identify and learn new vocabulary and concepts. Ask them to formulate ideas for how to present this information to classmates. Also ask them to speculate about what may have happened or been discussed in the sections before or after their portion.

AFTER READING

5. Have "expert" groups (those who have read the same material) come together and prepare for their "teaching" of the new material. This might involve preparing visuals (drawings, photos, Prezi or PowerPoint presentations, or videos), as well as an oral presentation. Conferencing with the teacher is acceptable.
6. Have students present their material and answer questions.

While jigsawing is typically used with expository material, this modification, Read a Book in an Hour, can be used with narrative material for the express purpose of engaging students with a literary piece that they might not otherwise read on their own. Often students in upper grades are required to read particular works of literature as part of state content standards. Students may not have either the confidence in themselves or the motivation to complete these required texts. Using this strategy, which adapts the jigsaw concept, allows these students to participate more fully in reading these texts. The anticipated benefit of this experience is that students will get a sense of the entire piece and thus have the schema necessary to read the book on their own, confident that they will be successful. And, much like book talk activities, by using high-quality literature this technique will increase students' interest and desire to read the entire book on their own. A sample Read a Book in an Hour lesson with suggestions for integrating other areas of the curriculum is presented in Figure 5.7.

Reader Response Activities

Support for reader response activities as part of a comprehensive program for comprehension instruction is based on the work of Lev Vygotsky (1978, 1986) and Louise Rosenblatt (1938, 1969, 1978, 1983, 1994). Vygotsky's work views comprehension as socially constructed through negotiation with text, readers, teachers, and other members of the classroom community; Rosenblatt's work views compre-

"Read a Book in an Hour": Example lesson and book contract activities.

figure **5.7**

Book: *The Summer of the Swans,* by Betsy Byars. Grade Level: 6th

Goals: To help students learn how to summarize and how to develop one key question from a passage; to encourage students to read *The Summer of the Swans* in its entirety on their own.

Content Standard(s): CCSS.ELA-Literacy.RL.6.2: Determine a theme or central idea of a text and how it is conveyed through particular details; provide a summary of the text distinct from personal opinions or judgments; and CCSS.ELA-Literacy.RL.6.3: Describe how a particular story's or drama's plot unfolds in a series of episodes as well as how the characters respond or change as the plot moves toward a resolution.

FACTORS TO BE CONSIDERED:

1. Motivation for the lesson cannot give away the story line.
2. Students should be grouped according to their reading abilities.
3. The number of chapters and the number of students should be compatible.
4. Books should have dramatic intensity and be of high literary quality; those that are very predictable are not good choices.

OTHER STORIES BY BETSY BYARS:

The Eighteenth Emergency and *Pinballs*

OTHER STORIES ABOUT DISABILITIES:

Take Wing, by Jean Little, and *A Racecourse for Andy,* by Patricia Wrightson

ANTICIPATORY SET/MOTIVATION:

Relate feelings of awkwardness, loneliness, or simply being different. "Is everyone the same? Is it wrong to be different? Are people always happy? Have you ever felt you weren't good enough? Or simply that you just can't fit in? I'd like to introduce you to a girl named Sara and let's see what problems she encounters and how she attacks and solves her problems."

THE PROCESS:

1. Pair students and assign chapters/sections.

2. Tell students that partners may move to another location while doing their paired reading but must return to their seats when the reading is completed.
3. Remind the class of the rules for partner reading, which include shoulder-to-shoulder reading and a *12-inch voice* (voice cannot be heard beyond 12 inches from mouth) maximum.
4. Read the first chapter to the entire group to establish setting.

SUMMARIZING:

5. Review the meaning of *to summarize.* Summaries should be no more than 2 minutes long.
6. Summarize the chapter and ask a prediction question for the upcoming section. Students are now ready to do their paired reading and prepare their summaries and a prediction question from their assigned section. *Note:* The prediction question is posed to the following group during the sharing phase.

THE PROCESS CONTINUES:

7. Once students have read their sections and prepared their summary and prediction question, allow the process to continue. This should take about 15 to 20 minutes depending on the reading abilities and the length of the chapters assigned.
8. Repeat the prediction question to the first group. The first group then addresses the question and answers, if possible, and summarizes their reading. (These summaries may be written down and read, read from a prepared outline, or merely recited from memory, depending on the grade level.) This group then asks their prediction question to the following pair.
9. Allow the process to continue until the last group has participated.
10. For the last chapter, either read it aloud or assign it to the students to read.

COMPREHENSION CHECK:

- Literal
  1. What made Charlie leave his home in the middle of the night?

(continued)

2. Why did Sara dislike Joe Melby?

3. What did Charlie lose while he was lost?

4. Why was Aunt Willie nervous when Frank came to pick up Sara's sister, Wanda?

- Inferential

  1. Is Sara happy at the end of the story? Why do you think so?

  2. Why did Sara decide to accept Joe Melby's invitation to Benny Hoffman's party?

  3. Why do you think Sara knew that Charlie had gone out in the night to see the swans and that he had taken the one he had into the forest?

- Critical

  1. What does it mean to care more about someone else than you care about yourself?

  2. Often characteristics are revealed about a person when he or she reacts to a situation. When Gretchen called Charlie a "retard," Sara squirted water on her. When Sara believed Joe had stolen Charlie's watch, she became angry at Joe and would not believe him when he denied being the thief. What do these incidents tell you about Sara?

  3. On page 140, Betsy Byars writes that Sara "suddenly saw life as a series of huge, uneven steps." What do you think the author meant by this?

  4. Could Charlie really relate to the swans? Why or why not?

- Creative

  1. Charlie found the place where the swans were to be beautiful and serene. Create and describe a place that you think would be like this, a place where you might go at a time like this.

  2. Create a character who is in a situation that makes him or her feel awkward or out of place. Describe the situation and help the character cope with his or her feelings.

  3. Describe Aunt Willie's next ride on a motor scooter. Will she ever ride solo?

  4. What happened to Sara at the party? Did she enjoy herself?

ENRICHMENT ACTIVITIES:

1. Reread the entire novel on your own.

2. Keep a diary for Sara during the summer that Charlie is lost. Write entries for her dated at the beginning of the summer, during Charlie's absence, and at the end of the summer. Show her cares and concerns. Does she mature?

EXTENSION ACTIVITIES TO CHOOSE FROM FOR BOOK CONTRACT:

- Art

  1. Using poster paints, mix the paints to create puce (brownish-purple) and then paint a picture using this new color.

  2. Create a mobile of scenes from *Summer of the Swans* (swans, lakes, puce tennis shoes, watch, Sara, Charlie, etc.)

- Science

  3. Prepare a research report on birds and swans.

  4. It became very cold the night Charlie was lost. Conduct a study of weather and why temperature drops at night. Record at least six daytime and six nighttime outdoor temperatures for a week, but try to use the same times of day.

- Math

  5. Graph the outdoor temperatures from their science work in choice #4.

  6. Solve math problems finding kilometers walked by Sara, Joe, and Charlie. (The problems use decimals and the directions north, south, east, and west.)

- Social Studies

  7. Author Betsy Byars used West Virginia for the location of her story. Conduct a study of the geography of West Virginia. Decide where in the state the story took place, and write a paper supporting this answer.

  8. Conduct research on disabilities. Then choose one and write a paper on that one disability.

hension as the result of the interaction, or transaction, between the reader and the text. Rosenblatt (1969) proposes a transactional theory in which the meaning of a text derives from the transaction between the text and the reader within a specific context. She eloquently described this concept many years prior to proposing the transactional theory:

> The special meaning, and more particularly, the submerged associations that these words and images have for the individual reader will largely determine what the work communicates to him. The reader brings to the work personality traits, memories of past events, present needs and preoccupations, a particular mood of the moment, and a particular physical condition. These and many other elements . . . determine his response to the peculiar contribution of the text. (1938, pp. 30–31)

The instructional frameworks and strategies that follow support the development of comprehension through independent reading. Students can respond to what they read in an infinite number of ways, and teachers are encouraged to incorporate use of technology and multimedia (Larson, 2009a, 2009b). Many teachers and students are already familiar with written forms of responding, such as journals, paraphrases, and summaries. Students can also write letters, emails, or blog posts to authors, or to a character in a story that they have read. Some students write as if they were the character in the story. Personal essays, poems, scripts for a readers theatre, and short stories are additional forms of written response. Response can be spoken as well. In addition to readers theatre, students might be asked to teach the text, discuss it in small groups, retell the text, make an audio recording, or role play. Engaging in panel discussions or in a student–teacher conference are also spoken ways of responding to text. Finally, visual responses to text might include drawings, photographs, videos, and the use of graphic organizers.

Sketch to Stretch   activity

In Sketch to Stretch (Short, Harste, & Burke, 1995), students create a simple line drawing that depicts their interpretation of the material they've just read. This sketch is then shared with a small group of peers who give their interpretations of each other's sketches. For an example lesson for students in grades 4–6, visit the suggested website. The guidelines are as follows:

Lesson using Sketch to Stretch

www.readwritethink.org/lessons/lesson_view.asp?id=229

1. Place students in groups of four or five. Ask them to think about the selection and draw a sketch of what the selection meant to them or what understanding they took away from the selection.

2. When the sketches are complete, have students in the group share them with the other group members.

3. Have the other group members give their interpretations of the sketch before the artist shares his. This activity is important because it allows readers who struggle with verbally oriented procedures to demonstrate understanding and alternative interpretations. Examples are presented in Figure 5.8.

To provide a technology component for this activity, students can use a drawing app to create their artwork and then post it to a class website, blog, or wiki. Available apps include Sketchbook Express, Paper, and Infinite Design.

figure **5.8** Example sketches for Sketch to Stretch.

Sketch for <u>Fox Song</u>

Sketch for <u>The Bracelet</u>

activity Going Beyond Visualizing

This activity encourages the reader to use all senses to comprehend and respond to text, not just visualizing. Direct readers to create mental images that involve all five senses when they read. Using the sentence starters I see . . . , I hear . . . , I feel . . . , I smell . . . , and I taste . . . , ask students to write, tell, or draw what they saw, heard, felt, smelled, and tasted as they were reading.

The sentences one fifth-grade student generated after reading a *National Geographic* article about sea turtles follow:

I see turtles trying to get to the water. Thousands.

I hear the sound of thumping against their flippers.

I can feel all of the sand kicking into my eyes.

Some turtles died so I can smell the rot.

I can taste other turtles' backs. I can taste sand flinging into my open mouth.

(HARVEY & GOUDVIS, 2000, P. 104)

Graphic organizers

Graphic organizers, defined in Chapter 4 as visual ways of representing a body of knowledge, can also be used to help students focus their thoughts for responding to text. In general, they help students

- categorize words, ideas, and characters.
- organize a sequence of events.
- compare what they read to something else.
- identify important elements in a text.
- examine the organizational pattern of the information or story read.

Graphic organizers can use only drawings or pictures, only written words, or some combination of both. Examples of a target organizer (so called because of its shape) and a conversational roundtable (Burke, 2000) are presented in Figure 5.9. Here, the target organizer compares two versions of the same story, and the conversational roundtable demonstrates story features. Another alternative would be to use drawings instead of words. Generally speaking, organizers are flexible enough to be used for a variety of purposes. For example, the target organizer could also be used for vocabulary development by placing a word such as *independence* in the center of the target and writing other words in the next level that represent varying aspects of this concept. In the outermost circle, synonyms, antonyms, definitions, explanations, or instances of use could be written. Likewise, the conversational roundtable could be used to explore essential and nonessential characteristics, with examples and nonexamples for the concept located in the center circle. Additional examples of graphic organizers can be found in Chapters 4 and 7.

Reading Comprehension and Technology

Helping students understand what they are reading is a challenge that's made even more complex as evolving technologies call for *new literacies* (O'Brien & Bauer, 2005). New literacies require new skill sets. Furthermore, today's technological tools are changing so rapidly that teachers continually need to stay up to date, learning new digital literacy skills and new literacy practices.

Multimodal experiences are different than reading a page of text. The comprehension process tends to grow more complex when text includes many different forms of media. As mentioned earlier, ebook features may include video, audio, hyperlinks, and interactivity. Even tech-savvy students who are more comfortable than their teachers at navigating the various features—expanding font size, engaging with the text through annotation or recording sounds and adding graphics, attaching pictures, captions, and other texts—may need to be taught how to navigate them logically and how to "read" them effectively to comprehend the text.

If school and classroom practices are not able to include the rich opportunities afforded by technology and new literacies (if we have "digital disconnect"), we may find our students unmotivated and unengaged. One example of a new literacy tool that can be easily adapted for classroom use is **blogging,** or the online publication of commentary on specific topics of interest (e.g., political, social, and so forth). Blogging can present opportunities for changing literacy practices in schools (Lankshear & Knobel, 2003); for example, many blogs allow readers to respond interactively to its content. The websites listed in the margin offer examples of blogging resources for the classroom.

● blogging

Regarding changing literacy practices, Coiro (2003) summarizes,

> Reading on the Internet is different, and our definition of reading comprehension needs to reflect those differences. Our job now is to envision new constructs of reading comprehension that introduce students to strategies for interacting with these new literacies. We must help students appreciate the distinctions of each one and also be willing to explore digital information environments together in more thoughtful ways. (p. 464)

The RAND Reading Study Group (2002) suggests the following definition for reading comprehension: "The process of simultaneously extracting and constructing meaning through interaction and involvement with written language" (p. 11). Although this definition seems similar to the traditional notion of reading comprehension, the report goes on to recognize a broad description of text, including electronic text and multimedia documents as well as conventional print. "Electronic

WWW●○○

Setting Up a Classroom Blog

http://kidblog.org/home/

http://edublogs.org/

http://www.teachhub.com/setting-classroom-blog

Check Out These Class Blogs

http://theedublogger.com/check-out-these-class-blogs/

7th Grade Science Blog

http://newliteracies.typepad.com/science_exchange

figure **5.9** Graphic organizers: Target organizer and conversational roundtable.

Target Organizer

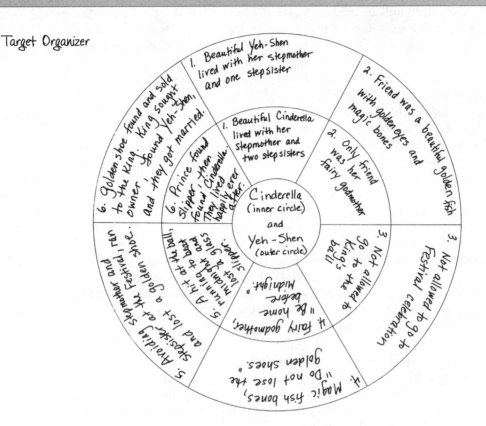

Conversational Roundtable

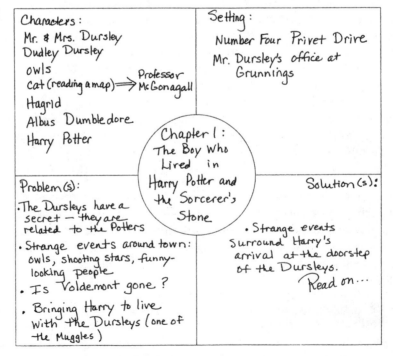

Characters:
Mr. & Mrs. Dursley
Dudley Dursley
owls
Cat (reading a map) ⟹ Professor McGonagall
Hagrid
Albus Dumbledore
Harry Potter

Setting:
Number Four Privet Drive
Mr. Dursley's office at Grunnings

Chapter 1:
The Boy Who Lived in Harry Potter and the Sorcerer's Stone

Problem(s):
· The Dursleys have a secret — they are related to the Potters
· Strange events around town: owls, shooting stars, funny-looking people
· Is Voldemont gone?
· Bringing Harry to live with the Dursleys (one of the Muggles)

Solution(s):
· Strange events surround Harry's arrival at the doorstep of the Dursleys.

Read on...

text can present particular challenges to comprehension, such as dealing with the nonlinear nature of hypertext, but it also offers the potential for supporting the comprehension of complex texts, for example, through hyperlinks to definitions or translations of difficult words or to paraphrasing of complex sentences" (p. 14). The use of electronic text requires skills and abilities that are different from those required for conventional, linear print (Coiro & Schmar-Dobler, 2005). Skill areas that are among the most important to online reading comprehension and the use of the Internet include: "identify important questions, locate information, analyze the usefulness of that information, synthesize information to answer those questions, and then communicate the answers to others" (Leu, Kinzer, Coiro, & Cammack, 2004, p. 1570). Additionally, Azevedo and Cromley (2004) provide evidence that instruction in comprehension monitoring (realizing when something one has just read has been understood or not, and making needed adjustments to ensure understanding) transfers well to learning in hypermedia.

Students who are self-regulated learners understand their strengths and weaknesses as learners.

Reciprocal teaching, a technique already presented in this chapter, is appropriate for reading comprehension instruction for online resources because it helps develop a high level of self-regulated learning. **Self-regulated learning** (SRL) is a process that requires awareness and application of learning strategies and extensive reflection and self-awareness. Pintrich (1995) describes self-regulation as the "active, goal-directed self-control of behavior, motivation, and cognition for academic tasks by an individual student" (p. 5). Students who are self-regulated learners understand their strengths and weaknesses as learners. They are skilled at recognizing the demands of the specific academic tasks required of them, and they know when they have mastered the tasks or not (Isaacson & Fujita, 2006). For the academic task of reading comprehension, this ability is referred to as *comprehension monitoring;* thus, comprehension monitoring is closely related to SRL.

- self-regulated learning

A large body of research findings exists supporting reciprocal teaching as effective for teaching reading comprehension strategies and improving reading comprehension, especially among adolescents (Palincsar & Herrenkohl, 2002; Rosenshine & Meister, 1994). Research by Leu, Castek, Hartman, et al. (2005), however, clearly supports the use of intensive small group instruction especially when using reciprocal teaching for developing online reading comprehension skills. Their research also found that, when it came to traditional measures of reading comprehension, groups that received special online instruction did not outperform groups that received instruction without online access; this perhaps indicates both the need for alternative measures for online reading comprehension and the fact that the skills used during online learning are different.

Troubleshooting

S tudents of all ages can have difficulty with reading comprehension for a variety of reasons. Comprehension will obviously be difficult if the reader cannot quickly and automatically pronounce many of the words that she is trying to read. In addition, the reader needs some prior knowledge of the topic being read to be able to adequately comprehend the material. Assuming the reader has access to material at an appropriate level of difficulty, she needs to be able to relate, or make connections, to the text for it to be meaningful. This is why the before-reading strategies are so important—to activate, build, or enhance background knowledge prior to beginning a lesson. Readers who have difficulty with comprehension often are not connecting to the text in a meaningful way. The following recommendations are for those students who have a difficult time making connections to the text.

Difficulty Making Connections Before Reading

anticipation guides ●

Students need to start thinking about connections to the text even before they begin to read. Used before reading, **anticipation guides** consist of a set of three to five statements that serve two basic purposes: (1) to activate the student's background knowledge for the topic by asking the student to either agree or disagree with the statement and then be prepared to explain her position, and (2) to provide guidance for the upcoming reading. Anticipation guides are also intended to arouse curiosity about the topic by presenting statements that are potentially controversial or challenging. Students become motivated to read the material to prove their choice or to resolve conceptual conflicts or lack of understanding. The anticipation guide can thus also serve as an after-reading activity, to revisit the statements and allow for changes in viewpoints.

You prepare an anticipation guide by

- reading the text to identify the major concepts students should learn.
- considering students' current knowledge about these concepts.
- creating statements in a way that students have sufficient knowledge to understand what they say, but not enough to conceptually understand the statements or the rationale behind them.
- listing the statements in a particular order—one that follows the order presented in the text is usual, but it's not mandatory.

Once completed, the anticipation guide can be presented as an individual handout accompanied by a visual; use an overhead transparency or image that's shown on an interactive whiteboard. Read aloud the directions and the statements for the students, who should respond individually to each statement by agreeing or disagreeing, and explaining why. In order to do this, students must make connections to their own background knowledge related to the topic they are about to read. A group discussion follows after you tally the responses for agreement and disagreement with each statement. Discussion should include at least one explanation for each point of view. Following this discussion, students read the material, keeping the anticipation guide in mind. After the reading, the students may return to the guide and respond once more. This time they will have the actual text to use to support or refute points expressed in the earlier discussion (Bean, Readence, Baldwin, 2011; Duffelmeyer, 1994). Figure 5.10 shows an anticipation guide for a book entitled *Outside and Inside You* (Markle, 1991), which is used with struggling readers to help them learn more about their bodies.

Difficulty Making Connections During Reading

Comprehension improves when students actively seek to connect the content of what they are reading with what they already have experienced or have learned (Brown, 2002). The strategy called "It reminds me of . . ." (Richards & Gipe,

Anticipation guide for use with *Outside and Inside You.*   *figure* **5.10**

Directions: Below are some statements about parts of your body. Read each statement carefully and write Agree or Disagree on the line before each statement. Be prepared to explain why you agree or disagree with the statement.

_____ 1. If you scrub too hard, you might wash your skin away.

_____ 2. Muscles are more important than bones.

_____ 3. You don't really see with your eyes, but with your brain.

_____ 4. It would be best if you just drank liquids to nourish your body.

1992) encourages students to make connections verbally between what they read and their background knowledge *while they are reading.* To be able to state what the passage "reminds me of . . . ," the student has to make a connection between the material and his own background knowledge.

Model this strategy by reading a portion of a text selection, stopping, and saying aloud, "It reminds me of . . .". Modeling works best if realistic fiction, a memoir, or a version of a familiar tale is used because these will be more likely to provide situations that readers can recall or relate to in their own lives. For example, the story *Fox Song* (Bruchac, 1993) tells of a young girl whose beloved grandmother has recently died. As the girl walks around her community, she is constantly reminded of the things they did together, and what she learned from her grandmother. After reading an early section of how sad the girl feels when she is told of her grandmother's death, you might say, "It reminds me of the time when I heard my mother on the phone with my grandmother. She had just learned that my grandfather—her father—had died. This sad, empty feeling just came over me." Then students are given the opportunity to respond to the same passage. You might also use just the cover of a book and consider what it reminds you of as a way of modifying this activity for use during prereading. After a few examples, students will soon be able to identify parts in other content with which they connect.

Similarly, you might introduce students to the double entry journal with the specific purpose of making connections to the text being read. Bromley (1993) defines a **double entry journal** as "one in which students keep two separate entries related to the same topic, idea, or activity" (p. 71). The main purpose of the double entry journal is to encourage students to make connections between the material they are reading and their own lives, another text they have already read, or world issues and current events outside their community. Introduce the double entry journal by first dividing a journal page into two columns and then selecting a quote from an assigned reading. Write the quote in the left column and then model a personal response in the corresponding right column. Then ask your students to read a portion of the material until they find a sentence that causes them to recall a particular event in their own lives. Direct them to write the sentence in the left column and their personal connections in the right column.

● double entry journal

It is easiest to introduce double entry journals using personal connections (i.e., text-to-self connections) as a way of responding to text. In addition, Herrell and Jordan (2002) suggest

As students become more proficient in responding to text, they can be taught to connect other books they have read to the text currently being read. They can also learn to relate current events to reading materials in this same way. In the process they practice writing skills. The discussions that follow the journaling are equally important because they support the students in understanding the impact of life experiences in the way text is interpreted and valued. (p. 99)

See Figure 5.11 for an example of a page from a double entry journal demonstrating a format for making connections to self, to text, and to the world (also see the following section for more on text-to-text and text-to-world connections).

Difficulty Making Connections After Reading

The possibilities for making connections following the reading are many. The simplest connections are most likely to be to our own experiences. These text-to-self connections come more naturally and are similar to the "it reminds me of . . ." during-reading connections. But we also can make connections to other things we

figure **5.11** Example page from a double entry journal for making connections.

BOOK	CONNECTIONS
Title: The Giver (Lois Lowry)	Text-to-Me/Text-to-Another Text/Text-to-World
Date: 3/13 Page(s): 1–2	Me ✓ Another Text ____ World ____
Then all the citizens had been ordered to go into the nearest building and stay there. IMMEDIATELY, the rasping voice through the speakers had said. LEAVE YOUR BICYCLES WHERE THEY ARE.	I remember one time when there was a tornado warning while I was at school. We all had to drop everything and go down to the cafeteria because there were no windows there. I was scared because I did not know what would happen.
Date: 3/14 Page(s): 5–7	Me ____ Another Text ____ World ✓
"I feel a little sorry for him," Jonas said, "even though I don't even know him. I feel sorry for anyone who is in a place where he feels strange and stupid."	I bet all the people who come here from other countries feel strange and stupid when they first come. We should think of ways to help the Mexican immigrants who are coming to our town feel welcome.
Date: 3/15 Page(s): 8–10	Me ____ Another Text ✓ World ____
"I know there's really nothing to worry about," Jonas explained, "and that every adult has been through it. . . . But it's the Ceremony that I'm apprehensive about."	This reminds me of the Harry Potter books and the Sorting Hat Ceremony for finding out what house new students would live with while at Hogwarts School.
Date: 3/16 Page(s): 18–19	Me ✓ Another Text ____ World ____
But her father had already gone to the shelf and taken down the stuffed elephant which was kept there. Many of the comfort objects, like Lily's, were soft, stuffed, imaginary creatures.	I still like to hug my stuffed dog when I'm feeling sad, so it is my comfort object.

have read, or to events that happen in the world. Some common types of text-to-text connections, from easiest to more difficult, include

- comparing characters, their personalities, and their actions.
- comparing story events and plot lines.
- comparing lessons, themes, or messages in stories.
- finding common themes, writing style, or perspectives in the work of a single author.
- comparing the treatment of common themes by different authors.
- comparing different versions of familiar stories. (Harvey & Goudvis, 2000, p. 73)

You can model text-to-text connections by choosing to share books that have similar themes, or that are two versions of the same story. It is best to model with the easier material first. For example, read the more familiar *Little Red Riding Hood* and then share *Lon Po Po*, a Chinese version of the same story (Young, 1989). These books would not be too difficult for struggling readers to grasp the connections. After practice with easy material, students will be better able to identify the similarities, and make connections, between more age-appropriate stories. A **T-chart** (a two-column chart for comparing information) can be used to list the connections, with you beginning the list and students contributing to it (see Figure 5.12 for an example using two books about the Holocaust).

● T-chart

As students become comfortable making text-to-self and text-to-text connections, they may naturally begin to make connections to more global issues, or they can be encouraged to make these text-to-world connections through modeling. Additionally, as Harvey and Goudvis (2000) point out, "Encouraging students to make text-to-world connections supports our efforts to teach students about social studies and science concepts and topics" (p. 75). They share an example of a fourth/fifth-grade teacher who introduced *The Lotus Seed* (Garland, 1997) to his students. This book relates the story of a Vietnamese family fleeing their home for the United States during the Vietnam War. Most students had little knowledge about, or direct experience with, the content of this book, but there was one particular text-to-self connection that enabled the teacher to illustrate a text-to-world connection. As the class discussed the book, one student shared, "My grandfather fought in Vietnam and he told me all about it." In response to this statement, another student looked rather confused and then looked back to a picture in the book that showed bombs falling on a rice paddy. She exclaimed, "You mean *we* were the ones dropping the bombs on Vietnam?" At this point the teacher interjected with a text-to-world connection and some information about the war: "The rice paddy is probably in North Vietnam and U.S. planes may have been doing the bombing. The North Vietnamese were fighting for communism and the South Vietnamese were fighting for freedom."

It is important to note that these connections can often overlap. It is not that crucial for students to accurately distinguish among what is a text-to-self, text-to-text, or text-to-world connection, or to come up with a long list of these connections. In the process of contemplating and making some connections, students begin to monitor their understanding, think about what they are reading, and thus enhance their comprehension. That is the purpose.

Summary

C omprehension is the reason we read. But comprehension cannot occur without the simultaneous use of all the language cue systems (semantic, syntactic, graphophonemic). That is, the reader has to construct meaning from the words that

figure **5.12** T-chart of text-to-text connections for *Hana's Suitcase* and *The Diary of a Young Girl*, two books about the Holocaust.

Hana's Suitcase (by Karen Levine)	*The Diary of a Young Girl* (by Anne Frank)
written about Hana by someone else (biography)	written as a diary by Anne herself—Anne received the diary on her 13th birthday, June 12, 1942 (autobiography)
Born Jewish on May 16, 1931, Hana Brady was 13 when she died on October 23, 1944.	Born Jewish on June 12, 1929, Anne Frank was 15 when her diary stopped on August 1, 1944.
Hana, her older brother George, and her parents lived in Nove Mesto, Moravia, Czechoslovakia.	Anne, her older sister Margot, and her parents lived in Amsterdam, Netherlands.
Hana's mother was arrested and sent to a women's concentration camp in Germany.	Fearing arrest, Anne's family made plans for a hiding place. They stored canned foods and books in the hiding place.
Soon after, Hana's father was arrested.	When Anne's father and sister received notices from the SS, it was time to hide.
Hana and George went to live with their aunt and uncle until ordered to report to a deportation center. Hana turned 11 while at the center.	On July 9, 1942, Anne's family went into hiding in the Secret Annex. They could no longer go outside. Friends helped them get food.
Hana and George were separated into housing for boys and for girls at a camp in Theresienstadt (or Terezin).	On July 13, 1942, another family of three, Mr. and Mrs. Van Daan and their son Peter, came to hide in the Secret Annex (their real name was Van Pels). Later, a dentist, Albert Dussel (Fritz Pfeffer) joined them to make eight people in the small annex.
Hana loved her mother very much and missed her terribly.	Anne's relationship with her mother was not very good, and it did not improve while they lived in their small space.
Hana spent her days in the camp attending art, music, and sewing classes. Art class was her favorite.	Anne spent her days in the annex doing schoolwork, reading, and being quiet.
Theresienstadt was becoming too crowded, and George was sent away.	Only days before they were found, Anna was hopeful about going back to school in October.
Four weeks after George went away, Hana was sent to Auschwitz, and the gas chamber.	Anne was taken to Bergen-Belsen at the end of October, 1944, where she died in late February or early March, 1945—about 3 months short of her 16th birthday.
George survived and returned to Nove Mesto to learn his parents and Hana were all dead. George shared Hana's story with students and teachers in Tokyo.	Otto Frank, Anne's father, was the only member of her family to survive. He made sure his daughter's diary was published. Anne's diary was first published in 1947. Otto Frank died in 1980.

have been decoded while simultaneously connecting what is read to prior knowledge as well as connecting new information to previously known information. It is a complex and arduous process best consummated through a program that offers guidance in specific comprehension strategies and many opportunities to apply them with quality literature as well as expository text. For a literacy program to be balanced and comprehensive, it must not only enable learners to decode text, but also offer them guidance in strategic reading and provide ample opportunities for independent reading using techniques such as those presented in this chapter.

Questions FOR JOURNAL WRITING AND DISCUSSION

1. Think about what you do when you read. What comprehension strategies did you use while reading this chapter? Make a list of the strategies you can identify. Then spend a few minutes reading a novel or other narrative material. Make a second list, this time of the strategies you used with the narrative text. Compare the two lists. Are there major differences between the two? Discuss the lists with your classmates.

2. Prepare an argument for why you should allow students in your classroom to have time to read self-selected material and discuss it in small groups. How would you change this argument for your administrator and for a parent?

3. How does your definition of reading impact the importance of comprehension instruction to your total reading program?

4. Reflect on a teacher you know who uses technology in creative and instructive ways for reading instruction with his or her students. With regard to technology, what is this teacher doing that is effective?

5. Locate examples of digital-text websites and construct a lesson using one of the sites and one of the instructional activities presented in this chapter.

Suggestions FOR PROJECTS AND FIELD ACTIVITIES

1. Choose several representative printed materials that students in grades 4–8 are expected to read. Determine their readability levels using the Fry Readability Graph, and look carefully at the demands of the text overall, considering sophistication and text complexities. Discuss this information with a classroom teacher. What other possible factors would make these materials more or less readable than the graph indicates?

2. Select one of the comprehension strategies from this chapter. Locate a reading selection that would be appropriate material for teaching this strategy. Teach the strategy to a small group of your classmates. Discuss their reactions. How would you modify your teaching for grade 4–8 students? What feedback helped you the most?

3. Teach a comprehension strategy to a small group of students or to an individual student. Did they have any problems with the lesson? Did you have any problems with the lesson? What did the students like and dislike about the strategy? Discuss the results with your class.

4. Observe a classroom teacher during reading lessons for at least five days (try to observe a full week, or different days). Make a list of all the activities the teacher and students engage in during this time. Keep track of how much time is spent on each activity. How much time was spent on direct teaching of comprehension strategies? How much time was spent on the application of these strategies? How much time was spent on actual reading by the students? What did you learn from these observations?

Altwerger, B., Jordan, N. C., & Shelton, N. R. (2007). *Rereading fluency: Process, practice, and policy.* Portsmouth, NH: Heinemann.

Anderson, R., Hiebert, E., Scott, J., & Wilkerson, I. (1985). *Becoming a nation of readers.* Washington, DC: National Institute of Education.

Aronson, E., & Patnoe, S. (2011). *Building cooperation in the classroom: The jigsaw method* (3rd ed.). London: Pinter & Martin.

Ash, K. (2010). Schools Test E-Reader Devices With Dyslexic Students. *Education Week.* Retrieved from Digital Directions, www.edweek.org/dd/articles/2010/10/20/01dyslexia.h04.html

Azevedo, R., & Cromley, J. G. (2004). Does training on self-regulated learning facilitate students' learning with hypermedia? *Journal of Educational Psychology, 96*(3), 523–535.

Beach, R. (1993). *A teacher's introduction to reader-response theories.* Urbana, IL: National Council of Teachers of English.

Bean, T. W., Readence, J. E., & Baldwin, R. S. (2011). *Content area literacy: An integrated approach* (10th ed.). Dubuque, IA: Kendall/Hunt.

Beck, I. L., McKeown, M. G., Hamilton, R. L., & Kucan, L. (1997). *Questioning the author: An approach for enhancing student engagement with text.* Newark, DE: International Reading Association.

Biancarosa, G., & Snow, C. E. (2006). Reading next: A vision for action and research in middle and high school literacy: A report to Carnegie Corporation of New York (2nd ed.). Washington, DC: Alliance for Excellent Education.

Brenner, J. (2012, April 27). Pew Internet: Teens. Retrieved from http://pewinternet.org/Commentary/2012/April/Pew-Internet-Teens.aspx

Bromley, K. (1993). *Journaling: Engagements in reading, writing and thinking.* New York: Scholastic.

Brooks, W. (2006). Reading representations of themselves: Urban youth use culture and African American textual features to develop literary understandings. *Reading Research Quarterly, 41,* 372–392.

Brown, R. (2002). Straddling two worlds: Self-directed comprehension instruction for middle schoolers. In C.C. Block & M. Pressley (Eds.), *Comprehension instruction: Research-based best practices* (pp. 337–350). New York: Guilford.

Bruchac, J. (1993). *Fox song.* (P. Morin, Illus.). New York: Putnam.

Burke, J. (2000). *Reading reminders: Tools, tips, and techniques.* Portsmouth, NH: Boynton/Cook.

Cecil, N. L. (1990). Read a book in an hour: A smooth transition to multi-chaptered texts. *Reading Improvement, 27*(3), 188–191.

Cecil, N. L. (1995). *The art of inquiry: Questioning strategies for K–6 classrooms.* Winnipeg, Manitoba: Peguis.

Childrey, J. (1980). Read a book in an hour. *Reading Horizons, 20,* 174–176.

Clarke, L. W., & Holwadel, J. (2007). "Help! What is wrong with these literature circles and how can we fix them?" *The Reading Teacher, 6*(1), 20–29.

Coiro, J. (2003). Reading comprehension on the Internet: Expanding our understanding of reading comprehension to encompass new literacies. *The Reading Teacher, 56,* 458–464.

Coiro, J., & Schmar-Dobler, B. (2005). Reading comprehension on the Internet: Exploring the comprehension strategies used by sixth-grade skilled readers as they search for and locate information on the Internet. Manuscript submitted to *Reading Research Quarterly.*

Cunningham, J. W. (1982). Generating interactions between schemata and text. In J. A. Niles & L.A. Harris (Eds.), *New inquiries in reading research and instruction* (pp. 42–47).Thirty-first Yearbook of the National Reading Conference. Washington, DC: National Reading Conference.

DaLie, S. O. (2001). Students becoming real readers: Literature circles in high school English classes. In B.O. Ericson (Ed.), *Teaching reading in high school English classes.* Urbana, IL: NCTE, 84–100.

Daniels, H. (2002). *Literature circles: Voice and choice in book clubs and reading groups* (2nd ed.). York, ME: Stenhouse.

Dantonio, M., & Beisenherz, P. C. (2001). *Learning to question, questioning to learn: Developing effective teacher questioning practices.* Boston: Allyn and Bacon.

Davey, B. (1983). Think aloud—Modeling the cognitive processes of reading comprehension. *The Reading Teacher, 27,* 44–47.

Demski, J. (2010). The device versus the book. *Campus Technology.* Retrieved from http://campustechnology.com/articles/2010/05/01/the-device-versus-the-book.aspx

Dobler, E., Johnson, D., & Wolsey, T. D. (2013). *Teaching the language arts: Forward thinking in today's classrooms.* Scottsdale, AZ: Holcomb Hathaway.

Draper, D. (2010a). Comprehension strategies: Making connections. Retrieved from https://curriculumdepot.wikispaces.com/file/view/Making_Connections_Strateg.pdf[0]

Draper, D. (2010b). Comprehension strategies: Visualizing. Retrieved from www.decd.sa.gov.au/northernadelaide/files/links/4_VisualisingBooklet.pdf

Duffelmeyer, F. A. (1994). Effective anticipation guide statements for learning from expository prose. *Journal of Reading, 37,* 452–457.

Duffy, G. G. (2002). The case for direct explanation of strategies. In C. C. Block & M. Pressley (Eds.), *Comprehension instruction: Research-based best practices* (pp. 28–41). New York: Guilford.

Duke, N. K., & Pearson, P. D. (2002). Effective practices for developing reading comprehension. In A. E. Farstup & S. J. Samuels (Eds.), *What research has to say about reading instruction* (pp. 205–242). Newark, DE: International Reading Association.

Englert, C. S., & Thomas, C. C. (1987). Sensitivity to text structure in reading and writing: A comparison between learning disabled and non-learning disabled students. *Learning Disabilities Quarterly, 10*, 93–105.

Fielding, L., & Pearson, P. D. (1994). Reading comprehension: What works. Educational Leadership, 51(5), 62–68.

Fountas, I. C., & Pinnell, G. S. (2001). *Guiding readers and writers grades 3–6: Teaching comprehension, genre, and content literacy.* Portsmouth, NH: Heinemann.

Garland, S. (1997). *The lotus seed* (T. Kiuchi, Illus.). New York: Harcourt.

Gipe, J. P. (2013). *Multiple paths to literacy: Assessment and differentiated instruction for diverse learners, K–12* (8th ed.). Upper Saddle River, NJ: Pearson.

Graesser, A. C., McNamara, D. S., & Louwerse, M. M. (2003). What do readers need to learn in order to process coherence relations in narrative and expository text? In A. P. Sweet, & C. E. Snow (Eds.), *Rethinking reading comprehension* (pp. 82–98). New York: Guilford.

Hadaway, N., Vardell, S., & Young, T. (2004). *What every teacher should know about English learners.* Boston: Pearson.

Harris, T. L. & Hodges, R. E. (1995). *The literacy dictionary: The vocabulary of reading and writing.* Newark, DE: International Reading Association.

Harvey, S., & Goudvis, A. (2000). *Strategies that work: Teaching comprehension to enhance understanding.* York, ME: Stenhouse.

Herrell, A., & Jordan, M. (2002). *50 active learning strategies for improving reading comprehension.* Upper Saddle River, NJ: Pearson Merrill Prentice Hall.

Isaacson, R. M., & Fujita, F. (2006). Metacognitive knowledge monitoring and self-regulated learning: Academic success and reflections on learning. *Journal of the Scholarship of Teaching and Learning, 6*(1), 39–55.

Jorm, A. (1977). Effect of word imagery on reading performance as a function of reader ability. *Journal of Educational Psychology, 69,* 46–54.

Kajder, S. (2010). *Adolescents' digital literacies: Learning alongside our students.* Urbana, IL: NCTE Press.

Keene, E. (2008). *To understand: New horizons in reading comprehension.* Portsmouth, NH: Heinemann.

Kiefer, B. Z. (1995). *The potential of picture books: From visual literacy to aesthetic understanding.* Englewood Cliffs, NJ: Merrill Prentice Hall.

Klingner, J. K., & Vaughn, S. (1996). Reciprocal teaching of reading comprehension strategies for students with learning disabilities who use English as a second language. *Elementary School Journal, 96*(3), 275–293.

Lankshear, C., & Knobel, M. (2003). *New literacies: Changing knowledge and classroom learning.* Buckingham, UK: Open University Press.

Larson, L. C. (2009a). e-Reading and e-responding: New tools for the next generation of readers. *Journal of Adolescent & Adult Literacy, 53*(3), 255–258.

Larson, L. C. (2009b). Reader response meets new literacies: Empowering readers in online learning communities. *The Reading Teacher, 62*(8), 638–648.

Leu, D. J. Jr., Castek., J., Hartman, D., Coiro, J., Henry, L. A., Kulikowich, J. M., & Lyver, S. (2005). *Evaluating the development of scientific knowledge and new forms of reading comprehension during online learning.* Final report submitted to the North Central Regional Educational Laboratory, a subsidiary of Learning Point Associates (LPA).

Leu, D. J., Kinzer, C. K., Coiro, J., & Cammack, D. (2004).Toward a theory of new literacies emerging from the Internet and other information and communication technologies. In R. B. Ruddell & N. Unrau (Eds.), *Theoretical models and processes of reading* (5th ed., pp. 1568–1611). Newark, DE: International Reading Association.

Leu, D. J., Zawilinski, L., Castek, J., Banerjee, M., Housand, B., Liu, Y., & O'Neil, M. (2007). What is new about the new literacies of online reading comprehension? In A. Berger, L. Rush, & J. Eakle (Eds.), *Secondary school reading and writing: What research reveals for classroom practices.* National Council of Teachers of English/ National Conference of Research on Language and Literacy: Chicago, IL.

Liang, L. A., & Dole, J. A. (2006). Help with teaching reading comprehension: Comprehension instructional frameworks. *The Reading Teacher, 59,* 742–753.

Markle, S. (1991). *Outside and inside you.* New York: Scholastic.

McKeown, R. G., & Gentilucci, J. J. (2007). Think-aloud strategy: Metacognitive development and monitoring comprehension in the middle school second-language classroom. *Journal of Adolescent and Adult Literacy, 51*(2), 136–147.

McMahon, S. I., & Raphael, T. E. (1997). The book club program: Theoretical and research foundations. In S. I. McMahon & T. E. Raphael (Eds.), *The book club connection: Literacy learning and classroom talk* (pp. 3–25). New York: Teachers College Press.

McTaggert, J. (2006). *The graphic novel: Everything you ever wanted to know but were afraid to ask.* Unpublished ms. available from author at www.theteachers desk.com.

National Governors Association Center for Best Practices (NGACBP) & Council of Chief State School Officers (CCSSO) (2010). Common Core State Standards: English Language Arts & Literacy in History/Social Studies, Science, and Technical Subjects. (Appendix A: Research Supporting Key Elements of the Standards; Appendix B: Exemplars of Reading Text Complexity, Quality, and Range & Sample Performance Tasks Related to Core Standards.) Washington, DC: National Governors Association Center for Best Practices, Council of Chief State School Officers.

Nation's Report Card: Reading 2011 (2011). Retrieved from http://nces.ed.gov/nationsreportcard/pubs/main2011/2012457.asp

O'Brien, D. G., & Bauer, E. B. (2005). New literacies and the institution of old learning. *Reading Research Quarterly, 40,* 120–131.

Ohlhausen, M., & Jepson, M. (1992). Lessons from Goldilocks: "Somebody's been choosing my books but I can make my own choices now!" *The New Advocate, 5,* 31–46.

Palincsar, A. (1987, January). Reciprocal teaching: Can student discussions boost comprehension? *Instructor,* 56–60.

Palincsar, A. S., & Brown, A. L. (1984). Reciprocal teaching of comprehension-fostering and comprehension-monitoring activities. *Cognition and Instruction, 1*(2), 117–175.

Palincsar, A. S., & Brown, A. L. (1986). Interactive teaching to promote independent learning from text. *The Reading Teacher, 39,* 771–777.

Palincsar, A. S., & Herrenkohl, L. R. (2002). Designing collaborative learning contexts. *Theory Into Practice, 41*(1), 26–32.

Pearson, P. D., & Gallagher, M. (1983). The instruction of reading comprehension. *Contemporary Educational Psychology, 8,* 317–344.

Pintrich, P. R. (1995). Understanding self-regulated learning. In P. R. Pintrich (Ed.), *Understanding self-regulated learning* (pp. 3–12). San Francisco, CA: Jossey-Bass.

Pressley, M. (2000). Comprehension instruction in elementary school: A quarter-century of research progress. In B. Taylor, M. Graves, & P. Van den Broek (Eds.), *Reading for meaning: Fostering comprehension in the middle grades* (pp. 32–51). New York: Teachers College Press.

Pressley, M. (2002). Comprehension strategies instruction: A turn-of-the-century status report. In C. C. Block & M. Pressley (Eds.), *Comprehension instruction: Research-based best practices* (pp. 11–27). New York: Guilford.

RAND Reading Study Group (2002). *Reading for understanding: Toward an R & D program in reading comprehension.* Santa Monica, CA: RAND.

Raphael, T. E. (1982). Question-answering strategies for children. *The Reading Teacher, 36,* 186–190.

Raphael, T. E. (2000). Balancing literature and instruction: Lessons from the Book Club Project. In B. Taylor, M. Graves, & P. Van den Broek (Eds.), *Reading for meaning: Fostering comprehension in the middle grades* (pp. 70–94). New York: Teachers College Press.

Raphael, T. E., & Au, K. H. (2005). QAR: Enhancing comprehension and test taking across grades and content areas. *The Reading Teacher, 59,* 206–221.

Raphael, T. E., & McMahon, S. I. (1994). Book club: An alternative framework for reading instruction. *The Reading Teacher, 48*(2), 102–116.

Richards, J. C., & Gipe, J. P. (1992). Activating background knowledge: Strategies for beginning and poor readers. *The Reading Teacher, 45,* 474–476.

Rosenblatt, L. (1938). *Literature as exploration.* New York: Appleton-Century. Reprinted, 1995. New York: Modern Language Association.

Rosenblatt. L. (1969). Towards a transactional theory of reading. *Journal of Reading Behavior, 1*(1), 31–51.

Rosenblatt, L. M. (1978). *The reader, the text, the poem.* Carbondale: Southern Illinois University Press.

Rosenblatt, L. M. (1983). *Literature as exploration.* New York: The Modern Languages Association of America.

Rosenblatt, L. M. (1994). The transactional theory of reading and writing. In R. B. Ruddell, M. R. Ruddell, & H. Singer (Eds.), *Theoretical models and processes of reading* (4th ed., pp. 1057–1092). Newark, DE: International Reading Association.

Rosenshine, B., & Meister, C. (1994). Reciprocal teaching: A review of the research. *Review of Educational Research, 64,* 479–530.

Scholastic (2010). 2010 kids and family reading report: Turning the page in the digital age. Retrieved from http://mediaroom.scholastic.com/themes/bare_bones/2010_Kfrr.pdf

Schrock, K. (2006). E-Readers: Can electronic books help reluctant readers? *Interactive Educator, 2*(2), 10–11. Retrieved from http://downloads01.smarttech.com/media/education/pdf/ ieautumn06.pdf

Short, C., Harste, J., & Burke, C. (1995). *Creating classrooms for authors and inquirers* (2nd ed.). Portsmouth, NH: Heinemann.

Stauffer, R. G. (1975). *Directing the reading-thinking process.* New York: Harper & Row.

Van den Broek, P. W. (1990). The causal inference maker: Towards a process model of inference generation in text comprehension. In D. A. Balota, G. B. Flores d'Arcais, & K. Rayner (Eds.), *Comprehension processes in reading* (pp. 423–445). Hillsdale, NJ: Erlbaum.

Van den Broek, P. W., Risden, K., Fletcher, C. R., & Thurlow, R. (1996). A "landscape" view of reading: Fluctuating patterns of activation and the construction of a stable memory representation. In B. K. Britton & A. C. Graesser (Eds.), *Models of understanding text* (pp. 165–187). Mahwah, NJ: Erlbaum.

Vygotsky, L. S. (1978). *Mind in society.* Cambridge, MA: MIT Press.

Vygotsky, L. S. (1986). *Thought and language* (A. Kozulin, Trans.). Cambridge, MA: MIT Press.

Wilhelm, J. D. (1997). *"You gotta BE the book": Teaching engaged and reflective reading with adolescents.* New York: Teachers College Press.

Young, E. (1989). *Lon Po Po: A Red Riding Hood story from China.* Daly City, CA: Philomel.

SIX

Writing Instruction

FOCUS QUESTIONS

- What are the components for an effective writing program in grades 4–8?
- What is writing workshop, and how can it help students become skilled and motivated writers?
- How can teaching the 6 + 1 traits of effective writing provide a common vocabulary for both narrative and expository writing?
- What are the main components of writing fluency?

The students in Mrs. McCray's fifth-grade class have just returned from lunch. They eagerly head for the back of the classroom where the individually decorated writing folders are stored. Each student has a folder in which papers are kept related to the writing projects currently being worked on. As the students retrieve their folders, they quickly sit down at their desks, arranged in small groups. Three students sit at computers, using a word-processing program to print out the final drafts of pieces they have been working on all week. Some students quietly discuss new writing ideas with classmates. Other students write intently, while still others share their drafts with their classmates—or "peer editors"—who offer suggestions about content or writing conventions, as requested by the author. Everyone is focused and clearly on task, yet working at their own pace.

At her desk, Mrs. McCray conferences briefly with several students; the rest of the students will be engaged in similar encounters over the remainder of the week. During these one- to two-minute sessions, Mrs. McCray asks individual students to talk about what they are writing, listens to them read a paragraph or two of their work, and questions them about what they are planning to do next. Hoa, for example, explains that yesterday she received valuable input from her peer editor, so she is now going to correct spelling mistakes and add a more exciting opening idea that will better "grab" her audience.

Other students are at the revising stage of writing. Jesse and Alyce sign up to meet with Mrs. McCray so that she can offer feedback about the strengths of their current work and ask questions about ideas that may be unclear. Sometimes Mrs. McCray also offers suggestions for improvement, and the two collaborators—the teacher and the author—decide if the suggestions are compatible with what the author is trying to say.

After a half hour, Mrs. McCray calls the whole class together in a circle in a large section of the room. Brianne and Raúl, who have just finished the writing they have been working on, are ready to sit in the "author's chair" to read their finished pieces to the rest of the class. Although a couple of classmates propose specific suggestions to each student, the rest of the class offers mostly praise and celebratory comments for the two completed writing projects—Brianne wrote a detailed description of Harriet Tubman's house that the class visited recently on a field trip, and Raúl wrote about an amusing autobiographical incident.

When all who wish to do so have shared their writing with the whole class, the students return to their desks and Mrs. McCray conducts a 10-minute minilesson. She usually focuses such lessons on writing strategies and skills that, from her charted observation of students' writing, she feels most students will find helpful and will allow them to move forward in their writing. Today, Mrs. McCray shows the students how to use quotation marks to express dialogue in conversation. She shows them a sample of a student's writing on an interactive whiteboard (examples are usually obtained from the preceding year's class). The writing is a conversation that is told second-hand, without the benefit of direct quotes. She guides students to see how much richer and more personal the writing seems with the addition of dialogue and quotation marks. For similar lessons, Mrs. McCray often shows excerpts from books the students are reading to demonstrate how published authors use the writing skills and strategies she is trying to depict.

How Instruction in Writing Has Changed

Our attitudes toward the teaching of writing have changed dramatically over the past 50 years. Many older adults recall writing homework compositions that were essentially a "one-shot deal." In those days, students would write a draft; turn it in to the teacher; and receive a grade, often based primarily on spelling, grammar, and handwriting. In the 1970s, researchers began to stop focusing solely on the writing *product* in such a simple manner and began to study how the entire *process* of writing can impact thinking. Among their most consistent findings was that students truly needed direct teaching at every stage of the writing process—to enable them to generate better ideas, to elaborate on those ideas, to organize their writing for a specific purpose or audience, to edit their work so that it was communicated effectively, and to develop their own style of writing (Block, 2001).

In the 1980s and 1990s, our knowledge expanded so that instruction went beyond assisting students to select topics, compose, and edit to eliminate errors.

In that era, students were instructed to adjust to new purposes and audiences and to revise their thoughts and ideas. Researchers of the time noted that "the problem with writing is not poor spelling, punctuation, grammar, and handwriting. The problem with students' writing is NO writing" (Stuart & Graves, 1987, p. 12). Today's researchers are still concerned with how little writing goes on in our schools (Applebee & Langer, 2009, 2011).

Instruction continues to move toward increasing students' abilities to generate thoughts and ideas and then, as a second but equally important concern, to communicate these ideas in written form, and to do so often. Moreover, for the student, writing requires specific kinds of critical thinking: questioning, citing evidence, evaluating content, and using one's own personal schema (Langer & Applebee, 1987, 2009). The Common Core State Standards recommend the following writing priorities: (1) students must be able to write "logical arguments based on substantive claims, sound reasoning, and relevant evidence"; (2) students must have mastered the ability to conduct research; and (3) across grade levels, students must be able to write in various genres including argumentative (opinion), narrative, and informational (NGACBP & CCSSO, 2010).

Today's teachers, more than ever before, consider the thinking processes that go into forming a final product and use the writing process as a vehicle to help students to think through the problems that all writers encounter. Mrs. McCray, the teacher in the chapter-opening vignette, is informed about current theories and research in the teaching of writing. She is also acquainted with the language arts framework and the standards—based on the CCSS—that her home state has set for grades 4–8. But what makes her students passionate about the hard work of drafting, revising, and editing a piece of writing is simply this: Mrs. McCray has created a literacy-centered classroom where reading and writing are not only connected but viewed as important life and career skills. This teacher gives her students plenty of opportunities to experience what it is like to share an engrossing writing topic with someone else. She is well aware that all the students in her class will be engaged with writing if they are allowed to explore a variety of topics in which they are interested. Above all, this teacher knows that it is all but impossible to resist the appreciation of a sincere and respectful audience (Cohle & Towle, 2001).

The Writing Process

Writers engage in a series of experiences to solve certain problems that are unique to a certain stage of writing; this is the writing process. It is exactly this problem-solving approach that makes the writing process more effective in creating thoughtful writers than more traditional approaches that focus solely on the finished product. By working through the writing process, with continuous and scaffolded support from a competent teacher/facilitator, students go through the stages published authors do; thus, they begin to think of themselves as authors themselves, a process that furthers their ability to construct meaning.

The writing process consists of five recursive stages, each of which should be explained and modeled for students (Gillet & Beverly, 2001). The stages are

1. planning/prewriting
2. composing/drafting
3. revising
4. editing
5. publishing

CONCEPT
guide

Although students will often follow the process through to the final reward of publication, *all* writing need not progress through each of these steps. At times, students may not be making progress with a piece of writing, or they may lose interest and decide to go in an entirely different direction with it. This can occur at any point in the writing process. Strive to make it clear that all writing does not have to be published. Student and teacher make the decision about publication together, after considering both the quality of the piece and how the student feels about it.

① Planning/Prewriting

The first stage of any writing effort is a "planning/prewriting" stage in which writers explore and then organize the ideas they feel passionate about—so much so that it will sustain the hard work to follow. This stage often includes a kind of mental *quick write* ● rehearsal that may emanate from a **quick write,** a rapid writing down of ideas about a topic. In most writing workshops, students in this stage are often allowed to select their own topics. Although this may seem easy because it is so wide open, it could leave many students wondering what to write about. Peha (1996) suggests having students take out a sheet of paper and divide it into two columns. In one column, students should make a list of all the things they really like; in the other, all the things they really detest. (This exercise can also be done electronically.) These topics can then lead to a whole-class discussion in which the teacher supports topic selection by making comments such as, "That sounds like a good topic to write about!" It is also a good idea for students to keep a list of topics (which can continue to grow) as part of their writing folder. Peha (1996) further suggests discussing with students exactly what makes an idea good enough to explore in written form. Tell students that their idea is worth pursuing if it is:

- *something you have strong feelings about.* What do you feel about the subject? Can you communicate those feelings to readers? How?
- *something you know a lot about.* What can you share with readers that they would be interested in knowing? What are the most important elements to tell readers?
- *something you are able to describe in great detail.* Why are these details important? Will they help readers see what you see and feel how you feel?
- *something your audience will be interested in.* Who is your audience? What could you tell them that will interest them most?
- *something your audience will feel was worth reading.* Will your audience learn something new from your piece? What will keep them reading all the way to the end?

Brainstorming

Another way to help students select ideas for writing is through brainstorming with a partner or with a larger group. This oral prewriting activity helps students, especially reluctant writers, bounce their ideas off other people and gain confidence that their idea is worth pursuing. Similarly, oral discussions on a topic before a writing workshop session can help students come up with their own intriguing ideas. For example, a teacher suggests a provocative topic such as, "What would it be like if everyone looked exactly the same?" Students then consider the pros and cons of such a scenario. Some muse that prejudice would disappear and people would be judged for their character rather than their looks; others suggest that such a world would be as boring as a garden with only one variety of flower. After much discussion, students are able to write a three-paragraph persuasive piece in which the first paragraph contains advantages of such a situation (the pros); the second, negatives (or cons); and the third, their own personal opinion.

An Effective Writing Program in Grades 4–8

Mrs. McCray and many other teachers across the country have found that it is possible to get students to become enthusiastic, capable writers with a writing program that is characterized by the following elements, which we elaborate on throughout the remainder of this chapter:

1. **Schedule plenty of time for writing.** Students need ample time to draft, share, and think about their writing. Donald Graves (2003) suggests that students write at least four days a week; less writing than that encourages poor habits, which often leads to a dislike of writing. Moreover, the time set aside should be predictable. When students know when they will be writing, they begin to anticipate and plan mentally for what they will write. Also, write with students; be part of the community of writers.

2. **Teach the writing process as a way to write.** The focus on the writing process is what writers think and do as they write. The process consists of prewriting/planning, composing and drafting, revising, editing, and publishing or sharing as a series of recursive cycles as students think through a piece of writing. Strive to model this process often with your own writing.

3. **Use writing workshop as a structure for writing.** Writing workshop encourages students to become a community of writers who write and share. You become a facilitator in the process.

4. **Provide feedback on students' writing through peer and teacher conferences.** When students are taught to provide critical feedback on each other's work, they become better able to evaluate their own writing. When students write for peers, even those who may be at a distant school, the quality of their work has been shown to be significantly better than if they write solely

for their teachers (Cohen & Riel, 1989). The teacher also provides information about each student's writing strengths and needs.

5. **Use the "6 + 1 traits" (Education Northwest, 1998/ 1999) to explain good writing in ways students can understand.** The important aspects of writing can be narrowed down to six essential traits—ideas, organization, voice, word choice, sentence fluency, and conventions—plus presentation, which can be taught to students so that they know exactly what good writing is and how to produce it themselves. Each trait can be discussed in minilessons and then practiced through authentic writing situations. Samples of students' writing or the writing of published authors can be used to point out how the samples exemplify, or do not exemplify, any one of the 6 + 1 traits.

6. **Develop clear, focused rubrics that are genre specific.** For example, for expository writing, create writing rubrics that assess supporting evidence, development, audience, cohesion, style, and conventions. Teach students what these terms mean and how to address them in their writing. In addition, consider working with your colleagues to develop a means to use these rubrics schoolwide and practice scoring student writing together. If any of your colleagues are unsure how to teach students to address an expository prompt, write an argument, and provide evidence to support it, use collaboration and professional development opportunities to help them provide better instruction. These interactions will help to identify schoolwide writing needs.

7. **Use authentic student writing as models and for assessment.** By examining real examples from students, teachers can show growth over time and identify upcoming instructional needs.

Clustering

Students may sketch a map of their ideas, or "cluster" them, to form a graphic outline that can then be filled in with details that flesh it out. Using the clustering technique, students start with their idea, which forms the nucleus of the cluster. Then, using a process akin to free association, they write down everything they can think of that relates to their topic. Many teachers report that this technique is helpful in assisting English learners and reluctant writers to plan their compositions effectively (Martinez, 1986). Figure 6.1 shows a cluster created

Education Northwest
http://educationnorthwest.org/resource

by a seventh-grader as she prepared to write her first draft of a four-paragraph essay about her sister, and the resultant essay. The same strategy can be used on the computer, using Inspiration software; this tool enables students to create graphic organizers—or "inspiration maps"—to help them plan and develop their writing.

figure **6.1** Cluster for "My Sister" and the resultant essay.

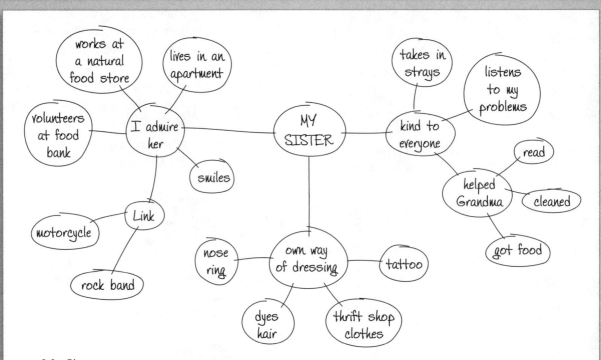

My Sister

The person I most admire in my family is my sister. My oldest sister, Jenna, is 20 years old and lives in an apartment with two other girls. She works at a natural food store and helps out at the food bank on weekends. She has a boyfriend named Link who rides a motorcycle and is in a rock band. When Jenna smiles, she lights up the room.

Jenna is always kind to everyone. When my grandma was sick, Jenna took time off from work to help her get groceries and clean her house. She read to her every single night. Also, Jenna takes in every stray animal that comes around and has always listened to my problems when I ask her to. Everyone is drawn to Jenna like a magnet.

My oldest sister has her own way of dressing. Some people say she looks like a punk, but I think she looks more like a rocker. She has a nose ring and a little wrist tattoo that looks like poison ivy. Even though she has a job, she wears old clothes that she buys at thrift shops. She changes her hair color about every month. It has been red, blue, and black. This month it is brown with red streaks. Jenna dresses for herself, not others.

When people first meet my sister they sometimes think she is weird. At times, they even call her names because she looks so different. Just because she looks different they should not judge her; they should take the time to get to know her. Her outside appearance may be strange, but inside she has a heart of gold. To know my oldest sister Jenna is to love her. If you met her you would see what I mean.

② Composing/Drafting

Composing, or drafting, is the stage in which writers develop their topic and actually translate their ideas into written form. A word-processing program is perfect for this stage, because later revisions can be easily accomplished. Students can use the Track Changes feature or create multiple copies of their writing at different stages so they can see what they have changed. Sometimes, in retrospect, one's original ideas may seem better than revised ones; thus, it is important for students to have access to those earlier ideas. If computers are not available, have students write their drafts on lined paper, using every other line, so that ample room is available for later revisions. Students should also be instructed not to erase but to draw one line through words or sentences they wish to change or delete; again, this will help them go back to see what they have changed.

③ Revising

Revising, in short, entails the "big changes." This is the step in the writing process that may require the most difficult work and generally encounters the most resistance. Revision requires reexamining content, word choice, and organization as well as rethinking the writing style with an emphasis on how effectively it communicates its intention to the audience.

Response guides

Revision can be initially introduced by showing students how to use a response guide to examine pieces of writing. A **response guide** offers specific compliments to and asks specific questions of the writer concerning the effectiveness of the writing. A sample response guide is shown in Figure 6.2. Students learn to read other students' writing more critically and effectively by framing the peer reviews using these starters, or frames.

• response guide

Using this or a similar response guide, you can display examples of bland or ineffective writing (decodable text is perfect for this purpose) on the interactive

---

Response guide.   *figure* **6.2**

COMPLIMENTS	QUESTIONS
I liked the part where . . .	Could you write an opening sentence to "grab" the reader?
You used some great words like . . .	
The imagery was effective in the sentence(s) . . .	Could you throw away these tired words . . . ?
I like the way you explained . . .	Is this paragraph all on one topic?
Your writing made me feel . . .	Do you need an ending that summarizes better?
I like the order you used in the piece because . . .	Are your paragraphs in the right order?
The dialogue was realistic when [the character] said . . .	Could you add more details to this part?
	I got confused in the part where . . .
Your writing made me more interested in this topic because . . .	Could you combine these sentences?
	Can you make this part clearer?
It was effective when you used _____ as an example.	Can you tell me more about . . . ?
	Could you leave this part out because . . . ?
I thought the most important part was . . .	

whiteboard and have students practice commenting on the writing by selecting appropriate phrases from the response guide. To extend this activity further, invite small groups of students to rewrite the piece and discuss with the class exactly how they have made the writing more effective.

Peer revising

peer revising ●

When students are adept at offering suggestions that are both helpful to the writer and appropriate to the piece of writing, they are ready to become active in peer revising. In **peer revising,** a writer who has drafted a piece selects a peer to provide constructive feedback in order to ensure the piece communicates its intent more effectively. By taking on the roles of author as well as revising peer, students not only get the benefit of an audience with whom to share their work, but also begin to learn how to evaluate a piece of writing objectively.

Cecil (2011) suggests that revising peers give their feedback to authors in written form using a format known as *PQP*, which stands for praise, question, and polish. Multiple copies can be made available to students so that when they are ready to share a draft and receive revision suggestions from a peer, this template makes the work easier. An example of a PQP form is shown in Figure 6.3.

④ Editing

During the editing stage of the writing process, the writer "cleans up" the spelling, punctuation, and other mechanics of the language that make the writing more accessible to readers. This step should take place only after the writer has

---

figure **6.3** PQP form for peer revising.

Author   Rachel   Title of Piece   Grandfather's watch

Peer Editor   John   Date   3/12

PRAISE: I particularly like these things about your piece of writing.

The beginning sentence made me really want to read on. I could really relate to what Nellie was feeling when she lost her watch. That happened to me once. I was actually worried she would get into trouble. By leaving the outcome until the end, you had me dying to find out what kind of punishment she would get.

QUESTION: These things were unclear to me.

Why didn't she just go back to the park and look for the watch? Wouldn't she have tried to do something about it? I also don't understand who Martin is. Is he her brother or just a friend?

POLISH: I have these suggestions to help make your piece even better.

Your dialogue is realistic but could you use another word besides said all the time. Maybe a word that explains more how Nellie is feeling. It might be helpful, also, to describe what Nellie looks like. You described other things about her so well that I care about her and would like to know if my mental image is correct.

made all the content changes he feels are necessary. During a minilesson, you and your students should make a list of grade-appropriate factors to look for in the editing stage; the list should then be prominently displayed in the classroom so that students can refer to it as they write and edit their work.

An example of a generic checklist is provided in Figure 6.4. Such a checklist can be used by the writer to edit his or her own writing as well as by a peer. The writer may ask the peer to look for specific problems or to look at the piece as a whole. The items on the checklist can be adjusted as needed to meet students' levels of writing sophistication.

⑤ Publishing

Publishing is the celebratory step in the writing process when you help students find many ways to share and disseminate their writing. This public phase of the writing process creates a sense of the real purpose of writing and allows students to feel genuine pride in their completed product. The more students publish their writing, the more they will develop a true sense of themselves as "authors," and the cycle begins to perpetuate itself. Soon, even reluctant writers become prolific.

Allowing students to enhance their efforts through visuals and sound and to provide attractive covers is part of the reward for the writer's accomplishment. Although the format may vary according to the type of piece, book form is one

---

Editing checklist.   *figure* **6.4**

AUTHOR: **PEER EDITOR:**

Author   Peer Editor

☐   ☐   1. Did I read the piece backwards, one sentence at a time, to check for spelling errors, sentence fragments, and run-on sentences?

☐   ☐   2. Did I use a dictionary, friend, spell checker, or other resource to find spelling errors?

☐   ☐   3. Did I check to make sure all proper nouns and the first word of each sentence are capitalized?

☐   ☐   4. Did I indent each paragraph?

☐   ☐   5. Did I make sure each sentence has the appropriate ending punctuation?

☐   ☐   6. Did I use commas appropriately? Are they used only for compound sentences, a list of items, an introductory word or phrase, to set off interruptions, to separate adjectives, or in dates?

☐   ☐   7. Do I need to add commas? Have I made sure commas are not separating complete sentences?

☐   ☐   8. Have I used apostrophes only for contractions or to show ownership?

☐   ☐   9. Have I used more complex punctuation (dashes, semicolons, hyphens, parentheses, etc.) correctly?

☐   ☐   10. Have I used common homonyms correctly, for example they're/their/there; your/you're; its/it's; too/two/to?

☐   ☐   11. Was I consistent in the use of either present or past tense in the entire piece?

☐   ☐   12. Was I consistent in my use of either first person or third person throughout the entire piece?

common way for students to publish their work. A laminated or cloth cover is appealing and sturdy enough to allow classmates to read the book many times. Or, students can decorate commercially made hard-cover blank books.

Besides sharing their final product with the class, other avenues for publication can help students feel that all their hard work was worthwhile. Work can be displayed on classroom bulletin boards and in special showcases around the school. Class or school newspapers are another way to highlight the work of individual students. Students can also post their work on a class website or wiki for the class to read, revise, and share. Student writing can be made even more public by inviting family members as well as teachers and students in other classes to view the writing posted online. Publishing websites for students (for example, Student Treasures) are also available to provide an even larger audience for student writing.

Student Treasures
www.studenttreasures.com

Writing Workshop

Writing workshops have been recommended by numerous researchers and practicing writing teachers (Atwell, 1998; Calkins, 2005; Hansen, 2001; Pritchard & Honeycutt, 2006; Smagorinsky, 2006). Descriptions of writing workshops appear in several seminal full-length books (see, e.g., Calkins, 1991; Calkins & Huron, 1987; Stuart & Graves, 1987). The workshop itself is a flexible plan that places students and teacher in a partnership for learning. Managing writing workshop cannot be reduced to a simple how-to formula; it is an ongoing, complex set of tasks that develop differently within the context of different classrooms (Peha, 1996).

Writing workshops that buzz with the activity of students working on a variety of tasks may, to an outsider, appear to be disorganized and chaotic. However, most of these classrooms are built on a firm, underlying structure. In most classrooms, writing workshop takes place two or three times a week, often alternating with a reading workshop or literature circles. The writing workshop approach to organizing a writing program can be conducted in three or four centers, or writing stations, through which students rotate to complete the writing stages discussed in the previous section. In smaller classrooms, as in the chapter-opening vignette, students can be completing all stages of writing at their desks. The writing workshop consists of four basic parts, and students' use of technology can enhance each part of the process.

① Minilessons

The minilesson is a focused lesson—typically done with the whole class—that usually lasts no more than 5 to 10 minutes. The content of this brief lesson is determined by what you have observed to be a writing need of most members of the class. Such lessons need not focus exclusively on isolated skills; instead, they could focus on a range of topics based on student needs. The only topics that should be addressed in these sessions are the 6 + 1 Traits of effective writing, discussed later in this chapter. Although there is no end to the possible topics for minilessons, here are examples of common topics that can be addressed:

- appropriate vocabulary and strategies for finding words
- how to determine when a paragraph is needed
- how to select specific tone or mood words to convey fear, sadness, and other emotions
- the conventions for a business letter or email
- procedures for writing workshop
- how to find and present evidence to support an argument

- how to select a topic that has relevance to the writer and the audience
- examples of imagery from young adult literature

To model the topic being addressed, prepare a good and/or poor example of the skill; this example might be obtained from literature that is familiar to students or from writing done by former students. Then discuss the example with the class.

② State-of-the-Class Conferences

For means of assessment and accountability, you may choose to build in a five-minute "state-of-the-class conference" once or twice a week to make sure you know exactly what each student will be doing during writing workshop. Using a chart such as the shown one in Figure 6.5, determine who is at what stage in the writing process and who might benefit from a teacher conference or a discussion about how to become "unstuck" from a certain stage or how to brainstorm for ideas. Additionally, because the stages in the writing workshop are not necessarily linear but recursive, you may feel that a student who is leaving out a certain step would benefit from going back to an earlier stage to work through a particularly problematic piece.

③ Writing and Conferencing

The majority of students' time in writing workshops—30 to 40 minutes, depending on grade level—is spent actually writing and talking about that writing in peer-editing conferences and/or teacher conferences.

Students may select a revising peer and schedule a conference with that individual or a small group at any time when informal feedback is needed. The purpose

State-of-the-class chart. *figure* 6.5

NAMES:	MON.	TUES.	WED.	THURS.	FRI.
José	1stD	S	R	2ndD	(3)
Brianne	1stD	S	2ndD	(2)	T
Jennifer	P	1stD	(2)	P	2ndD
Hoa	T	R	2ndD	S	(1)
Svetlana	(1)	(1)	1stD	P	2ndD
Garrett	P	2ndD	R	(3)	S

	CODE		CODE
Prewriting	(1)	Drafting	D
Peer editing	P	Proofreading	(2)
Sharing with group	S	Revising	R
Teacher conference	T	Illustrating	(3)

of the conference could be for formulating and planning an idea, helping with revisions, or for specific proofreading as the writer gets ready to edit a piece.

The teacher in a writing workshop acts as a co-collaborator—not as the "authority"—who also writes and shares pieces of work and ideas. During the writing time, the teacher may hold individual or small group conferences that have been previously scheduled by signing up on the class bulletin board or online. Writing conferences should be brief (usually between one and four minutes) and concentrate on a specific piece the writer is doing or finishing. During the conference, you can answer questions and help solve writing problems. In addition, you might do the following:

1. Ask for more information about the content of the piece.
2. Restate or mirror the student's ideas.
3. Share similar writing experiences you have had.

Comments during the conferences should take a positive, encouraging tone, focusing on particularly effective writing and pointing out to the student what has made it effective (Graves, 2003). When significant problems occur, concentrate on only one or two in any one session, making a note to check on progress in those areas in the next conference. Finally, students should take an active role in the conference by asking their own questions about the pieces they are working on.

If no conferences are scheduled, walk around the room and engage in "writer's talk" (e.g., "What an interesting observation" or "The way you described the werewolf made me just shudder!"), prompting, encouraging, and lending support. Carry a notebook or tablet device to jot down anecdotal records (see Chapter 2) on student progress, which will provide information about what to address in future minilessons.

No one correct organizational scenario exists for writing workshop, because each workshop tends to be different from the one before. Some days, most students conference with each other or with the teacher in an attempt to bounce their ideas off others; other days, students work at drafting or revising their ideas while the teacher talks to individual students at their desks. The key concepts to remember are flexibility and decision making based not on curriculum but on the demonstrated needs of your students.

④ Group Sharing

Group sharing is an oral activity done to celebrate a finished piece, similar to publishing, and is usually done in front of the whole class (often in a special "author's chair"). The purpose is not to obtain feedback to create a better piece but to get group appreciation, suggestions for future pieces, and celebratory comments for the completed piece and all the hard work that it entailed. Although the time allotted for this sharing is ordinarily brief—five minutes or so—it is incredibly important and should never be omitted because sharing work:

- gives students a real reason to write—to impress an audience.
- allows revising peers to see how their ideas had an effect on a piece.
- builds a sense of community when done in a safe environment.
- makes literacy public.
- shows the interconnectedness between the two processes of reading and writing. (Graves, 2003)

⑤ Using Technology in the Writing Process

The various stages of the writing process are valuable for teaching students how to write, but students who lack the skills of good handwriting and appropriate spelling can often allow these conventions to interfere with bringing their thoughts and ideas to publication. Technology can help in each stage of the writing process.

In the planning stage, students can use online tools and resources to further their understanding of a topic. Then, working electronically, they can generate ideas and explore the topic they are writing about. They can prewrite, create maps and webs, brainstorm, or free associate without worrying about hurriedly producing pages so rough they are unreadable even to the author. Working electronically can help students avoid frustration by allowing them to explore ideas without fear of mistakes, which might lead to extra effort. Students can easily delete or add material and move sentences and paragraphs without erasing or starting all over again.

Revising, perhaps the hardest stage to "sell" to any student, is far more manageable when students can easily incorporate suggested word changes, add or delete paragraphs, or even extensively rewrite certain parts of the piece. Because revising is more easily done electronically, and doesn't entail having to rewrite the whole piece, students are more open to the constructive feedback of the teacher and revising peers.

Editing also becomes easier when done electronically. The spell checker and thesaurus built in to most programs can be valuable tools to students, helping them to find misspellings as well as choose among many synonyms to express their ideas in more powerful ways. In addition, some programs contain a grammar check that can help students, especially English learners, structure their sentences more effectively.

Finally, the wide variety of fonts available allows all students—even those with the poorest handwriting—to produce neat, professional-looking pieces of writing. Writing can be further enhanced with photographs, clip-art, sound, and video found online or created by the student.

Teaching the 6 + 1 Traits of Effective Writing

The **6 + 1 Trait Writing** framework was developed by Education Northwest (previously the Northwest Regional Educational Laboratory; 1998/1999) to create an easy-to-understand language that helps teachers describe to students just what it is that makes good writing effective. 6 + 1 Trait Writing is not a program but, rather, a common vocabulary for describing quality in writing, both narrative and expository. With 6 + 1 Trait Writing, students learn the traits that make quality writing work. They come to know exactly what good writing is and how to produce it themselves. They do this by comparing their own efforts as writers with those set forth in the high standards of the 6 + 1 Trait Writing criteria. Thus, they are encouraged to become steeped in the real purpose of writing as a medium for communication and to understand that the primary purpose of the various subskills (e.g., grammar, spelling, punctuation) is to enhance written communication.

● 6 + 1 Trait Writing

6 + 1 Trait Writing represents the most basic knowledge we need to impart to students about what good writing is—in all genres—and how they may go about producing it. The traits are as follows:

① ideas
② organization
③ voice
④ word choice
⑤ sentence fluency
⑥ conventions
⊕ presentation

See Figure 6.6 for a 6 + 1 Trait guide to revision.

figure **6.6** 6 + 1 Trait Writing guide to revision.

IDEAS

- ☐ Does my paper have a clear, focused idea?
- ☐ Did I use details to elaborate?

ORGANIZATION

- ☐ Does my piece have a clear introduction, middle, and conclusion?

VOICE

- ☐ Does my piece have a spark, a mood, a personality, a specific tone—formal or informal—that expresses what I want the reader to feel?

WORD CHOICE

- ☐ Did I use a variety of interesting words?

SENTENCE FLUENCY

- ☐ Do my sentences sound smooth? When I read the piece to myself, does it flow?

CONVENTIONS

- ☐ Did I check my capitals, periods, and spelling (editing for conventions)?

PRESENTATION

- ☐ Does my writing look neat and professional?

Based on the 6 + 1 Trait writing assessment model from Education Northwest. Copyright © 1998 Christopher-Gordon Publishers.

① Ideas

In order to be effective writers, students need to understand that the *ideas* they come up with are the most important element of their writing. Ideas are the fundamental core of a writer's message, the content of the piece, or the theme that—together with the supporting details and images—enriches and develops the writing by building new insight in a way that holds the reader's attention.

Evidence of the writer's ideas can be found dispersed throughout the piece. However, the general "idea" is more than simply the main idea or topic sentence; it also consists of the careful fleshing out or elaboration of the topic, the quality and quantity of the details, and how these supporting sentences help convey and clarify the writer's message.

The best ideas come from our own lives, from the unique as well as the mundane aspects of our lives. But just writing about our lives does not guarantee an effective piece of writing. A piece of writing also has to have a specific purpose that makes readers so aware of its significance that they want to continue reading.

You can facilitate the free flow of ideas by holding brainstorming sessions with students or by offering provocative prompts, such as "What is one thing you've done that you will never regret?" or "What would the world be like if everyone looked exactly alike?" (See the section on "Planning/Prewriting," above, for additional suggestions.) You may also help students grasp the importance of ideas and what they should look like by posing the following questions, which will help them analyze their own ideas as well as others':

- Does the writing make sense?
- Do I know the topic well?
- Have I included interesting details?
- Does the writing have a clear purpose?
- Does the writing make you want to continue reading?

② Organization

Students need to understand that good writing constitutes much more than just an endless flow of freely associated thoughts. For writing to be truly effective, it must demonstrate strong organization, or a logical sequence of ideas, which means that it begins with a purposeful, enticing lead sentence and terminates with a satisfying, thought-provoking ending. In between, the writer carefully links each new detail or development with the larger picture, building to a turning point or key revelation. Strong transitions are provided, so the reader never feels lost. Similarly, a section or paragraph of the piece should exist only if it has a specific function to perform, such as stating the theme, advancing the plot, providing more information about a character, or citing evidence to support an argument.

You can introduce the idea of structure by initially introducing expository frames for expository writing (see Chapter 7) and story grammars for narrative writing. To help your students understand how the internal structure of a piece is important, pose the following questions, which will help them analyze the organizational structure of their own and others' work:

- Will my beginning grab the reader's attention?
- Do all of the sections or paragraphs have a purpose and hang together?
- Does the writing build up to a key point?
- Is the writing in a logical sequence that is easy to follow?
- Does the piece feel finished at the end?
- Will it make the reader think?

③ Voice

Students need to understand that the heart and soul of a piece of writing is its voice. That **"voice,"** or life force, is the writer's personality emerging through words. When a writer has especially strong feelings for the chosen topic, the result is a piece that explodes with energy, and the reader feels close to both the writing and the writer. It is perhaps the most fundamental element of 6 + 1 Trait Writing, because all the others flow from it. From the writer's own voice come chosen ideas and a unique way of organizing those ideas. Word choice flows from voice, for the words we select are part of who we are. Sentence fluency, especially, emanates from a complex interaction of the words and phrases we choose. Even conventions such as the way a writer decides to use an exclamation point to show emphasis are part of the exclusivity that is voice.

If students never find their voice, they will never really discover who they are as writers. Without this trait, they will be forever guessing when it comes to selecting topics, organizing ideas, choosing words, and revising for clarity and style. Confusion will lead to frustration, and frustration will lead to fear. When students fear writing—because they think they have nothing to say or they are afraid to say what they think in a way that makes them feel comfortable—they do less of it, which decreases their chances of ever becoming good at writing.

• voice

When a writer has especially strong feelings for the chosen topic, the result is a piece that explodes with energy and the reader feels close to both the writing and the writer.

Students can find their voice when a teacher values their unique perspective and urges them to tell their own stories— stories that all students have to tell. For students to find their voice, the teacher must expect, and actually require, a diversity of opinions within the class. A strong voice, however, usually develops over time with much practice, reflection, and feedback from a knowledgeable writing coach.

You can introduce the idea of voice by closely examining each student's writing to find the part that is unique and personal to the student who wrote it and holding that up as an example of "voice." Students must understand that, even if they all start with the same topic, no two pieces of writing should be the same because no two writers are exactly the same. Students can be invited to reflect on why the writing works and what was done to make it sound just like the person who wrote it. A strong voice can also be demonstrated to students by examining the voice of familiar authors, such as Gary Paulsen, Judy Blume, or Rick Riordan.

To help students use their own voice in a piece of writing, pose the following questions, which will help them analyze the use of voice in their own writing as well as in other writing:

- Does this writing sound like me?
- Is this what I really think and feel?
- Could a reader feel my commitment to the topic?
- Do I know why I am writing and who my audience is?
- Do I want to share this writing with someone?

④ Word Choice

word choice ●

Appropriate **word choice** is the artistic element of writing that involves using fresh and colorful language to fascinate the reader and make certain passages memorable and worthy of reading aloud. Word choice emanates from a love of language and a desire to select words that express the exact image, impression, or mood the writer is feeling or that clearly and accurately explain a concept or support an argument.

Word choice becomes apparent when a writer's language describes an event, feeling, or topic in such a manner that readers feel they have received new insights into the mundane; with such writing, it seems clear that no other words or phrases would have worked as perfectly. Word choice is much more than simply effective adjectives or phrases; it entails many factors, such as unusually vivid descriptions and sensory impressions ("a white carpet of fresh snow"), strong and specific verbs ("enveloped by the gloom"), effective use of colloquial language ("He hogtied the critter and threw him into the truck"), and even the occasional use of invented words ("He went vavooming down the slide") when they add to the image needed.

Perhaps the most effective way to help students become aware of subtleties in language choice is to give them plenty of experiences with good literature, both fiction and nonfiction. While conducting a guided reading lesson or reading aloud to students, point out excellent word choice as it is encountered: "Oh, I can really see that sunset!" or "Wow! I feel as though I were there, don't you?" or "I never thought of it that way!" Help students practice word choice by having them transform simple sentences, orally or in written form, into ones that vividly depict a situation. For example, they could transform the simple sentence "The boy ran" into "The tiny, freckle-faced boy ran swiftly through the field, fearing the angry bull would make a meal of him." You can also help students choose appropriate words and phrases by posing the following questions, which will help them analyze their own word choices as well as those of others:

- Is this the best way I can say this?
- Do my words and phrases create mind pictures?
- Have I tried new ways to say everyday things?
- Are my verbs powerful?
- Do any of my words and phrases linger in my mind?
- Would any of my phrases be interesting to hear when read aloud?

⑤ Sentence Fluency

Writing fluency is that intangible essence that separates excellent writing from the ordinary. It is the careful crafting of sentence structures into graceful sentences so that paragraphs flow smoothly and effortlessly. While effective word choice is part of this trait, **sentence fluency** is more than just the individual words chosen. It is the entire effect of the way the sentences sound when read aloud, including such features as parallel construction, easy transitions between paragraphs, alliteration, and the variety of lengths and constructions of the sentences—all of which provide a sense of aesthetic satisfaction to the reader.

● sentence fluency

Sentence fluency takes time and practice for students to develop because, more than any of the other traits, it depends heavily on students' ability to hear the difference between awkward writing that is hard to follow and understand, and crisp, smooth writing that communicates the writer's intent with an economy of words.

As with attuning students' ears to effective word choice, sentence fluency can best be fostered by reading aloud often to them with expression and gusto, and pointing out examples of excellent writing when they appear. Point out the use of alliteration ("pink poppies"), conversational style ("Aaaahhh, I wish I weren't so tired!"), and similes ("as brown as the tired desert"), as well as pleasing and consistent rhythm in pieces of writing. You can also demonstrate how *you* write, modeling how you think through the process. In addition, with an interactive whiteboard, students can practice rewriting awkward sentences so they more clearly and concisely convey intended ideas. Finally, help students write fluent sentences by posing the following questions, which will help them analyze their sentence fluency and that of others:

- Do my sentences vary in length?
- Do my sentences "flow" as I read them aloud?
- Do I use alliteration and/or similes to make my sentences interesting?
- Does the writing flow easily from sentence to sentence?
- Do the sentences begin in different ways?
- Are the sentences powerful and memorable?

⑥ Conventions

The most important traits of writing are, arguably, the ones just covered because they concern the core of what the writer has to say. Conventional correctness, however, should not be overlooked, because it constitutes the tools of the trade that help bring the writing to others in a uniform manner that readers expect. **Conventions** include grammar, spelling, paragraphing, capitalization, punctuation, and all the mechanics of the language that are often corrected in the editing process.

● conventions

Conventions are more than the window dressing used to make our writing correct, or a list of simple rules to be obeyed. They should in fact be presented as "tools," not "rules." Combined, they are a systematic set of symbols to facilitate communication between writer and reader. Conventions have meaning, just as words do, and it is a skillful writer who takes advantage of a full range of these meaning-making tools and situations to communicate most effectively with the reader.

While more materials exist for the teaching of conventions than for all the other traits combined, evidence shows that assigning worksheet after worksheet on grammar usage, punctuation, and the like, out of context, is ineffective in teaching students to write; such undue focus often interferes with what the writer has to say (Weaver, 1996). Individual conventions, such as the proper use of capital letters, should be taught in short minilessons and reinforced continually by showing writers how important it is for their writing to be readable and telling them how much readers appreciate being able to clearly understand what they have written. Noden (2011) offers wonderful ideas about how to create activities specifically designed to help students make grammar and stylistic changes in their writing. Appropriate or good use of conventions should be pointed out as they occur, rather than negative ones. Students also need to hear that the more they read and write, the more proficient they will become at using conventions appropriately. You can help students use conventions properly by posing the following questions, which will help them proofread their writing and that of others:

- Have I used capital letters correctly?
- Is all the punctuation in the right place?
- Are all the words spelled correctly?
- Have I used a resource to help spell unfamiliar words?
- Did I indent the start of each paragraph?
- Are my sentences logical and grammatically correct?

+1 Presentation

For years, teachers and readers alike have indicated that the format of a piece of writing—the spacing, handwriting, layout, graphics, and so forth—influenced their ability to read and fairly assess for the traits. Now, instead of not covering those presentation issues, teachers discuss them and integrate them into the 6 + 1 Trait Writing model. Not all teachers cover this trait, but many educators find it useful as today's students use a great variety of presentation formats to practice and develop their writing skills.

Inspiring Students to Write

Motivation, instruction, feedback, and opportunity all contribute to students' enthusiasm for writing. This section suggests tools teachers can use to create a writerly classroom environment. Writing workshop and 6 + 1 Trait Writing provide multiple writing opportunities and means for assessment; however, writing, like any other skill, requires continual practice to hone and refine its many nuances. The crafting necessary for good writing can be developed through daily writing for real purposes, with continual feedback from caring peers and adult coaches. The following sections concern three practices that can help students become engaged writers who write for authentic purposes.

1. The use of dialogue journals, offering a vehicle through which students can use writing in much the same way as they use conversations with friends.

2. The opportunity to write a narrative piece that is both longer and more comprehensive than the ordinary story writing assignment.

3. Writing poetry through the use of literacy scaffolds, which offers students the opportunity to express their creative thoughts and ideas.

Writing informational text is a fourth practice that can help students become engaged writers who write for authentic purposes; it is discussed in Chapter 7.

① Dialogue Journals

Of the many journal-writing formats, the one that provides students with the most helpful feedback about their writing is the **dialogue journal,** also known as the interactive journal (Cecil, 1994a). The "dialogue" part of the name simply means that, in this journal, a running dialogue is carried on between the teacher and each individual student. The journal can be maintained in a notebook or online, perhaps in blog format. The student begins the dialogue by writing down anything that is of interest to him, and the teacher simply responds to what the student has expressed. The teacher may comment on the student's ideas, use thoughtful questions to ask for elaboration, or paraphrase what the student has said to validate and affirm the student's ideas. The teacher and no one else (unless the student initiates sharing with someone else) reads what the student has written.

● dialogue journal

To launch the idea of dialogue journals in the classroom, it is often helpful to write two or three questions on the whiteboard to inspire students, such as, *What are your favorite things to do on a Saturday morning?* or *Which famous sports figure do you admire and why?* Advising students that these topics are only possibilities for writing and not mandates frees those who already have their own diary-like writing agenda, which can include problems, goals, fears, or just a recording of the things they have recently been doing. Ideally, students should have some time set aside for journal writing every day, beginning with a few minutes and increasing to 15 or 20 minutes or more as they find more and more to say in their dialogue.

Justification for adding dialogue journal writing to an already overcrowded literacy curriculum is compelling; in this age of teacher accountability, it is worth examining. First, students who participate in such a program develop a much more positive attitude toward writing. If sessions are frequent, endure for most of the school year, and include nonjudgmental feedback from the teacher, even reluctant writers will be more favorably inclined toward writing and will write much more (Cecil, 2007).

Second, students become more confident as they begin to believe in the power of their writing ability and look forward to the teacher's comments, rather than dreading the proverbial "sea of red marks" common in traditional writing programs. As they realize their thoughts and ideas have merit, their self-perception as writers will increase. In addition, the nonthreatening nature of dialogue journals makes them particularly appropriate for English learners. Such learners are too often fearful of being publicly ridiculed for their lack of oral and written fluency (Peyton & Reed, 1990). In their journals, however, they can write in their home language or "code switch," by using words from both their native language and their newly acquired language.

Third, students receive important writing practice through journal writing and, as a result, they become more fluent writers. As in any activity—skiing, texting, riding a bicycle—writing improves with continual practice. Moreover, through the teacher's modeling and questioning (see Figure 6.7), students begin to recognize just what details to include to make their writing more effective. Additionally, through modeling, the teacher is able to provide certain "teachable moments" when students need to use an unaccustomed grammatical construct or to spell an unfamiliar word, as with the word *Hawaii* in Figure 6.7.

Students become more confident as they begin to believe in the power of their writing ability.

figure **6.7** Dialogue journal entry (fourth grade).

No, I have never been to Hawaii, Kim, but I have always wanted to go there. Did you get to do any snorkeling? Yes, I noticed your lovely tan!	We had such a fun time in ~~Hawiiy~~ Hawie Mrs. Cecil. Were you ever thare? I got sun bruned like a ~~los~~ lobstor. Did you notis Mrs. Cecil. I can't wait to go back thare.
Snorkeling is fun, isn't it, Kim? How did you learn? Did your mother teach you? Was it difficult? What else did you do in Hawaii?	Yes we got to ~~sm~~ snorkel when we were in Hawaii. It was so neat! There were so many fish with all difrint colors. I never saw anything like that befor.
I'm sorry you are being bothered, Kim. I will change your seat and speak with Meg. No, I am not angry with you! ☺	You know, Mrs. Cecil. You were telling me to stop talking today in math class. but it wasn't me. Meg was talking. Meg keeps bothing me. Please move her seat. Dont be mad at me please, Mrs. Cecil??
I have one daughter, Kim. Like you, I am sure she thinks I am mean sometimes. It is hard being a Mommy!	Mrs. Cecil, do you have any children? I wish I was your child. Instead of your student. My mother is to mene. I think you are probly never mene to your children?
Kim, the important thing is that you have now told the truth. Sometimes it's hard to tell the truth. No, I am not angry, but please don't do it again, okay? ☺	Now I want to tell you something o.k. Last weak when I was absint I was'nt sick. I ~~jus~~ just made that up becuase I wanted to stay home and watch Scuby Do. Im sorry, Mrs. Cecil. Are you angry now???? Do'nt be.

Finally, students begin to see an authentic use for writing for their own purposes rather than to fulfill a teacher-directed assignment. In the informal venue of their own private journals, many students find that writing can be a most cathartic experience—especially when they are using it to vent strong feelings and emotions. As students get older, they find, too, that writing can be a positive outlet to defuse potentially explosive situations ahead of time because they can examine their written feelings before they act on them. In this age of sporadic violence in school, the importance of such a constructive outlet should not be underestimated.

② Extended Narrative Text

Students who have had the experience of writing an extended form of narrative text, such as an original episodic novel or a multi-chaptered novelette, come away with a tremendous feeling of accomplishment and a sense of pride at having produced a complex set of characters who have evolved with time and effort. These characters become real to them in much the same way as any characters do to adults who have just finished reading a satisfying novel.

To initiate the writing of a novelette, it is often helpful to provide an extensive outline of what possible chapters could look like. Outlines might focus on themes related to a certain emotion, such as greed, jealousy, love, or hope. Or, after reading a number of Greek and Roman myths with students, teachers can create an outline of the adventures of a hero or heroine who is similar to those in the myths. After reviewing the basic elements of narrative structure, the teacher can invite students to write chapters describing their main characters and their struggles and resolutions, or use the longer format to explain a natural phenomenon, such as tornadoes or hurricanes.

After distributing guidelines, such as the ones offered in Figure 6.8, have students brainstorm a list of possible ideas for the first chapter. For example, for the first item listed in Figure 6.8 (Invent and describe a character), imagined characters

---

Writing a novelette. *figure* **6.8**

1. Invent and describe a character; physical characteristics, habits, likes, dislikes, traits. (characterization)

2. Provide your character with a history: What has his or her life been like up to now? Who were his or her parents? What sort of childhood did he or she have? What were his or her friends like? (background)

3. Describe where your character lives. (setting)

4. Describe a typical day in the life of your character.

5. Your character is going to leave town; describe what led to this decision.

6. Just before leaving town, your character receives advice from someone; re-create this scene in dialogue.

7. The first day out of town your character meets someone strange; describe this person and what makes him or her strange.

8. This person asks your character to do something, but your character is not sure if he or she should. What was your character asked to do and what goes through his or her mind?

9. Your character decides to do what has been asked; describe the decision and its consequences.

10. Some time later, your character turns up in a large city with very little money. Your character decides to find a job. Describe the search for a job and the job he or she finally secures.

11. Describe a typical day on the job.

12. Despite the fact that your character likes the job, he or she is fired. Describe this scene, making clear why he or she was fired.

13. Your character is depressed and inattentive. As a result, he or she has an accident. Describe it.

14. Your character is taken to a hospital and learns that he or she is not expected to live. Describe this scene and your character's feelings about the imminence of death.

15. Despite the doctor's predictions, your character recovers and decides the city is not for him or her. Your character moves to a small town where he or she lives for a year. Describe this period.

16. While living in this small town, your character sees a number of things he or she believes ought to be changed. What are they?

17. In order to bring about changes in the town, your character decides to run for mayor. Describe the campaign.

18. Your character wins the campaign and begins to inaugurate changes; however, he or she encounters difficulties. What are they? How are they resolved? How will you end the novelette? (Cecil, 1994a)

may range from a girl modeled on Susan B. Anthony who is fighting for women's rights to a boy based on the persona of Martin Luther King, Jr., and his championing of peaceful resistance. Students will be inspired to select an idea to work up for their own chapter, or choose another that comes to mind. It is crucial that the teacher remind students that there are no right or wrong characters, only many ideas, each of which can be an interesting beginning for a novel.

After the class brainstorming session, students select a character and then flesh out the chapter with class ideas as well as ideas of their own. Students can then be paired with a revising peer during writing workshop to share their chapters and receive praise, questions, and suggestions for improvement. New chapters are usually written weekly or biweekly, with revisions and teacher and peer conferences occurring in between. However, by the second or third chapter, the class brainstorming, and even the outline, become less and less important as students become closer to their characters and look forward to expanding them wherever the characters decide to go. The excitement of the deepening development of the character and plot becomes a unique source of motivation.

When all of the chapters are completed, through the joint efforts of the author, the teacher, and the author's editorial partners—which can take anywhere from a few weeks to several months—students are eager to do the final editing and illustrating. A minilesson can address the fact that a title should be chosen with great care, not only to catch the reader's attention but also to capture the essence of the novelette. Completed novelettes can then be posted on the class website or professionally bound. Finally, authors can read some or all chapters aloud to the class and receive appreciative comments, and the teacher can explore other venues to share students' accomplishments, such as reading the novelettes to another class or taking a field trip to a convalescent home to read to the residents.

High-quality young adult literature can be the inspiration for writing in particular styles and genres. Teachers can foster this inspiration by calling attention to interesting phrases, word choice, dialogue, character development, and foreshadowing in books that are read aloud to students or those that are read by students in their literature circles (see Chapter 5). If books are wisely chosen, students will have excellent models from which to draw for their own writing. Some high-quality novels can be found through recommendations from the school librarian or from professional organizations such as the International Reading Association or the American Library Association. An additional source is a list of Newbery Medal books. The Newbery Medal is awarded each year by the American Library Association to the author of the most distinguished contribution to literature for children published during the preceding year.

Some titles that we have found to be particularly useful for modeling the traits of a well-crafted novelette are listed in the box on the facing page.

③ Poetry

The entire spectrum of students—from gifted to the difficult-to-motivate to English learners—can be encouraged to create poetry through the use of literacy

scaffolding ●
literacy scaffold ●

scaffolds. **Scaffolding** is a support mechanism by which students are able to accomplish more difficult tasks than they could without assistance. The **literacy scaffold** is a kind of formula for writing a poem by imitating, to a greater or lesser degree, an existing poem. By simplifying the process of writing a poem—a process that can seem threatening and esoteric to many—students can see that, once they are given the structure, they are freed to fill in their own creative thoughts and ideas. The eight steps discussed in the following activity guide the teacher and students through the process (Cecil, 1994b).

Models for the Well-Crafted Novelette

Balliett, B. (2004). *Chasing Vermeer.* Scholastic.

Bartolettei, S. C. (2005). *Hitler youth: Growing up in Hitler's shadow.* Scholastic.

Berry, D., & Pearson, R. (2004). *Peter and the starcatchers.* Hyperion Books for Children.

Collins, S. (2003). *Gregor the overlander.* Scholastic.

Creech, S. (2004). *Heartbeat.* Joanna Cutler Books.

Cremer, A. & Levithan, D. (2013). *Invisibility.* New York: Philomel Books.

Cummings, P. (2004). *Red kayak.* Dutton Children's Books.

Dessen, S. (2011). *What happened to goodbye.* Penguin Group.

DiCamillo, K. (2003). *The tale of Despereaux.* Candlewick.

Farmer, N. (2004). *The sea of trolls.* Atheneum.

Funke, C. (2002). *The thief lord.* Translated by O. Latsch. Scholastic.

Holub, J. (2005). *An innocent soldier.* Translated by M. Hoffmann. Scholastic.

Hunter, E. (2013). *A hidden enemy.* HarperCollins.

Ibbotson, E. (2004). *The star of Kazan.* Dutton Children's Books.

McKernan, V. (2005). *Shackleton's stowaway.* Knopf.

Mochizuki, K. (1997). *Passage to freedom: The Sugihara story.* Lee & Low.

Oppel, K. (2004). *Airborn.* Eos.

Palacio, R. J. (2012). *Wonder.* Knopf.

Patneaude, D. (2004). *Thin wood walls.* Houghton Mifflin.

Ryan, P. M. (2004). *Becoming Naomi Leon.* Scholastic.

Selznick, B. (2011). *Wonderstruck.* Scholastic.

Weeks, S. (2004). *So B. it: A novel.* Laura Geringer Books.

Woodson, J. (2003). *Locomotion.* Putnam.

Zusak, M. (2006). *The book thief.* Knopf.

Writing Poetry Using a Literacy Scaffold  activity

1. Provide a literacy scaffold, or temporary writing framework, created from the work of a poet students admire, such as Shel Silverstein or Jack Prelutsky. Or you can choose another selection (see Figure 6.9(a)).

2. Read examples of other students' work, or your own, that contain the structure or scaffold (save other students' work from previous classes).

3. Guide students through the poem and ask them to identify its structure, as well as the particular conventions (punctuation, spacing, capital letters, and so forth) that the poem employs.

4. As a group, brainstorm some topics for a poem that the whole class can contribute to using the scaffold.

5. Brainstorm some words or phrases that could be used in the poem.

6. On an interactive whiteboard, write a group poem on the chosen topic, using the scaffold and brainstormed words and phrases.

7. Individually, or in pairs for the reluctant, invite students to write their own poems using the literacy scaffold. (*Note:* More "seasoned" poets should feel free to deviate from the literacy scaffold.)

8. Have students follow the remaining steps in the writing process to revise, edit, share, and publish their work in either written or audio form. An example of a poem written by fourth-graders using this process is shown in Figure 6.9(b).

Figure 6.10 shows a sample and two poems created by older students using a different scaffold but with this same process.

---

figure **6.9** (a) Sample poem to be used as a literacy scaffold and (b) an example poem created by fourth-grade students using the same scaffold.

(a)

Bees

Bees are buzzy,
Bees are bold.
   Boisterous, bashful.
   Belligerent, bold.
   Beautiful, bellicose,
   Bewildering, bright.
Bees are bold,
Bees are buzzy.

(b)

Snakes are sneaky,
Snakes are slim.
   Slithery, slimy.
   Somber, slinky.
   Scaly, sneaky.
   Simple, sassy.
Snakes are slim.
Snakes are sneaky.

---

figure **6.10** Career poem.

DESCRIPTION: This is a three-stanza poem that extols the virtues of a particular career or trade. In it, the poet muses about the tools of that career or trade. The brief verses follow this format:

The song of the [*tool used in the job*]
Is [*adjective describing the tool*]
As they [*action of the tool*]
[*Rhyme with line two*].

Repeat twice.

—Adapted from *Busy Carpenters,* by James S. Tippett

THE FARMER (student's career poem #1)

The song of the pitchfork
Is fine
As they get the hay in
Just barely in time.

The song of the reaper
Is grand
As they grow food to eat
From the rich land.

The song of the tractor
Is loyal
As they plow the fields
And till the soil.

—*Sabrina, grade 7*

FIRE FIGHTER (student's career poem #2)

The song of the fire truck
Is speed
As they rush to the fire
And help people in need.

The song of the water hose
Is kind
As they put out the flames
And save people they find.

The song of the siren
Is caring
As they spend their whole lives
Doing deeds that are daring.

—*Jim, grade 8*

Cecil, N. L. (1997). *For the Love of Poetry: Literacy Scaffolds, Extension Ideas, and More.* Winnipeg, Manitoba: Portage & Main.

The following box presents a scaffolding example for incorporating technology with reading and writing poetry, using a Shel Siverstein poem.

A Multimodal Approach to Writing Poetry

Mrs. Frank has been discussing poetry. Today she asks her fifth graders what they know about the poet Shel Silverstein before introducing him using material from his website and from his YouTube channel, in which he reads his poetry; this allows students to see how he sounds. Using other YouTube videos, Mrs. Frank also shows an interview and several clips of him playing the guitar, which her students enjoy.

Next, Mrs. Frank asks the students how their parents or caregivers would describe their kids' bedrooms at home. On an interactive whiteboard, she types the words the students call out for the class to see. *Disaster, messy, gross* are first to be heard. A few say *neat* and *organized,* but not many. While they laugh and chat about their bedrooms, Mrs. Frank places the words "disaster," "messy," and "gross" into a three-column graphic organizer on the screen. She asks the class to give her some phrases to describe what created the mess. Students call out, "My stinky socks lie on the floor," "school papers all around the room," and "candy wrappers under my bed." Mrs. Frank types these in as the students talk, and then she asks them to place the description under the word that best seems to fit. They place both the "stinky socks" and the "candy wrappers" under *gross* and "school papers" with the word *messy.*

After this quick categorization, students watch two YouTube clips of students reciting the Shel Silverstein poem "Messy Room" as they film their messy rooms. The teacher hands out clickers, and students weigh in on whether or not their rooms are similar to the ones shown on the clips. Because this technology tallies and then presents data, the students see that of the 29 members of the class, 15 reported having a room like those shown on screen. Examining the results, the students determine and discuss what percentage of the class have messy rooms at home.

In the next class session, Mrs. Frank shows students the entire poem "Messy Room" using the whiteboard. After they have read the poem together, she invites students to use it as a scaffold to create a class version of the poem, using the words and phrases from the graphic organizer they created earlier. Having already created multimedia presentations with the class, she asks her students to jot down new ways to make a multimedia presentation out of their class poem that captures its essence. Ideas are shared, and one is selected. Students agree to create a Prezi presentation with animation features to swing words in, dropping them down into a big mess on the floor of the room shown on the slide. They discuss which words should appear in a larger font by their importance or level of filth, and which font would look best with a particular image they have found (e.g., underwear hanging on a lamp).

Next, students discuss the meaning of the poem itself and how they can capture that meaning in their animation. How can they make the words create the mess in the room? They discuss the features of the Silverstein poem they used as a scaffold, such as repetition, and why the author uses that technique. As with the original poem, the class poem begins and ends with "Whoever's room this is should be ashamed"; the students develop ideas about how to make the words look ashamed by "floating in" rather than flying in like the other words. They discuss adding background music; they wonder if they should use Shel Silverstein's own guitar playing to bring a bit more of the author into the poem, or should use a song that feels "messy" to them, one with lots of noise.

At every point in the discussion, Mrs. Frank listens and types, moving around the words of their poem and asking for feedback as she does so, while the students brainstorm more ways to present it. After working on their multimedia presentation for some time, the class turns off the overhead lights to watch their creation. As the opening screen comes up with an empty box of a room, the class is silent. As the poem's words start to swing in, the students whisper with excitement. At the end of the poem, they cheer for their clever work, and Mrs. Frank is pleased with their ability to look at the stylistic features of the poem and explain its meaning better through the visual images.

WWW○○○

Shel Silverstein
www.shelsilverstein.com
www.youtube.com/user/ShelSilversteinBooks

WWW○○○

Examples: Student Readings of "Messy Room"
https://www.youtube.com/watch?v=Q2f9kDZ8g5c
https://www.youtube.com/watch?v=FX6xEoQVuCE

Enhancing Writing Using Technology Tools

Digital writing formats can be simple, such as posting to a blog, or quite complex, such as making use of multimedia and the mobile devices students use daily. Many teachers ask students to write in multimodal environments. Mrs. Frank, for example, asked her students to enhance their class poem by using multimedia tools, experimenting with font size and shape, and including animation features—all of which added a unique voice to their work.

Writing digitally allows students more choice and provides a greater variety of tools for self-expression. Students can pursue ideas that are interesting to them and play with various genres in one document. They have choices about sharing their documents publically or privately—or not at all—but sharing publicly encourages students to write with an extended audience in mind, one beyond the teacher and the school. Digital writing makes it easy to project writing outside the classroom walls, to share with audiences locally and globally.

In addition, using technology while writing allows for a more social dynamic. Students can collaborate on a piece of writing by posting their work on a class wiki or website or sending it among themselves electronically. They can seek feedback, or help and support; they can take place in shared conversations about the piece.

Troubleshooting

Nothing is more satisfying to most students than taking a piece of writing that they have successfully drafted, revised, edited, and illustrated; sharing it with a trusted audience; and then receiving celebratory comments. However, a variety of factors can make writing a dreaded chore for many students. Following are some suggestions for this common dilemma.

No Confidence

Reluctant writers with little or no confidence in their ability to write—especially English learners who are just coming to terms with a new language—may initially prefer to draw pictures of their ideas in the prewriting stage. They can be invited to share these pictures orally with trusted peers or the teacher. Additionally, after using the writing process as discussed in this chapter, such students can be shown sentences that illustrate the strengths and limitations in their own writing and be told how to correct or avoid specific problems.

Students' perception of themselves as writers does affect their mastery in writing. In one study, students who felt they were good at writing had less anxiety and dislike for the task, and their writing fear or apprehension was related to their ability to write well (Pajares, Johnson, & Usher, 2007). Students respond best to honest and immediate feedback. With boosted self-efficacy, students are better able to internalize feedback and are motivated to make positive changes in their writing.

No Ideas

Often in writing workshop, when students are given free rein to choose their own topics, some will complain that they do not know what to write about. Providing specific prompts ("What would you do with a million dollars?") and story starters (see Figure 6.11)—provocative lead-in sentences that pique a student's imagination—can sometimes be helpful. When a student is "stuck" with a piece of writing and complains that she doesn't know what comes next, a helpful technique is to read the student's work and then offer a snippet of an idea that can lead the student to a new

Story starters.   *figure* **6.11**

1. It was the most hideous, monstrous thing I had ever seen.

2. Who would think a tree branch could let go so suddenly?

3. Bringing a Martian home for dinner was something I never thought I'd be doing.

4. I don't suppose you ever spied on someone, at least not for weeks at a time, but I did.

5. I had always hated school until that day when . . .

6. Haunted house stories are a dime a dozen but, I promise you, this one will top them all.

7. The best friend I ever had was not a human but a . . .

8. We had always made fun of her.

9. Moving to the ranch had seemed like such a good idea until that morning when we all had our assigned chores to do.

10. There was blood all over the doorstep that morning when I went out to start my paper route.

11. A helium-filled balloon—especially a very large one—is not an easy thing to carry on a very windy day.

12. He was the tiniest little man (horse, dog, etc.) you ever saw and he was sitting right on my desk.

13. It looked like a very ordinary lamp—a little crooked perhaps, and rather dirty.

14. It was way too big to be a hen's egg, so what was it doing in the chicken coop?

15. I always thought jumping rope was a silly thing to do until my little sister challenged me to try it.

16. Skateboards can get you places in a hurry, as I found out that day.

17. It had been raining for a week and now the road had disappeared.

18. Making someone come back to life after being dead for years is a very scary thing to do.

19. The map was very old, and the paper cracked as I opened it.

20. Stowing away on a cruise ship is not easy but well worth the hassle.

21. "There's no such thing as a werewolf," I said as I watched the hairs on my hands grow longer.

22. "Of course I'll be all right!" I told my parents as they went off on vacation.

23. Summer camp is not all it's cracked up to be. Especially Camp Gitchigumi . . .

24. The little puppy sat by the window looking in at the warm fire.

25. "Three wishes," said the strange old lady, "and use them with great care!"

26. "Zap!!!" There was that annoying sound again. What *was* it???

27. There was no one there when I answered the doorbell, but there sat a very large package with a huge bow.

28. I have always loved to play jokes on people.

29. It had arms like a monkey, fur like a leopard, and a very human face.

30. "Of course I'm not afraid!" I told my friends as we ventured into the rainforest.

set of possibilities. For example, a student writing about a mirror in an attic may imagine a picnic area on the other side of the mirror but be unable to come up with an idea about what could happen there. The teacher might suggest, "I see a squirrel scurrying away into the woods and . . . ," and then walk away, promising to check back later to see how the student is doing. Often, a tiny nudge of this sort will remove the block. Finally, teachers should not hesitate to tell students an important truth about writing: More often than not, inspiration occurs *during* writing rather than before it. In other words, as they simply take the leap and begin to write something, most students find that the fear dissipates as the ideas generated beget more ideas.

Too Many Ideas

Although it may not seem like much of a problem, certain students will have so many ideas that they will become overwhelmed, or even paralyzed, by indecision. In this case, an early-idea mental-rehearsal conference with a peer or the teacher can be help-ful in assisting the student to pick a topic. For example, the student would talk about some of his ideas and the peer or teacher might ask questions or encourage the stu-dent to write about a particular idea. Also of help can be a discussion with the student about her experiences and resources. Most writers suggest that the best topics to write about are those about which one has the most information and personal experience. Therefore, although a student may wish to write about wild Shetland ponies, space flight, or getting lost at the mall, the last may be the best suited topic.

Unfamiliar Organizational Patterns

Each writing discourse has its own organization and conventions. Each time a new genre of writing is introduced to students, teachers must model and then rein-force it. Because writing is organized in culturally specific ways (Gibbons, 2002), English learners often have an especially difficult time with unfamiliar genres. For example, they may organize their thoughts differently, or they may be used to cir-cular structures rather than the linear or hierarchical structure used most often in U.S. culture. Minilessons about writing structures and genres can be helpful to all students, but English learners, in particular, may benefit from initial class collabo-rations before writing independently. They thus have the opportunity to review the new writing structure or genre, practice using the writing process, become familiar with the necessary academic language, and balance their energy between wanting to express their ideas and worrying about the correct conventions.

No Interest in Writing

Students may enter a classroom with a decided aversion to writing—especially those who have not yet been through the confidence-building adventure of a writ-ing workshop. Such students need to be encouraged to write and to experience the rewards of writing.

Sometimes reluctance to write emanates from a history of having received numer-ous discouraging corrections on the conventions of writing, including spelling, grammar, and punctuation, as well as marks for poor penmanship (if not produced electronically). If this is where the problem lies, the teacher can intervene by recording the student's ideas and first draft, emphasizing the difference between the mere physi-cal act of writing and the actual creating/composing, for which the student is still held responsible. A similar strategy is to allow the student to dictate ideas into a recording device and then transfer those ideas to the word processor, using the spell check and grammar aids. Finally, pairing students who prefer oral activities over solitary ones for brainstorming discussions, and then having them write the initial draft together, is a collaborative way to lessen feelings of isolation and spur interest in writing.

Summary

In a balanced and comprehensive literacy program, writing is not seen as mere-ly the prosaic sum of its parts. Writing, like reading, is viewed as a tool for considering the world, or as a vehicle for sorting out and clarifying one's thinking. The more students reformulate content, the more their thinking and writing abilities grow. In the process, students play with words, organize their ideas into sentences and paragraphs, and express their innermost thoughts to increase their personal sig-nificance and self-awareness. Moreover, through a well-constructed writing program, students learn to harness skills that will enable them to examine their ideas and determine whether those ideas can stand up to analysis by their peers.

The writing process, employed in the self-directed setting of the writing workshop, shifts the emphasis from the finished product to the problem-solving stages all writers go through as they gather and organize ideas, draft them, and refine and polish their pieces with the help of others. Because the teacher is not the only person evaluating the final product, the students, as revising peers, become astute at discerning what does and does not constitute good writing. Reading and writing become reciprocal partners as students write and then read their own writing and that of other students.

To further help students understand what constitutes good writing, the 6 + 1 Trait Writing framework is used in a balanced and comprehensive literacy program. Using this framework, students explore the important components of ideas, organization, voice, word choice, sentence fluency, conventions, and presentation. Teachers use writing samples that either exemplify the trait being discussed or that lack the trait and thus are not effective. In either case, students receive valuable information as to what makes writing work. They extend this information to their own writing and to that of their peers.

Arguably, a large majority of the problems that writers experience can be alleviated by having them write often; as active young authors become more engaged in writing, they desire to communicate their ideas more clearly. Daily dialogue journals and frequent writing of novelettes are but two means to supplement the ample writing practice offered by writing workshops.

Finally, teachers of a balanced and comprehensive literacy program must convey to students the fundamental axiom that was proffered by Robert Frost: "There is no art to writing but having something to say."

To be sure, the writing process takes much effort and concentration. Students must be gently guided through the process and encouraged to continue when they become discouraged or frustrated with the many revisions that every piece of writing needs. With the assistance of a teacher who truly believes that everyone has something to say, a writing revolution can occur in every classroom. Eventually, all students will have the confidence to produce a worthwhile piece of writing that they are proud of and eager to share with the world.

Questions FOR JOURNAL WRITING AND DISCUSSION

1. Write a piece of fiction, nonfiction, or poetry for a group of students in grades 4–8. Note the process you went through to arrive at the finished product. How might you use your piece of writing in a writing workshop to teach writing more effectively?

2. Reflect on your own experiences with learning to write in school. Describe any positive experiences that helped you to become a better writer, and describe any negative experiences that may have hindered your development and/or motivation to write. How do your experiences relate to the ideas presented in this chapter?

3. After observing writing instruction in a grade 4–8 classroom, record your thoughts on what took place. Did the teacher follow the writing process as discussed in this chapter, or did she use a different approach? How did the students feel about the writing they were doing? What did you think about the quality of their writing (if you were able to read any)? Do you think the writing approach used in this class will have a positive and lasting effect on these students?

Suggestions FOR PROJECTS AND FIELD ACTIVITIES

1. Arrange to visit a middle school classroom during writing workshop. Listen to the conversation that accompanies the composing process. Take notes on what you hear. How did "talk" facilitate the writing process?

2. Ask a small group of students what they prefer to read and what they prefer to write: fiction (stories, novels), nonfiction (informational texts, biographies, arguments), or poetry. Is there a difference between the genres students choose to read and what they choose to write? Why might this be so?

3. Survey a small group of students about their computer literacy. How comfortable are they with using the computer as a writing tool? How accessible are computers to these students when they are writing? How many use Inspiration, Prezi, or other multimedia tools while writing? How often do they actually publish and share their work online? Is their audience limited to class members only, or is it open to a wider group?

REFERENCES

Applebee, A., & Langer, J. (2011). Snapshot of writing instruction in middle and high schools. *English Journal, 100*(6), 14-27.

Applebee, A. N., & Langer, J. A. (2009). What's happening in the teaching of writing? *English Journal, 98*(5), 18–28.

Atwell, N. (1998). *In the middle: New understandings about writing, reading, and learning* (2nd ed.). Upper Montclair, NJ: Boynton/Cook.

Block, C. C. (2001). *Teaching the language arts: Expanding thinking through student-centered instruction* (3rd ed.). Needham Heights, MA: Allyn & Bacon.

Calkins, L. M. (1991). *Living between the lines.* Portsmouth, NH: Heinemann.

Calkins, L. M. (2005). *The nuts and bolts of teaching writing.* Portsmouth, NH: Heinemann.

Calkins, L., & Huron, S. (1987). *The writing workshop: A world of difference.* Portsmouth, NH: Heinemann.

Cecil, N. L. (1994a). *Freedom fighters: Affective teaching of the language arts.* Salem, WI: Sheffield.

Cecil, N. L. (1994b). *For the love of language: Poetry for ALL learners.* Winnipeg, MB: Peguis.

Cecil, N. L. (2007). *Focus on fluency: A meaning-based approach.* Scottsdale, AZ: Holcomb Hathaway.

Cecil, N. L. (2011). *Striking a balance: A comprehensive approach to early literacy* (4th ed.). Scottsdale, AZ: Holcomb Hathaway.

Cohen, S., & Riel, B. (1989). The effect of distant audiences on students' writing. *American Educational Research Journal, 26,* 143-159.

Cohle, D. M., & Towle, W. (2001). *Connecting reading and writing in the intermediate grades.* Newark, DE: International Reading Association.

Common Core Initiative (2013). Retrieved from www.corestandards.org/resources/key-points-in-english-language-arts.

Education Northwest (1998/1999). *Assessment and accountability program.* Portland, OR.

Gibbons, P. (2002). *Scaffolding language, scaffolding learning: Teaching second language learners in the mainstream classroom.* Portsmouth, NH: Heinemann.

Gillet, J. W., & Beverly, L. (2001).*Directing the writing workshop: An elementary teacher's handbook.* New York: Guilford Press.

Gipe, J. P. (2013). *Multiple paths to literacy: Assessment and differentiated instruction for diverse learners, K-12* (9th ed.). Upper Saddle River, NJ: Merrill Prentice Hall.

Graves, D.H. (2003). *Writing: Teachers and children at work* (20th ed.). Portsmouth, NH: Heinemann.

Hansen, J. (2001). *When writers read* (2nd ed.). Portsmouth, NH: Heinemann.

Langer, J. A., & Applebee, A. N. (1987, 2009). *How writing shapes thinking: A study of teaching and learning.* Urbana, IL: National Council of Teachers of English.

Martinez, E. B. (1986). It works! In C. B. Olson (Ed.), *Practical ideas for teaching writing as a process.* Sacramento: California State Department of Education.

National Governors Association Center for Best Practices (NGACBP) & Council of Chief State School Officers (CCSSO). (2010). Common Core State Standards: English Language Arts. Washington DC: National Governors Association Center for Best Practices, Council of Chief State School Officers.

Noden, H. R. (2011). *Image grammar: Using grammatical structures to teach writing* (2nd ed.). Portsmouth, NH: Heinemann, Boynton/Cook.

Pajares, F., Johnson, M., & Usher, E. (2007). Sources of writing self-efficacy beliefs of elementary, middle, and high school students. *Research in the Teaching of English, 42*(1), 104-120.

Peha, S. (1996). *The compleat writing teacher.* Unpublished manuscript.

Peyton, J. K., & Reed, L. (1990). *Dialogue journal writing with nonnative English speakers: A handbook for teachers.* Alexandria, VA: Teachers of English to Speakers of Other Languages.

Pritchard, R. J., & Honeycutt, J. (2006). Process writing. In C. MacArthur, S. Graham, & J. Fitzgerald (Eds.), *Handbook of writing research* (pp. 275-290). New York: Guilford.

Smagorinsky, P. (Ed.). (2006). *Research on composition.* New York: Teachers College.

Stuart, V., & Graves, D. (1987). *How to teach writing.* Urbana, IL: National Council of Teachers of English.

Weaver, C. (1996). *Teaching grammar in context.* Upper Montclair, NJ: Boynton/Cook.

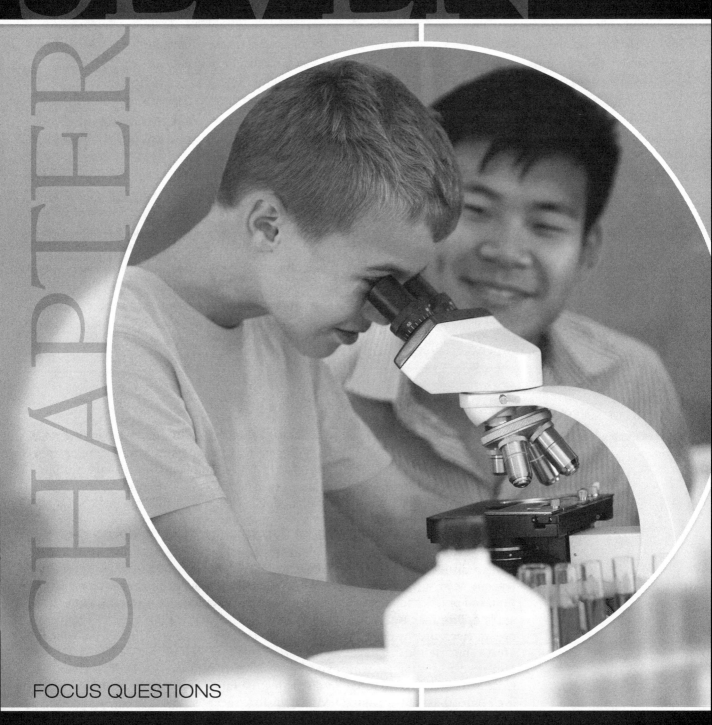

SEVEN

Literacy in the Content Areas
LEARNING FROM INFORMATIONAL TEXT

CHAPTER

FOCUS QUESTIONS

- What is the difference between a content area approach and a disciplinary approach to teaching literacy?
- Why is it important to use expository material to teach content area literacy strategies? How is content area text different from narrative text?
- What are some effective techniques for teaching expository reading and writing?
- What do students need to know about researching in the content areas?

"Okay, now I will read the passage again, but this time I want you to write down some more key words or phrases to add to those you just wrote," Mrs. Martinez explains.

She then reads the same section of the seventh-grade social studies text that she had just read—this being the third time. The first time she read the passage, she directed students to just listen. The second time, she directed them to listen for key words or phrases—those words or phrases they thought were most important to the material. This time, they will listen for some key words or phrases they may have missed earlier. Mrs. Martinez is using a strategy called *dictoglos* (Wajnryb, 1990) to help her students, especially her English learners, to understand the structure and language of expository text and to collaborate with others to learn specific content area knowledge.

After she finishes reading, Mrs. Martinez walks around the room looking at students' papers and asks, "Did everyone note some more key words and phrases? All right. Now take your paper and pencil and get with your assigned partner." She waits while quietly counting to 30, knowing that it takes her students about 30 seconds to move their chairs in order to work with their partners. She continues, "Discuss your notes with your partner and try to re-create the text you just heard me read. Expand your notes and try to rewrite the text just as you heard me read it. You have 15 minutes to work on it."

Mrs. Martinez again moves around the classroom, making sure each pair of students is clear about what they are doing. After 15 minutes she says, "Okay, now join together with one other pair of students near you so that there are four of you working together."

After another quiet count of 30 seconds, Mrs. Martinez continues with her directions: "Combine all of your notes and again try to re-create the text you heard me read. Try to make what you write as close to what I read as you can. After about 10 minutes, I will ask you if you need an additional 5 minutes. If not, I will ask for volunteers to read what you have come up with, and we will then discuss your work. Be thinking about what parts of the text are hard to re-create. We will analyze why some parts are harder than others to recall, and ways we might be able to remember those parts better."

What Is Content Area Literacy?

content area literacy ●

Content area literacy refers to the use of reading, writing, speaking, listening, viewing, and visually representing as tools for integrating and learning subject matter. Students are often expected to learn subject matter through reading, taking notes and outlining, listening to their teachers lecture, reading and understanding charts or graphs, or viewing a documentary. But they may not be taught *how* to learn in these ways. Learning informational material is different from reading or writing stories. A significant difference lies in the fact that stories are narrative material and informational text is expository material, and each type has its own distinctive structure. When teaching students to learn from informational, or content area, text, we must use expository material for modeling, demonstration, and practice to make sure students can identify the various text structures and apply appropriate strategies to other informational text. While most of the literacy strategies already introduced in this book are applicable for use in the content areas—and should be integrated into content area instruction—these strategies also need to be taught with expository material (Alfassi, 2004). The Common Core State Standards (CCSS), in discussing the range and content of student reading, state that "By reading texts in history/social studies, science, and other disciplines, students build a foundation of knowledge in these fields that will also give them the background to be better readers in all content areas. . . . Students also acquire the habits of reading independently and closely, which are essential to their future success" (NGACBP & CCSSO, 2010a, p. 10).

In this chapter, we present those strategies that are most effective for content area literacy. See the box on the facing page for an overview of the research for best practices in content area instruction.

Synopsis of Research on Best Practices

Before presenting strategies that are especially effective for literacy instruction in specific content areas, we offer the following overview of research on best practices in content area instruction, based on work by Zemelman, Daniels, and Hyde (2012).

BEST CLASSROOM STRUCTURES FOR CONTENT AREA INSTRUCTION

- Integrative units: multiweek chunks of curriculum organized around topics (e.g., whales) or themes (e.g., perseverance)

- Small group activities: less teacher talk; more active student involvement within continually shifting groupings (e.g., pairs, threes, study teams, group investigations) organized around skill needs, interests, or random assignment

- Representing-to-learn: a broadening of writing as a way to show what has been learned, including sketch books, maps, and other artistic and graphic representations

- Classroom workshop: a long, regularly scheduled chunk of time during which the focus is on doing the subject—such as doing writing, doing reading, doing math, doing history, doing science—rather than just hearing or reading about it. Student choice about what books to read, projects to complete, or topics to pursue, and frequent conferences between teacher and students are the two major elements of workshops. The typical time breakdown is 5 minutes for each student to share what will be worked on during the workshop; 30 minutes of workshop time, including conferences; and 10 minutes of each student sharing what was done that day.

- Authentic experiences: genuine real-world issues that are addressed similar to service-learning (see Chapter 10), beginning with student interest or natural curiosity for solving a problem or answering questions (e.g., homelessness—reasons for it and ways to help)

- Reflective assessment: use of observation, interviews, questionnaires, artifacts, portfolios, and rubrics with the intent to monitor growth and help students set goals, keep track of their own work, and evaluate their efforts (see Chapter 2)

BEST PRACTICES FOR MATH

- use of manipulatives
- cooperative groups
- discussion
- questioning
- justification
- writing about math
- problem solving
- word problems with everyday problems and applications
- connecting to other subjects
- understanding key concepts
- estimation
- spatial sense
- collecting/organizing data
- tables, graphs
- use of multiple assessment techniques (written, oral, demonstration)

BEST PRACTICES FOR SOCIAL STUDIES

- provision of choices about what to study in depth
- inquiry and problem solving
- student decision making
- participation in community/school affairs
- cooperative groups
- integration of other curriculum areas
- getting to know cultures
- open expression of ideas (e.g., class meetings)

BEST PRACTICES FOR SCIENCE

- hands-on activities
- observation
- hypothesizing
- reflection
- questioning
- thinking
- problem solving
- in-depth study of a few important thematic topics
- integration of reading, writing, and math
- collaborative small group work
- use of literature circles

What Is Disciplinary Literacy?

Content literacy and disciplinary literacy are related, but disciplinary literacy goes beyond content literacy. Content area reading focuses on teaching the reading and study skills that will help students better understand and remember the material (such as textbooks) in their content area classes. The disciplinary literacy approach to learning, on the other hand, helps students read discipline-specific material that goes beyond the textbook and focuses more on *what* is being taught; it teaches students content from the discipline. Using the disciplinary literacy framework, students learn like mathematicians, scientists, historians, or computer technologists; read and write with more specificity; use models of reading from the disciplines; do more probing; and acquire more insight into the discipline's literature (Moje, 2008; Shanahan & Shanahan, 2008). Since each discipline offers its own challenges, demands, and literacy distinctions, the focus for teachers should be on the discipline's academic language, which is markedly exact and concise.

Writing in the disciplines also differs. Demonstrate to students how to write in a manner similar to that used by professionals in a given discipline by showing them examples of discipline-specific writing: for example, a lab report or abstract in a scientific journal, or an article, published in a journal of history, that was based on original research in an Italian archive. Comparing and contrasting various types of content area writing helps students write to learn, whereas analyzing specific kinds of writing in a discipline has a different goal: to allow students to better understand it and to then be able to write in that discipline using familiar models. Following are examples of content area writing and writing in the disciplines; in both, the task is for the writer to persuade the reader:

- *Content area writing examples:* When writing a letter to the editor, writers share their opinions, experiences from other sources, and/or personal experiences to argue a point or take a clear stance to substantiate their thoughts. They may use formal or informal language, depending on their goal. As another example, an expository essay for a social studies class may cite evidence to support a claim and use logical reasoning and language that is more formal and objective than the more stylized language likely to appear in a letter to the editor. Formal language creates a more distanced stance.

- *Writing in the disciplines example:* In a lab report, the writer assumes authority by stating a hypothesis and proving or disproving it with specific and concise language and logical appeal. The writer must use statistics, facts, observations, and other persuasive methods to support the results.

Literacy and Content Standards vs. Discipline-Specific Literacy Activities

All teachers play a role in enhancing students' literacy. In all content areas, teachers should prepare students to read increasingly complex and sophisticated materials as required by the Common Core State Standards (NGACBP & CCSSO, 2010b). Since each discipline has its own text types or genres, which increase in complexity as grade levels increase, students should engage with these texts and learn to navigate them for comprehension. In addition, content areas also have standards that incorporate and overlap with literacy standards; in fact, the CCSS require content areas to include literacy:

The Standards set requirements not only for English language arts (ELA) but also for literacy in history/social studies, science, and technical subjects. Just as students must learn to read, write, speak, listen, and use language effectively in a variety of content areas, so too must the Standards specify the literacy skills and understandings required for college and career readiness in multiple disciplines. (NGACBP & CCSSO, 2010b, p. 3)

National associations devoted to specific disciplines have also developed content area standards. Note the terminology used in the following content area standards that reference literacy activities:

- National Curriculum Standards for Social Studies (National Council for the Social Studies, 2002) include reference to the following literacy tasks: "identify, describe, and examine," "compare and analyze," "consider the connections," and so forth. This subject area also has discipline-specific literacy processes. In history, rhetorical competency includes the ability to apply three processes (from Stahl & Shanahan, 2004, with some examples from Moje, 2008):

  - *Corroboration,* which involves such skills as comparing and contrasting documents and looking for patterns to create new understandings from facts and events presented.

  - *Sourcing,* which involves considering how the bias of a document affects its content; examining the significance of evidence, sources, or events; reading and understanding the accounts of others and their biases and credibility; and more.

  - *Contextualization,* which involves situating a text in its temporal, spatial, and ideological contexts, to include locating and using evidence from the past, placing events into time periods and explaining their commonalities, and presenting historical accounts.

- The National Science Education Standards (NSES) include reference to the following literacy tasks: pose a question, carry out an investigation, critique and communicate its results (National Academies, 1996). The inquiry-based question should guide the learning to come. Prereading activities provide students the opportunity to learn about the concept under study. In a more disciplinary approach, teachers ask students to describe the problem they are studying and state what they already know about it, as well as to make predictions or hypotheses about it and the outcome of the study they will pursue.

- National Council of Teachers of Mathematics (NCTM) Standards include reference to the following literacy tasks: interpret and comprehend word problems; develop, record, explain, critique strategies for solving computational problems; understand patterns and describe verbally; and formulate questions that can be addressed with data and collect, organize, and display relevant data to answer them. This critical thinking and inquiry-based content area also has certain discipline-specific literacy tools for making sense of mathematics. These include manipulatives as well as printed symbols and graphic representations that all must be "read" as text in mathematics. To problem-solve in math, teachers establish connections among pictures, written symbols, oral language, real-world situations, and manipulatives. Using proofs as one example, mathematicians identify and analyze them, and then present or publish them; if students can read and make sense of mathematical proofs in math class, this will help to prepare them for the real work in the discipline.

NCTE/IRA Standards for the English Language Arts

www.ncte.org/standards/ncte-ira

The same terminology is found in national literacy standards: critical thinking, formulating questions, and communicating results are the same literacy tasks that are expected in the literacy standards (see the NCTE/IRA Standards for the English Language Arts).

Themed units are an effective way to integrate literacy instruction and to use the inquiry tools necessary for learning in the content areas. One possible set of inquiry tools for students follows (Sierra-Perry et al., 1996, p. 37):

- identifying interesting and meaningful topics and questions to pursue;
- gathering quality source materials appropriate to their questions, interests, and abilities;
- gleaning information from these sources;
- organizing this information;
- responding to this information;
- sharing what they've learned; and
- pacing themselves for success.

Furthermore, as Kane (2011) notes, "Wide and varied opportunities for reading, writing, listening, speaking, and viewing can help students meet national content knowledge standards and benchmarks . . . a standards-based curriculum can use literacy strategies not as add-ons, but as integral to content teaching itself" (p. ix).

Reading in the Content Areas

We often assume that, once students learn to read, they can read just about anything. However, we must realize that not all reading tasks are alike. For example, the cognitive demands placed on readers by expository text differ from those placed by narrative text: they are not necessarily more difficult, but they are different. Readers must be taught how to recognize these differences and how to actively engage with expository text.

Students reading in any content area must also be able to identify when they are having difficulty accessing the material. As they read, students may skip information contained in charts, tables, graphs, or text. In such cases, they are simply not attending to their comprehension. They may lack metacomprehension when they read a difficult passage of text, and not realize they did not understand. When readers do experience metacognition, they are aware when they do not comprehend the material.

Strategies to help students when they struggle with content information include the following:

- Model how you read and comprehend text in a content area. Read aloud part of a difficult passage and, as you go, reflect on what you are reading.
- Teach students to pause and reflect on new or difficult vocabulary words and make predictions of their meanings based on context or derivations, or on related words.
- Ask students questions as you read together, and encourage them to ask questions of each other before, during, and after the reading occurs.
- Encourage students to use their reading strategies (context clues, identifying new words and finding their meanings, and the other strategies we've discussed).
- Most important, promote metacognition in the disciplines. Ask students to slow down when they read, to acknowledge when they do not understand the materials, and to strategize how to resolve questions and confusion.

Following is information about the texts that are used in content area classrooms and additional strategies for teaching students how to actively engage with them.

Content Area Materials

Reading in the content areas involves learning how to read a variety of discourse patterns and understanding the different text structures associated with a particular content area. When planning lessons, one strategy that might be helpful for examining and selecting content area texts is FLIP.

The FLIP Strategy   activity

This strategy, originally developed as a before-reading strategy, can also be used by teachers when preparing content area lessons to determine the friendliness (F), language (L), interest (I), and prior knowledge (P) of a reading selection (Schumm & Mangrum, 1991). The steps for this strategy, as presented by Sadler (2001), involve asking yourself the following questions:

Step 1 (F): To determine the text's *friendliness* for your students, ask yourself:
- Which features of the content area material are easy to understand?
- Which features need further explanation (e.g., use of headings, sidebars, graphs)?

Step 2 (L): To determine the difficulty of the *language* for your students, ask yourself:
- What terms might students have difficulty understanding?

Step 3 (I): To determine your students' likely *interest,* ask yourself:
- How much interest will my students have in this topic?
- How might their interest affect their level of involvement?
- How might I enhance their interest?

Step 4 (P): To determine students' *prior knowledge* about the text's topic, ask yourself:
- Do I know what my students already know about this topic?
- What methods will I use to find out?

For example, suppose your students are about to start a new science unit on light. The related chapter in their science textbook is "The Nature of Light." Examine this material and apply the FLIP strategy (Sadler, 2001, p. 38):

F The text is divided into sections with questions.
L Go over words such as *opaque, translucent,* and *transparent.*
I Think how fast light moves!
P Ask what students already know about light.

Note that you can also teach students to use the FLIP strategy—have them ask themselves these various questions—before they attempt their content area reading. The following sections provide more information related to helping students learn from content area materials.

Types of texts used across the curriculum

Textbooks have traditionally been a central focus of most content area classes, from elementary grades through the college level (Cuban, 1991; Gottfried & Kyle, 1992), but they are certainly not the only materials appropriately used across the

The use of literature, including graphic texts, has the potential for enhancing the interest students have in a topic.

curriculum. Nonfiction trade books; nonfiction children's and young adult literature, including picture books (e.g., *Sweet Clara and the Freedom Quilt*, 1993) and certain graphic books/novels (e.g., *Fagin the Jew*, 2003); and electronic text provide useful tools for learning content and learning to read critically. They also can motivate and enrich content area teaching and learning. The nonfiction trade books available today are beautifully illustrated and cover a wide range of content area topics. Resources such as *Celebrating Children's Choices: 25 Years of Children's Favorite Books* (Post et al., 2000), *Nonfiction Matters: Reading, Writing, and Research in Grades 3–8* (Harvey, 1998), *Teaching with Picture Books in the Middle School* (Tiedt, 2000), *The Power of Picture Books in Teaching Math, Science, and Social Studies: Grades PreK–8* (Columba, Kim, & Moe, 2009), *Integrating Literature in the Content Areas* (Kane, 2008), and *Using Literature in the Middle Grades: A Thematic Approach* (Moss, 1994) provide a wealth of information about specific book titles for use in the content areas.

Fictional picture books and graphic books, as well as novels, must also be considered for use in the content area classroom. For example, older students interested in social justice issues will find that picture books dealing with such subjects as homelessness (*Fly Away Home*, Bunting, 1991), the Holocaust (*Rose Blanche*, Gallaz & Innocenti, 2003), and the effects of the atom bomb (*Sadako*, Coerr & Young, 1993) make an impact not easily made through the denser, more text-heavy accounts found in history books. Likewise, graphic novels such as *Good-bye, Chunky Rice* (Thompson, 2006) and *Pedro and Me* (Winick, 2000) convey important messages in a way that is accessible to the most reluctant readers. (See Chapter 5 for more information about graphic novels and Appendix A for suggested picture books and graphic novels.)

Several valuable websites offer listings of materials, activities, supplies, and lesson plans, as well as links to extensive electronic text material for content area themes. For example,

- **http://scholastic.com/MagicSchoolBus/theme/index.htm** lists materials, supplies, and activities related to popular science themes. For example, one activity that is part of the "Life Science" theme looks at the food chain, and an activity that is part of "Environment" looks at the importance of recycling.

- **www.carolhurst.com** includes a collection of reviews of great books for kids; appropriate grade-level usages; ways to use these books in the classroom; and collections of books and activities on particular topics, curriculum areas, and themes.

Many content area teachers use both fiction and nonfiction literature as a way to introduce challenging subject area content. For example, historical fiction can be used to introduce and clarify a unit on World War II. Books such as *Friedrich* (Richter, 1970) or *The Boy in the Striped Pajamas* (Boyne, 2006), novels written from the perspective of non-Jewish boys about the persecution of Jewish neighbors and friends in Nazi Germany, may be read aloud to students, and their responses to the characters and events may be written in journals and referred to at relevant points during the study of World War II.

Teachers may choose to use several books across a wide range of reading ability levels and genres on a particular topic (e.g., ocean life, rainforests, the Holocaust, the stars, civil rights). These books are made available for students to search for answers to questions they have about the particular topic (see the discussion of data charts later in this chapter). Using literature has the potential to enhance the interest students have in a topic and also helps teachers address curriculum standards related to providing students with a variety of genres for individual content areas such as social studies, science, and mathematics. See Appendix A and Tables 5.1 and 5.2 in Chapter 5; see also Kane (2008, 2011) for extensive bibliographies of children's and young adult literature appropriate to the content areas.

Expository text structures

The structure of expository text differs from the structure of narrative text. Stories represent the structure of **narrative text.** Stories have characters, settings, problems, key events, and resolutions. These elements work together to impart a message or theme, and sometimes to present a moral or lesson. The purpose of **expository text** is to explain, describe, or persuade. Expository material has a content focus and provides information and ideas. Representative examples of expository writing include news stories, reports, case studies, comparison/contrast papers, and historical accounts. Expository writing is organized according to a variety of structures. The most common of these structures are: description, cause/effect, comparison/contrast, time/order, problem/solution, enumeration, and persuasion.

● narrative text

● expository text

- *Description, commonly found in informational text, provides characteristic features of the topic:* "Eels are characterized by their snakelike shape, lack of spines in the fins, and the absence of ventral fins."
- *Cause/effect tells of events and what happens as a result:* "The Pilgrims were not used to such long, hard winters. Many Pilgrims became sick—so many that by spring about 50 percent of the population was dead."
- *Comparison/contrast directly discusses two related topics, giving their essential characteristics, and often employs similes to help readers make connections to more familiar concepts:* "Hurricanes usually form over warm, tropical water, whereas tornadoes usually form over land. When tornadoes approach, people often say the sound is like that of a fast-moving train."
- *Time/order (also called sequence) presents a chronological, historical accounting of events:* "Archaeologists have learned that the evolution of man began with . . ., then . . ., followed by . . ."
- *Problem/solution presents real-life events that require research in seeking a solution:* Wetlands are valuable nursery areas for aquatic and land animals. They can even filter out some kinds of pollution . . . but developers are planning to build on these wetlands. What can be done to satisfy developers while maintaining these animals' homes?"
- *Enumeration (can also include sequence) presents listings, step-by-step directions, or stages of development:* "Amphibians first lay their eggs in clumps in quiet water or on moist leaf mold. Then the eggs hatch into larvae, or tadpoles. The tadpoles develop legs and grow into frogs."
- *Persuasion offers a statement that is a proposition—a statement that can be argued as accurate—and support for that proposition:* "The school bond referendum should be passed, and this is why . . ." Examples of persuasive writing include reviews of books, music, and films; editorials; letters to the editor; and position papers.

It is important to locate these structures within the expository materials that students will be using. Provide modeling and have small groups work together to find other examples within their classroom materials.

Content Area Reading Strategies/Activities

After examining the content area material, you might plan for students to use one or more of the following content area reading strategies/activities before, during, or after reading, as indicated.

Before reading

The two-minute preview (Stephens & Brown, 2000). Time spent previewing a content area selection before reading it helps students prepare adequately for what might be difficult, complex, or technical material. Previewing the material places the student in an active role right from the start. A checklist such as the one in Figure 7.1 can be used to guide the previewing; specific items might change depending on the purpose of reading and the nature of the material. Students can work alone or in pairs for two minutes, jotting down their responses on the preview form. Following this, the teacher might suggest a strategy for reading the selection, based on the structure of the material.

Skimming and scanning. Reading rate quite naturally varies depending on the text's readability level, the subject matter (whether it is narrative or expository text), and the purposes for reading. For example, you might read a mystery novel at a rapid pace, but you might read more slowly and deliberately when studying a social studies chapter to prepare for a quiz. Even proficient adult readers may read in a slow, laborious manner when confronted with material that contains highly technical

figure **7.1**   Two-minute preview checklist.

☐ **Introduction.** What is the selection about?

_____

_____

☐ **Headings.** What are the topics in this selection?

_____

_____

☐ **Graphics and other visuals.** Can I interpret this information?

_____

_____

☐ **Margin notes.** Are there notes in the margins? What kind of information do they contain?

_____

_____

☐ **Summary.** Is it a clear and concise overview of the selection? What is one key idea in the summary?

_____

_____

vocabulary, or if the text addresses subjects of which they have little background knowledge. Students need direct instruction in knowing when to adjust their rate according to the text and their purposes for reading.

Two types of in-class silent reading require a variation from normal reading rate, as they are often done for purposes other than simple pleasure reading: skimming and scanning. **Skimming** is reading that is done rapidly, but purposefully, to get a general idea what a selection is about. Readers engaged in skimming will be expected to get the main idea of the selection as well as a few supporting details. A reader is **scanning**, however, when she is looking for some specific information—such as when she is reading the blurb on the back of a book to decide if she wants to read it, or when she is scanning a web page before clicking on a link to another page.

- skimming

- scanning

Skimming and scanning are critical skills for increasing comprehension because they show students that reading rate is not a constant but changes depending on the purposes for which one is reading. In addition, both skimming and scanning are discrete reading skills that encourage students to push themselves to read at a faster than normal rate while still attending to comprehension.

An effective way to have students practice skimming is to incorporate it as a regular routine when introducing new chapters in content-area material. Use the following procedure:

- Before beginning the chapter, ask students to look through or skim the chapter to get a general idea of what it might contain. Tell them to pay particular attention to the introduction, section titles, boldfaced words, and the summary.

- Invite them to jot down their ideas about the chapter's possible content and then share those ideas with the rest of the class.

- Later, when students have finished reading the chapter, ask them to revisit their ideas to see if they were correct.

- This activity can eventually be timed to emphasize for students that skimming should be done more rapidly than normal reading.

Scanning abilities can be fostered by encouraging students to locate specific information from reference material, such as a TV guide, a section of the newspaper, an encyclopedia, a website, or an almanac. For example, using the website for a local television station or community, ask students to find the phone number of the nearest pizza restaurant. Or, students can scan news articles to find out the what, why, where, and when of a recent event. To enhance student interest and increase speed, make the activity into a teamed competition, pairing a skilled reader with one who may need more assistance.

Before, during, and after reading

Anticipation guides. A simple anticipation guide—a before-reading tool—may provide three to five statements and ask students to indicate whether they agree or disagree with each statement. Students then read the text and either confirm or rethink their choices.

1. There are about 1,500 active volcanoes. <u>disagree</u>
2. Mount St. Helens is a dormant volcano. <u>agree</u>
3. Mauna Loa is the world's most active volcano. <u>agree</u>
4. Once a volcano is dormant it can never erupt again. <u>agree</u>

Anticipation guides can be extended to include an additional part that is completed during or after the reading. In an extended anticipation guide (Duffelmeyer & Baum, 1992), students determine whether or not the text offers support for their agree/disagree choices, indicating yes or no and stating why. For the preceding example, students asked to extend their thinking during or after reading might provide the following information:

1. No support. I disagreed, but the article says there are about 1,500 active volcanoes.

2. Yes, the text supports it. I agreed, and the article says that when a volcano is between eruptions it is dormant. Since Mount St. Helens is not erupting now, it is dormant.

3. No support. I agreed that Mauna Loa is the most active volcano, but it is actually Kilauea, in Hawaii.

4. No support. I agreed that a dormant volcano never erupts again, but a volcano that never erupts again would be called extinct. Mount St. Helens erupted in 1980 after being dormant for about 120 years.

text-based collaborative learning ◦

Text-based collaborative learning.   Text-based collaborative learning is an effective technique for helping all students (including those with learning disabilities in inclusive settings, as well as English learners) actively engage with expository material (Klingner et al., 2004; Langer, 2001). In text-based collaborative learning, students work with a partner or in a small group to discuss, question, clarify, and perform writing tasks, involving expository text. Follow these steps to initiate text-based collaborative learning.

1. Introduce the subject of the text material and provide sufficient background information.

2. Have students collaborate to notice how information in the text is organized (e.g., multiple sections and subheadings within chapters; a proposition with supporting paragraphs).

3. Encourage students to ask questions about what they're about to read (e.g., who, what, when, where, why, how).

4. Then, have students prepare general outlines, using the text's headings and subheadings, before they begin the reading. Students can now begin their reading with a purpose, better prepared to understand what they're about to read or to ask questions to help with their understanding.

5. As students read silently, recommend that they write notes about unknown words, confusing sections, or answers to their questions, and have them start to fill in their general outlines.

6. Following the reading, have students return to the text with their partner or small group and discuss their notes in an effort to clarify any questions they may have.

www◦◦◦

Reciprocal Teaching Plus
www.readingonline.org/articles/
art_index.asp?HREF=ash

Extension: Ash (2002) describes an extension, Reciprocal Teaching Plus, which engages students in critical evaluation of the text after reading. This strategy also uses peer support to clarify students' understanding of the text.

Reading "with the grain" and "against the grain."   This concept may seem to apply primarily to persuasive or editorial writing, but understanding it can help students read more critically overall. When students are asked to read "with the grain," they are reading to understand the piece and the author's point of view, reading through an author's eyes (Bartholomae & Petrosky, 1993; Bean, Chappell, & Gilliam, 2011). When reading "against the grain," however, students are asked look more closely at the piece, exploring underlying context and cultural influences, questioning aspects such as the author's point of view, logic, intentions, and possible biases. Students can increase their critical literacy by reading both with and against the grain.

Study systems. Having a study system helps students develop an awareness of their own abilities to understand and learn information from expository material. Several systems are available that students can explore and perhaps modify to suit their personal preferences. Most of these systems stem from, or are modifications of, the classic study strategy of **SQ3R—Survey, Question, Read, Recite, Review** (Robinson, 1946). Briefly, to *survey,* the student reads the title, introductory paragraph, main headings, and chapter summary and then examines any illustrations. To *question,* the student rephrases the main headings into questions to be answered during reading. The student then proceeds to *read,* with the purpose of answering the questions. To *recite,* the student simply recites the answers to the questions out loud. Finally, to *review,* the student tries to recall answers to questions as well as the general structure of the material, from memory. As students are introduced to a study strategy, they may find that a variation of that strategy works better for them. Students might be more willing to use a study system if they have participated in creating a personalized system. Some examples of study systems and their acronyms follow:

● SQ3R—Survey, Question, Read, Recite, Review

PLAE =	Preplan, List, Activate, Evaluate (Simpson & Nist, 1984)

PLAN =	Predict, Locate, Add, Note (Caverly, Mandeville, & Nicholson, 1995)

PORPE =	Predict, Organize, Rehearse, Practice, Evaluate (Simpson, 1986)

PQRST =	Preview, Question, Read, Summarize, Test (Spache, 1963)

REAP =	Read, Encode, Annotate, Ponder (Eanet & Manzo, 1976)

SCAIT =	Select key words, Complete sentences, Accept final statements, Infer, Think (Wiesendanger & Bader, 1992)

SQ3R =	Survey, Question, Read, Recite, Review (Robinson, 1946)

SQRQCQ = Survey, Question, Read, Question, Compute, Question (Fay, 1965)

STAR =	Skim and set purpose, Think, Anticipate and adjust, Review and retell (Stephens & Brown, 2000)

Study Strategy Tryout ⊚ **activity** ⊚

To try out a study strategy, follow these steps:

1. Model the use of several of the previously listed study systems.
2. Discuss with students what the strategies seem to have in common, and invite students to use them when reading informational text.
3. After students have had an opportunity to try various strategies, discuss which ones seemed most helpful.
4. Encourage students to create their own combinations of study systems that work best for them. Some student-created systems might look like the following (Stephens & Brown, 2000, p. 113):

    GOAL = Glance through, Order information, Adjust, Learn by retelling

    LAFF = Look over, Ask questions, Find answers, Follow through by reviewing and retelling

---

After reading

Retelling. Just as retellings are done for narrative comprehension, effective retellings can be done for expository text as well. They can be fostered with these guiding questions (Hoyt, 1999, p. 125):

- What is the topic?
- What are the most important ideas to remember?
- What did you learn that you did not already know?
- What is the setting for this information?
- What did you notice about the organization and text structure?
- What did you notice about the visuals, such as graphs, charts, and pictures?
- Can you summarize what you learned?
- What do you think was the author's purpose for writing this material?

See Appendix C.9 for a self-assessment tool based on these questions.

Writing in the Content Areas

We often assume that if we teach students to write about their personal experiences or to write stories, they will then be able to transfer those abilities to writing in the content areas. But students must have opportunities to write in response to expository text, to use writing as a tool for learning, and to write in expository modes (i.e., to inform, describe, persuade, or explain) in order to develop these skills. **Informational writing,** often called "expository writing," allows students to explain ideas, objects, and processes to a reader in an understandable way while at the same time improving the writer's own knowledge and understanding of the topic.

informational writing •

Each discipline tends to have its own purposes for writing; for example,

- science essays identify, describe, explain, and hypothesize
- history essays analyze, compare, contrast, trace, and identify causal relationships
- English essays interpret, analyze, compare, contrast, and evaluate

When students are given appropriate instruction regarding the structure of informational text and a topic they find interesting, they are fully capable of coping with the complex organizational challenges inherent in writing informational text. Indeed, students as young as 6 or 7 years of age can be successful in writing informational text. As an example, Read (2005) found that when first- and second-grade students were allowed to write on topics of their own choosing and were invited to write collaboratively, they worked out any content problems aloud and provided feedback to each other regarding content organization and print conventions.

Choosing a topic about which to write is often easier for students when doing informational writing as opposed to narrative writing (Read, 2005). We hear less of "I don't know what to write about!" because students can choose from so many topics they can become interested in. Students enjoy researching and then writing about their discoveries on a wide variety of topics, including wild and domestic animals, cars, other cultures and ancient civilizations, volcanoes, and planets, to name just a few. See the box accompanying this discussion for websites that can spur interest in informational topics. Some of the sites are directed at student learners, while others offer educational tools for teachers.

As indicated by many states' content standards, we now expect students to be able to write in a variety of genres. The techniques described in the following sections can help guide teachers in planning instruction for writing in the content areas. In addition, scoring rubrics for assessing expository writing, like those found in Appendix C.18, are valuable tools.

Websites for Informational Text

Children's Book Council (CBC), www.cbcbooks.org

This site provides lists of outstanding trade books for young people in the areas of social studies and science.

Cleveland Rock & Roll Hall of Fame, http://rockhall.com/education/inside-the-classroom

This site offers lesson plans that integrate music with history and literature.

Defenders of Wildlife, www.defenders.org

The programs addressed here focus on the extinction of animal species and the destruction of their environment. The website is committed to protecting endangered plants and wild animals.

Eisenhower National Clearinghouse, www.goenc.com

This clearinghouse is dedicated to identifying superior curriculum resources, creating high-quality professional development materials, and improving science and math learning in K–12 classrooms.

Endangered Species Coalition, www.stopextinction.org

This group is the watchdog for the Endangered Species Act of 1973. The website disseminates information and provides discussions about environmental, scientific, and conservation issues related to the ESA.

Fish America Foundation, www.fishamerica.org

This organization has assisted more than 700 grassroots organizations to enhance fish production and increase water quality throughout North America.

Greenpeace, www.greenpeace.org

This activist organization is dedicated to achieving change in environmental and conservationist issues through direct action and international conferences.

The History Place, www.historyplace.com

This site provides information about history that can be used as background for any social studies unit; especially good for discussing U.S. presidents.

Journey North, www.learner.org/jnorth

This site includes information about an online project and resources for the study of seasonal change. Children from all 50 states and Canada have taken part in the project.

Kids Web Japan, http://web-jpn.org/kidsweb/index.html

Introduces American children to Japan, including Japanese lifestyle, pictures, and legends. Managed by the Japan Center for Intercultural Communications.

Knowledge Adventure, http://knowledgeadventure.com/home

This site features educational games on all subjects for all ages.

Magic School Bus, http://scholastic.com/MagicSchoolBus/index.htm

This site includes content area materials and activities for students and is also a resource for teachers, librarians, and parents.

My Hero Project, www.myhero.com/home.asp

This site allows students to read about many heroes worldwide and celebrate the best of humanity as they come to understand what it means to make a difference.

National Geographic for Kids, http://kids.nationalgeographic.com/kids

This site is run by the National Geographic Society, so it includes their incredible photographic resources; Games, videos, and more are intended for kids of all ages.

New York Philharmonic Kidzone, www.nyphilkids.org/main.phtml

The activities on this site include videos about instruments, composing music, games, and puzzles.

Smithsonian for Kids, www.si.edu/Kids

This site helps students explore the "seriously amazing" resources of the Smithsonian.

Student Science, https://student.societyforscience.org/sciencenews-students

This site offers a wide variety of science news for students, including biology, astonomy, physics, chemistry, and much more.

Writing Expository Paragraphs/Essays

The expository paragraph or essay presents information about a topic. The main purpose of this mode of discourse is to explain or inform, to tell readers something they may not know, and to tell them in a way that they will understand (see Figure 7.2). It allows students to explain ideas, objects, or processes while at the same time improving their own knowledge and understanding of the topic.

Instead of having a somewhat loose beginning, middle, and end, as in narrative structure, the expository paragraph/essay has a somewhat more rigid organization and is organized according to one of the patterns discussed earlier in this chapter (e.g., description, cause/effect, and so on). Essentially, expository writing has a distinct organization that students can be taught; it typically follows this format:

1. *Thesis statement.* In an essay, the thesis statement occurs at the beginning of the piece and indicates the author's attitude or position on a topic. It tells the reader why the piece is being written. *Example:* Spiders play an important role in controlling certain insect populations.

2. *Topic sentence.* In a paragraph, the topic sentence tells the reader what the paragraph is going to be about. *Example:* Insects differ from spiders in several ways.

3. *Transition phrases.* Important words that signal new ideas often are called transition phrases. They are the "glue" that holds the essay's paragraphs together and tend to be related to the expository text structure a writer is

---

figure **7.2** Example passages for contrasting expository and narrative writing.

GIVING INFORMATION
(Explaining)

The dolphin may look like a fish, but this friendly sea creature is really a mammal. First of all, dolphins have lungs just like we do. They must come to the surface of the water to breathe and get oxygen from the air. Fish can take oxygen from the water. Like other mammals, dolphins have backbones and are warm blooded. Finally, they nurse young dolphins on milk just like a cow might nurse a calf. The dolphin's streamlined body and its big, strong tail might resemble a fish, but don't be fooled; it's definitely a mammal.

TELLING A STORY
(Narrating)

I was excited to see the dolphins, my favorite animal.

"Go closer to the tank," my father said.

I looked into the water and saw the beautiful animals swimming together. Someone was feeding them fish.

"I wish I could swim with the dolphins," I said.

"Maybe someday you will," said my father.

Just then one of the dolphins swam close to us and suddenly we were as wet as could be! We laughed and laughed.

using (see the earlier discussion of text structures). *Examples:* Words and phrases such as *first, second, finally, on the other hand, nevertheless,* and *in a similar way* are examples of phrases that help readers to realize that a new idea is about to be introduced.

4. *Examples, evidence, and explanations.* The essence of any expository piece is in the details. After providing a topic sentence or thesis statement, the writer must elaborate and support it using various tools, depending on the organizational structure being used; these tools include explanation, examples, reasons, facts, and evidence. *Example:* The first difference is that insects have six legs, while a spider has eight.

5. *Conclusion.* The expository piece is tied together with a conclusion that reminds the reader of the topic sentence/thesis statement. Because supporting information has been given via examples, evidence, or explanations, the conclusion is stated slightly differently than the original statement. *Example:* People should be careful about killing off the spiders in their yards and gardens because spiders are useful in controlling the population of harmful bugs.

Writing Persuasive Essays and Arguments with Support

Two purposes of expository writing are to persuade and to argue. A classroom can provide many opportunities for authentic persuasive writing; for example, a writer may try to persuade readers to adopt a viewpoint concerning environmental or safety issues facing the school or neighborhood that students recognize and want to do something about. Writing an argument differs from persuasive writing, however. In argumentative writing, a claim is presented and supported with evidence, but alternative claims, with supporting facts, also need to be discussed objectively. Although it may be clear which perspective the writer favors, other claims are presented and discussed. From school issues (should physical education be required? should school cafeterias have vending machines?) to national and international issues (climate change, U.S. funding of the international space station), the topics that students can explore and for which they can be taught to write argumentative essays are endless.

The CCSS emphasize reading, understanding, and writing arguments. For example, standard 6-8.1 for writing in grades 6–8 in history/social studies, science, and technical subjects states that students are expected to be able to do the following:

1. Write arguments focused on discipline-specific content.
   a. Introduce claim(s) about a topic or issue, acknowledge and distinguish the claim(s) from alternate or opposing claims, and organize the reasons and evidence logically.
   b. Support claim(s) with logical reasoning and relevant, accurate data and evidence that demonstrate an understanding of the topic or text, using credible sources.
   c. Use words, phrases, and clauses to create cohesion and clarify the relationships among claim(s), counterclaims, reasons, and evidence.
   d. Establish and maintain a formal style.
   e. Provide a concluding statement or section that follows from and supports the argument presented. (NGACBP & CCSSO, 2010c, p. 64)

This standard—pertaining to argumentation—provides a map for instructors who are teaching the argumentative writing skills that students need to forge ahead in school. These skills must come from experiences in each discipline, as students read, write, and speak in the specific content areas; defending their assertions; supporting their claims; presenting alternate perspectives; and providing evidence and analysis to show their critical thinking.

activity — Proposition/Support Outline for Persuasive Writing

This strategy helps students

- write more persuasively;
- read material of an editorial nature more critically (Buehl, 2009);
- build the analytical-thinking skills so important for functioning in the world at large;
- use supporting evidence effectively and thus prepare them for argumentative writing.

Six steps are involved in the strategy:

1. Discuss the difference between facts and opinions with students. Brainstorm examples of each, and have students define the terms in their own words. Some examples might be the following:
   - The temperature today is 78 degrees. (Fact)
   - It feels warm today. (Opinion)
   - Everybody enjoys eating pizza. (Opinion)
   - There are 13 boys and 11 girls in our class. (Fact)
   - Dogs are the best pets. (Opinion)
   - Ten students in our room have a dog for a pet. (Fact)
2. For students, define the term *proposition* as "an opinion represented by a statement that is put forth as being true or accurate." Give an example, such as, "Wearing school uniforms increases student achievement." Have students brainstorm other examples of possible propositions. Then ask students, in small groups, to think of arguments they could make to support one of these propositions. Introduce the Proposition/Support Outline (see Figure 7.3) and model the five ways used to support propositions: facts, statistics, examples, expert authority, and logic and reasoning.
3. Practice analyzing an author's persuasive piece using the outline. (Carefully choose a piece of writing that clearly features the elements in the outline.) For example, students might work in pairs to analyze an editorial that appeared in the local newspaper detailing how the loss of a local wetland area would cause flooding in surrounding communities. Students should be prepared to share the clues that helped them determine the facts, statistics, examples, expert authority, and logic and reasoning elements of the editorial.
4. Discuss the quality of the support presented in the material. Is it convincing? Does the piece rely on only one means of support (e.g., logic and reasoning)? Do the statistics seem reliable? Are the examples far-fetched? Is more than one expert authority cited?
5. Use the outline to critique editorials, prepare for a class debate, guide independent research, or to write an argument.
6. To help students make the transition from persuasive to argumentative writing, bring in an argumentative essay on the same topic as the persuasive essay. Ask students to note the differences in the two types of essays.

Example of a proposition/support outline.   *figure* **7.3**

PROPOSITION/SUPPORT OUTLINE FOR RAINFORESTS

PROPOSITION: The loss of rain forests will lead to an environmental disaster.

SUPPORT: 1. Facts
                 ● Rain forests use carbon dioxide.
                 ● There is increased carbon dioxide in the earth's atmosphere.
                 ● The rain forests contain many endangered plant and animal species.
                 ● Deforestation leads to widespread soil erosion in many areas.
                 ● The burning of fossil fuels puts carbon dioxide into the environment.

              2. Statistics
                 ● More than one acre of rain forest disappears every second.
                 ● Four million acres (larger than the state of Connecticut) disappear every year.
                 ● Fifty to 100 species are destroyed with each acre of forest cleared.
                 ● If present trends continue, deforestation could wipe out or severely damage nearly 60% of the Amazon rainforest by 2030.

              3. Examples
                 ● India has almost no remaining rain forest.
                 ● Current plans target eliminating much of the Congo's rain forest.
                 ● Run-off from deforestation in Indonesia threatens their coral reefs and diminishes the fish population.
                 ● Cutting of rain forests in Bangladesh and the Philippines has led to killer floods.

              4. Expert Authority
                 ● Computers predict doubling of carbon dioxide in the 21st century, raising temperatures by 3 to 9 degrees.
                 ● The National Center for Atmospheric Research believes increased carbon dioxide results in the greenhouse effect and global warming.
                 ● Environmentalist leader Al Gore calls the greenhouse effect our most serious threat ever.

              5. Logic and Reasoning
                 ● Warmer temperatures will harm crops and increase energy costs.
                 ● More people will starve because of less food and increased population growth.
                 ● The polar glaciers will continue to melt and raise the sea level, flooding coastlines.
                 ● Many species useful to humans will disappear.
                 ● More sections of the world will become uninhabitable deserts due to soil loss, erosion, overgrazing, and overcultivation.

Source: Adapted from Buehl, D. (2009), *Classroom Strategies for Interactive Learning,* 3rd ed. Reprinted with permission of Doug Buehl and the International Reading Association.

Writing Summaries

Quite often, students in grades 4–8 are asked to write summaries of what they have read as a way of demonstrating their comprehension of the material. A summary should provide only the main points from the material without interpretation or commentary. Additionally, summaries are not retellings; in a retelling the student tries to include as much information as possible, whereas in a summary the goal is to be concise. These summaries may be kept in a notebook or in an online folder and then used as a way to prepare for unit tests.

For most students, writing a summary is not an easy task. When asked to summarize what they have read, students often use personal criteria for deciding what is important to include, or they use a "copy and delete" method (Friend, 2000/2001); this means they copy or paraphrase some sentences and leave out others, again for personal reasons. Students need instruction on how to determine what is most important and then how to summarize that information concisely. The best way to determine what is most important is to look for repeated information. When an argument is repeated, or when reference is made to the same topic or idea, even if different words or phrases are used, that is a clue that the information is important.

Depending on the length of the material being read, the summary might range from one sentence to a paragraph, or several paragraphs; it should not be more than about one-third the length of the original piece. A good summary should be concise, with a minimum of details and with nothing repeated. Only the most central ideas are included, which are written in the student's own words.

◎ activity ◎   **Writing a Summary**

Have students practice writing an effective summary using the passage below. Follow these steps:

1. Have students preview, think, and read. Ask students to preview the entire passage and think about what they expect to learn. Then have them read the passage.
2. To prepare students to write their summary, have them look for repeated information by asking themselves: What is the author talking about? What is the author trying to say about this topic? This will be the main idea, or the thesis, of the passage.
3. Have students ask the same two questions given in step 2 about each paragraph or group of paragraphs. Ask them to write out that idea in their own words in one sentence—leaving out details, examples, or stories, and giving only the most important idea.
4. Have students continue this process for the entire reading selection.
5. Ask students to check their summary sentences against the passage, ensuring that they gave the most important ideas rather than the details. Have them make sure that nothing is repeated; that the sentences are their own words; and that their first sentence gives the overall main idea, or thesis, of the entire selection, with the following sentences supporting the meaning of the first sentence.

PASSAGE FOR "WRITING A SUMMARY" ACTIVITY

Animals' Body Coverings

Every animal's body covering is an adaptation that helps the animal survive. Feathers protect birds and help them fly. The fur or hair that covers most mammals helps keep them warm. Some mammals have sharp hairs that are used for protection. Others have whiskers that they use as sense organs. Many fish are covered with scales that protect them from disease and other animals that live in the water. A reptile's scales protect it from injury and from drying out.

Many animals have body coverings that are camouflage to help them hide. For example, a tiger's fur is striped. The stripes help the tiger blend in with the light and shadows of the tall grass in its environment. Toads—with their bumpy, brownish skin—look like pebbles on the forest floor. A chameleon's color changes to match its surroundings. The dark skin on an alligator's back makes it blend into the swamps where it lives. (Adapted from Lesson 2, "How Do Animals' Body Parts Help Them Meet Their Needs?" on the Science page of Quizlet.com.)

The following statements are sample student responses to the passage using the steps listed above for writing a summary.

1. I expect to learn about the different body coverings of animals.
2. The author keeps talking about the body coverings of animals, and how they help the animal survive.
3. The author is describing how body coverings can help animals blend in with their environment.
4. Animals have body coverings that help them survive by keeping them warm and protecting them from other animals, from injury, or from weather. Body coverings also help animals blend in with their environment so they can hide from their enemies.

Digital Storytelling

One way for students to connect writing with reading and speaking in the content areas is through digital storytelling. *Digital storytelling* combines the art of telling stories with multimedia for teaching, learning, or conveying information in a technological format. Digital media such as images, audio, video, and animation can enhance both stories and content area presentations. Digital storytelling revolves around a specific content area topic or theme and may serve a variety of purposes, such as creating a personal narrative of a historical figure, recounting a historical event, or informing or instructing about a particular topic. Both students and teachers can create and use these digital stories in the learning process.

Digital storytelling provides students with opportunities to strengthen their writing voice and their comprehension as they retell stories or events or construct their own text, based on content area topics. As one example, Glen Bull, a professor at The University of Virginia, developed the website PrimaryAccess with his team. The site is a tool that allows school students to combine their own writing with historical images from primary sources and audio narration to create short online documentary films linked to social studies learning standards. Using the PrimaryAccess site, a group of middle school students told stories from the Civil War—a story of a slave, for example—in their words and, in many cases, added pictures and original documents from the era, as well as period music and other multimedia. These stories were shared with the class and made public. Students created their scripts after researching to learn more about their topic; they then revised and edited until the digital stories were ready to be made public. Similar work has taken place at University of California, Berkeley, which houses the Center for Digital Storytelling; and at Tufts University, where its Digital Stories in the Classroom site helps "students integrate their personal experiences with a larger understanding of race, class, and culture in their community. It also exposes them to the views and personal history of their peers, pulling the concepts from class

WWW○○○

**Tufts University
Digital Storytelling**

www.welcomeproject.org/
content/digital-stories

https://www.facebook.com/
events/153775301326168/

*Digital Storytelling
Resources*

AudioBoo

http://audioboo.fm/

**Center for Digital
Storytelling**

http://storycenter.org/

Primary Access

www.primaryaccess.org/

Sound Portraits

www.soundportraits.org/

Storify

http://storify.com

StoryCorps

http://storycorps.net

VoiceThread

www.voicethread.com

WEVideo

www.wevideo.com

text out of the books and into the seat next to them, making the issues discussed undeniably real" (Inside Tufts, 2011).

In creating digital documentaries, students embed facts and events in a narrative context, retelling and summarizing material and increasing their learning about a topic as well as their writing, speaking, and visual literacy skills. Additional sources for digital storytelling are listed in the margin.

Using Expository Text Structures in Writing

As students experience the variety of structures used in expository material through their reading (see the definitions in the earlier section on "Expository Text Structures"), ask them to use these various structures in writing sessions as well.

Read/Organize/Write (ROW)

A strategy such as **ROW,** or Read/Organize/Write (Stephens & Brown, 2000), is a useful framework for helping students move from locating each of the various text structures in their reading—one at a time—to identifying the characteristics of that structure, to writing their own selection for each of the text structures as they learn them. The steps for using ROW are as follows:

1. Present a short, clear example of one of the expository text structures for the class to read. (**Read**)
2. Guide students in developing a working definition of the text structure (see the earlier discussion) and perhaps a graphic organizer that represents that structure. (**Organize**)

ROW ●

3. Using a current topic, have students write an expository piece using a particular expository text structure. (**Write**)

Cubing

cubing ●

Cubing (Cowan & Cowan, 1980) is a strategy that requires students to explore a topic from six viewpoints: describe, compare, associate, analyze, apply, and argue. Typically, cubes are created to show what has been learned about a topic or to review a topic being studied. However, they can also be used to help students respond in writing to expository text, and thus to learn forms of expository writing.

For a content area topic the students have chosen or that the teacher has assigned, students answer key questions—some of which may represent the structure of expository text—using the six sides of a cube. They write their answers on each side, taking about three to five minutes. (See Figure 7.4 for a sample cube for writing about the topic of statistics.) Some sample questions are:

- What is it like [describe]?
- What is it similar to or different from [compare/contrast]?
- What does it make you think of [associate]?
- How is it made or what is it composed of [analysis]?
- How is it used [application]?
- What are some arguments for or against it and support for each [persuasion]?

Students can use these cubes as springboards for longer writing assignments. Small groups can also work together and then compile their information into a group paper. Additionally, these cubes can be used to jigsaw content area information (see Chapter 5) and then shared so that all students have access to the information for review purposes.

Cubing for expository writing about statistics.   *figure* **7.4**

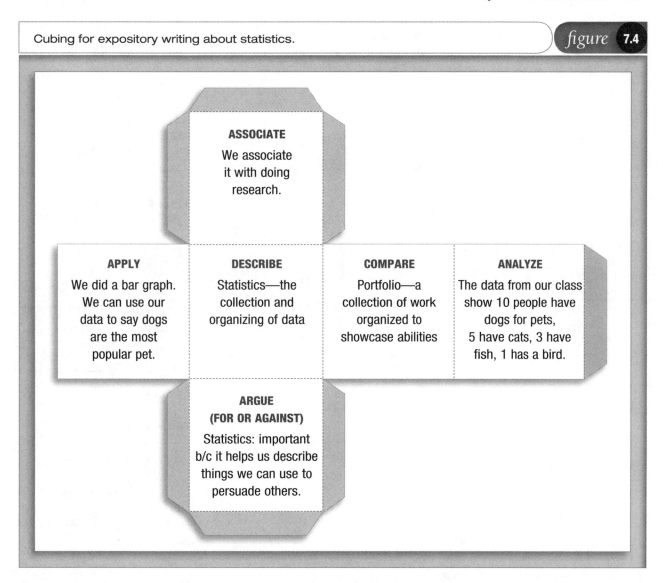

ASSOCIATE
We associate it with doing research.

APPLY
We did a bar graph. We can use our data to say dogs are the most popular pet.

DESCRIBE
Statistics—the collection and organizing of data

COMPARE
Portfolio—a collection of work organized to showcase abilities

ANALYZE
The data from our class show 10 people have dogs for pets, 5 have cats, 3 have fish, 1 has a bird.

ARGUE (FOR OR AGAINST)
Statistics: important b/c it helps us describe things we can use to persuade others.

Graphic organizers

Graphic organizers—maps, clusters, webs, Venn diagrams, T-charts, think-links, sequence charts, or outlines—provide a visible structure that can assist the writer with expository forms. With the appropriate use of symbols and/or arrows, graphic organizers can be constructed to correspond to the patterns found in expository text. As the examples in Figure 7.5 show, a student wishing to write about Abraham Lincoln's life might use a **time/order** or **sequence chart,** to indicate chronological order. Another student who is going to write about the causes of the Civil War would use a cause/effect web. Someone writing to compare or contrast two events or concepts could use a **T-chart** (a two-column chart that resembles a lower-case t) or a **Venn diagram** (two overlapping ovals to show both similarities and differences) to organize their thoughts. Simple **topic and details maps** help to organize paragraphs about a single topic. A student whose essay describes a science concept might use a weblike organizer such as a *concept and examples web* to present characteristics of the concept with examples. A student explaining the steps to follow for solving a math problem could use a *listing* (enumeration, an ordered category of elements) or a *flowchart* format (a visual description of a process).

- time/order or sequence chart

- T-chart
- Venn diagram
- topic and details map

figure **7.5** Examples of graphic organizers for expository text patterns.

TIME/ORDER CHART

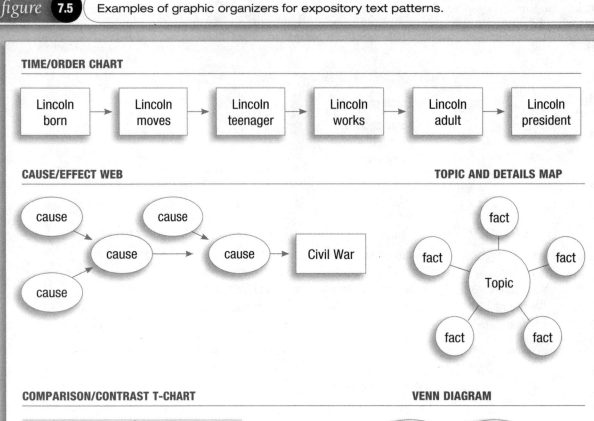

Lincoln born → Lincoln moves → Lincoln teenager → Lincoln works → Lincoln adult → Lincoln president

CAUSE/EFFECT WEB **TOPIC AND DETAILS MAP**

cause, cause, cause, cause, cause → Civil War

Topic — fact, fact, fact, fact, fact

COMPARISON/CONTRAST T-CHART **VENN DIAGRAM**

TRIANGLE	SQUARE
3 sides	4 sides
3 angles	4 angles
	4 right angles
Sides can be different lengths	Sides are the same length

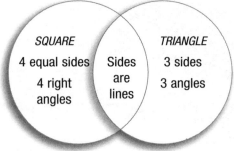

SQUARE — 4 equal sides, 4 right angles | Sides are lines | TRIANGLE — 3 sides, 3 angles

ENUMERATION CHART **CONCEPT AND EXAMPLES WEB**

How to Solve Multiplying Fractions

1. Multiply the numerators.
2. Multiply the denominators.
3. Whole numbers act as numerators with a denominator of 1.
4. Reduce the fraction to a whole or mixed number.

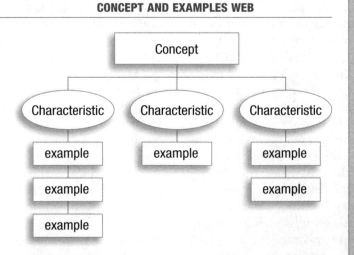

Concept — Characteristic, Characteristic, Characteristic

example, example, example / example / example, example

Graphic organizers are used to help students represent and understand text and then be able to put their ideas into words. As students move from reading to thinking about the reading to writing about what they've read, it is critical that they understand the material. Unfortunately, graphic organizers are often used only once and for only one purpose. If they are used multiple times, however, they help students to go back and access their previous thinking; this helps students put their thoughts into words. Once students have gleaned important information from a text and have added it to a graphic organizer, they can then revisit that information and write about it more easily. The following activity suggests ways to use a graphic organizer as an introduction to a planned unit on whales and dolphins.

Multiple Uses of a Graphic Organizer   ◎ activity ◎

Have students read about whales and dolphins to become acquainted with key vocabulary and background information. This will help prepare them for more difficult reading later, written from a variety of perspectives and for various purposes. The following steps can be used to prepare students for the writing assignment.

1. Begin by having your students read the entire passage shown in Figure 7.6 and confirm that they understand it, before you start to break down the passage into chunks. (For our purposes, Figure 7.6 uses two shades of gray boxes, light gray for comparison words/phrases and dark gray for contrast words/phrases. Later, you would provide students with passages that are not highlighted.)

2. After discussing the passage and asking students if they are at all confused by it, begin to read it more critically with your students. During this reading, model how you identify words that show comparisons between dolphins and whales. For example, select some of the more obvious embedded comparison words or phrases, such as *alike* in the first sentence and *in common* from the second sentence.

3. Ask students to create a list of other words that are used to compare. Generate a class list, and add some yourself if they need your support. Words that you might use in your list are: *both, same, similar, also, like, just as, similarly,* and *as well as.* You may even want to suggest a few higher-level comparison words, such as *uniform, copy,* and *replica.*

4. Have the students find and highlight all the comparison words in the text and note what is being compared.

5. Using a graphic organizer such as a Venn diagram, have students list the similarities between whales and dolphins.

6. Ask students to return to the passage to find differences between the two animals. Ask them to highlight or underline words that contrast, or show differences.

7. Discuss the words that indicate differences, and have students write them down. Examples of contrast words and phrases are: *differences, contradicts, disagrees, dissimilar, compared, inverse, opposite, contrary, neither, unlike, than, not like,* or *not the same.* Other signal words or phrases for contrast are: *though, although, however, on the other hand,* and *but.*

8. Have students complete the following two tasks: (a) Create a list of words that show contrast and (b) complete their graphic organizer with the differences listed.

9. Give students their writing assignment; for example, to explore and write about the habitats of sea mammals or the ethics of keeping whales and dolphins captive.

figure **7.6** Sample passage for comparison/contrast.

Dolphins and whales are even more alike than many people think. Some scientists consider dolphins to be a kind of whale because they have so many things in common. Belonging to the cetacean family, whales and dolphins are ocean mammals that have lungs and blowholes, which sit atop their heads to allow them to breathe. Both dolphins and whales have hair instead of scales, and they have live babies instead of laying eggs. Baby dolphins and whales, born near the top of the water so they can breathe easy from birth, almost immediately after birth learn to swim. The babies are nursed by their mothers. Whales grow bigger and are heavier than dolphins as a whole, though some smaller whales, like the beluga, can be roughly the same size as dolphins. Both dolphins and whales have teeth, but they are shaped differently and are used for different purposes. Unlike dolphins, whales have baleen in their mouths, which filter out small fish and other unwanted things. For survival, both make and pick up on sounds, although they do this in different ways. Whales make high-pitched sounds like whistles to warn other whales of pending danger or to show them directions. Dolphins, on the other hand, make echo sounds, which are transmitted in the ocean. While whales and dolphins have many traits in common, they do have many differences, as well.

10. Before they begin to write, students should practice using language to discuss whales and dolphins by using sentence frames. Sentence frames will prepare them to transfer their writing from notes in a graphic organizer to longer sentences in academic language. Model the use of the sentence frame. Explain that the graphic organizer states that both the dolphin and whale are mammals and both have blowholes, which provides a start for their writing. Here is another frame to provide practice using academic language to describe comparisons with the students:

> Both _____ & _____ are/have _____.
>
> _____ is like _____ because _____.
>
> _____ is similar to _____ in multiple ways, including _____, _____, and _____.

After modeling and having students practice writing with the graphic organizer listing comparisons, have them do the same for the contrasts. Then students can move to addressing the prompt. (See Chapter 6 for more on the writing process.)

Probable passages

An adaptation of probable passages (Wood, 1984), a strategy more commonly used to assist in the writing of narrative material, can also provide support for students who struggle when writing expository text. The strategy again uses a writing frame to help students understand and use expository text structures. The steps in this strategy are as follows:

1. Identify the most significant concepts or terms that appear in the content area material currently being studied. Write these terms on the interactive whiteboard (see Figure 7.7).

2. Supply an incomplete writing frame representing one of the various expository writing structures. (Model use of this strategy with each of the structures over a series of days.) For example, see the writing frame in Figure 7.7.

3. Prior to their reading the material, present to students the writing frame and the key vocabulary from the topic. Tell students this strategy is intended to help them learn the key vocabulary of the discipline and better comprehend the material they are about to read, as well as to help them write about the topic in the expository style.

4. Read and discuss the vocabulary with students. Invite students to think about where and how these words might be used in the writing frame. They could also use nonlisted words to complete the writing frame.

5. Work with students to develop a probable passage. By writing in words and phrases, they will complete the writing frame.

6. Have students read a section of the related expository material.

Probable passage: sample terms/vocabulary, writing frame, and passage.

figure **7.7**

KEY CONCEPT: Blue Whale (terms/vocabulary)

Characteristics and Features:

breathing hole, or nostril	krill, a shrimplike creature	100 feet
up and down strokes	dorsal fin	arm bones
flukes	blowhole	flipper bones
mammal	blubber	two hours
largest creature	30 elephants	four-ton tongue
baleen	stringy plates of whalebone	few minutes

Probable Passage (writing frame)

This selection tells us about the blue whale. The blue whale is the _____ ever to live on Earth, weighing more than _____ and becoming _____ long. It is not a fish but a _____. It breathes through a _____, which is the same thing as a _____. The blue whale eats four tons of _____ every day in summer. When it eats, about 400 _____, called baleen, hang down from the upper lip. The _____ traps anything the blue whale catches. Then the whale's _____ forces water in and out of the mouth, making the food go down the throat. In winter the blue whale survives on its own body fat. A thick layer of _____ under the skin helps to keep in body heat.

As the whale roams the oceans it uses its _____, the muscular tail flippers, in _____ to propel itself through the water at about 20 miles per hour. The whale also has a boneless _____, _____, and _____ to help it move and stay in an upright position. Because it is a mammal and needs air to breathe, the whale must come to the surface every _____, although it can hold its breath for up to _____.

(continued)

figure **7.7**   Probable passage: sample terms/vocabulary, writing frame, and passage, *continued.*

The Blue Whale (actual passage)

This selection tells us about the blue whale. The blue whale is the largest creature ever to live on earth, weighing more than 30 elephants and becoming 100 feet long. It is not a fish but a mammal. It breathes through a blowhole, which is the same thing as a breathing hole, or nostril. The blue whale eats four tons of krill, a shrimplike creature, every day in summer. When it eats, about 400 stringy plates of whalebone, called baleen, hang down from the upper lip. The baleen traps anything the blue whale catches. Then the whale's four-ton tongue forces water in and out of the mouth, making the food go down the throat. In winter the blue whale survives on its own body fat. A thick layer of blubber under the skin helps to keep in body heat.

As the whale roams the oceans it uses its flukes, the muscular tail flippers, in up and down strokes to propel itself through the water at about 20 miles per hour. The whale also has a bone-less dorsal fin, arm bones, and flipper bones to help it move and stay in an upright position. Because it is a mammal and needs air to breathe, the whale must come to the surface every few minutes, although it can hold its breath for up to two hours.

7. After reading and discussing the material, have students look back at the probable passage and modify it to accurately reflect the information presented in the material (see the actual passage shown at the end of Figure 7.7). After several teacher-directed sessions, students can work on their own, in pairs, or in small groups, to develop and share probable passages.

Researching in the Content Areas

A nother important aspect of content area literacy is learning how to find out what you want to know. In essence, this is what research is all about. The CCSS6-8.8 Writing Standards for Literacy in History/Social Studies, Science, and Technical Subjects asks students to "draw evidence from literary or informational texts to support analysis, reflection, and research" and to "gather relevant information from multiple print and digital sources (*primary and secondary*), using search terms effectively; assess the credibility and accuracy of each source; and quote or paraphrase the data and conclusions of others while avoiding plagiarism and following a standard format for citation" (NGACBP & CCSSO, 2010c, p. 66). To do this effectively, students must become strategic as they search for information. Students need to read and assess material critically, questioning the text and the authorial stance. As discussed earlier, they must read "against the grain." They must evaluate sources, references and citations, and possible biases; they must satisfy themselves regarding the integrity of a text. The following sections describe some strategies to encourage and promote effective research.

Locating Information

When students search for information that helps to answer their questions about particular topics, they need several underlying skills. In addition to basic alphabetizing skills, online search skills, and knowledge of how to use various book parts, students need to be able to categorize the information they will seek and find. For example, if students are trying to learn more about the habitat of the polar bear, which involves weather, they need to recognize that information about weather can also be found under the category heading of "climate"; another possible relevant heading might be "global warming." Recognizing potentially useful category headings and key words is critical for students using reference books and online resources.

As a first step before students begin their research, teachers may wish to list possible information sources—and make sure their use has been modeled first. The great variety of possible research sources include websites, almanacs, atlases, biographies, dictionaries, encyclopedias, magazines and newspapers (both print and online), maps, museum exhibits, reference books, photographs, published interviews, podcasts, television programs, thesauri, videos, and experts who may be contacted. As stated previously, students need to evaluate the integrity of all the sources they use. (See also "Evaluating the Reliability of Sources" on p. 241.)

Bay Area Writing Project teachers attest to the effectiveness of the *I-Search process,* or "hunting story," for teaching the research skills students will need throughout their academic lives (Olson, 1986). I-Search can help to motivate writers because it is inquiry-based, with students formulating the questions they'd like to answer. I-Search calls for emotional involvement by the researcher and is driven by the desire to know the answer (Macrorie, 1988). Although the concept of I-Search predates the widespread use of the Internet, the process is enhanced by its ability to provide access to so many online resources.

I-Search Process
activity

Freedman (1986) teaches the I-Search process in three stages: (1) identifying the topic to be studied, (2) searching for information, and (3) writing the report. She advises teachers who are introducing the I-Search technique in their classroom to use the following procedure:

1. Begin with a before-writing exercise in which students write statements about topics of interest to them and then generate a list of things they would like to know about the topic. For example, one topic might be dinosaurs. Students might pose questions such as,

   "When did dinosaurs live?"

   "Where did they live and what did they eat?"

   "Did they kill people?"

   "What caused them to become extinct?"

2. After several ideas, students can select one topic of special interest to explore. This brainstorming activity helps to stimulate thinking and ensures that all students will have a topic that they care enough about to spend time gathering information about it.

3. Show students how to search for information through the use of the many resources available to them.

4. Give students a structure to help them plan, organize, and write up their information so that they can share it with others. The I-Search reporting format is shown in Figure 7.8.

figure 7.8 The I-Search reporting format.

1. *Statement of the problem:* What do I want to know? (establish key questions)

   When did dinosaurs live?

   Why did they die out?

2. *The hunting process:* Where will I find information about my topic? (list possible resources)

   The Internet

   Encyclopedias in the library

   Books in the classroom

3. *Summary of findings:* What did I learn about my topic? (compose written summary)

   Dinosaurs lived many millions of years before the first human being appeared on earth. Although many cartoons show humans and dinosaurs together, that never really happened. Most dinosaurs were plant eaters, although some others were meat-eaters and hunted other, smaller dinosaurs. No one really knows for sure why dinosaurs became extinct. Some scientists think it was because of disease, while others believe an ice age, which caused the world to become very cold, killed them. Though we often imagine that they were ferocious and that we would fear them, we will never know, because no human EVER saw a live dinosaur!

4. *Conclusion:* How can I best share my information? (create multimedia presentation)

   I will use a PowerPoint presentation of the information and include some clip art of dinosaurs.

Online Search Skills

As discussed in Chapter 5, reading online is a skill students need to develop as they use the Internet to research school assignments. Another critical aspect of using online resources is the ability to perform searches that will lead to useful and high-quality information.

Before beginning online searches, Henry (2006) recommends introducing students to the way search engines are organized (e.g., text matching, categories) and the way they work (e.g., word frequency, sponsored links; see the NoodleTools site listed in the margin for ideas of search engines for specific needs). She states, "once students have a good grasp of the organization of various search engines, they are much more successful in conducting searches and reading information" (p. 617). Henry goes on to describe an instructional framework, called SEARCH, which represents the research findings both for locating information in written text and for searching information online. The SEARCH acronym delineates the following skills related to online searching:

WWW○○○

Choosing the Best Search for Your Information Need

www.noodletools.com/debbie/ literacies/information/5locate/ adviceengine.html

Inspiration

http://www.inspiration.com/ Inspiration/examples

1. Set a purpose for searching.
2. Employ effective search strategies.
3. Analyze search-engine results.
4. Read critically and synthesize information.
5. Cite your sources.
6. How successful was your search?

Current instructional techniques—such as I-Search (discussed above) and clustering (see Chapter 6)—and certain software products (e.g., Inspiration) that help students activate prior knowledge and brainstorm terms and key words, will enhance your students' search strategies.

Once the searching begins, students also need to learn how to determine whether they should follow up with the many links found during their search. Coiro (2005) describes a critical-thinking activity for helping students learn to predict which websites hold the most promise for providing answers to their questions. (An adaptation of this activity follows below, using the questions found in the data chart presented in Figure 7.9.)

Students must develop the ability to perform online searches that lead to useful and high-quality information.

Sample data chart for ocean features.

figure **7.9**

Research Group: <u>Ocean Features</u> (other groups are Ocean Plants and Ocean Animals)

Source	How many oceans are there?	How deep are the oceans?	What is on the ocean floor?	How much water is in the ocean?	Why is ocean water salty?	What causes waves?	What are tides?
1.							
2.							
3.							

Online Search Using a Data Chart

activity

A **data chart** serves as an organizational structure for keeping track of research questions, notes, and information gleaned from several sources. These charts can be kept by individual students or small cooperative study groups, or posted for whole-class contributions. They can also be used as listening or viewing guides for students who are gathering information from resources such as a television documentary or a recorded interview. A sample chart, using questions generated from brainstorming the topic of ocean life, is presented in Figure 7.9. The completed

● data chart

data chart can reveal relationships among concepts and help students get an over-all picture of the topic being studied. These charts serve students well as study guides before exams or as guides for writing informational papers or creating web pages, or preparing an oral presentation.

This activity "encourages students to stop, think, and make predictions about which Web sites to explore" (Coiro, 2005, p. 31).

1. Before presenting the activity to the class, conduct an online search for information relevant to the topic (see the earlier box on Websites for Informational Text for site suggestions; in our example, we'll use the study of ocean features, as in our data chart). Capture the first few entries from the search with a screen-capture program. (See Figure 7.10.)

2. Provide students with a visual that includes the first few results of the online search and a set of questions that "guide students to critically examine each entry on the list, noticing text and screen features embedded within the website addresses, website annotations, and file extensions after each hyperlinked resource" (Coiro, 2005, p. 31). See Figure 7.11.

3. Have small groups of students discuss their answers to each question and exchange strategies for deciding how to navigate online. The website evaluation tool shown in Appendix C.20 can be used to analyze the sites once they are visited.

---

figure **7.10** Internet search results.

Internet search activity: Use these questions to guide your small group discussion.

figure **7.11**

QUESTIONS AND ANSWERS	HOW DO YOU KNOW?	WHY IS THIS IMPORTANT TO KNOW?
1. How many websites were found using these search key words? Answer: 1,010,000	The line at the top of the page says, "Results 1–10 of about 1,010,000."	One million sites are too many to look at. Try using different key terms to make the results list shorter. Maybe try ocean features and resources as key terms.
2. Which website contains information about the topic you are studying? Answer: Site 2	The description says, "topics include ocean bottom features" as the first item listed. Site 1 includes the word "ocean" but it is not the main topic.	Reading the description saves time because it gives clues about what is in the website and what the website is mostly about.
3. Which site appears to be least helpful? Answer: Site 4	This is a link to a specific school in Ocean, New Jersey	Sometimes the results will include a site that might use only one of the words used in the key word search, like the word "ocean." This word might be used in the title, but the site has nothing to do with ocean features.
4. Which URL seems most likely to be available over the next several months? Answer: The URL for DLESE Find a Resource	The URL tells me it is an organization (.org), which is probably going to be around longer than a URL that includes ~ followed by someone's name, which indicates a personal site.	Looking carefully at the URL can give clues about who developed the site and whether it is a reliable source.

Evaluating the Reliability of Sources

In addition to learning how to use evolving tools for research, students must also learn how to determine the reliability of the sources they locate. Students tend to believe what they read, especially online, so our goal must be to train them to identify false or misrepresented information and to use honed searching skills to recognize credible and helpful materials. In a 2010 study, Scholastic found that 39 percent of students ages 9–17 said they believed the information they found online was always correct. Unfortunately, much of the information students access and read online may be inaccurate or even fabricated. Students simply don't realize how easy it is to publish online.

Kathy Schrock's "Guide to Everything" is a terrific resource for classroom teachers using, or having their student use, online resources. Schrock provides a wealth of information for educators, including previewed websites on a wide variety of topics. She has also developed a set of critical evaluation questions in both English and Spanish for elementary, middle, and secondary students to use when reviewing websites. (See the "Critical Evaluation" link on the lefthand side of her site.) Figure 7.12, a compilation of several checklists, provides another set of evaluation

www○○○

Kathy Schrock's Guide to Everything
www.schrockguide.net/

figure **7.12** Guidelines for evaluating websites.

The set of questions that follows is a compilation of several checklists developed for evaluating websites and is intended to be used by the classroom teacher.

AUTHOR CREDIBILITY

- Who is the author/source or producer?
- What is the authority or expertise of the individual or group that created this site? With what organization is the author of the website affiliated?
- Is there a way to contact the author or supply feedback?

  Tips: Check the header and footer information to determine the author and source.

  In the URL, a tilde (~) usually indicates a personal web directory rather than being part of the organization's official website.

  To verify an author's credentials, you may need to consult some printed sources such as *Who's Who in America* or the *Biography Index.*

ACCURACY AND RELIABILITY

- Is the information accurate?
- How current is the information? Is a date of publication provided? When was the website last revised? How frequently is the resource updated?
- Is the information presented in an objective, balanced manner?
- Is the information well written? Does the text follow basic rules of grammar, spelling, and composition?
- Are the sources of information stated? Can the information be verified?
- Does the information contradict something already known or learned from another source?
- Has the site been reviewed or ranked by an online reviewing agency?

SCOPE

- What is the primary purpose of the site (e.g., advertising, information)? Is the purpose of the resource clearly stated? Does it fulfill its purpose?
- Does the site contribute something unique on the subject?
- Is the material covered adequately?
- Is the site appropriate for the intended audience? Is it interactive enough to make students think?
- Are excerpts from texts provided or are entire texts available?

- Is the information available in other formats?
- Is the information factual or opinion?
- Does the site contain original information or simply links?
- Is a bibliography of print or web resources included?

FORMAT AND NAVIGATION

- Can you find your way around and easily locate a particular page from any other page?
- Is response time fast?
- How many links does it take to get to something useful?
- Is the arrangement of links uncluttered?
- If there are links to other sites, do they work? How up-to-date are the links?
- How many links lead to a dead end?
- How stable is the connection to the site?
- Do parts of it take too long to load?
- Does the site require additional software or hardware?
- Is the site open to everyone on the Internet, or do parts require fees?
- Can nonmembers still have access to part of the site?
- Must a name and password be registered before using the site?
- Is there a text alternative? Text only? Can the graphics be turned off?
- Do illustrations, video, or audio add value to the site?
- Is the site conceptually exciting? Does it do more than can be done with print?
- Do the multimedia, graphics, and art serve a function or are they decorative?
- What is the quality of the multimedia or graphic images? Do these images enhance the resource or distract from the content?
- Are the individual web pages concise, or does one have to scroll extensively?
- Does the site have its own search engine?
- Is the site easily browsable or searchable?

SOURCES

http://www2.lib.unc.edu/instruct/evaluate/?section= websites

www.widener.edu/about/campus_resources/ wolfgram_library/evaluate/original.aspx

http://library.usm.maine.edu/research/researchguides/ webevaluating.html

questions intended for teacher use. A field trip to a public or university library, and talking with the reference librarian, can provide further instruction in using online resources and the multitude of other resources available (Gipe, 2013). Finally, as stated earlier, you'll find a useful "Web Evaluation" tool in Appendix C.20.

Troubleshooting

I t is common for students who have made good progress in their literacy development up to the fourth grade to then start to show signs of difficulty. The increased attention to subject matter knowledge, as opposed to narrative materials, causes some students to struggle. Use of the content reading interview (Figure 7.13) might help to identify students who need extra attention in this area. However, it is the lack of familiarity with expository text structure that is generally the basis for difficulty. The following section presents some ways to deal with this common difficulty.

Content reading interview.   *figure* **7.13**

1. How much do you read in _____(content area)_____
   What do you read? Why?

2. When you are reading in _____(content area)_____ and come to something you don't know, what do you do?
   Do you ever do anything else?

3. Who is the best reader you know in _____(content area)_____?
   What makes him or her a good reader in _____(content area)_____?

4. How good are you at reading your _____(content area)_____ book(s)?
   How do you know?

5. What is the hardest part about answering the questions in the book(s) used in _____(content area)_____?

6. If you needed to study a chapter in _____(content area)_____ so you could remember the information, how would you do it?

7. Have you ever tried _____(name a study strategy)_____?
   Tell about it.

8. What do you have to do to get a good grade in _____(content area)_____ class?

Source: Adapted from Wixson et al., 1984.

Lack of Familiarity with Expository Text Structures

Students who have sufficient abilities in reading narrative material need to recognize that these same abilities can be applied to the more unfamiliar structures of expository material. In some ways, developing these new skills in reading expository material is like learning a new language—the language of expository text. Providing opportunities to use the patterns of content area language through all the language arts areas will accelerate both learning the content knowledge and learning the structure of expository text language. Students need to become comfortable with the unfamiliar language patterns and structures associated with various subject areas.

Because we know that native-English-speaking students begin to have difficulty in their literacy development when content area material is the focus, it is no surprise that English learners might also experience difficulty. As the "In the Classroom" example of the dictoglos strategy demonstrates, it is especially valuable, when working with English learners, to integrate the language arts areas of reading, writing, listening, speaking, viewing, and visually representing with the goal of achieving cognitive academic language proficiency (CALP); that is, the language of school. Learning the technical terms associated with each academic area is critical (Pilgreen, 2006).

---

activity   Dictoglos

1. Select an expository passage from a textbook or nonfiction trade book and read it aloud to the class.
2. While you are reading, have students write down key words and phrases.
3. Have students work in pairs to rewrite the text, as they heard it, from their notes.
4. Have the pairs join together to form groups of four and repeat step 3.
5. Ask for volunteers to read their re-created passages.
6. Lead a discussion about the material in the passage that students found hard to re-create; what can you suggest that would make this material easier to remember?

As indicated earlier in this chapter, graphic organizers can be especially helpful to readers struggling in content area literacy. The use of such visuals can help both English learners and native English speakers alike understand expository text structures and comprehend organization patterns. When students are asked to read large quantities of material, some may have difficulty and feel they are overwhelmed with information. The visual format of a graphic organizer helps to make the information comprehensible, but it must also be used within a context where academic language (e.g., main idea, supporting details, "WH"—who, what, where, when, why, how—words) matches the academic concepts.

herringbone strategy ●   Another type of graphic organizer is the **herringbone strategy**, a graphic, structured outlining technique that helps readers organize the most important information from expository material. The herringbone structure (see Figure 7.14) reminds them of what information to look for while they are reading. Six basic questions are asked: Who? What? When? Where? How? and Why? In addition, readers are asked to determine the main idea. Students can easily reproduce

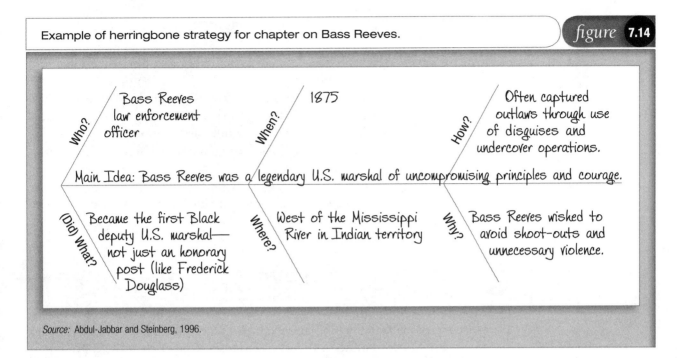

Example of herringbone strategy for chapter on Bass Reeves.

figure **7.14**

Source: Abdul-Jabbar and Steinberg, 1996.

the herringbone form in their notebooks or electronic folders and record their answers there while they read informational texts. After several sessions of teacher modeling, students are ready to begin completing their own herringbone forms. Students may notice that they may not find answers to all of the questions in the selection they are reading. This situation leads to the recognition that they will need a variety of sources to learn as much about a topic as possible. Alvermann, Phelps, and Gillis (2007) report that students became more successful with using the herringbone technique over time, so teachers need to provide regular opportunities for its use.

Summary

This chapter has presented a wealth of information about the nature of content area literacy and the relationship of literacy standards and content area standards, as well as many examples for instruction in content area reading, writing, and researching. The most important aspect of content area literacy instruction is to use expository material to teach the strategies that will help students most with informational text. Recognizing that expository text is different from narrative text, as well as *how* it is different, will help students understand that they will need to adjust their typical reading behaviors, such as reading fast, and do more stopping, thinking, and reviewing of informational material.

At the middle levels, students shift from a one-classroom, one-teacher classroom, where teachers integrate literacy skills throughout the day in content areas, to discipline-specific classes, where an expert teaches a particular discipline in isolation. In this type of classroom, students become historians and scientists, and engage in questions and learning that is specific to that discipline. Thus, the teachers are not necessarily teachers of reading; instead, they are discipline experts. But even content area teachers must ensure their students can access and comprehend their texts and materials; these teachers must also strive to be effective teachers of literacy.

Questions FOR JOURNAL WRITING AND DISCUSSION

1. Explain the difference between content area literacy and disciplinary literacy and provide an example of each.

2. Identify key concepts that students need to know in a math, science, or social studies text being used in a local school district. What kind of activities could you design that would enhance students' comprehension of these concepts?

3. Discuss the value of metacomprehension or comprehension monitoring abilities for reading in the content areas.

4. You have a friend whose son was given an open-ended homework assignment that requires this student to demonstrate his knowledge about the topic "ocean animals." Your friend and her son have no idea what to do or where to start. How could you help?

Suggestions FOR PROJECTS AND FIELD ACTIVITIES

1. Model for students how to organize ideas into a graphic organizer, as with this chapter's whales and dolphins example. Then ask students to write about the information using the skills they have developed; have them practice moving from the brief points in the graphic organizer to writing complete sentences to describe, compare, and contrast the ideas. With new material, let the students try the technique. Question them regarding the effectiveness of the technique of moving from graphic organizer to fleshed-out writing. Did they feel the strategy was helpful? Why or why not?

2. Prepare a paragraph frame based on a content area selection read by a student. Discuss the detail sentences with a student who typically has difficulty with expository text material. Have the student sequence the detail sentences and then complete the paragraph frame. Reflect with the student on the effectiveness of this technique. Did the student find this strategy helpful? Why or why not?

3. Choose a topic or theme that is widely discussed in your local school districts (e.g., rain forests, conservation, the planets, geometry in our daily lives), and prepare an annotated bibliography of fiction and nonfiction materials (not just text materials) that span a wide range of reading ability levels for this topic/theme.

REFERENCES

Abdul-Jabbar, K., & Steinberg, A. (1996). Bass Reeves. In *Black profiles in courage: A legacy of African American achievement* (pp. 112–139). New York: William Morrow.

Alfassi, M. (2004). Reading to learn: Effects of combined strategy instruction on high school students. *Journal of Educational Research, 97,* 171–184.

Alvermann, D., Phelps, S., & Gillis, V. R. (2007). *Content reading and literacy: Succeeding in today's diverse classrooms* (5th ed.). Boston: Pearson Education.

Ash, G. E. (2002). Teaching readers who struggle: A pragmatic middle school framework. *Reading Online, 5*(7). Available: www.readingonline.org/articles/art_index. asp?HREF=ash.

Bartholomae, D., & Petrosky, A. (Eds.) (1993). *Ways of reading* (3rd ed.). Boston: St. Martins Press.

Bean, J. C., Chappell, V. A. & Gillam, A. M. (2011). *Reading rhetorically*. New York: Pearson/Longman.

Boyne, J. (2006). *The boy in the striped pajamas*. Oxford, UK: David Frickling Books.

Buehl, D. (2009). *Classroom strategies for interactive learning* (3rd ed.). Newark, DE: International Reading Association.

Caverly, D., Mandeville, T., & Nicholson, S. (1995). PLAN: A study-reading strategy for informational text. *Journal of Adolescent & Adult Literacy, 39,* 190–199.

Coiro, J. (2005). Making sense of online text. *Educational Leadership, 63*(2), 30–35.

Columba, L., Kim, C. Y., & Moe, A. J. (2009). *The power of picture books in teaching math, science, and social studies: Grades preK–8* (2nd ed.). Scottsdale, AZ: Holcomb Hathaway.

Cowan, G. & Cowan, E. (1980). *Writing*. New York: Wiley.

Cuban, L. (1991). History of teaching in social studies. In J. Shaver (Ed.), *Handbook of research on social studies teaching and learning* (pp. 197–209). New York: Macmillan.

Duffelmeyer, F. A., & Baum, D. D. (1992). The extended anticipation guide revisited. *Journal of Reading, 35,* 654–656.

Eanet, M. G., & Manzo, A. V. (1976). REAP—a strategy for improving reading/writing study skills. *Journal of Reading, 19,* 647–652.

Fay, L. (1965). Reading study skills: Math and science. In J. A. Figurel (Ed.), *Reading and inquiry*. Newark, DE: International Reading Association.

Freedman, A. (1986). Adapting the I-Search paper for the elementary classroom. In C. B. Olson (Ed.), *Practical ideas for teaching writing as a process*. Sacramento: California State Department of Education.

Friend, R. (2000/2001). Teaching summarization as a content area reading strategy. *Journal of Adolescent & Adult Literacy, 44*(4), 320–329.

Gipe, J.P. (2013). *Multiple paths to literacy: Assessment and differentiated instruction for diverse learners, K–12* (7th ed.). Upper Saddle River, NJ: Pearson.

Gottfried, S. S., & Kyle, W. C., Jr. (1992). Textbook use and the biology education desired state. *Journal of Research in Science Teaching, 29,* 35–49.

Harvey, S. (1998). *Nonfiction matters: Reading, writing, and research in grades 3–8*. York, ME: Stenhouse.

Henry, L. A. (2006). SEARCHing for an answer: The critical role of new literacies while reading on the Internet. *The Reading Teacher, 59,* 614–627.

How Do Animals' Body Parts Help Them Meet Their Needs? From *Science*, Chapter 2, Lesson 2. Retrieved from http://quizlet.com/9317782/science-chapter-2-lesson-2-how-do-animals-body-parts-help-them-meet-their-needs-flashcards/#

Hoyt, L. (1999). *Revisit, reflect, retell: Strategies for improving reading comprehension*. Portsmouth, NH: Heinemann.

Inside Tufts (2011). Tufts University Digital Storytelling. Retrieved from welcomeproject.org/content/digital-stories https://www.facebook.com/events/153775301326168/

Kane, S. (2011). *Literacy and learning in the content areas* (3rd ed.). Scottsdale, AZ: Holcomb Hathaway.

Kane, S. (2008). *Integrating literature in the content areas: Enhancing adolescent learning and literacy*. Scottsdale, AZ: Holcomb Hathaway.

Klingner, J. K., Vaughn, S., Arguelles, M. E., Hughes, M. T., & Leftwich, S. A. (2004). Collaborative strategic reading: "Real world" lessons from classroom teachers. *Remedial and Special Education, 25,* 291–302.

Langer, J. A. (2001). Beating the odds: Teaching middle and high school students to read and write well. *American Educational Research Journal, 38,* 837–880.

Macrorie, K. (1988). *The I-Search Paper*. Portsmouth, NH: Heinemann.

Moje, E. B. (2008). Foregrounding the disciplines in secondary literacy teaching and learning: A call for change. *Journal of Adolescent & Adult Literacy, 52*(2), 96–107

Moss, J. G. (1994). *Using literature in the middle grades: A thematic approach*. Norwood, MA: Christopher-Gordon.

National Academies (1996). *National science education standards*. Washington, DC: Author. Retrieved from www.nap.edu/openbook.php?record_id=4962

National Council for the Social Studies (NCSS) (2002). *National standards for social studies teachers, vol. I.* Retrieved from http://downloads.ncss.org/NCSSTeacherStandardsVol1-rev2004.pdf

National Governors Association Center for Best Practices (NGACBP) & Council of Chief State School Officers (CCSSO). (2010a). *College and Career Readiness Anchor Standards for Reading*. Washington DC: National Governors Association Center for Best Practices, Council of Chief State School Officers.

National Governors Association Center for Best Practices & Council of Chief State School Officers. (2010b). *Common Core State Standards for English Language Arts & Literacy in History/Social Studies, Science, and Technical Subjects*. Washington DC: National Governors Association Center for Best Practices, Council of Chief State School Officers.

National Governors Association Center for Best Practices & Council of Chief State School Officers. (2010c). *Writing Standards for Literacy in History/Social Studies, Science, and Technical Subjects 6–12*. Washington D.C.: National Governors Association Center for Best Practices, Council of Chief State School Officers.

Olson, C. B. (Ed.). (1986). A sample prompt, scoring guide, and model paper for the I-Search. In *Practical ideas for teaching writing as a process*. Sacramento: California Department of Education.

Pilgreen, J. (2006). Supporting English learners: Developing academic language in the content area classroom. In T. A. Young & N. L. Hadaway (Eds.), *Supporting the literacy development of English learners* (pp. 41–60). Newark: DE: International Reading Association.

Post, A. D., with Scott, M., & Theberge, M. (2000). *Celebrating children's choices: 25 years of children's favorite books*. Newark, DE: International Reading Association.

Read, S. (2005). First and second graders writing informational text. *The Reading Teacher, 59,* 36–44.

Richter, H. P. (1970). *Friedrich*. Translated from the German by Edite Kroll. New York: Holt, Rinehart & Winston.

Robinson, F. P. (1946). *Effective study*. New York: Harper and Bros. (Also 1970, 4th ed. New York: Harper & Row.)

Sadler, C. R. (2001). *Comprehension strategies for middle grade learners: A handbook for content area teachers*. Newark, DE: International Reading Association.

Scholastic Media Room (Sept. 29, 2010). *New study on reading in the digital age: Parents say electronic, digital devices negatively affect kids' reading time*. Retrieved from http://mediaroom.scholastic.com/node/378

Schumm, J. S., & Mangrum, C. T. (1991). FLIP: A framework for content area reading. *Journal of Reading, 35,* 120–124.

Sierra-Perry, M., with Ewing, J., Foertsch, D., & Sierra, S. (1996). *Standards in practice grades 3–5.* Urbana, IL: National Council of Teachers of English.

Simpson, M. L. (1986). PORPE: A writing strategy for studying and learning in the content areas. *Journal of Reading, 29,* 407–414.

Simpson, M. L., & Nist, S. L. (1984). PLAE: A model for planning successful independent learning. *Journal of Reading, 29,* 218–223.

Shanahan, T. & Shanahan, C. (2008). Teaching disciplinary literacy to adolescents: Rethinking content-area literacy. *Harvard Educational Review 78*(1), 40–59.

Spache, G. (1963). *Toward better reading.* Champaign, IL: Garrard.

Stahl, S., & Shanahan, C. (2004). Learning to think like a historian: Disciplinary knowledge through critical analysis of multiple documents. In T. Jetton & J. Dole (Eds.), *Adolescent Literacy Research and Practice* (pp. 94–118). New York: Guildford Press.

Stephens, E. C., & Brown, J. E. (2000). *A handbook of content literacy strategies: 75 practical reading and writing ideas.* Norwood, MA: Christopher-Gordon.

Tiedt, I. M. (2000). *Teaching with picture books in the middle school.* Newark, DE: International Reading Association.

Wajnryb, R. (1990). *Grammar dictation.* Oxford, UK: Oxford University Press.

Wiesendanger, K. D., & Bader, L. (1992). SCAIT: A study technique to develop students' higher comprehension skills when reading content area material. *Journal of Reading, 35,* 399–400.

Wixson, K. K., Bosky, A. B., Yochum, M. N., & Alvermann, D. E. (1984). An interview for assessing students' perceptions of classroom reading tasks. *The Reading Teacher, 37*(4), 346–352.

Wood, K. D. (1984). Probable passages: A writing strategy. *The Reading Teacher, 37,* 496–499.

Zemelman, S., Daniels, H., & Hyde, A. (2012). *Best practice: Bringing standards to life in America's classrooms* (4th ed.). Portsmouth, NH: Heinemann.

EIGHT

Fluency

FOCUS QUESTIONS

- Why does reading fluency decline around grade 4, and what can be done to improve it?
- What are the components of reading fluency, and how are they taught?
- How is reading fluency assessed?
- What are the components of writing fluency and how are they taught?
- How is writing fluency assessed?

Mrs. Diaz wants to provide her fifth-grade students with an authentic approach to increasing their fluency skills as well as a highly motivational reason for repeatedly reading a passage. In a professional-development workshop, she learns about the revised radio reading activity. This provides students with the opportunity to become radio announcers and then allows them to assume the role of "audience," a chance to listen critically in order to engage in subsequent discussion. For an extension activity, she plans to ask students to create podcasts of their radio reading, using the class computers, to provide additional motivation for rereading.

In preparing for the lesson, Mrs. Diaz needs to find a short piece of literature, written at her students' independent reading level. She selects *An American Plague: The True and Terrifying Story of the Yellow Fever Epidemic of 1793* by Jim Murphy (2003). After considering several other trade books and selections from the class's basal reader, she chooses this one because it contains the drama and excitement she thinks will motivate her students to muster their best reading expression.

After her students have read the book, Mrs. Diaz has them help her summarize its key points using a story grammar. She then divides her class into groups and also divides the book into small sections, giving a book section to each member of the group. She then has students rehearse their selections for the upcoming radio program by reading it out loud several times at school, or at home for a parent or caretaker.

Next, she models the writing of open-ended questions so her students will be equally challenged in their role as audience members of the radio program. She models asking an open-ended question with this example, "What would you have done during the epidemic: Would you have been one of those who stayed to help the city during the crisis, or one of those who left to protect themselves? What caused you to decide this?" She then asks her students to create one such open-ended question to ask their audience for the reading selection they have been assigned.

On the day her students are to perform their radio readings, Mrs. Diaz models reading a passage aloud, as a radio announcer might, while her students listen with their books closed. Then she asks her students to form their groups. The readings begin with the student who has been assigned the first section of the book reading the passage as a radio announcer might. After each student finishes reading the assigned section, he or she asks the other group members to answer open-ended questions about the material.

After all students have finished the readings in their groups, Mrs. Diaz invites them to take turns recording their readings over the next few weeks during center time.

Introduction

T he importance—academically, socially, and vocationally—of the ability to read and write with ease in contemporary society cannot be emphasized enough. In their Reading: Foundational Skills standards, grades K–5, the CCSS emphasize students being fluent readers by fifth grade. Therefore, teachers need to support the development of smooth, accurate, and prosodic oral reading (Rasinski, Blachowicz, & Lems, 2012). The use of oral prosody and voice helps the reader stay engaged with the text and helps make the words more understandable (Paige, Rasinski, & Magpuri-Lavell, 2012).

As with reading, fluency in writing should be a fundamental goal of every literacy program. All writers, through their thinking and problem solving, learn about both writing and reading and how they are connected (Shanahan, 1988). Writers in grades 4–8 are learning how to think like authors, which helps them as they read and evaluate what other authors have written. As writers get older, they learn the importance of using exactly the right word or sentence to communicate their intended meaning. This way of thinking about words and sentences also applies to reading. Thus a strong focus on fluent writing is an important component in literacy programs—especially for children who are struggling with reading (Rasinski, Padak, & Fawcett, 2010).

Increasing Reading Fluency

As students advance through the grades, the texts they are expected to read contain increasingly complex linguistic and syntactical features. A reader who up to now has been able to read with **fluency**—that is, speed, accuracy, and prosody (or appropriate pacing, intonation, expression)—may suddenly begin to read more slowly, or less accurately, and with less confidence. In fact, reading rate charts do show a drop-off at grade four, when reading requires more emphasis on expository text (see Figure 8.1).

● fluency

The structure of the texts that students now encounter is often different from that of earlier text. Students need to learn new functions for some words. They need to learn what is preferred and what is to be avoided in inflection and syntax. The use of more varied punctuation will likely reduce fluency until those new patterns can be practiced. Teachers would do well to read aloud to students to model these new patterns (Richardson, 2000).

Students also need to spend time reading so they can gain experience and practice with the more complex forms of written language. A minimum of 20 minutes per day of silent reading—more if possible—will go a long way toward providing the necessary practice for increasing fluency. In schools with higher achievement levels, students spend more than 75 percent of the time scheduled for reading instruction actually reading. Thus, if instruction were scheduled for 100 minutes, then students

---

Reading rate ranges for instructional-level reading.

figure **8.1**

Reading rate is measured in words read correctly per minute. This rate is used to evaluate automaticity of word recognition. Words per minute (WPM) is determined by multiplying the number of words in the passage by 60 and then dividing by the number of seconds taken to read the passage. This measure can be used with both oral and silent reading; use of a stopwatch is recommended. For silent reading, direct the student to indicate when he or she is starting to read, and to look up when he or she has finished the selection. National norms for oral reading fluency are available at www.readnaturally.com/pdf/oralreadingfluency.pdf.

INSTRUCTIONAL LEVELS	ORAL RATE RANGE	SILENT RATE RANGE
Preprimer	13–35 WPM	NA*
Primer	28–68 WPM	NA
First	31–87 WPM	NA
Second	52–102 WPM	58–122 WPM
Third	85–139 WPM	96–168 WPM
Fourth, Fifth	78–124 WPM	107–175 WPM
Fifth, Sixth	113–165 WPM	135–241 WPM
Seventh, Eighth	128–177 WPM	180–290 WPM

*NA = not available.

would actually be reading for 75 minutes of that time, not working with a group or with the teacher on skill lessons (Allington & Cunningham, 2006).

No matter what grade level is involved, students' comprehension of text is improved when they are taught to read in meaningful chunks, phrasing well and using appropriate expression (Herrell & Jordan, 2006). Although this is easier for some students than others, almost all students can benefit from this instruction. A lesson on sentence-level "chunking" (breaking words into pronounceable chunks) is especially valuable for struggling readers and English learners. Listening to teachers or students who are proficient readers, as they model good phrasing and expression, often helps students to better understand that good reading is not necessarily fast reading; they learn that it should be paced and phrased so that it sounds meaningful. Asking students to read aloud in class, having never seen the material before, puts them on the spot. For those who feel they are not good readers, this might make them anxious. In addition, students may spend time looking ahead in the reading and counting off to see which passage they will read rather than paying attention to the reading being done by a classmate. Therefore, to keep students on task during read-aloud time and, more important, to maintain a supportive classroom environment, give students the chance to practice the material ahead of time.

Providing opportunities for repeated readings of familiar text is a vital component to sound instruction in the fostering of reading fluency. Provide opportunities for students to read aloud, to hear models read with prosody, and to hear themselves. Poetry reading, readers theatre scripts, and texts in a variety of genres are critical in building the reader's confidence and reading rate. *Choral reading* involves a more proficient student reading along with another student in unison. In this case, the more proficient reader models speed and accuracy for the other reader. *Echo reading* provides a model, as well. In this situation, the more proficient reader starts by reading a small section of the text, and then the second reader reads the same text again. Another way for students to hear themselves read is to have them read aloud into a recording device, cell phone, or other device they can use to hear themselves reading. Yet another option, if students are slow readers, is to ask them to build their speed through *timed-repeated readings*. In this case, a teacher asks students to read a piece of text for meaning, then reread it more quickly three to five more times to encourage them to feel more confident in their reading and their increase in speed, and also to begin to recognize the words in the passage more quickly and automatically. It's important to remember, however, just because a student reads quickly and gives the appearance of fluency does not mean they comprehend or retain what they have read. Therefore, it is critical that a student read for comprehension in addition to automaticity. Fluency works in tandem with comprehension in a balanced approach, and teachers must assess both aspects of a student's reading.

Observation and planned interventions by the teacher in the form of modeling place value on fluency and encourage students to focus more deliberately on this important aspect of literacy, which will also allow them more energy to expend on the comprehension of written material (Kuhn & Stahl, 2003).

Provide opportunities for students to read aloud, to hear models read with prosody, and to hear themselves.

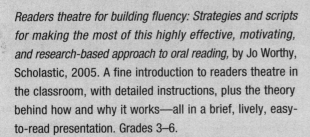

Readers Theatre

Readers theatre for building fluency: Strategies and scripts for making the most of this highly effective, motivating, and research-based approach to oral reading, by Jo Worthy, Scholastic, 2005. A fine introduction to readers theatre in the classroom, with detailed instructions, plus the theory behind how and why it works—all in a brief, lively, easy-to-read presentation. Grades 3–6.

Stories on stage: Children's plays for readers theatre, with 15 play scripts from 15 authors, including Roald Dahl's The Twits *and Louis Sachar's* Sideways Stories from Wayside School (2nd ed.), by Aaron Shephard, Shepard Publications, 2005. The premier collection of readers theatre scripts, with adaptations of stories by a variety of authors. www.shepardpub.com

Folktales on stage: Children's plays for readers theatre, with 16 play scripts from world folk and fairy tales and legends, including African, Chinese, Southeast Asian, Indian, Middle Eastern, Russian, Scandinavian, and Native American, by Aaron Shepard, Shepard Publications, 2004.

Scripts based on Shepard's own picture books and stories. www.shepardpub.com

From the page to the stage: The educator's complete guide to readers theatre, by Shirlee Sloyer, Teacher Ideas Press, 2003. Just what the subtitle says, plus sample scripts. www.teacherideaspress.com

Institute book of readers theatre: A practical guide for school, theater, & community, by William Adams, Institute for Readers Theatre, 2003. A university-level textbook that can be used with middle school students from a pioneer of readers theatre.

Playbooks for Young Readers by Aaron and *Playbooks for Tween Readers by Aaron.* Each book includes adaptations of three of the author's scripts into Playbook format, which features illustrations, color-coding, and diverse reading levels for small groups of students or for families. For ages 5–10 and 8–13, respectively. Available in both print and electronic formats: www.eplaybooks.com

Readers Theatre

One effective strategy for improving fluency and oral reading that many students find motivating is readers theatre. Sloyer (1982) defines readers theatre as "an interpretative reading activity for all the children in the classroom. Readers bring characters to life through their voices and gestures. . . . Readers theatre becomes an integrated language event centering upon oral interpretation of literature" (p. 3). As such, readers practice oral reading and address all the areas of fluency (speed, accuracy, prosody) through "rehearsals" of the material to be read before an audience. To provide an appealing performance, readers must not only comprehend the material and read it accurately, but must also dramatize the interpretation through appropriate intonation and expression. See the box above for readers theatre resources, and see the activity below for a suggested procedure.

readers theatre

Readers Theatre   activity

In this type of group-reading activity, a narrator speaks directly to the audience, establishing the basic premise of the story and linking the various segments. The text for the narration is created with the help of the students. The narrator also simplifies the language and abstract concepts. The other actors read the characters' dialogue, and each actor may take the part of more than one character. The success of the readers theatre production depends on the oral aspects of the presentation rather than on acting skills or props. The actors read their parts fluently and use facial expressions and tone of voice to convey the emotions and moods. Action is merely suggested; the audience members must visualize the activity in their mind's eye. Readers theatre usually omits stage properties, lights, and costumes, so that nothing distracts the audience's attention from the characterization.

The story chosen should require a minimum of rewriting, or students could use a prepared readers theatre script. The kind of story best adapted for readers theatre contains characters who have multidimensional features and unique personalities. The language of such a story should be thought provoking, colorful, and rhythmic. The plot should have an element of conflict and/or suspense. The completed script may be made into a laminated booklet and placed in a learning center for students to enjoy as a free-time oral reading activity. The websites listed in the margin offer free readers theatre scripts. Also see the previous box for additional resources.

The development of a script requires two distinct steps: (1) selecting material with strong dramatic appeal, and (2) adapting the selection to bring about a positive audience response. Almost any piece of literature containing a great deal of dialogue will do, but folktales are especially well suited to the vehicle.

One adaptation of readers theatre is to create audiobooks, which are recorded literature selections for an unseen audience. Using this method, small groups of students select a piece of quality literature and practice reading it until they have become fluent and expressive, adding sound effects and including various voices for different characters. Teachers could ask local businesses to contribute the literature as well as the recording media. The audiobooks together with the books and biographies of the different readers could then be sent to children's hospitals in the surrounding area as a class service-learning project.

For classes seeking more formal productions, stories can also be adapted into more traditional plays in which the physical actions of the characters are acted out. The following seven steps briefly outline a more spontaneous process for creating an adaptation of readers theatre that allows students to use their own words to bring literature to life:

1. After setting a purpose for listening, read the story aloud for comprehension. Then have students reread the story aloud with as much dramatic intensity as they can.

2. Have several students relate the story in sequence from memory with the aid of an appropriate graphic organizer (see Chapter 5).

3. Select a scribe to write down the story, section by section, in the students' own words. Distribute copies of this new version to each student, thus providing each with a "script." (In a traditional play, this script is memorized; in readers theatre, it is simply read.)

4. Have small groups of students act out, or "block," each section of the play as another student reads it.

5. As a group, discuss how different characters might talk, walk, look, and behave. The roles of all characters should be considered in this discussion—from narrator to those involved in crowd scenes.

6. While the play is in the rehearsal stage, tell the music teacher the theme of the upcoming performance and ask her to select several songs that might enhance the script. Also ask the art teacher if she would be willing to set aside some class time to help students create simple props or scenery to enhance the setting.

7. Encourage students to design invitations that reflect the theme of the performance and allow them to distribute the invitations to those who will be in the audience (e.g., parents or caregivers, classmates, other classes within the school).

WWW●●●

Scripts for Readers Theatre

Aaron Shepard's Readers Theatre Page
www.aaronshep.com/rt/RTE.html

Readers Theater Scripts and Plays (for younger students)
http://teachingheart.net/readerstheater.htm

Storycart Press
www.storycart.com

Use of Phrase Markings

Phrase marking (Fox, 2003) improves students' expression by helping them read in meaningful word groups. This is accomplished by having the teacher physically mark the phrase boundaries in text, through the use of colored highlighters or slashes, or by rewriting sentences using spaces between the phrases (see Figure 8.2). The student reads the text while adhering to the word groupings the teacher has identified.

Using Phrase Markings to Increase Fluency   **activity**

The student can be encouraged to mark the phrase boundaries in a new passage, thinking aloud through the appropriate phrasing with the assistance of the teacher. Specifically, the following steps can be followed to use phrase markings to increase fluency.

1. Preview the passage to be read. Discuss the title, make connections with the student's background, and have the student make predictions about the passage.

2. Read the first sentence to the student. Make slashes where the ends of groupings would be and then read the sentence again, showing the student how the slashes indicate where you pause in the reading. Mark up several more sentences in this fashion.

3. Next, ask the student to read the next sentence silently. Invite her to make slashes where the word group should end. She then reads the sentence aloud, according to how the phrase has been marked.

4. Discuss where the student placed the slashes and if the sentence was indeed broken into meaningful units.

5. The teacher and student then take turns reading a sentence and marking the phrases using slashes or highlighting them using colored markers. The student may reread the passage several times to practice good phrasing.

6. Finally, ask the student, "What was that passage about?" and prompt her to summarize the passage, including components of narrative structure if fictional text is used, or relevant facts and details if nonfiction material is used.

A phrase-marked passage.   *figure* **8.2**

> The wounded cowboy/ could not move. /He struggled for a while/ and then lost consciousness./ Rambo, his dog,/ licked the cowboy's face/ with his tongue./ He tried to get/ the unconscious man/ to answer him/ but the cowboy/ did not stir./ Rambo finally ran/ to the road/ and howled./ Every once in a while/ he would trot back/ to the wounded man/ and try to wake him.

Fluency-Oriented Reading Instruction

One group activity for assisted reading combines teacher-assisted reading with partner reading. This promising intervention program, *fluency-oriented reading instruction (FORI)*, connects the research-based practices of repeated readings with independent, silent reading within a three-part classroom program, set up and partially assisted by the teacher.

The three components of FORI are

- a reading lesson that includes teacher-led, repeated oral reading and partner reading
- a free reading period at school
- prescribed at-home reading

This fluency intervention program produced gains of almost two years in second-grade students (Stahl, 2002; Stahl, Heubach, & Cramond, 1996), and should also be effective with older students.

◉ activity ◉   Using Fluency-Oriented Reading Instruction

The following are the steps in FORI.

1. The teacher initiates the activity by modeling the reading of a story or passage, modeling correct expression, phrasing, and attention to punctuation. Although the passage can be fiction or nonfiction, it should be highly motivational and on the students' independent reading level.

2. After the reading, the teacher solicits the students' responses to the selection, gauging their appreciation for the story and making sure that they understand what has been read.

3. The teacher then reviews key vocabulary and concepts and has students engage in comprehension activities built around the reading. For example, the students might make a recording of themselves orally retelling the sequence of events in an expository piece about penguins in small share groups, or they might act out scenes from a story about a wounded knight, one group at a time.

4. The students then take the selection home and—with prior instructions to parents or other caregivers (e.g., "Simply listen to your child read this passage and provide positive feedback.")—read it aloud an additional time.

5. The following day, have students reread the selection in pairs. One student reads a page as the other student monitors the reading. Then the partners switch roles for another page. This continues until the text is finished.

6. After the partner reading, the teacher leads extension activities that can cross the curriculum, such as having the students research the continent of Antarctica after reading an expository piece on penguins.

7. In the independent reading phase of FORI, time is reserved later in the day for students to select their own reading material, at their independent reading level. During this time they practice the skills leading to reading fluency in a nonstructured way. Optionally, they may do oral reading with partners.

Oral Recitation Lesson

The oral recitation lesson (ORL) is another fluency instruction intervention that contains the key ingredients of effective fluency instruction and provides teacher assistance and modeling (Hoffman, 1987; Hoffman & Crone, 1985). Like the other teacher-assisted techniques described here, it too has been reported to lead to increased gains in fluency, but it also has a major focus on comprehension and appears to improve scores in that component of literacy as well (Reutzel & Hollingsworth, 1993).

The ORL can be used in both whole-group and small-group situations, and contains both direct and indirect instruction.

Initiating an Oral Recitation Lesson   ◉ **activity** ◉

The following steps are recommended in initiating an ORL.

1. The teacher reads a story to the students and then leads the class in discussing and analyzing it.
2. From the discussion, the teacher helps the students to create a story map or story grammar summarizing the key elements in the story.
3. Using the story map or story grammar, each student creates a written summary of the story.
4. The teacher then selects certain segments of the story and models reading them aloud again, calling attention to different features of fluent oral reading, such as effective oral expression.
5. The students imitate the teacher's reading, both individually and chorally.
6. Individual students "perform" the reading of self-selected parts of the story for small groups of their fellow students, while the impromptu audience offers praise and positive comments.
7. For ten minutes daily, the students practice reading portions of the story by themselves, using a kind of "whisper reading." The teacher listens to each student, checking progress using anecdotal notes.

Fostering Writing Fluency

As stated earlier, fluency in writing, as well as in reading, should be a fundamental goal of every literacy program. Writers who achieve fluency are more likely to have a continuous flow of ideas. Fluent writers quickly get to work on assigned writing tasks and therefore have considerably more practice than their less-fluent counterparts, who may spend endless time struggling to think of topics about which they can write. This problem can be remedied by engaging students in writing for authentic purposes, which was explored in Chapter 6. The following discussion and activities will also help to improve writing fluency.

Two main components comprise **writing fluency**: the speed with which students write, and the automaticity of the conventions of writing—spelling in particular—which allow them independence and confidence when drafting their ideas (Cecil, 2007).

Fluency in writing should be a fundamental goal of every literacy program.

Speed

Writing speed can be increased through free writing. *Free writing* is a form of quickwrites designed to alleviate writers' anxieties about penmanship and the correctness of language conventions in drafts (Norton, 2004).

◎ activity ◎   Free Writing

- Tell students that they will be writing nonstop for a specified amount of time (e.g., two to five minutes).
- Instruct them that they should not be concerned with erasing, crossing out, or requesting help with spelling. Explain that the idea is that they should be relaxed when writing and allow their ideas to flow. At the end of the designated writing time, ask individual students to share their writing with the group.
- To make this activity faster and more engaging, ask students to reread their writing and underline a key phrase or sentence they are most interested in reading to the group. This means that students will have a sentence to share that they have personally selected and prepared, which keeps them from feeling put on the spot. As students share quickly around the room, everyone is included and has a chance to read the sentence that is most important to them.
- Another option is to invite listeners to ask questions and offer comments and suggestions that may help authors clarify or further develop their work.
- As an extension to free writing, listeners may be invited to respond to authors' messages in written form; for example, in one speed-writing session, a student might share her personal narrative about her grandmother, who recently underwent an operation and died. The other students, after hearing the sad tale, might immediately respond by writing sympathy cards to the bereaved granddaughter (Gipe, 2013).

Free-writing techniques can be used to respond to stories that have been read, but they may also be used to have students write about what they have been learning in science, social studies, or other content areas. The teacher reads and responds to the writing and notes the correct versions of misspelled words at the bottom of the page so that students will notice the corrected spelling. Sometimes, the teacher may encourage students to revise and edit their speedwriting and produce a final, published copy, but the primary goal is to develop writing fluency rather than to create polished compositions.

Automaticity

To become "automatic" in their writing, students must have a command of the conventions of writing so that they can spend more energy on their ideas than on the actual formulation of text. They must also be aware of strategies that help them think through problems and concerns that all writers encounter as they are composing a piece of writing. The following sections offer some suggestions that can be used to help students develop automaticity in their writing, demonstrate how to model fluent writing behavior, and provide strategies that students can use when they possess limited spelling prowess.

Teacher modeling

A comprehensive program of writing instruction should provide daily demonstrations and minilessons, modeling how writers use the conventions of language and think through many different kinds of writing strategies. Teachers can then offer (1) guided practice sessions in which students will use the new skills with the assistance of a proficient writer and (2) independent writing sessions in which students have the opportunity to practice their newly acquired skills. Such sessions show students how fluent writers think through the myriad writing decisions that authors must make, and what they do when they discover problems. After each such session, allow students to gain valuable practice in implementing these writing tools until they become second nature. Students can then be said to have reached the stage of automaticity in writing.

Spelling automaticity and handwriting flow

Of all the conventions necessary for writing fluency and automaticity, spelling problems especially tend to slow down and "inhibit many students who would otherwise be imaginative, intelligent writers" (Silva & Yarborough, 1990, p. 48). To become fluent writers, students must be able to spell words automatically and, if writing a document by hand, must be able to rapidly form letters. Just as disfluent readers read word by word and decode many words, disfluent writers write slowly, word by word, and have to stop to sound out the spelling of many words. In fact, some disfluent writers write so slowly that by the time they get to the end of a sentence, they have forgotten what it is they were writing!

Using a spellcheck feature when writing on a computer offers students a way to ensure that their spelling is correct, although they need to be taught that the feature will not catch all errors. Spellcheck can also help students develop a spelling conscience.

Although students need to practice automatically forming their letters quickly and legibly when writing by hand, a balance between using a computer and writing longhand helps to diminish the frustration associated with a lack of fine motor skills.

Troubleshooting

Every learner's ability to read aloud can be enhanced through ample practice and performing before a group of caring and supportive peers. However, teachers will need to address special concerns when fostering fluency in English learners.

Lack of Verbal English Skills

Technology can help in developing all students' reading fluency; it can also help English learners by providing mechanisms for fluent reading. Examples of technology that are motivational and current include scaffolded text where students can see and hear text and recognize familiar stories such as translations of popular literature. Websites that can help English learners develop their verbal skills include:

Milcuentos, www.milcuentos.com. This Spanish-language site features young people reading stories and displays artwork made by young artists. This website has a few known stories like Little Red Riding Hood, for example, but few titles overall and few authors that students will recognize. The site has good language models; the words are shown on the screen.

International Children's Library, http://en.childrenslibrary.org. This site offers many titles in Spanish and other languages. Some of the authors are popular, but there are few popular translated titles. There is no read-aloud component, but the book pages, which have no moving graphics, do resemble the actual book's pages.

Summary

The Common Core State Standards place great emphasis on students being fluent readers by fifth grade. However, as students in grades 4–8 encounter text structures that are different from the familiar narrative structures of primary-grade materials, fluency levels may drop off. Students' comprehension of text is improved when they are taught to read in meaningful chunks, phrase well, and use appropriate expression. Teacher modeling of fluent reading is helpful, as is providing time for students to practice reading these more complex materials. Writing fluency, including the ability to write with speed and automaticity, is also vital for students as they progress through the grades.

Questions FOR JOURNAL WRITING AND DISCUSSION

1. What is your understanding of the nature of reading fluency? Do you believe more fluent reading can lead to enhanced comprehension? Why or why not?
2. What is your understanding of the nature of writing fluency? Do you believe that developing writing fluency can lead to more and better writing? Why or why not?

Suggestions FOR PROJECTS AND FIELD ACTIVITIES

With a classroom teacher's help, identify a fluent reader and a disfluent reader. Observe each student reading a passage. Describe the differences between their reading. What would you predict their relative comprehension abilities to be, based on their oral reading? Check your perceptions with the students' teacher.

REFERENCES

Allington, R. L., & Cunningham, P. M. (2006). *Schools that work: Where all children read and write* (3rd ed.). Boston: Allyn & Bacon.

Cecil, N. L. (2007). *Focus on fluency: A meaning-based approach*. Scottsdale, AZ: Holcomb Hathaway.

Fox, B. J. (2003). *Word recognition activities: Patterns and strategies for developing fluency*. Upper Saddle River, NJ: Merrill/Prentice Hall.

Gipe, J. P. (2013). *Multiple paths to literacy: Assessment and differentiated instruction for diverse learners, K–12* (9th ed.). Upper Saddle River, NJ: Merrill/Prentice Hall.

Herrell, A. L., & Jordan, M. (2006). *50 strategies for improving vocabulary, comprehension, and fluency: An active learning approach*. Boston: Allyn & Bacon.

Hoffman, J. V. (1987). Rethinking the role of oral reading in basal instruction. *Elementary School Journal, 87,* 367–373.

Hoffman, J. V., & Crone, S. (1985). The oral recitation lesson: A research-derived strategy for reading basal texts. In J. A. Niles & R. A. Lalik (Eds.), *Issues in literacy: A research perspective. Thirty-fourth Yearbook of the National Reading Conference* (pp. 76–83). Rochester, NY: National Reading Conference.

Kuhn, M. R., & Stahl, S. A. (2003). Fluency: A review of developmental and remedial practices. *Journal of Educational Psychology, 95,* 3–21.

Murphy, J. (2003). *An American plague: The true and terrifying story of the yellow fever epidemic of 1793* . New York: Clarion Books.

Norton, D. (2004). *The effective teaching of the language arts* (6th ed.). New York: Merrill.

Paige, D. D., Rasinski, T.V., & Magpuri-Lavell, T. (2012). Is fluent, expressive reading important for high school readers? *Journal of Adolescent & Adult Literacy, 56*(1), 67–76.

Rasinski, T., Blachowicz, C., & Lems, K. (2012). *Fluency instruction: Research-based best practices* (2nd ed.). New York: Guilford.

Rasinski, T., Padak, N., & Fawcett, G. V. (2010). *Teaching children who find reading difficult* (4th ed.). Upper Saddle River, NJ: Merrill/Prentice Hall.

Reutzel, D. R., & Hollingsworth, P. M. (1993). Effects of fluency training on second graders' reading comprehension. *Journal of Educational Research, 86*, 325–331.

Richardson, J. S. (2000). *Read it aloud!* Newark, DE: International Reading Association.

Shanahan, T. (1988). The reading-writing relationship: Seven instructional principles. *The Reading Teacher, 41*, 636–647.

Silva, C., & Yarborough, B. (1990). Help for young writers with spelling difficulties. *Journal of Reading, 34*, 48–53.

Sloyer, S. (1982). *Reader's theatre: Story dramatization in the classroom*. Urbana, IL: National Council of Teachers of English.

Stahl, S. A. (2002, November). Fluency: Instruction and assessment. PowerPoint presentation presented at A Focus on Fluency Forum, San Francisco.

Stahl, S. A., Heubach, K., & Cramond, B. (1996). *Fluency oriented reading instruction* (NRRC Report no. 79). College Park, MD: National Reading Research Center.

CHAPTER NINE

Differentiating Instruction
for Diverse Classrooms

FOCUS QUESTIONS

- What is differentiation, and why is it important in today's classrooms?
- When differentiating instruction to meet the needs of diverse learners, what curricular components can be modified?
- What are some of the major groups of diverse learners for whom differentiated instruction is especially important?
- What specific adaptations can be made for these diverse learner groups?

Marcia, a special education student, and Jason, an advanced learner, both of whom are in the fifth grade, are working together to research the Tasmanian devil—its habitat, eating habits, and physical characteristics. Their teacher, Mrs. Hooper, has given her students the choice of studying one particular animal that is real but also "exotic." Marcia and Jason both wished to study the Tasmanian devil, so they are working together on this research project, which will culminate with a creative presentation of the information they have learned. While searching for information online, Jason does most of the reading. Marcia's strengths are more apparent in the creative areas of art and designing. She also likes cooking, so she suggests creating recipes for a pretend restaurant that caters to Tasmanian devils. During a brief sharing time, Marcia and Jason solicit feedback from their classmates on their ideas for the recipes and the restaurant. Marcia shares some recipes she has created for Tas's Cave Café, which is open only for dinner since Tasmanian devils are nocturnal creatures. She describes a poultry item she has created that includes fried grubs as a side dish. She explains that Tasmanian devils eat grubs, small mammals, and birds. Jason relates how he realized their menu needed prices, and since Tasmanian devils live on Tasmania, an island south of Australia, he needed to figure out what the food costs would be in Tasmanian currency. He says he enjoyed converting American dollars and cents to Tasmanian money, giving as an example the poultry dish Marcia created, which is listed at $6.95 US or $7.48 AUD (Australian currency). Peer feedback comes in the form of both compliments and suggestions. Classmates say that they really like the idea of the restaurant and suggest that it will improve the presentation if Marcia and Jason include more specific information on what Tasmanian devils look like.

Why Differentiate Instruction?

Today's classrooms, like Mrs. Hooper's, are places of great diversity. All classrooms are academically diverse, but classrooms are also diverse in other ways. Some students come to school speaking first languages other than English. Some are academically gifted. Others experience a variety of physical and neurological challenges—including cerebral palsy; vision or hearing deficits; disorders that affect communication, including autism; and cognitive learning disabilities, such as dyslexia and attention deficit hyperactivity disorder (ADHD). Still others demonstrate behavioral maladjustments or health and environmental issues associated with extreme poverty. Nearly all of these students have academic, behavioral, physical, or social needs, or combinations of needs, that require instructional adaptations within the classroom setting (Lewis & Doorlag, 2011). Fortunately, many recommended instructional adaptations are effective for all learners—not just those with special needs. A teacher might spend more time on a specific subject or may scaffold information to a greater degree with certain students or content; however, the intent is to reach the needs of all the learners in the classroom.

Frey and colleagues (2009) recommend *guided practice* as an effective teaching method. In this recursive model, the teacher teaches to the whole class and also works with the whole class to check for understanding; then, students work in small groups to evaluate their learning. When students are ready to be independent, the teacher checks each student for understanding as he or she completes assignments pertaining to the topic. In guided practice, the differentiation occurs in every step; the teacher takes care to communicate information in ways all students can understand, checks that they are able to do the task well, and waits until they are able to perform or comprehend the task independently before assigning it for individual work. The teacher uses formal and informal assessments to determine when to spend more time on a particular lesson, uses additional scaffolds, provides other models, or asks students to work independently to demonstrate their knowledge. It is from their analysis of assessments that teachers recognize the needs of the learners in their classrooms.

Unfortunately, many teachers are not prepared to recognize the needs of the diverse learners in today's classrooms. The two main goals for this chapter are: (1) to provide information about how to differentiate instruction in ways that help all students learn and grow, and (2) to discuss the important characteristics and special adaptations for several diverse learner groups. Teachers must learn to recognize students' special needs. How they perceive themselves as learners affects their self-esteem, and teachers need to understand that in order to guide their learning (Glazer, 1998). It is important to explain to the entire class that everyone learns differently, but we are all capable of learning. Students may be doing different assignments on occasion, but these assignments may be differentiated based on particular learning needs.

The Concept of Differentiated Instruction

In the previous section we asked, Why differentiate instruction? It should be clear that no one approach or learning activity will meet the needs of all students in one classroom. Yet, the classroom teacher is responsible for providing a learning environment in which all students can achieve their full potential.

According to Tomlinson (1999, p. 12), a teacher who differentiates instruction embraces the following principles:

- Respect the readiness level of each student.
- Expect all students to grow, and support their continual growth.
- Offer all students the opportunity to explore essential understandings and skills at degrees of difficulty that escalate consistently as they develop their understanding and skill.
- Offer all students tasks that look—and are—equally interesting, equally important, and equally engaging.

Figure 9.1 presents an overall look at the concept of **differentiated instruction,** in which all students' needs are taken into account. Notice that several of the strategies mentioned throughout this book are also strategies employed by teachers who use differentiated instruction; indeed, most strategies can be implemented with a wide variety of students.

> differentiated instruction

Differentiated instruction is a way to meet the needs of all students, including those with special needs, because different tasks can take into account the nature of those needs. It is not necessary to differentiate every lesson; however, particular points within an instructional unit or topic of study can be differentiated based on students' readiness for the topic, materials, or skills needed; their interests; their abilities; and/or their learning profiles.

Any classroom will have students who are capable of reading material at or above their grade level, as well as those who struggle with reading and need easier materials. The class may also have a few nonreaders. Likewise, not all students are interested in reading the same topics. Students have different abilities, both physical and mental; see the discussion of particular special needs later in this chapter. Finally, they have different learning profiles. These profiles include personality traits (e.g., shy, gregarious, sensitive); learning styles (visual learner, auditory learner, kinesthetic learner); and students' personal profiles of intelligences, or degrees to which they reflect linguistic, spatial, bodily-kinesthetic, logical-mathematical, musical, intrapersonal, interpersonal, or naturalist intelligences (Gardner, 1983, 1999). Attempts to match students' learning profiles with school tasks may help students initially with tasks that are completely new and unfamiliar; to match the learning environment to a student's developmental level perfectly and regularly will likely arrest the student at that level, however (Hunt, 1971). In other words,

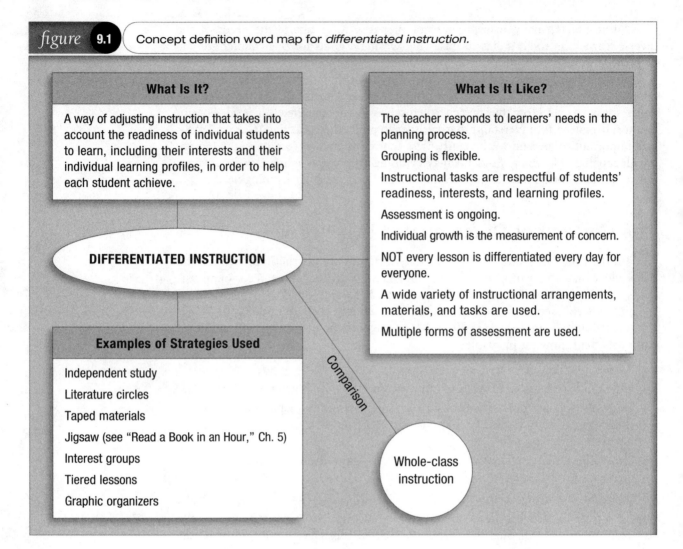

figure **9.1**   Concept definition word map for *differentiated instruction*.

What Is It?

A way of adjusting instruction that takes into account the readiness of individual students to learn, including their interests and their individual learning profiles, in order to help each student achieve.

What Is It Like?

The teacher responds to learners' needs in the planning process.

Grouping is flexible.

Instructional tasks are respectful of students' readiness, interests, and learning profiles.

Assessment is ongoing.

Individual growth is the measurement of concern.

NOT every lesson is differentiated every day for everyone.

A wide variety of instructional arrangements, materials, and tasks are used.

Multiple forms of assessment are used.

DIFFERENTIATED INSTRUCTION

Examples of Strategies Used

Independent study

Literature circles

Taped materials

Jigsaw (see "Read a Book in an Hour," Ch. 5)

Interest groups

Tiered lessons

Graphic organizers

Comparison

Whole-class instruction

a certain amount of discomfort is a good thing and leads to growth. Joyce, Weil, and Calhoun (2000) make this point clear:

> For example, gregarious students are initially the most comfortable with social models and can profit from them quickly. However, the less-gregarious students were in the greatest need of the models least comfortable for them. Hence, the challenge is not to select the most comfortable models but to enable the students to develop the skills to relate to a wider variety of models, many of which appear, at least superficially, to be mismatched with their learning styles. . . . If environment and the student are too much in harmony, the student is permitted to operate at a level of comfort that does not require the challenge of growth. (p. 401)

Thus, it is important that teachers know their students' learning profiles in order to match instruction with those profiles occasionally, and also to know where students need to expand their ways of learning and knowing.

Planning and Implementing a Differentiated Lesson

The most important aspect of planning a differentiated lesson is to establish clear goals for students. According to Tomlinson (1999), "During planning, a teach-

Learning Styles Index

www.ncsu.edu/felder-public/
ILSpage.html

**Multiple Intelligences
Inventory**

http://surfaquarium.com/
MI/inventory.htm

er should generate specific lists of what students should know (facts), understand (concepts and principles), and be able to do (skills) by the time the unit ends" (p. 40). To write a lesson plan that differentiates for student needs, include the concept or broad idea to be taught, standards addressed, objectives and ways to assess whether these objectives have been met, pre-assessment information about the students' abilities and prior knowledge about the topic, and grouping considerations. Then, using what you know about your students' specific readiness levels, interests, and learning profiles, develop a set of engaging activities that provide the varied learning opportunities that the students need. Finally, identify several options for students to demonstrate what they have come to know, understand, and are able to do at the conclusion of the unit. After the lesson, take the time to reflect on what has been done and still needs to be done for students' understanding and learning.

All components need not be differentiated for every lesson. In fact, it may be best to think about differentiating instruction by looking at just one curricular component that can be modified to meet students' needs. Thus, we can look at

- differentiating the content, or what students will learn and the materials they will use.
- differentiating the process, or the activities students will engage in to understand key ideas and use essential skills.
- differentiating the product, or how students will demonstrate what they understand and can do as a result of the lesson.

Differentiating the content. One example of differentiating content would be varying the spelling words that students need to learn. Based on a pretest, some fifth-grade students may show they need to work with third-grade words, while others top out with a ninth-grade word list. The teacher could use the same procedures for presenting and practicing spelling words with all students, but the words themselves would be appropriate for individual readiness levels. In other words, the students would not all be learning the same words, but they would be learning words appropriate to their needs, and they would be practicing and being tested on them in the same way.

Differentiating the process. This same teacher could also differentiate the process, or the activities students use to learn the spelling of certain words. For example, based on their learning profiles some students will best learn their words by writing each word with a crayon and then tracing it while spelling it out loud to get a sensory impression of the word. Other students may simply need to look at the whole word and then practice saying and writing it in order to learn the spelling.

Differentiating the product. Finally, the product could differ as well. In addition to the written spelling test, students with a particularly strong bodily-kinesthetic intelligence could perform a "cheerleader spelling" of the words, leading a small group of students in spelling out the words (Rogers, 1999). Teachers can encourage students to move around while also attending to critical thinking. For example, ask students to choose sides on a controversial

Teachers may differentiate the content, the process, or the product to enhance learning for diverse student needs.

topic to debate and defend, and then have each group move to different areas of the classroom depending on which side they chose; ask them to discuss and explain why they chose the side they did, and have them listen to one another. Similarly, students can create multimedia presentations to respond to text or to share information with the class; they could then give it to classmates to review, post it to a blog, or publish it for a more global audience. Also, students can create posters, songs, or skits to differentiate a product for class.

Achieving Differentiation Through Tiered Activities

tiered activities ●

A teacher can use **tiered activities** to design and adapt a single lesson plan to meet the varied needs of class members as well as provide specific instructional aid to individual students; that is, versions of activities are designed to provide the same essential understandings but address a variety of learning needs. "Tiered activities are very important when a teacher wants to ensure that students with different learning needs work with the same essential ideas and use the same key skills. For example, a student who struggles with reading or has a difficult time with abstract thinking nonetheless needs to make sense of the pivotal concepts and principles in a given chapter or story" (Tomlinson, 1999, p. 83). The following teacher guidelines are useful for developing tiered activities:

1. Identify the concept that will be the focus of the lesson.
2. Think about your students. Know their talents, interests, abilities, and learning profiles.
3. Create one activity that is interesting, requires high-level thought, and clearly focuses on elements that require students to use a key skill to understand a key idea.
4. Draw a ladder, with the top rung representing a very high skill level and understanding and the bottom rung a low skill level and understanding. Decide where, on the ladder, your activity fits. Is it too challenging for the advanced students, or will it challenge the less-advanced students? In this way, you will see who needs another version of the activity.
5. Revise the activity to create versions that will meet the needs of all your students. This might mean varying the material students use, or varying the ways in which students will express their learning.
6. Match a version of the activity to each student based on his or her needs.

In their companion books, *Differentiation in Practice: A Resource Guide for Differentiating Curriculum Grades K–5* and *Differentiation in Practice: A Resource Guide for Differentiating Curriculum Grades 5–9*, Tomlinson and Eidson (2003a, 2003b) provide models of differentiated units of study. The models include many examples of how teachers at all grade levels prepare tiered activities for lessons across the curriculum. For instance, one teacher shares tiered writing prompts based on the readiness levels of her students. The more detailed example that follows demonstrates a content area differentiated lesson in science with tiered activities at three different readiness levels.

Sixth-Grade Science Example: The Biosphere

Mr. Caday's sixth-grade students are studying the biosphere. They understand the meanings of words such as *organism* and *environment*; in the chapter they have just read in their textbook, they have been introduced to new vocabulary, including *atmosphere, energy, environmental factors,* and *biosphere.* The essential understanding that Mr. Caday wants his students to have is to be able to name and describe the four conditions necessary for most life on Earth—presence of water, an atmosphere, light, and temperature.

Mr. Caday knows his students well. Of the 28 students in his class, nine are reading at grade level, nine above grade level, seven are two years below grade level, and three read well below grade level. Of the three reading below grade level, two are English learners. One student in the class is learning disabled and has been diagnosed with ADHD. Another student has cerebral palsy, but he is in the group who read above grade level. He uses a wheelchair and a special communication device for reading and writing. Through observation, Mr. Caday notes those students who learn better through visual means (the majority) and those who prefer auditory and kinesthetic activities. Mr. Caday also surveys his students, using the survey referred to in the margin, to help him identify their multiple intelligences profile. All of Mr. Caday's students can use context clues to determine word meanings, and they all enjoy word puzzles. They are a close group, and everyone gets along well, although there is the occasional misunderstanding.

Mr. Caday works at an urban school in a high-poverty area, so his students are unfamiliar with agricultural land uses. He has developed a small experiment as his "ladder" activity. On Friday, he plans to give each student four sandwich bags, some rye grass seed, four cotton balls—two dampened with water and two dry—and some masking tape. He will have each student "plant" the seeds and cotton balls inside the sandwich bag. Students will write their names on a piece of tape to identify their bags. Then Mr. Caday will collect one wet bag and one dry bag from each student and place these in a dark cabinet. The other bags will be taped to the windows of his classroom. Mr. Caday will ask his students to predict what will happen over the weekend to the seeds in both bags. Then, as some seeds sprout, Mr. Caday will ask students to predict what will happen to these sprouts under a variety of other conditions.

Mr. Caday places this activity in the middle of his ladder. He feels it is not challenging enough for his advanced students, but it is physically challenging for the student with cerebral palsy (this student will not be able to plant his seeds). Mr. Caday likes using real-life objects with his non–English speakers but needs to think about how he will help them understand the directions for planting and predicting. He will have his advanced students identify as many permutations of the experiment as they can to test the four conditions for life. He will create a poster that uses pictures and symbols to direct the English learners but will encourage them to give short oral explanations of what happened to the seeds. Finally, he will ask for a volunteer to help the student with cerebral palsy complete the physical aspects of the experiment.

Mr. Caday also wants to assess what his students learn from this activity. Since he differentiated the process for his students with these tiered activities, Mr. Caday realizes that he will need to use tiered assessment, allowing students to adequately show their understanding of the four conditions necessary for life as demonstrated in the experiment. Therefore, he wants to differentiate the product, or how his students will demonstrate what they learned.

Mr. Caday will ask his advanced students to analyze their data on the permutations they set up, prepare charts to show the results of these permutations, and write a summary report of their findings. The majority of the students will prepare timelines for each day the seeds "grow" within the sandwich bags and what happened in each of the four bags. They will then write a summary report discussing their findings as related to the four conditions for life. The English learners will draw their results to share and explain their results orally. The stu-

WWW○○○

Multiple Intelligences Inventory
www.surfaquarium.com/MI/inventory.htm

dent with cerebral palsy will orally dictate his daily observations and explain these findings in writing using his assistive communication device for both oral dictation and writing.

Figure 9.2 shows the "ladder" of Mr. Caday's differentiated activity. Figure 9.3 shows the poster he used to represent the grass seed experiment.

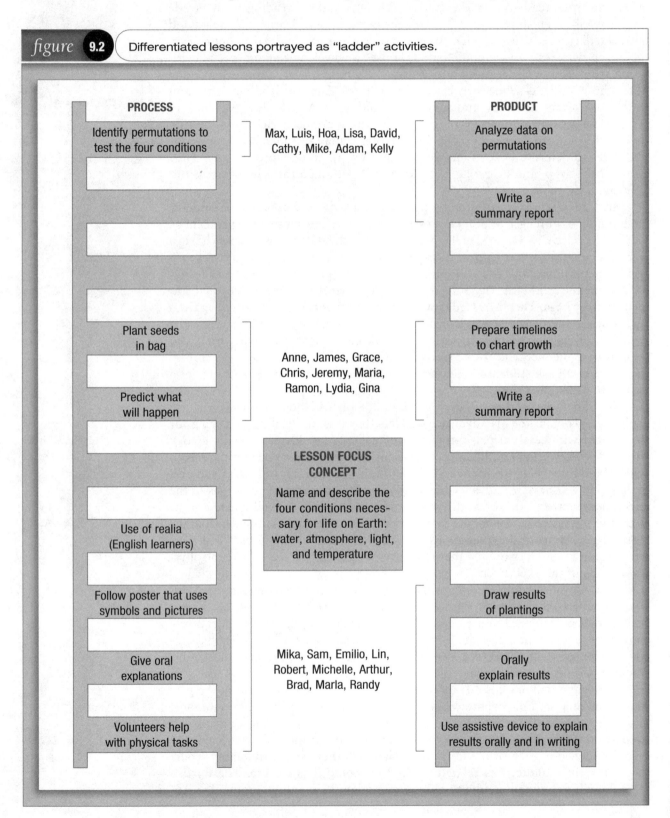

figure 9.2 Differentiated lessons portrayed as "ladder" activities.

PROCESS

Identify permutations to test the four conditions

Plant seeds in bag

Predict what will happen

Use of realia (English learners)

Follow poster that uses symbols and pictures

Give oral explanations

Volunteers help with physical tasks

Max, Luis, Hoa, Lisa, David, Cathy, Mike, Adam, Kelly

Anne, James, Grace, Chris, Jeremy, Maria, Ramon, Lydia, Gina

Mika, Sam, Emilio, Lin, Robert, Michelle, Arthur, Brad, Marla, Randy

LESSON FOCUS CONCEPT

Name and describe the four conditions necessary for life on Earth: water, atmosphere, light, and temperature

PRODUCT

Analyze data on permutations

Write a summary report

Prepare timelines to chart growth

Write a summary report

Draw results of plantings

Orally explain results

Use assistive device to explain results orally and in writing

Visual representation of the grass seed experiment.

figure 9.3

Diverse Learner Groups

As stated earlier, today's classrooms are remarkably diverse. In a sense, all learners are diverse, as each learner is unique, with his or her own set of learning needs. However, in this section we are concerned with those learners who benefit most from focused, differentiated instruction. Typically these include students (1) whose native language is something other than English, (2) who are identified as gifted (3) or learning disabled, (4) who demonstrate disorders that affect communication, (5) who are physically challenged in some way, or (6) who demonstrate behavioral disorders. The remainder of this chapter discusses each of these diverse learner groups.

① Students Who Are Linguistically Diverse (English Learners)

Characteristics

Linguistic diversity is a reality in our public schools, where English learners aim to achieve biliteracy, the ability to read and write in two or more languages. According to Kindler (2002), more than 450 languages are spoken in U.S. schools. In addition, approximately 10 percent of preK–12 students are considered English learners (National Center for Education Statistics, 2012). A U.S. Census Bureau survey from 2009 reported that 21.1 percent of students between 5 and 17 years of age speak another language at home. This number varies by location: In the western United States, the number who speak another language at home increases to roughly 34 percent, while in the Midwest this number is roughly 12 percent. In the South and Northeast, roughly 20 percent speak a language other than English at home (U.S. Census Bureau, 2009).

Spanish speakers are currently the largest group of bilingual individuals in the United States; roughly 70 percent of the students between the ages of 5 and 17 who speak another language at home speak Spanish (U.S. Census Bureau, 2009). Other languages spoken at home include German, French, Chinese, and Italian (U.S. Census Bureau, 2007). But many other languages are represented in classrooms today: Arabic, Bengali, Filipino, Greek, Hebrew, Hmong, Hungarian, Japanese, Korean, Polish, Portuguese, Russian, Somali, Ukrainian, Vietnamese, and others. Linguistic diversity, moreover, is not limited to foreign languages. Native American languages and English dialects, such as African American Vernacular English (AAVE), are also represented in many classrooms. In all cases, however, students who have a solid foundation in at least one language more easily learn another language. In the United States, having this foundation contributes to academic success.

When students acquire English as a second language, their speech may sound different from that of native English speakers. Phonological features of languages differ and impact English learners in their production of certain sounds. Some English sounds do not exist in other languages and may present difficulty or confusion for speakers of these languages. For example, a student whose native language is Spanish might say "chip" for "ship," or "sip" for "zip." A student who speaks AAVE might say "sick" for "six," or "birfday" for "birthday." Other sound differences for some of the many languages in today's schools are presented in Figure 9.4.

Adaptations

August and Shanahan (2006) point out that the research on acquiring literacy in a second language is limited. But they also state that "becoming literate in a second language depends on the quality of teaching, which is a function of the content coverage, intensity or thoroughness of instruction, methods used to support the special needs of second-language learners and to build on their strengths, how well learning is monitored, and teacher preparation" (p. 3). The professional literature does provide general principles, or best practices, that to keep in mind in order to be supportive of your English learners. As condensed from Barnitz (2006, pp. 55–58), these principles include:

- Respect natural differences in languages and dialects.
- Use methods that bridge cultural background knowledge and whatever materials are being read.
- Contextualize instruction on language structures and skills within the composing and comprehending process. Contextual supports include scaffolding

Problematic sounds for English learners.

figure **9.4**

LANGUAGE	SOUNDS EITHER NOT PART OF THE LANGUAGE OR PROBLEMATIC
Chinese	b ch d dg g oa sh s th v z f j l m n ng l-clusters r-clusters
French	ch ee j ng oo th a h oy s schwa
Greek	aw ee i oo schwa
Italian	a ar dg h i ng th schwa v l-clusters end clusters
Japanese	dg f i th oo v schwa h l r sh s w l-clusters r-clusters
Korean	b l oa ow p r sh t th l-clusters r-clusters
Spanish	dg j sh th z b d h m n ng r t v w y s-clusters

in the form of simplified language, teacher modeling, visuals, graphic organizers, hands-on learning, and cooperative learning groups.

- Use authentic materials from the learner's community.
- Design literature-based instruction for developing language competence.
- Use technological and other communicative arts to facilitate oral and written language acquisition.
- Facilitate authentic, functional communication.
- Base literacy assessment on authentic language and literacy tasks and events: that is, a multidimensional approach to assessment that includes alternative assessments and modifications to traditional assessments (Lenski, Ehlers-Zavala, Daniel, et al., 2006).
- In interpreting assessment data, be sensitive to cultural and linguistic variation.

These general principles serve as a basis for curriculum and lesson planning. In addition, Abate (2004) provides four specific recommendations for working with English learners.

1. *Know your students.* Find out something about their culture, first language, English proficiency levels for both oral and written language, educational experiences, learning styles, and interests. Communicate with their parents, with the ESL teacher if there is one, and with other classroom teachers. Examine their student records.

2. *Create lessons with clear goals and expectations.* The Sheltered Instruction Observation Protocol (SIOP) Model of sheltered instruction (Echevarria, Vogt, & Short, 2013) and the Four-by-Four Model (Mora, 2006) are both appropriate approaches for meeting the instructional needs of English learners (see further discussion later in this section).

3. *Group students by readiness levels and the complexity of the learning task.* Identify which aspects of learning tasks are imperative and which are negotiable. Learning tasks can also be categorized along spectrums that include simple to complex, concrete to abstract, single-faceted to multi-faceted, highly structured to loosely structured, or fast-paced to slow-paced (Tomlinson, 2001).

WWW○○○

Differentiated Instruction

http://www.ascd.org/research-a-topic/differentiated-instruction-resources.aspx

ESL Online Meeting Place

www.Eslcafe.com

Considering the complexity level of the learning task allows for "planning that is tiered so as to allow students to experience success while being challenged to achieve higher levels of language mastery and content knowledge" (Mora, 2006, p. 33). (Recall the guidelines for differentiated instruction from earlier in this chapter; see also the online references cited in the marginal note.)

4. *Implement effective strategies.* These might include using learning centers, graphic organizers, and supplemental texts.

General approaches for adapting instruction to better meet the needs of the English learner include cooperative learning and sheltered instruction.

Cooperative learning. This is an approach in which students work together to achieve a common goal. English learners will find working cooperatively with native English speakers useful because they will need to learn to communicate orally with each other. Through cooperative learning, English learners can acquire competence in oral language because of the increased opportunities for "comprehensible input" from their peers (Krashen, 1987).

comprehensible input •

Comprehensible input refers to communicating with language learners (providing "input") in such a way that they are able to make connections between concepts known in their native language and those same concepts in the unknown language for the purpose of learning that new language; it also involves modifying the new information in ways that are both linguistic and nonlinguistic in nature. The use of such modifications is called *scaffolding* (see Chapters 5 and 6). Linguistic supports include using less complex sentence structures, as well as "slower speech rates, clear articulation, less slang, fewer idioms, and a greater use of high-frequency vocabulary" (Krashen, as cited in Pilgreen, 2006, p. 43). Nonlinguistic supports are real

realia •

objects (**realia**), visuals, videos, storyboarding, movement (total physical response, or TPR), role plays, and collaborative or cooperative learning. For example, an instructor can make the new vocabulary word *ecstatic* more comprehensible by happily shouting "hurray" and jumping in the air. This action would be an example of TPR. Another example using visuals and a concept organizer can be seen in Figure 9.5. Providing comprehensible input is critical when teaching content area material and is a major consideration in sheltered English instruction.

Four-by-Four Model
http://prezi.com/jzm39iq9i67d/
four-by-four-thematic-planning-
activities-and-strategies/

Sheltered instruction. The major approaches associated with sheltered instruction are SDAIE (Specially Designed Academic Instruction in English) and ELD (English Language Development). SDAIE emphasizes *content learning* through modifications in instructional strategies, whereas ELD emphasizes English *language learning,* vocabulary development, and listening and speaking tasks using the content material as a vehicle. Two examples of instructional models employing sheltered English are the Four-by-Four Model and the SIOP (Sheltered Instruction Observation Protocol) Model.

Four-by-Four Model •

The **Four-by-Four Model** uses content area themes and a matrix (see Figure 9.6) of four levels of language development skills (i.e., listening, speaking, reading, writing) and four levels of language proficiency (i.e., beginning, early intermediate, intermediate, early advanced) to provide an instructional framework for planning learning tasks and activities.

SIOP Model •

In the **SIOP Model,** each lesson has separate language and content objectives that link to grade-level subject curriculum and standards. For examples of lesson plans adapted to the SIOP Model, visit the sites listed here.

The goal of sheltered English instruction is to teach English language skills to students at the same time they are learning specific subject matter knowledge (Echevarria, 2004). In all sheltered English instructional approaches, you need to examine the content of the lesson to identify and select key concepts or terms that

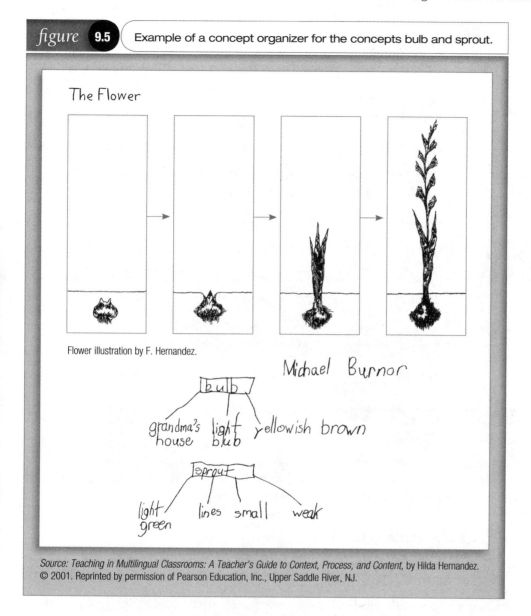

figure **9.5**   Example of a concept organizer for the concepts bulb and sprout.

The Flower

Flower illustration by F. Hernandez.

Michael Burnor

bulb

grandma's   light   yellowish brown
house   bulb

sprout

light   lines   small   weak
green

Source: Teaching in Multilingual Classrooms: A Teacher's Guide to Context, Process, and Content, by Hilda Hernandez.
© 2001. Reprinted by permission of Pearson Education, Inc., Upper Saddle River, NJ.

are critical to the lesson. Then teach these systematically in ways that maximize students' ability to comprehend: that is, ways that use Krashen's (1987) notion of comprehensible input. For example, using graphic organizers, as discussed in several chapters throughout this book, would be very appropriate. These structures provide visible and manipulable input that enables English learners to connect concepts and ideas to a new language for the purpose of learning that new language. In the case of grades 4–8, English academic language, or the language of school (e.g., *paragraph, caption, table, summarize, outline, compare and contrast, main ideas, details, implications*) is the *new* language. See Coxhead (2000) and Pilgreen (2006) for academic word lists.

Hernandez (2001) shares several types of organizers that are especially useful for English learners: realia, verb, noun, concept, and episodic. These organizers can be posted to provide a visual reference for students. Anything and everything should be used to create a context for the content information to make it understandable. In addition to realia, pictures, sketches, gestures, body language, demonstrations, and dramatic enactments will all provide for "comprehensible input." For example, for the sentence "Her facial expression was as sour as a lemon," students can be

WWW●●●

**SIOP Model
Lesson Plans**

www.cal.org/siop/lesson-
plans/index.html

www.washoe.k12.nv.us/staff/
ell/siop/elementary-lesson-plans

figure **9.6**   Matrix of the Four-by-Four thematic planning model.

LEVEL 1: Beginning language proficiency	LEVEL 2: Early intermediate language proficiency	LEVEL 3: Intermediate language proficiency	LEVEL 4: Early advanced language proficiency
Listening	Listening	Listening	Listening
LEVEL 1: Beginning language proficiency	LEVEL 2: Early intermediate language proficiency	LEVEL 3: Intermediate language proficiency	LEVEL 4: Early advanced language proficiency
Speaking	Speaking	Speaking	Speaking
LEVEL 1: Beginning language proficiency	LEVEL 2: Early intermediate language proficiency	LEVEL 3: Intermediate language proficiency	LEVEL 4: Early advanced language proficiency
Reading	Reading	Reading	Reading
LEVEL 1: Beginning language proficiency	LEVEL 2: Early intermediate language proficiency	LEVEL 3: Intermediate language proficiency	LEVEL 4: Early advanced language proficiency
Writing	Writing	Writing	Writing

given a bit of lemon to taste as they look in a mirror. Examples from the students' own backgrounds should be included as well. Helping students personally identify with the topic will make the learning more meaningful to them.

② Students Who Are Gifted and Talented

Characteristics

Gifted and talented students have extraordinary intellectual abilities, or they demonstrate exceptionally high achievement in particular academic areas or in the visual or performing arts as compared with their peer group. These students represent all cultural, ethnic, and socioeconomic backgrounds. Moreover, individual states identify, classify, and implement programs for gifted and talented students in a variety of ways. Frequently, intellectually gifted students are identified by very high scores on standardized tests and high achievement levels in school. Their linguistic abilities are usually highly developed compared with their peers. Hyperactivity may also be a sign of giftedness; students who are gifted often display high levels of activity as a result of boredom or intense interest in an activity. See Figure 9.7 for characteristics of intellectually gifted children.

Students are also classified as creatively gifted and talented if they excel in the visual or performing arts. These talents usually become apparent when a student is relatively young. Davis (1995) lists 12 categories as representative of creative individuals: "original, independent, risk taking, aware of creativeness, energetic, curious, has a sense of humor, attracted to complexity, artistic, open-minded, needs time alone, and intuitive" (as cited in Mastropieri & Scruggs, 2000, p. 148). Further information about recognizing giftedness in students can be found online.

WWW○○○

National Association for Gifted Children

www.nagc.org

GT World

www.gtworld.org

Council for Exceptional Children

www.cec.sped.org

Few students will display all of the characteristics in a given list; however, when clusters of these characteristics are present, they do serve as fairly reliable indicators. These characteristics are best used as signals to indicate that a particular student might warrant closer observation and could require specialized educational attention, pending a more comprehensive assessment by a qualified specialist.

GENERAL BEHAVIORAL CHARACTERISTICS

- Many typically learn to read earlier with a better comprehension of the nuances of the language. As many as half of the gifted and talented population have learned to read before entering school. They often read widely, quickly, and intensely and have large vocabularies.

- They commonly learn basic skills better, more quickly, and with less practice.

- They are frequently able to pick up and interpret nonverbal cues and can draw inferences which other children have to have spelled out for them.

- They take less for granted, seeking the "hows" and "whys."

- They display a better ability to work independently at an earlier age and for longer periods of time than other children.

- They can sustain longer periods of concentration and attention.

- Their interests are often both widely eclectic and intensely focused.

- They frequently have seemingly boundless energy, which sometimes leads to a misdiagnosis of "hyperactive."

- They are usually able to respond and relate well to parents, teachers, and other adults. They may prefer the company of older children and adults to that of their peers.

- They are willing to examine the unusual and are highly inquisitive.

- Their behavior is often well organized, goal directed, and efficient with respect to tasks and problems.

- They exhibit an intrinsic motivation to learn, find out, or explore and are often very persistent. "I'd rather do it myself" is a common attitude.

- They enjoy learning new things and new ways of doing things.

LEARNING CHARACTERISTICS

- They may show keen powers of observation, exhibit a sense of the significant, and have an eye for important details.

- They may read a great deal on their own, preferring books and magazines written for youngsters older than themselves.

- They often take great pleasure in intellectual activity.

- They have well developed powers of abstraction, conceptualization, and synthesizing.

- They generally have rapid insight into cause–effect relationships.

- They often display a questioning attitude and seek information for the sake of having it as much as for its instrumental value.

- They are often skeptical, critical, and evaluative. They are quick to spot inconsistencies.

- They often have a large storehouse of information regarding a variety of topics which they can recall quickly.

- They show a ready grasp of underlying principles and can often make valid generalizations about events, people, and objects.

- They readily perceive similarities, differences, and anomalies.

- They often attack complicated material by separating it into its components and analyzing it systematically.

(continued)

figure **9.7**   Characteristics of intellectually gifted learners, *continued.*

CREATIVE CHARACTERISTICS

- They are fluent thinkers, able to produce a large quantity of possibilities, consequences, or related ideas.

- They are flexible thinkers able to use many different alternatives and approaches to problem solving.

- They are original thinkers, seeking new, unusual, or unconventional associations and combinations among items of information. They also have an ability to see relationships among seemingly unrelated objects, ideas, or facts.

- They are elaborative thinkers, producing new steps, ideas, responses, or other embellishments to a basic idea, situation, or problem.

- They show a willingness to entertain complexity and seem to thrive in problem situations.

- They are good guessers and can construct hypotheses or "what if" questions readily.

- They are often aware of their own impulsiveness and the irrationality within themselves and show emotional sensitivity.

- They have a high level of curiosity about objects, ideas, situations, or events.

- They often display intellectual playfulness, fantasize, and imagine readily.

- They can be less intellectually inhibited than their peers in expressing opinions and ideas and often exhibit spirited disagreement.

- They have a sensitivity to beauty and are attracted to aesthetic dimensions.

Source: Whitmore, J. R. (1985). Characteristics of intellectually gifted children (Digest 344). *Digests on the gifted* (pp. 1–2). Reston, VA: The Council for Exceptional Children.

Adaptations

Just because a student has exceptional abilities does not mean he can realize his full potential without specially adapted educational programs. Gifted and talented students may struggle in the general education program because they have special learning needs that are not fully met there (Lewis & Doorlag, 2011). The most common educational approaches for gifted and talented students are acceleration and enrichment. **Acceleration** simply means moving students through the curriculum at a faster pace than general education students. This could mean beginning school early, skipping grades, testing out of classes, or providing more ability-appropriate curriculum. Acceleration often means students do not remain with their age peers. **Enrichment** simply means expanding on the curriculum. The same subjects may be studied in greater depth, or after-school programs may provide instruction in additional subjects or content not typically found in the curriculum (e.g., chess, finance policies in state government). Enrichment programs generally keep gifted students in their general education classrooms with their age peers. Both accelerated and enrichment programs can be provided within the regular classroom, in resource classes, in university classes, or through flexible scheduling or mentoring programs. General classroom teachers would do well to heed the advice of Kennedy (1995, pp. 233–234) when they find gifted students in their classrooms:

- Resist policies requiring more work of those who finish assignments quickly and easily. Instead, explore ways to assign different work.

- Seek out supplemental materials and ideas that extend, not merely reinforce, the curriculum.

- Deemphasize grades and other extrinsic rewards.

acceleration

enrichment

- Encourage intellectual and academic risk taking.
- Help all students develop social skills to relate well to one another.
- Take time to listen to responses that may at first appear to be off target.
- Provide opportunities for independent investigations in areas of interest.
- Be aware of the special needs of gifted girls (i.e., they can achieve high-level career goals and succeed in math and science).

③ Students Who Are Learning Disabled

Characteristics

Students with a cognitive **learning disability** (LD) are typically average and bright learners who nevertheless have difficulty processing information. These processing problems may be in the area of perception, attention, memory, or expressive language. Students who have a learning disability do not typically have hearing or visual impairments, physical or health issues, emotional disturbances, or environmental, cultural, or economic disadvantages—yet they perform poorly in school. They are often unfairly labeled and described in negative terms such as "neurologically impaired," "deficient," or "perceptually handicapped." They can be quite puzzling to their teachers. They often have poor strategies for learning because they learn differently and need to be taught alternative learning skills that take advantage of their individual strengths. As Mooney and Cole (2000) relate, it is important to remember that students with LD are bright and have many strengths, often in creativity, intuition, and emotional understanding.

In addition to performing poorly in school subjects, students with LD may lack the skill to communicate appropriate social messages, making group work difficult, and they often have a high activity level and difficulty paying attention. As a result, they are frequently diagnosed as having ADHD, which can lead to a misplaced focus on behavioral issues rather than cognitive issues.

 learning disability

WWW○○○

Resources Supporting Students with Special Needs

www.specialconnections.ku.edu

Adaptations

Because their difficulties are unique, students with learning disabilities present a special challenge to classroom teachers. You will need to use collaboration, creative thinking, and problem-solving strategies to best help these students. Mastropieri and Scruggs (2000, pp. 83–84) provide an extensive list of adaptations to consider when teaching students with cognitive learning disabilities; an abbreviated version follows:

- Adapt the physical environment to provide a distraction-free workplace that will help students focus their attention (e.g., rearrange seating positions, provide quiet space within the classroom, keep desks away from potentially troublesome stimulation).
- Model organization (e.g., a place for everything and everything in its place; show what an organized desk, notebook, or computer desktop looks like).
- Structure daily routines and schedules (e.g., make a list of what to do first, second, etc.).
- Adapt instructional materials (e.g., make assignments more compatible with literacy skills and organizational abilities—see the section on differentiated instruction earlier in this chapter).
- Teach study skills (e.g., how to schedule time, keep an assignment calendar, and use study strategies).

- Adapt instruction (e.g., use of SCREAM variables: structure, clarity, redundancy, enthusiasm, appropriate pace, maximized engagement; or HOTS, a creative instructional program that uses Socratic dialogue, technology, and dramatic techniques; see the website listed in the margin for more information).
- Vary presentation formats (e.g., verbal instruction, visual aids, realia, field trips, websites, podcasts, audiobooks, and videos).
- Question students frequently (e.g., ask students to rephrase information in their own words, checking for understanding).
- Provide clear directions and accessible goals (e.g., use short, concise sentences, reminders for long-term assignments, regular monitoring).
- Teach students how to learn (e.g., model how to use learning strategies).
- Use peer tutors (e.g., classmates can provide assistance or additional practice).
- Conduct periodic reviews (e.g., recall previously taught content and relate to new information being learned).
- Adapt evaluation procedures (e.g., use alternatives to standard assessments, such as drawings, sketches, or dramatic enactments).

Higher Order Thinking Skills

www.hots.org

Now that ADHD is recognized as a cognitive learning disability rather than a behavioral disorder, educators need to address the learning needs of these students. In terms of designing lessons, Tannock and Martinussen (2001) suggest learning strategies that:

- include a system for remembering, such as a mnemonic device;
- are worded simply, which would also help English learners;
- begin with action words; and
- use words that are familiar to the students.

In addition, consider new forms of learning environments whenever possible. For example, project-based learning and problem-based learning (see Chapter 10) are viable alternatives for students with cognitive learning disabilities, and ones that can enhance motivation levels for all learners.

Assistive technology professionals are researching how digital technologies can help those who are learning disabled. For example, one project focused on the use of text-reader software with computer-readable school texts. Text-reader software "uses synthetic speech to read text aloud while the same text is highlighted on a computer screen" (Hasselbring & Bausch, 2005/2006, p. 73). Teachers found that their students with disabilities more often reread text passages for clarity when using this software. More research is needed, however. Boone and Higgins (2007) state that

Students with a cognitive learning disability are typically average and bright learners who nevertheless have difficulty processing information.

mere access to the content is inadequate as an AT [assistive technology] unless that access is mediated with instructional design supports appropriate for the specific disability of the user. This point is especially relevant for the large population of students who may have a combination of physical and cognitive disabilities. And although the traditional AT intervention of providing an alternate medium or format of the content for such an individual would be helpful, difficult vocabulary, poor organization, and distracting elements often remain. It still would not provide the access to learning that many educators have identified [is needed]. (p. 138)

The majority of students with learning disabilities are not placed in special classes but remain in the regular classroom with some part-time help from a resource teacher. It is imperative that you strive to recognize these students' unique strengths and do your best to help them learn.

④ Students Who Have Disorders that Affect Communication

Characteristics

Disorders that affect communication affect a student's ability to interact with teachers and peers. Generally, communication disorders involve language and speech disorders. **Language disorders** are characterized by the inability to use the oral and/or written symbols of language. Students have trouble expressing themselves either orally or in writing; grammatical patterns are not used appropriately; students' vocabulary is limited; and they have difficulty following directions. **Speech disorders** are characterized by frequent and severe difficulty in pronouncing certain sounds (articulation) or speaking fluently (stuttering). **Autism** is a condition that affects communication skills. The 1990 Individuals with Disabilities Education Act (IDEA) defined autism as "a developmental disability significantly affecting verbal and nonverbal communication and social interaction, generally evident before age 3." Some children with autism do not speak at all, while others simply repeat back what they hear (echolalic speech). Students with **Asperger's syndrome,** a milder form of autism, have more developed communication abilities and are often highly intelligent, but they have difficulty interacting socially. For obvious reasons, students with disorders that interfere with communication may have difficulty becoming fully functioning members of the classroom community.

● language disorders

● speech disorders
● autism

● Asperger's syndrome

Adaptations

Because they are able to participate in most aspects of the curriculum, students with disorders that affect communication generally remain in regular classroom settings for their instructional needs. The possible exception is students with autism. For working with students with autism in regular classrooms, Wood, Lazzari, and Reeves (1993, p. 115) provide some suggestions:

● Structure the learning environment so that it is predictable and consistent. This includes the physical structure of the classroom as well as routines, schedules, and teacher behavior.
● Design instructional programs to provide ways to help children learn to communicate. Remember that verbal communication is but one way to communicate; provide students with alternatives such as signing, writing, [or] using the computer.
● Since students with autism have difficulty managing their own behavior without structure, develop individual and group behavior plans that stress positive behavior management and set forth clear instructions, rules, and consequences.
● Work closely with the family to ensure consistency between school and home and other settings in approaches, methods of interaction, and response to students.

WWW●●●

Communication Disorders
www.comeunity.com/disability/
speech/index.html

If literature circles are part of the classroom curriculum, one young adult novel that would help classmates better appreciate what it means to be autistic is *The Curious Incident of the Dog in the Night-Time* (Haddon, 2003; see Table 5.2 in Chapter 5 for more information). Discussing this book can help students generate ideas for better engaging a student with autism in the regular classroom setting.

A specialist will help students with severe speech impairments develop speech skills. As the classroom teacher, you will need to reinforce the work of the specialist by providing opportunities for students to practice their new skills in a safe, risk-free environment. Through modeling appropriate grammar, providing language models through quality literature, and emphasizing vocabulary development, you will be assisting the student with a communication disorder.

Additionally, you cannot allow peers to tease or ridicule students who make speech errors. Building a classroom atmosphere that is respectful of all learners, and recognizes that everyone has strengths and areas that need to be developed, is crucial not only for students with disorders that affect communication but also for all members of the classroom community. When students with communication difficulties do speak, they need to be listened to carefully. You need not correct their speech but instead model the appropriate articulation or word order in responding to the student. Attention to the content of what was said is most important.

augmentative communication system ●

For those students with more severe disorders, special devices, called **augmentative communication systems,** may be used to help them communicate. One such device is the *communication board,* or *language board* (Johnston, Tulbert, & Sebastian, 2000). The board (which can be just a piece of paper with pictures pasted on) contains pictures of common objects or representative pictures for common activities that the student can simply point to in order to convey her ideas. Pictures could be of faces that show the emotions of happiness or sadness; clothing items; food and beverages; buildings such as school, home, or church, or rooms in the home; and the words *yes* and *no.*

assistive technologies ●

As mentioned earlier, **assistive technologies** (AT) are available to provide access to information to students with communication disorders and learning disabilities (Boone & Higgins, 2007). These devices may have larger than normal keys, or keys with wider spaces between them so the desired keys are easier to locate and hit. Letter keys might appear in alphabetical order, or the keys may feature pictures or words rather than letters. Some devices actually "talk" by using prerecorded speech when a particular key is pressed.

⑤ Students Who Are Physically Challenged

Characteristics

Students with physical challenges represent a large group of today's school population. In addition to the obvious challenges of a visual or hearing impairment, other physical challenges include severe allergies, arthritis, asthma, cerebral palsy, congenital anomalies (e.g., albinism, cleft lip, spina bifida), diabetes, epilepsy, hemophilia, HIV/AIDS, leukemia and other cancers, muscular dystrophy, rheumatic fever, and Tourette's syndrome, as well as impairments resulting from a traumatic brain injury. (For more detailed explanations of these conditions, visit the websites listed on the facing page.) Because such a wide variety of conditions can cause physical challenges—the preceding list names only a few—there is no concise list of characteristics; however, in general, these physical challenges are just that: physical. Students with one or some combination of physical disability are quite capable of performing well intellectually. For example, some individuals who have cerebral palsy with severe motor impairments are intellectually gifted. No relationship exists between the degree of physical impairment and intellectual ability. What can happen is that students may experience excessive absences or fatigue as a result of certain physical impairments, and learning problems can begin in this way. Students who are "medically fragile"—that is, their participation in school requires heart monitors, oxygen tanks, suctioning units, or special medical support—are regularly being placed in general classroom settings. **Individualized education programs (IEPs)** are then developed. IEPs help the teacher, support personnel, parents, and the student understand their respective responsibilities toward meeting educational and medical needs.

● individualized
education programs

Adaptations

For students with visual or hearing impairments, special arrangements within the learning environment can be made. For example, using technology, visuals, and special seating can allow maximum visual access to information for those with hearing impairments. For those with visual impairments, three-dimensional models, oral presentations, and wide, clear aisles are helpful. In addition, the structure of certain teaching procedures may need to be adapted, such as directly facing a student who is hearing impaired to allow for lipreading or using American Sign Language; for a student with a visual impairment, provide both printed materials in a large print or Braille format and extra time in order to read these materials. Technological devices can also be used, such as amplification devices for those with hearing impairments and Braillewriters for students who are blind.

For most of the physical impairments that your students may have, you will first need to learn more about the particular condition. Again, as with visual and hearing impairments, the physical arrangement of the classroom may need to be adapted to allow students with mobility difficulties to have easy access to all classroom areas and activities. Although the Americans with Disabilities Act should have remedied many issues, other areas of the school should also be checked for accessibility (e.g., curb cuts in the sidewalks, handrails at the appropriate height, wide door openings, nonslip surfaces on the floors, toilet accessibility, and water fountains at a variety of heights). Students needing wheelchairs may also need a lapboard for writing. Crutch holders can be attached to the sides or backs of chairs. For students with muscular impairments, papers can be taped to their desk, or pencils attached to the desk by a string and thumbtacks. Some students may need to record their responses orally rather than write them. A plastic ruler serves the student with poor muscle control better than a paper bookmark (Glazzard, 1982). Sometimes simple modifications are all that is necessary.

WWW●●●

**More about Physical
Impairments**

Visual impairment:
http://www.lighthouse.org/navh

Hearing impairment:
www.nad.org

Cerebral palsy:
http://cerebralpalsy.org/

Muscular dystrophy:
www.mda.org

Spina bifida: www.sbaa.org

Brain injury: www.biausa.org

Epilepsy:
www.epilepsyfoundation.org

Diabetes: www.diabetes.org

AIDS: www.aids.org

American Academy of Pediatrics:
www.aap.org

Others:

http://www2.ed.gov/parents/
needs/speced/edpicks.jhtml

http://education.qld.gov.au/
curriculum/learning/students/
disabilities/resources/information/
pi/pi.html

⑥ Students Who Have Behavioral Disorders

Characteristics

There is no one definition of behavioral disorder, nor does any single pattern of behavior identify a student as having a behavioral disorder. Behaviors range from extreme withdrawal to extreme aggression. It is common for classroom teachers, especially in grades 4–8, to be the first to recognize atypical behaviors and to begin the referral process (Lewis & Doorlag, 2011). A **behavioral,** or conduct, **disorder** is generally identified when a student's behavior deviates significantly from what is recognized as normal, occurs often and/or intensely, and occurs over time (Nelson, 1993). It is common for behavioral disorders to negatively impact the student's academic achievement, and it is possible that the student also has a learning disability. In fact, the behavioral disorder could be the result of poor academic performance brought about by the learning disability. Students with behavioral disorders are often described as hyperactive, distractible, or impulsive, and these students experience difficulty because they do not have appropriate social and study skills. Instruction focused on these two areas should improve their chances of success in the classroom.

● behavioral disorder

Adaptations

Because study skills are discussed elsewhere in this book, suggestions for improving social skills (also called life skills) and classroom conduct are presented here. Enlist the school counselor or psychologist to help a student with a behavioral disorder. Additionally, inform the student's parents or caregivers of the types of interventions being implemented at school so they can respond to their child in ways that are consistent with what the school is trying to achieve. General suggestions for helping students with behavioral disorders include:

- Establish an open, accepting classroom environment.
- Clearly state class rules and consequences.
- Stress positive behaviors and focus on student successes.
- Reward positive behaviors and state the behavior that is being rewarded.
- Provide extra opportunities for student success.
- Use good judgment, and be patient and tolerant.
- Teach self-control, self-monitoring, and conflict resolution using role playing and examples.
- Select activity partners carefully.
- Have alternative activities available.
- Allow groups of one.
- Use behavioral contracts. (Mastropieri & Scruggs, 2000, p. 98)

It is important to have a consistent approach when reacting to students' inappropriate behavior. For example, rather than immediately reprimanding negative behavior, say to the student in a normal tone of voice, "Stop and think about what you just did. What should you have done? Now, try to do this more appropriately." By using these same words each time students behave inappropriately, you will help students begin to take responsibility for their actions and to "learn that making good choices about their behavior is in their own best interest" (Mastropieri & Scruggs, 2000, p. 221).

Some students will benefit from more formalized procedures. In potentially volatile situations, students may be asked to go to **time-out** so that they have a chance to cool down and think about their behavior. Time-out can be a location in the classroom, or a designated location within the school. Occasionally, students may need to be escorted to a time-out location. Most schools have policies and procedures in place for such situations. A debriefing activity should occur after any cool-down periods. This can be a verbal conversation such as that in Figure 9.8, or students can be asked to complete a **think sheet** like the one in Figure 9.9, which can serve as a way of documenting behaviors and any positive changes that occur over time.

Students with behavioral disorders often lack basic knowledge of social skills. For example, they may not understand the components of a conversation—knowing how to join, start, maintain, or end the conversation—or that it's not polite to interrupt. Or they may not know how to ask for clarification, make a request, or exhibit politeness. "Play" skills are social skills that include being able to share with others, encourage and praise others, and invite others to join in the activity. Classroom skills include being on task, completing tasks, following directions, and trying to do the best one can. Self-help skills include good grooming (being clean and neat) and good table manners and eating behaviors. Commonly, students with behavior disorders lack knowledge of problem-solving, or coping, skills such as staying calm, thinking of possible solutions, choosing best solutions, taking responsibility for their actions, handling name calling and teasing, and avoiding trouble.

WWW ●●●

Positive Behavioral Interventions and Support
www.pbis.org

time-out ●

think sheet ●

Debriefing following time-out.

figure **9.8**

Teacher:	Raúl, your time-out is over. But before you join the class, I want you to tell me what happened. Why were you sent to time-out?
Raúl:	[Raúl shrugs his shoulders, indicating he doesn't know.]
Teacher:	Okay, well, just tell me what happened.
Raúl:	Luis and Mike were pointing at me and laughing. I said, "What are you laughing at?" and they just kept laughing. So I threw my pencil at them and told them to stop it.
Teacher:	Did you have to go to time-out because Luis and Mike were laughing at you?
Raúl:	No.
Teacher:	No, you were sent to time-out because you threw the pencil.
Raúl:	Yes.
Teacher:	Do you know why it is not okay to throw pencils at other people?
Raúl:	The point could hit them in the eye and hurt them.
Teacher:	That's right. Our classroom needs to be a safe place for all of us, so we cannot throw things at other people. Tell me what you can do the

next time someone points at you or laughs at you.

Raúl: Ignore them.

Teacher: That's a good idea. If you ignore them they will probably just get bored and stop. What else could you do, if you think you will not be able to ignore them?

Raúl: Tell you.

Teacher: Okay, you could tell me and then I could try to help you not get into trouble, and also stop the people who are teasing you. Can you remember to try these ideas the next time something like this happens?

Raúl: Yeah.

Teacher: You don't have to throw things at people. Ignore them or come tell me if you are having a problem with somebody. You need to control your own behavior. I really like you, Raúl, and I want you to do well in school. Can you try these ideas?

Raúl: Yeah.

Teacher: Great! Okay, let's go back to class now. I know you will do better.

Social skills instruction begins with the teacher explaining and discussing the targeted social skill. Then the teacher needs to operationalize the targeted social skill (e.g., sharing, being a "good sport," handling name calling) by demonstrating both appropriate and inappropriate behavior while students observe and identify the skill.

Teacher: This is an example of how to get the markers you need to create your poster: "Please may I have the red and blue markers?" This is *not* the way to get the markers: "Give me those markers!" or just grabbing the markers.

The teacher then describes a situation for students to role play, with the teacher's guidance, during which students can offer suggestions or give examples of appropriate behavior:

Teacher: Pretend you are on the playground and you kicked the soccer ball into a group of students by mistake, but they grab the ball and won't give it back to you. How should you act?

Students: We could say, "Please give the ball back to me" or "I'm sorry I kicked the ball too hard—it was my mistake. Could I please have the ball back?"

Teacher: Good suggestions! These ideas are examples of appropriate behavior.

As actual situations occur in the classroom, remind students of the role plays and their behavior rewarded when they act in socially appropriate ways without being reminded.

| figure | 9.9 | Think sheet for use with students behaving inappropriately. |

THINK SHEET

Name of student: _____

Teacher: _____   Date: _____

This is what I did:
_____
_____

This is the rule I broke:
_____
_____

I behaved this way because:
_____
_____

This is who I bothered when I behaved this way:
_____
_____

This is what I could have done instead:
_____
_____

Student signature: _____   Date: _____

Summary

All students, including those with special needs, deserve the best education that teachers can provide. No one best method will meet the needs of the wide variety of students found in today's classrooms. If anything, diversity is increasing. As a teacher, viewing this diversity as a positive development should help you meet the challenge that comes with it in terms of helping all students move forward in their development. In this chapter, we first provided some guidelines for implementing instruction that is differentiated in an attempt to meet all learners' needs, along with a sixth-grade science example to illustrate these guidelines. Then, we provided brief descriptions of various categories of learners as they are classified by the U.S. educational system. We also presented information related to instructional adaptations appropriate to each learner type.

Questions FOR JOURNAL WRITING AND DISCUSSION

1. What is differentiation and why is it important?
2. How do teachers create a tiered activity?
3. Design an instructional program to address the needs of linguistically diverse students. What materials would be appropriate? What techniques would you

use and why? How will your program help to meet the emotional needs of the students?

4. Write about a time when you had difficulty learning something. What were your feelings? How were you finally able to learn? How might this experience impact your teaching?

ⓢuggestions FOR PROJECTS AND FIELD ACTIVITIES

1. Find a lesson plan online at ReadWriteThink.org (www.readwritethink.org/classroom-resources/lesson-plans/) that relates to a literacy lesson in grades 4–8. Select three of the groups of diverse learners discussed in the chapter and plan ways to differentiate the lesson for their special needs, including differentiation by content, process, and product.

2. Interview a student whose first language is not English. Ask the student how he came to learn English. Ask about the student's attitudes toward both English and his native language. Try to discover some of the problems the student experienced when translating from one language to another. Then use the information from this interview to identify the unique features of the student's language (phonology, syntax, structure, semantics, and lexical questions). What differences and similarities of language do you have with this student?

3. Over a period of three to five days, observe a student with one of the special needs discussed in this chapter. What can this student do well, and what seems to be difficult for her? Summarize your observations, and make suggestions about how you could differentiate instruction to meet the needs of this particular student.

4. Begin to develop an annotated bibliography of novels and reference books, articles, poems, websites, videos, or other materials that deal with students who have overcome adversity due to learning disabilities, physical challenges, language diversity, behavioral issues, or social problems caused by giftedness or by conditions of poverty. Sharing such materials with students in similar situations can be a form of bibliotherapy. (The article by Landrum [2001] can help you get started.)

REFERENCES

Abate, L. (2004, Spring/Summer). Differentiating instruction for limited English proficient students. *BETAC Interchange, 12*(2), 1, 3.

August, D., & Shanahan, T. (Eds.). (2006). Executive Summary: Developing literacy in second-language learners. *Report of the National Literacy Panel on Language Minority Children and Youth.* Mahwah, NJ: Erlbaum.

Barnitz, J. G. (2006). Linguistic diversity perspectives for literacy instruction. In J. P. Gipe, *Multiple paths to literacy: Assessment and differentiated instruction for diverse learners, K–12* (6th ed., pp. 44–64). Upper Saddle River, NJ: Merrill Prentice Hall.

Boone, R., & Higgins, K. (2007). The role of instructional design in assistive technology research and development. *Reading Research Quarterly, 42,* 135–140.

Coxhead, A. (2000). A new academic word list. *TESOL Quarterly, 34*(2), 213–238.

Davis, G. A. (1995). Identifying the creatively gifted. In J. L. Genshaft, M. Bireley, & C. L. Hollinger (Eds.), *Serving gifted and talented students: A resource for school personnel* (pp. 67–82). Austin, TX: Pro-Ed.

Echevarria, J. (2004). Improving comprehension of expository text for English language learners. PREL Focus on Comprehension Forum. Retrieved from www.prel.org/programs/rel/rel.asp with link to Focus on Comprehension, Topic 4.

Echevarria, J., Vogt, M. E., & Short, D. (2013). *Making content comprehensible for English learners: The SIOP model* (4th ed.). Upper Saddle River, NJ: Pearson.

Fisher, D., & Frey, N. (2008). *Better learning through structured teaching: A framework for thegradual release of responsibility.* Alexandria, VA: Association for Supervision and Curriculum Development.

Frey, N., Fisher, D., & Everlove, S. (2009). *Productive group work: How to engage students, build teamwork, and promote understanding.* Alexandria, VA: Association for Supervision and Curriculum Development.

Gardner, H. (1983). *Frames of mind: The theory of multiple intelligences.* New York: Basic Books.

Gardner, H. (1999). *Intelligence reframed: Multiple intelligences for the 21st century.* New York: Basic Books.

Glazer, S. M. (1998). *Assessment IS instruction: Reading, writing, spelling, and phonics for ALL learners.* Norwood, MA: Christopher-Gordon.

Glazzard, P. (1982). *Learning activities and teaching ideas for the special child in the regular classroom.* Englewood Cliffs, NJ: Prentice Hall.

Hasselbring, T. S., & Bausch, M. E. (2005/2006). Assistive technologies for reading. *Educational Leadership, 63*(4), 72–75.

Hernandez, H. (2001). *Multicultural education: A teacher's guide to linking context, process, and content* (2nd ed.). Upper Saddle River, NJ: Merrill/Prentice Hall.

Hunt, D. E. (1971). *Matching models in education.* Toronto: Ontario Institute for Studies in Education.

Johnston, S. C., Tulbert, B. L., & Sebastian, J. P. (2000, May). Vocabulary development: A collaborative effort for teaching content vocabulary. *Intervention in School and Clinic, 35,* 311–315.

Joyce, B., Weil, M., with Calhoun, E. (2000). *Models of teaching* (6th ed.). Boston: Allyn & Bacon.

Kennedy, D. M. (1995). Plain talk about creating a gifted-friendly classroom. *Roeper Review, 17,* 232–234.

Kindler, A. L. (2002). *Survey of the states' limited English proficient students and available educational programs and services, 2000–2001 Summary Report.* Washington, DC: National Clearinghouse for English Language Acquisition and Language Instruction Educational Programs.

Krashen, S. D. (1987). *Principles and practices in second language acquisition.* Upper Saddle River, NJ: Prentice Hall.

Landrum, J. (2001). Selecting intermediate novels that feature characters with disabilities. *The Reading Teacher, 55*(3), 252–258.

Lenski, S. D., Ehlers-Zavala, F., Daniel, M. C., & Sun-Irminger, X. (2006). Assessing English-language learners in mainstream classrooms. *The Reading Teacher, 60,* 24–34.

Lewis, R. B., & Doorlag, D. H. (2011). *Teaching students with special needs in general education classrooms* (8th ed.). Upper Saddle River, NJ: Merrill/Prentice Hall.

Mastropieri, M. A., & Scruggs, T. E. (2000). *The inclusive classroom: Strategies for effective instruction.* Upper Saddle River, NJ: Merrill/Prentice Hall.

Mooney, J., & Cole, D. (2000). *Learning outside the lines.* New York: Simon & Schuster.

Mora, J. K. (2006). Differentiating instruction for English learners: The four-by-four model. In T. Young and N. Hadaway (Eds.), *Supporting the literacy development of English learners* (pp. 24–40). Newark, DE: IRA.

National Center for Education Statistics. (2012). Fast Facts, 2010–2011. U. S. Department of Education. Available: https://nces.ed.gov/FastFacts/display.asp?id=96

Nelson, C. M. (1993). Students with behavioral disorders. In A. E. Blackhurst & W. H. Berdine (Eds.), *An introduction to special education* (3rd ed., pp. 528–561). New York: HarperCollins.

Pilgreen, J. (2006). Supporting English learners: Developing academic language in the content area classroom. In T. Young & N. Hadaway (Eds.), *Supporting the literacy development of English learners* (pp. 41–60). Newark, DE: International Reading Association.

Rogers, L. K. (1999). Spelling cheerleading. *The Reading Teacher, 53,* 110–111.

Tannock, R., & Martinussen, R. (2001). Reconceptualizing ADHD. *Educational Leadership, 59*(3), 20–25.

Tomlinson, C. A. (1999). *The differentiated classroom: Responding to the needs of all learners.* Alexandria, VA: ASCD.

Tomlinson, C. A. (2001). *How to differentiate instruction in mixed-ability classrooms* (2nd ed.). Alexandria, VA: ASCD.

Tomlinson, C. A., & Eidson, C. C. (2003a). *Differentiation in practice: A resource guide for differentiating curriculum, grades K–5.* Alexandria, VA: ASCD.

Tomlinson, C. A., & Eidson, C. C. (2003b). *Differentiation in practice: A resource guide for differentiating curriculum, grades 5–9.* Alexandria, VA: ASCD.

U.S. Census Bureau (2007). The 2007 statistical abstract: The national data book, Table 222. Available online: www.census.gov/prod/2006pubs/07statab/educ.pdf.

U.S. Census Bureau (2009). Children who speak a language other than English at home. Available online: www.census.gov/compendia/statab/2012/tables/12s0236.pdf

Whitmore, J. R. (1985). Characteristics of intellectually gifted children (Digest 344). *Digests on the gifted (pp.1–2).* Reston, VA: The Council for Exceptional Children.

Wood, J. W., Lazzari, A., & Reeves, C. K. (1993). Educational characteristics and implications. In J.W. Wood (Ed.), *Mainstreaming* (2nd ed., pp. 78–120). New York: Merrill/Macmillan.

FOCUS QUESTIONS

- What are some ways in which we engage in literacy outside the classroom?
- How can we develop motivation for engaging in literacy?
- Why is service learning a valuable organizational/curricular element for grades 4–8?
- Why is it important to teach media literacy skills?
- What are some characteristics of a school that emphasizes information literacy?

"Let me share with you the ways I used literacy this weekend," Mr. Fortier begins. "Then I will ask you to think about your weekend and how you engaged in literacy outside the classroom." Mr. Fortier proceeds to give his eighth-graders a detailed account:

"I got up Saturday morning and looked at the clock, which read 7:46. Then I read the newspaper while having breakfast. Later, I checked the TV listings to see if there was a football or basketball game that I wanted to watch. Seeing I had plenty of time before the game started, I decided to put together a bookcase I had purchased. The directions were clearly written, and I finished the project in about an hour. Next I made a grocery list for the week and went to the store. I am careful about what I eat, so I first checked the labels before buying several new items I have been wanting to try. When I returned home, I put the groceries away, and watched the Sacramento Kings basketball game on TV. After the game, I turned on the computer and paid a few bills. I also checked my email and some social networking sites and corresponded with some friends who live far away. While online, I searched for a website comparing kitchen appliances. I need to buy a new refrigerator, so I decided to gather information so I can make a wise decision. Before turning off my computer, I attempted the *New York Times* crossword puzzle online. For dinner, I wanted to try a new dish, so I read the recipe, gathered the ingredients, and prepared the meal. After dinner, I checked the TV listings again but didn't see anything appealing, so I decided to read a novel instead. On Sunday, I attend religious services, so when I awoke I first looked at the clock to determine which service I would be able to attend and then got dressed. At the service I read through the weekly bulletin and used the hymnal to sing along with the choir. After services, I like to eat breakfast out, so I drove to one of my favorite breakfast places. At the restaurant I studied the menu and chose pancakes. On the way home, I bought the Sunday newspaper, which kept me busy for the next few hours. After a light lunch, I began to grade papers and prepare lessons for Monday. I developed a graphic organizer for one lesson, searched online for resources related to our upcoming WebQuest, and explored a few lesson plan sites for ideas to include in my own lessons. A new friend had invited me over for Sunday dinner, so I checked my GPS to find the best route to my friend's house. On the way there, I watched the street signs closely so I would not miss my turns. After dinner, I returned home and read my novel some more before watching the nightly news and going to bed."

Mr. Fortier then draws a four-column chart on the whiteboard. The headings are: Informational, Recreational, Occupational, and Environmental (Goodman, 1996). He and his students begin to classify the ways he used various literacy skills (i.e., reading, writing, listening, speaking, viewing, visually representing) during his weekend.

Mr. Fortier then directs his students to think back to their own weekends, list all the literacy activities they can remember, and create similar charts of their own, considering their current occupation as "student."

Literacy Skill	Informational	Recreational	Occupational	Environmental
Reading	• Read newspaper • Read directions for bookcase • Read food labels • Found/read website for kitchen appliances • Read recipe • Read bulletin • Read menu	• Read TV listings • Read email • Read social media sites • Read novel • Used hymnal	• Read and graded papers • Read information to help prepare WebQuest lesson	• Read clock • Read scores on TV • Read labels to gather ingredients for recipe • Read restaurant sign • Read street signs
Writing	• Wrote grocery list	• Wrote and sent email • Attempted NY Times crossword puzzle	• Completed online banking fields • Wrote lesson plan • Wrote comments and grades on student papers	

(continued)

Literacy Skill	Informational	Recreational	Occupational	Environmental
Listening	• Listened to TV news	• Sunday services • Listened to choir • Listened to the announcers for Kings' basketball game		
Speaking	• Ordered breakfast	• Sang from hymnal • Visited with new friend over dinner		
Viewing	• Watched TV news	• NY Times crossword puzzle online • Watched Kings play on TV	• Viewed online sites to prepare WebQuest	• Interpreted GPS map
Visually Representing			• Developed graphic organizer for lesson	

Expanded Goals for Literacy Instruction

Literacy is a continuum of skills—including reading, writing, speaking, listening, viewing, visually representing, and critical thinking—applied in a social context to enable a person to function effectively in a particular group and community (Harris & Hodges, 1995). In this sense, literacy goes far beyond the classroom walls. Students engage in literacy practices outside of school hours, but what they do outside the classroom on their own time is often not recognized in school or by teachers. In one study (Smith & Wilhelm, 2002), boys who demonstrated literate activities outside of school (for example, reading books and buying magazines about professional wrestling and drawing and labeling wrestling moves) but who were not engaged with the academic reading and writing tasks assigned to them were not considered literate. Essentially, since our students' literacy skills can be developed both in and out of school, we must promote multiple methods for motivating students to engage with literacy activities.

As students progress through the grades, literacy instruction goals change from ones that focus on learning to read, to ones that include reading to learn. But we want students to do more than simply be able to read and read to learn; we also want them to *want* to read and to recognize the value of literacy in their everyday lives. To continue developing their competencies in literacy, students must engage in literate activities (reading, writing, speaking, listening, viewing, and visually representing) beyond the classroom setting. Elsewhere in this book we have presented information on strategies for a variety of literacy competency areas, such as vocabulary; comprehension of narrative and expository text; and content area literacy. In this chapter, the emphases are on providing students with engaging opportunities to participate in activities that promote literacy in and out of school and in real-world (authentic) informational aspects of literacy, and on establishing lifelong literacy habits. The goals of literacy instruction, therefore, must expand to include

1. developing motivated literacy learners
2. establishing lifelong literacy habits

Each of these goals will be discussed in detail.

① Developing Motivated Literacy Learners

Creating interest and fostering positive attitudes in your literacy learners is an important part of motivating them. A motivated reader is an engaged reader (Edmunds & Bauserman, 2006; Gambrell, 1996; Guthrie, 2001; Wigfield & Guthrie, 1997); student motivation and engagement with reading can impact reading achievement (Gambrell, 2011), and a lack of motivation stands in the way of reading success.

One can be extrinsically or intrinsically motivated, although these two forms of motivation are not mutually exclusive. When readers focus on completing a task to receive incentives, grades, or praise, or do it for reasons of competition, they are *externally motivated*. When they want to read for themselves, they are internally or *intrinsically motivated*. Individuals are more likely to be lifelong readers when they are intrinsically motivated. Examples of ways to develop more intrinsically motivated readers include the following:

- offer readers a variety of books at home and at school (Gambrell, 2011; Young & Moss, 2006);
- provide opportunities for students to select their own readings (Duncan, 2010; Lesesne, 2003), giving them some control over their own enjoyment and learning (Gaskins, 2008);
- make sure students have time to read (Allington, 1994; Gambrell, 2011);
- provide a community of readers with whom students can hold conversations about their reading; when reading is a social activity, students tend to be engaged, especially when those activities are relevant to their own lives (Gambrell, 2011; Strommen & Mates 2004);
- praise students and give them a sense that they are successful and capable readers; teachers' praise is an important motivator for creating readers who read for pleasure (Gambrell, 2011).

Attitudes toward reading and writing can be generally positive or negative, or they may vary depending on the subject area (Mathewson, 1985). In other words, an individual might enjoy reading or writing about historical events but have negative feelings about reading or writing scientific material. When readers are interested in what they are reading, their comprehension is positively affected (Alexander, Kulikowich, & Jetton, 1994; Mathewson, 1994; McKenna, 1994). Thus, it is important for teachers to help their students develop both positive attitudes and varied reading interests to help them to become effective, motivated readers and writers.

Researchers have shown that reading motivation decreases as students advance in grade level (Eccles, Wigfield, Harold, et al., 1993; Marsh,

To continue developing their competencies in literacy, students must engage in literate activities (reading, writing, speaking, listening, viewing, and visually representing) beyond the classroom setting.

1989). However, this same body of research also concludes that this decline results, in part, from changes in school and classroom environments. In reality, then, this is a hopeful finding because educators can control those environments. Next we consider several approaches for increasing student motivation.

Provide a responsive classroom culture

Oldfather (2001) suggests a responsive classroom culture as an effective environment for increasing motivation. Common characteristics of responsive classrooms include the following:

- Teachers give reasons for particular activities or topics of study.
- Teachers discuss with students the value of what is being learned (e.g., How might this skill be useful to you in the future?).
- The environment is one in which learning is more important than getting the right answer.
- The atmosphere encourages risk taking.
- Each student's contribution of ideas is expected and responded to.
- The teacher and students participate together as learners.
- Desks are arranged to support group work.
- Samples of student work fill the room.
- The curriculum is developed thematically, incorporating students' interests and suggestions.
- Topics often relate to large issues, current events, or environmental concerns.
- Students read self-selected books as well as materials from the core curriculum.
- Writing is a daily activity and often a favored activity.

Several techniques already discussed in Chapter 5, such as literature circles, in-school book clubs, and the use of graphic novels, would likely be found in a responsive classroom. These activities provide ways for teachers to lead students to read quality literature. You can find some other innovative ideas at the website noted here.

WWWooo

Innovative Ideas
www.theteachersdesk.com

Offer incentives

Since not all readers are intrinsically motivated, at least at first, offering incentives may help students become more interested in reading. Several studies demonstrate that using tangible incentives, such as prizes, under certain conditions can enhance intrinsic motivation. If a valued reward (extrinsic motivation) is offered (1) when the level of initial interest is low, (2) when the attractiveness of the activity will become apparent after engaging in it over time, or (3) when a certain level of mastery needs to be attained, then the reward may lead to intrinsic motivation (Lepper, Greene, & Nisbett, 1973; McLoyd, 1979). Verbal praise and positive feedback increase intrinsic motivation because of their informational value.

Student choice is also a powerful incentive and is the likely reason that sponsored reading programs and approaches such as book clubs and literature circles are successful. Students like to be in charge of choosing what they read. In fact, the research is most clear on the strong positive correlation between choice and the development of intrinsic motivation (Ivy & Broaddus, 2001; Oldfather, 1993; Paris & Oka, 1986; Pitcher, Albright, DeLaney, et al., 2007; Rodin, Rennert, & Solomon, 1980; Turner, 1995).

WWWooo

Book Adventure
www.bookadventure.com

Book-It!
www.bookitprogram.com

Work with differing levels of motivation

Even within responsive classrooms, some students are not motivated intrinsically but choose to be positive about the learning activity, are open minded, search for the worthwhileness of the activity, observe other classmates' interest in the activity, plunge ahead into the activity, and in doing so become motivated and fully participate. Others will do the activities but are motivated only by some type of reward system to complete their work. This lack of intrinsic motivation probably occurs with all students at some time or another. Finally, there are those students who are not motivated and who do not participate. This situation involves avoidance or perceived helplessness. Avoidance occurs when the student finds reasons for not getting around to the work, perhaps after several attempted starts. The more serious situation—perceived helplessness—often involves physical symptoms, such as feeling ill, or an excessive need to move. These students feel anxious and less than competent; they need special accommodations for completing assignments, such as a choice of tasks, freedom to move in order to complete a task, or hands-on activities. Timed tests are usually a disaster. Teachers who respond to these students with care and empathy, and who take actions to alleviate anxiety, will best serve this group.

② Establishing Lifelong Literacy Habits

To promote lifelong literacy skills, provide your students with authentic reasons for engaging in literacy activities, help them develop media literacy skills, connect literacy to popular culture, and participate in out-of-school book clubs.

Authentic reasons for literacy activities

WWW●●●

**More About
Authentic Learning**

http://prezi.com/ctbmwraepxdk/
10-characteristics-of-authentic-
learning-activities/

http://net.educause.edu/ir/
library/pdf/eli3009.pdf

One aspect of helping students develop lifelong literacy habits is to provide classroom experiences that relate to the types of authentic literacy activities they will engage in as adults and citizens living within a community (see also the section on Real-World Classroom Activities later in this chapter). Figure 10.1 presents a list of criteria to help determine whether a learning activity is authentic.

Shelley Harwayne (2000) shares a letter that she wrote to the families of students in the Manhattan New School about the authentic literacy activities taking place in her classroom. Relevant portions of that letter appear here:

> Dear families,
>
> . . . [*I responded by suggesting that literacy needs to be long lasting and making a promise:*] Your children will not only know how to read and write, but more importantly they will choose to read and write.
>
> [*I went on to explain this heartfelt promise.*] Your children will choose to read and write—has implications for classroom practice. It is no longer enough in the reading classroom for students to be able to answer questions at the end of a chapter or fill in the blanks on a worksheet. . . . Instead, we have much higher expectations. Students throughout the grades are being asked to read a wide range of beautifully crafted authentic materials and to read them deeply and critically, discovering new meanings, making personal interpretations, connecting one text to another, and even reading as a writer intent on borrowing techniques for their own writing.
>
> . . . Writing no longer means simply following a teacher's specific instructions. We are no longer asking for 250 words on "Your Summer Vacation." Instead, students throughout the grades are working much harder and learning a great deal more. Students are filling journals, discovering important and original ideas, shaping and revising those ideas into appropriate forms, and editing those drafts into publishable finished works that do real work in the real world. Students are sending letters, crafting picture books for younger students, performing original plays for their peers, publishing non-fiction texts for their class libraries, etc. . . . (pp. A-11–A-12)

Criteria for authentic learning tasks.   *figure* **10.1**

1. *Authentic learning activities have real-world relevance.* Activities match as nearly as possible the real-world tasks of professionals in practice.

2. *Authentic learning activities are purposely ill defined, requiring students to define the tasks needed to complete the activity.* Problems inherent in the activities are loosely structured and open to multiple interpretations, with solutions not readily apparent. Learners must make decisions about what tasks and subtasks are required to seek solutions to the problem.

3. *Authentic learning activities comprise complex tasks to be investigated by students over a sustained period of time.* Activities are completed in days, weeks, and months rather than minutes or hours. They require a significant investment of time and intellectual resources.

4. *Authentic learning activities provide the opportunity for students to examine the task from different perspectives, using a variety of resources.* The use of a variety of resources rather than a limited number of teacher-selected references requires students to examine the problem from several theoretical and practical perspectives, and to distinguish relevant from irrelevant information.

5. *Authentic learning activities provide the opportunity to collaborate.* Collaboration is integral to real world

tasks; seldom does an individual working alone solve real world problems.

6. *Authentic learning activities provide the opportunity to reflect.* Activities need to enable learners to make choices and reflect on their learning both individually and socially.

7. *Authentic learning activities can be integrated and applied across different subject areas and lead beyond domain-specific outcomes.* Activities encourage interdisciplinary perspectives and allow diverse roles and expertise rather than a single well-defined field or domain.

8. *Authentic learning activities are seamlessly integrated with assessment.* The manner of assessment for the major task reflects real world assessment, rather than separate, artificial assessment removed from the nature of the task.

9. *Authentic learning activities create polished products valuable in their own right rather than being preparation for something else.* Activities culminate in the creation of a whole product rather than being an exercise in preparation for something else.

10. *Authentic learning activities allow competing solutions and diversity of outcome.* A range of diverse and multiple solutions of an original nature are anticipated, rather than a single correct response obtained by the application of rules and procedures.

Adapted from Reeves, Herrington, & Oliver (2002). *Authentic activities and online learning,* p. 564. Available at http://researchrepository.murdoch.edu.au/7034/1/authentic_activities_online_HERDSA_2002.pdf

Authentic literacy projects—such as *project-based learning* and *problem-based learning*—that relate to real-world issues and problems can capture the interest of reluctant learners in ways that the standard curriculum cannot do. Although these two terms are often used interchangeably and have similar approaches, project-based learning is more closely aligned with thematic teaching, while problem-based learning is more focused on suggesting solutions to real-world problems.

Project-based learning. In **project-based learning,** students work collaboratively to engage in learning activities that are interdisciplinary, student centered, and integrated with real-world issues. Students are usually asked to produce a project or creation to show what they have learned. Project-based learning can help to develop collaborative group skills on a small scale—perhaps only one or two other students—while engaging students in a highly motivating and meaningful project. This type of small-scale collaborative learning can be particularly beneficial for students with special needs. For example, although students with cognitive learning disabilities often find group work difficult, a project-based learning activity can ease them more gradually

● project-based learning

into collaborative group work; students begin with one simple task and one well-chosen partner and then move toward working on tasks with small teams.

The fundamentals of project-based learning are:

1. Group students into small teams to work on an in-depth project for three to eight weeks.
2. Introduce a complex entry question that establishes the project and what students need to discover, and then scaffold the project with activities and new information that deepen the work.
3. Schedule the project's timeline, through plans, drafts, timely benchmarks, and finally the team's presentation. The presentation audience may be the class, students from other classes, or an outside panel of "experts" drawn from parents, caregivers, and the community.
4. Provide timely assessments and/or feedback on the project for content, oral and written communication, teamwork, critical thinking, and other important skills. (Pearlman, 2006, p. 52)

The many benefits of project-based learning include the following:

Project-Based Learning
www.edutopia.org/project-based-learning

- Deep understanding of subject matter
- Increased motivation and self-directedness
- Increased interpersonal skills
- More effective oral and written communication skills
- Improved research, problem-solving, and critical thinking skills

More information on project-based learning can be found on the Edutopia site.

problem-based learning ●

Problem-based learning. **Problem-based learning** is another approach that provides students with authentic learning activities. It organizes curriculum and instruction around real-world problems or carefully designed scenarios that mirror real-world problems. In small groups, students gather information and apply knowledge from multiple disciplines in their quest for solutions. Guided by the teacher acting as a facilitator, students develop critical-thinking, problem-solving, and collaborative skills as they identify problems, formulate questions and hypotheses, seek out resources, conduct data searches, perform experiments, propose solutions, and determine a "best fit" solution linked to the conditions of the problem. This process involves all six literacy components—reading, writing, speaking, listening, viewing, and visually representing. Problem-based learning enables students to embrace complexity, find relevance and joy in their learning, and enhance their capacity for creative and responsible real-world problem solving (Gordon, 1998).

Problem-Based Learning
www.studygs.net/pbl.htm

Example middle school science problem-based learning unit. A seventh-grade science class is engaged in a unit on the environment. The initial question deals with the environmental health of a local stream. Working in groups of four or five, the students are directed to assess the health of this stream in order to prepare a formal PowerPoint presentation for the local Sewage and Water Board and the School Board, recommending ways to keep the stream healthy. The students work with local water experts and research ways to assess the health of the stream. Elements of authentic learning as described in Figure 10.1 can be readily identified in what the students are learning (W. U., personal communication, January 6, 2006).

WebQuests
http://webquest.sdsu.edu/webquestwebquest-ms.html

WebQuest ●

WebQuests can also serve as examples of problem-based learning and represent student-centered learning in an online setting. A **WebQuest** challenges students to explore the Internet for information related to a particular problem or inquiry. For information on learning to develop WebQuests and for intermediate and middle school examples, visit the website provided here.

Developing media literacy skills

Lifelong literacy also includes developing the skills to be discriminating media users. **Media literacy** skills enable students to "access, analyze, evaluate, and create messages using media in various forms" (Hobbs, 2005, p. 58); at the same time, using media is also one way to increase students' motivation in literacy. Media literate individuals think critically about what they see, hear, and read in books, newspapers, magazines, advertisements, and music; on television, radio, movies, and online; and through other technologies (Hobbs, 2001). A teacher can foster critical literacy in relation to the media by having students read reviews of films that they may typically watch without making judgments. For example, you may show a clip from the Disney film *Mulan* and have students think about its authenticity in terms of the Chinese culture and the values it portrays. Students can then read the article "A Mean Wink at Authenticity: Chinese Images in Disney's *Mulan*" (Mo & Shen, 2000). In this article, the authors give details backing their claims that the film is culturally inauthentic, contains distortion and stereotypes, and is guilty of using racially coded language. Students can then reconsider the movie based on the article's comments or those of another reviewer.

The PBS Video website is an excellent resource for finding films for various grade levels and subject areas. Figure 10.2 provides guiding questions to help students think critically about a feature or documentary film. The related activity encourages students to think about how the media portrays people and cultures.

A media literate person can also interpret messages whether they are in print, audio, video, or multimedia. By learning to recognize how the media influence information, and by analyzing and thinking critically about the messages the creators of mass media send, students become savvy consumers and informed participants in a democratic society. For additional outcomes of increased media literacy skills, see Figure 10.3.

● media literacy

PBS Video Catalog
www.pbslearningmedia.org/

Media Literacy
www.medialit.org
www.acmecoalition.org

Guiding questions for viewing a documentary or feature film.   *figure* **10.2**

- What (or whose) point of view is represented in this film? How might the story be told differently using another's point of view?

- What content information did you learn from this movie? How does it connect with other things you've learned in this class or on your own?

- What do you see as a pervasive motif, or overall theme, to this movie? Is it well developed? How did the screenwriter or director convey this theme?

- Reflect on how you made sense of this film. Were there points of confusion for you? Did you combine what you were seeing and hearing with background information you already knew? What surprises did you become aware of as you watched?

- Which characters are well developed? Which were simple, and which were complex? Did any characters grow or change over the course of the story?

- What was the importance of the setting? What elements contributed to the successful portrayal of the setting?

- What symbols, archetypes, and/or motifs did you find? Were they effective for you?

- Discuss the use of special effects. Evaluate the film in terms of music, artistic quality, and crafting.

- What values are portrayed in this film? Did you feel it was preachy or manipulative? In what ways? What did you learn about people, human nature, or societies?

- If you also read the book (assuming there is one), which did you prefer? What differences did you notice? What characteristics were prominent or effective in each mode of presentation?

- What would you say to a friend who asked you about this movie?

Source: S. Kane, (2011). *Literacy & Learning in the Content Areas,* 3rd ed. Scottsdale, AZ: Holcomb Hathaway. Used with permission.

figure **10.3** Potential outcomes of increased media literacy skills.

Media literacy . . .

1. empowers individuals to make independent judgments about media consumption.

2. focuses attention on the elements involved in the media communication process.

3. fosters an awareness of the impact of the media on the individual and society.

4. develops strategies with which to analyze and discuss media messages.

5. promotes awareness of interactive media content as a "text" that provides insight into our contemporary culture and ourselves.

6. cultivates enhanced enjoyment, understanding, and appreciation of media.

7. challenges interactive media communicators to produce effective and responsive media messages.

Source: Silverblatt, A. (2000, September). Media literacy in the digital age. *Reading Online*, *4*(3). Available online at www.readingonline.org/newliteracies/lit_index.asp?HREF=/newliteracies/silverblatt/index.html.

activity Media Portrayals of People and Cultures (COOPER & MORREALE, 2003)

This activity encourages students to think about how people and life in the United States are represented in the media. It raises the issue of stereotypes, allowing students to begin to question media representations and images with regard to various preconceived standards. They will learn to read physical and behavioral cues (clothing, hairstyles, communication styles) to interpret characterizations.

1. Pose the following scenario and questions to students:

> Some students from another country are planning a visit to our town. These students have never been to the United States before and have decided to try to learn what they can through watching American television and movies. What might surprise them about our town if they are expecting it to be like what they've seen in movies and on TV?

Prepare a video to show a sampling of television content by channel surfing, spending several seconds on each channel, to help students think about questions involving stereotypes. The channel surfing video should be made using content that students are likely to be viewing.

2. List your students' impressions as they respond to the following questions:
   a. Do you think the foreign students will get an accurate picture of what our town and people are like?
   b. What might surprise them if they are expecting our town to be like the movies and TV?
   c. What will they expect in terms of our quality of life? Rich, poor, or in between?
   d. What will they think about the way we look and dress?
   e. What will they expect our houses to be like?
   f. Do you think they will expect to find a lot of crime and violence?
   g. What will they think about how women and girls behave? Boys and men? People of different races and ethnic groups (stereotypes)?
   h. What will they think of how we solve problems?

    i. What will they think of the kind of humor we have and the jokes we make?

    j. Will they think we are polite or rude?

    k. What will they think about any extraordinary powers we might have?

3. Point out to students the discrepancies between what they thought the visitors would expect based on media images and representations and what they think their town and its people are really like. Raise the question of whether these media characterizations might affect the way they think about themselves and their own lives in comparison to what they see through media.

4. Have students report on differences between real-life people and situations and those reflected through media. Ask for explanations concerning the differences between media people and situations and real people and situations. Ask students to define and give examples of stereotypes. Develop a chart divided into two categories: Media and Reality. Have students generate ideas for characteristics and categorize them, noting which ones represent stereotypes.

Connecting literacy to popular culture

Students in grades 4–8 reject literacy tasks that lack purpose and interest (Pitcher et al., 2007). When limited to textbooks and whole-class activities, students miss opportunities to engage in authentic literacy tasks. Expanding our concept of "text"—to include other print material, such as newspapers and graphic novels, as well as text and email messaging and nonprint media, such as television shows, films, websites, and songs—will increase engagement in literacy tasks (Phelps, 2006). "When we connect literacy to popular culture, our students can understand difficult content in new ways, as well as learn to question the media they are presented with on a daily basis" (Norton-Meier, 2005, p. 608). In addition, Fukunaga (2006) states, "we may be able to find students' potential literacy skills and their multiple identities by paying attention to their activities with popular culture texts and the Internet" (p. 219).

Emailing and text messaging are examples of authentic literacy tasks that motivate learners to engage in encoding, decoding, interpreting, and analyzing, among other literacy processes. Lewis and Fabos (2005) found that when emailing, students used font color, font size, and emoticons to communicate sarcasm and visually represent emotional content. Students also gave a great deal of thought to word choice and shorthand. Students demonstrated themselves to be strategic language users in order to communicate their intended messages. Instructional strategies such as dialogue journals and reading response logs can be easily adapted to make them candidates for use with emailing and text messaging.

Song lyrics are another example of an artifact from popular culture that can be quite useful for literacy lessons. Using song lyrics by the performers they enjoy can help students connect their own experiences with the lesson objective. For example, instead of teaching students about poetry techniques in the usual ways, you might use the lyrics of some of their favorite songs and raps (Weinstein, 2007) to demonstrate the various poetry techniques. Have students find lyrics from current songs as examples of the techniques; the box on the following page offers examples to begin with. As the examples show, song lyrics can also be used to develop vocabulary (e.g., synonyms, descriptive words, polysemantic words) and critical analysis skills (e.g., uncovering intended meanings or political meanings).

Another example from popular culture involves using visual images that permeate our lives. Identifying such images can help students understand difficult concepts or new content and learn to read critically and interpret meaning. Norton-Meier (2004) refers to the "bumper sticker curriculum," although you can use any commonly found message signs, such as highway billboards or even tagging and graffiti writing (MacGillivray & Curwen, 2007). Using a collection of bumper

WWW●●●

**History Behind
Song Lyrics**

www.readwritethink.org/lessons/
lesson_view.asp?id=812

Making Connections Between Poetry Techniques and Popular Song Lyrics

Hyperbole: a great exaggeration
> *Example:* I feel the weight of the world on my shoulder. (Black Eyed Peas, "Where Is the Love?")

Repetition: words or phrases are repeated
> *Example:* This girl is on fire / This girl is on fire (Alicia Keys, "This Girl Is on Fire")

Assonance: repetition of the vowels without repetition of consonants, often used as an alternative to rhymes in verse
> *Example:* It just ain't the same, always unchanged, new days are strange, is the world insane (Black Eyed Peas, "Where Is the Love?")

Consonance: repetition of consonant sounds
> *Example:* Man you gotta have love just to set it [anger] straight, take control of your mind and meditate, let your soul gravitate to the love. (Black Eyed Peas, "Where Is the Love?")

Rhyme: sound-alike endings in words
> **End rhyme:** words rhyme at the end of lines
> *Example:* I don't want to be left behind / Distance was a friend of mine. (Kelly Clarkson, "Catch My Breath")

Internal rhyme: words rhyme in the middle of the line
> *Example:* Princess on the steeple and all the pretty people (Bob Dylan, "Like a Rolling Stone")

Additional poetry techniques to have students look for in song lyrics:

Simile: comparing two things using "like" or "as"
> *Example:* Her eyes are blue like the sky.

Metaphor: comparing two things without using "like" or "as"
> *Example:* Lies are a friend of some.

Personification: giving human-like characteristics to an inanimate object
> *Example:* The stars winked at me.

Alliteration: consonants at the beginning of words are repeated
> *Example:* Bees are buzzy, bold, boisterous, and belligerent.

Onomatopoeia: words sound like the actual word
> *Example:* The burning wood snapped, crackled, and popped.

stickers (easily found online), students can first examine them for visual appeal. The ensuing discussion leads to questions that advertisers might ask: for example, "How big do letters need to be to be read by people in the car behind you?" (Norton-Meier, 2004, p. 262). Then the discussion can move to the message the bumper sticker conveys. Students can discuss, question, and critique the use of print and visual images to comment on how the creators of the bumper stickers (or other signs) seek to influence or manipulate their thinking. Bumper sticker messages, such as those in the short list that follows, give some idea of the kinds of intellectually challenging lessons that could occur.

> I Will Not Tolerate Intolerance
> The Best Things in Life Are Not Things
> A Nation of Sheep Will Beget a Government of Wolves
> I Think Therefore I Doubt
> People Who Know the Least Always Seem to Know It the Loudest

Participating in out-of-school book clubs

Although book clubs can take place in school and out of school, this section focuses on out-of-school book clubs or student-run before- or after-school clubs, much like adult book clubs. (Information on the in-school or classroom book club model can be found in Chapter 5.)

Student-run book clubs provide time for students to talk about the books of their choice in an authentic and meaningful way, and they help students to become more engaged and motivated in their reading. Book clubs seem to be particularly successful for middle school students who are unmotivated to read. Whittingham & Huffman (2009) report that middle school students who reported disliking reading and who had low confidence in their reading ability increased their self-efficacy and enthusiasm (and talking about what they had read) after participating in the book club. Many schools anecdotally report that their out-of-school book club programs motivate students to read more and with greater interest than when reading in a traditional classroom setting.

The book club experience offers several motivating factors. As mentioned earlier, students are motivated readers when they are allowed to select the books they read; it also helps when parents are involved and when reading is done in a positive social environment. Choice seems to be a critical factor in a successful book club. While some book clubs assign or designate the book, optimal book clubs for student motivation are those where students determine their own selections (Duncan, 2010; Lesesne, 2003), and where students feel they have control of their own enjoyment and learning (Gaskins, 2008). Books clubs can take place among peers, on or off school grounds, before or after school. In addition, mother–daughter or father–son book clubs are popular (Hudson, 2009).

Service Learning: Taking Literacy Beyond the Classroom

It is the "real work in the real world" part of Shelley Harwayne's (2000) letter, cited earlier, that brings us to our next focus. Teachers and students are often involved in doing real literacy work within their communities, and this work is referred to as **service learning.** The term is generally defined as "a teaching strategy that combines classroom curriculum with community service, to enrich learning, teach civic responsibility, and strengthen communities" (National Commission on Service-Learning, 2002). Students of all ages, from all backgrounds, and from all over the world have become involved in service-learning projects. Of course, service-oriented organizations such as Boy Scouts and Girl Scouts have been doing this kind of community service work for many years. More recently, however, there has been a groundswell of interest in viewing service learning as part of what school is, or should be, about. Many organizations, such as the National Youth Leadership Council (NYLC), have websites that share current resources and ways for teachers and students to be involved in various and ongoing projects. Research on sites such as the National Service Learning Clearinghouse show the importance of service learning by revealing the many benefits for schools and communities as well as for students. Participation in effective service-learning programs is linked to:

● service learning

- higher scores on state achievement tests (Davila & Mora, 2007).
- improved grades and increased attendance (Epstein & Sheldon, 2002; State of Tennessee's Department of Education, 2008)
- increased classroom participation (David, 2009)
- improved problem-solving skills (State of Tennessee's Department of Education, 2008)
- fewer behavioral problems (State of Tennessee's Department of Education, 2008)
- improved student attitude toward helping others (Cofer, 2006)
- increased civic engagement (Billig, Root, & Jesse, 2005; Kahne & Sporte, 2008).

WWW○○○

Service-Learning Projects

www.nylc.org/
www.servicelearning.org

Especially relevant here is the potential of service learning to motivate disengaged students. For students who see little relevance between the school curriculum and their own lives, service learning highlights the relevance. Projects weave together such curricular areas as literacy, math, social studies, science, and health and nutrition. "Service learning puts academics into action because it puts learning into an authentic context. It engages young people in addressing real problems in their communities, not just fictitious problems in a textbook" (Glenn, 2002, p. 3). Two examples of service-learning projects are discussed below. They demonstrate the interweaving of several academic curricular areas, including literacy.

Gardens are popular service-learning projects and can be connected to many content area studies, including science, math, and social studies.

Garden Project: Chenowith Elementary School

This garden project was tended by all students at Chenowith Elementary School, where 80 percent of the students are on free or reduced-price lunch. To begin the project, parents, caregivers, teachers, and students all worked together to create six raised beds. The art teacher and his fourth- and fifth-grade students painted over graffiti-filled walls to create beautiful, butterfly-filled murals surrounding the garden. The administrative assistant for the school, a master gardener, showed students how to take care of the soil and the plants. The students, however, were the ones who grew the plants from seeds, watered and weeded the garden, harvested the flowers and vegetables, and made compost to fertilize the soil. Keeping careful records of when things were planted, where, and how often they were watered; counting days until plants were ready to harvest; and measuring for location of seeds and amount of fertilizer all involved literacy and math. The students harvested the vegetables and flowers and delivered them to senior citizens. They also led tours of the garden and described the elements of the butterfly garden, herb garden, and garden of plants native to their area. The teachers noted that this project was particularly beneficial for their English learners (Fredericks, Kaplan, & Zeisler, 2001).

Gardens such as the one at Chenowith Elementary School are popular service-learning projects. One such project led to the publication of *The Edible Schoolyard* (Learning in the Real World, 1999). This book and the website for the Edible Schoolyard are good resources for those who are interested in pursuing the curricular possibilities of such projects. First Lady Michelle Obama's Let's Move program has also inspired interest in real-world gardens used in education.

WWW○○○

Edible Schoolyard
http://edibleschoolyard.org/
news-events/news

Let's Move
www.letsmove.gov/
gardening-guide

History of the Community Project: Horace Mann Academic Middle School

As the sixth-graders at Horace Mann began a language arts assignment to write a paper on the history of their community (the Mission District in San Francisco), they found that little information was available on a specific stage of development, called the "fifth stage" by historians, that was most important to the students in understanding their community. The students and their teacher decided to address this shortage of information by talking with the people who were a part of the community's development. In so doing, they addressed an impressive list of academic skills. The students began by identifying the tasks they would need to do and the supplies they would need. They proceeded to write a project budget and develop a grant proposal to acquire what they needed. They then began to create a "living history" by talking with individuals identified as "community heroes." To prepare, students developed interview questions and interviewing skills. After hearing the stories of the heroes and compiling their biographies, the students created a mural to document the missing fifth stage and to celebrate the accomplishments of everyday heroes. Throughout the project, students needed to engage in multiple writing tasks, such as writing biographies, letters to community members, and the grant proposal. They also learned proper telephone skills through the numerous calls they made to invite speakers and gather information. The finished mural covers almost four city blocks, depicts 28 community heroes of the Mission District, and required much planning, measuring, and artistic designing (Learning In Deed, 2002).

Real-World Classroom Activities

Service learning is not the only way to add relevance to the curriculum and motivate and engage students. Other types of authentic, or real-world, activities can be used in the classroom to demonstrate that what students learn in school has direct application in their own lives. Although some activities may only simulate real-world experiences, they give students the opportunity to do what real workers do (e.g., scientists, teachers, or any other working professional). They also offer students the chance to assume responsibility and to work in teams. For example, while on the playground some students noticed the earthworms living in the nearby vacant lot. They were fascinated with these worms, so their teacher took advantage of this high level of interest and suggested that they find out more about the kind of habitat earthworms require. This led to an extended study of earthworms both in a classroom setting and outside in the field. The experience was authentic scientific inquiry, and students acted as true researchers; they asked questions, gathered data, manipulated variables, discovered answers, and asked follow-up questions. A sampling of additional real-world activities follows.

Bike Repair   activity

Most students either own or are familiar with bicycles. A number of bike-related activities can be accomplished within a classroom setting that allow students to practice the skills of reading comprehension, following directions, reasoning, and descriptive writing. This is one such activity.

1. Gather a few bike repair manuals.
2. Ask a local bike dealer or students if they have a used or broken bike they can donate to the class for disassembling.
3. Gather a few simple tools: vise grips, adjustable wrench, screwdrivers, pliers, hammer, steel wool, oil can, lubricating spray, rags, oil.
4. Have students work on the bike (i.e., disassemble and then try to reassemble it) during several class meetings and keep a log of what they have done and why. This provides a record of the repair effort and requires students to write an explicit account.

Additional bike-related activities include obtaining bike registration (writing to the local police department or to the official trade association of the bicycle industry for information on how to set up a one-day bike registration drive); seeking information on local and national biking groups; and locating, reading, and sharing contents of bicycling magazines.

◎ **activity** ◎ Job Market

The local business community is a great resource for materials that can provide relevant and exciting learning experiences for older students.

1. Ask local businesses for sample job application forms and hints for interviewing. Fast-food restaurants, supermarkets, and discount stores will be the most likely businesses where students may find part-time jobs. Many businesses have application forms available online.
2. Invite managers to speak to students about the importance of following directions when filling out job applications, and ask them to share interviewing techniques.
3. Have students fill out job application forms as neatly and accurately as possible.
4. Go over the forms with students as they work and then again when they finish to check spelling and accuracy.

◎ **activity** ◎ Developing Discriminating Consumers of Media

Food labels are an environmental artifact that can provide an authentic literacy task related to an important life skill. This activity, on learning to read nutrition labels on food packages, is a valuable and interesting critical literacy lesson that will help develop sophisticated consumers.

1. Have students examine the nutrition labels of popular food products.
2. Have them study the recommended serving size compared with the amount they might consume when eating the product. As an example of what to have students look for, a pint of "fat-free" sorbet shows the serving size to be one-half cup, with four servings per container and 130 calories per serving.
3. Using multiplication, have them determine if they are ingesting more calories than they realize. For example, if they decide to eat the entire pint of sorbet (4 servings) or six cookies instead of two (3 servings), they need to know to multiply the number of calories by the number of servings they are consuming (e.g., 4 x 130 = 520 calories).

Point out that how information is presented—in this case, label design—impacts what they notice. Serving size information appears above a wide line (often solid black) separating it from information about the number of calories (e.g., 130) and other nutrition information contained in each serving. This important information is followed by another wide line (often solid black). The use of the two solid wide lines draws the eye to the nutritional information and away from the serving size recommendation.

Have students compare a variety of foods that have fat-free, sugar-free, gluten-free, and "regular" labels; this activity is likely to prove enlightening to them. Fat-free labeling, for example, can be misleading, as these foods often have more sugar and an even higher calorie count than the "regular" product might have. Such a lesson can lead to discussions of (1) how other types of information are presented and how the presentation influences our understanding of the message, and (2) how we must be critical consumers of information.

◎ **activity** ◎ Reading Can Save You Money

Students are already full participants in the consumer culture. You are providing a useful service to them when you teach critical-reading and thinking skills as they relate to reading and responding to advertisements as well as making wise purchases. Constructing a lesson such as the following helps students to become smart consumers.

1. Browse for misleading advertisements in popular magazines or online. Depending on your students and their interests or perceived concerns, these could be related to weight reduction, skin problems, astrology, or hobbies.
2. Collect (or print out) and laminate about 50 advertisements.
3. From this group, choose a few to be mounted on poster board for all to see.
4. As a readiness activity, have students share their own experiences related to misleading or deceptive offers, or other responses to advertisements that they, or family members, have personally experienced.
5. Using the mounted advertisements, discuss the misleading ads.
6. With students working in pairs, have each pair choose two additional ads from the 50 that were laminated. Have each pair read these aloud to each other, discuss them, and analyze them using a set of prepared questions (Figure 10.4).
7. Have students share their ad analyses in a whole-class discussion.

WWW●○○

Get Media Smart
http://pbskids.org/dontbuyit

Questions for analyzing misleading advertisements.	*figure* **10.4**

1. What is the product being advertised?
2. What is the eye-catching line? Write it down exactly so you can read it to the class.
3. What does the advertiser want you to believe you will get?
4. What do you think you really will get for your money?
5. What is the total amount of money that this product will actually cost?
6. What do you think are the outright lies, if any, in this advertisement?

The World When You Were Born

activity

An activity that integrates history with reading comprehension, skimming, and reference skills, The World When You Were Born fosters personal interest in a particular period of history. The more general message of this activity is that history is made every day. As students will learn, we are either making history or reacting to past history.

1. Find a resource (for example, Picturing the Century: One Hundred Years of Photographs from the National Archives) that provides excellent photographs and enough text to give an idea of what life was like during a particular decade.
2. Design a set of questions for students to answer that helps them understand what life was like when they were born and when they were growing up. Figure 10.5 gives examples, but questions and answers will vary based on age level.
3. To provide more depth, have students do further research on their decade or on what the world was like when their parents were born.
4. After the research, share memories with students and discuss the part of their lives that is already a part of history.

WWW●○○

Picturing the Century
www.archives.gov/exhibits/
picturing_the_century/galleries/
galleries.html

figure **10.5**   History questions for the 2000s.

1. What is significant about smartphones?

2. By what name is Joseph Ratzinger better known?

3. What happened on September 11, 2001?

4. How did Justin Bieber become famous?

5. What scandal has affected baseball and other professional sports, causing athletes to be suspended?

6. What are "digital natives"?

7. Prince Charles' eldest son married and had a child with whom?

8. In regard to immigration, who are the DREAMers?

9. What tragic event happened on August 29, 2005?

10. What films won the Academy Award for Best Animated Feature from 2003 to 2012?

ANSWER KEY:

1. Smartphones are handheld computers and phones with online access that are also personal tools through which people can easily stay connected to peers.

2. Pope Benedict XVI, who succeeded Pope John Paul II in April 2005 and resigned in February 2013.

3. Middle Eastern terrorists hijacked four airplanes, crashing them into targets in New York City and Washington DC; the fourth plane crashed in a field in Pennsylvania.

4. Bieber, a Canadian pop musician, was discovered on YouTube in 2008 by an American talent agent.

5. The steroid scandal; some athletes have acknowledged taking steroids to enhance performance and some have been stripped of records in addition to being suspended from play.

6. A label attached to young individuals born during or after the introduction of digital technologies; these individuals typically have a greater understanding of digital technology and its tools.

7. Kate Middleton married Prince William on April 29, 2011, at Westminster Abbey in London.

8. Young immigrants who would meet the requirements of the Development, Relief, and Education for Alien Minors Act, should it be passed.

9. Hurricane Katrina hit New Orleans, flooding the city.

10. 2003, *Finding Nemo;* 2004, *Incredibles;* 2005, *Wallace and Gromit: The Curse of the Were Rabbit;* 2006, *Happy Feet;* 2007, *Ratatouille;* 2008, *WALL-E;* 2009, *Up;* 2010, *Toy Story 3;* 2011, *Rango;* 2012, *Brave*

Into the Real World: Information Literacy

n 2000, Carmen Luke noted that "book- and print-based literacies, and the industrial model of schooling built around book culture, are no longer wholly adequate in a changing information, social, and cultural environment" (424). In our world today, information is expanding at an exponential rate along with enormous technological advancements. We live in the Information Age; knowledge, rather than agriculture or manufactured goods, is the most precious resource in the United States. Thus, people who are **information literate**—who know how to locate, acquire, and use information—are America's greatest resources.

The American Library Association Presidential Committee Report on Information Literacy (ALA, 1989) describes what we need to do as educators:

To be information literate, a person must be able to recognize when information is needed and have the ability to locate, evaluate, and use effectively the needed information. Producing such a citizenry will require that schools and colleges appreciate and integrate the concept of information literacy into their

information literate ●

www●●●

Information Literacy Lessons and Ideas
www.informationliteracy.org

learning programs and that they play a leadership role in equipping individuals and institutions to take advantage of the opportunities inherent within the information society. Ultimately, information literate people are those who have learned how to learn. They know how to learn because they know how knowledge is organized, how to find information, and how to use information in such a way that others can learn from them. They are people prepared for lifelong learning, because they can always find the information needed for any task or decision at hand. (p. 1 of 13)

Educators realize that the people who most need to be information literate—such as at-risk students, illiterate adults, English learners, and those who are economically disadvantaged—are the least likely to have the learning experiences or the access to information that will enable them to improve their situation. For example, these individuals are most vulnerable when they need to make decisions about health care for their families; find affordable insurance; locate and select nursing care for an elderly parent; or purchase, finance, or insure a car. A school's emphasis on textbooks, workbooks, and lectures is not sufficient to provide the learning experiences needed for the Information Age. At the very least, providing students with the technological skills to find information should be an additional focus in grades 4–8. Such a focus will actively involve students in

- knowing when they need information
- identifying information needed to address a given problem or issue
- finding needed information and evaluating the information (see the sections "Locating Information" and "Online Search Skills" in Chapter 7)
- organizing the information
- using the information effectively to address the problem or issue at hand (ALA, 1989, p. 6 of 13)

In addition to the activities already described in this chapter and the chapter on literacy in the content areas (see Chapter 7), the following items describe what education might be like if information literacy were a central, rather than peripheral, focus in school.

1. The school would be more interactive in the following ways:
   - Students interact with teachers, other students, multiple information resources, and their community in pursuit of questions that interest them personally.
   - Students engage in long-term quests for answers to real and serious social, scientific, aesthetic, or political problems.
   - Quests involve searching print, electronic, audio, and video information; interviewing people in and outside of school; reading original sources; and doing extended writing.
   - Learning is more self-initiated and more intellectually and emotionally demanding when asking important questions; gathering data; reducing and synthesizing data; and analyzing, interpreting, and reporting information in a variety of forms.
   - The results of student projects are prominently displayed.
   - Discussion and debate about substantive, relevant issues pervade the halls, playgrounds, and cafeteria, as well as the classroom.
   - Questions such as "How do you know that?" "What evidence do you have for saying that?" and "How can we find out?" are commonplace.
   - Global online connections among students, educators, and literary figures are possible and encouraged.

2. Teachers would be team members, coaches, and guides:
   - Teachers focus on arousing curiosity, asking the right questions, leading serious debate and discussion, and modeling inquiry.
   - Together with librarians, media resource people, and instructional designers, teachers ensure that student projects are challenging, interesting, and productive learning experiences.
   - Class sessions include less lecturing and more coaching and guiding.
3. Evaluation would reflect the interactive nature of the school:
   - Interactive tutoring software provides useful diagnostic information to help teachers and students understand student needs.
   - A broad range of literacy indicators, including knowing appropriate information sources and the ability to perform information searches, are assessed.
   - Assessments would relate specifically to ways students use their minds and achieve success as information consumers, analyzers, interpreters, evaluators, and communicators of ideas.

In general, most schools are far from placing an emphasis on information literacy. Those who engage in the service-learning projects discussed earlier probably come closest. However, as the strategies and activities presented throughout this book demonstrate, it is possible to develop literacy in ways that are compatible with the demands of our world. Cooperative learning, comprehension skills, research skills, and writing in a variety of genres are all necessary skills in the Information Age.

Summary

This chapter discussed motivation, lifelong literacy habits, involvement in real-world aspects of literacy, and information literacy. No one way exists for developing motivation for literacy activities, and motivation can vary depending on the task. However, by engaging students in meaningful and relevant work, such as service-learning projects and real-world applications that require the need for literate activity, chances improve of developing motivation and a lifelong habit of reading and writing—two major goals of literacy instruction in grades 4–8. Techniques for encouraging students to read quality literature, select their own books, and become involved in service-learning activities within their own communities can move students from needing extrinsic rewards for doing literate work, to being more intrinsically motivated. As a teacher, you should strive to do whatever it takes to help your students become literate individuals, especially beyond the classroom.

Questions FOR JOURNAL WRITING AND DISCUSSION

1. Recall a time when you were highly motivated to complete a task. Write about your feelings and try to explain why you were so motivated. Share your reasons with a group of classmates and compile a list of common characteristics for what motivates all of you.
2. How do you choose a book to read for pleasure? How do you choose a book to read for information? How would you direct a student to locate a book to read for pleasure?
3. Develop a list of activities you could use in the classroom, or as potential service-learning projects, that would involve students in doing real literacy work.

4. How would you explain to parents or caregivers (or to a principal) your reasons for using artifacts of popular culture (e.g., television shows, song lyrics, films, websites, magazines) in your classroom?

Suggestions FOR PROJECTS AND FIELD ACTIVITIES

1. Interview a student and use one of the reading attitude or interest surveys found in Appendix C (or develop your own set of questions to ask). Analyze the results to draw some conclusions about the student's level of motivation. Then, if possible, observe this student within the classroom setting. Do the survey results match the student's actions?

2. Complete for yourself a chart similar to the one Mr. Fortier made with his students in the chapter's opening scenario. Then complete a similar chart with a group of students. Have a discussion with them on why it is important to be literate in today's world.

3. View a sitcom that is popular with your students. Analyze the program for how various groups of people are portrayed. Identify any stereotypes presented. Then plan a lesson that will help your students critically analyze television's influence on personal and societal values.

REFERENCES

Alexander, P. A., Kulikowich, J. M., & Jetton, T. L. (1994). The role of subject-matter knowledge and interest in the processing of linear and nonlinear texts. *Review of Educational Research, 64*, 201–252.

Allington, R. L. 1994. The schools we have, the schools we need. *The Reading Teacher 48*(1): 14–29.

American Library Association. (1989). *Presidential Committee on Information Literacy Report* [Online]. Available at http://www.ala.org/acrl/publications/whitepapers/presidential.

Billig, S., Root, S., & Jesse, D. (2005). *The impact of participation in service-learning on high school students' civic engagement.* Denver, CO: RMC Research Corporation.

Brozo, W. G., & Flynt, E. S. (2008, October). Motivating students to read in the content classroom: Six evidence-based principles. *Reading Teacher, 62,*(2), 172–174.

Cofer, J. (1996). Service-learning: Does it affect attitudes, grades and attendance of students who participate? (Report No. SO 030 860). Frankfort, KY: Franklin County Schools.

Conway, J. M., Amel, E. L., & Gerwien, D. P. (2009). Teaching and learning in the social context: A meta-analysis of service learning's effects on academic, personal, social, and citizenship outcomes. *Teaching of Psychology, 36*(4), 233–245.

Cooper, P., & Morreale (2003). *Creating competent communicators: Activities for teaching, 7–12.* Scottsdale, AZ: Holcomb Hathaway.

David, J. L. (2009). Service learning and civic participation. *Educational Leadership, 66*(8), 83–84. Retrieved from www.ascd.org/publications/educational_leadership/archived_issues.aspx

Davila, A. & Mora, M. (2007). *Civic engagement and high school academic progress: An analysis using NELS data.* College Park: University of Maryland School of Public Policy, Center for Information and Research on Civic Learning and Engagement (CIRCLE).

Duncan, S. P. (2010). Instilling a lifelong love of reading. *Kappa Delta Pi Record, 46*(2), 90–93.

Eccles, J. S., Wigfield, A., Harold, R., & Blumenfeld, P. S. (1993). Age and gender differences in children's self- and task perceptions during elementary school. *Child Development, 64*, 830–847.

Edmunds, K. M., & Bauserman, K. L. (2006, Feb). What teachers can learn about reading motivation through conversations with children. *The Reading Teacher, 59* (5), 414–424.

Epstein, J. L., & Sheldon, S. B. (2002). Present and accounted for: Improving student attendance through family and community involvement. *The Journal of Educational Research, 95*(5), 308–318.

Fredericks, L., Kaplan, F., & Zeisler, J. (2001). *Integrating youth voice in service-learning.* Learning In Deed issue paper produced by Education Commission of the States' Initiative and Learning in Deed, the W. K. Kellogg Foundation's Service Learning Initiative [Online]. Available at www.ecs.org.

Fukunaga, N. (2006). Those anime students: Foreign language literacy development through Japanese popular culture. *Journal of Adolescent & Adult Literacy, 50*, 206–222.

Gambrell, L. (1996). Creating classroom cultures that foster reading motivation. *Reading Teacher, 50*, 4–25.

Gambrell, L. (2011). Seven rules of engagement: What's most important to know about motivation to read. *Reading Teacher, 65*(3), 172–178.

Gaskins, I. W. (2008). Ten tenets of motivation for teaching struggling readers—and the rest of the class. In R. Fink and S. J. Samuels (Eds.), *Inspiring reading success: Interest and motivation in an age of high-stakes testing* (pp. 98–116). Newark, DE: International Reading Association.

Glenn, J. (2002, June). Service-learning puts academics into action. *Education Update, 44*(4), 1, 3.

Goodman, K. S. (1996). *On reading.* Portsmouth, NH: Heinemann.

Gordon, R. (1998). Balancing real-world problems with real-world results. *Phi Delta Kappan, 79,* 390–393.

Guthrie, J. T. (2001, March). Contexts for engagement and motivation in reading. *Reading Online, 4*(8).

Harris, T. L., & Hodges, R. E. (Eds.) (1995). *The literacy dictionary: The vocabulary of reading and writing.* Newark, DE: International Reading Association.

Harwayne, S. (2000). *Lifetime guarantees: Toward ambitious literacy teaching.* Portsmouth, NH: Heinemann.

Hobbs, R. (2001, Spring). The great debates circa 2001: The promise and the potential of media literacy. *Community Media Review,* 25–27.

Hobbs, R. (2005). What's news? *Educational Leadership, 63*(2), 58–61.

Hudson, C. (2009). *Book by book: The complete guide to creating mother-daughter book clubs.* Berkeley, CA: Seal Press.

Ivy, G., & Broaddus, K. (2001). Just plain reading: A survey of what makes students want to read in middle school classrooms. *Reading Research Quarterly, 36,* 350–377.

Kahne, J. E., & Sporte, S. E. (2008). Developing citizens: The impact of civic learning opportunities on students' commitment to civic participation. *American Educational Research Journal, 45*(3), 738–766.

Kane, S. (2011). *Literacy and learning in the content areas* (3rd ed.). Scottsdale, AZ: Holcomb Hathaway.

Learning In Deed. (2002). *Service-learning profiles* [Online]. Available at www.learningindeed.org/slcommission/horace.html.

Learning in the Real World. (1999). *The edible schoolyard.* Berkeley, CA: Center for Ecoliteracy.

Lepper, M. R., Greene, D., & Nisbett, R. E. (1973). Undermining children's intrinsic interest with extrinsic reward. *Journal of Personality and Social Psychology, 28,* 124–137.

Lesesne, T. S. (2003). *Making the match: The right book for the right reader at the right time, grades 4–12.* Portland, ME: Stenhouse.

Lewis, C., & Fabos, B. (2005). Instant messaging, literacies, and social identities. *Reading Research Quarterly, 40,* 470–501.

Luke, C. (2000). New literacies in teacher education. *Journal of Adolescent & Adult Literacy, 43,* 424–435.

MacGillivray, L., & Curwen, M. S. (2007). Tagging as a social literacy practice. *Journal of Adolescent and Adult Literacy, 50*(5), 354–369.

Marsh, H. W. (1989). Age and sex effects in multiple dimensions of self-concept: Preadolescence to early adulthood. *Journal of Educational Psychology, 81,* 417–430.

Mathewson, G. C. (1985). Toward a comprehensive model of affect in the reading process. In H. Singer & R. B. Ruddell (Eds.), *Theoretical models and processes of reading* (3rd ed., pp. 841–856). Newark, DE: International Reading Association.

Mathewson, G. C. (1994). Model of attitude influence upon reading and learning to read. In R.B. Ruddell, M. R. Ruddell, & H. Singer (Eds.), *Theoretical models and processes of reading* (4th ed., pp. 1131–1161). Newark, DE: International Reading Association.

McKenna, M. C. (1994). Toward a model of reading attitude acquisition. In E. H. Cramer & M. Castle (Eds.), *Fostering the love of reading: The affective domain in reading education* (pp. 18–40). Newark, DE: International Reading Association.

McLoyd, V. C. (1979). The effects of extrinsic rewards of differential value on high and low intrinsic interest. *Child Development, 50,* 1010–1019.

Mo, W., & Shen, W. (2000, spring). A mean wink at authenticity: Chinese images in Disney's "Mulan." *New Advocate, 13*(2), 129–142.

National Commission on Service-Learning. (2002). *Learning in deed: The power of service-learning for American schools, Final Report* [Online]. Available at www.servicelearning.org/library/resource/4647.

Norton-Meier, L. A. (2004). The bumper sticker curriculum: Learning from words on the backs of cars. *Journal of Adolescent & Adult Literacy, 48,* 260–263.

Norton-Meier, L. A. (2005). Trust the fungus: Lessons in media literacy learned from the movies. *Journal of Adolescent & Adult Literacy, 48,* 608–611.

Oldfather, P. (1993). What students say about motivating experiences in a whole language classroom. *The Reading Teacher, 46,* 672–681.

Oldfather, P. (2001). *When students do not feel motivated for literacy learning: How a responsive classroom culture helps* [Online]. Available at http://curry.virginia.edu/go/clic/nrrc/rspon_r8.html.

Paris, S. G., & Oka, E. R. (1986). Self-regulated learning among exceptional children. *Exceptional Children, 53,* 103–108.

Pearlman, B. (2006, June). New skills for a new century. *Edutopia.* (pp. 50–53). Available: http://cell.uindy.edu/docs/NewSkillNewCentury.pdf

Phelps, S.F. (2006). Introduction to Part I: Situating adolescents' literacies. In D. E. Alvermann, K. A. Hinchman, D. W. Moore, S. F. Phelps, & D. R. Waff (Eds.), *Reconceptualizing the literacies in adolescents' lives* (2nd ed., pp. 3–4). Mahwah, NJ: Erlbaum.

Pitcher, S. M., Albright, L. K., DeLaney, C. J., Walker, N. T., Seunarinesingh, K., Mogge, S., et al. (2007). Assessing adolescents' motivation to read. *Journal of Adolescent & Adult Literacy, 50,* 378–396.

Reeves, T. C., Herrington, J., & Oliver, R. (2002). Authentic activities and online learning. p. 564. Available: www.herdsa.org.au/wpcontent/uploads/conference/2002/papers/Reeves.pdf

Rodin, J., Rennert, K., & Solomon, S. (1980). Intrinsic motivation for control: Fact or fiction. In A. Baum, J. E. Singer, & S. Valios (Eds.), *Advances in environmental psychology II* (pp. 64–86). Hillsdale, NJ: Erlbaum.

Silverblatt, A. (2000, September). Media literacy in the digital age. *Reading Online, 4(3).*

Smith, M. W., & Wilhelm, J. D. (2002). *"Reading don't fix no Chevys": Literacy in the lives of young men.* Portsmouth, NH: Heinemann.

State of Tennessee's Department of Education. (2008). An evaluation report of student attitude and behavior changes to the Tennessee Department of Education and Volunteer Tennessee on the Learn and Serve America School-based Program. Volunteer, TN: Laird.

Strommen, L. T., & Mates, B. F. (2004). Learning to love reading: Interviews with older children and teens. *Journal of Adolescent & Adult Literacy, 48,* 188–200.

Turner, J. (1995). The influence of classroom contexts on young children's motivation for literacy. *Reading Research Quarterly, 30,* 410–441.

Weinstein, S. (2007). A love for the thing: The pleasures of rap as a literacy practice. *Journal of Adolescent and Adult Literacy, 50(4),* 270–281.

Whittingham, J. L. & Huffman, S. (2009). The effects of book clubs on the reading attitudes of middle school students. *Reading Improvement, 46(3),* 130–136.

Wigfield, A. & Guthrie, J. (1997). Relations of children's motivation for reading to the amount and breadth of their reading, *Journal of Educational Psychology, 89* (3), 420–422.

Young, T. A. & Moss, B. (2006). Nonfiction in the classroom library: A literacy necessity. *Childhood Education, 82(4),* 207–212.

FOCUS QUESTIONS

- What should teachers know about the home backgrounds of their students?
- How can teachers forge a relationship with parents or caregivers that facilitates the literacy development of their students?
- What should parents be told about literacy development in grades 4–8?

At the beginning of the school year, eleven-year-old Lydia's mother, a single parent from the Caribbean, is reluctant to come to Parent–Teacher Conferences with Lydia's teacher, Ms. Janos. Mrs. Baptiste, who is originally from St. Croix, in the U.S. Virgin Islands, had to drop out of school at the age of 16 to care for younger siblings and now feels intimidated by the thought of going to an educational institution so different physically and culturally from those with which she is familiar. Mrs. Baptiste returns neither the teacher's phone calls nor notes sent home with Lydia. Unperturbed, Ms. Janos decides to make a home visit. She asks Lydia to arrange a time, at her mother's convenience, when she can pay a social visit. The two women meet one Friday afternoon and, over tea and Johnny cakes that Mrs. Baptiste has baked, discuss nothing about school; instead, they chat about their shared affection for the Lydia. The next time Mrs. Baptiste is invited to a conference, she is less hesitant, having positive memories of the human connection that she and Ms. Janos have forged.

On this particular evening, Ms. Janos smiles warmly as she greets Lydia's mother at the door of her classroom. She asks Mrs. Baptiste to sit down, and the two briefly exchange pleasantries. Then Ms. Janos shares Lydia's progress reports and discusses her improvement in reading and writing. She shows Mrs. Baptiste a portfolio of Lydia's writings. Ms. Janos discusses the work and compares pieces from the beginning of the year to a piece Lydia wrote recently and had asked to have included in her portfolio. Mrs. Baptiste is impressed. Ms. Janos describes exactly what literacy skills Lydia has mastered thus far and explains her plans for continuing to meet Lydia's instructional needs.

The conference ends, as such conferences often do, with Mrs. Baptiste asking what she can do to help her child to become a more successful student. However, she then frowns and lowers her head as she reveals that she herself is barely able to read. Ms. Janos assures Mrs. Baptiste that she can do a great deal to further her daughter's academic career. First, Ms. Janos admires the fact that Mrs. Baptiste and her daughter have a close relationship and converse so easily. She explains that such talk is crucial to literacy development. Second, she suggests that Mrs. Baptiste have Lydia read to her whenever it is convenient and that both of them discuss what was read. Finally, she tells Mrs. Baptiste that, in later meetings, she will offer a few specific tips and ideas of learning activities to help achieve selective objectives. But, for today, enough has been accomplished. Lydia's mother leaves the classroom feeling reassured that her lack of a formal education will in no way impede her daughter's progress. Indeed, she now understands that she has already done much that is useful, and she is pleased to learn that, simply by listening, she will be furthering Lydia's growth in reading. A true partnership has been formed.

Literacy Growth at Home

L iteracy was once defined as the ability to read and write. It was considered a set of neutral and objective skills independent of social context or ideology (Street, 1995; Verhoeven & Snow, 2001). Ethnographic research, however, has shed light on a wide range of culturally specific literacy practices among different communities. This research suggests that literacy involves much more than simply encoding and decoding symbols and is much more complex and difficult to define (Bowman, 2002; Delgado-Gaitan, 2001; Heath, 1983; Valdés, 1996).

Moreover, literacy extends beyond the acquisition of reading and writing skills to include speaking, listening, viewing, and visually representing, and it entails the ability to use these skills in a socially appropriate context. Our concept of literacy has also evolved to include the wide array of skills required to function in a technological society. We now use the term *literacy* to refer to a wider domain of activities, from media literacy and computer literacy to citizenship literacy (Anstey & Bull, 2006; Kinzer & Leander, 2003; Wilson, 2002). Are parents and caregivers equipped to support their children in learning the basics of literacy—especially the "new literacies" of the twenty-first century—at home?

Every teacher hopes for a class full of students whose caretakers care about and support their literacy growth. Teachers know, intuitively and through research, that such students will have a much easier road to becoming readers and writers. Indeed, research consistently identifies and reports strong correlations between parents reading to and with their children and the students' later success in literacy (Anderson, Hiebert, Scott, et al., 1985; Chomsky, 1972; Froiland, Peterson, & Davidson, 2013; Laosa, 1982; Lonigan, Shanahan, & Cunningham, 2008; National Center for Family Literacy, 2002; Teale & Sulzby, 1986). Specifically, success in literacy was found to be related to the amount of time parents give to sharing books with their children (Lonigan et al., 2008), and the number of young people's books in the home (Froiland et al., 2013).

Other research has attempted to identify the essential nature of what transpires when parents and students read together and what makes these interactions so beneficial. Lancy and Bergin (1992) found that students who are more fluent and positive about reading came from families that viewed reading as fun, kept stories moving with a "meaning-seeking" rather than a purely "decoding" orientation, and encouraged questions and humor while reading together.

Teachers have long been telling parents simply to "read to your child!" but perhaps this advice has been misguided in the light of research findings. For example, Lancy, Draper, and Boyce (1989) describe the parents of good readers as using *expansionist strategies*, which include adding personal information and explanations, or scaffolding, as their children grapple to understand stories. For example, a father might start reading a story with his child and then make guesses as to what will happen next, modeling the comprehension strategy of making predictions. Over time, this father takes a less active role and encourages the child to use these strategies when reading. This is especially useful with a story that has been read multiple times. According to Lancy et al. (1989), when a child experiences difficulty, the parent of a good reader tends to make a mild joke of it, thus diffusing anxiety, whereas the parent of a less adept reader treats a decoding error as a serious infraction, sometimes even covering up an illustration in order to prevent "cheating."

Statistics on Students and Their Home Environment

- Parental literacy is one of the single most important indicators of a child's success. The National Assessment of Education Progress (NAEP) has concluded that youngsters whose parents are functionally illiterate are twice as likely as other students to be functionally illiterate themselves.

- By age four, children whose families are of a lower socioeconomic status (SES) will have heard 32 million fewer words than those whose families are of a higher socioeconomic status.

- Some 30 million adults in the United States have extremely limited literacy skills. If one teacher could teach 100 adults to improve their reading skills, we would need 300,000 teachers to meet the need.

- The Latino population is the largest minority in the United States and has the highest school dropout rate. More than two in five Americans of Latino or Hispanic origin, age 25 and older, have not graduated from high school. (National Center for Family Literacy, 2007)

Understanding Differences in Home Practices

Although the statistics in the box (p. 315) on students and their home environment may appear alarming, they are no reason to give up hope. An understanding of the literacy practices that *do* occur in the homes of at-risk students can help teachers learn from and build upon those practices.

Because many teachers come from middle-class backgrounds, they may tend to believe that the most effective home literacy practices are those they recall experiencing in their own homes. For many teachers, the image that most often comes to mind when they think of literacy in the home is of a young child sitting on the lap of a parent who is reading from a large story book. Such an image sets up the notion that parents who do not read books to their children in this manner are laying the groundwork for a lack of progress in literacy. However, it is important to consider the wide range of literacy practices that may occur in students' homes. This approach allows us to build more effectively upon the literacy experiences that students from a host of backgrounds bring to school (Thomas, Fazio, & Stiefelmeyer, 1999).

In fact, it appears that literacy in the home and community is very much a part of a person's culture. Moreover, each community has its own special literate traditions. Shirley Brice Heath's (1983) seminal investigation of two different African American communities showed how literacy may vary widely depending on the cultural context of students' homes and communities. The first community she observed had fewer reading materials, but there seemed to be a collaborative approach to literacy. In the second community, a higher value was placed on literacy in terms of people's statements, but this was not necessarily reflected in their actions. The two communities held differing beliefs about how their children would learn to read and write; however, neither community's literacy concepts and practices matched well with the concepts and practices of the formal literacy taught in school.

It is critical for teachers to keep in mind that most parents and caregivers—regardless of income level or cultural or ethnic background—value education for their children. However, different parents may have differing perceptions of what it means to be literate, and they may not always be aware of the most effective methods to foster literacy development in their children. Several researchers have reported that many low SES families place a high value on literacy. For example, Taylor and Dorsey-Gaines (1988), studying inner-city parents whose children had succeeded in school, noted that parents had made extraordinary sacrifices and efforts in the interest of their children's education, despite the parents' limited educational levels. Fitzgerald, Spiegel, and Cunningham (1991), in a study of both low- and high-income parents, reported that many low-income families rate the value of education higher than the high-income families do.

Studies on reading improvement among Latino students underscore the importance of parents reading aloud to and with their children. Ortiz and Ordoñez-Jasis (2005) found that Latino parents enjoy choosing books and sharing them with their children if they find the materials interesting, valuable, and relevant to their lives. Therefore, these researchers suggest that teachers include in their classroom libraries "multicultural literature that reflects the rich and diverse realities of Latino families" (p. 116). Although this study looked only at Latino families, the same principles certainly hold true for families from other cultures. Middle-school teachers should select books that reflect the a variety of traditions, celebrate the richness of the many cultures, tell personal stories about people who share experiences and values similar to those of their students, and address relevant social issues and concerns (see Appendix A for some suggestions). Inviting students to discuss what they have read with their families encourages strong home-school connections. If the students are then encouraged to share their parents' responses to the readings, students and their parents begin to believe that the teacher respects their culture and background.

Also helpful are programs that model instructional strategies that parents who are themselves English learners can use with their own children. These often prove to be successful in building connections between home and school; see the home literacy activities mentioned later in this chapter. In another study on parental literacy practices, Baker, Sonnenschein, Serpell, et al. (1994) reported that parents in low SES families spend much time explicitly instructing their children in the work and practice elements of reading, whereas middle-income parents use a more playful approach, through stories and play. In these families, literacy is presented and modeled as an enjoyable pastime and an important avenue through which to understand the world. Knowing that this difference might occur, emphasize to all parents that students who find literacy learning painful tend to avoid books and reading, whereas those who learn to enjoy reading for its own sake are more likely to ask for books and read recreationally, thus becoming more successful (Baker, Serpell, & Sonnenschein, 1995).

Be aware that all parents participate in some sort of literacy activities with their children (Froiland, Peterson, & Davison, 2013). True, some parents may have problems with reading and writing, or English may not be their first language, but nearly all still engage in a wide range of literacy activities in the course of their daily lives. In his research, Barton (1997) found many examples of parents who experienced difficulties with some forms of written communication who nonetheless kept diaries, maintained household accounts, wrote poetry, took phone messages, and sent letters. These parents dealt with shopping lists, bills, forms, recipes, junk mail, and TV listings. (If you recall, the chapter-opening vignette for Chapter 10 offered additional examples of everyday literacy activities.) For the most part, adults who admit to problems with reading and writing are ordinary people leading ordinary lives; if they have children, they are like all parents in that they are deeply concerned about their children's education.

Educators have moved beyond thinking of just the mother as the key partner in literacy with the schools. We now include the father, siblings, grandparents, and the other relations and family friends whom students often cite as important in their literacy lives. Additionally, focusing exclusively on parent-child relations excludes important social agencies and community resources that may enhance literacy behaviors.

Educators are also moving beyond the notion that parents should read only to young children. We recognize that homes are significant places where myriad literacy practices can occur from infancy all the way up to the teenage years, and that parents can often learn from their children, too. Literacy learning can be a symbiotic event within families. Finally, rather than ask parents to replicate what teachers do in schools, teachers instead try to support the practices parents are already doing, in their homes, to promote literacy (Barton, 1997).

Communicating with Parents and Caregivers

In this section, we first provide important information that should be communicated to parents and caregivers about their student's literacy learning. Then we discuss the many ways teachers can communicate with the home.

What Parents Should Know About Literacy in Grades 4–8

Certain basic understandings about the nature of literacy, if understood by parents, will positively influence any assistance they offer their children. For example, simple naming of words, or "word calling," is not true reading; until a meaning-ful communication is taking place between the author and the reader, real reading, according to an accepted definition of that process, has not taken place. Inform parents of the following factors that influence that communication and lead to what we call *reading comprehension.*

First, comprehension is affected by decoding skills. When students do not obtain meaning from the printed page, it may be that their attention is too intent-ly focused on trying to recognize individual words. It is difficult to understand the gist of a passage as a whole if one is spending a large amount of time struggling to identify its components. It is essential that students develop fluency in word recog-nition to attain maximum comprehension. Some parents may not realize that both decoding and comprehension lead to proficient reading and may need to have this pointed out to them.

Second, comprehension is affected by experience. Essentially, what the reader absorbs from the printed page is in proportion to the experiences that he or she brings to it. Both comprehension and interpretation are based on past as well as present experiences; the wider and deeper a reader's past experiences, the more basis that reader has for drawing conclusions and, thus, the better will be the reader's comprehension and interpretation. No amount of school teaching can offset a lack of experience, so it is important for parents to provide their chil-dren with a wide range of experiences and to discuss those experiences at length. This activity also helps to expand a child's vocabulary. A simple maxim can be shared with parents: *The more a student brings to a book, the more that student will take from it.*

Finally, comprehension is affected by fluency of language development in the language of instruction. Comprehension is dependent on the ease with which the reader decodes printed symbols into already mastered oral language patterns. If oral language is inadequate, there will be no fluency. Underlying reading is a spoken language into which written words must be translated. Inadequacy in language fluency in general, and in knowledge of the meaning of English words specifically, will limit comprehension. However, knowledge of reading strategies and meaning-acquiring techniques in one language transfers to another. Linguistically diverse parents who do not speak English but who are literate in their native language, therefore, can help their children with reading comprehension through modeling and discussions of how they think through the reading process.

Parent–Teacher Conferences

Good communication between the home and the school, right from the start of each new school year, is essential in any balanced and comprehensive literacy pro-gram. Because most educators are aware of the need for good communication, many schools provide several parent–teacher conference days when teachers are available to talk with parents and caregivers about students' progress. The parent-teacher conference can be a fruitful time for the teacher to explain in clear terms the literacy program and how a student is progressing within the program. More-over, it is the ideal time to let the parents know how much their partnership is needed to reinforce the notion upon which a balanced and comprehensive litera-cy program is based: that literacy activities are both important in the world and enjoyable. After teachers have explained the literacy program, many parents will want to know how they can help their child at home. They often need reassurance that their concern for their children is appropriate and that they possess the abil-ity to take part in the school-home partnership. What brings parents to school?

When both the school district and individual schools make a concerted effort to let parents and caregivers know that they are wanted and needed, and that the school has valuable information to share about their child's literacy needs, they will come—provided that flexible scheduling makes attendance possible. Schools must also make clear that they respect and value the information and insights parents might share about their children and their particular needs. Therefore, schools must take a positive approach and work with the strengths and needs of families. Local radio and television stations, websites, and newspapers can help publicize the need for caring adults to meet with their children's teachers. In addition, a local chamber of commerce can be asked to send letters to all area employers requesting that they allow parents and caregivers to take time off from work to attend partnership conferences.

Conference scheduling is vitally important. Teachers should offer a variety of times for the conferences because some parents cannot come to school during the regular school day. In order for this arrangement to be successful, the district's administrative unit must be fully committed to the partnership concept and arrange for teachers to receive compensation for their efforts.

Conferences can be productive and pleasant for both teachers and parents if teachers follow a few simple procedures. Begin the conference with a friendly and relaxed greeting. Adopt the tone of a friendly acquaintance, reinforcing the idea, in every way possible, that you are all on the same team. If the parents speak little or no English, arrange to have an aide or community member available to translate, or invite an older English-speaking sibling to perform this important task. In advance, ask the student to teach you a few phrases (e.g., "How are you?" or "I am very pleased to meet you.") in his or her home language to make the parents feel welcomed. Begin and end the conference on a positive note, addressing what is noteworthy and unique about the student. The following points are helpful to consider in regard to parent–teacher conferences:

1. Set up the conference with the parents' comfort in mind. Rather than sitting behind a desk, as an authority figure, choose a room arrangement in which all adults can sit side by side to create a more equal setting.

2. Understand that parents have a right to their anxiety. It is quite normal for them to wonder how their child compares with her peers.

3. Inform parents about the student's strengths and instructional needs while sympathizing with their concerns. "Don't worry" is a phrase that has little value and should be avoided.

4. Refrain from being judgmental; instead, actively listen to parents, always seeking common ground. Instead of blaming them for what may not have occurred in the home, praise them for their concern and desire to help, engendering a feeling of true partnership.

5. Focus on specific constructive suggestions rather than vague generalities. "Your child needs help breaking down words into syllables" is much more helpful than "Your child is not reading well."

6. Discuss the student's progress using examples, such as actual progress forms, test results, or samples of the student's work.

7. Accept parents' questions and provide clear, honest responses.

8. Thank parents for attending and let them know that you are available for additional conferences if they have further concerns.

Finally, offer parents specific activities they can do at home, such as those offered in the next section, to help the student with any deficiencies or to enhance reading interest and proficiency.

Encourage parents to explore with their children the kinds of questions that provoke critical and creative thinking.

Working with Parents to Help Their Children

The most commonly heard question during conferences—which crosses all ethnic, cultural, and socioeconomic lines—is, "What can I do to help my child become a better reader?" While this chapter offers a general idea of what kinds of practices are helpful, parents are also asking for some specific activities that they can do to help their children succeed at literacy. Many teachers tell parents simply, "Turn off the TV or computer and have your child read for 15 minutes every day." This is excellent advice, and if every parent did this there would no doubt be fewer reading failures; however, for parents who are capable and willing, they may undertake several other activities with their children that will go even further to help students comprehend well and enjoy reading. Many teachers have had great success conducting two or three activity workshops each academic year, each focusing on one activity. Three such activities are discussed next. Having refreshments or a potluck can draw many parents; after a brief social period, the format of the evening can consist of providing simple instructions followed by practicing the activity in small groups. This ensures that parents will have the confidence to try the activity at home with their own children.

Home literacy activity: Questioning

Encourage parents to explore, with their children, the types of questions that extend and provoke critical and creative thinking; this will follow up the critical-thinking strategies that have been introduced in class. Instruct parents to follow every paragraph or so with a thought-provoking question that can *not* be answered with a simple yes or no. Tell them that questions such as "Why do you think . . . ?" and "What if . . . ?" almost always fulfill this purpose.

Begin the workshop by brainstorming a list of questions that will be useful for expanding comprehension and discussing the kind of responses they will likely generate. Then follow the instruction by giving everyone a short story containing several paragraphs. Have parents contribute appropriate questions for each paragraph and praise all responses. If a contributed response is not appropriate, accept it and then rework it into a useful question. Example: A parent offers, "Did the boy go into the woods?" (the answer is given in the paragraph). This response can be accepted and then slightly modified into, "Why do you think the boy went into the woods?" Readers must then consider the information in the story, compare it with what they know of the world, and create an answer.

Home literacy activity: Parent think-aloud

Parents who already read with their children can learn to extend the activity into a comprehension-modeling practice by using think-alouds. Explain that, as its name implies, this activity is one in which the parent shares aloud everything she is thinking as a paragraph is read, including these mental processes:

- *Making predictions:* "I bet Jerry will ask for his dog back."
- *Imaging:* "Ooh—that meadow reminds me of the field behind Mr. Darrow's farm where we used to hike, remember?"

- *Generalizing:* "So I guess these polar bears hibernate like the grizzlies we were reading about last week."
- *Using the context to figure out the meaning of unknown words:* "It says an Alaskan lifestyle is the *antithesis* of a Californian lifestyle. Since it seems they are way different, I'll bet *antithesis* means the opposite."

Using a piece of writing intended for adults, model how parents might do a think-aloud by slowing down their thinking and offering a window to into their thought processes. Invite parents to add their observations about the passage to yours, praising comments that would be particularly helpful for students to have modeled. Pass out a passage to each attendee and have pairs practice reading a paragraph out loud, sharing their meaning-gaining thought processes as they do so. Have them switch roles after each paragraph so that both get a chance to practice the technique. Finally, encourage parents to try this activity at home as they are doing shared reading. Explain that children can be invited to share their thoughts with their parents as they understand the point of the activity.

Home literacy activity: Dyad reading

A third activity is one that is especially effective for informational text and, thus, will help parents be of assistance when their child has reading to do in the content areas such as science and social studies. Explain to parents that dyad reading is a way to have their child read aloud and be sure the child understands what she is reading. Instruct them that if only one text is available, as is often the case with content area textbooks, the parent and child should sit side by side and take turns reading aloud, rotating after every paragraph. When the reader has finished the paragraph, he will summarize it for the listener, who will then add any material that the reader may have overlooked. They then switch roles for the next paragraph. To introduce this activity, explain the steps as you model them with a partner or parent who has been briefed in advance. It is helpful to model the activity using just one text, because this is the way it will be used at home; for the purpose of the demonstration, however, the passage may be reproduced so that all of the attendees have a copy. Additionally, explain to parents that an effective summary is a shortened version of the original—no more than a third in length—that contains the main idea as well as important details. Answer any questions parents may have about the steps of the procedure. Hand out new informational passages to pairs of parents and have them practice doing dyad reading, rotating roles after each paragraph. Encourage them to use this technique at home whenever their child has homework that requires reading in the content areas.

Other Communication with Parents

Besides conducting regularly scheduled conferences and workshops, teachers can keep parents informed in a variety of ways. One way is through a monthly newsletter or email. An attractive, simply written newsletter can help explain the literacy program and help avoid misunderstandings and confusion. The newsletter can also be a vehicle through which to convey or reiterate the previously discussed suggestions for home reading. Additionally, any questions that parents have been asking, or those that frequently come up every year, can be addressed.

Progress notes are a more personal way to keep parents informed. At frequent intervals, short notes can be written about a student in a positive, congratulatory tone when she has completed a book, asked an incisive question, or written an especially interesting piece. Such notes might also include a few open-ended questions for parents to ask about a story that has been read in class, or some vocabulary to discuss with their child. Parents might also be asked to listen to their child read a passage from a book he has recently finished so they can share in the experience of completing a book and celebrating success.

One way to bring parents to the school for a special occasion other than the formal parent-teacher conference is a reading festival. Any number of activities can be planned that have parents, students, and invited community members coming together to share favorite books, articles, websites, and stories. Parents can be asked to bring in their favorite age-appropriate book to read with the class, if they wish. Community members—especially those role models whom youngsters do not ordinarily associate with reading, such as firefighters, sports figures, and police officers—can be invited to read with small groups of children, or choral reading can be done with adults and students taking appropriate, or reverse, roles. Art activities can be planned, such as creating and playing reading games, or constructing dioramas or murals in connection with a favorite book. Such a festival works well in collaboration with a book fair or a book swap. The book fair can be organized with the help of a local bookstore or a paperback book publisher such as Scholastic. A book swap, on the other hand, requires less advance planning and can be arranged simply by asking students to bring in old books and magazines from home. They can then take turns reading the blurbs on the back covers and swap them, while teachers help parents match books to readers by interest and reading levels.

What Is Family Literacy?

National Center for Families Learning
http://familieslearning.org/

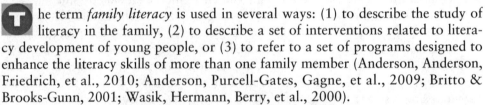

he term *family literacy* is used in several ways: (1) to describe the study of literacy in the family, (2) to describe a set of interventions related to literacy development of young people, or (3) to refer to a set of programs designed to enhance the literacy skills of more than one family member (Anderson, Anderson, Friedrich, et al., 2010; Anderson, Purcell-Gates, Gagne, et al., 2009; Britto & Brooks-Gunn, 2001; Wasik, Hermann, Berry, et al., 2000).

The ways in which parents interact with their child are paramount to the student's burgeoning literacy abilities, but some parents may require more assistance than teachers can offer in a traditional school-based workshop. Research increasingly supports the notion that parent–child literacy interactions are often more complex than just reading to children and providing them with literacy materials. In fact, simply telling a parent to read to a child may lead to quite different behavior than the teacher intended, depending on the parent's background. Home-school programs need to be nonthreatening and the activities enjoyable. Easy-to-use materials should be introduced to students in school first (Morrow, Kuhn, & Schwanenflugel, 2007). To help families improve the literacy of all members, family literacy programs have evolved.

Family Literacy Programs

For the past 25 years, educational policies have promoted family literacy programs in schools and community-based organizations. Family literacy appears in government legislation including the Elementary and Secondary Education Act, Reading Excellence Act, Workforce Investment Act, Community Services Block Grant Act, and the Head Start Act (National Center for Family Literacy, 2002). The development of family literacy programs draws on multiple academic fields, among them adult literacy, English learning, child literacy education—in particular, the field of emergent literacy and special education—early childhood development, cognitive psychology, and parent education.

Family literacy programs were created to help adults develop literacy skills while promoting the learning success of their children. Reading together builds confidence for low-literacy parents who might be reluctant to read to other adults, provides a positive model of literacy for their children, and fosters parent–child bonding. By supporting adult literacy, early childhood education, and parenting skills, family literacy programs aim to break the cycle of intergenerational illiteracy.

Family literacy programs generally address the following interrelated components:

The ways in which parents interact with their children are paramount to students' growing literacy.

- Adult literacy, basic skills, and life skills: To increase motivation, skills, and knowledge; to help parents find work or prepare for further training.
- Early childhood education: To help children prepare for academic and social success in school.
- Parent education and support groups: To allow parents to share questions, concerns, and strategies with their peers and counselors.
- Parent-child interaction: To provide role models and structured situations for positive parent-child interactions.

See the box on the next page for online resources for family literacy.

The federal government has set up a series of family literacy programs, such as Even Start, designed both to increase the literacy skills of the parents and to provide positive strategies and attitudes for enhancing a student's literacy at home. Programs are targeted for speakers of English as a first or second language and are located in a variety of settings, such as libraries, schools, colleges/universities, and family centers. A wide variety of activities take place, ranging from discussion groups to activities for parent-child interactions, as well as direct teaching of literacy skills for the parent leading to the attainment of a high school diploma.

In literacy programs aimed at both students and adults, there are various perspectives on what family literacy should be. Most initiatives act directly on the need most adult participants have to help their children become literate, while many also stress the vital role of community in education. Additionally, family literacy, in general, provides the possibility of assisting adults in ways that need not be constrained by intimidating traditions of formal education but, instead, actually draw on the knowledge that each family already possesses. Most educators working with families realize that there is no single road to becoming literate and that they must seek parents' help parents to ascertain what positive practices are already occurring in the home.

In one study, Kyle and colleagues (2005) found that teachers' home visits helped them understand their students and their families better, while also helping families enhance the literacy in their homes. Working in a low SES area, teachers went to students' homes to reflect on the connections between learning in school and experiences and contexts in the home. While teachers did provide more instruction to their students, the main outcome of teachers' visits was their acquisition of a greater understanding of students and their families and their provision of specific literacy support and direction. They also found that impoverished families did not value education any less than any other group; rather, education was valued and family-centered literacy activities were taking place (Kyle, McIntyre, Miller, et al., 2005).

Family Literacy Websites

Home schooling, www.home-school.com *and* http://home schooling.about.com

Sites provide information and resources for home-schooling families. Services include software, a curriculum exchange, e-pals, a home school magazine, curriculum reviews, and subject reference links.

PBS It's My Life, http://pbskids.org/itsmylife/parents/resources/middleschool.html

It's My Life is funded by the Corporation for Public Broadcasting to create safe, educational online activities for students aged 9 to 12. Parents and their children can read informative articles, share stories, play games, and get advice from experts.

International Reading Association, www.reading.org

An organization of teachers, librarians, researchers, parents, and others dedicated to promoting literacy for all.

National Center for Families Learning, http://families learning.org/

National Center for Families Learning provides referrals for family literacy programs at a local level.

Reading Is Fundamental, www.rif.org

Develops and delivers children's and family literacy programs that help prepare children for reading and them motivate school-aged children to read. Trains literacy providers, parents, and others to prepare all students to become lifelong readers.

This study promoted teachers' understandings about students, because teachers may be skeptical or even hostile toward students' home environments as they are related to literacy or school values. Students may speak a language at home that is not the same as the language of school, which may cause families to feel imposed on by schools and be made to feel inferior for their use of their native language at home. This is especially true for those families who sense they have been marginalized for speaking a language that is not the dominant one of the school and community (Reyes & Torres, 2007). Taking the lessons learned from Kyle and colleagues (2005), teachers should make sure that students and their families feel part of the literacy process. Teachers, given time and resources, benefit from home visits, and families benefit from learning specific ways to help their children progress.

It appears that long-term, community-based family literacy programs can be an important adjunct to the relationship the classroom teacher builds with the parent or caregiver. The classroom teacher can support such programs by acknowledging that literacy is an issue whose domain is not exclusive to the school.

Troubleshooting

Getting parents and caregivers the help they need for general literacy interactions at home is the focus of family literacy programs. But what about parents with whom the teacher has been totally unable to communicate? Certainly, the value of the parent-teacher conference to discuss specific issues related to students' literacy progress cannot be underestimated. Therefore, this section addresses several factors that preclude some parents' attendance at any school functions.

Interfering Work Schedules

Most schools have several parent-teacher days when teachers are available to talk with parents or caregivers about their child's progress. While this can be an ideal time to talk about the student, most parents work during the day and for various compelling reasons some may not be able to take time off to attend these important sessions. Because it is inappropriate—and impossible—for the teacher to evaluate parents' priorities and work responsibilities, some schools try to rectify the problem with flexible scheduling. Having some conference slots later in the day or in the evening (with the teachers given the morning to prepare) has been helpful in many schools. Teachers who have adopted this flexible plan report being successful in reaching parents who had previously not attended conferences due to job conflicts.

Reluctance to Attend School Functions

Some parents and caregivers may be reluctant to attend school functions because they feel uncomfortable in the school environment. They themselves may not have done well in school, and for them anything related to school holds unpleasant memories. Furthermore, parents from some cultural groups may hold the teacher in high esteem and may be hesitant as a result of being unfamiliar with the language and customs; they may fear embarrassing themselves in a formal academic environment. These parents are often the ones teachers wish to see in regard to their child's reading habits and attitudes. One suggestion to alleviate this problem is for the teacher—like Ms. Janos in the chapter-opening vignette— to visit the family in their home. A handwritten note or brief telephone call saying the teacher will be in the area on a particular day and requesting to visit for a chat is rarely refused. During this visit, nothing educational need be discussed, but the teacher should look for common ground with the parents; usually the adults' concern for the student is sufficient. A teacher's warm and down-to-earth attitude often forges an initial rapport that makes the parents' attempt to attend the next conference more likely.

Lack of a Common Language

A third barrier for parents is a tendency on the part of many teachers to use the technical "jargon" of literacy. Some parents refrain from attending meetings and conferences because they believe that they will not understand the teacher's academic language; unfortunately, at times teachers are to blame for this concern. Educators have acquired a large vocabulary of very specific literacy terminology. *Dyslexia* is one such difficult-to-define term, which might be better defined for parents more simply as "a problem with your child's reading," followed by a clear explanation of what the problem is, how it is being corrected in class, and how the parents might best help the student at home. Other literacy concepts can also be discussed in lay terms, with the outcome being that the parents feel they are capable of understanding what the teacher is talking about and be able to help. To invite parents to be true partners in the education of their child is to convince them they can communicate as equals.

Summary

To suggest that the relationship among the child, the parents or caretakers, and the school is a "triangle affair" is certainly nothing new. But it is not always appreciated just how much communication and sensitivity are required to make this relationship work optimally so that there is a true synergy among the student, the home, and the school. Teachers often need to be the prime movers, envisioning innovative ways to get parents—from all cultural and linguistic backgrounds—to school, or in some cases, even visiting them in their homes. Teachers need to make parents or caregivers feel at ease by talking to them in clear terms about the progress of their son or daughter and finding ways to explain how the goals of a balanced and comprehensive literacy program can be reinforced at home. Teachers also must be aware of research that supports the notion that parents, regardless of income or background, care about their children's success in literacy and only need to be guided to the best practices to augment the school's literacy program. Finally, teachers need to be aware of family literacy programs in their community that may offer possibilities for parents not only to help their children but also to further their own educational prowess. Such programs add another dimension to the relationship, letting parents and children know that the entire community sees literacy as a positive and worthwhile activity, and reminding everyone: "It takes a village to educate a child."

Questions FOR JOURNAL WRITING AND DISCUSSION

1. Recall from your childhood any literacy activities that took place in your family. How do you think these activities might have influenced your later academic success?

2. After reading this chapter, why do you think some educators object to labeling the children of parents of a lower socioeconomic status "at risk"? How might you respond to a colleague who claims that "these parents don't really care about their children's literacy development"?

3. What do you think parents should know about the literacy development of students in grades 4–8?

Suggestions FOR PROJECTS AND FIELD ACTIVITIES

1. Arrange to sit in on a parent-teacher conference. To what extent were the suggestions in this chapter followed? What do you feel might have made the parents or caregivers more comfortable?

2. Read a short story to a small group of students using either the questioning or the think-aloud activity. Do you feel sharing such an activity with parents is preferable to telling them simply to "read to your child"? Why or why not?

3. Find out if there are any family literacy programs in your area. If there are, visit a center to determine what its programs offer and how often they are used by the parents of students in your community. Share your findings with others in your class.

REFERENCES

Anderson, J., Anderson, A., Friedrich, N., & Kim, J. (2010). Taking stock of family literacy: Some contemporary perspectives. *Journal of Early Childhood Literacy* 10(1), 33–53.

Anderson, R. C., Hiebert, E. H., Scott, J. A., & Wilkinson, I. (1985). *Becoming a nation of readers: The report of the Commission on Reading.* Washington, DC: The National Institute of Education.

Anderson, J., Purcell-Gates, V., Gagne, M., & Jang, K. (2009). Implementing an intergenerational literacy program with authentic literacy instruction: Challenges, responses, and results. Vancouver: University of British Columbia.

Anstey, M., & Bull, G. (2006). Teaching and learning multi-literacies: Changing times, changing literacies. Newark, DE: International Reading Association.

Baker, L., Serpell, R., & Sonnenschein, S. (1995). Opportunities for literacy learning in the homes of urban preschoolers. In L. Morrow (Ed.), *Family literacy: Connections in schools and communities* (pp. 236–252). Newark, DE: International Reading Association.

Baker, L., Sonnenschein, S., Serpell, R., Fernandez-Fein, S., & Scher, D. (1994). *Contexts of emergent literacy: Everyday home experiences of urban prekindergarten children* (Research report). Athens, GA: National Reading Research Center, University of Georgia and University of Maryland.

Barton, D. (1997). Family literacy programmes and home literacy practices. In D. Taylor (Ed.), *Many families, many literacies: An international declaration of principles.* Portsmouth, NH: Heinemann.

Bowman, B. (2002). Love to read: An introduction. In B. Bowman (Ed.), *Love to read: Essays in developing and enhancing early literacy skills of African American children* (pp. vii–ix). Washington, DC: National Black Child Development Institute.

Britto, P. R., & Brooks-Gunn, J. (2001). The role of family literacy environments in promoting young children's emerging literacy skills. Concluding comments. *New Directions for Child and Adolescent Development, 92,* 91–99.

Chomsky, C. (1972). Stages in language development and reading exposure. *Harvard Educational Review, 42,* 1–33.

Delgado-Gaitan, C. (2001). *The power of community: Mobilizing for family and schooling.* New York: Rowman & Littlefield.

Fitzgerald, J., Spiegel, D. L., & Cunningham, J. W. (1991). The relationship between parental literacy level and perceptions of emergent literacy. *Journal of Reading Behavior, 13*(2), 191–212.

Froiland, J. M., Peterson, A., & Davison, M. L. (2013). The long-term effects of early parent involvement and parent expectation in the USA. *School Psychology International, 34,* 33–50.

Heath, S. B. (1983). *Ways with words: Language, life, and work in communities and classrooms.* New York: Cambridge University Press.

Kinzer, C. K., & Leander, K. (2003). Technology and the language arts: Implications of an expanded definition of literacy. In J. Flood, D. Lapp, J. R. Squire, & J. M. Jensen (Eds.), *Handbook of research on teaching the English language arts* (2nd ed., pp. 534–545). Mahwah, NJ: Lawrence Erlbaum.

Kyle, D., McIntyre, E., Miller, K., & Moore, G. (2005). Family connections: A basis for teacher reflections and instructional improvement. *The School Community Journal, 15*(1): 29–50.

Lancy, D. F., & Bergin, C. (1992). *The role of parents in supporting beginning reading.* Paper presented at the annual meeting of the American Educational Research Association, San Francisco.

Lancy, D. F., Draper, K. D., & Boyce, G. (1989). Parental influence on children's acquisition of reading. *Contemporary Issues in Reading, 4*(1), 83–93.

Laosa, L. M. (1982). School, occupation, culture, and family: The impact of parental schooling on the parent-child relationship. *Journal of Educational Psychology, 74*(6), 791–827.

Lonigan, C. J., Shanahan, T., Cunningham, A., & with the National Early Literacy Panel and National Early Literacy Panel. (2008). Impact of shared-reading interventions on young children's early literacy skills. Developing early literacy: Report of the National Early Literacy Panel (pp. 153–170). Washington, DC: National Institute for Literacy.

Morrow, L. M., Kuhn, M. R., & Schwanenflugel, P. (2007). The family fluency program. *The Reading Teacher, 60,* 322–333.

National Center for Family Literacy. (2007). *Family literacy: A strategy for educational improvement.* Louisville, KY: National Governors Association. Retrieved from www.bridges4kids.org/articles/2002/12-02/NGAliteracy 12-02.pdf.

Ortiz, R. W., & Ordoñez-Jasis, R. (October, 2005). Leyendo juntos (Reading together): New directions for Latino parents' literacy involvement. *The Reading Teacher, 59,*110–121.

Reyes, L., & Torres, M. (2007). Decolonizing family literacy in a culture circle: Reinventing the family literacy educator's role. *Journal of Early Childhood Literacy, 7*(1), 73–94.

Street, B. V. (1995). *Social literacies: Critical approaches to literacy in development, ethnography and education.* New York: Longman.

Taylor, D., & Dorsey-Gaines, C. (1988). *Growing up literate: Learning from inner-city families.* Portsmouth, NH: Heinemann.

Teale, W. H., & Sulzby, E. (1986). Home background and young children's literacy development. In *Emergent literacy: Writing and reading.* Norwood, NJ: Ablex.

Thomas, A., Fazio, L., & Stiefelmeyer, B. L. (1999). *Families at school: A guide for educators.* Newark, DE: International Reading Association.

Valdés, G. (1996). *Con respeto: Bridging the distances between culturally diverse families and schools.* New York: Teachers College Press.

Verhoeven, L., & Snow, C. E. (2001). Literacy and motivation: Bridging cognitive and sociocultural viewpoints. In L. Verhoeven & C. Snow (Eds.), *Literacy and motivation: Reading engagement in individuals and groups* (pp. 1–23). Mahwah, NJ: Lawrence Erlbaum.

Wasik, B. H., Hermann, S., Berry, R. S., Dobbins, D. R., Schimizzi, A. M., Smith, T. K., et al. (2000). *Family literacy: An annotated bibliography.* Chapel Hill: University of North Carolina.

Wilson, K. K. (2002). *Promoting civic literacy.* (ERIC Document Reproduction Service No. ED 466924).

TWELVE

Literacy in Grades 4-8
ORCHESTRATING A BALANCED AND COMPREHENSIVE PROGRAM

FOCUS QUESTIONS

- How do teachers' classroom practices emanate from their philosophy of teaching?
- How does a teacher effectively organize a classroom for literacy instruction?
- What does a typical day in an integrated classroom look like?

Mr. Fortney's fifth- and sixth-graders are studying the World War II era in their integrated language arts/social studies class. One group of students is reading and discussing Donna Jo Napoli's award-winning *Stones in Water* (1999), a novel about a young Italian boy who is torn from his family and taken to a Nazi work camp. It is an intense, gripping tale that engages students and allows the teacher to tie in the reading with all other subject areas.

Every day, the students meet in small literature circles to discuss the book. The students in each group read an assigned chapter for homework and are responsible for a specific role in the literature circle. Today, all of the students appear eager to talk about the chapter they have just read. Dmitra, the summarizer in one of the groups, begins by offering an animated review of the major points in the chapter. Ezran, the investigator, uses a map to explain where in Germany the work camp was located and explains that during the war Germany and Italy fought on the same side. Leann, the vocabulary enricher, shows a set of 3 x 5 cards on which she has written words that she didn't know. She teaches the others the words *pummeled, squirmed, throbbed,* and *yelp* by acting them out; for the word *grotesque,* she draws a picture of a hideous monster, and for the word *wrath,* she tells a story of a time her uncle became very angry when someone stole his mail. Leann then adds these vocabulary words to a word wall that is posted in the classroom. Lailani, a shy Pakistani girl who speaks little English, is the illustrator; she displays her picture of Roberto giving his food to the hungry little girl, a key incident in the chapter. The discussion director, Carlos, asks questions he has designed to encourage thinking and interacting among group members, such as "Do you think you could have given up your food for a friend like Roberto did?" Finally, the literary luminary, Brett, shares his favorite part of the chapter aloud—when Enzo calls the guard names, knowing the guard does not understand his dialect—and tells the group how visualizing the scene made him laugh out loud.

Later, the students use their social studies textbook to learn more about World War II. They work in groups to read the three sections of the chapter. They then report back to each other, and Mr. Fortney helps to direct their focus to the main ideas in each section as he lists them on the whiteboard. Students in each group make a chart listing the main ideas and adding details based on their section of the chapter. Later, they present their information to the class, wherever possible connecting information from the textbook to ideas gleaned from the novel.

To exhibit what they have learned, the students in Mr. Fortney's class create an interactive museum about the Holocaust. Working in small groups, they create displays on the events leading up to World War II, the rise of Adolph Hitler, and what anti-Semitism meant in Germany in the 1930s and 1940s as well as what it means today. Students work together to research their chosen topics using the classroom and school libraries as well as online resources. They engage museum visitors—including parents and caregivers, other classes, and community members—through the use of a Prezi presentation, a time-line mural, a dramatic performance based on the novel, and a panel discussion on the effects of religious intolerance.

To assess learning, Mr. Fortney and his students had developed a five-point rubric to evaluate their contributions to the museum display. By creating and discussing this rubric before initiating the reading and research, the students knew exactly what was expected of them. Foreknowledge of desired goals, as well as numerous ways to attain them, helps all students in Mr. Fortney's class succeed.

Introduction

Many schools for grades 4–8 are departmentalized; that is, students receive daily instruction from several different teachers because each teacher specializes in a single subject. The instructional content of each academic subject requires teachers who are experts in the area; instruction may be of higher quality when teachers can take special pride in their subject-matter discipline and can concentrate on preparing a limited number of outstanding lessons that are then offered to several different classes each day.

In this text, we are not advocating for any particular grade structure or "label" (i.e., middle school, junior high, intermediate) for schools that educate students in the 9 to 13 age range. We agree with middle grades reformer Hayes Mizell (2002):

It's not the sign in front of the building that matters, it's what is going on inside. Is the school focused on high achievement and success for all students? Have its leaders and supporters taken into account the unique developmental needs of this remarkable age group? All schools with middle grades should be judged by their academic excellence, their developmental responsiveness and their social equity. (p. 119)

The Common Core State Standards promote high achievement in schools, with the ultimate goal being success in college and career. Therefore, the middle grades matter—a lot. According to one study, "a student's middle grades experience *strongly impacts* the odds of graduating from high school" (Balfanz, 2009, emphasis added). An issue brief from the MetLife Foundation reports that "*Sixth graders* who failed math or English/reading . . . had only a 10% to 20% chance of graduating high school on time. In a study of *middle schoolers,* less than 1 out of every 4 students with at least one of these 'off-track indicators' graduated high school in five years or less" (2011, emphasis added). Indeed, students cannot hope to become college and career ready by the end of high school if they are not well on their way by middle school. Therefore, it is critical for students in the middle grades to receive instruction that prepares them for the rigors of high school and beyond.

We have chosen to present Mr. Fortney's outstanding classroom as one that we believe models this excellent environment. His classroom, though certainly not the only possible model of excellence, exemplifies how literacy and the content areas can be artfully integrated.

Mr. Fortney has been teaching a fifth- and sixth-grade combination classroom at Oak Point Middle School for 13 years. Oak Point, which includes grades 4–8, is located in an urban area in northern California. Most of the students at Oak Point come from working-class families, and more than 70 percent of the students qualify for the free lunch program. Seven of the students in Mr. Fortney's class are English learners, and all speak some English. Nine different cultures are represented in the classroom.

The class is for the most part self-contained, but with some team teaching. Mr. Fortney works in a team with two other teachers, which is fairly typical of classrooms in grades 4–8. Before the school year begins, the team meets to make program decisions and to discuss matters such as scheduling and curricular responsibilities. The classrooms comprising Mr. Fortney's team are made up of approximately 15 fifth-grade students and 15 sixth-grade students each. When the sixth-graders move on to seventh grade, 15 new fifth-grade students take their place. The students are with the same teachers for two years, which allows for continuity of teaching.

Mr. Fortney has read widely from the current literature on literacy, and when describing his program he frequently refers to topics in that literature. When we asked him to describe the literacy program he and his colleagues have developed, this is what he told us:

> The literacy program we have developed over the years reflects the unique challenge we encounter as middle school teachers. Our literacy goal for our students is to have them become actively engaged with text. Our students are required to analyze, identify, define, explain, and critique what they read rather than merely understand it, as was expected in earlier grades. But besides the cultural and linguistic differences in our students, the variability in reading ability is extreme in most students by grades 5 and 6. For example, one of my students, a 10-year-old, reads at an eleventh-grade level and typically reads an entire Harry Potter novel over several free reading periods, while another, 11 years old, struggles with anything higher than second-grade material. He finds it difficult to decode

even short articles and displays very little interest at all in reading and writing; his only passion is basketball, so we build on that.

This discrepancy in abilities and motivational levels presents a pressing obstacle for me and my colleagues: How do we meet the needs of all our students, given this formidable range of ability and interest? Given that current thinking in middle school instruction is to move away from traditional heterogeneous grouping of students toward whole-group and flexible group instruction, meeting the needs of the students becomes even more challenging. My colleagues and I are continually honing the methods and resources we use to best address the literacy needs of each of our students while taking into account the state standards we are expected to address.

A Classroom Climate Conducive to Literacy

Despite the challenges facing Mr. Fortney and his colleagues, the "methods and resources" this team of teachers is using appear to be working. They have experienced success with their literacy program as measured by improving standardized test scores—which meet and exceed the state average every year—and also evidenced by the fact that their students appear to have acquired a genuine love for reading and writing. Reading and writing attitude surveys, administered at the beginning and end of every school year, suggest that students' attitudes have strongly improved, and reading logs and book circulation indicate that by the end of the year, most students are choosing to read as a favorite free-time activity. How do they manage such success with students at an age when interest in literacy often declines?

The answer to that question lies, in part, in the way Mr. Fortney and his colleagues make decisions about classroom instruction. Any changes in the curriculum that the teachers have developed are usually precipitated by a combination of three factors:

1. Their ongoing assessment of students informs them that change is in order.
2. They have read about a strategy or observed an activity that they feel might be beneficial to help them reach their instructional goals.
3. They have reviewed research in a respected journal, such as *The Reading Teacher,* that provides compelling evidence that a literacy practice is effective and should be implemented.

As an example of their responsiveness to current research, Mr. Fortney explains that their philosophy of teaching draws on four factors taken from motivational theory (Brophy, 2010):

1. setting objectives and teaching to state standards
2. providing for differentiated instruction
3. implementing powerful activities and assignments
4. teaching for depth and connections

Setting Objectives

Mr. Fortney and his colleagues plan their curriculum based not on content but on desired student knowledge and behaviors. When these teachers sit down at the end of a school year to decide what and how they will teach students in the coming year, they think first of how next year's students will think and behave differently at the end of that school year. Mr. Fortney confesses that when he first started teaching, he planned lessons and units based solely on the content included in the textbook and the activities he found helped students master this content. Essentially, he realized later, he was allowing the authors of the textbook to dictate his goals. Over time, he began to see that his teaching must start with *his* goals—including the attitudes, knowledge, skills, and values he wants his students to come away with—and plan curriculum that will help students reach these goals. Today, Mr. Fortney and his colleagues plan their curriculum around the most important ideas they want their students to understand.

Providing for Differentiated Instruction

Mr. Fortney and his colleagues organize instruction around the premise that all students can learn, but each student's needs are unique and, therefore, each will need a different amount of time and effort to complete assignments. They also offer their students multiple ways to access material and a variety of means by which students can complete an assignment. For example, students choose from a number of books to complete a book contract. The book contract is a self-contained set of information, through and beyond activities that relate to a particular book (see Chapter 5). The books for each book contract come in a range of reading and interest levels, and students can choose from a variety of writing, art, technology, and research activities in order to respond personally to the text. In some cases, the books for a particular assignment all relate to one concept or era in the social sciences, such as a unit on China. Mr. Fortney has chosen books that range from second- to eighth-grade reading levels, yet each book covers the essential information about the Chinese culture and customs that will lead to later whole-class discussion. In addition to the book contract, students sometimes take part in literature circles, where each student assumes a role to help other classmates clarify and deepen their understanding of the chosen text (see the chapter-opening vignette and Chapter 5).

All students can learn, but each student's needs are unique.

As another example of differentiated instruction, Mr. Fortney makes wide use of collaboration for research projects, offering students a variety of ways to contribute to the final project—from a mural of rural Chinese life to a PowerPoint presentation to a ballad based on a Chinese fairytale. Such an approach not only ensures the engagement of all learners but taps into the wide range of learning styles and preferences and types of intelligences found in most classrooms.

Finally, Mr. Fortney forms many flexible groups so students who share the need for a reading skill or strategy will be taught as effectively as possible. Groups are deliberately impermanent and, because they exist for a specific purpose, will then be disbanded as soon as he has completed the lessons planned for the group. When Mr. Fortney, through ongoing assessment (see Chapter 2), observes that a student is falling behind or is having particular difficulty, he or she receives individualized instruction—one-on-one sessions with the teacher.

Implementing Powerful Activities and Assignments

Mr. Fortney and his colleagues understand that the most powerful activities and assignments are built around powerful ideas, such as "freedom" or "oppression." Mr. Fortney shares his belief that the key to an activity's effectiveness is that it prompts students to actively think about and apply key ideas, preferably with conscious awareness of the pre-established learning goals mentioned earlier. Contrary to the practice of some teachers, Mr. Fortney believes that an appropriate activity is not one that merely has students all doing something quietly; instead, it should have them all thinking and talking about what they are doing as they move toward the attainment of an important goal.

Ultimately, Mr. Fortney also believes that the success of any activity depends not only on the quality of the activity itself, but also on the teacher-student debriefing that occurs into, through, and beyond the time period in which students are responding to the activity's demands. Mr. Fortney and his colleagues maximize the impact any activity has on their students by introducing activities in ways that clarify their cognitive and affective goals and create the desire to accomplish those goals through constant student buy-in. Then, as students work on the activity, Mr. Fortney monitors their progress and provides appropriate feedback. Throughout the days we visited, Mr. Fortney led students through many types of postsharing of and reflection on the insights that they had gained as a result of ongoing activities.

Finally, Mr. Fortney and his colleagues go to great lengths to involve parents and caregivers in their children's instruction. When they found that few parents were coming to open houses and back-to-school night events, they began to think of more creative ways to reach parents. An early-morning doughnuts-and-coffee social, for example, allowed parents to drop in before work to chat with the teachers and view the interactive museum and an iMovie production the students had created. Additionally, the teachers email parents brief newsletters containing schedules of classroom activities and suggestions for family reading that would complement current units.

Teaching for Depth and Connections

Mr. Fortney is aware that, in recent years, the findings of research on effective teaching and the instructional guidelines issued by national and state subject-matter specialists have stressed the importance of teaching for thorough understanding, or "mastery." Students who have learned content deeply have mastered the content itself and then retain it in a form that will make it usable when it is needed. Mr. Fortney provides clear explanations and modeling of new ideas—so students can see how the new content is important—and then helps them see how the new ideas connect with ones with which they are already familiar. He encourages this connection through discussions and debates and helps students apply the new information in problem-solving or decision-making contexts. For example, for literature circles on the topic of immigration, he makes sure they can choose from a wide range of trade books, of varying reading levels, that describe the immigration experience of various groups and told from various perspectives. Integrated math and social studies lessons center around creating bar graphs tracking groups of immigrants; to integrate music into the lesson, Mr. Fortney finds songs that represent the travails of many immigrant groups. Finally, students are encouraged to find online articles concerning recent immigrants, which the class discusses; students then individually write personal essays based on the discussion. Those students whose families have recently come to the United States share how their experiences differ from those of immigrants from the nineteenth and early twentieth centuries.

When researching older immigration patterns, the class uses the Best of History Websites. This site features links that have been compiled and organized by world regions and time periods; many of these links take users to sites that have been created to help teachers align units in social studies/history with the Common Core State Standards (Common Core: History—Immigration, 2013). Immigration

www●●●

Best of History Websites

www.besthistorysites.net

links, for example, provide resources, assessments, and support for teachers, like Mr. Fortney, who are interested in a standards-aligned unit on this topic.

Organizing the Classroom for Instruction

Another challenge facing Mr. Fortney and all other instructors in his overcrowded urban school is using classroom space most effectively and comfortably. Mr. Fortney takes time with students at the beginning of the school year to discuss the room set-up, gathering their input so that they feel ownership of their classroom. They also offer suggestions concerning its organization. While the amenities found in Mr. Fortney's classroom are not in all schools, certain organizational features can be attained in most classrooms.

Materials and Equipment

Desks, chairs, and tables throughout the room are movable so that they can be reorganized based on the demands of a particular activity. The room also contains pillows, an arm chair, an old comfortable couch, and area rugs to further define space and indicate appropriate settings for particular projects, such as reading, research, interviewing, illustrating a piece of writing, or simply skimming for information. Students' works are displayed on walls, bulletin boards, hanging mobiles, chart paper, and occasionally on easels. Additional materials and equipment are borrowed or purchased according to the needs of the subjects being studied and the realities of the limited school budget.

Centers

Besides bookshelves filled with books and reference materials, Mr. Fortney's classroom has several centers (see Figure 12.1). Some centers are permanent, while others are temporary according to the unit being studied and are dismantled once the unit of study is finished. For example, a recent unit on the rain forest required that tables be moved to certain corners of the room so that students would have access to science and social studies resources such as maps, a terrarium, and examples of flora and fauna. Permanent centers include the classroom library, the reading area, the art center, and the writing center, which includes the computer corner.

The writing center contains many items needed for writing and art activities, ranging from lined paper and stationery to elaborate computer paper and wallpaper samples. Writing utensils are similarly extensive to invite forays of fancy, including gel pens, ink pens, and even fine-line markers. The focal point in the writing center is the colorful mailbox. Students write letters to the teacher, or to other students about classroom concerns, or with positive comments to brighten their days. In this classroom, negative comments are not allowed in the mailbox.

Adjacent to the writing center is the computer corner. The computers allow students to access information though online searches and to share that information with others. With the computers, students engage in writing activities that include drafting and revising with an online partner, either from class or from somewhere else. Tutors volunteer to be online revisers or mentors, also referred to as penpals, and the reading and writing they do with the students is helpful and certainly authentic. The online tutors have been trained to ask good probing questions of Mr. Fortney's students rather than feel obligated to discuss every error the students make. Recent additions to the computer corner are a few tablets that the school has purchased. Students use the tablets for some of the same reading and

figure **12.1**   Diagram of Mr. Fortney's classroom.

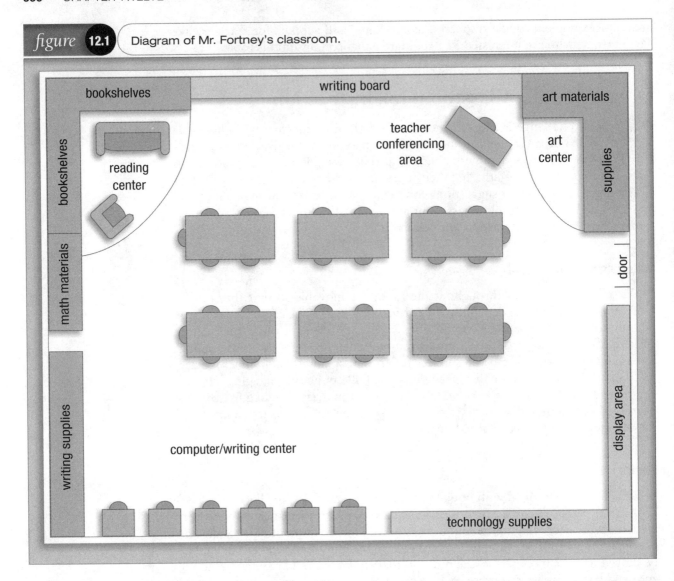

writing activities they do on the desktop computers, but they also use them for taking photographs, engaging with literacy apps, and recording audio and video.

Mr. Fortney is understandably proud of his extensive classroom library, which is located in a carpeted corner of the room and contains a comfortable couch, armchair, and pillows. Two shelves line the corner walls and are filled with books from his personal collection, supplemented by books from the school or city library depending on the subject areas being studied. Mr. Fortney has amassed more than one thousand trade books on a wide variety of topics during his teaching career—through commercial book clubs, garage sales, auctions (both live and online), library sales, and gifts from friends and family. These books range in readability level from low second grade to high school and include both narrative and informational texts from every literary genre. They also reflect the various cultures found in the classroom and the local community, and some are in the home languages of the class's English learners. Audiobooks, magazines, catalogs, newspapers, and graphic novels find their way onto these shelves, and students can be seen browsing in the reading area during any free time they have during the day as well as before and after school.

Finally, the classroom has a well-stocked art center. Because the school does not have an art teacher, Mr. Fortney incorporates art activities with the students' language arts and social studies activities. The center is stocked with materials for coloring, painting, drawing, sculpting, and craft making as well as a few digital cameras. Students also use the equipment in the computer center to enhance their work visually.

Devising an Instructional Plan

everal important attributes are evident in Mr. Fortney's and his colleagues' organization—curriculum content, space, time, and students:

- These teachers are committed to the idea of a homeroom, so students feel that one person is mainly responsible for them; moreover, the teachers appreciate this way of sharing the administrative duties.
- The team goes to great lengths to set aside large blocks of time so a topic can be covered in the depth it requires.
- These teachers center their instruction around broad unifying themes containing essential questions that will help drive the investigation. Additional essential questions for the theme discussed in the chapter's opening vignette, for example, are: "Why did the Holocaust happen?" and "How can prejudices such as anti-Semitism be eliminated?"

A typical school day in Mr. Fortney's fifth/sixth grade at Oak Point Middle School looks like this:

[9:00–11:15 Homeroom]

9:00	Journal writing/silent reading/computer buddies
9:30	Directed reading-thinking activity (DRTA)
10:15	Language arts/social studies/writing workshop
11:15	Math
12:00	Lunch/recess
12:40	Physical education or library, alternating
1:20	Integrated curriculum block: science, art, music, and health, combined with reading, writing, listening, speaking, viewing, and visually representing
2:30	Homeroom: debriefing discussions
2:45	Dismissal

From this schedule, you can see that students remain with their homeroom teacher for more than two hours in the morning and then return in the afternoon. Mr. Fortney's fifth- and sixth-grade students stay with him from 9:00 until 11:15. The team teachers and the students like these large blocks in the schedule because they require fewer disruptive "downtimes" between classes and allow for more substantive relationships between teacher and student. The larger blocks also allow teachers to delve into a topic in greater depth, using extended time to make connections with other curricular areas. Finally, the blocks offer time for students to work in small groups in a self-directed manner, allowing the teacher to work closely with those students needing individual assistance.

Students split into grade-level groups for math and physical education. In the afternoon, the integrated curriculum blocks allow each member of the team to teach in his or her area of greatest expertise; Mr. Fortney's undergraduate minor was in the physical sciences, and he has always enjoyed this field, while the other two teachers in the team prefer teaching health and art.

The large amount of time for the language arts and the integrated curriculum block provides an opportunity for the team to illustrate the interconnectedness of reading, writing, listening, speaking, viewing, and visually representing. The literature-based focus of both blocks of time allows for integration of content as well as flexibility in instruction; when more time is needed in science one day, for example, that subject can spill into the health and art time periods, or even the language arts period, without causing a problem. These team teachers are always looking for—and finding—unique opportunities to connect reading and writing to the other content areas, as well as to state standards and mandated content area material.

This team has found that the literature-based approach is highly motivational. Meeting to discuss what they have read, as described in the opening vignette, helps students develop rich schemata while responding enthusiastically to text in their own words. Mr. Fortney also finds that it is natural for him to model and talk about appropriate behavior with respect to literature, because he is able to share his own personal book club experiences with his students. Additionally, literature circles appear to have an advantage with students in this age range because they are unable to avoid being participants in the small group discussions, and other group members hold each other accountable for completing their assigned roles. Finally, a clear advantage to the literature circles approach is that students are able to select their own books. While the teacher usually selects all the texts that relate to the broad theme, such as immigration, students have the freedom to choose which of the trade books they would like to read, thus increasing the likelihood that they will choose a book that is of interest and at their level of reading ability. Novel study can also be effective (see Chapter 5).

Although unplanned events often interfere with Mr. Fortney's instructional plan (fire drills, assemblies, absences, parties, guest speakers, etc.), one would expect to see an activity similar to the one described in the opening vignette. Following is a brief description of his fifth/sixth-grade students' daily routine.

9:00–9:30 Journal Writing/Silent Reading/Computer Buddies

When students enter the classroom, they immediately take out their self-selected books and their double-entry journals (see Chapter 5). Because some of Oak Point's students have chaotic home lives, these students appreciate the predictability of having a certain time of the day that rarely varies. As they read the books they have selected from the classroom library, they often stop and write down in the first column of their journal a phrase or paragraph that catches their attention because it resonates with the character's feelings or actions. Then students explain, in the second column, how they personally relate to the particular excerpt. Some students have signed up to use the classroom computers to email their computer buddy, a university preservice teacher. Mr. Fortney has set up this arrangement so that his students can have authentic electronic dialogues about the books they are currently reading. Both parties agree to read the same book, and then students enthusiastically "discuss" their reading with their university counterpart, who adds her own insights about the text.

9:30–10:15 Directed Reading–Thinking Activity (DRTA)

Mr. Fortney and his team are aware of the importance of direct instruction in reading and study strategies. Therefore, they set aside a time when reading comprehension, vocabulary skills, and comprehension strategies are modeled for students through many of the instructional strategies discussed throughout this book. This day, Mr. Fortney prepares students to read an online news story about a Holocaust survivor who lives nearby and has been reunited with a sister she had not seen since both were in Auschwitz. Mr. Fortney uses several paragraphs to show students how the meaning of the words *corroboration* and *universal* can be gleaned by using the context. The students pair off and use reciprocal questioning to read, summarize, predict, and clarify each paragraph. Then the pairs share their ideas with the whole class as the paragraph is displayed on the whiteboard.

10:15–11:15 Language Arts/Social Studies/Writing Workshop

Students get into their groups and quickly attend to the business of sharing their responses to the reading they did the night before. Besides *Stones in Water* (see the opening vignette), students are reading *The Diary of Anne Frank, The Upstairs Room,* and *Number the Stars.* After doing literature circles, students in one group devise a short reader's theatre presentation to share with the rest of the class so that other groups will get a sense of the other books being read. Very often, Mr. Fortney states, students will opt to read all four books being used in the literature circles, for recreational reading outside of school. On this day, Mr. Fortney conducts a minilesson on the use of quotation marks in dialogue, the sixth of an ongoing set of lessons designed to teach students to become more effective writers through the use of the 6 + 1 Traits writing framework. Students then incorporate this new learning in an essay about the importance of the Holocaust in today's world, which is assigned for homework. Tomorrow, students may peer edit these essays in writing workshop, which occurs every other day at this time. At regular intervals, Mr. Fortney returns to the essential questions for a whole-class discussion on the Holocaust and how it has impacted recent events.

11:15–12:00 Math

Mr. Fortney and his team believe in adding an oral language component to all math activities by asking students to articulate their answers to word problems as well as computations and equations. Additionally, Mr. Fortney often checks for understanding by using "quick writes," in which students are asked to paraphrase, in written form, their understanding of a math procedure that has just been taught, providing a check on how effectively the concept has been taught and understood.

12:00–12:40 Lunch and Recess

12:40–1:20 Physical Education/Library

Three days a week, students go to physical education; the other two days, they are taken to the library, where the media specialist often provides a lesson on some aspect of study skills such as using a variety of online resources to augment a report. Because students are allowed to borrow books during a portion of library time, Mr. Fortney is always available to "match books to readers," using his observations and the data from running records to determine reading levels, and the results of his reading interest inventory to get an idea of exactly what books might interest each student.

1:20–2:30 Integrated Curriculum Block

The integrated curriculum block time is an exciting time to channel the energy of middle school students through the implementation of cross-curricular thematic units, innovative teaching

Integrated studies help students connect knowledge across content areas.

and learning, and a strong focus on the language arts. For the next four weeks, the students in Mr. Fortney's class will be doing a unit called "Biomes of the World," studying the interactions between living things and their environment. Assessments are completed at the end of the group presentations using a teacher-made rubric and a self-evaluation rubric for the group and for individual students. The unit contains the following components that address his state's science and language arts curriculum standards to which Mr. Fortney adheres:

- View and discuss videos on deserts, forest, marine, freshwater, grassland, and tundra habitats *(viewing; oral language)*
- Take a field trip to an environmental camp; summarize learning *(informational writing)*
- Use "Project Wild" conservation educational program materials *(science, reading, applying)*
- Participate in the "Oh Deer" game from Project Wild, allowing students to see and chart the cycle of deer populations in an ecosystem *(science, math)*
- Explore NASA Earth Observatory websites and record information *(computer skills, media literacy, summarizing)*
- Create a PowerPoint or Prezi presentation on symbiosis *(oral presentation, computer skills, visually representing)*
- Read and discuss *There's an Owl in the Shower*, by Jean Craighead George, using buddy reading *(reading, oral discussion)*
- Dissect owl pellets; label and classify them *(science, categorizing, classifying)*
- Create a "biome in a box" depicting characteristics of an assigned biome *(art, visually representing, science, describing)*
- Research their biome and present findings via posters, dioramas, skits, diagrams, and the "biome in a box" *(art, visually representing, summarizing, drama)*
- Adopt and research a zoo animal at the city zoo *(research, technology, informational writing)*
- On a desktop or table computer, write a story about an imaginary creature and its habitat; create hypothetical adaptations for it *(science, creative writing, computer skills)*

Project Wild
www.projectwild.org

Oh Deer
www.projectwild.org/
documents/ohdeer.pdf

2:30–2:45 Homeroom/Debriefing Session

Returning to their homerooms at the end of the day, students have a chance to reflect on what they have learned during the day, through either small-group discussion, quick writes, whole-group share, or question-and-answer sessions in which individual students ask for clarification concerning a concept or an assignment about which they feel unsure.

Summary

Throughout this book, we have explored ways to teach literacy in a comprehensive way that includes direct instruction in the skills of writing conventions, reading comprehension, decoding, and vocabulary enrichment while also focusing on responding to literature in personal, meaningful, and joyous ways. The skills of literacy, while absolutely necessary, are part and parcel of the more critical task—realizing what reading can mean and how it can make readers feel. To that end, many activities were included throughout that were designed for making text meaningful and using text as a springboard to substantive writing activities.

Yet learning about specific strategies—seeing only individual pieces of the big picture—is not totally satisfactory. Particularly if one has not yet taught, it is vital to see how a gifted teacher manages to orchestrate all of the elements into a total program. And this program must meet the required state and national standards while also meeting the needs of the heterogeneous collection of students, with various strengths and needs, who now face teachers in most classrooms.

Although literacy instruction might be implemented in many possible ways, we chose to showcase one teacher in one team's approach. This team has had success despite major challenges of poverty in homes, limited home support, several home languages, and a wide range of ability levels. Based on the substantiation of test scores as well as an impartial observer's examination, the students appear to be learning the skills of literacy and to be able to apply them to the content areas in a rich and rewarding way.

Finally, Mr. Fortney's classroom, for us, stood out in another, more fundamental way: it was impossible to miss the zest for teaching and the love for all aspects of literacy, and learning in general, modeled in this veteran teacher's classroom. He eagerly shared with us his involvement in reading and writing activities outside the classroom. With students, he often refers to books he is reading, or a poem or article he has recently written. Moreover, this teacher is integrally involved in his profession through conducting in-service workshops for colleagues; attending professional conferences; and, on occasion, discussing current journal articles in the teachers' lounge. His passion for learning is contagious and is clearly "caught" by the students with whom he works.

A balanced and comprehensive literacy program can be a reality when a competent and caring teacher puts forth the time and effort it takes to create a program that connects content areas with the language arts in deep and meaningful ways, and offers important ideas that students can wrap their minds around through engaging activities. Mr. Fortney's classroom truly embodies these goals.

Questions FOR JOURNAL WRITING AND DISCUSSION

1. Reflect on a teacher you know who appears to be highly effective in teaching students to read for knowledge and enjoyment. In light of this chapter, what do you believe makes this teacher effective? What do you believe makes Mr. Fortney such an effective teacher of intermediate literacy? What are the similarities between the two teachers? Differences?

2. Brainstorm a list of ways you can ensure that the students in your class will read not only for knowledge but also for enjoyment. Share and discuss this list with the others in your class. What do you consider the most effective methods?

3. Discuss the provisions that must be made so that linguistically and culturally diverse learners may succeed. How do you believe such provisions affect the native English speakers in the class?

Suggestions FOR PROJECTS AND FIELD ACTIVITIES

1. Arrange to observe a middle grades classroom. Make notes about the environment, the classroom climate, and the literacy activities in which the students engage. Your observation should be as objective as possible. Compare your experience with the other members of your class and include in your discussion your personal responses to the classroom you observed.

2. Interview someone who teaches grades 4–8. Ask this teacher how decisions are made in his classroom about changing instruction. For this teacher, which

seems to be the most potent reason for changing a classroom practice: (a) what research says, (b) what other teachers say, (c) what the district policy is, or (d) what assessment tells the teacher?

3. Make a sketch of what you consider to be an ideal classroom for grades 4–8, including furniture, materials, equipment, and storage space most suited to what you believe to be a balanced literacy environment. Compare your sketch to Figure 12.1. How is yours different? Why? Share your sketch with others in your class, discussing the benefits and drawbacks of each design. Websites such as Classroom Architect can help with classroom design.

Classroom Architect

http://classroom.4teachers.org/

REFERENCES

Balfanz, R. (June, 2009). Putting middle grades students on the graduation path: A policy and practice brief. Retrieved from www.amle.org/BrowsebyTopic/At-riskRTI/AtDet/TabId/181/ArtMID/783/ArticleID/314/Putting-Middle-Grades-Students-on-the-Graduation-Path.aspx

Brophy, J. (2010). *Motivating students to learn* (3rd ed.). Boston: McGraw-Hill.

Common Core: History—Immigration (2013). Retrieved from http://schools.nyc.gov/NR/rdonlyres/B46D0228-1BB5-4E44-A3CB-3A5C81334461/138140/NYCDOE_G4_LiteracySS_NYCImmigration_Final.pdf

Metlife Foundation (2011). Afterschool alert issue brief. Retrieved from www.metlife.com/assets/cao/foundation/MSBrief_2010-4.pdf

Mizell, H. (2002). *Shooting for the sun: Middle school reform.* New York: Edna McConnell Clark Foundation.

Napoli, D. J. (1997). *Stones in water.* New York: Puffin Books.

Multicultural Literature

T he following books are suitable for introducing students to a variety of cultures in a respectful and informative way.

Adoff, A. (2011). *Roots and blues: A celebration* (R. G. Christie, Ill.). Clarion / Houghton Mifflin Harcourt. (African American)

Boyce, F. C. (2011). *The unforgotten coat.* Candlewick. (Mongolian)

Bruchac, J. (1997). *Lasting echoes: An oral history of Native American people* (P. Morin, Ill.). Harcourt. (Native American)

Delacre, L. (1996). *Golden tales: Myths, legends, and folktales from Latin America.* Scholastic. (Latino American)

de la Peña, M. (2011). *A nation's hope: The story of boxing legend Joe Louis* (K. Nelson, Ill.). Dial. (African American)

Diakité, B. W. (2010). *A Gift from childhood: Memories of an African boyhood.* Groundwood Books. (African)

Dolphin, L. (1997). *Our journey from Tibet: Based on a true story.* Dutton. (Asian American)

Ekoomiak, N. (1990). *Arctic memories.* Holt. (Native American)

Filipovic, Z. (1993). *Zlata's diary: A child's life in Sarajevo.* Viking. (European American)

Frazier, S. T. (2010). *The Other half of my heart.* Yearling. (African American)

Gonzalez, C. D. (2012). *A thunderous whisper.* Knopf books for young readers. (Spanish)

Greenfield, E. (2011). *The great migration: Journey to the north.* (J. Spivey Gilchrist, Ill.). Amistad / HarperCollins. (African American)

Hughes, D. (2010). *Missing in action.* Simon Pulse. (American Indian)

Hurmence, B. (1982). *A girl called boy.* Clarion. (African American)

Jaffe, N. (1995). *Older brother, younger brother: A Korean folktale* (L. August, Ill.). Penguin. (Korean)

Mazer, A. (Ed.). (1993). *America street: A multicultural anthology of stories.* Persea. (Many cultures)

Morpurgo, M. (2010). *Shadow.* Feiwel & Friends. (Afghani)

Morpurgo, M. (2011). *An elephant in the garden.* Feiwel & Friends. (German)

Myers, W.D. (1997). *Harlem* (C. Myers, Ill.). Scholastic. (African American)

Napoli, D.J. (1997). *Stones in water.* Puffin. (Jewish/Italian)

Normandin, C. (Ed.). (1997). *Echoes of the elders: The stories and paintings of Chief Lalooska.* DK. (Native American)

Nye, N. (1997). *Habibi.* Simon & Schuster. (Arabic American)

Orlev, U. (1991). *The man from the other side.* Houghton. (Jewish/Polish)

Smith, I. (2010). *Half spoon of rice: A survival story of the Cambodian genocide* (S. Nhem, Ill.). East West Discovery Press. (Cambodian)

Wood, N. (Ed.). (1997). *The serpent's tongue: Prose, poetry, and art of the New Mexico pueblos.* Dutton. (Native American)

Literature Across the Curriculum

The following books can be used as a launching point or as an enhancement for a unit of study in a particular curriculum area.

Arnold, C. (2000). *Easter Island: Giant stone statues tell of a rich and tragic past.* Clarion. (Archaeology)

Aronson, M. & Parker, M. (2010). *If stones could speak: Unlocking the secrets of Stonehenge.* National Geographic Children's Books. (Archaeology)

Blackwood, G. (2000). *Shakespeare's scribe.* Dutton. (Language arts)

Brown, M. (2011). *Pablo Neruda: Poet of the people* (J. Paschkis, Ill.). Henry Holt. (Literature)

Buettner, D. (1997). *Africatrek: A journey by bicycle through Africa.* Lerner. (Geography)

Burleigh, R. (2012). *George Bellows: Painter with a punch!* (G. Bellows, Ill.). Abrams Books for Young Readers. (Art)

Campbell, S. C. (2010). *Growing patterns: Fibonacci numbers in nature* (S. C. Campbell, R. P. Campbell, photos). Boyds Mills Press. (Math)

Carter, D. A., & Diaz, J. (1999). *The elements of pop-ups: A pop-up book for aspiring paper engineers.* Simon & Schuster. (Art)

Cerullo, M. M. (2000). *The truth about great white sharks* (J. L. Rotman, Ill.). Chronicle. (Science)

Cerullo, M. M. & Roper, C. F. E. (2012). *Giant squid: Searching for a sea monster.* Capstone Press. (Biology)

Creech, S. (2000). *The wanderer.* (D. Diaz, Ill.). Cotler/HarperCollins. (Writing)

Demi. (1997). *One grain of rice: A mathematical folktale.* Scholastic. (Math)

Elkins-Tanton, L. (2010). *The Earth and the moon. Facts on file.* (Science/ Astronomy)

Fleming, C. (2011). *Amelia lost: The life and disappearance of Amelia Earhart.* Schwartz & Wade. (History)

Fradin, D. B. (2000). *Bound for the North Star: True stories of fugitive slaves.* Clarion. (History)

Fradin, J. B. & Fradin, D. B. (2011). *Tornado!: The story behind these twisting, turning, spinning, and spiraling storms.* National Geographic Children's Books. (Earth science)

Gardner, R. (2011). *Recycle: Green science projects for a sustainable planet.* Enslow. (Science/Environment)

Gondosch, L. (2011). *How did tea and taxes spark a revolution?: And other questions about the Boston Tea Party*. Lerner Classroom. (History)

Green, D. (2012). *The elements*. Scholastic Reference. (Science)

Jackson, D. M. (2000). *The wildlife detectives: How forensic scientists fight crimes against nature*. Houghton Mifflin. (Science)

Jones, C. F. (1999). *Yukon gold: The story of the Klondike goldrush*. Holiday House. (History)

Matthews, T. L. (1999). *Always inventing: A photobiography of Alexander Graham Bell*. National Geographic Society. (Science)

Monceau, M. (1994). *Jazz: My music, my people*. Knopf. (Music)

Montgomery, S. (2010). *Kakapo rescue: Saving the world's strangest parrot* (N. Bishop, photos). HMH Books for Young Readers. (Science/Biology)

Moore, C. (2011). *From then to now: A short history of the world* (A. Krystoforski, Ill.). Tundra Books. (History)

Nagda, A. W., & Bickel, C. (2000). *Tiger math: Learning to graph from a baby tiger*. Holt. (Math)

Rochelle, B. (Ed.). (2001). *Words with wings: A treasury of African-American poetry and art*. HarperCollins. (Poetry/Art)

Ross, S. (2011). *Into the unknown: How great explorers found their way by land, sea, and air* (S. Biesty, Ill.). Candlewick. (Geography/History)

Roth, S. L. & Trumbore, C. (2011) *The mangrove tree: Planting trees to feed families*. Lee & Low Books. (Science/Environment)

Sheinkin, S. (2012) Bomb: *The race to build—and steal—the world's most dangerous weapon*. Flash Point (Science)

Stanley, D. (2000). *Roughing it on the Oregon Trail* (H. Berry, Ill.). Cotler/HarperCollins. (History)

Vigna, G. (1999). *Jazz and its history*. Baron's. (Music/History)

Walker, P. and Wood, E. (2010). *Space and astronomy experiments*. Facts on File. (Science/Astronomy)

Literature to Provoke Discussion

The following books concern relevant, provocative issues and would be useful for engaging students in grades 4–8 in lively discussions.

Aylette, J. (1990). *Families: A celebration of diversity, commitment, and love*. Harper & Row. (Diverse family configurations)

Fenner, C. (1998). *The king of dragons*. McElderry. (Homelessness)

Fleishman, P. (1991). *The borning room*. HarperCollins. (Intergenerational relationships)

Krull, K. (1999). *They saw the future: Oracles, psychics, scientists, great thinkers, and pretty good guessers* (K. Brooker, Ill.). Atheneum. (Parapsychology)

Macy, S., & Gottesman, J. (Eds.). (1999). *Play like a girl: A celebration of women in sports*. Holt. (Sexism)

Pettit, J. (1993). *My name is San Ho*. Scholastic. (Stepfamilies)

Rosen, M. J. (1995). *Bonesy and Isabel*. Harcourt Brace. (Death of a pet)

Strachan, I. (1990). *Flawed glass*. Little, Brown. (Disabilities)

Woodson, J. (2001). *The other side* (E.B. Lewis, Ill.). Putnam. (Racism)

Books to Promote Visual Literacy

G raphic novels and picture books can promote not only visual literacy but also independent reading and content learning. Following are books that can be used for these purposes and are appropriate for grades 4–8.

GRAPHIC NOVELS (list adapted from S. Kane, 2007)

Amir (2011). *Zahra's paradise* (Khalil, Ill.). First Second.

Avi. (1993). *City of light, city of dark: A comic book novel* (B. Floca, art). Orchard Books.

Bradbury, R. (2003). *The best of Ray Bradbury: The graphic novel.* iBooks.

Briggs, R. (1998). *Ethel & Ernest: A true story.* Knopf.

Crane, S. (2005). *The red badge of courage* (W. Vansant, Ill.). Puffin Graphics.

Curry, P., & Zarate, O. (1996). *Introducing Machiavelli.* Totem Books.

Eisner, W. (1986). *Will Eisner's The big city.* Kitchen Sink Press.

Eisner, W. (2003). *Fagin the Jew: A graphic novel.* Doubleday.

Factoid Books. (1999). *The big book of Grimm, by the Brothers Grimm as channeled by J. Vankin and over 50 top comic artists!* Paradox Press.

Garza, X. (2011). *Maximilian and the mystery of the guardian angel: A bilingual lucha libre thriller.* Cinco Puntos Press.

Gerszak, R. with D. Hunter (2011). *Beyond bullets: A photo journal of Afghanistan.* Annick Press.

Giardino, V. (1997). *A Jew in Communist Prague: 1. Loss of innocence.* NBM Comics Lit.

Gonick, L., & Outwater, A. (1996). *The cartoon guide to the environment.* HarperCollins.

Harder, J. (2004). *Leviathan.* Comics Lit/NBM.

Harris, S. (1989). *Einstein simplified: Cartoons on science.* Rutgers University Press.

Lyga, B. (2011). *MangaMan.* (C. Doran, Ill.). Houghton Mifflin Harcourt.

Martin, M. (2005). *Harriet Tubman and the underground railroad.* Capstone Press.

Martin, M. (2005). *The Salem witch trials.* Capstone Press.

McKissack, P. C. (2011). *Never forgotten.* (L. Dillon, D. Dillon, Ill.). Schwartz & Wade.

Myers, W. D. (2011). *We are America: A tribute from the heart* (C. Myers, Ill.). HarperCollins.

Olson, K.M. (2005). *The assassination of Abraham Lincoln.* Capstone Press.

Pomplun, T. (Ed.). (2004). *Graphic classics: Edgar Allan Poe* (2nd ed.). Eureka Productions.

Reed, G. (2005). *Mary Shelley's Frankenstein: The graphic novel.* Penguin/Puffin.

Robbins, T. (2011). *Lily Renee, escape artist: From Holocaust survivor to comic book pioneer* (A. Timmons, M. Oh, Ill.). Graphic Universe.

Sartrapi, M. (2003). *Persepolis: The story of a childhood.* Pantheon Books.

Shanower, E. (2004). *Sacrifice.* Image Comics.

Spiegelman, A. (1997). *Maus: A survivor's tale.* Pantheon.

Thompson, C. (2006). *Good-bye, Chunky Rice*. Pantheon.

Winick, J. (2000). *Pedro & me: Friendship, loss, and what I learned*. Henry Holt.

Yezerski, T. F. (2011). *Meadowlands: A wetlands survival story*. Farrar Straus Giroux.

Young, E. (2011). *The house Baba built: An artist's childhood in China*. Text as told to Libby Koponen. Little, Brown.

PICTURE BOOKS

Ambrose, S. (2001). *The good fight: How World War II was won*. Atheneum.

Barasch, L. (2005). *Ask Albert Einstein*. Farrar, Straus & Giroux.

Bunting, E. (1991). *Fly away home*. Clarion.

Carey, C. (2000). *The Emancipation Proclamation*. Child's World.

Close, C. (2012). *Chuck Close: Face book*. Abrams Books for Young Readers.

Coerr, E., & Young, E. (1993). *Sadako*. Putnam.

Craats, R. (2000). *The science of sound*. Garth Stevens.

Feelings, T. (1995). *The Middle Passage: White ships/black cargo*. Dial.

Fielding, B. (2011). *Animal eyes*. EarlyLight Books.

Hopkinson, D. (2003). *Sweet Clara and the freedom quilt*. Knopf Books for Young Readers.

Jackson, D. (1996). *The bone detectives: How forensic anthropologists solve crimes and uncover mysteries of the dead*. Photos by C. Fellenbaum. Little, Brown.

King, M. (1997). *I have a dream*. (Paintings by 15 Coretta Scott King Award and Honor Book Artists.) Scholastic.

Kodama, T. (1995). *Shin's tricycle*. Walker Books.

Lember, B. (1997). *The shell book*. Houghton Mifflin.

McEwan, I., & Innocenti, R. (2004). *Rose Blanche*. London: Red Fox.

McKissack, P. C. (2011). *Never forgotten* (L. Dillon, D. Dillon, Ill.). Schwartz & Wade.

Murphy, P. (2004). *Grace Hopper: Computer whiz*. Enslow.

Nivola, C. A. (2011). *Orani: My father's village*. Farrar, Straus and Giroux.

Riley, J. (2005). *The nervous system*. Lerner.

Sloan, C. & Buigues, B. (2011). *Baby mammoth mummy frozen in time: A prehistoric animal's journey into the 21st century*. Photographs by Francis Latreille. National Geographic Children's Books.

Strother, R. (2011). *B is for blue planet: An earth science alphabet* (B. Marstall, Ill.). Sleeping Bear Press.

Summer, L. (2001). *The march on Washington*. Child's World.

Tang, G., & Briggs, H. (2001). *The grapes of math: Mind-stretching math riddles*. Scholastic.

Recreational

The following books can form a foundation for a classroom library for the purpose of recreational reading in grades 4–8. These books were selected by teachers or students for their overall appeal to all readers.

Almond, D. (2000). *Kit's wilderness*. Delacorte.

Applegate, K. (2012). *The one and only Ivan*. HarperCollins.

Ayres, K. (2000). *Silver dollar girl*. Delacorte.

Baker, J. (1987). *Where the forest meets the sea*. Greenwillow.

Blume, J. (1972). *Tales of a fourth-grade nothing*. Dutton. (And other books by this author)

Buchanan, J. (2001). *Hank's story*. Farrar, Straus & Giroux.

Curtis, C. P. (1999). *It's Bud, not Buddy*. Delacorte.

Cushman, C. (1995). *Catherine called Birdy*. Clarion.

Deutsch, B. (2010). *Hereville: How Mirka got her sword*. Amulet Books.

Howe, D., & Howe, J. (1979). *Bunnicula: A rabbit-tale of mystery*. Atheneum. (And other books in the series)

L'Engle, M. (1962). *A wrinkle in time*. Farrar, Straus & Giroux. (And other books by this author)

Lemieux, M. (1999). *Stormy night*. Kids Can Press.

Lowry, L. (1989). *Number the stars*. Houghton Mifflin.

Naylor, P. R. (1991). *Shiloh*. Atheneum.

O'Connell, C., & Jackson, D. M. (2011). *The elephant scientist* (C. O'Connell, T. Rodwell, photos). HMH Books for Young Readers.

Patterson, K. (1977). *Bridge to Terabithia*. Crowell.

Rocklin, J. (2012). *The five lives of our cat Zook*. Amulet Books.

Rylander, C. (2011). *The fourth stall*. Walden Pond Press.

Schlitz, L. A. (2010). *The night fairy* (A. Barrett, Ill.). Candlewick.

Schlitz, L. A. (2012). *Splendors and gloom*. Candlewick.

Sommer, S. (2011). *Hammerin' Hank Greenberg: Baseball pioneer*. Boyds Mills Press.

Spinelli, J. (1998). *Wringer*. HarperCollins.

Tomecek, S. (2010). *Sports (Experimenting with everyday science)*. Chelsea House.

Venkatraman, P. (2011). *Island's end*. Putnam.

Wang, G. (2011). *The garden of Empress Cassia*. Puffin.

Wilder, L. I. (1953). *Little house in the big woods*. Harper & Row. (And other books in this series)

Wolitzer, M. (2011). *The fingertips of Duncan Dorfman*. Puffin.

Yep, L. (2000). *Dream soul*. HarperCollins.

Appendix (B)

The following websites will be especially helpful for teachers of literacy. The sites include lesson plans in the language arts, as well as ideas for curriculum integration with other subject areas. Some of the sites can also be used by learners in the classroom and at home. Many of the sites have both teacher and student links.

http://gws.ala.org/

The American Library Association's Great Websites for Kids links to hundreds of worthwhile sites for learners of all ages. Topics include Animals, The Arts, Literature & Languages, History & Biography, Sciences, and Mathematics & Computers.

http://a4esl.org

This site includes grammar quizzes, crossword puzzles, and Internet scavenger hunts designed especially for students who are English learners.

www.rockhall.com

This site is for the Cleveland Rock & Roll Hall of Fame. It offers programs for teachers that integrate music with history and literature.

www.awesomelibrary.org

More than 33,000 carefully reviewed resources are organized by school subject for teachers, young children, teenagers, and parents. The top 5 percent education websites are included.

http://bookadventure.com

This site provides a child-oriented reading program designed to encourage students in grades K–8 to read more often, for longer periods of time, and with greater understanding, offering stories, contests, quizzes, and awards.

https://www.ceismc.gatech.edu/

This easy-to-use, award-winning site provides busy K–12 teachers with annotated links to source material, lesson plans, and classroom activities.

www.education-world.com

Found on this site are a variety of lesson plans, activities, and current news integrating the language arts with all disciplines.

www.pearsondigital.com

A provider of digital learning solutions focused on the art and science of teaching and on helping all learners reach their potential.

http://englishonline.tki.org.nz/

Originating in New Zealand, this site for K–12 English teachers is part of a professional development program comprising unit plans created by teachers throughout New Zealand and covering all grade levels.

www.free.ed.gov/

Sponsored by more than 30 federal agencies, this site provides a host of learning resources such as reading activities, famous paintings, historical documents, web-based tools, and ask-an-expert services.

www.scholastic.com

Teacher lesson plans and classroom activities are provided here. Specific materials for current books, such as the Harry Potter series, address the books, the authors, and the stories.

www.kidsplanet.org

This site provides a bibliography of books about specific species of animals, a large database of wolf-related curriculum designed for integrated language arts units, and much more.

www.rhlschool.com/reading.htm

This site offers weekly worksheets, mostly for upper-elementary and middle school students, for teachers to copy and use at no charge.

http://libguides.ivytech.edu/content.php?pid=59157&sid=3756619

Offered here is a plethora of information about children's and young adult's authors and illustrators.

www.eduplace.com

This site provides classroom resources for teachers, including graphic organizers and online links.

www.poetry.com

On this site students can post their poems, enter poetry contests, use the world's most comprehensive rhyming dictionary, and read hundreds of poems by other students and accomplished poets.

http://people.ucalgary.ca/~dkbrown/

The Children's Literature Web Guide is devoted entirely to young adult and children's literature.

www.artsconnected.org/

A database of educational materials for using the arts in the classroom.

http://ctell.uconn.edu/cases/newliteracies.htm

Using 12 principles of effective literacy instruction, the Case Technologies to Enhance Literacy Learning (CTELL) group designs and assesses CTELL cases to inform preservice teacher education on best practices.

www.smithsonianeducation.org

The Smithsonian Center for Education and Museum Studies links educators, families, and students to hundreds of online resources. Educators will find ideas for lesson plans and field trips in addition to websites and related publications.

www.readwritethink.org

This IRA- and NCTE-sponsored site presents educators and students with the highest quality practices and resources in reading and language arts instruction.

www.loc.gov

The Library of Congress website provides resources for kids and families as well as teachers.

Fluency

READERS THEATRE

www.aaronshep.com/rt/RTE.html
www.teachingheart.net/readerstheater.htm
http://users.humboldt.edu/jfloss/rt-eval.html

TEACHING FLUENCY THROUGH POETRY

www.poetry4kids.com

FLUENCY CALCULATOR

http://teacher.scholastic.com/reading/bestpractices/assessment/OFAcalc.htm

Vocabulary

VOCABULARY INSTRUCTION

www.vocabulary.com

CHAPTER BOOKS TO READ ALOUD

www.kinderkorner.com/readalouds.html

VOCABULARY LESSON PLANS

http://lessonplancentral.com/lessons/Language_Arts/Vocabulary/index.htm

OTHER VOCABULARY DEVELOPMENT

www.techteachers.com/vocabulary.htm

Appendix C

How the Tools in this Appendix Are Organized:

NAME: _____   GRADE: _____   DATE: _____

1. What do you like to do most when you have spare time?

    _____

2. What do you usually do after school?

    _____

    . . . in the evenings?

    _____

    _____

    . . . on weekends?

    _____

    _____

    . . . on vacations?

    _____

    _____

3. Do you have brothers or sisters? If so, what activities do you like to do with them?

    _____

    _____

    _____

4. Are your parents/grandparents from a different country? Which one? What language do they speak?

    _____

5. What is the best movie/video you have ever seen? What did you like about it?

    _____

    _____

6. What is your favorite television show? What do you like about it?

    _____

    _____

7. Do you ever listen to the news on television?

    _____

8. What is your favorite sport and who is your favorite sports figure?

    _____

9. What songs/music do you like?

    _____

    _____

10. Do you take any special lessons? Describe them.

_____

_____

11. Do you have any pets? If not, what kind of animal(s) do you like or wish to own?

_____

12. If you could meet anyone in the world, who would you choose?

_____

13. What kind of job would you like to do?

_____

14. Which of the following do you enjoy reading? (circle all that apply)

magazines	newspapers	catalogs
comic books/strips	books	manuals
graphic novels	ebooks	

15. What kinds of books appeal to you? (circle all that apply)

fantasy	true stories	action/adventure
biographies	mysteries	romance
how to	humor	historical fiction
autobiography	books in a series	poetry
travel books	books based on TV characters	science fiction

16. What book is your all-time favorite? Why?

_____

_____

17. Do you like to have someone read to you?

_____

18. Do you prefer to read alone or with someone?

_____

19. What books would you like to own?

_____

_____

20. Which of the following describe the kinds of books you most enjoy? (circle as many as apply)

scary	sad	believable
adventurous	informative	unbelievable
insightful	humorous	characters like me
helpful	historical	characters unlike me

Attitude surveys address students' perceptions of reading and writing as processes and their perceptions of themselves as readers and writers. An interview format is appropriate for providing the teacher with this information. The interview might include some of the following key questions:

- Do you like to read (write)?
- What is your favorite book (or who is your favorite author)?
- When do you read (write)?
- Do you think you are a good reader (writer)? Why or why not?
- Who is the best reader (writer) you know? Why?
- When you do not understand what you've read, what do you do?
- Would you rather read (write) or play sports?
- Would you rather read (write) or watch a movie?
- Would you rather read (write) or play a video game?
- Would you rather read a story or write a story?
- Would you rather read (write) or do nothing?
- Would you rather read (write) or paint?
- Would you rather read (write) or do math homework?
- Would you rather read (write) or help with the chores?

Open-ended statements are also used to assess attitudes. For example, the student might be asked to complete the following sentences:

What I like most about reading is

_____

_____

I think writing

_____

_____

Most books

_____

_____

My writing

_____

_____

When my teacher reads

_____

_____

Adapted from Gipe, J. P. (2006). *Multiple Paths to Literacy: Assessment and Differentiated Instruction for Diverse Learners, K–12* (6th ed, p. 137). Upper Saddle River, NJ: Merrill-Prentice Hall.

appendix C.3 Reading Attitude Survey—Handout Format

NAME: _____ DATE: _____

Directions: Check the circle for each of your choices.

○ I like reading a lot.
○ Reading is O.K.
○ I'd rather do other things.

What kinds of books do you like to read? Check as many as you like.

○ realistic fiction   ○ picture books
○ poetry   ○ true facts
○ fantasy   ○ folktales and fables
○ myths   ○ mysteries
○ historical fiction   ○ plays
○ biographies (about real people)   ○ science fiction
○ graphic novels   ○ ebooks
○ (write any other kind you like here)

_____

_____

_____

How do you choose something to read?

○ I listen to a friend   ○ I look to see if it's easy enough
○ I look at the front cover   ○ I look to see if it's hard enough
○ if it's part of a series I like   ○ I read the back cover or jacket flap
○ I read the first few pages   ○ I follow my teacher's suggestion
○ if I liked other books by that author

When do you prefer to read?

○ in my spare time
○ at home
○ as part of my class work

How do you like to read?

○ with friends
○ with kids who read about the same as I do
○ by myself
○ with my teacher in the group

Description

The *Denver Reading Attitude Survey* provides an indication of students' engagement in reading activities, their perception of the importance and utility of reading, and their confidence in themselves as readers. The survey includes a few items from the National Assessment of Educational Progress.

Instructions for Administering

So that the results of the survey are not affected by variations in reading ability, read each item aloud. Students respond to each item by circling the letter of their response.

Spanish and English versions are available. Students should complete the survey in the language they are most confident using.

Explain that the purpose of the survey is to learn students' honest feelings about reading in and out of school. Emphasize that this is not a test; there are no right or wrong answers, and the results will have no effect on grades.

As you read the items, clarify them and answer questions as needed. Also draw attention to each change in the response format.

NAME: _____ GRADE: _____

TEACHER: _____ DATE: _____

Make a circle around the answer that is most true for you.

How often do you do each of the following things?

	Almost every day	Once or twice a week	Once or twice a month	A few times a year	Never or hardly ever
1. Get so interested in something you're reading that you don't want to stop.	A	B	C	D	E
2. Read the newspaper.	A	B	C	D	E
3. Tell a friend about a good book.	A	B	C	D	E
4. Read on your own outside of school.	A	B	C	D	E
5. Read about something because you are curious about it.	A	B	C	D	E
6. Read more than one book by an author you like.	A	B	C	D	E

7. What kind of reader do you think you are?

   A. A very good reader.

   B. A good reader.

   C. An average reader.

   D. A poor reader.

   E. A very poor reader.

(continued)

Denver Reading Attitude Survey, CONTINUED   **appendix** C.4

The following statements are true for some people. They may or may not be true for you, or they may be true for you only part of the time. How often is each of the following sentences true for you?

	Almost always	More than half the time	About half the time	Less than half the time	Never or hardly ever
8. Reading helps me learn about myself.	A	B	C	D	E
9. I feel good about how fast I can read.	A	B	C	D	E
10. Reading helps me understand why people feel or act the way they do.	A	B	C	D	E
11. I believe that reading will help me get ahead when I am no longer in school.	A	B	C	D	E
12. I feel proud about what I can read.	A	B	C	D	E
13. Reading helps me see what it might be like to live in a different place or in a different way.	A	B	C	D	E
14. Being able to read well is important to me.	A	B	C	D	E
15. I can understand what I read in school.	A	B	C	D	E
16. Other people think I read well.	A	B	C	D	E
17. I learn worthwhile things from reading books.	A	B	C	D	E

appendix **C.5** Encuesta Sobre Lectura de Denver

NOMBRE: _____ GRADO: _____

MAESTRO/A: _____ FECHE: _____

Encierre en un círculo la letra de la respuesta que sea mas cierta para usted.

¿Con que frecuencia hace cada una de las siguientes cosas?

	Casi cada día	Una o dos veces por semana	Una o dos veces por mes	Varias veces por año	Nunca o casi nunca
1. Se interesa tanto en la lectura que no puede dejar de leer.	A	B	C	D	E
2. Lee el periódico.	A	B	C	D	E
3. Le plactica a un(a) amigo(a) de un buen libro.	A	B	C	D	E
4. Lee libros de texto (como por ejemplo de ciencias sociales o naturales).	A	B	C	D	E
5. Lee algo por curiosidad.	A	B	C	D	E
6. Lee más de un libro de algún escritor que le guste.	A	B	C	D	E

7. ¿Qué tipo de lector se considera usted?

    A. Excelente lector.

    B. Buen lector.

    C. Lector regular.

    D. Lector con problemas.

    E. Lector con muchos problemas.

(continued)

Las siguientes declaraciones se refieren a ciertas personas. Estas declaraciones no necesariamente son aplicables a usted, o serán ciertas solo en algunas ocasiones. ¿Con qué frecuencia es cada una de las siguientes declaraciones cierta para usted?

	Casi siempre	Más de la mitad del tiempo	Como la mitad del tiempo	Menos de la mitad del tiempo	Nunca o casi nunca
8. La lectura me ayuda a aprender de mi mismo(a).	A	B	C	D	E
9. Me gusta la rapidez con la que leo.	A	B	C	D	E
10. La lectura me ayuda a entender por qué la gente se siente o actuá de la manera en que lo hace.	A	B	C	D	E
11. Pienso que la lectura me ayudará a salir adelante cuando ya no esté en la escuela.	A	B	C	D	E
12. Me siento orgulloso(a) de lo que puedo leer.	A	B	C	D	E
13. La lectura me ayuda a ver cómo sería vivir de otra manera o en otro lugar.	A	B	C	D	E
14. El poder leer bien es importante para mi.	A	B	C	D	E
15. Entiendo mi lectura escolar.	A	B	C	D	E
16. Otra gente piensa que yo leo bien.	A	B	C	D	E
17. Aprendo cosas que valen la pena a través de libros.	A	B	C	D	E

appendix C.6 Running Record Form

STUDENT: _____ DATE: _____

TEACHER: _____ READING LEVEL: _____

STORY: _____

NUMBER OF ERRORS: _____ PERCENTAGE: _____

RUNNING WORDS: _____ LEVEL FOR STUDENT: EASY, INSTRUCTIONAL, FRUSTRATION

COMMENTS:

Analysis of errors and self-corrections

TEXT

INFORMATION USED

Page of text	E M S V	SC M S V

Checklist for Observations of Progress Toward Standards*   appendix C.7

NAME: _____   GRADE: _____

STANDARDS	CONTEXT	DATE OBS.	CONTEXT	DATE OBS.	CONTEXT	DATE OBS.
CCSS.ELA-Literacy. CCRA.R.1 Read closely to determine what the text says explicitly and to make logical inferences from it; cite specific textual evidence when writing or speaking to support conclusions drawn from the text.						
CCSS.ELA-Literacy. CCRA.R.2 Determine central ideas or themes of a text and analyze their development; summarize the key supporting details and ideas.						
CCSS.ELA-Literacy. CCRA.R.3 Analyze how and why individuals, events, or ideas develop and interact over the course of a text.						
CCSS.ELA-Literacy. CCRA.R.4 Interpret words and phrases as they are used in a text, including determining technical, connotative, and figurative meanings, and analyze how specific word choices shape meaning or tone.						
CCSS.ELA-Literacy. CCRA.R.5 Analyze the structure of texts, including how specific sentences, paragraphs, and larger portions of the text (e.g., a section, chapter, scene, or stanza) relate to each other and the whole.						
CCSS.ELA-Literacy. CCRA.R.6 Assess how point of view or purpose shapes the content and style of a text.						
CCSS.ELA-Literacy. CCRA.R.7 Integrate and evaluate content presented in diverse media and formats, including visually and quantitatively, as well as in words.						
CCSS.ELA-Literacy. CCRA.R.8 Delineate and evaluate the argument and specific claims in a text, including the validity of the reasoning as well as the relevance and sufficiency of the evidence.						
CCSS.ELA-Literacy. CCRA.R.9 Analyze how two or more texts address similar themes or topics in order to build knowledge or to compare the approaches the authors take.						
CCSS.ELA-Literacy. CCRA.R.10 Read and comprehend complex literary and informational texts independently and proficiently.						

*The standards used in this checklist are the English Language Arts Standards, College and Career Readiness Anchor Standards for Reading. Any state standards could be used, and the checklist can be made grade-level specific using state standards and the grade-level specific CCSS.

Source: National Governors Association Center for Best Practices (NGACBP) & Council of Chief State School Officers (CCSSO). (2010). English Language Arts Standards, College and Career Readiness Anchor Standards for Reading. Washington D.C.: National Governors Association Center for Best Practices, Council of Chief State School Officers.

appendix C.8   Reading Observation Checklist

NAME: _____   GRADE LEVEL: _____   TEACHER: _____

CONTENT STANDARDS	DATE						COMMENTS
Reads narrative text with fluency							
Reads expository text with fluency							
Identifies main events of the plot							
Makes inferences using text							
Makes inferences using illustrations							
Identifies structural patterns in expository text:							
–compare and contrast							
–cause and effect							
–order (enumeration or sequential)							
Asks questions							
Makes predictions							
Monitors own understanding							
Applies appropriate fix-up strategies							
Creates mental images while reading							
Retells to include salient points							
Makes text-to-self connections							
Uses clues to determine word meanings:							
–word clues							
–sentence or paragraph clues							
–background knowledge							

| Informational Text Retelling Self-Assessment | appendix C.9 |

NAME: _____

SELECTION: _____

1. What is the topic?

2. What are the most important ideas to remember?

3. What did you learn that you did not already know?

4. What is the setting for the information?

5. What did you notice about the organization and text structure?

6. What new vocabulary did you learn?

7. What did you notice about the visuals, such as graphs, charts, and pictures?

8. Can you summarize what you have learned?

9. What do you think was the author's purpose for writing this material?

Adapted from L. Hoyt (1999). *Revisit, reflect, retell: Strategies for improving reading comprehension.* Portsmouth, NH: Heinemann.

Directions: Dictate the following words in groups of five. After saying each word, use it in a sentence. Then repeat the word. You may wish to stop your assessment at the end of a set if students seem frustrated with a particular group of words. Possible script: "I want you to spell some words. You have not had the chance to study these words, but I want you to spell them the best that you can. Some might be easy for you, and some might seem hard. If you think you don't know how to spell the word, just listen carefully to the word, say it to yourself, and then write down all the sounds you hear."

SET ONE

1. drawing   Joey was drawing a picture of a dog. *drawing*
2. trapped   The animals were trapped in their cages. *trapped*
3. waving   Mom was waving hello to us from the car. *waving*
4. powerful   The alligator's jaws are powerful. *powerful*
5. battle   The Battle of the Bands is this Saturday. *battle*

SET TWO

6. sailor   Christopher Columbus was a sailor. *sailor*
7. lesson   Pat has a piano lesson every Tuesday. *lesson*
8. pennies   Save your pennies for a rainy day. *pennies*
9. fraction   One-fourth is a fraction. *fraction*
10. distance   The distance for the race is three miles. *distance*

SET THREE

11. visible   The Big Dipper is visible without a telescope. *visible*
12. confusion   There was confusion over who was in charge. *confusion*
13. discovery   The scientists made a great discovery. *discovery*
14. resident   You are a resident of planet Earth. *resident*
15. fortunate   I was fortunate to win the grand prize. *fortunate*

SET FOUR

16. pleasure   Reading a good book brings me pleasure. *pleasure*
17. puncture   He used a sharp pencil to puncture a hole in the balloon. *puncture*
18. confidence   The speaker showed confidence when on stage. *confidence*
19. decorator   They hired a decorator to help them fix up their house. *decorator*
20. opposition   There was too much opposition to the idea and so most people voted against it. *opposition*

(continued)

Student Record Sheet for Developmental Comparisons

NAME: _____

DATE: _____ SPELLING LEVEL: _____

STAGE

1. _____ _____
2. _____ _____
3. _____ _____
4. _____ _____
5. _____ _____
6. _____ _____
7. _____ _____
8. _____ _____
9. _____ _____
10. _____ _____
11. _____ _____
12. _____ _____
13. _____ _____
14. _____ _____
15. _____ _____
16. _____ _____
17. _____ _____
18. _____ _____
19. _____ _____
20. _____ _____

NAME: _____

DATE: _____ SPELLING LEVEL: _____

STAGE

1. _____ _____
2. _____ _____
3. _____ _____
4. _____ _____
5. _____ _____
6. _____ _____
7. _____ _____
8. _____ _____
9. _____ _____
10. _____ _____
11. _____ _____
12. _____ _____
13. _____ _____
14. _____ _____
15. _____ _____
16. _____ _____
17. _____ _____
18. _____ _____
19. _____ _____
20. _____ _____

How to Analyze Students' Spellings

1. Look at the student's spelling for each word. Match the spelling with the spelling in the Scoring Chart (p. 368), or find the spelling that comes closest.
2. Write an abbreviation of the matching spelling stage beside each of the words on the Student Record Sheet for Developmental Comparisons.
3. The stage that appears most often is the label that will be used as the spelling level for that administration date. Administer the same words again three to four months later for a comparison.

REFERENCES

Bear, D. R., Invernizzi, M., Templeton, S., & Johnston, F. (2000). *Words their way: Word study for phonics, vocabulary, and spelling instruction.* Upper Saddle River, NJ: Merrill.

Fiderer, A. (1995). *Practical assessments for literature-based reading classrooms.* New York: Scholastic Professional Books.

appendix C.10 Spelling Inventory, CONTINUED

Scoring Chart for Spelling Inventory

Directions: Locate the spelling in the lists below that matches or comes closest to the student's spelling. Look straight up at the heading for the spelling stage represented by that spelling in the developmental continuum. Write that stage on the student record sheet.

Spelling Developmental Continuum for Intermediate Grades

| TRANSITIONAL | | SYLLABLES AND AFFIXES | | | DERIVATIONAL RELATIONS | | |
Middle	Late	Early	Middle	Late	Early	Middle	Late
draing	drauing	drawing					
trapt	traped	trappt	trapped				
waiving	weighving	waveing	waving				
pauerfle	pouerful	powerfle	powerfel	powerful			
batul	batil/batel	batle/battul	battle				
saler	sayler/saylor	sailer	sailor				
lisin	lesen/lesin/leson	lessin/lessen	lesson				
penes/penez	penknees/penees	penys/pennys	pennies				
	frakshun		frackshun	fracktion	fraction		
dizdance	disdance	distanz	distans	distance			
vizabull	vizabel	vizabul	vizable	visable	visible		
confushon	confushun/confution	confustion	conffusion	confusetion	confussion	confusion	
diskuverie	diskkuveree	discuveree	discovere	discoverie	discovery		
resatin	reserdent	rezudint	resadent/resedint	reseadent	resedent	residant	resident
	forhnat/frehnit	foohinit	forchenut/fochininte	fortunet	fortunate		
	plasr/plager/plejer	pleser	plesour	plesher	plesure/pleasur	pleasure	
	pucshr/pungchr/puncur	pucker/punksher	punchure	puncure	punture	puncsure	puncture
	confadents	confadence	confedense	confedence	confidince	confidense	confidence
	dector/decrater	decerator	decarator	decreator	decoratore	decorater	decorator
	opasishan/opozcison	opasitian	opasition	oppisition	oposision	oposition	opposition

Developmental Spelling Test (The "Monster Test")   appendix C.11

An easily administered 10-word checklist, such as the following developmental test devised by Gentry (1985), makes it possible for teachers to assess children's developmental spelling level.

	WORDS	PRECOMMUNICATIVE SPELLINGS	SEMI-PHONETIC SPELLINGS	PHONETIC SPELLINGS	TRANSITIONAL SPELLINGS	CORRECT SPELLINGS
1.	monster	random letters	mtr	mostr	monstur	monster
2.	united	random letters	u	unitid	younighted	united
3.	dress	random letters	jrs	jras	dres	dress
4.	bottom	random letters	bt	bodm	bottum	bottom
5.	hiked	random letters	h	hikt	hicked	hiked
6.	human	random letters	um	humm	humin	human
7.	eagle	random letters	el	egl	egul	eagle
8.	closed	random letters	kd	klosd	clossed	closed
9.	bumped	random letters	b	bopt	bumpt	bumped
10.	type	random letters	tp	tip	tipe	type

From Gentry, J. Richard (1985). You Can Analyze Developmental Spelling. *The Early Years* (9), 44–45. Reprinted with permission.

appendix C.12   Checklist for Assessing the Nifty-Thrifty-Fifty

NIFTY-THRIFTY-FIFTY*	TRANSFERABLE	CHUNKS
1. ___ antifreeze	1. ___ anti	
2. ___ beautiful		2. ___ ful (y - i)
3. ___ classify		3. ___ ify
4. ___ communities	4. ___ com	4. ___ es (y - i)
5. ___ community	5. ___ com	5. ___ y
6. ___ composer	6. ___ com	6. ___ er
7. ___ continuous	7. ___ con	7. ___ ous (drop e)
8. ___ conversation	8. ___ con	8. ___ tion
9. ___ deodorize	9. ___ de	9. ___ ize
10. ___ different		10. ___ ent
11. ___ discovery	11. ___ dis	11. ___ y
12. ___ dishonest	12. ___ dis	
13. ___ electricity	13. ___ e	13. ___ ity
14. ___ employee	14. ___ em	14. ___ ee
15. ___ encouragement	15. ___ en	15. ___ ment
16. ___ expensive	16. ___ ex	16. ___ ive
17. ___ forecast	17. ___ fore	
18. ___ forgotten		18. ___ en (double t)
19. ___ governor		19. ___ or
20. ___ happiness		20. ___ ness (y - i)
21. ___ hopeless		21. ___ less
22. ___ illegal	22. ___ il	
23. ___ impossible	23. ___ im	23. ___ ible
24. ___ impression	24. ___ im	24. ___ sion
25. ___ independence	25. ___ in	25. ___ ence

(continued)

Checklist for Assessing the Nifty-Thrifty-Fifty, CONTINUED   appendix C.12

NIFTY-THRIFTY-FIFTY*	TRANSFERABLE	CHUNKS
26. ___ international	26. ___ inter	26. ___ al
27. ___ invasion	27. ___ in	27. ___ sion
28. ___ irresponsible	28. ___ ir	28. ___ ible
29. ___ midnight	29. ___ mid	
30. ___ misunderstand	30. ___ mis	
31. ___ musician		31. ___ ian
32. ___ nonliving	32. ___ non	32. ___ ing (drop e)
33. ___ overpower	33. ___ over	
34. ___ performance	34. ___ per	34. ___ ance
35. ___ prehistoric	35. ___ pre	35. ___ ic
36. ___ prettier		36. ___ er (y - i)
37. ___ rearrange	37. ___ re	
38. ___ replacement	38. ___ re	38. ___ ment
39. ___ richest		39. ___ est
40. ___ semifinal	40. ___ semi	
41. ___ signature		41. ___ ture
42. ___ submarine	42. ___ sub	
43. ___ supermarkets	43. ___ super	43. ___ s
44. ___ swimming		44. ___ ing (double m)
45. ___ transportation	45. ___ trans	45. ___ tion
46. ___ underweight	46. ___ under	
47. ___ unfinished	47. ___ un	47. ___ ed
48. ___ unfriendly	48. ___ un	48. ___ ly
49. ___ unpleasant	49. ___ un	49. ___ ant (drop e)
50. ___ valuable		50. ___ able (drop e)

Source: Word list from Cunningham, P. M., & R. L. Allington. *Classrooms That Work: They Can All Read and Write,* 5/e, © 2011. Printed and electronically reproduced by permission of Pearson Education, Inc., Upper Saddle River, NJ.

appendix **C.13** Scoring Rubric for an Oral Presentation

CRITERIA	NEEDS WORK (1)	MAKING PROGRESS (2)	DOING GREAT (3)	ABOVE AND BEYOND (4)	SCORE
Speaking	Monotone; speaker seemed uninterested in material.	Little eye contact; fast speaking rate, little expression, mumbling.	Clear articulation of ideas, but apparently lacks confidence with material.	Exceptional confidence with material displayed through poise, clear articulation, eye contact, and enthusiasm.	1 2 3 4
Creativity	Delivery is repetitive with little or no variety in presentation techniques; lacks visuals.	Material presented with little interpretation or originality; visual aids fail to grab attention and/or fails to communicate information.	Some apparent originality displayed through use of original interpretation of presented materials visually and/or orally.	Exceptional originality of presented material and interpretation both visually and orally.	1 2 3 4
Content	Results are unclear and information appears randomly chosen.	Results are clear, but supporting information is not available.	Results are very clear; many relevant points, but they are unaddressed.	Exceptional use of material that clearly relates to a focused thesis; abundance of varied supportive materials.	1 2 3 4
Clarity	No apparent logical order of presentation; unclear focus.	Content is loosely connected; transitions lack clarity.	Sequence of information is well organized for the most part, but more clarity with transitions is needed.	Development of thesis is clear through use of specific and appropriate examples; transitions are clear and create a succinct and even flow.	1 2 3 4
Presentation Length	Greatly exceeding or falling short of allotted time.	Exceeding or falling short of allotted time.	Remained close to the allotted time.	Presented within the allotted time.	1 2 3 4

DELIVERY (Total Possible: 36 points)

① ② ③ ④   Student used a different form to communicate to the group other than simply screen reading.

① ② ③ ④   Student used each slide as a lead into the wealth of additional information he or she found on the topic.

① ② ③ ④   Student maintained eye contact with the audience, seldom returning to notes.

① ② ③ ④   At conclusion of presentation, student checked for understanding via questions, oral quiz, written assessment, etc.

① ② ③ ④   Student used allotted time effectively; the pacing of the presentation was appropriate.

① ② ③ ④   Information was presented in a logical and interesting sequence that the audience could follow.

① ② ③ ④   Student used a clear voice and correct, precise pronunciation of terms so all audience members could hear the presentation.

① ② ③ ④   Each member of the audience was given a handout to accompany the presentation.

① ② ③ ④   Audience was engaged throughout the presentation; if engagement waned, the presenting student managed to reengage the audience.

GRAPHICS (Total Possible: 20 points)

① ② ③ ④   The presentation included a minimum of 10 slides.

① ② ③ ④   The presentation included a variety of text fields, graphics, audio, video, and transitions.

① ② ③ ④   The presentation had a professional look with an overall graphical theme appealing to the audience, with each slide visually neat and incorporating a variety of layouts.

① ② ③ ④   Student's graphics explained and reinforced screen text and oral presentation.

① ② ③ ④   Text fields were not overly crowded with text, and used a readable font and font size.

(continued)

appendix C.14 Scoring Rubric for a Multimedia Presentation, CONTINUED

CONTENT (Total Possible: 28 points)

① ② ③ ④ All material was thoroughly proofread and without careless errors.

① ② ③ ④ All information was well researched and well written, and reflects the student's own voice.

① ② ③ ④ All flaws pointed out by the instructor and/or peer reviewers in drafts have been corrected.

① ② ③ ④ Material showed strong understanding of major ideas and displayed evidence of critical thinking.

① ② ③ ④ Presentation included a title page.

① ② ③ ④ Presentation included a bibliography following specified citation rules.

① ② ③ ④ Student demonstrated full knowledge of the topic by answering all class questions with explanations and elaborations.

TECHNICAL SKILL (Total Possible: 16 points)

① ② ③ ④ Student can access the presentation and all linked and embedded materials and has saved the presentation and has also made a backup copy of the presentation to insure against any disaster.

① ② ③ ④ Student was facile at operating all equipment used during the presentation.

① ② ③ ④ An electronic form of the presentation has been given to the instructor via thumb drive, server, email, or other means.

① ② ③ ④ The handout each member of the audience received includes an area to take notes.

TOTAL POINTS = _____ **of 100**   Delivery = 36   Graphics = 20   Content = 28   Technical Skill = 16

Circle Y for "Yes" and N for "No" after each question about your listening habits and attitudes.

1. I like to listen to others.   Ⓨ Ⓝ

2. I listen even if I do not like the person who is talking.   Ⓨ Ⓝ

3. I listen even if I do not like the topic.   Ⓨ Ⓝ

4. I treat all people the same when I listen to them—whether or not they are friends, family, adults, children, male, female, or from a different country.   Ⓨ Ⓝ

5. I stop what I am doing so that I can give the speaker my full attention.   Ⓨ Ⓝ

6. I look at the speaker.   Ⓨ Ⓝ

7. I let the speaker finish what she/he is saying before I begin talking.   Ⓨ Ⓝ

8. I sometimes repeat back to the speaker what she/he said to see if I got it right.   Ⓨ Ⓝ

9. I ask questions if I don't understand an idea.   Ⓨ Ⓝ

10. I try to improve my listening.   Ⓨ Ⓝ

Source: Cooper, P. & Morreale, S. (Eds.) (2003). *Creating competent communicators,* p. 95. Scottsdale, AZ: Holcomb Hathaway.

appendix **C.16** Editing Checklist

| | PEER | |
| AUTHOR | EDITOR | |

○ ○ 1. Did I read the piece backward, one sentence at a time, to check for spelling errors, sentence fragments, and run-on sentences?

○ ○ 2. Did I use a dictionary, friend, spell checker, or other resource to find spelling errors?

○ ○ 3. Did I check to make sure all proper nouns and the first words of each sentence are capitalized?

○ ○ 4. Did I indent each paragraph?

○ ○ 5. Did I make sure each sentence has the appropriate ending punctuation?

○ ○ 6. Did I use commas appropriately? Are they only used for compound sentences, lists of items, introductory words or phrases, to set off interruptions, to separate adjectives, or in dates?

○ ○ 7. Do I need to add commas? Have I made sure commas are not separating complete sentences?

○ ○ 8. Have I used apostrophes only for contractions or to show ownership?

○ ○ 9. Have I used more complex punctuation (dashes, semi-colons, hyphens, parentheses, etc.) correctly?

○ ○ 10. Have I used common homonyms correctly, for example they're/their/there; your/you're; its/it's; too/two/to?

○ ○ 11. Was I consistent in the use of either present or past tense in the entire piece?

○ ○ 12. Was I consistent in my use of either first person or third person throughout the entire piece?

Student Self-Assessment Checklist for Effective Writing — appendix C.17

NAME: _____

TITLE OF WORK ASSESSED: _____

Did I . . . ?

○ have a plan before I started writing?

○ write complete sentences that are not run-on sentences?

○ write some compound sentences that are connected with *and, or,* or *but?*

○ write a good topic sentence for each paragraph?

○ write supporting sentences that help support the topic sentence in each paragraph?

○ write accurate nonfiction that is also interesting?

○ provide good transitions between paragraphs?

○ write a story that has a beginning, a middle, and an end?

○ write a story with a problem and a solution?

○ describe the main character well?

○ include dialogue in my story?

○ use correct punctuation in any dialogue?

○ use interesting and vivid words?

○ confer with others to revise?

○ edit my drafts?

appendix C.18   Scoring Rubric for Expository Essay

CRITERIA	NEEDS WORK (1)	MAKING PROGRESS (2)	DOING GREAT (3)	ABOVE AND BEYOND (4)	SCORE
Understanding of Material	Apparent misunderstanding of material.	Limited understanding of material displayed by vague, unclear language.	Developing understanding of material.	Clear understanding of material displayed by clear, concrete language and complex ideas.	1 2 3 4
Structural Organization	Essay lacks logical progression of ideas.	Essay includes brief skeleton (introduction, body, conclusion) but lacks transitions.	Essay includes logical progression of ideas aided by clear transitions.	Essay is powerfully organized and fully developed.	1 2 3 4
Sentence Fluency (Flow)	Repetitive sentence patterns. There are no connecting words between sentences. Many sentences run into each other.	Sentence patterns are generally repetitive, with occasional variance. There are usually connecting words between sentences, where appropriate. Some sentences should be merged; others should be made into two or more sentences.	Sentence patterns are generally varied, but sometimes variations seem forced and inappropriate. There are connecting words between sentences, where appropriate. Each sentence contains a complete thought; there are no run-on sentences.	Varied and interesting sentence patterns. There are connecting words between sentences, where appropriate. Sentences are complete thoughts, with no run-ons.	1 2 3 4
Support	Few to no solid supporting ideas or evidence for the essay content.	Some supporting ideas and/or evidence for the essay content.	Support lacks specificity and is loosely developed.	Specific, developed details and superior support and evidence in the essay content.	1 2 3 4
Mechanics	Frequent errors in spelling, grammar, and punctuation.	Errors in grammar and punctuation, but spelling has been proofread.	Occasional grammatical errors. Spelling has been proofread.	Nearly error free. Reflects thorough proofreading for grammar and spelling.	1 2 3 4

Self-Assessment Scoring Rubric for a Writing Project — appendix C.19

TARGET:

STUDENT:

REQUIREMENTS	FANTASTIC (4)	NICE JOB! (3)	OKAY (2)	NEEDS IMPROVEMENT (1)	SELF-ASSESSMENT	TEACHER'S ASSESSMENT
Cover Page	Includes title, author, and an appropriate illustration.	Includes two of the three required elements.	Includes one of the three required elements.	Does not include any of the three required elements, or is missing.		
Book Pages	Each page includes all required elements. Examples: (1) target word (2) word used in context (3) three facts about word (4) illustration for the word	Most pages include at least three required elements, and frequently four elements.	Many pages include two required elements, with several including three or four elements.	Many pages include only one or two required elements, or some pages are missing.		
Author Page	Includes author name, background information, an illustration or photo.	Includes two of the three required elements.	Includes one of the three required elements.	Does not include any of the three elements, or is missing.		

My strengths are:

What I need to work on:

appendix C.20   Web Evaluation Form

The Likert scale items that follow are intended for use by students.

NAME OF WEBSITE: _____   DATE: _____

URL: _____

Circle the number you think best reflects each item.   *(1 = Poor, 5 = Excellent)*

CONTENT					
1. The title of the site is accurate.	1	2	3	4	5
2. Additional resource links are included.	1	2	3	4	5
3. The information is helpful.	1	2	3	4	5
4. There is much good content, and the site will be revisited.	1	2	3	4	5
5. This site ranks high compared with other sites having similar content.	1	2	3	4	5

CREDIBILITY					
1. A contact person or email address is given, as well as the host school, institution, or organization.	1	2	3	4	5
2. The site indicates when it was last updated.	1	2	3	4	5

TECHNICAL ELEMENTS					
1. The links all work.	1	2	3	4	5
2. Graphics download quickly (within about 30 seconds).	1	2	3	4	5
3. A text alternative is offered when there are heavy graphics.	1	2	3	4	5

DESIGN					
1. The use of graphics and color makes the site visually appealing.	1	2	3	4	5
2. It is easy to move from page to page.	1	2	3	4	5
3. The links are clear and easy to find.	1	2	3	4	5
4. The text is easy to read with pages of appropriate length.	1	2	3	4	5

Add the total number of points for this website and write it in the blank below.

TOTAL SCORE: _____ /70

INTERPRETATION

If a website receives a score between 63 and 70, it is considered an excellent website.

If a website receives a score between 49 and 62, it is considered an above average website.

If a website receives a score between 35 and 48, it is considered an average website.

A website receiving a score below 35 is not well constructed and should not be used.

A Teacher's Self-Evaluation for Literacy Instruction · appendix C.21

NAME: _____ DATE: _____

	YES	SOMEWHAT	NO
1. I can list whole-group, small-group, and individual activities for the development of reading.	○	○	○
2. I can make a basic developmental reading lesson plan.	○	○	○
3. I know the components deemed necessary for a comprehensive, balanced reading program.	○	○	○
4. I can correctly write objectives (with three parts) for lessons.	○	○	○
5. I can describe and list at least 10 techniques for motivating students to read.	○	○	○
6. I can explain how listening, speaking, reading, writing, viewing, and visually representing are related.	○	○	○
7. I understand the usage of authentic reading materials and how literature-based reading supports this.	○	○	○
8. I can develop and employ tools for diagnosing reading ability, including portfolios.	○	○	○
9. I am familiar with the reading material adopted by the State of _____ for use in grade 4–8 classrooms.	○	○	○
10. I know the terminology used by reading teachers (e.g., guided rdg., shared rdg.), including abbreviations (IRI, DRTA, IRA).	○	○	○
11. I can develop and analyze types of questions to get at various levels of comprehension and analyze students' answers.	○	○	○
12. I can identify and demonstrate techniques for teaching word analysis skills.	○	○	○
13. I can identify and demonstrate techniques for developing students' vocabulary.	○	○	○
14. I can list and develop techniques for teaching the various comprehension skills.	○	○	○

(continued)

appendix C.21 A Teacher's Self-Evaluation for Literacy Instruction, CONTINUED

	YES	SOMEWHAT	NO
15. I can plan and describe activities to aid special need students (e.g., gifted, physical handicap, special ed.).	○	○	○
16. I can plan and describe activities to aid students with language differences.	○	○	○
17. I can identify sources (websites, journals, magazines) for instructional materials and teaching strategies.	○	○	○
18. I can list activities for *meaningful* seatwork or learning centers to supplement the basic reading program.	○	○	○
19. I can define basic linguistic terminology and describe the contribution of phonics to reading acquisition.	○	○	○
20. I can use diagnostic techniques to identify the strengths and weaknesses in reading of the students in a class and devise a differentiated lesson for identified areas of need.	○	○	○
21. I can plan reading lessons that are interdisciplinary.	○	○	○
22. I know the professional organizations and journals that have reading as their focus.	○	○	○
23. I am familiar with the purpose of the state framework, district benchmarks, and social improvement plan.	○	○	○
24. I know various methods of presenting a young adult book to students whether one copy or multiple copies are available.	○	○	○
25. I enjoy reading and can be a good role model for students.	○	○	○
26. I know the components of writing workshop and could incorporate it in my classroom.	○	○	○
27. I can design a literature-based three-day reading unit plan that includes reinforcement and enrichment tasks.	○	○	○

Appendix D

WORD LISTS

D.1 Nifty-Thrifty-Fifty Words

D.2 Transfer Words for the Nifty-Thrifty-Fifty

Nifty-Thrifty-Fifty Words | appendix **D.1**

1. antifreeze
2. beautiful
3. classify
4. communities
5. community
6. composer
7. continuous
8. conversation
9. deodorize
10. different
11. discovery
12. dishonest
13. electricity
14. employee
15. encouragement
16. expensive
17. forecast
18. forgotten
19. governor
20. happiness
21. hopeless
22. illegal
23. impossible
24. impression
25. independence
26. international
27. invasion
28. irresponsible
29. midnight
30. misunderstand
31. musician
32. nonliving
33. overpower
34. performance
35. prehistoric
36. prettier
37. rearrange
38. replacement
39. richest
40. semifinal
41. signature
42. submarine
43. supermarkets
44. swimming
45. transportation
46. underweight
47. unfinished
48. unfriendly
49. unpleasant
50. valuable

Here are just some of the words students should be able to decode, spell, and discuss meanings for by using parts of all fifty words:

conform	relive	declassify	powerlessly
conformity	repose	decompose	powerlessness
inform	reclassify	deform	superpower
informer	revalue	deformity	finalize
informant	recover	prearrange	finalizing
information	rediscover	resign	finalization
misinform	electrical	resignation	weighty
uninformed	displease	designation	weightier
formation	discontinue	significant	weightiest
formal	disposal	significance	weightless
transform	musical	freezer	undervalue
transformation	continual	freezing	friendlier
performer	employer	freezable	friendliest
responsibility	employment	subfreezing	friendliness
responsive	unemployment	underclass	unfriendliness
responsiveness	unemployed	overexpose	unpleasantness
honesty	employable	underexpose	historical
dishonesty	unemployable	superimpose	historically
honestly	difference	undercover	expressive
legally	consignment	forecaster	impressive
illegally	nationality	forecasting	repressive
responsibly	nationalities	forecastable	invasive
irresponsibly	internationalize	miscast	noninvasive
arranging	interdependence	antidepressant	invasiveness
rearranging	depress	overture	hopefully
placing	depression	empower	hopelessly
replacing	depressive	empowerment	predispose
misplacing	deport	powerful	predisposition
report	deportation	powerfully	deodorant
reporter	deportee	powerfulness	beautician
refinish	devalue	powerless	electrician

Monday. Display the five new words on a word wall large enough to be seen by students from their seats. **Word walls** are charts or bulletin boards on which important vocabulary words are placed, usually alphabetically, to be referred to during word study activities (see below). Use thick, bold permanent markers for printing the words. Model the decoding of these five words.

Write a sentence using a new word on the board:

If your pet licks the <u>antifreeze</u> off the garage floor, it could become very sick, and even die.

Teacher: The underlined word contains a word you might already know and a prefix. A prefix is a word part that is added to the beginning of a word. Can anyone tell me the word without the prefix? (If not, draw a circle around "freeze" and ask again.)

Then discuss the meaning of the word, and other words that begin with "anti." Continue this process for the other four words of the day.

Tuesday. Come back to the five words introduced on Monday. Practice the five new words by saying the letters and syllables in these words as a rhythmic chant, almost like a song, or a cheer that a cheerleader might lead at a football game. For example, antifreeze might develop into

a - n - t - i anti
a - n - t - i anti
a - n - t - i anti
anti antifreeze

Again, the meanings of the affixes and the whole word should be discussed.

Wednesday. Return to the five words introduced on Monday. Examine the composition of each of the five new words. Focus on how the spelling of the root words may change when an affix is added. Have each student create a written chart such as the following:

WORD		PARTS	SPELLING CHANGES
antifreeze	=	anti + freeze	no changes
beautiful	=	beauty + ful	y changes to i
classify	=	class + ify	no changes
communities	=	com + unity + es	m doubles, y changes to i
community	=	com + unity or com + unit + y	m doubles

Then ask questions about these words to focus on their meanings or other special characteristics:

1. Which word is the opposite of ugly?
2. Which word means the opposite of freezing?
3. Which two words have unity as their root?
4. How do you write the plural of community?
5. Which word tells what you do when you group things that are similar?

Students should check the spellings of the words they wrote using the word wall.

Thursday. Chant again (see Tuesday) the five new words introduced on Monday. Now help students see how knowing these words can help them recognize and spell other words they may not yet know. Using related forms of the words taught (see Appendix D.2), ask students to decode, spell, and discuss meanings for these words. For example, have students pronounce *declassify,* note its spelling (add "de" to "classify"), and talk about its meaning as undoing what had been done, or classified. Other words to use could be *classification, freezer, subfreezing, beautifully, powerful, hopeful, communication, mystify,* and *certify.*

Friday. Cover up the word wall. Administer a spelling test on the five new words, or include these in a weekly spelling test. The format might proceed as follows: Say the word, use the word in a sentence, and repeat the word. Then go on to the next word. Students can correct their own papers by writing the correct spelling from the word wall next to any misspelled words.

After 10 weeks all of the words will have been learned. Because these 50 words contain morphological patterns for so many other words, they should be overlearned. The various elements will then be recognized and recalled automatically when needed during reading and writing. The transfer words in Appendix D.2 contain parts of the Nifty-Thrifty-Fifty words. Many other words can also be used as transfer words.

You can use this general pattern when teaching the morphology and etymology of words:

1. Begin with the known and move to the unknown.
2. Provide a means for making the transfer. Talk through the process. With practice and repetition, the process becomes internalized.
3. Discuss related words so that knowledge increases in an exponential way as opposed to just one word being studied at a time.
4. Value the content of particular disciplines by using the critical language in that discipline as a means of teaching a functional skill—word analysis.

academic language The language that teachers and students use for imparting information, acquiring new knowledge and skills, describing abstract ideas, and developing content area and conceptual understanding.

acceleration Progress through the curriculum at a faster rate.

accuracy The ability to recognize words correctly.

achievement test A formalized test that measures the extent to which a person has assimilated a body of information or possesses a certain skill after instruction has taken place.

affixes Bound morphemes that change the meaning or function of a root or stem to which they are attached, as the prefix *ad-* and the suffix *-ing* in *adjoining.*

alliteration A pattern in which all words begin with the same sound.

alphabetic principle The principle that there is a one-to-one correspondence between phonemes (or sounds) and graphemes (or letters); letters represent sounds.

analog A strategy of comparing patterns in words to ones already known.

anecdotal notes Written observations taken by the teacher —usually on a clipboard—of literacy-related behaviors in an authentic literacy context.

anticipation guide A prereading tool used to activate schemata and engage readers.

antonyms A pair of words that have opposite meanings.

Asperger's syndrome A mild form of autism.

assessment The process of gathering information about students' abilities using a variety of means and tools, both formal and informal.

assistive technologies Electronic devices, equipment, or products designed or modified specifically to improve the functional capabilities of individuals with severe communication disorders and other disabilities.

augmentative communication system Any system or device designed to enhance the communication abilities of individuals who are nonverbal or have speech too difficult to understand.

authentic assessment Assessment representing literacy behavior in the community and in the workplace.

autism A disability characterized by extreme withdrawal and underdeveloped communication or language skills.

automaticity Fluent performance without the conscious deployment of attention.

basal reader series A coordinated, graded set of textbooks, teacher's guides, and supplementary materials from which to teach reading.

basic words Commonplace words that are the building blocks of everyday language.

behavioral disorder A disability in which students are characterized by inappropriate school behavior.

big book An enlarged version of a book used by the teacher for mediated reading instruction so that students can track the print and attention can be focused on particular phonemic elements.

blend A consonant sequence before or after a vowel within a syllable, such as *cl, st,* or *br;* the written language equivalent of a consonant cluster.

blogging The online publication of commentary on specific topics of interest (e.g., political, social, and so forth).

book clubs Another term for (see) literature circles.

book contract An individual contract of literacy activities based upon a self-selected book.

book talk Brief teaser that teacher presents to interest students in a particular book.

CALP An acronym for cognitive academic language proficiency, or the language of school.

camouflage A vocabulary-enriching activity in which learners must try to disguise a chosen word by creating an oral story using several words above their normal speaking vocabulary. The other students must try to guess the hidden word.

clarifying table A graphic organizer used to help children understand the meaning of complex terms.

closed sorts Word sorts that classify words into predetermined categories.

cloze test An assessment device in which certain words are deleted from a passage by the teacher, with blanks left in their places for students to fill in by using the context of the sentence or paragraph.

code switching The use of English for known words and the home language for words not yet acquired in English.

cognitive academic language proficiency (CALP) Skill in academic language, or the language of school.

compound words A word composed of two separate words that have meaning on their own, such as *baseball* and *lipstick*.

comprehensible input New information that is modified to enable an English learner to make connections to already known information.

comprehension The interpretation of print on a page into a meaningful message that is dependent on the reader's decoding abilities, prior knowledge, cultural and social background, and monitoring strategies—the "essence of reading."

comprehension monitoring The reader's awareness of whether what is being read makes sense and, when it does not, his or her ability to make adjustments to improve comprehension.

concept-oriented reading instruction (CORI) An integrated curriculum approach.

concepts about print Concepts about the way print works, including directionality, spacing, identification of words and letters, connection between written and spoken language, and the function of punctuation.

construct validity When test items assess the skills, knowledge, and understandings that most experts agree comprise the area being tested.

constructivist model of learning A learning theory suggesting that students are active learners who organize and relate new information to their prior knowledge.

content area literacy Reading, writing, speaking, listening, viewing, and visually representing with a focus on the bodies of knowledge in the academic curriculum; e.g., English, science, social studies, mathematics.

content standards Stated expectations of what students should know and be able to do in particular subjects and grade levels.

content validity When test items assess the ability needed to perform the behaviors expected in the course or curriculum.

context clues The syntactic and semantic information in the surrounding words, phrases, sentences, and paragraphs in a text.

context–relationship procedure A strategy utilized to help students integrate new words into their meaning vocabularies.

contract spelling Children have a written agreement with the teacher each week to learn specific words.

controlled vocabulary A system of introducing only a certain number of grade-level appropriate words before the reading of each basal story, with periodic review.

conventional spelling stage The final stage of spelling development, in which the student has mastered the basic principles of English orthography and spells most words correctly.

conventions (writing) Tools of writing, including grammar, spelling, paragraphing, capitalization, punctuation, and all the mechanics of the language that are often corrected in the editing process.

conversation clubs Small, student-led groups established to enhance oral language in an informal, enjoyable setting.

cooperative learning An instructional model in which students work together as a team to complete activities or assignments.

correct spelling stage See conventional spelling stage.

criterion-referenced assessment An assessment designed to reveal what a student knows, understands, or can do in relation to specific objectives or standards.

criterion-referenced test A test for which scores are interpreted by comparing the test taker's score to a specified performance level rather than to the scores of other students.

critical analysis As a component of comprehension, the ability of readers to actively engage and to interpret text critically, uncovering intended meanings, discovering biases, and producing a cultural understanding of the text.

critical reading Reading to evaluate the material being read.

cubing A writing scaffold used for students to model how to organize a six-paragraph essay.

cuing systems The four language systems that readers rely upon for cues as they seek meaning from text: graphophonic (based on letter–sound relationships), syntactic (based on grammar or structure), semantic (based on meaning), and pragmatic (based on social and cultural norms).

curriculum-based assessment The process of matching the curriculum to the content standards assessed in a testing program to ensure that teachers will cover the material assessed.

data chart A table or grid for recording answers to specific research questions (columns) gathered from a variety of sources (rows).

decodable text Beginner-oriented books that contain the same letters or word patterns currently being studied, or those previously taught.

decoding The translation of written words into verbal speech for oral reading or mental speech for silent reading.

deduction The process of helping students construct meaning by going from the general to the particular, through explanation.

derivational relations stage A spelling stage characterized by the ability to recognize and spell bases and roots correctly. Correlates to an advanced stage of reading and writing.

developmental spelling stages Stage-like progressions through which students advance when learning to spell, characterized by increasingly complex understandings about the organizational patterns of words, including precommunicative, prephonetic, phonetic, transitional, and conventional spelling stages.

diagnosis The act, process, or result of identifying the nature of a disorder or disability through observation and examination, often including the planning of instruction and the assessment of the strengths and needs of the student.

diagnostic test Age-related, norm-referenced assessment of specific skills and behaviors students have acquired compared with other students of the same chronological age.

dialogue journals Journals that provide a means of two-way written communication between learners and their teachers, in which learners share their thoughts with teachers (including personal comments and descriptions of life experiences), and the teachers, in turn, write reactions to the learners' messages. Also called interactive journals.

differentiated instruction Instruction designed to meet the needs of all students by adjusting content, process, or product.

direct instruction Teacher control of the learning environment through structured, systematic lessons; goal setting; choice of activities; and feedback.

directed reading thinking activity (DRTA) A time-honored format for guiding students as they read selections, usually from basal reading programs.

directionality of print The concept that, in English, writing goes from left to right and from top to bottom. Directionality of print varies among languages.

directive context Text that provides helpful clues for figuring out word meanings.

discussion Oral communication in an informal setting, involving an exploration of an issue or topic; problem solving by cooperative thinking.

double entry journal This journal uses a two-column format for entries of two types of student response to text.

dramatic play Play that simulates real experiences with no set plot or goal.

dyad reading A paired reading activity in which students alternately read aloud or listen and summarize what their partner has read.

dyslexia A developmental reading disability, presumably congenital and often hereditary, that may vary in degree from mild to severe.

echo reading A strategy where a lead reader reads aloud a section of text and others follow immediately after it, or echo the leader's reading.

editing The process of reviewing text in draft form to check for correctness of the mechanics and conventions in writing.

electronic portfolio A compilation of work stored digitally; gives students the option of storing a great deal of information electronically, including items such as work samples, photos, art, and even oral reading samples; sound, music, and video clips can also be included to enhance the portfolio. Electronic portfolios also give students the ability to connect sections of a portfolio through hyperlinks, allowing access to a variety of artifacts that might show how specific goals have been met.

emergent literacy A person's developing awareness of the interrelatedness of oral and written language that occurs from birth to beginning reading.

encoding Transferring oral language into written language.

engagement A process involving a complex set of ongoing activities that occur in the classroom.

English learner A person who is in the process of acquiring English as a second language.

enrichment Strategies designed to deepen appreciation for reading selections.

environmental print Print that is encountered outside of books and that is a pervasive part of everyday living.

ESL (English as a second language) A program for teaching English language skills to those whose native language is not English.

etymology The study of the history of words.

evaluation Making a judgment about assessment data or assigning a score or grade to assessment data.

experience–text relationship A lesson format for narrative text that helps students develop prior knowledge and relate it to what they read.

experiential background The fund of total experiences that aid a reader in finding meaning in printed symbols.

experimental spellings Unconventional spellings, or approximations, resulting from an emergent writer's initial attempts to associate sounds with letters.

expository frame A basic structure for expository text designed to help students organize their thoughts for writing or responding to text.

expository structure Content organized around a main idea and supporting details.

expository text A text written in a precise, factual writing style.

expressive writing Personal writing that expresses emotion, such as diaries or letters.

FLIP strategy A strategy readers use to examine a text for reader-friendliness, language, interest, and degree of prior knowledge needed to understand the text.

fluency Achieving speed and accuracy in recognizing words and comprehending text, and coordinating the two.

fluent reader A reader whose reading accuracy and rate meet or exceed normal expectations with respect to age, ability, and grade level; an independent reader.

formal assessments Commercially designed and produced tests given on single occasions.

formal (standardized) test A testing instrument for which readability and validity can be verified; the results of these tests are based on right or wrong answers, and individual scores are interpreted against national norms.

formative assessment Classroom-based measures intended to provide feedback to learners on areas needing improvement.

Four-by-Four Model A "sheltered English" (see below) instructional model that addresses four developmental levels of language proficiency (beginning, early intermediate, intermediate, early advanced) and four literacy skills (reading, writing, speaking, listening) through the use of content themes.

frustration level A level of reading difficulty at which a reader is unable to cope; when reading is on the frustration level, the reader recognizes approximately 90 percent or fewer of the words encountered and comprehends 50 percent or fewer.

general-utility words More complex words that are used often by proficient readers and speakers but tend not to be specific to any particular subject.

GIST (generating interactions between schemata and text) A strategy used by readers to summarize text.

Goldilocks strategy Students examine a book to determine if it is "too easy," "too hard," or "just right" for them to read.

grade-level equivalency score A conversion of a score on a test into one that tells how a student compares with others in the same grade; e.g., a grade equivalent score of 4.5 on a reading test would suggest that the student is reading as well as students in the normative sample who are in the fifth month of fourth grade.

graded word list A list of words at successive reading levels.

grand conversation A response to text strategy whereby students share personal connections to the text, make predictions, ask questions, and show individual appreciation.

grapheme A written symbol that represents a phoneme.

graphic novels Book-length comic books.

graphic organizer A visual representation of facts and concepts from a text and their relationships within an organized frame.

graphophonic cues Cues based on sound or visual similarities.

group profile A listing of scores on a specific reading or writing skill that allows the teacher to view the strengths and weaknesses of the whole class for purposes of reteaching and reporting to parents and others.

guided reading A teacher-mediated instructional method designed to help readers improve skills, comprehension, recall, and appreciation of text.

herringbone strategy A graphic organizer used with expository text to show who, what, when, where, why, and the main idea for a passage.

heterogeneous literature groups Literature circles based not upon reading ability level, but on self-selection of a particular book.

high-frequency words Words common in reading material that are often difficult to learn because they cannot be easily decoded.

high-stakes assessments Assessment tools mandated by the state or district in which the teachers work that are often used to determine how well students are doing compared with other students in the district, state, or nation and to help decide whether certain programs will be funded.

holistic approach A whole-to-parts approach in which meaning is considered to be more critical than the underlying skills of reading.

holographic stage The earliest language acquisition stage, in which one word is used to represent a concept or idea.

impromptu speech A short speech given on a topic with little or no preparation.

independent level A level of reading difficulty low enough that the reader can progress without noticeable obstructions; the reader can recognize approximately 98 percent of the words and comprehend at least 90 percent of what is read.

individual dictation A strategy in which the student dictates a message while the teacher writes it down, sounding out the words in front of the student.

individualized education program (IEP) A written educational plan specifying a special student's annual goals, current levels of educational achievement, and short-term instructional objectives; prepared by a team that includes the student's parents, teachers, and often the student.

induction The process of helping students to construct meaning by going from the particular to the general, with the help of examples.

informal assessment A nonstandardized measurement in which a teacher seeks to learn about what a student is able to do in a certain area of literacy, interprets the results, and uses those results to plan instruction.

informal reading inventory An informal assessment instrument designed to help the teacher determine a student's independent, instructional, frustration, and reading capacity levels.

informal speaking Oral language of a nonacademic, conversational nature.

information literate Knowing how to locate, acquire, and use information.

informational books Nonfiction books that provide factual information about a topic; expository text.

informational writing Often called "expository writing," allows students to explain ideas, objects, and processes to a reader in an understandable way while at the same time improving the writer's own knowledge and understanding of the topic. Writing purpose may be discipline-specific.

instructional level A level of difficulty low enough that the reader can be instructed by the teacher during the process; in order for the material to be at this level, the reader should be able to read approximately 95 percent of the words in a passage and comprehend at least 75 percent.

interactive electronic books Computerized programs that allow learners to read books on a computer while responding to questions about the text, exploring various aspects or sidelines of the text, and often even adapting the text.

interactive oral reading A method for teaching vocabulary in which adults read aloud to learners, stopping on occasion to discuss individual words.

interactive (story) writing A mediated writing experience used to assist emergent readers in learning to read and write. With help from the teacher, students dictate sentences, and the teacher verbally stretches each word so the students can distinguish sounds and letters. Students use chart paper to write the letter while repeating the sound.

interest and attitude inventory An informal assessment device that allows teachers to discover how their students feel about reading and about themselves as readers.

interest groups Students are organized according to a common interest in a topic or book selection.

interest inventory A list of questions used to assess a student's preferences in a particular area.

intervention The corrective instructional program the teacher devises as a result of assessment.

interview An oral language activity consisting of asking another person a specific set of questions.

jigsaw grouping A collaborative learning technique in which individuals become "experts" on one portion of text and share their expertise with a small group, called their home group. Each member of the home group becomes an "expert" on a different part of the text and shares his new knowledge with the group so that each group member will get a sense of the whole text.

journals Journals are kept by students in the same way artists keep sketch books. Students write in them regularly to record life events of their choosing or, for very beginning writers, to complete sentence stems offered by the teacher. At the beginning reader stage, journals are often accompanied by illustrations and are rarely corrected.

K-W-L Plus strategy A process intended to help students organize learned information into a coherent paragraph or research report; typically involves a chart with column headings such as "What We Know," "What We Want to Know," and "What We Learned." The "Plus" refers to using additional categories of information, perhaps to write summaries or reports.

language arts The global term for reading, writing, listening, speaking, viewing, and visually representing.

language disorders Communication disorders that involve poor speech or language performance due to various factors, including voice quality, speech fluency, and sound production.

language experience approach (LEA) An approach in which reading and the other language arts are interrelated and the experiences of students are used as the basis for the material that is written and then used for reading.

learning center A location within the classroom in which students are presented with instructional materials, specific directions, clearly defined objectives, and/or provisions for self-evaluation.

learning disability A condition in which a person with average or above intelligence is substantially delayed in academic achievement because of a processing disorder, not because of an environmental, an economic, or a cultural disadvantage.

learning logs Journals students use to summarize a day's lesson and to react to what they have learned.

letter name/alphabetic stage Spelling characterized by literally matching letters to sounds in a linear sound-by-sound fashion.

letter name stage See phonetic stage.

listening vocabulary The words a person is able to understand aurally; also known as receptive vocabulary.

literacy The competence to carry out the complex reading and writing tasks in a functionally useful way necessary to the world of work and life outside the school.

literacy scaffold A temporary writing structure.

literal comprehension Understanding those ideas that are directly stated.

literary sociogram A diagram used to help students understand the complexity of the relationships among characters in a story or chapter.

literature circles Small, student-led book discussion groups that meet regularly in the classroom to read and discuss self-selected books.

literature double response journal A special type of reading log with quotes from a story or informational book in the left column and a personal reflection on the quote in the right column.

literature response groups Same as literature circles and analogous to writing response groups; in literature response groups, students discuss the work of published authors; in writing response groups, they discuss the work of their peers.

long vowels Vowels that represent the sounds in words that are heard in letter names, such as the /a/ in *ape*, /e/ in *feet*, /i/ in *ice*, /o/ in *road*, and /u/ in *mule*.

look-say method An early meaning-based method of reading instruction requiring students to use the context alone to figure out words they did not know.

low-utility words Less frequently encountered words that are usually found in particular content areas.

masking Using a sliding frame or other device to help students focus on a particular word or part of a word.

Matthew effect The phenomenon that suggests that skilled decoders get better at reading while poor decoders tend to fall further behind.

meaning vocabulary That body of words the meaning of which one understands and can use.

media literacy The skill of thinking critically about what one sees, hears, and reads when presented through a wide variety of media.

mediated reading Large or small group instruction in which the teacher guides the students in selected reading skills.

metacognition A person's awareness of her own thinking and her conscious efforts to monitor this awareness.

metacognitive strategies Techniques for monitoring one's own thinking.

metacomprehension Understanding what you know about how you comprehend; self-knowledge about your own comprehension processes.

metalinguistic ability The conscious awareness of sound, meaning, and the practical nuances of language.

minilesson A short lesson on procedures, concepts, strategies, or skills taught based on teacher observation of the need for it.

miscue An unexpected reading response (deviation from text).

miscue analysis A procedure that lets the teacher gather important instructional information by providing a framework for observing students' oral reading and their ability to construct meaning.

mock interviews Pretend discussions with deceased or fictional figures.

modeling Showing an instructional strategy through teacher demonstration.

morning message Students observe as the teacher writes a meaningful morning message on the board about a specific event that is planned for the day, or an interesting question. It is used as an instructional tool for discussing skills that the students are learning, such as conventions of writing or phonic elements.

morpheme The smallest meaning-bearing linguistic unit in a language.

morphology The aspects of language structure related to the ways words are formed from prefixes, roots, and suffixes (e.g., "re-heat-ing") and are related to each other.

motivation The incentive to do something; a stimulus to act.

multicultural Classrooms are multicultural settings when students from a variety of cultures learn together daily, making it necessary to know how students' perceptions, knowledge, and demeanor are shaped by their experiences at home and in their own community.

narrative text Text that contains the structural features of a story.

nondirective context Text that does not provide helpful context clues for determining a word's meaning.

nonstage theory A theory that suggests that unskilled and skilled readers use the same strategies to figure out unknown words.

norm-referenced test A test designed to yield results interpretable in terms of the average results of a sample population.

norm (normative) group A large number of students chosen to represent the kinds of students for whom an assessment device is designed.

norms Statistics or data that summarize the test performance of specified groups, such as test takers of various ages or grades.

novel study The in-depth reading and interpretation of a novel or a group of related novels or stories.

one-to-one correspondence The concept that letters or combinations of letters correspond directly with certain sounds in the English language.

ongoing assessment Assessment that occurs within daily lessons and over time, usually through observation and anecdotal notes.

onset All the sounds of a word that come before the first vowel.

open sort A type of picture or word sort in which the categories for sorting are left up to the student.

oral recitation lessons (ORL) Three-part lessons designed to increase oral reading fluency.

oral report A presentation (often using multimedia) of information for an audience of classmates.

oral synthesis Hearing sounds in sequence and blending them together to make a word; sounding out.

orthographic knowledge Understanding of the writing system of a language, specifically the correct sequence of letters, characters, or symbols.

parent packets Folders containing early reading and writing reinforcement activities that can be completed at home with a student's parents or caregivers.

paragraph frame A scaffold for helping students write paragraphs; transition words are provided, and students fill in the substantive content words.

partner reading Also known as buddy reading. Oral reading with another student.

peer editor A student assigned to help a classmate evaluate a piece of writing and to provide helpful questions and suggestions.

peer revising A process in which a writer has a peer provide constructive feedback to ensure that a piece communicates its intent effectively; the writer may in turn act as peer editor for the other student. Feedback may follow the PQP (praise, question, polish) format.

percentile scores Raw scores that are converted to percentiles so that comparisons can be made. Percentiles range from 1 to 99, with 1 being the lowest.

performance descriptors The criteria that help communicate to teachers and students the standards that will be used to evaluate students' work.

phoneme The smallest unit of sound in a language.

phoneme blending Blending individual sounds to form a word.

phoneme counting Counting the number of sounds in a word.

phoneme deletion Omitting the beginning, middle, or ending sounds of a word.

phoneme isolation Identifying the beginning, middle, and/or ending sounds in a word.

phoneme substitution Substituting beginning, middle, or ending sounds of a word.

phonemic awareness The ability to hear, identify, and manipulate individual sounds in spoken words.

phonemic segmentation The process of separating sounds within a word.

phonetic stage The third stage of spelling development, in which consonants and vowels are used for each spoken syllable.

phonics Instruction in the association of speech sounds with printed symbols.

phonics generalizations Rules that help clarify English spelling patterns.

phonology The study of the sound system of language.

picture walk An instructional strategy in which the teacher guides students through the text by looking at and discussing the pictures before reading the story.

play centers Areas of the classroom containing inviting props and set aside for spontaneous dramatic play.

polysemantic words Words that can have different meanings depending on the context in which they are used.

portfolio Place to collect evidence of a student's literacy development. It may include artifacts collected by the student, the teacher, or both.

portmanteau word Word created from a combination of two existing words (e.g., motel = motor + hotel).

precommunicative stage The initial stage of spelling development, in which the student scribbles random letters with little concept of which letter makes which sound.

predictable texts Books that use repetition, rhythmic language patterns, and familiar patterns; sometimes called pattern books.

predictive questions Questions designed to activate students' prior knowledge before they read in order to focus their attention on key ideas as they read.

prefixes Meaningful chunks attached to the beginnings of words, such as re + play = replay.

preliterate stage See prephonetic stage.

prephonetic stage The second stage of spelling development, in which the student becomes aware of the alphabetic principle.

prewriting The initial creative and planning stage of writing, prior to drafting, in which the writer formulates ideas, gathers information, and considers ways in which to organize a piece of writing.

primary language The first language a student learns to speak, or the student's home language.

problem-based learning Organizes curriculum and instruction around authentic real-world problems with a focus on solving these problems as if the students were working in the area being studied.

process-oriented assessment A teacher's direct observations of students' reading and writing abilities for the purpose of noting which specific behaviors or strategies students use.

productive questioning Involves the use of students' responses to carefully crafted questions in guiding the development of conceptual thinking.

professional teaching standards Standards related to how well the teacher performs.

project-based learning Provides an alternative learning environment in which students work collaboratively to explore real-world issues in depth and to create a project that represents their learning.

QARs (question–answer relationships) A strategy in which students become aware of their own comprehension processes, particularly the importance of the knowledge they bring to text and their role as active seekers rather than passive receivers of information through reading.

quick write An activity in which students rapidly write down ideas about a topic.

r-controlled vowels Vowels that occur in a syllable preceding an *r* and in which the vowel sound is modified, such as the /r/ in car.

readability An objective measure of the difficulty of written material.

readers theatre A form of drama in which participants read aloud from scripts adapted from stories and convey ideas and emotions through vocal expression. This oral interpretation strategy helps students see that reading is an active process of constructing meaning. Unlike a play, there is no costuming, movement, stage sets, or memorizing of lines.

reading The construction of meaning from coded messages through symbol decoding, vocabulary awareness, comprehension, and reflection.

reading buddies A social reading activity in which students read and reread books with a partner who may help them with unfamiliar words and encourage them to continue reading.

reading capacity level The highest level of material that students can understand when the passage is read to them.

reading interest inventory An informal assessment device used to determine a student's interests so that the teacher can match appropriate reading material to the student.

reading process The steps a reader goes through to construct meaning from what the author has written.

reading product Some form of communication that results from the reading process.

reading rate Speed of reading, often reported in words per minute.

reading readiness The level of preparedness for formal reading instruction.

reading response journal A journal in which readers record their first reactions to something they have read.

reading vocabulary The words a person is able to understand in written form; part of receptive vocabulary.

realia Concrete pictures and other items used to show the meaning of words and concepts.

reciprocal teaching A technique to develop comprehension and metacognition in which the teacher and students take turns predicting, generating questions, summarizing, and clarifying ideas in a passage.

recreational reading An independent reading activity for motivating voluntary reading interest and appreciation rather than instruction.

reliability When a test consistently measures the same behavior with each administration of the test.

repeated readings The process of students rereading a selection for a different purpose and thinking again about what they have read. Rereading helps improve a reader's speed, accuracy, expression, comprehension, and linguistic growth.

response guide A set of suggestions designed to help peer editors provide helpful feedback to student writers.

retelling The process of teachers analyzing students' retellings of text to gauge their level of comprehension and use of language. In examining the retellings, teachers look for the number of events recalled, how students interpret the message, and how students use details or make inferences to substantiate ideas.

revising The process of changing a piece of writing to improve clarity for its intended audience and to make certain that it accomplishes its intended purpose.

rime The first vowel in a word and all the sounds that follow.

role playing A form of dramatic play that involves having students act the part of another student or a fictional character.

root word A word to which prefixes and/or suffixes are added to create new, but related, words.

roots Base words.

ROW Read, organize, write: a strategy used to help students write summaries.

rubber-banding The process in which the teacher stretches out all the sounds in a word so learners can pay attention to each phoneme or sound.

running records A procedure for analyzing students' oral reading and noting their strengths and weaknesses when using various reading strategies.

scaffolding A support mechanism by which students are able to accomplish more difficult tasks than they could without assistance.

scanning Processing text quickly, looking for some specific information—such as reading the blurb on the back of a book to decide if you want to read it, or when scanning a web page before clicking on a link to another page.

schema A preexisting knowledge structure developed about a thing, a place, or an idea; a framework of expectations based on previous knowledge.

scoring rubric A tool describing the levels of performance a student must demonstrate related to a particular achievement goal, whether it is written or oral.

self-monitoring The mental act of knowing when one does and does not understand what one is reading.

self-regulated learning A learning process that requires awareness and application of learning strategies and extensive reflection and self-awareness; students who are self-regulated understand their strengths and weaknesses as learner. Closely related to *comprehension monitoring*.

semantic cues Meaning clues.

semantic feature analysis An instructional activity in which students select a group of related words and then create a chart to classify them according to distinguishing characteristics.

semantic field A range of similarity among words.

semantic gradient A vocabulary-enriching activity that allows students to discuss the many shades of meaning of words, beginning with a word and ending with its opposite.

semantic map A graphic representation of the relationship among words and phrases in written material.

sentence fluency The careful crafting of sentences so that paragraphs flow smoothly and effortlessly.

sentence stems The first two or three words of a sentence followed by blank spaces offered to students to support initial attempts at writing.

sentence strips Rectangular pieces of tag board or construction paper upon which are written individual sentences from a story students have read.

service learning Curriculum projects that involve and enhance the surrounding community.

shared reading A mediated technique whereby the teacher reads aloud while students follow along using individual copies of the book, a class chart, or a big book.

sheltered English Lessons taught in a multisensory, multi-intelligence way to ensure understanding by English learners.

short vowels Vowels that represent the sound of /a/ in *apple*, /e/ in *end*, /i/ in *igloo*, /o/ in *octopus*, and /u/ in *bus*.

showcase portfolio A collection of artifacts taken from the working portfolio that demonstrates excellence in achievement.

sight vocabulary Words that the reader recognizes immediately, without having to resort to decoding.

sight word A word that is immediately recognized as a whole and does not require word analysis for identification.

SIOP Model SIOP (Sheltered Instruction Observation Protocol) is a "sheltered English" instructional model that delineates both language and content lesson objectives linked to subject area and curriculum standards.

6 + 1 Trait writing The important aspects of writing, including ideas, organization, voice, word choice, sentence fluency, conventions, and presentation.

skimming Reading that is done rapidly, but purposefully, to get a general idea what a selection is about. Readers engaged in skimming will be expected to get the main idea of the selection as well as a few supporting details.

speech disorders Disabilities characterized by deficits in speech, receptive language, and/or expressive language.

SQ3R (Survey, Question, Read, Recite, Review) A study strategy that asks readers first to survey the material and form questions based on that survey, then to read, restate in their own words, and review or rehearse what was read to help their comprehension and memory of the material.

Squire's model The notion that reading and writing are related because they place similar demands on one's thinking.

stage theory A theory that suggests that students go through three stages in acquiring literacy: the "selective cue stage," the "spelling-sound stage," and the "automatic stage."

standard deviation A number describing the variability in scores as indicated by their distance from the mean, or average.

standard error of measurement A number representing the error associated with a test.

standardized reading tests Achievement tests that are published; norm-referenced, group-administered, survey tests of reading ability.

standardized testing The use of norm-referenced tests to measure reading and writing skills as well as their subskills.

standards Broad curricular goals containing specific grade-level targets or benchmarks. They represent systematic ways for educators to ask themselves, What is it that we want our students to be able to know? and What do we want them to be able to do?

standards-based performance assessment Assessment tasks designed to show what has been learned as it relates to a particular content standard.

stanine scores Scores that have been converted into nine equally spaced groups, with 1 being the lowest.

story frame A basic outline for a story designed to help students organize their ideas about what they have read.

story grammar A set of rules that defines story structures.

strategic reader model A view of reading instruction that focuses on teaching readers a wide variety of strategies to use before, during, and after reading.

structural analysis Examination of words for meaningful parts (affixes, contractions, endings, compound words).

structured listening activity An activity in which students listen to a story accompanied by visuals that support the action in the story, and then retell the story with the help of the visuals.

suffix A meaningful chunk attached to the end of words, such as play + ing = playing.

summative assessment A compilation of summary data provided at the end of a program, units of study, or other intervals to report progress.

sustained silent reading (SSR) A program for setting aside a certain period of time daily for self-selected, silent reading. During SSR time, each student chooses material to read for a designated period of time, typically 10–15 minutes for beginning readers. Everyone, including the teacher, reads without interruption.

syllabication Breaking words into syllables; "chunking."

syllable juncture stage See syllables and affixes stage.

syllables The units of pronunciation that include a vowel sound.

syllables and affixes stage Spelling stage characterized by considering the conventions of preserving pattern-to-sound relationships at the place where syllables meet.

synonyms Groups of words that have the same, or very similar, meanings.

syntactic cues Clues derived from the word order, or grammar, of the sentence.

T-chart A two-column list used to compare the information in the column heads.

talk-to-yourself chart A chart to help students self-assess their ability to read and spell new words.

teachable moments Opportunities for spontaneous, indirect teaching that occur when teachers respond to students' questions or when students otherwise demonstrate the need to know something.

teacher observational portfolio A progress file containing observations and informal assessments of students' reading and writing behaviors and accomplishments.

telegraphic stage The language acquisition stage in which an idea or concept is represented by two words.

text-based collaborative learning A process in which students work with a partner or small group to clarify expository text.

think-aloud A strategy in which the teacher models aloud for students the thinking processes used when reading or writing.

think, pair, and share A cooperative learning strategy in which students listen to a question, think of a response, pair to discuss with a partner, and then share their collaboration with the whole class.

think sheet A written format used to help students with behavioral disorders devise better choices for ways to behave.

tiered activities Activities that are modified to meet the differentiated needs of learners.

time/order chart Sequencing to show chronological order.

time-out Removing a student who is acting disruptively from the immediate vicinity of instruction for a specified period of time, or until she can return and behave appropriately.

topic and details maps Charts showing relationships of details to main topic.

tracking Indicating understanding of the one-to-one correspondence of spoken and written words by finger-pointing.

trade book Any book that can be purchased by the general public in bookstores, through mail-order houses, online, or at book fairs.

transactional model A perspective of early reading instruction from cognitive psychology and psycholinguistic learning that views students as bringing a rich prior knowledge background to literacy learning.

transfer words Words containing elements that are also found in many other words.

transitional reader A reader who is aware of letter pattern units, or word families, and frequently occurring rimes.

transitional stage The fourth stage of spelling development, in which the student is able to approximate the spelling of various English words.

transmission model A perspective of early reading instruction from behavioral psychology that views children as empty vessels into which knowledge is poured.

validity The degree to which a test measures what it purports to measure.

Venn diagram A set of overlapping circles used to graphically illustrate the similarities and differences of two concepts, ideas, stories, or other items.

vicarious experiences Indirect experiences, not involving the senses.

viewing The interpretation and analysis of visual media.

visual literacy The ability to interpret the meaning of visual images as well as to construct effective visuals in order to convey ideas to others.

visually representing The process of communicating through visual images such as photographs, drawings, video presentations, cartoons, and other image types.

vocabulary The words that a person knows and uses.

voice The writer's personality emerging through words.

web A graphic organizer used to involve students in thinking about and planning what they will study, learn, read about, or write about within a larger topic.

WebQuest An inquiry-based and student-centered technique that challenges students to explore the Internet for information related to a particular topic or problem.

within word stage See transitional stage.

word attack An aspect of reading instruction that includes intentional strategies for learning to decode, sight read, and recognize written words.

word bank A collection of sight words that have been mastered, usually recorded on index cards.

word building An activity in which students arrange letter cards to spell words, practicing phonics and spelling concepts.

word choice The element of writing that involves using fresh and colorful language to make certain passages memorable and worthy of reading aloud.

word consciousness Students' awareness of new words and their desire to learn them and then to use them when speaking and writing.

word families Set of words formed from common rimes by onset substitution.

word hunt An activity in which students search for words that correspond to a certain pattern that has been identified by them or by the teacher.

word map A visual illustration of a word showing its meaning by offering examples, explaining what it is and what it is not.

word play The manipulation of sounds and words for purposes of language exploration, practice, and pleasure.

word sort An activity in which students sort a collection of words into two or more categories.

word study Analyzing words to discover the regularities, patterns, and rules of English orthography needed to read and spell.

word wall A chart or bulletin board on which are placed, alphabetically, important vocabulary to be referred to during word study activities.

wordless books Picture story books without words.

working portfolio A collection of completed work samples or works in progress that may be chosen for placement in a showcase portfolio.

writing fluency Abilities that allow writers to achieve a continuous flow of ideas; comprises two main components—the speed with which students write, and the automaticity of the conventions of writing—giving writers independence and confidence when drafting their ideas.

writing folder A folder where students keep rough drafts in various stages of the writing process and other daily compositions or reports, topics for future writing, and notes from minilessons.

writing process The process by which a piece of writing is completed for publication, involving prewriting, drafting, revising, editing, and publishing.

writing prompts Motivational ideas or structures that are offered by the teacher to inspire students to write.

writing workshop A writing program that implements the writing process by having students write on topics that they choose themselves, assuming ownership of their writing and learning.